America the Beautiful Curriculum Package

America the Beautiful by Charlene Notgrass is a one-year American history, geography, and literature course designed for students in grades 5-8. Daily lessons guide your child chronologically through American history, highlighting key events, people, and places.

All of the instructions for how to use the course are included in Part 1 and Part 2, so you do not need a separate teacher's manual. At the beginning of each weekly unit, an introductory page gives an overview of the unit, a list of the lessons, and a list of what additional books the student will be using while studying that particular unit. Following the unit introduction are five lessons, one to be read each day. While this course is designed for children in grades 5-8, younger children can listen to the lessons and participate in the family activities.

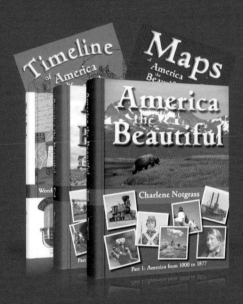

Your child can read the daily lessons on his own or you can read the lessons aloud. The lessons are richly illustrated with color and black-and-white historical photographs, illustrations, and artwork. At the end of each lesson is a list of four to six activities. You may choose which activities to assign. Depending on how many activities you assign, most students will need 45-90 minutes to complete one lesson.

The full curriculum package includes:

- *America the Beautiful Part 1*
- *America the Beautiful Part 2*
- *We the People*
- *Maps of America the Beautiful*
- *Timeline of America the Beautiful*
- *America the Beautiful Answer Key*

Ten works of literature are assigned in the *America the Beautiful* curriculum to give your child a richer perspective on the various time periods studied. Two optional additional resources are the *Student Workbook* and *Lesson Review,* each of which provides a way to review material in each lesson. The *Answer Key* that comes with the curriculum package has all of the answers needed for grading.

For more information, visit notgrass.com or call 1-800-211-8793.

America the Beautiful

Part 2: America from the Late 1800s to the Present

Charlene Notgrass

America the Beautiful
Part 2: America from the Late 1800s to the Present
by Charlene Notgrass

ISBN 978-1-60999-039-8 (hardcover)

Unless otherwise noted, scripture quotations taken from the
New American Standard Bible, Copyright 1960, 1962, 1963, 1971, 1972, 1973,
1975, 1977, 1995 by the Lockman Foundation Used by permission.

Lesson and Family Activities by Bethany Poore

Cover design by Mary Evelyn McCurdy
Interior design by Charlene Notgrass

Printed in the United States of America

Notgrass Company
975 Roaring River Rd.
Gainesboro, TN 38562

1-800-211-8793
www.notgrass.com
books@notgrass.com

Table of Contents
Part 2

Go West!

After the corruption of the Grant administration, America wanted their government to be reformed. Presidents Hayes, Garfield, and Arthur worked to make that happen. In the late 1800s, Andrew Carnegie began giving away his immense fortune to spread knowledge around the country through his beautiful Carnegie libraries. Americans and immigrants from Europe began pouring into the West to take advantage of the land offered through the Homestead Act. The Ingalls from Wisconsin were one of these homesteading families. One of their daughters grew up to be the famous author Laura Ingalls Wilder, who wrote the Little House books about life as a pioneer. During this time, American soldiers served at frontier forts such as Fort Larned in Kansas.

Garfield/Arthur Campaign Plate

Lessons in Unit 16

Lesson 76 – Our American Story: Reformers in the White House: Hayes, Garfield, and Arthur
Lesson 77 – An America Landmark: Carnegie Libraries
Lesson 78 – Daily Life: Homesteading in the American West
Lesson 79 – An American Biography: Laura Ingalls Wilder, Pioneer and Author
Lesson 80 – Daily Life: Frontier Soldiers

Books Used in Unit 16

- *Maps of America the Beautiful*

- *Timeline of America the Beautiful*

- *We the People*

- *Little Town on the Prairie* by Laura Ingalls Wilder

Reformers in the White House: Hayes, Garfield, and Arthur

Inauguration of Rutherford B. Hayes

By 1876 Americans were ready to put the Civil War behind them. Democrats had regained control of most of the former Confederate states. Southerners wanted all Union troops out of their states. Even northerners were unhappy with the Republicans. They did not like the way Republicans had treated Andrew Johnson or the corruption of the people who had served with President Grant.

When time came to elect a new President, Democrats chose New York Governor Samuel Tilden. Republicans chose Civil War veteran and Ohio Governor Rutherford B. Hayes. The vote was close; results were disputed in three southern states. Congress set up a commission of eight Republicans and seven Democrats to decide the real winner in those states. Two days before inauguration day the commission voted that Hayes had won in those three states. Many believe that Democrat and Republican leaders made a secret deal, with Democrats agreeing that Hayes had won and Republicans agreeing to remove the last Federal troops from the South.

The election of Rutherford B. Hayes began to heal a nation torn apart during the Civil War and Reconstruction. Though the election was the most corrupt in American history, Hayes himself was honest, moral, and upstanding. He brought good changes to the Presidency. Look at the photo above. Hayes began making the government more honest. Hayes fired Chester Arthur, a customs collector in New York, because of illegal activities happening there, even though Arthur was a Republican. His decisions helped the national economy. Still, since the Democrats controlled Congress, Hayes was not able to make major changes in how the government conducted business. When Hayes left office, Alexander Stephens, former Vice President of the Confederacy, said he had never seen a President leave power "so well-spoken of." Read about Hayes' life on page 441.

Rutherford Birchard Hayes
America's Nineteenth President
March 4, 1877 - March 4, 1881

Hayes was born in Delaware, Ohio. His family had been in America since the 1680s, having settled in New England. Hayes' father died ten weeks before he was born, so he was raised by his mother. She taught him to read and write. He and his sister Fanny were quite close. Fanny shared Shakespeare and the poetry of Sir Walter Scott with him. The children attended public and private schools. His family called him "Rud."

A wealthy uncle helped Hayes go to Harvard Law School. He moved to Cincinnati, where he became a successful lawyer. Back in Delaware, Ohio, Mrs. Hayes befriended Lucy Webb and wanted her son to marry her. When Lucy came to Cincinnati to go to school, Hayes decided that his mother was right. Rutherford and Lucy married in 1852. They are pictured above. Lucy was a strong Methodist who believed in abolition and temperance (not using alcohol). After they married, Hayes regularly attended church with her and gradually began to embrace her views. The couple had eight children. Two

Hayes and His Sons

are pictured at left with their father. Hayes was deeply saddened when his sister died in 1856. He said she was his "dearest friend of childhood" and the "confidante of all my life."

Though he had never served in the military when the Civil War began, Hayes quickly volunteered to fight for the Union. He was almost 40 years old and the father of three children with a fourth child on the way. He became an officer and learned his job well. Hayes bravely led his men into battle and was wounded five times. In 1864 he was elected to the U.S. House of Representatives, even though he was away fighting in the war. By the time Congress went into session, the war was over. After serving in the House of Representatives, Hayes served two terms as Governor of Ohio.

In 1876 Hayes was elected as the nineteenth President of the United States. By the time he entered the White House, he had become a teetotaler, meaning he drank no alcohol at all. People later refered to his wife as "Lemonade Lucy" since the couple did not serve alcohol.

Mrs. Hayes brought fun to the White House. Once the house was so full of guests that one of the oldest boys who was home from college had to sleep in a bathtub. Among their guests were future President William McKinley and his wife Ida, as well as Helen Herron, who later married future President William Howard Taft.

Lucy had a beautiful voice and accompanied herself on the guitar. She and other musicians brought popular, folk, and classical music to the White House. On Sunday evenings, Mrs. Hayes commonly led a "sing." Civil War hero General Sherman joined in singing gospel songs.

At Christmas, the two youngest Hayes children handed out presents to all the White House employees. After celebrating their first Christmas at the White House, the Hayes celebrated their twenty-fifth wedding anniversary on December 30. They invited relatives, close friends, and the White House staff. During the party, the Hayes repeated their wedding vows.

After Hayes left the presidency, he worked for equality, tax-funded education, and prison reform. After his dear Lucy died in 1889, his only daughter Fanny became his companion. Rutherford B. Hayes died in 1893.

President Hayes did not seek to be re-elected in 1880. Republicans nominated another religious man, Senator James Garfield from Ohio. He was also a Civil War veteran. Democrats chose still another Civil War veteran, Winfield Scott Hancock. Again the election was close, but Garfield was the clear winner.

Only four months after Garfield's inauguration, a mentally unstable man shot him at a Washington train station. Apparently, the man had been turned down for a government job. Garfield was badly wounded. Though he survived for several weeks, he died in September. Read about the life of James Garfield below.

James Abram Garfield
America's Twentieth President
March 4, 1881 - September 19, 1881

James Abram Garfield was born in 1831 on a farm in Ohio. His father died while James was still a baby. James earned money to attend school and then college by working as a carpenter, a teacher, and a janitor.

At age 18, he trusted in Jesus and was baptized. Like his parents, he worshiped with Christians who were part of the Disciples of Christ. This religious movement began during the Second Great Awakening and tried to base their practices on the example of the New Testament church. In his early twenties Garfield served as a minister.

Garfield began courting Lucretia "Crete" Rudolph, a school classmate. She taught school while he completed Williams College. After college, he began teaching English, history, geology, and mathematics. In 1858 James and Lucretia married. Five of their seven children survived to adulthood.

When the Civil War began, Garfield organized the 42nd Ohio Infantry and quickly became a colonel. He showed bravery in battle. After leading his small brigade to victory over Confederates in the Battle of Middle Creek, he was in control of eastern Kentucky. He made a brave ride under fire at the Battle of Chickamauga. By then he was a major general. For a while, he served as Chief of Staff for General Rosecrans, commander of the Union Army of the Cumberland. See his photo at right.

In 1863 Garfield was elected to the House of Representatives without campaigning. He left the war and went to Washington, where he served in the House for sixteen years. At first Garfield supported the harsh policies of the Republican Party meant to punish the South, but later he became less radical.

James Garfield's mother was the first mother to attend her son's inauguration. She moved into the White House with his family. Garfield was a strong man of over six feet in height, while his mother was frail. He personally carried his mother up and down the White House stairs.

When Garfield died, his daughter Mary and four sons—Harry, James, Irvin, and Abram—were all eighteen or younger. They and their mother returned to Ohio. Lucretia raised the children well. She was a widow for 36 years. Mary grew up to marry Garfield's presidential secretary. She became active in community affairs in New York and in California. Harry became a professor of politics at Princeton and later president of Williams College. Harry also served in Woodrow Wilson's administration. James served in President Theodore Roosevelt's cabinet. Irvin became a lawyer in Boston and Abram was an architect in Cleveland, Ohio.

After James Garfield died, Vice President Chester A. Arthur became President. America was shocked that another President had been assassinated just sixteen years after Lincoln. Many believed that the way government jobs were given was part of the reason.

At that time, thousands of Federal government jobs were given to people who had supported the winning candidate during a presidential election. Every time the President changed, many people left government jobs and others took their places. Jobs were based on who you knew rather than on whether you did a good job.

Congress passed the Civil Service Act in 1883. This act required that some Federal jobs be filled with people who did well on a test. It was a start in the right direction. Though Arthur had overseen a corrupt customs office in New York, he worked against dishonesty in the Federal government and increased the number of jobs that were based on skill rather than on who you knew. Abraham Lincoln's son, Robert Todd Lincoln, was Secretary of War under both Garfield and Arthur. Learn about the life of President Arthur below.

Chester Alan Arthur
America's Twenty-First President
September 19, 1881 - March 4, 1885

Chester Alan Arthur was born in a log cabin in Vermont in 1829. His father was a strong abolitionist and a Baptist preacher. The family moved often while Arthur's father preached for different congregations in Vermont and New York. Chester learned to read and to write at home before going to school. After college he taught school and read law. He passed his bar exam when he was 25 years old and began working for a New York law firm which defended the rights of blacks.

In 1859 Chester married Ellen Lewis Herndon. She was 22 and he was 30. They had two children who survived to adulthood.

Arthur had joined the New York militia in 1858. He continued serving during the Civil War, attaining the rank of brigadier general. He was responsible for securing provisions and housing for several hundred thousand soldiers. Arthur gained a reputation for working efficiently. He longed to serve in combat. However, his wife had family members in the Confederacy and his sister was married to a Confederate official, so he did not push for this kind of role.

Arthur retired from the Army in 1863 and went back to the practice of law, which made him wealthy. He also worked for a corrupt New York politician. As the duty collector for the Port of New York under President Grant, he earned a salary plus kickbacks, which were secret, illegal payments from companies that did business with the Port Authority.

Mrs. Arthur died of pneumonia in 1880, so Arthur was a widower when he became President. As President, Arthur used the organizational skills he had learned during the Civil

War. He paid close attention to details. Arthur continued the Civil Service reforms begun by Hayes and Garfield.

President Arthur enjoyed luxury. He remodeled the White House, which had fallen into disrepair. He was also an avid fisherman. In 1883 he and several others toured Yellowstone. In the picture at left, Arthur is seated in the center. The man with the dark beard on his left is Robert Todd Lincoln. Arthur became ill a few months before he left the Presidency and died the following year.

When Grant left the presidency, Americans were tired of people favoring their friends and not acting with justice toward everyone. They were tired of people using their political positions to get rich. People wanted fairness, which God had commanded in the Old Testament:

Now then let the fear of the Lord be upon you; be very careful what you do, for the Lord our God will have no part in unrighteousness or partiality or the taking of a bribe.
2 Chronicles 19:7

Activities for Lesson 76

Thinking Biblically – Read Deuteronomy 16:18-20. In your notebook, write a paragraph about why it is important for leaders to practice justice and what damage is done by taking bribes.

Vocabulary – Look up each of these words in a dictionary and read their definitions: corrupt, moral, equality, unstable, frail

> **Please note:** In the vocabulary assignments, we have used simple forms of the vocabulary words. In some lessons, a vocabulary word appears in a different form from the form used in the vocabulary assignment. For example, in this lesson the word corrupt is used in both the adjective form corrupt and its noun form corruption. In some cases a verb might appear in the past tense in the lesson. Keep this in mind when you look back in a lesson to find vocabulary words.

Literature – Read "How Arthur Was Inaugurated" in *We the People*, page 81, and "Surprise," "Springtime on the Claim," and "The Necessary Cat" in *Little Town on the Prairie*.

Timeline – In *Timeline of America the Beautiful* next to 1883, write: Congress passes the Civil Service Act.

Student Workbook or Lesson Review – If you are using one of these optional books, complete the assignment for Lesson 76.

Carnegie Libraries

The first libraries in America were private. Wealthy people often had small libraries in their homes. Wealthy colonists sometimes contributed to a social library. Together they

Library Hall was built in Philadelphia in 1790. After being torn down in the 1880s, it was rebuilt in the 1950s.

bought books, which they shared with one another. Such libraries still exist in places such as Philadelphia, New York City, and Charleston, South Carolina.

After the American Revolution, women continued the tradition of creating circulating libraries to share books with one another. In the early 1800s, library societies sometimes concentrated on collecting books about certain subjects. For instance, mechanics or seamen might have their own libraries. Sometimes business owners supported these libraries to give young men opportunities to increase their knowledge.

In the last half of the 1800s, people who wanted to help new immigrants and the poor began to organize free libraries. They believed that libraries would give people something better to do than drink and gamble. However, by the 1880s, only a few places had public libraries. This changed when a wealthy businessman, Andrew Carnegie, started giving away millions of dollars to build libraries for the public to use.

Carnegie grew up in Dunfermline, Scotland. See the drawing at right. His father

Dunfermline, Scotland, Where Carnegie Lived as a Child

was a weaver who helped create the Tradesmen's Subscription Library. As a child, Andrew listened to men read aloud and discuss books borrowed from that library. The elder Carnegie's weaving business suffered when people began to get more and more of their fabric from factories. He sold his family's belongings and emigrated to Allegheny, Pennsylvania, a suburb of Pittsburgh.

Young Andrew went to work when he got to America. First he worked in a textile factory. Later he became a messenger boy for a telegraph company. While working there, he met Colonel James Anderson, who opened his personal library every Saturday to any working boy in the city who wanted to borrow a book. Carnegie decided that if he ever became wealthy, he would provide opportunities like this to other poor workers.

Philanthropist Andrew Carnegie

In the following fifty years, Andrew Carnegie became very wealthy. While working as a messenger, he taught himself how to send telegrams. This helped him get a job with the Pennsylvania Railroad when he was eighteen. He worked there for twelve years, taking on jobs of increasing importance. Meanwhile, he began to invest in other businesses. In 1865 Carnegie left the railroad and began to manage a company that built iron railroad bridges to replace wooden ones. In the 1870s, he created the Carnegie Steel Company. In 1901 he sold the company for $250 million and retired. See his photo at left.

Andrew Carnegie spent the rest of his life giving away money. He believed that wealthy men should not live extravagantly; instead they should provide a moderate living for their families and give the rest of their riches away to help others. Carnegie chose seven types of organizations as worthy of support: churches, libraries, medical centers, meeting and concert halls, public baths, public parks, and universities. He later added scientific research, the spread of knowledge, and the promotion of world peace to his list.

Carnegie said that a library was the best possible gift to give a community because it gave people a chance to improve themselves. He believed that even though those who went to libraries were a small percentage of the entire population, they were the ones who would help their communities the most.

From 1886 to 1896, Carnegie donated money to build fourteen community centers in six cities. These buildings had libraries and recreational facilities such as swimming pools and billiard tables. At right is the billiard room of the Carnegie Library of Homestead in Munhall, Pennsylvania. Of this library, Carnegie said:

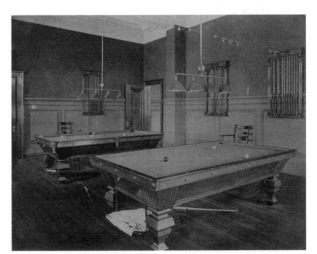

Billiard Hall in the Carnegie Library in Munhall, Pennsylvania

> The building has rightfully in the center as the focus 'The Library' — Music Hall upon the right and the Working Man's Club upon the left. These three [are the] foundations from which healing waters are to flow for the Instruction, Entertainment and Happiness of the people. Recreation of the working man has an important bearing upon his character and development. . . .

After 1896 Carnegie gave gifts that helped 1,406 towns build buildings that were just libraries. Most Carnegie libraries are in the Midwest, but cities in forty-six states received help. See photos at right. After 1916 Carnegie stopped building libraries and began to help train people to work in them.

By the time Carnegie died in 1919 at age 84, he had given away almost ninety percent of his accumulated wealth.

A generous man will be prosperous,
And he who waters will himself be watered.
Proverbs 11:25

Activities for Lesson 77

Thinking Biblically – Copy 1 Timothy 6:17-19 into your notebook.

Map Study – Complete the assignment for Lesson 77 on Map 3 "American Landmarks" in *Maps of America the Beautiful*.

Literature – Read "Colonel Anderson and Books" in *We the People*, pages 82-83, and "The Happy Days," "Working in Town," and "The Month of Roses" in *Little Town on the Prairie*.

Timeline – In *Timeline of America the Beautiful* next to 1886, write: Andrew Carnegie begins giving money to start libraries.

Student Workbook or Lesson Review – If you are using one of these optional books, complete the assignment for Lesson 77.

Carnegie Free Library in Union, South Carolina

University of Kentucky Carnegie Library

Women's Reading Room at the Carnegie Library and Music Hall in Allegheny, Pennsylvania

Carnegie Library in Guthrie, Oklahoma

Homesteading in the American West

During the Civil War, Congress passed and President Lincoln signed into law the Homestead Act of 1862. In the following decades, private citizens received a total of about 275 million acres of land, which amounts to about 10% of the total land

Homestead Drawing from the U.S. Bureau of Land Management

in the United States. The Homestead Act stayed in effect until it was repealed in 1976. Even then people had ten more years to claim homesteads in Alaska. During the 124-year history of the Homestead Act, about two million people filed a claim and about 783,000 were successful.

When the Homestead Act was passed, most Americans lived east of the Mississippi River or near the west coast. Vast lands lay in between. Government officials and business leaders wanted people to settle on those lands that Native Americans used for hunting.

Advertisement Encouraging People to Move to South Dakota

Representatives from railroads and Western towns even went to Europe to encourage people to come to America and begin homesteads. Newspapers published articles encouraging people to try it. At left is an advertisement encouraging people to come to South Dakota.

The drawing above illustrates the dreams of the early homesteaders. They wanted a family, a farm, and freedom. Though a few homesteads were in the East, most were in the West. Here is a list of states that had homesteaders, beginning with the state with the most homesteads down to the one with the least: Montana, North Dakota, Colorado, Nebraska, Oklahoma, South Dakota, Kansas, New Mexico, Minnesota, Arkansas, Wyoming, California, Oregon, Idaho, Washington, Alabama, Missouri, Dakota territory (before North and South Dakota became states),

Wisconsin, Florida, Mississippi, Louisiana, Arizona, Michigan, Utah, Iowa, Nevada, Alaska, Ohio, Illinois, and Indiana. The numbers of homesteads in each state differed greatly: Montana had 151,600 homesteads, while Ohio had thirty. In Colorado, Montana, Nebraska, North Dakota, and Oklahoma, a third or more of the total land area was given to homesteaders. The state with the highest percentage of land given to homesteaders was Nebraska, with 45% of the land.

Earning a Homestead

The earliest homestead claims were for 160 acres. To qualify for a homestead, a man or woman had to be the head of a household or be at least 21 years old. The first step was to file a claim at the Land Office nearest the desired land. The homesteader had to pay a $10 filing fee to place a temporary claim on the land and also give the land agent a $2 commission. During the next five years, he or she had to farm the land, live on it, build a home, and make improvements.

At the conclusion of those five years, the homesteader had to find two neighbors who would vouch for his honesty in claiming that he had completed these requirements. This was not always easy, since homesteads were sometimes far apart. He also had to pay the remaining fee of $6. After meeting these two requirements, the homesteader received a patent stating that he owned the land. The patent had the signature of the President of the United States. Homesteaders often displayed these patents on the walls of their homes. The chart above shows how many final patents were issued in the decades between 1871 and 1960.

Homestead Patents Received Per Decade, 1871-1960

Decade	Patents
1871-1880	64,515
1881-1890	192,880
1891-1900	225,743
1901-1910	372,002
1911-1920	439,710
1921-1930	161,896
1931-1940	40,211
1941-1950	4,592
1951-1960	3,856

Many homesteaders were farm workers from the East who had no land of their own or immigrants who had just arrived in America. Some were former slaves. A few were women. The offer of a homestead was a great attraction for people wanting to own land.

*Homesteader's Outhouse
Near the Tetons*

Successful homesteaders needed perseverance and resourcefulness. Most homesteads were in the Great Plains, where weather was sometimes severe. Blizzards came in the winter and extreme heat in the summer. Families suffered from loneliness. They lived far from other people, so they had to know how to do many things for themselves. See homestead scenes at left and on page 450.

Still, many found success and enjoyed the simple pleasures of homestead life. They loved their freedom, the beautiful scenery, and the blessings of being with their families. They made their own

449

Above and Right: Two Early Homestead Claims near the Teton Mountain Range in Wyoming

entertainment by singing and playing musical instruments. As others moved close by, they enjoyed getting together for social gatherings. They worked together to form communities and to build churches and schools. Shopkeepers came and built stores. Store goods came from the East on railroad cars.

Interior of a Homesteader's Home near Williston, North Dakota

The First Homesteader

About 400 people filed for homesteads on January 1, 1863, the first day they were available. Daniel Freeman is considered to be the first, since he filed his claim at 12:10 a.m. in Brownville, Nebraska. Freeman had moved to Nebraska from Illinois. After arriving there, he began writing letters to Agnes Suiter. She had been engaged to his brother who had died during the Civil War. In one of his letters, Daniel proposed. Agnes accepted, and in 1865, Freeman went back to Illinois, married her, and brought her to his homestead.

At first the Freemans lived in a small log cabin. They surrounded it with several outbuildings. The family later built a two-story brick home. The Freemans planted a hedgerow of Osage Orange trees to serve as a fence to keep animals out of their fields. Some of these are still growing today. The Freemans hired tenant farmers. Along with the Freemans, they grew fields of corn, oats, and wheat and orchards with apple and peach trees.

Daniel and Agnes had eight children. Some of the children also built homes on the farm. Daniel died in 1908. Agnes continued to live on the claim. She enjoyed caring for her grandchildren there. Mrs. Freeman lived on the homestead until shortly before her death in 1931. The Freeman land in Beatrice, Nebraska, is now the site of the Homestead National Monument. It is overseen by the National Park Service.

The Kansas Fever Exodus

After President Hayes removed Federal troops from the South, conditions grew worse for some African Americans. Many decided to leave the South and become homesteaders in Kansas. Though some blacks, especially those from Tennessee, had begun to migrate to Kansas soon after the Civil War, a great exodus occurred in 1879.

In January of 1879, a Minnesota Senator introduced a resolution in the U.S. Senate encouraging black migration out of the South. Blacks already living in Kansas wrote letters to friends and family in the South encouraging them to come. Newspaper articles spoke of better conditions in Kansas. Facing political discrimination and poor economic opportunities where they were, black families began to move west. Many rode steamboats to St. Louis but did not have resources to go further. Local ministers and business leaders worked together to help them survive. They also helped the travelers continue their journey to Kansas. Whites from other states sent aid also.

In 1879 about 6,000 freed slaves and their families migrated to Kansas from Texas, Louisiana, and Mississippi. The African American population of Kansas was about 16,250 in 1870. By 1880 it had risen to about 43,110. Some established the all-black town of

Nicodemus, Kansas, Around 1885

Nicodemus, pictured at left. Its peak population was about 700. Today it is a National Historic Site.

Soddies and Dugouts

Homesteaders on the Great Plains had to make do with a lack of lumber. Some homesteaders found enough trees to build a house, but many used sod. Sod is grass with roots and dirt attached. Settlers cut three-foot slabs of sod that were four inches thick. They laid the sod with the grass side down, stacking them like building blocks. Settlers usually built one-room dwellings with wooden doors and window frames. Some sod houses, or soddies,

were built into the side of a hill, while others were built free-standing. Some people added glass windows and more rooms. A few were one and a half stories. Isadore Haumont built the two-story soddy pictured at right. Built in about 1884, it stood until 1967.

Haumont Family with Two-Story Soddy in Nebraksa

Pioneer women found sod homes difficult to keep clean; and they did not enjoy sharing their homes with mice, insects, and snakes. Nevertheless, people on the Great Plains lived in sod houses well into the 1900s.

Some families dug into hillsides to build dugout homes. The photo at top left on the next page shows the entrance to a dugout. The two photographs beside it were taken on the inside of this home.

Exterior and Interior Photographs of a Dugout near Campbell, Wyoming

Solomon D. Butcher was born in 1856. When he was twenty-four years old, he and his family came to Nebraska and filed a homestead claim. Though he admired the determination of other homesteaders, he decided that it was not a life he would choose. Instead, he became a photographer. Between 1886 and 1912, he made over 3,000 photographs, including the one of the two-story Haumont house on page 451 and the picture at right. In this photo the family has brought out a rocking chair

Solomon Butcher Photograph of a Family with Their Soddy

and another chair, the little girl at left holds a doll, and the baby is in a cart. Notice the windmill on the roof of the building next to the house.

Famous Homesteaders and Their Descendants

From 1956 to 1970, your grandparents and great-grandparents probably watched television newscasts with Chet Huntley. He was the son of homesteaders in Montana. He returned to Montana after he retired. Your grandparents and great-grandparents also probably watched a musical program on television called *The Lawrence Welk Show*, which played on ABC from 1955 until 1971 and then into the early 1980s in syndication. Lawrence Welk was the son of German homesteaders in Strasburg, North Dakota. Wa gi ma wub was a chief of the Bois Forte Band of Ojibwe who lived from 1835 to 1937. He was a homesteader in Minnesota.

African American inventor and teacher George Washington Carver was a homesteader in Kansas. Before receiving the patent for his homestead, Carver left Kansas and went to college in Iowa. He became the first African American to teach at Iowa State Agricultural College. Later he moved to Alabama to teach at Tuskegee Institute, which was founded by another great African American leader of the 1800s, Booker T. Washington. While at Tuskegee, Carver discovered 325 uses for peanuts, 108 uses for sweet potatoes, and 75 uses for pecans. Most of his discoveries are still in use today.

The Last Homesteader

In 1974 Kenneth Deardorff, a Vietnam veteran from California, filed a claim for an 80-acre homestead in Alaska. He and his family lived on the land and worked it for ten years. In 1988 he received his patent. Deardorff built his home and other farm buildings from white spruce trees growing on the property. He fished for salmon and hunted for moose and other wild animals. On many mornings, he found grizzly bears in his yard when he woke up. The only ways to get to and from his home were by boat or dog sled.

Notice the corner of a homesteader's log house below. The quality workmanship shows that the builder had great patience and skill, because the logs fit together so well. The only homesteaders who succeeded were those who were patient and worked hard:

I passed by the field of the sluggard and by the vineyard of the man
lacking sense, and behold, it was completely overgrown
with thistles; its surface was covered with nettles, and its stone wall
was broken down. When I saw, I reflected upon it; I looked, and
received instruction. "A little sleep, a little slumber, a little folding of
the hands to rest," then your poverty will come as a robber
and your want like an armed man.
Proverbs 24:30-34

*Detail of a Homesteader's
Log House*

Activities for Lesson 78

Vocabulary – In your notebook, write the following sentences and fill in each blank with one of these words: perseverance, resourcefulness, hedgerow, tenant, exodus.

1. The old farm has a _____ of thorny bushes that is still in good shape.
2. The long math lesson was a test of my _____.
3. When my brother stirred up their hill with a stick, the ants began a forced _____.
4. My grandfather has a _____ in his apartment house that won't pay his rent.
5. Though we were snowed in on Dad's birthday, Mom's _____ gave us a great party.

Literature – Read "Summer on the Homestead" in *We the People*, pages 84-85, and "Nine Dollar" and "Fourth of July" in *Little Town on the Prairie*.

Creative Writing – Imagine that you live in 1875 and your family has decided to go west in a covered wagon to claim a homestead. In your notebook, write a letter to your grandparents telling them about the decision, what you're worried about, and what you're looking forward to about living on a homestead.

Timeline – In *Timeline of America the Beautiful* next to 1863, write: The first homestead claim is filed.

Family Activity – Make a Homestead Map. See page 961 for instructions.

Student Workbook or Lesson Review – If you are using one of these optional books, complete the assignment for Lesson 78.

Laura Ingalls Wilder, Pioneer and Author

In 1880 forty-four-year-old Charles Phillip Ingalls filed a claim for a homestead in Dakota Territory. Ingalls was born in 1836 near Cuba, New York. His parents were Lansford and Laura Ingalls. Charles was a descendant of one of the Englishmen who sailed to America on the *Mayflower*. When he was nine years old, his family moved to the frontier, first to Illinois and then to Wisconsin. There he met Caroline Lake Quiner and her family.

Caroline was born in Wisconsin in 1839. Generations before, Caroline's ancestors had come to America from Scotland. Twenty-four-year-old Charles and twenty-one-year-old Caroline were married in 1860, not long before the beginning of the Civil War.

Laura Ingalls as a Young Woman

In 1863 Charles and Caroline moved into a "Little House in the Big Woods," near Lake Pepin in Wisconsin. Lake Pepin is actually a wide part of the Mississippi River along the border between Wisconsin and Minnesota. In 1865 they had their first child, a girl they named Mary Amelia. Two years after that, they had another girl, Laura Elizabeth. When Laura was in her sixties, she began to write books about her childhood on the American frontier. The first, *Little House in the Big Woods*, was published in 1932, when Laura was sixty-four. Laura wanted children to know what it was like when she was a little girl. Eight of her books were published during her lifetime, the last in 1943, when she was seventy-six.

Though Laura's books are considered children's fiction, they are based on her real life. She omitted some of her family's experiences, especially the sad ones. After she was a famous author and in her eighties, she wrote a letter to her young readers to answer some of their most common questions. In the letter Laura said, "I lived everything that happened in my books." Here is a brief history of the Ingalls family, as told in Laura's books. The title of each of the next eight sections is the title of one of her books. The picture above was taken when Laura was a young woman.

Little House in the Big Woods

In Laura's first book, she told about her early childhood in Wisconsin. Laura describes a happy little girl who enjoys her life with her family. Pa farms, traps, and hunts. Ma is a gentle and kind mother and homemaker. Music was important in the Ingalls family. They all sang and Pa played the fiddle. In the big woods, the Ingalls family enjoyed visits with grandparents, aunts, uncles, and cousins. Laura was just two years old when Pa sold his home and land, put his family and their belongings in a covered wagon, and moved to Kansas; so in writing this book, Laura depended on stories she had heard from her parents.

Meanwhile, a boy named Almanzo Wilder was growing up back East. At that point in her life, Laura didn't know that one day she would marry the man who had spent his childhood as a . . .

Farmer Boy

Almanzo Wilder was born in 1857 in Malone, New York, in the foothills of the Adirondack Mountains. Almanzo lived in the same house until he was a teenager, when his family moved to Spring Valley, Minnesota. Almanzo, his brother Royal, and his sister Eliza Jane later became homesteaders near De Smet, South Dakota. There they met the Ingalls family. The photograph at right was taken when Laura's husband was a young man.

Laura and Almanzo had been married over forty years when Laura wrote *Farmer Boy*. Almanzo told her stories of his childhood and even drew diagrams of the family's farm buildings for her.

Almanzo Wilder as a Young Man

Little House on the Prairie

. . . is the home Pa built for his family in Kansas after they left the big woods. Ma helped him along with Mr. Edwards, a neighbor who lived nearby. Like the Ingalls, he had recently moved to the area. Mr. Edwards came from Tennessee.

While the Ingalls were in Kansas, Ma homeschooled Mary and Laura. She taught them to read and helped them learn Bible verses. She also taught them how to sew and do chores. Ma and Pa taught them important lessons by always making them obey. At nighttime, when the schoolwork, chores, and play were finished for the day, the family gathered to listen to Pa play the fiddle.

Though Laura does not mention it in the book, she and Mary gained another sister while they lived in the little house. Here Ma gave birth to Caroline Celestia, whom they called Carrie. Though Laura tells about their move away from Kansas, she doesn't tell that the family returned to Wisconsin for three years. In 1874 they set out again in their covered wagon and moved into a dugout . . .

On the Banks of Plum Creek

Plum Creek is near the town of Walnut Grove, Minnesota. Mary and Laura walked across the prairie to school in Walnut Grove. The Ingalls family joined the Congregational Church there. After a while, Pa was able to build his family a proper home. Confident that he would earn money from his crops, he borrowed money to complete the house.

Unfortunately, the Ingalls experienced hard times when a plague of grasshoppers ate their crops. Pa walked over two hundred miles to the east to find work. Though Laura does not mention him in any of her books, a baby brother, Charles Frederick, was born while the Ingalls family lived on Plum Creek. Laura is also silent about their move to Burr Oak, Iowa. Between the time they left Plum Creek and moved to Burr Oak, her baby brother died.

In Burr Oak, the Ingalls family lived for a while in a hotel owned by some of their friends. Laura and Mary worked as waitresses and washed dishes. They also went to school. Pa and Ma wanted to get their girls away from the hotel, so they moved first to some rented rooms over a store and later to a small house. The Ingalls' fifth child, Grace Pearl, was born while they lived in Burr Oak.

After two years, the family was able to move back to Walnut Grove. Soon afterwards, Mary became ill and lost her sight. Pa told Laura that she would have to become Mary's eyes. Afterwards, Mary used all of her other senses to know and to feel the world around her, while Laura described what she saw with her eyes. After several years in Walnut Grove, the Ingalls family moved to South Dakota . . .

By the Shores of Silver Lake

Pa got a temporary job with a railroad company that was building a track in South Dakota. It was a position with much responsibility. Pa was the paymaster; he would hand out pay to each of the men working on the railroad. He went ahead to South Dakota to begin his job. Several months later, Ma, Mary, Laura, Carrie, and Grace joined him. This time the girls did not go in a covered wagon. They rode on a train.

The Surveyor's House in De Smet, South Dakota

When the railroad surveyor left for the winter, the Ingalls lived in his house to protect the equipment. The house is pictured above. The Ingalls soon found that they could earn money by running a boarding house for homesteaders passing through the area. Night after night people showed up at the little surveyor's house needing food and shelter for the night as they headed westward.

A town was going up nearby, so Pa decided to buy a city lot and put up a store that he could rent to a shopkeeper. The family lived there for a few months and then, in 1880, Pa filed his claim for a homestead. He built a house and a stable, plowed and sowed his fields, and planted five cottonwood trees, one for each of his girls. One of the Ingalls' cottonwood trees is pictured at right. Homesteaders only had to live on their claims for part of the year, so Pa moved his family into their store in town each winter. Charles Ingalls is considered the first resident of the town of De Smet, South Dakota. The town was named for Pierre-Jean De Smet (see page 400). When Laura wrote about one of those winters in town, she called it . . .

Pa planted this cottonwood tree on the Ingalls homestead outside of De Smet, South Dakota.

The Long Winter

Today most people depend on trucks, barges, and trains to bring food to stores, where they purchase what they need. Though many homesteaders raised crops in the summer and saved them for the winter in 1880, the town of De Smet and the homesteads around it had not been there very long. Townspeople and the homesteaders who moved to town for the winter depended on the railroad to bring at least some of their food from the East to stock the stores.

That winter the first blizzard came early—in October. The citizens of De Smet experienced one blizzard after another. Laura and Carrie went to school at the beginning of the winter. The De Smet schoolhouse was close to Pa's store. One time the girls were at school when a blizzard came and they were barely able to find their way home.

Many miles east of De Smet, snow piled so high on the railroad track that the train could not get through. Townspeople used up most of the food in the stores. They were afraid they would starve. Men in De Smet had heard that a settler several miles away had a large amount of wheat. Almanzo Wilder and Cap Garland, another young man from De Smet, went out onto the wide, white prairie to find that man and his wheat. They could easily have lost their way and frozen to death. They found the man, bought wheat from him, and made it back to town. Their heroic efforts kept the town from starving. The train could not reach De Smet until May, eight months after the first blizzard.

To stay warm, the Ingalls family burned twisted prairie grass in their stove. For Laura, one of the saddest things about that winter was that Pa's hands became stiff and swollen from twisting the prairie grass, and for a while he couldn't play his fiddle. After surviving *The Long Winter*, the Ingalls family moved back to the homestead for the summer. Laura enjoyed the country life on the homestead and the winters when her family moved back to the . . .

Little Town on the Prairie

Ma learned about the Iowa School for the Blind (now the Iowa Braille and Sight Saving School) and wanted Mary to be able to go there. After months of saving, the Ingalls family was able to send her to school. They kept in close contact through letters and enjoyed her visits back home.

Laura grew to be a teenager on the Ingalls homestead and in De Smet. She became close friends with some of the girls in her class. She went to church and social events. One evening after an event, Almanzo Wilder surprised her by asking to walk her home. Almanzo was ten years older than Laura. Laura did not consider him one of her peers but thought of him as a friend of her father. Laura's mother thought she was too young to have a suitor, but Pa had a deep respect for Almanzo and said it was all right.

Laura was a good student. Ma had always hoped one of her girls would become a teacher. Though Laura did not want to teach, she knew it was a way to help her parents. She wanted to help with the expenses of sending Mary to school. Laura took an exam to qualify as a teacher, and she passed. She left school so she could become a teacher.

Soon Laura came to the part of her life she called . . .

These Happy Golden Years

Laura taught at three different schools. One was far away, so she had to board with a homesteader who lived nearby. His wife hated her life in the West and made things miserable for Laura. Laura spent a hard winter there teaching in the tiny Brewster School, pictured at right. Almanzo took his horses and sleigh down every Friday to bring her back to her parents' home for the weekend.

Laura had not yet decided she wanted Almanzo for a beau, and she made that clear to him. He continued to court her. Almanzo and Laura spent many Sunday afternoons during warm weather taking long buggy rides across the surrounding prairies. During these rides Laura grew to love Almanzo and finally agreed

Reproduction of the Brewster School

to marry him. On the last night that Laura spent at home with Ma, Pa, Grace, and Carrie, Pa played the old songs on his fiddle. Laura and Almanzo, whom Laura called Manly, were married in 1885, when she was 18 and he was 28.

The Writer from Rocky Ridge Farm

In 1894 Laura, Almanzo, and their little daughter Rose moved away from De Smet in a covered wagon. Laura was twenty-seven years old, Almanzo was thirty-seven, and Rose was seven. They moved to a farm in the Ozark Mountains of Missouri. Laura wrote all of her books on the farm they called Rocky Ridge. She first became an author when she wrote articles for the *Missouri Ruralist*. In 1919 she wrote an article, "The Farmer's Wife Says," for the national women's magazine *McCall's*. Her daughter Rose encouraged her to write about her childhood, so she wrote an autobiography called *Pioneer Girl*.

Laura could not find a publisher for it so she began to write the series now known as the Little House books. The first book, *Little House in the Big Woods*, became popular. Laura continued to publish a new book about every two years, and readers were eager to find out what happened next. Laura was careful to be accurate. She wrote to Grace to find out the names of wildflowers near De Smet. She even went to Kansas to try to find the site of their house on the prairie.

Laura became a famous person, and she received many letters from her fans. She traveled and made speeches. Laura received many awards for her books, including Newbery Honor awards. The Association for Library Service to Children began honoring authors and illustrators who create significant literature for children with the Laura Ingalls Wilder Award. Laura received the first award in 1954.

Laura's Letter to Children

In the letter Laura wrote to her young readers when she was in her eighties, she told about her life after *These Happy Golden Years*. She told about how she and Almanzo lived for a while near De Smet in the home Almanzo had built for her. She told about moving to Rocky Ridge. There they cleared the fields and built their own home, using wood and stone from their own land. It is pictured below. They worked hard until they had a good farm of two hundred acres. Laura and Almanzo had cows, hogs, and, according to Laura, "the best laying flock of hens in the country." In the first years after they moved to the Ozarks, they went horseback riding and buggy riding for fun, just as they had when they were courting in South Dakota. They read books, played music, and went to church socials. In later years, they took rides in their Chrysler automobile.

Tourists in Front of the Home That Laura and Almanzo Wilder Built on Rocky Ridge Farm

When they grew older, Laura and Almanzo traveled back to De Smet to see their old friends. She said they recognized faces everywhere, but they were surprised that their friends were old and gray—like she and Almanzo were.

In her letter to readers, Laura told of how she and Almanzo had been married for 63 years when he died in 1949 at the age of 92. She told about their daughter Rose Wilder Lane, who had become a novelist.

Laura also told about what happened to the members of her family. She said that her Ma and Pa had stayed on their homestead for a while before they moved permanently to town where Pa worked as a carpenter. Laura spoke of Mary who lived with Ma and Pa after she graduated from the College of the Blind. She said that Mary was always cheerful and busy, spending her time working, reading, and playing music.

Laura told about Carrie, who worked for the De Smet newspaper and then married a man who owned a mine. Carrie and her husband lived in Keystone, South Dakota, in the Black Hills. You will learn about the Black Hills in Lesson 104. Grace married a farmer, and she and her husband lived near De Smet. Laura outlived her parents and all of her sisters.

In all of Laura's books, she liked to tell about Pa's fiddle. She talked about it in her letter, too. She said that every year someone played Pa's fiddle in a public concert. They played the songs he used to play.

As in her books, Laura took the opportunity in her letter to talk about important things. She said that the real things haven't changed. She spoke of being honest and truthful, making the most of what we have, being happy with simple pleasures, being cheerful, and having courage when things go wrong. She said that the reason great improvements had been made in living was because every American has been free to pursue his happiness. She said that as long as Americans were free they would continue to make their country more and more wonderful.

Charles Ingalls is seated in the center. He is surrounded from left to right by Caroline, Carrie, Laura, Grace, and Mary.

During her long life, Laura witnessed dramatic changes in the way Americans live. Laura traveled on a covered wagon when she was a little girl, and when she was 87 years old, she flew on an airplane to visit her daughter Rose in Connecticut. Laura had hoped she would reach the age of ninety, and she died at home three days after her ninetieth birthday in 1957. In Laura's small Bible on the table beside the rocker where she sat to read was a list of Bible references written in her handwriting. The last one said, "And make Psalm 51 your prayer." It begins:

> Be gracious to me, O God, according to Your lovingkindness;
> According to the greatness of Your compassion blot out my transgressions.
> Wash me thoroughly from my iniquity and cleanse me from my sin.
> Psalm 51:1-2

Activities for Lesson 79

Thinking Biblically – Read Psalm 51, a favorite scripture of Laura Ingalls Wilder.

Vocabulary – In your notebook, write a definition for each of these words: diagram, plague, paymaster, surveyor, swollen. Compare your definitions with those in a dictionary.

Literature – Read "Thanksgiving Time" in *We the People*, pages 86-87, and "Blackbirds" in *Little Town on the Prairie*.

Timeline – In *Timeline of America the Beautiful* next to 1894, write: The Wilder family moves to Mansfield, Missouri.

Student Workbook or Lesson Review – If you are using one of these optional books, complete the assignment for Lesson 79.

Frontier Soldiers

Frontier Soldier Reenactors at Fort Larned, Kansas

As more Americans moved into the West, the U.S. Army built forts to help keep peace between the settlers and Native Americans who shared the land. The U.S. government made treaties with Indian tribes. Some of these defined what land belonged to Native Americans and what land was available for American settlers. Soldiers at the forts helped keep settlers off of the land that belonged to Native Americans. This is why the Ingalls family had to leave their little house on the prairie in Kansas (see page 455). The soldiers also worked to keep peace between tribes. Some forts were set up so that Native Americans could come there to get items the U.S. government had promised to give them. The frontier forts also helped keep peace along trails and during the building of railroads.

Sadly, the U.S. government often failed to keep the promises it made in treaties with the Indians. Indian warriors and U.S. soldiers fought many battles from the 1840s to the 1880s. Frontier forts were used as military headquarters and as supply depots during that time. The last major conflict was at Wounded Knee in South Dakota in 1890, during the presidency of Benjamin Harrison.

Fort Larned

The National Park Service oversees the Fort Larned National Historic Site in Larned, Kansas. Fort Larned is one of the best preserved and restored frontier forts. Here visitors can learn what it was like to participate in fort activities during the 1800s. Fort Larned is located along the Pawnee Fork of the Arkansas River.

Fort Larned was a frontier fort from 1859 to 1878. In 1859 the U.S. Army established Camp Alert. Men were housed in dugouts and tents. When Camp Alert was moved two and a half miles away, it was renamed Fort Larned. From 1866 to 1868 the Army built ten buildings out of native sandstone. The walls of the buildings were from two to two and a

461

half feet thick. Nine of the buildings are still standing. The buildings surround the parade ground. The flag flying today at Fort Larned has 37 stars, because the National Park Service is showing what fort life was like there in 1867. See the flag and parade ground at left.

Parade Ground at Fort Larned

The tenth building at the fort was the blockhouse, which has been reconstructed. The parade ground, all building exteriors, and more than forty interior rooms have been restored to show what daily life was like in a frontier fort. As seen in the photograph below, the area around Fort Larned has remained rural. This also helps visitors feel what it was like long ago.

Like most Western frontier forts, Fort Larned had no wall or stockade surrounding it. The Pawnee River surrounds the fort on three sides. This provided some protection and the wide, open prairie allowed soldiers to see possible attackers a long distance away. Native Americans never attacked the fort, but there often were enough Native Americans nearby that people could not leave the fort without a military escort. Tribes in the area included Arapahos, Comanche, Kowa, and Southern Cheyenne. At times Pawnee, Plains, Apache, and Sioux entered the area, too.

Fort Larned Beside the Pawnee River

Fort Larned is in the vast prairie of western Kansas. It was about mid-way on the Santa Fe Trail, which went from Independence, Missouri, to Santa Fe, New Mexico. Freight traffic was heavy on the 800-mile long trail. Fort Larned and other forts protected mail coaches, freight caravans, and passengers. When wagon trains traveled the Santa Fe Trail, they sometimes camped near the fort but not inside it.

The fort had an Indian Agency which tried to work out peaceful solutions to conflicts between Native Americans and settlers. The agency distributed commodities promised to the Indians in treaties, items such as food, domestic animals, and agricultural tools.

The town of Larned was founded in the 1870s. The Federal government sold Fort Larned in 1884, and it became a cattle and horse ranch. The fort became part of the National Park Service in 1966. All of the photographs in this lesson are modern ones taken at the restored fort. The people in the photos are reenactors who show what life was like at the fort in the 1800s.

Demonstrating Native American Culture

462

The Blockhouse

The blockhouse was originally built to protect residents at the fort from attack. It had gun slits so that soldiers could shoot from inside. Under the blockhouse was a tunnel that led to a well. If soldiers were ever under a siege, they would still be able to get water without going outside. The fort never had to use it this way. The blockhouse became a place to imprison soldiers needing discipline and to store supplies. See photos at right.

Reconstructed Blockhouse

Civilians at Fort Larned

Fort Larned used the services of many civilians, just as military forts do today. These civilians received high salaries to do blacksmithing, woodworking, and other crafts in this remote area. The Army also hired women to serve as laundresses. See the blacksmith, blacksmith shop, and workshop below.

Some officers brought their wives and children to the fort. A few enlisted soldiers brought their families as well.

Tunnel Under Blockhouse

Blacksmith Shop

Providing Food, Water, and Other Supplies

In addition to its well, Fort Larned had easy access to water from the river. The fort had to store food and other goods needed by the soldiers and civilians who lived there. Since the fort was so isolated, keeping it supplied was a

Ladies at the Fort

challenge. The wife of a major who was stationed at Fort Larned said, "It was indeed a work of art and genius to get up a respectable meal . . . . We really had to invent dishes from what we could procure."

Perishable food items were stored in a commissary. The fort bakery made fresh bread each day. However, they believed that it was healthier to eat it after it sat for two or three days on drying racks. See commissary and bakery on page 464.

Workshop

Bakery

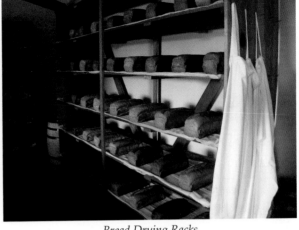

Bread Drying Racks

Today a commissary is where military personnel can purchase supplies for their own personal use. In 1824 the U.S. Army began allowing officers to purchase personal items at the same price the Army paid. Beginning in 1841, officers could purchase goods for their families. These privileges were expanded in 1867, so that enlisted men could also make these purchases.

At right below is pictured the quartermaster storehouse where the fort's non-perishable supplies were stored. Here were boots, flags, furniture, horse equipment, shoes, uniforms, wagons, and wagon parts. Today it is home to this rare 1835 Conestoga wagon. Many Conestoga wagons made the journey along the Santa Fe Trail. The wagon was also called a prairie schooner because it is a shaped like a boat.

Commissary

Conestoga Wagon in the Quartermaster Storehouse

Arms

Soldiers at the fort needed small arms as well as cannons. For a while they used rifles like the Springfield rifles pictured at right. They used the Mountain Howitzer cannon shown on page 465. Because of its relatively small size, it was easier to move than other cannons.

Springfield Rifles

Mountain Howitzer Cannon

Barracks Porch

Hospital

Housing

Officers and their families lived in the officers' quarters. Pictured below are rooms where lieutenants and captains lived. Soldiers with lower ranks lived in barracks like the one shown at the bottom of the page. A barracks porch is pictured below the cannon. The average number of men serving at the fort at one time was between 200 and 250. Wives and families of enlisted men stayed in adobe or sod houses that stood behind the barracks.

Quarters for Lieutenants and Captains

Hospital

Forts needed hospitals like the one shown above. Doctors took care of soldiers wounded in battle and those who got sick. More soldiers died of disease than from combat.

Famous People at Fort Larned

Enlisted Men's Barracks

Famous Western personalities William "Buffalo Bill" Cody, General Philip Sheridan, General Winfield Scott Hancock, and mountain man Kit Carson spent time at the fort, as did Lieutenant Colonel George Custer. Custer became well-known for his major defeat at the Battle of the Little Bighorn in 1876, the battle in which he lost his life.

Buffalo Soldiers

Soldier Reenactors

After the Civil War, Congress created four new cavalry regiments. Two of these, the 9th and 10th U.S. Cavalry units, were all African American units. White officers commanded America's first African American professional soldiers to serve during peacetime. Both units were sent to the West. The 10th Cavalry unit served for two years at Fort Larned.

The African American soldiers who served in the West were called "Buffalo Soldiers." The source of the nickname is unclear. Some believe that Plains Indians called them this out of respect for their fighting abilities. It is estimated that more than 12,000 African American men served in the military during the late 1800s.

When the apostle Paul wanted to encourage Timothy to stand firm, he told him:

> Suffer hardship with me, as a good soldier of Christ Jesus.
> 2 Timothy 2:3

Activities for Lesson 80

Literature – Read "Mary Goes to College," "Miss Wilder Teaches School," and "Snug for Winter" in *Little Town on the Prairie*.

Creative Writing – Write one page in your notebook describing how a settler would react to the presence of a frontier fort in his neighborhood, and then how a Native American would react to it.

Timeline – In *Timeline of America the Beautiful* next to 1859, write: Camp Alert, forerunner of Fort Larned, is built in Kansas.

Student Workbook or Lesson Review – If you are using one of these optional books, complete the assignment for Lesson 80. If you are using the Lesson Review, take the quiz for Unit 16.

Americans Move from the Farm to the Factory

Democrat Grover Cleveland became President in 1885. He was followed by Benjamin Harrison in 1889. Then came Grover Cleveland again in 1893! The beauties God created in Yosemite and Sequoia National Parks have awed generations of Americans and visitors from other countries. Thomas Edison opened up many new possibilities for people in America and all over the world when he invented a way to make electric lighting available in people's homes. Chicago, America's Windy City, hosted the World's Columbian Exposition in 1893 to celebrate the 400th anniversary of Columbus discovering America.

An 1884 illustration of a torchlight procession in New York City. Each man has attached to his hat an Edison incandescent lamp powered by a generator in the middle of the group.

Lessons in Unit 17

Lesson 81 – Our American Story: Democrats Make a Comeback
Lesson 82 – God's Wonders: God Created the Beauties of Yosemite and
                Sequoia National Parks
Lesson 83 – An American Biography: Thomas Edison, Inventor
Lesson 84 – An American Landmark: Chicago, the Windy City
Lesson 85 – Daily Life: The World's Columbian Exposition

Books Used in Unit 17

- *Maps of America the Beautiful*

- *Timeline of America the Beautiful*

- *We the People*

- *Little Town on the Prairie* by Laura Ingalls Wilder

Democrats Make a Comeback

America made many changes in the late 1800s. The economy moved from being based mainly on farming to being based mainly on industry. Cities grew as people moved from farms and small towns. Many immigrants also settled in cities when they arrived from Europe.

By the late 1800s, railroads could take farm goods and factory products across the country. Mail order catalogs became popular. Americans did not have to buy only what was grown by farmers or made by craftsmen near where they lived. They could look at catalogs at home, order goods by mail, and have them shipped across the country. See right.

Some business owners became greedy. While their factories grew larger and their wealth increased, they did not

Ordering from a Catalog

always treat their workers fairly. Individuals formed organizations called unions to try to help factory workers get more pay and have better working conditions. Sometimes union members refused to work until the business owner agreed to make the changes they wanted. This action is called going on strike.

Grover Cleveland Serves as President

In 1884 the Democratic Party nominated New York Governor Grover Cleveland as its candidate for President. Cleveland was a reformer who had fought for honesty in the government of New York. The Republican candidate was James G. Blaine from Maine. The election was very close, but Democrat Grover Cleveland was victorious. Cleveland was the first Democrat to be elected President since before the Civil War, when James Buchanan had won in 1856. (President Andrew Johnson was a Democrat, but he was not elected; he became President after the assassination of Abraham Lincoln.)

President Cleveland continued the reforms begun by Hayes, Garfield, and Arthur. He doubled the number of government jobs that were based on a person's ability. He made positive changes in the way the Federal government treated Native Americans, and he gave back some of their land. Some Native Americans were able to become American citizens and gained the right to vote. Railroad companies had a long history of corruption. Cleveland helped to make sure that they treated citizens and other businesses fairly.

Benjamin Harrison Serves as President

In 1888 the Democrats again nominated Cleveland. Republicans nominated Senator Benjamin Harrison from Indiana. Again the election was close, but this time Benjamin Harrison won. The most important law enacted during Harrison's presidency was the Sherman Antitrust Act of 1890. At the time, some large American businesses were working together in a way that made it difficult for small businesses to compete with them. These large businesses worked together secretly to raise prices. The Sherman Antitrust Act made some of these actions illegal. This helped businesses and consumers.

New States Admitted

1889 North Dakota
1889 South Dakota
1889 Montana
1889 Washington
1890 Idaho
1890 Wyoming

Six states entered the Union during Harrison's presidency: North and South Dakota, Montana, Washington, Idaho, and Wyoming. Read about President Harrison's life below.

Benjamin Harrison
America's Twenty-Third President
March 4, 1889 - March 4, 1893

Benjamin Harrison was born in 1833 in Ohio. He was the grandson of President William Henry Harrison and the great-grandson and namesake of Benjamin Harrison, a signer of the Declaration of Independence. Harrison grew up near his grandfather's estate and spent hours reading in his library. After learning at home with tutors, Harrison went to a preparatory school in Cincinnati and then to Miami University in Ohio. He married his college sweetheart, Caroline Lavinia Scott, in 1853 (pictured above left). They had one son and one daughter. Harrison studied law, became an attorney, and practiced in Indianapolis.

Harrison became a member of the new Republican Party, campaigning for John C. Fremont in 1856 and for Abraham Lincoln in 1860. Harrison entered military service in 1862. He rose to the rank of Brigadier General. He was with General Sherman when Union forces entered Atlanta. After the war, Harrison returned to his law practice in Indianapolis. From 1881 to 1887, Harrison represented Indiana as a U.S. Senator.

Harrison was the last Civil War general to serve as President. While he was President, he spent as much time as possible with his family. He usually left his office at noon. When the Harrisons moved into the White House, their son Russell (age 36), daughter Mary (age 32), and their families moved into the White House, too. Harrison loved playing with his grandchildren. Once he chased their goat, Old Whiskers, down the street carrying his top hat. When Harrison ran for a second term, he lost. When he lost, he told his family that he felt like he had been released from prison.

Caroline died of tuberculosis just two weeks before the 1892 election. In 1896 Harrison married his wife's niece, Mary Scott Lord Dimmick (pictured above right). He wrote two books, *This Country of Ours* (1897) and *Views of an Ex-President* (1901). Harrison died in 1901 at his home in Indianapolis, leaving his widow with their four-year-old daughter.

The Populists

Farmers wanted to be able to influence government decisions that affected them. They began to organize into groups to increase their influence. Some were called Grangers or The Grange. See poster at right. In many states, Grangers and other farm groups were called the Populist Party. Populist means "standing for the people." A national Populist Party was formed in 1891.

Cleveland Serves as President Again

In 1892 the presidential election was a rematch between Republican Benjamin Harrison, the incumbent, and former Democratic President Grover Cleveland. The Populists also nominated a candidate for President. Though the Populist candidate received over a million votes, the election was actually another close race between Harrison and Cleveland. This time it was the Democrat Cleveland who won. President Cleveland is the only U.S. President to serve two terms that were not consecutive. When you see a list of Presidents, Cleveland is listed twice; he is officially the twenty-second President and the twenty-fourth. Not until 1913 would another Democrat serve in the White House.

The new Populist Party sent five U.S. Senators and several Representatives to Washington, D.C., and they elected three state governors. About 1,500 Populists also won seats in various state legislatures.

Poster Promoting the Grange, 1873

The Panic of 1893

Soon after Cleveland was elected to a second term, America entered a serious economic recession. Many banks and businesses failed. Millions of people lost their jobs. Most people at that time, including President Cleveland, did not believe it was the responsibility of the Federal government to give assistance in such a situation. The economy improved and the Panic of 1893 ended by 1897. Utah became the forty-fifth state in 1896. Read about the life of President Cleveland on page 471.

New State Admitted
1896 Utah

Stephen Grover Cleveland
America's Twenty-Second and
Twenty-Fourth President
March 4, 1885 - March 4, 1889 and
March 4, 1893 - March 4, 1897

Stephen Grover Cleveland was born in New Jersey in 1837. His father was a Presbyterian minister. When the future President was four years old, his family moved to New York state. There he was educated at home and in village schools. Early in his life, he dropped his first name and was thereafter called Grover. His father died when he was sixteen. Cleveland moved to New York City to work with his brother at the New York Institute for the Blind. There he began a lifelong friendship with hymnwriter Fanny J. Crosby.

President Cleveland never graduated from college, but he studied law and became an attorney. Cleveland practiced law and held local political offices, including county sheriff and mayor of Buffalo, New York. He worked to clean up political corruption in local government. In 1882 he was elected Governor of New York. Two years later, Cleveland received the Democratic nomination for President.

Cleveland entered the presidency in 1885 as a bachelor. His sister Rose served as his First Lady. Cleveland became one of America's hardest-working Presidents. He usually worked until after midnight, sometimes until two or three o'clock in the morning. He paid for his own expenses and rejected usual presidential luxuries like the presidential yacht. He hated the fancy White House cooking, and said he would prefer pickled herring, Swiss cheese, and a pork chop.

In 1886 Cleveland became the first and only President to be married in the White House. His bride was Frances Folsom, the daughter of his former law partner. He was 49; she was 21. Rose Cleveland planned their simple June wedding. Frances Cleveland became one of the most popular First Ladies in American history. Women copied her fashions. Businesses attached her name and face to their products. People bought millions of scarves, postcards, and other objects decorated with pictures of Frances and her husband.

At right is an 1888 poster with pictures of the Clevelands. The text reads, "The City of Saint Louis Welcomes the National Democratic Convention." Cleveland won the nomination in 1888 but lost the election. When the Clevelands left the White House, Frances told a servant that they would be back in four years. Her prediction was correct. When the Clevelands returned to the White House in 1893, they had a baby daughter named Ruth. Ruth became popular across the country. The Clevelands had four more children.

After Cleveland left office, he invested in the stock market and practiced law. He wrote a book, *Presidential Problems*, became a trustee of Princeton University, and gave speeches.

Grover Cleveland died in 1908. His youngest child was only five years old. Cleveland's last words were, "I have tried so hard to do right."

National Democratic Convention Poster, 1888

At left is a stereoscopic photograph of President Cleveland. Cleveland devoted himself to his family and his country. In his policies, he was concerned with justice. This is a quality that God wants us all to have, especially people who are leaders:

The king gives stability to the land by justice,
But a man who takes bribes overthrows it.
Proverbs 29:4

*Grover Cleveland at His Desk in
Princeton, New Jersey*

Activities for Lesson 81

Map Study – Complete the assignments for Lesson 81 on Map 20 "The Lower 48" in *Maps of America the Beautiful*.

Vocabulary – Write a definition for each of these words: reformer, consumer, incumbent, recession, trustee. Look in the lesson for clues for the meaning of the words. When you are finished, look in a dictionary to check your definitions.

Literature – Read "Sears and Roebuck Catalog, 1897" and "Wedding in the White House" in *We the People*, pages 88-91, and "School Days" and "Sent Home from School" in *Little Town on the Prairie*.

Creative Writing – In your notebook, write two or three paragraphs that compare living in the country with living in the city.

Timeline – In *Timeline of America the Beautiful* next to 1893, write: An economic panic hits the United States.

Student Workbook or Lesson Review – If you are using one of these optional books, complete the assignment for Lesson 81.

God Created the Beauties of Yosemite and Sequoia National Parks

In Yosemite National Park, God shows His magnificent handiwork in granite cliffs, clear rivers and streams, tall waterfalls, groves of giant sequoias, and even glaciers. Here He creates spectacular views that change in every season. At right are some of Yosemite's granite peaks with Half Dome rising above the others. A lone cross-country skier swishes past on a nearby snow-covered upland.

Yosemite National Park is on the western edge of the Sierra Nevada Mountains in southern California. The park is about the size of Rhode Island. Nearby is Mount Whitney, the highest peak in the continental United States.

Cross-Country Skier in Yosemite

Yosemite Valley has some of the park's most beautiful views. The Merced River meanders through the valley. Look at the picture of the Merced River and Half Dome at left. Half Dome rises almost 5,000 feet above the valley floor.

The Granite Mountain Called Half Dome and the Merced River

Yosemite Valley covers seven square miles. Here visitors can walk through meadows and forests and see many of the cliffs and waterfalls that make the area famous. Standing in Yosemite Valley, visitors can see Three Brothers, El Capitan, and Cathedral Rocks, all pictured on this page.

Around the valley, beautiful waterfalls drop down from the granite precipices. Yosemite Falls, at 2,245 feet high, is the tallest waterfall in America and one of the tallest in the world. It is really three falls: Upper Yosemite Falls, the Middle Cascades, and the Lower Yosemite Falls. The photo at right shows the Upper and Lower Falls. Bridalveil Falls thunders in spring when the water flow is heavy and sways in the breeze when the water flow slows. Horsetail Falls appears to be on fire at sunset when the light reflects off of the falls. Other falls seen from the valley are Ribbon Falls, Nevada Falls, and Vernal Falls.

Yosemite Falls

El Capitan, c. 1865

Cathedral Rocks, 1865

Ecosystems of Yosemite National Park are varied because the highest point in the park is two miles higher than the lowest point. In summer visitors can see morning frost in the higher elevations and on the same day feel the temperature rise above ninety degrees in lower

Three Brothers Mountain

elevations. The park gets significant snowfall in the winter, which provides water for the park's waterfalls, rivers, and lakes.

Yosemite has grasses, rushes, and sedges, plus over one thousand species of flowering plants and ferns. It has thirty-seven different kinds of trees, including groves of giant sequoia trees. It is home to about ninety types of mammals, including the Sierra Nevada bighorn sheep, mountain lion, California wolverine, black bear, bobcat, mule deer, seventeen species of bats, and over thirty species of rodents.

Native Americans in Yosemite Valley

Native Americans lived in Yosemite Valley for centuries (see photo on page 11).The Miwok were there when the first known whites entered the area in 1851. Photographer Edward Curtis took the pictures of the Miwok man and woman at right.

Whites Enter Yosemite Valley

When whites entered Yosemite Valley in 1851, they came with the intention of driving the Indians away. One of the men with the party was a young doctor, Lafayette Bunnell. He was amazed at the beauty he saw. He called the area Yosemite, thinking mistakenly that it was the name of the local Indian tribe.

Miwok Man on the Merced, 1924

Miwok Woman with Sifting Basket, 1924

Nevada Falls, 1865

Four years later James Mason Hutchings led another group of whites into the Valley. Hutchings believed that he could make his fortune by bringing tourists to see California's beauty. He decided to build a hotel in Yosemite Valley. Hutchings came back in 1859 with a photographer. News of the valley's beauty spread, but because of the difficulty of getting there, only 653 people made the trip between 1855 and 1864. The photo of Nevada Falls at left was taken in 1865.

At the urging of conservationists (people who want to conserve natural resources), President Abraham Lincoln signed a bill in 1864 giving Yosemite Valley and the nearby Mariposa Grove of giant sequoias to the State of California. This was the first time the Federal government had taken

475

any step to protect natural beauty so that all Americans could enjoy it. Only eight years later, America would set aside the Yellowstone region as its first national park.

John Muir Works to Make Yosemite a National Park

John Muir and his family emigrated from Scotland to Wisconsin in 1849, when Muir was eleven years old. As a young man, Muir studied botany and geology at the University of Wisconsin, worked in industry, and drew botanical sketches while walking from Indiana to Florida.

John Muir later traveled by sailing ship around Cape Horn to San Francisco and then walked to the Sierra Nevadas. At first he worked as a sheepherder in the high country. In 1869 he came to Yosemite Valley to build a sawmill for James Mason Hutchings. In his free time, he explored the wonders of Yosemite. He came to love Yosemite and began a lifelong commitment to protect this and other American treasures. See photo of Muir at right.

John Muir, 1872

This is what John Muir said about Yosemite Valley:

> The far-famed valley came suddenly into view throughout almost its whole extent: the noble walls, sculptured into endless variety of domes and gables, spires, and battlements and plain mural precipices, all a-tremble with the thunder tones of the falling water. The level bottom seemed to be dressed like a garden, sunny meadows here and there and groves of pine and oak, the river of Mercy sweeping in majesty through the midst of them and flashing back the sunbeams.

In 1873 Muir began to write for *Harper's Weekly* and other magazines, telling about the amazing beauties of the natural world. His articles made him famous and also helped people think about what God had placed in America and how to protect these places so that their children and grandchildren would be able to see them, too.

Yosemite Falls from Glacier Point Trail, 1901

John Muir and others began working to make Yosemite a national park. They succeeded in 1890. Notice the photo from 1901 at left. At first the U.S. Army protected Yosemite. They wore traditional trooper hats. Later this became the hat worn by park rangers in all of America's national parks.

Muir's work helped to protect Glacier Bay in Alaska, Mount Rainier in Washington, and the Grand Canyon and Petrified Forest in Arizona. In 1903 Muir accompanied President Theodore Roosevelt on a three-day camping trip in Yosemite. See the photo at top of page 477. Muir helped Roosevelt become an even more committed conservationist.

Sequoia National Park

A few miles south of Yosemite is the only area in the world where giant sequoia trees grow naturally. Part of this area is now Sequoia National Park. Sequoia National Park is also home to Mount Whitney. At 14,494 feet, it is the tallest mountain in the continental United States. The only mountain in the U.S. that is higher is Alaska's Mount McKinley. Mount Whitney is not far from Death Valley, home to Badwater Basin, the lowest point in the United States.

The giant sequoia tree is named for the inventor of the Cherokee syllabary. It is a species of the redwood tree. A different species of redwood is the coastal redwood which grows naturally only in a small area near the coast

President Theodore Roosevelt and John Muir at Yosemite in 1903

of northern California and southern Oregon. Many of these trees are protected in California's Redwoods National Park. Though coastal redwoods grow taller, the giant sequoia is the world's largest tree. See examples below.

Giant sequoia trees are generally between 165 and 280 feet tall and 18 to 24 feet in diameter. They have been known to grow to a height of 311 feet and a diameter of 57 feet! The largest living giant sequoia is in Sequoia National Park, and it is also the largest tree in the world. This tree is called the General Sherman. It is 275 feet high and 25 feet across. Giant sequoias can live for thousands of years. The General Sherman is thought to be more than 2,000 years old. The oldest known giant sequoia tree began growing about 1,500 years

Giant Sequoias in Sequoia National Park

before the birth of Christ.

The bark of a giant sequoia is very thick, as much as three feet thick at the base. The bark protects the tree from fires. The giant sequoia is an evergreen which produces cones. Giant sequoias can have as many as 11,000 cones at one time. The number of cones helps assure germination of new trees. Seed cones can remain green for up to twenty years. The thick bark, number of cones, and length of time the seed cones remain green make the giant sequoia a very hearty tree.

Large numbers of giant sequoia trees were once cut for lumber. The wood resists decay, but it is brittle. The trees often shatter when they fall. The wood has been used as fence posts, shingles, and even matches. Believing these uses to be wasting such magnificent trees, conservationists worked to have the groves protected.

General Grant, the Nation's Christmas Tree

In 1924 Charles E. Lee of Sanger, California, stood beside a little girl at the General Grant tree, pictured at right. The girl said, "What a wonderful Christmas tree it would be!" The following year Sanger organized a ceremony at the tree at noon on Christmas Day. He wrote to President Calvin Coolidge, who designated the General Grant as the Nation's Christmas Tree in 1926. Each year the Chamber of Commerce in Sanger sponsors an annual "Trek to the Tree" on the second Sunday in December.

Giant sequoias stand tall and strong for centuries. God uses trees to illustrate people who trust in Him:

The General Grant

Blessed is the man who trusts in the Lord and whose trust is the Lord.
For he will be like a tree planted by the water, that extends its roots by a stream
and will not fear when the heat comes; but its leaves will be green,
and it will not be anxious in a year of drought nor cease to yield fruit.
Jeremiah 17:7-8

Activities for Lesson 82

Thinking Biblically – Read Psalm 148. In your notebook, draw a pencil sketch of one of the photographs in this lesson and write one or two appropriate verses from Psalm 148 under it.

Map Study – Complete the assignment for Lesson 82 on Map 2 "God's Wonders" in *Maps of America the Beautiful*.

Literature – Read "Galen Clark of Yosemite" in *We the People*, pages 92-93, and "The School Board's Visit" and "Name Cards" in *Little Town on the Prairie*.

Timeline – In *Timeline of America the Beautiful* next to 1890, write: Yosemite becomes a national park.

Student Workbook or Lesson Review – If you are using one of these optional books, complete the assignment for Lesson 82.

Thomas Edison, Inventor

Thomas Alva Edison was born in Milan, Ohio, in 1847. He was the youngest of seven children born to Samuel and Nancy Edison. Samuel was from Canada. His grandfather had moved to Canada during the American Revolution because he supported England. Nancy's father had served in the Continental Army during the Revolution.

When Thomas Edison was seven years old, his family moved to Michigan where he spent the rest of his childhood. In Michigan, Thomas went to school for a few months, but his teachers thought he was slow. He left school, and his mother taught him at home. Thomas came to love reading, which he enjoyed the rest of his life. He also liked to do experiments in the basement.

Edison enjoyed his mother teaching him. When he grew up, he said, "My mother was the making of me. She was so true, so sure of me; and I felt I had something to live for, someone I must not disappoint." As an adult, Edison also talked about his views of education. He did not like schools that taught children to memorize facts. He thought schools cast the brain into a mold instead of encouraging children to think. Edison thought children should observe nature and make things with their hands.

Thomas Edison, About Age 14

At age twelve, Edison began working. He sold newspapers and snacks on a train. At age fifteen, Edison saved a little boy from being hit by a train, and the boy's father helped him learn to be a telegraph operator. As part of his work, Edison took messages for the Union Army during the Civil War.

Edison enjoyed taking things apart to see how they worked and creating new devices. His first patented invention was an electric vote recorder. When it failed to be successful, he moved to New York. There he improved a machine that the stock market used. By age 23, he owned a company that manufactured his stock ticker. He also made improvements in the telegraph, enabling it to send as many as four messages at one time.

Edison's mother died in 1871. Later that year, Thomas married Mary Stilwell. He and Mary had three children. In 1876 Edison moved to Menlo Park, New Jersey, where he built a famous laboratory. He is often called the "Wizard of Menlo Park" because of what he invented there. Edison hired immigrants from all over the world to help him at his laboratory. He called them "muckers."

Sound Recordings

Today we hear recorded sounds almost everywhere. We can listen to music, speeches, and sermons. We don't have to just read what a President says; we can hear a recording of his voice actually saying it. Music plays on loudspeakers in restaurants and stores. Little babies listen to soothing lullabies recorded especially for them. Children listen to educational songs to learn math or history. Teenagers and young adults listen to music on personal listening devices. Adults listen to books as they commute back and forth to work. Almost everywhere we hear the varied ringtones of cell phones.

Before 1877 there was no recorded sound—anywhere. No one could hear a song being sung unless a real person was singing nearby. All that changed when Thomas Edison figured out how to record sound. He invented the first machine that could record a person's voice and play it back. It was called a phonograph. The first recorded words were the voice of Thomas Edison reciting "Mary Had A Little Lamb." Imagine your world with no sounds except those made by real people, real animals, and the clang and clatter of everyday life. The phonograph was Edison's favorite invention. He called it his "baby" and continued to improve it for fifty-two years.

Story about Edison from Frank Leslie's Illustrated Newspaper, *January 10, 1880*

The Light Bulb and Electric Power Plants

Another of Edison's most famous inventions was his incandescent electric light bulb, which he invented in 1879. Scientists had been working on this for at least fifty years, but Edison kept trying until he invented one that worked consistently. Not only did he invent a workable light bulb, Edison designed electric power plants and wiring that brought electricity to people's homes.

Think about your home, all its power outlets, and all the gadgets your family plugs into them. How would your life be different without them? Thomas Edison's inventions began to change life for Americans and for people in developed countries all over the world. At left is a full-page story about Thomas Edison and Menlo Park from an 1880 issue of *Frank Leslie's Illustrated Newspaper*.

Glenmont in West Orange, New Jersey

Thomas Edison's first wife died in 1884 when he was 37 years old. The following year he met Mina Miller, the daughter of a fellow inventor. She was nineteen. Edison liked to tell that he taught Mina how to use Morse code and that the two had secret conversations when other people were around. He also said that one day, he tapped her a proposal of marriage and she tapped back, "Yes." They married in 1886 and had three children.

Mina Edison wanted a country home, so Thomas bought a 29-room mansion called Glenmont with thirteen and a half acres in West Orange, New Jersey. Edison had used the Menlo Park laboratory for ten years, but he now built a new one in West Orange. It was one of the largest laboratory complexes in the world—ten times larger than Menlo Park. One of his new labs is pictured below. Edison and his "muckers" worked day and night. Once Edison himself worked for three days straight, with only short naps.

Among other inventions, Edison created the first talking doll; it had a tiny phonograph inside. He also experimented with X-rays. Not only was Edison an inventor; he was also a good businessman. First he and his employees invented. Then he figured out a way to manufacture his invention in one of the factories that surrounded his lab.

One of Edison's Laboratories in West Orange, New Jersey

Making Movies

Thomas Edison began to work on a device that "does for the eye what the phonograph does for the ear." People had been taking photographs for several decades, but Thomas Edison invented motion pictures (or movies). He made his first demonstration in 1891. Two years later he began to produce movies as a business. As he had done with the light bulb, Edison developed the complete system; he invented ways to film movies and to show them.

Edison, the Genius

In 1928 the U.S. Congress voted Thomas Edison a special medal of honor to recognize his lifetime of achievements. The world called Thomas Edison a genius, but he knew that it takes hard work to make a dream become a reality. Edison liked to say, "Genius is 1% inspiration and 99% perspiration." Thomas Edison took advantage of his circumstances, even the fact that he was hard of hearing. He believed that not hearing well was an advantage because it was easier for him to concentrate on his work.

Edison enjoyed a close friendship with Henry Ford, who invented the assembly line. Like Edison, Ford was leading America into the modern age. Ford's assembly line made automobiles affordable for many Americans. In 1929 America celebrated the fiftieth

Thomas Edison (left), Naturalist John Burroughs, and Henry Ford at Edison's Home in Florida, 1914

anniversary of the incandescent light bulb. As part of the celebration, Ford gave a banquet at Greenfield Village in Edison's honor. President Herbert Hoover attended the banquet. Greenfield Village was Ford's new American history museum, where he had a complete restoration of Edison's laboratory at Menlo Park. Edison and Ford are pictured together at left.

Thomas Edison died in 1931 at the age of eighty-four. During his lifetime, he received 1,093 United States patents, more than anyone else in American history. Edison illustrated the value of diligence:

A lazy man does not roast his prey,
but the precious possession of a man is diligence.
Proverbs 12:27

Activities for Lesson 83

Thinking Biblically – Read Proverbs 10:4, 12:24, 13:4, and 21:5. Choose one of these to copy in your notebook. Write one or two paragraphs about how Thomas Edison is an example of diligence.

Vocabulary – Write a paragraph using all of these words: laboratory, gadget, patent, manufacture, genius. Consult a dictionary if you need help with their definitions.

Literature – Read "One of My Closest Friends" in *We the People*, pages 94-95, and "The Sociable," "Literaries," and "The Whirl of Gaiety" in *Little Town on the Prairie*.

Timeline – In *Timeline of America the Beautiful* next to 1879, write: Thomas Edison invents the incandescent light bulb.

Family Activity – Create a "Thank You, Thomas Edison!" Book. See pages 962-963 for instructions.

Student Workbook or Lesson Review – If you are using one of these optional books, complete the assignment for Lesson 83.

Chicago, the Windy City

In 1630 the Illinois tribe settled in the area near the mouth of the Chicago River, on the southwestern shore of Lake Michigan. The name "Chicago" means striped skunk. The Miami and Illinois tribes also used this word for wild leeks. Since wild leeks grew near the Chicago River, Indians began to use the word as their name for the river.

A Modern View of Chicago with the Chicago River, Taken from Over Lake Michigan

French explorers came about forty years later. They began using the name Chicago to refer to the land at the mouth of the Chicago River. French Jesuit missionaries operated the Mission of the Guardian Angel in the area during the last few years of the 1600s.

Jean-Baptiste Point DuSable is considered the first permanent resident of Chicago. He was a fur trader from Haiti. DuSable built a mansion and an estate in the Chicago area around 1790. He moved away ten years later. Chicago's Museum of African American History is named the DuSable Museum in his honor.

Around 1800 the United States government acquired a piece of land at the mouth of the Chicago River from local Native Americans. They built Fort Dearborn there in 1803. Soldiers and their families lived inside the fort. Fur traders, including those employed by Astor's American Fur Company, lived north of the river. South of the fort were a few homes and businesses. Indians destroyed Fort Dearborn in 1812; the Army rebuilt it in 1816.

As seen in the picture at right, Chicago had only a small number of homes and businesses in 1820; but the village began to grow. A Baptist preacher came to Chicago in 1825 and a Methodist church was established in 1831.

In 1830 a street system was designed for the Chicago settlement. In 1831 ferry service began across the Chicago River and the following year a bridge was constructed.

CHICAGO IN 1820.

Chicago: From Town to Major City

In 1833 Chicago was incorporated as a town within Cook County, Illinois. By 1890 it had grown to be the second largest city in the United States. In some ways the history of Chicago is like the history of other cities, but in other ways it is unique.

One important factor in Chicago's growth is its geography. God created a wide open plain next to Lake Michigan. Chicago had plenty of room to build homes, businesses, roads, and railroads on land that was flat. Here the Chicago River empties into the lake. Both Lake Michigan and the Chicago River have provided the city with water, which people have used in many ways. The water also gave Chicagoans a way to transport goods made in Chicago and the surrounding area.

This lesson will feature a timeline of the growth of Chicago. The timeline will help us learn about how American cities have grown and give us some clues about why Chicago became the "Heart of America," a nickname that refers to Chicago's role as a transportation center. Chicago has many nicknames. Another is "The Windy City." Its location beside Lake Michigan causes it to experience a great deal of windy weather.

Chicago was a town for only four years. During this time, St. Mary's Catholic Church was formed and Chicagoans founded the Chicago Bible Society to spread God's word. Residents enjoyed their first local theatrical performance. The first school of music opened. Entrepreneurs built the first ship constructed in Chicago and opened the city's first slaughterhouse. Kind people founded the Cook County Almshouse to help the poor.

Chicago was incorporated as a city in 1837. In 1838 the city hosted its first ballet performance. Chicago would soon grow into a major center for grain shipments. The first large grain shipment left the city in 1839.

The 1840s

Chicago had a population of 4,470 in 1840. Early in the decade, the city's first hospital was founded. Several religious institutions began, including the first Jewish synagogue, the German Lutheran-Missouri Synod, an African Methodist Episcopal congregation, and the first Catholic school. Chicago's first orphanages were established in the 1840s.

Chicago Board of Trade, 1900

Chicago's telegraph service started and the *Chicago Tribune* newspaper began publication.

As Chicago continued to be a center for selling grain raised by farmers in the Midwest, the Chicago Board of Trade was established to coordinate grain sales to markets in the East. At left is a photograph of the Board of Trade in 1900. In 1847 Cyrus McCormick, the great inventor of plows and reapers, moved to Chicago and built a successful reaper factory.

Shipping on the Chicago River

The location was ideal, since so many farmers lived in the Midwest.

The city's first railroad was built in the 1840s, and the Illinois and Michigan Canal was completed. The canal connected the Chicago River and the Illinois River. Since the Illinois River empties into the Mississippi, the canal made it possible to send goods to New Orleans. See photo of the Chicago River at left.

The 1850s

By 1850 Chicago's population had grown to 29,963. That year the first horse-drawn omnibuses began service. By the end of the decade, street railways were being used with horses pulling cars along the rails. In 1850 gas lighting was installed in Chicago. In 1853 Cook County built a new courthouse and Chicago built a new city hall. In 1855 Chicago established its first official police department. Three years later, its policemen began to wear uniforms instead of regular clothes and the city began to pay firemen a salary.

In 1855 Chicago became the world's largest port for grain shipments. That year the Chicago, Rock Island, and Pacific Railroad formed. Three years later the North Chicago Rolling Mill Company was built to produce steel and iron rails for railroads.

The city's first opera and first orchestra were organized in 1850. The first baseball game in Chicago was played the following year. The city hosted the Illinois State Fair in 1855. Northwestern University was founded in 1851, and Chicago Medical College (later Northwestern University Medical School) in 1859.

During the 1850s, the First Congregational Church was organized. Two Christian schools, Wheaton College and Chicago Theological Seminary, were founded. In 1853 a Young Men's Christian Association (YMCA) began. St. James Episcopal Church was completed in 1857.

Old Fort Dearborn was still standing during this decade. Notice the 1856 drawing of Fort Dearborn at right. The drawing also includes an industrial building, a lighthouse, and a steamboat.

Fort Dearborn and Surroundings, 1856

The 1860s

In 1860 Chicago was home to 112,172 people. That year the city hosted the Republican Party's national convention, the first of many political conventions to be held in Chicago. The party nominated Abraham Lincoln for President; five years later his funeral train would come through Chicago.

During the 1860s, Chicago's first steel mill opened. The Pullman Palace Car Company began to build railroad cars near Chicago. The Borden's milk condensing factory was built

Two Views of Union Stock Yard

Chicago White Stockings Baseball Cards
Adrian "Cap" Anson, 1887 and 1888

in nearby Elgin in 1866. The Union Stock Yard was established to transport beef. See two views at left. In 1868 the first shipment of refrigerated beef to be transported by railcar arrived.

In 1861 eight Protestant groups formed the Old Ladies Home to provide a retirement home for elderly women. Cook County Hospital opened in 1866. Two years later the first Jewish hospital was founded in Chicago.

The Lincoln Park Zoo opened in 1868.

The 1870s

In 1870 Chicago's population was 298,977. In 1871 the Chicago White Stockings baseball club was organized. They later came to be called the Chicago Cubs. See the baseball cards at lower left. That same year a group of farmers formed a grange organization in Chicago. They called it the Order of Patrons of Husbandry.

The most remembered event of the decade occurred on October 8. See box below.

The Great Chicago Fire

On October 8, 1871, a fire broke out in a barn owned by Mr. and Mrs. Patrick O'Leary. That day the wind was blowing at gale-force. The barn fire grew into what is called the Great Chicago Fire. It burned a three-and-a-half square mile section in the heart of Chicago. Eighteen thousand buildings were destroyed. One hundred thousand Chicagoans lost their homes. The city received help from around the world and quickly rebuilt. Builders began using steel and iron to make buildings less vulnerable to fire. In just twenty-two years, Chicago was ready to invite the world to visit. See Lesson 85.

As Chicago was rebuilding after the Great Fire, the city hired its first African American police officer. Montgomery Ward and Company sent out the world's first mail order catalog. In 1879 Chicagoans organized the Chicago Bicycle Club and played the city's first recorded game of football. The Chicago Public Library opened in 1872. The Art Institute of Chicago began in 1879. It has become one of the world's premier art institutions.

The 1880s

By 1880 the population of Chicago had reached 503,185. In 1882 the Chicago City Railway cable car system began operation. Three years later a new city hall and courthouse opened, as did the ten-story Home Insurance Building, Chicago's first skyscraper. The Chicago Conservatory of Music and Dramatic Art was founded in 1884.

Chicagoans formed their first soccer league in 1883, and in 1887 it hosted America's first pro heavyweight wrestling championship.

During that decade, the Children's Memorial Hospital and the Presbyterian Hospital opened. The Journal of the American Medical Association began. The Salvation Army organized a chapter in Chicago in 1885. In 1889 Moody Bible Institute was established. Moody and other organizations made Chicago a center for missionary training. The Catholic population of Chicago continued to grow. By 1889 the city had sixty convents.

Ryerson Laboratory at the University of Chicago

The 1890s

In 1890 Chicago was recognized as the second largest city in the United States with 1,099,850 people. Chinese immigrants there began a Chinese newspaper in 1893.

During the decade, Chicago's first oil refinery opened as did the Chicago Ship Building Company. In 1891 William Wrigley began selling soap and including free baking powder. Later he gave chewing gum away with his soap. The popularity of the chewing gum caused him to switch to making gum. In 1896 a Chicago company began to sell caramel-coated popcorn under the name Cracker Jack. The company had been started by German immigrants two decades before. In 1912 they began putting a small toy in every box.

Both the University of Chicago and the Chicago Symphony Orchestra were founded in 1891. The Art Institute of Chicago constructed its art museum and the Field Museum of Natural History opened. See photos of the University of Chicago above and the Field Museum at right. In 1893 Chicago hosted the World's Columbian Exposition. See Lesson 85.

In 1895 Sears, Roebuck and Company moved to Chicago. By the late 1890s, Chicago was the bicycle-building center of America. The Arnold

Field Museum of Natural History, 1905

Schwinn Company formed there that year. Notice the broken bicycle on page 488. The blacksmith has horseshoes on the floor while looking at the newer invention that is turned upside down in front of him.

By 1900 Chicago's population had grown to 1,698,575. That year a new professional baseball team was organized. They called themselves the Chicago White Stockings, just as Chicago's first professional baseball team had done. The name was later shortened to the White Sox. See the baseball card at lower right.

About 170 people in Chicago owned a car in 1900, just one out of every 10,000 Chicagoans. However, the rest of its well-developed transportation system made it possible for Chicago businesses and industries to send goods all over the world. That same transportation system made it possible for Chicago to send Christian missionaries all over the world, too.

A blacksmith attempts to repair a bicycle.

Go therefore and make disciples of all the nations,
baptizing them in the name of the Father and the Son and the Holy Spirit,
teaching them to observe all that I commanded you;
and lo, I am with you always, even to the end of the age.
Matthew 28:19-20

Activities for Lesson 84

Map Study – Complete the assignment for Lesson 84 on Map 3 "American Landmarks" in *Maps of America the Beautiful*.

Literature – Read "Burned Out of House and Home" in *We the People*, page 96, and "The Birthday Party," "The Madcap Days," and "Unexpected in April" in *Little Town on the Prairie*.

Creative Writing – Write a letter in reply to the one from Justin you read in *We the People*.

Timeline – In *Timeline of America the Beautiful* next to 1871, write: Much of Chicago is destroyed by fire.

Student Workbook or Lesson Review – If you are using one of these optional books, complete the assignment for Lesson 84.

Freddy Parent
Chicago White Sox, 1911

The World's Columbian Exposition

American leaders wanted to organize a World's Columbian Exposition to commemorate the 400th anniversary of Columbus sailing to the New World. St. Louis, New York City, Washington, D.C., and Chicago lobbied for the opportunity to host the exposition. Community leaders from these cities gathered ideas and resources and lobbied the U.S. Congress to choose their city. In the end, Congress chose Chicago.

Exposition Halls

The exposition was held in 1893 and was modeled after London's Crystal Palace Exhibition of 1851. Exposition planners chose architects to design fourteen ornate exposition buildings. One would house exposition offices; the others would house thousands of exhibits. These structures looked like palaces. Most were coated with plaster of Paris and painted white. The collection of buildings was dubbed the White City. See photo below.

Forty-three American states and territories as well as twenty-three foreign countries also erected buildings to showcase their exhibits. These exhibit halls varied greatly from the fourteen great buildings erected by exposition planners. Virginia built a reproduction of George Washington's home, Mount Vernon; Massachusetts, a reproduction of John

Scene from the Grounds of the World's Columbian Exposition

Four Boys Enjoy the Exposition

Hancock's home; and Florida, a reproduction of St. Augustine's Fort Marion. Vermont reproduced Pompeii, an ancient Roman town. In all the fair boasted two hundred buildings.

Arriving at the Exposition

Twenty million visitors paid fifty cents for admission into the World's Columbian Exposition. Visitors came from across America and from foreign countries. Some guests entered the fair on foot through the street entrance. Others came by boat and entered the fair from a pier on Lake Michigan. Most arrived at the fairgrounds by train. Four young attendees are pictured above.

The Palace of Mechanic Arts

Exhibits at the Exposition

Guests explored the grounds of the exposition with its many waterways, like the Venetian Canal shown on page 491. They walked past beautiful buildings like the Palace of Mechanic Arts at left. Inside the buildings, they saw halls crammed with exhibits. Most of the large "palaces" had one large exhibition room with a high ceiling.

The exhibition room in Machinery Hall was 435,500 square feet, bigger than seven football fields! Inside were Eli Whitney's cotton gin, the exposition's power plant with its forty-three steam engines, and numerous other mechanical devices.

Unusual exhibits at the fair included a U.S. map made of pickles, a 22,000-pound cheese from Canada, John Quincy Adams' baby clothes, a California redwood tree, a full-scale model of an ocean liner, the first locomotive in the United States, an

Trained animals line up with trainers and clowns.

ancient Etruscan chariot, a medieval knight made of prunes, a necklace belonging to Pocahontas, a giant aquarium, the real Liberty Bell, a Liberty Bell made of oranges, and trained animals. See the trained animals above.

Art masterpieces from America and Europe were displayed, including works by Winslow Homer, John Singer Sargeant, Mary Cassatt, and Augustus Renoir. Guests could view the manuscript of *Jane Eyre* in Charlotte Bronte's own handwriting as well as costumes from around the world. Visitors could also listen to the music provided by the Columbian Chorus and the Columbian Orchestra.

Long Boat on the Venetian Canal at the World's Columbian Exposition

The Mines and Mining building had a model of the Statue of Liberty made entirely of salt and a statue of an actress made entirely of silver. The Horticultural Building had eight greenhouses. Among the brightly-colored exhibits were a recreated Mexican desert, a Japanese garden, and 16,000 varieties of orchids. Fairgoers could walk through Wooded Island with its five hundred thousand pansies and one hundred thousand roses. Even the Wooded Island had exhibits: a Hunter's Cabin that honored Davy Crockett and Daniel Boone and a group of buildings exhibiting 12th, 16th, and 18th century Japanese architecture.

Exposition Meetings

More than seven hundred thousand people listened to addresses given at meetings called World Congresses. Speakers presented 5,978 addresses! Speakers included future presidential candidate William Jennings Bryan and future President Woodrow Wilson.

The Electricity Building

The most popular spot at the exposition was the Electricity Building. One exhibit was a large home fitted with all of the household electrical appliances one could buy at the time. Here visitors saw electric lamps, elevators, fans, sewing machines, burglar alarms, stoves, laundry machines, and irons. Also in the Electricity Building were the kinetoscope, an individual motion picture viewing station invented by Thomas Edison, as well as his 82-foot Tower of Light with over 18,000 light bulbs.

The Exposition Midway

On the Midway, fair visitors stepped into hanging cars and got an aerial view of the 633-acre fairgrounds on the giant wheel designed by George Washington Ferris. It is pictured at lower right. They also took rides in a hot-air balloon that was tethered to the ground. They walked through the Moorish Palace, with its funhouse mirrors and wax museum. They swam in the Natatorium. Visitors went sleighing on an 875-foot long track covered with artificial ice and snow.

Attendees strolled through models of an Austrian village, an Algerian village, Old Vienna, a street in Cairo, a Chinese village, an East Indian bazaar, a glass factory, and the Penobscot village pictured on page 30. They could also see models of the Eiffel Tower and St. Peter's Basilica, a diorama of Hawaii's Kilauea volcano, an ostrich farm, and dancers from Brazil. The German village held eight thousand guests. Two German military bands gave concerts daily.

George Washington Ferris' Invention Became Known as the Ferris Wheel

After Sundown

When the sun went down, visitors watched a water and music show featuring colored fountains. They waited for the

The Illuminated World's Columbian Exposition

park to be lit by electricity. Particularly spectacular were the thousands of electric lights that decorated the gilded dome of the exposition's Administration building. Notice the nighttime scenes above and on page 494. Every night fireworks went up over Lake Michigan.

After they finished enjoying the Midway and learning from the speeches and exhibits, some visitors headed to a performance of Buffalo Bill's Wild West Show, which was playing just outside the exposition grounds.

Impact of the World's Columbian Exposition

The World's Columbian Exposition began in May and continued through October of 1893, but it had a lasting impact on America. Henry Ford saw an internal combustion engine while visiting the fair. It inspired him to dream about designing a horseless carriage. Americans who visited the fair or who just saw it on postcards and in newspapers and magazines remembered it for the rest of their lives. Many of the exhibits went to museums around the country, including some to the Smithsonian. Fair exhibits helped start Chicago's Field Museum. A 140-room fair building became Chicago's Museum of Science and Industry.

We might wish to go back in time to see the displays of the World's Columbian Exposition, with so many items from so many places together at one time. However, if we open our eyes and look around us, we can see more wonderful displays day after day. God displays His handiwork every day on the earth and in the heavens.

O Lord, our Lord,
How majestic is Your name in all the earth,
Who have displayed Your splendor above the heavens!
Psalm 8:1

Activities for Lesson 85

Vocabulary – Find each of these words in a dictionary: lobby, ornate, dub, pier, manuscript. Choose the definition that corresponds to the way the word is used in this lesson. Copy the words and definitions into your notebook.

Literature – Read "The Glories of the Fair" in *We the People*, pages 97-98, and "Schooltime Begins Again," "The School Exhibition," and "Unexpected in December" in *Little Town on the Prairie*.

Creative Writing – Imagine that you are chairing the committee to design and execute a display from your state for the World's Columbian Exposition. In your notebook, write 1-2 pages of detailed ideas. Think of how your display could showcase your state's cities, natural areas, historic sites, famous citizens (that lived before 1893), and farm products. Describe some appropriate souvenirs and food items that you could sell. Include a simple sketch of your display.

Timeline – In *Timeline of America the Beautiful* next to 1893, write: The World's Columbian Exposition is held in Chicago.

Student Workbook or Lesson Review – If you are using one of these optional books, complete the assignment for Lesson 85. If you are using the Lesson Review, answer the questions on *Little Town on the Prairie* and take the quiz for Unit 17.

The Illuminated World's Columbian Exposition

America Enters A New Century

While President McKinley prepared to lead America into the new century, American troops fought a war with Spain. In the early 1900s, farmers in the Midwest learned how to grow large amounts of grain in America's Breadbasket. Immigrants arrived by the thousands at Ellis Island, being welcomed by the Statue of Liberty. John Philip Sousa wrote patriotic marches and entertained Americans with his band. A tiny minority of Americans, like the Vanderbilt family, lived like royalty in America's grandest mansions.

Lessons in Unit 18

Lesson 86 – Our American Story: America Fights a War with Spain
Lesson 87 – God's Wonders: God Created America's Breadbasket
Lesson 88 – An American Landmark: The Statue of Liberty and Ellis Island
Lesson 89 – An American Biography: John Philip Sousa, Patriotic Composer
Lesson 90 – Daily Life: The Vanderbilts in Their Grand Mansions

Books Used in Unit 18

- *Maps of America the Beautiful*

- *Timeline of America the Beautiful*

- *We the People*

Dutch children at Ellis Island, c. 1905

America Fights a War with Spain

Members of the Republican Party believed they had a good chance to put a Republican back in the White House in 1896. During the Panic of 1893, Americans lost jobs, businesses failed, and banks closed. When these things happen, the President and his political party usually get the blame, either for causing them to happen or for not doing enough to fix the problems. Since Democrat Grover Cleveland was in office while Americans suffered during the panic, he was blamed.

McKinley Campaign Poster, 1896

The Election of 1896

In 1896 Republicans nominated Ohio's Governor William McKinley. When the Democrats met for their national party convention in Chicago, they nominated William Jennings Bryan, a former member of the House of Representatives from Nebraska. Bryan gave a powerful speech at the convention. The speech was called "Cross of Gold." Both McKinley and Bryan were good and honest men.

President McKinley Giving a Speech in Quincy, Illinois

During the 1800s, men running for the presidency did not campaign for themselves as they do today. They let their supporters do that. In the 1896 campaign, McKinley gave speeches from the front porch of his home in Ohio. Notice his campaign poster above. Bryan, on the other hand, broke tradition by giving about six hundred speeches in twenty states.

McKinley won the election. He was the last Civil War veteran to be elected President. After he became President, McKinley traveled across the country meeting the people he served, making speeches, and attending ceremonies. At left he is shown giving a speech in Quincy, Illinois. He traveled more than any President up until that time.

"Separate But Equal"

The economy improved after McKinley became President. However, conditions continued to be difficult for African Americans. The Civil War had been over for thirty years, but most blacks still did not enjoy the same rights that whites had. In several southern states, blacks could not vote. In some places they had to pay a tax before they could vote. It was called a poll tax. Some states required voters to be literate (able to read and write), and many blacks had not learned these skills.

Across America blacks and whites were kept segregated. Segregation laws had been passed to keep people with different skin colors apart. In many places blacks and whites could not attend the same schools or ride in the same passenger railroad cars.

In 1896 the U.S. Supreme Court made a decision in the *Plessy v. Ferguson* case. In their decision, the Court said that segregation was legal. They said that blacks and whites could be kept separate as long as the facilities they had were of equal quality. This practice became known as "separate but equal." In reality, most facilities for blacks were inferior; but this was often ignored by whites.

America's Relationship to the World

The major question that President McKinley faced was how the United States would be involved in the world. Some leaders of American industry wanted the United States to have colonies in other parts of the world as did England, Germany, and France. Some Americans were afraid America would be left behind economically. Items that an industry uses to make its products are called raw materials. American industrialists wanted to get raw materials more easily from other parts of the world. They also wanted more people in other parts of the world to buy their products.

American Christians were interested in the rest of the world because they wanted to share the gospel with people in other countries. In 1900 about 18,000 Americans were serving as foreign missionaries.

While McKinley was President, some Chinese attacked foreigners living in China, including many missionaries. This was called the Boxer Rebellion. President McKinley sent 2,000 American troops to China to help control the situation. Twice he intervened in Nicaragua to protect American property there. However, McKinley's major foreign relations problem involved Spain.

The Spanish-American War of 1898

Ninety miles south of Florida is the island of Cuba. At that time, it was controlled by Spain, but Spain was not managing it well. Some Cubans decided to revolt, and many Americans supported them. The Spanish government treated the rebels harshly. President McKinley wanted to show Spain that America was serious about supporting freedom and justice. In 1898 he sent a battleship, the USS *Maine*, to the harbor in Havana, Cuba. While sitting in the harbor, the *Maine* blew up and sank. More than two hundred fifty American sailors died. No one knows for sure why the ship blew up, but many Americans blamed Spain and wanted the United States to go to war against Spain. They cried, "Remember the

Colonel Theodore Roosevelt and His Rough Riders
After the Battle of San Juan Hill

Maine!" President McKinley tried to use his ambassadors and diplomats to keep America out of a war with Spain, but his efforts did not succeed.

On April 20, 1898, the U.S. Congress declared that Cuba was independent. It gave the President authority to use military force to make Spain leave Cuba. Congress promised that the American military would leave Cuba when the U.S. was convinced that Cuba was truly independent.

American forces invaded Cuba. McKinley's Assistant Secretary of the Navy was future President Theodore Roosevelt. He resigned his post to lead a military unit called the Rough Riders into Cuba. Roosevelt and his Rough Riders participated in the Battle of San Juan Hill to help take control of the harbor in Santiago, Cuba. See photo above. African American Buffalo Soldiers also played an important role in the battle.

In August Spain and the United States signed an armistice which ended the fighting. Later that year they signed a treaty which ended the conflict. The United States gained control of Cuba and Puerto Rico in the Caribbean Sea as well as Guam and the Philippines in the Pacific Ocean.

The United States suddenly had a world empire. It soon experienced some of the problems of having an empire. Some Filipinos did not want to be ruled by the Spanish, but they did not want to be ruled by Americans either. (Filipino is the term for someone who is a native of the Philippines.) The U.S. military fought with them until 1902. The United States sent a territorial Governor to the Philippines, future President William Howard Taft.

The 1900 Election

After he returned home from the Spanish-American War, Theodore Roosevelt was elected Governor of New York in 1898. In 1900 President McKinley was again nominated as the Republican presidential candidate. Roosevelt was nominated as the vice-presidential candidate. See campaign poster at right. The Democrats nominated William Jennings Bryan again. Once more McKinley was victorious.

The Assassination of William McKinley

McKinley was inaugurated for his second term in March of 1901, becoming the first President of the new century. In late summer, he attended the Pan-American Exposition in Buffalo, New York, which was in part a celebration of the new century. It also celebrated

McKinley Campaign Poster, 1900

America's power and influence in the world. Like the World's Columbian Exposition in 1896, it displayed electrical power and other marvels of the new century. On September 6, President McKinley gave a speech at the exposition. Later that day, he stood in a receiving line to shake hands with visitors. A Polish American from Detroit who opposed all government authority shot McKinley. Secret Service agents wrestled the man to the ground as McKinley said, "Go easy on him, boys." The President was taken to the house were he had been staying. Eight days later the President died from his gunshot wound. Read about the President's life below.

William McKinley
America's Twenty-Fifth President
March 4, 1897 - September 14, 1901

William McKinley was born in Ohio in 1843. He was the seventh of eight children. His parents were committed to training their children well while providing them with a happy childhood. His mother was a devout Christian who taught him to pray and to be courteous and honest. His father taught him to have a respectful attitude and to work hard. As a child, William enjoyed fishing, horseback riding, hunting, ice skating, and swimming. As a youth, McKinley thought he would become a Methodist minister. He studied hard at a local Methodist seminary before entering Allegheny College in Pennsylvania. Illness and difficult finances allowed him to stay for only one term.

When the Civil War began, McKinley joined the Twenty-Third Ohio Volunteer Infantry. He entered as a private and became a valiant soldier. He rose to become a commissioned officer, serving under Colonel Rutherford B. Hayes. McKinley considered Hayes to be his mentor. This relationship continued for the rest of McKinley's life. By the end of the war, McKinley was a brevet major.

After the war, William McKinley returned to Ohio, went to Albany Law School, passed the bar exam in 1867, and began working as a lawyer. He met Ida Saxton at a picnic in 1869. Ida was a Sunday School teacher. She was interested in art, architecture, and current events. She was employed at the bank her father owned. William and Ida were married in 1871. During the first five years of their marriage, Ida McKinley gave birth to two daughters. One died at four months and the other at four years. Her mother also died during this time. Ida never fully recovered from these losses, and she also developed epilepsy. Sometimes her health improved, but it was often poor. William McKinley served her as a devoted husband.

Before his election to the presidency in 1896, McKinley served as county prosecutor, a member of the U.S. House of Representatives, and Governor of Ohio. McKinley personally suffered during the Panic of 1893 because he had co-signed a loan taken out by a friend, who went bankrupt during the panic. As Governor, McKinley worked to smooth relationships between labor (workers) and those who owned and managed companies.

McKinley lived as a Christian gentleman. While serving as President, he continued to be sensitive to the needs of his wife. Ida McKinley was able to participate in both of her husband's inaugurations. In the White House, he had his wife sit by his side at dinners. This was a major change in previous custom. Though often ill, Mrs. McKinley was able to give him excellent advice. Sometimes she was able to participate in events, but sometimes she had to sit quietly in a chair. While serving in the White House, McKinley usually spent his evenings answering letters, taking walks, going on carriage rides, or playing cards with his wife or with his personal secretary. McKinley enjoyed dressing up. He always wore a carnation in his lapel. Sometimes he gave it away to show his affection to people. One favorite outfit was a boiled white shirt with starched collar and cuffs, pin-striped trousers, a black frock coat, and a black satin tie.

Ida McKinley accompanied her husband to his final speech. She left the exposition afterward to rest. Mrs. McKinley was not with the President when he was shot. After the shooting, the President said to his private secretary, "My wife, be careful, Cortelyou, how you tell her—oh, be careful." An ambulance rushed the President to a hospital nearby. Doctors believed he would recover, but his wounds got infected and he died eight days later. Ida survived him by six years.

William McKinley remembered his mother's teaching and often prayed before making important decisions. He prayed before he decided to go to war with Spain and only agreed to do so because he thought it was necessary to help Cuba gain its freedom. According to witnesses present at his death, McKinley's last words were the words to the hymn, "Nearer, My God, to Thee." The poster of McKinley with his wife and mother at right was made after his death.

In remembering his mother's teaching, William McKinley was obeying God:

McKinley with His Wife and Mother

> My son, observe the commandment of your father
> And do not forsake the teaching of your mother;
> Bind them continually on your heart;
> Tie them around your neck.
> Proverbs 6:20-21

Activities for Lesson 86

Map Study – Complete the assignments for Lesson 86 on Map 21 "The Spanish-American War" in *Maps of America the Beautiful*.

Vocabulary – Write five sentences in your notebook, using one of these words in each: poll, literate, segregation, gospel, armistice. Check in a dictionary if you need help with their definitions.

Literature – Read "Old Glory" in *We the People*, page 99.

Creative Writing – Why did some Americans want colonies in other parts of the world? What are some of the good and bad results of larger, richer countries establishing colonies in smaller, poorer countries? Write one page answering these questions in your notebook.

Timeline – In *Timeline of America the Beautiful* next to 1898, write: The Spanish-American War is fought.

Student Workbook or Lesson Review – If you are using one of these optional books, complete the assignment for Lesson 86.

God Created America's Breadbasket

A Modern Grain Harvest

When God created the land we call America, He included some of the best farmland in the world. The farmlands of Illinois, Indiana, Iowa, Kansas, Michigan, Minnesota, Missouri, Nebraska, North Dakota, Ohio, South Dakota, and Wisconsin are called America's Breadbasket. Here God provides long growing seasons with hot summers to make plants grow rapidly. God gave the region fertile soils and placed essential minerals in them. See harvest at left and crop below.

Though the area experiences occasional droughts, the region's total amount of rainfall is usually about the same every year. God sends most of the rain between April and the start of November, just when farmers need it. God also placed water in underground layers called aquifers. Farmers can dig wells to use this water, too.

Field of Sunflowers Near Fargo, North Dakota

The state with the most land dedicated to farming is Nebraska. Iowa is second. Many fields in America's Breadbasket are huge, like the field of sunflowers on page 501. Most of the land in America's Breadbasket is flat or gently rolling, making it easy to plant, care for, and harvest crops. Flat fields in Indiana are pictured at right.

Rectangle Farm Fields at a Crossroads in Indiana

Crops of the Breadbasket

The Midwest is ideal for growing corn, and it is the main crop in the region. By the end of the twentieth century, corn had become the most important agricultural product in the United States. Corn grows so fast here that some farmers think they can hear it growing. God has designed every corncob to have an even number of rows, usually fourteen or sixteen. Each row has forty to fifty kernels each, making the average ear have between 560 and 800 kernels! Other important crops grown in America's Breadbasket include wheat, oats, soybeans, sorghum, barley, and sunflowers. See barley, oats, and products made from them below.

Farming specialties have developed in some places. Wisconsin and central Minnesota are ideally suited for dairy farming. The Great Lakes moderate the weather in Michigan, making it a good place for growing fruit. Fruit trees in Michigan tend to blossom after the last frost of spring. The main fruit crops there are apples and sour cherries. Grapes are important, too.

Corn

Barley, Oats, and Products Made from Them

Becoming America's Breadbasket

When Major Stephen Long led an expedition through the plains of Kansas, Nebraska, and Oklahoma in 1819 and 1820, he said: "I do not hesitate in saying that the entire area is almost wholly unfit for cultivation, and of course uninhabitable by people depending upon agriculture for their subsistence." To Long, the only purpose of this "Great American Desert" was a buffer zone in case Mexico decided to invade America.

Long was completely mistaken. Before Americans began farming the region, much of it was covered with many varieties of thick prairie grass. Farmers soon learned that land that grows prairie grasses well is also good for growing grains. Such large amounts of treeless land were good places to grow large fields of grain.

The homesteaders who settled in America's Breadbasket came from other parts of America and from European countries such as Germany, Russia, Sweden, and Norway. What immigrants learned before coming to America benefited others who lived

Tractor, Plow, Horse-Drawn Wagon, and Horse-Drawn Tank in South Dakota, 1910

here. For example, Russian Mennonites brought Turkey Red winter wheat seeds to Kansas from Russia in 1874. Soon this variety became the dominant kind of wheat grown in Kansas. In 2007 Kansas grew 375 million bushels of wheat. Turkey Red winter wheat makes up half of it.

Inventions designed in the 1800s made it easier for homesteaders to farm in the region. The steel-tipped plow, invented by John Deere of Vermont, made it easier to break up the prairie sod. Windmills helped to bring up water from underground aquifers. Mechanical reapers, like those Cyrus McCormick was making in Chicago, greatly increased what one man could harvest. Farmers first used oxen to pull their farm equipment. By the 1870s, horses and mules had taken the place of most of the oxen. Farmers later used steam engines to power their farm equipment. In many places, farmers did not have to buy every machine that was available because men took the machines from farm to farm. After the gasoline-powered engine was perfected in the 1890s, it became the dominant source of power for farm machinery. Notice the farm equipment above.

Storage, Transportation, and Markets

Businessmen built grain elevators, like those below. These could store large amounts of the grain that farmers grew. With such abundant grain, farmers could provide food for distant places in America and around the world. Railroads took the grain to markets.

Grain Storage Elevators and Freight

As cattle drivers drove cattle to northern markets after the Civil War, they found good grazing lands along the way. Much of the land on the Great Plains that could not grow grain became pasture land for large herds of cattle.

The need to transport grain helped cities like Cincinnati, Ohio; Chicago, Illinois; and Kansas City, Missouri grow. From these cities, products could be sent on to other cities in the East and to international ports like New Orleans. Businessmen also built factories so the grain could be turned into products for consumers.

Today farmers pay attention to grain markets around the world. They use computers in their homes and barns to keep track of the markets. They use this information to decide the best time to harvest their grain in order to receive the best prices.

Grains Waiting to Be Shipped to Foreign Ports

People created in God's image used the talents and resources God gave them to find ways to make America's Breadbasket a farmer's paradise. Today this region helps to feed not only the United States, but much of the rest of the world. Notice the sea containers of grain above. Jesus tells us that God cares for us and makes sure we have food, but He also taught us that spiritual food is more important than food that feeds our bodies. He told His disciples that He had food to eat that they did not know about. He tells us:

Do not work for the food which perishes, but for the food which endures to eternal life, which the Son of Man will give to you, for on Him the Father, God, has set His seal.
John 6:27

Activities for Lesson 87

Thinking Biblically – Read Ruth 2 to learn about farming during Old Testament times and how someone showed great generosity with his grain crops.

Map Study – Complete the assignment for Lesson 87 on Map 2 "God's Wonders" in *Maps of America the Beautiful*.

Vocabulary – In your notebook, write the following vocabulary words and the letter of the definition that goes with each word: mineral, aquifer, moderate, subsistence, buffer.

a. a protective barrier
b. an underground layer of rock, sand, or gravel that contains water
c. naturally occurring substances usually obtained from the ground
d. a way of obtaining what is essential to life
e. to decrease the strength or intensity of

Timeline – In *Timeline of America the Beautiful* next to 1874, write: Russian Mennonites bring Turkey Red winter wheat seeds to Kansas.

Student Workbook or Lesson Review – If you are using one of these optional books, complete the assignment for Lesson 87.

The Statue of Liberty and Ellis Island

Clockwise from Top Left: Liberty Island, The Statue of Liberty, Ellis Island, and the Ellis Island Immigration Station

In the harbor of New York City are two of America's most treasured symbols of freedom and opportunity: the Statue of Liberty and the immigration station on Ellis Island. Here millions of people have been inspired by the ideas of freedom and liberty.

Immigrants, soldiers returning from Europe after World War II, and modern tourists from America and around the world have all experienced the same exhilaration when seeing the Statue of Liberty. Lady Liberty has become the most recognizable symbol of freedom in the world. While Ellis Island was active as an immigration station, over twelve million immigrants stepped off ships and walked into its Great Hall. They entered Ellis Island with dreams of a new life of freedom and opportunity in America. See photos above.

The Story Behind "Liberty Enlightening the World"

In 1865 sculptor Frederic Auguste Bartholdi and Edouard Laboulaye, chairman of a French abolitionist society, were at a dinner party in France. Laboulaye believed that the United States had proved democracy successful by surviving the Civil War. At the dinner party, he suggested that if a monument to U.S. independence were created, it should be a joint work between the people of America and the people of France. Several years later, as the one hundredth anniversary of American independence approached, Laboulaye encouraged Bartholdi to look into creating a monument. See the photo of Bartholdi below.

Bartholdi began to sketch ideas for a liberty monument. The sculptor toured the United States in 1871 promoting his idea. In 1875 Laboulaye formed a committee to oversee the project. The committee approved Bartholdi's plaster model and began raising six hundred thousand francs to complete the project. Laboulaye sent a formal request to President Grant asking that the committee be allowed to erect the monument, officially named "Liberty Enlightening the World."

Frederic Bartholdi, 1880

Bartholdi began working on the statue. First he created the hand and torch. This portion was sent to the United States where it was displayed at the Centennial Exposition in Philadelphia in 1876. It was later shipped to New York where it was displayed at Madison Square Garden.

President Grant signed a bill in 1877 stating that the monument would be placed on Bedloe's Island in New York harbor. Americans began raising money for a pedestal on which the statue would stand. In 1878 the head and shoulders were completed and displayed at an exposition in Paris. Alexander Gustav Eiffel, who later built the Eiffel Tower, designed the inner framework of the statue.

"Liberty Enlightening the World" was completed in 1884. That year the cornerstone was laid for the pedestal on Bedloe's Island. In 1885 the statue was taken apart and put into crates to travel by ship to America. The ship almost sank in a storm on the way, but the statue arrived safely in June. In November Bartholdi came to the United States. In 1886 Americans completed the pedestal. A decision was made to light the torch with electricity. In October of 1886 Bartholdi held a formal dedication on Bedloe's Island. President Grover Cleveland presided over the ceremony. When the statue was erected, it was the tallest structure in New York City. It became known affectionately as the Statue of Liberty.

Emma Lazarus was a descendent of Jewish immigrants from Portugal. She lived in New York City. In 1883 she wrote a sonnet about the statue called "The New Colossus." In 1903 a bronze plaque of the poem was placed inside the statue's pedestal.

Facts about the Statue of Liberty

The Statue of Liberty is encased with 3/32-inch thick copper. The thickness of the statue is about the same as a stack of two pennies, also made of copper. Since it is covered with

The Current Torch

copper, the statue has turned green. Copper naturally oxidizes to form a green patina. In many places the patina is as thick as the copper itself. The patina protects the copper from wearing away.

Bartholdi made the statue a woman because in ancient Greece and Rome liberty was often represented by a woman. It is believed that the woman's face is modeled after Bartholdi's mother Charlotte. Lady Liberty is gigantic. From the ground to the tip of the flame, she is three hundred five feet and one inch tall. Lady Liberty's eyes are each two feet and six inches across; her nose is four feet and six inches long; her mouth is three feet wide; her right arm is forty-two feet long; her index finger is eight feet long; and her waist is thirty-five feet wide! The steel inside the statue weighs 120 tons and the copper weighs thirty-one tons.

The Statue of Liberty has been standing outside in the weather for over one hundred years. When the wind blows fifty miles per hour, she sways up to three inches. The torch sways up to six inches. Since the Statue of Liberty is made of copper, it attracts lightning and is hit several times each year.

The original torch is now on display in a lobby at the base of the statue. It was replaced in 1986 when the entire statue was carefully restored. The new torch is made of copper, covered with 24-karat gold leaf. In the daytime the torch shines when sunlight reflects off the gold. See above. At night sixteen floodlights illuminate the torch.

Lady Liberty wears a crown with twenty-five windows which symbolize gemstones. The crown's rays represent heaven's rays shining over the world. There are seven rays to symbolize the seven seas and the seven continents of the world. See photo at right. She holds a tablet which represents a book of law. On the tablet are the Roman numerals for July 4, 1776.

The Statue of Liberty became a National Monument in 1924. It became part of the National Park Service in 1933. Before this the Lighthouse Board and the War Department took care of the statue. In 1956 Bedloe's Island was renamed Liberty Island. Nearby Ellis Island was added to the National Monument in 1965.

Lady Liberty

Ellis Island Welcomes Immigrants to America

On January 1, 1892, Ellis Island officially opened as an immigration station. The first immigrant processed there was Annie Moore, a fifteen-year-old girl from County Cork, Ireland. She arrived in the United States on the USS *Nevada*. At left is a bronze statue of Annie Moore.

In the late 1800s, thousands of immigrants were coming to America from Europe. Many came first to New York harbor. The U.S. government wanted to make sure that people entering the country had adequate finances, did not have legal problems, and were healthy. First and second class passengers were examined while still onboard their ships. Government officials believed that there was less risk that those immigrants would be poor or sick. If first or second class passengers were found to have legal or medical problems, they were sent to Ellis Island for further examination. See the photo of a person undergoing a legal inspection below.

Statue of Annie Moore

Most of the immigrants who came to Ellis Island had traveled as third class or steerage passengers (steerage passengers had traveled together in a large open area in the bottom of a ship). When immigrants entered the main building, they came into the Registry Room (or Great Hall), pictured below. Here doctors examined them quickly. The doctors became very good at diagnosing many problems in their "six-second" examinations. Those who were sick with minor ailments were cared for in a complex of hospitals on the island.

Legal Inspection

After the immigration officials decided that a person qualified legally, medically, and financially, the immigrant was allowed to enter the United States. Many of the immigrants worried about whether they would pass all the required examinations, but ninety-eight percent were admitted. Others were sent back home. See a badge, hat, and desk used by the United States Immigration Service on page 509.

Immigrant Inspection in the Great Hall

Dining Hall

Government officials allowed businesses called concessionaires to sell food and other items. Notice the dining hall at left and the concessionaire plate and cash register at right.

Before Ellis Island opened, immigrants who came into New York were processed by state officials and not by the Federal government. From 1855 to 1890, New York processed immigrants at Castle Garden, a fort built for the War of 1812. When the number of immigrants rose in the late 1800s, Castle Garden could not handle them all.

The United States had purchased Ellis Island from the state of New York in 1808. President Benjamin Harrison designated it as the site of a new immigration station in 1890. The original island had only 3.3 acres. Between 1890 and 1892, it was greatly expanded by the use of landfill. As more facilities were added, the island grew to 27.5 acres. Much of the dirt came from excavation done to create the New York City subway system.

Plate and Cash Register Used by Ellis Island Concessionaires

The Ellis Island immigration station was built during the height of the homesteading era, when millions came to America to get free land or to settle in America's growing cities. After it opened, construction workers tried to keep up with the needs of more and more

Desk, Badge, and Hat Used by United States Immigration Service

509

immigrants, building hospital buildings, dormitories, kitchens, and wards for those with contagious diseases. They also built corridors to protect employees and patients from strong winds on New York harbor.

Ellis Island

New York was not the only place that immigrants entered the United States, but the Statue of Liberty and Ellis Island have become lasting symbols of immigration. The main use of Ellis Island as an immigration station was between 1892 and 1924. The busiest year at Ellis Island was 1907, when workers processed 1.25 million immigrants. As the way immigrants came to the United States and how they were processed changed, Ellis Island was no longer needed as an immigration station. It was used for other purposes until it was closed in 1954. It was opened to tourists in 1976.

In the words of Emma Lazarus, the Statue of Liberty speaks to the world, saying, "Give me your tired, your poor, your huddled masses yearning to breathe free." America has offered freedom to millions. Jesus offers the truest freedom to everyone:

Come to Me, all who are weary and heavy-laden, and I will give you rest.
Take My yoke upon you and learn from Me, for I am gentle and humble in heart,
and you will find rest for your souls.
Matthew 11:28-29

Activities for Lesson 88

Thinking Biblically – Read Jeremiah 22:3. Write one paragraph in your notebook about the way God wants us to treat strangers, aliens, or immigrants.

Map Study – Complete the assignment for Lesson 88 on Map 3 "American Landmarks" in *Maps of America the Beautiful*.

Literature – Read "Gains at Ellis Island" in *We the People*, page 100-101.

Creative Writing – Imagine that you are in charge of immigration to the United States. What questions would you ask an incoming immigrant to help keep Americans safe? Make a list of at least ten questions in your notebook.

Timeline – In *Timeline of America the Beautiful* next to 1886, write: The Statue of Liberty is unveiled.

Student Workbook or Lesson Review – If you are using one of these optional books, complete the assignment for Lesson 88.

John Philip Sousa, Patriotic Composer

John Philip Sousa

For over one hundred years, the sight of fireworks on the Fourth of July and the sounds of "The Stars and Stripes Forever" have gone hand in hand. John Philip Sousa, pictured at left, wrote songs that made Americans swell with pride. When great numbers of immigrants were coming to America, his music helped bind Americans together. It still does.

John Philip Sousa was born in 1854 in Washington, D. C., the son of immigrants. His father was John Antonnio Sousa, who was born in Spain of Portuguese parents. His mother was Maria Elisabeth Trinkhaus. She was born in Bavaria in Germany. John Philip grew up around the music of a military band; his father was a trombonist in the U.S. Marine Band.

When John Philip was around six years old, he began to study at a private music conservatory. He studied alto horn, baritone, cornet, flute, piano, trombone, violin, and voice. His father gave him additional instruction on the trombone. Even as a child, he could play a musical score almost perfectly the first time he saw it. He also had what is called perfect pitch.

During the Civil War, his parents took him to visit wounded soldiers. Being in Washington at this time gave him the opportunity to hear military bands. When he was ten or eleven, his father began taking John Philip to Marine Band rehearsals, where he was allowed to play the triangle, cymbals, or the alto horn.

Sousa and "The President's Own"

When John Philip was thirteen years old, he was tempted to run away with a circus band. His father enlisted him as an apprentice musician for the Marines. The younger Sousa continued to take music lessons. He studied musical composition, harmony, and violin. When Sousa was eighteen years old, he published his first musical composition, "Moonlight on the Potomac Waltzes."

John Philip Sousa was discharged from his apprenticeship with the Marines at age twenty-one. He began to give performances on the violin. He worked as a violinist in

Washington and Philadelphia. By the time he was twenty-five years old, he was conducting on Broadway in New York City. It was there that he met Jane van Middlesworth Bellis in 1879. They were married later that year.

John Philip took his new bride to Washington in 1880. At age twenty-six, he became the leader of the U.S. Marine Band. The U.S. Marine Band is known as "The President's Own." Sousa conducted the band during the presidencies of Hayes, Garfield, Cleveland, Arthur, and Harrison. Under his leadership, the Marine Band became one of the world's finest bands.

Sousa's Band

In 1892 Sousa left the Marine Band so he could bring quality music to millions of people. His new civilian band began performing in September of 1892. Within months it became respected as one of the finest bands in the world, on a par with the world's leading orchestras. Bands were very popular in America during the late 1800s and early 1900s. Small towns had their own bands. A band is similar to an orchestra, but it has no string instruments. Instead, it has a higher percentage of woodwind instruments.

Sousa is credited with the idea for a new musical instrument, the Sousaphone. He said that while he conducted the Marine Band, the band used a BB-flat bass tuba. Sousa thought the instrument was fine for parades but was too prominent for concerts. He spoke with J. W. Pepper, who manufactured instruments in Philadelphia. He gave Pepper the idea of making a bass instrument in which the bell could be pointed upward for indoor concerts. Pepper called the new instrument the Sousaphone.

Sousa hired the highest quality musicians and soloists and paid them well. Through the years, some of the world's most famous artists performed with him. Each year his band toured America. He became the first American superstar. When his band came to a small town, the day was declared Sousa Day. Schools and businesses shut down for the day. Notice the crowd attending a concert at Chautauqua, New York, pictured below.

Audiences enjoyed watching Sousa conduct his band. His posture was straight and tall. He kept his feet firmly in one place, but his arms, wrists, hands, and head led his band with emotion. It was easy for the audience to see his hands, because he wore a new pair of white gloves at every concert.

Sousa was good at choosing which music to play at a concert and the order in which to play it. He believed that people came to hear music, not to hear him talk, so the program was packed with music with very few pauses. When other bands were going out of business after movies and radio came to America in the 1920s, the Sousa Band still played

The Sousa Band performs at Chautauqua, New York.

to standing room only crowds. John Philip Sousa also kept up with news events and sometimes changed his program at the last minute to bring a piece of music to his audience that would be meaningful at the time. Shortly after the death of President McKinley, the Sousa Band played the first part of a concert in Ohio. When it came time for intermission, the audience saw him raise his baton. To a hushed and tear-filled crowd, Sousa led his band in "Nearer, My God, to Thee."

People the world over flocked to see Sousa and his band. It performed at the 1900 Paris Exhibition. See the picture at right. Sousa took his band on a world tour in 1910 and 1911. Starting and ending in New York, they performed in Great Britain, the Canary Islands, South Africa, Australia, New Zealand, the Fiji Islands, the Hawaiian Islands, Canada, and the United States. In addition to the world tour, the band made four tours of Europe.

The Sousa Band performs at the 1900 Paris Exhibiton.

The Sousa Band played both popular and classical songs. When attending a Sousa performance, audiences were assured of hearing every piece played to perfection. When performing Sousa made pleasing his audience his first priority. Sousa believed that by entertaining his audiences, he could introduce them to good music. He carried music to many people; his band performed 15,498 times between 1892 and 1931. In the photo at left, he conducts on a city street.

Sousa Conducts on a City Street

Sousa, the Gentleman

From childhood John Philip Sousa was industrious and optimistic. He had great talent and the self-discipline to put his great talent to use. In all he did, he tried his hardest and succeeded. Sousa was a humble man who was tolerant of other people. He had a wonderful disposition. People enjoyed being around him. He sought to share his love of country with other Americans.

Sousa's personal morals were extremely high. One of his managers said that he gave the impression of trying to be the most honorable man who ever walked on the face of the earth. Sousa was curious and eager to learn. His home had a library of three thousand books, and he wrote several novels. He enjoyed riding horses and other outdoor activities.

Sousa generously contributed his time and energy to projects, such as the National School Band Contests, the National Music Camp, and the American Bandmasters Association, of which he was Honorary Life President.

Sousa had deep respect for his mother, who encouraged him to follow her teachings. Keeping Sunday as a special day was especially important to her. He did not write songs on Sunday. He arranged several hymns and played them only during Sunday concerts. He wore a white uniform when performing on Sunday; on the other six days, he usually wore black.

Sousa's concert schedule often kept him away from home. This was difficult for his wife and three children. However, he did enjoy his time at home. He was good at engaging his family in conversation around the dinner table. Notice photos of family members on this page.

John Philip and Jane Sousa

Sousa, the Composer

In addition to leading his band, Sousa continued to write music. He wrote many kinds of music. In his lifetime, he wrote over two hundred songs for operettas. His first successful operetta was called *El Capitan*. It debuted in 1895. He also wrote seventy other vocal works. All his life he studied the music of other composers. He believed that Johann Sebastian Bach was the best composer in history.

Sousa the composer is remembered as "The March King." While serving as the conductor of the Marine Band, he wrote "The Washington Post March." It became the most popular song in America and in Europe. Sousa and his wife went on a European vacation in 1896. On the way back to America, he wrote "The Stars and Stripes Forever." It became his most famous march. Sousa believed that a march should "make goose pimples chase each other up and down your spine."

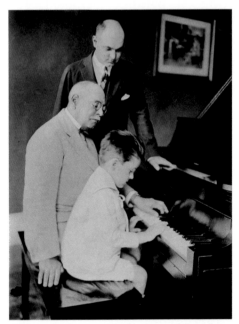
John Philip Sousa with His Son and Grandson

Sousa had an amazing memory. He composed songs in his head and wrote them down from memory. He often wrote in ink, making few changes or corrections. Sometimes he sent a musical piece to his publisher without ever having heard it played on the piano.

The Library of Congress has autographed manuscripts of most of John Philip Sousa's songs. Sousa worked to help fellow composers with copyright laws. He went before Congress twice to try to protect the rights of people who wrote music, so that they were able to benefit financially from their work and not have their compositions stolen by other people. He was one of the first members of ASCAP, the American Society of Composers, Authors, and Publishers. ASCAP protects the rights of its members by making sure they are paid when someone performs their work.

Lieutenant Sousa

During World War I, John Philip Sousa joined the U.S. Naval Reserve. He was sixty-two years old. He was given the rank of lieutenant and was paid a salary of $1 per month. He organized a band at the Great Lakes Naval Training Station. At right he is pictured leading the Great Lakes Navy Band.

Sousa continued to work tirelessly. He said, "when you hear of Sousa retiring, you will hear of Sousa dead." On March 6, 1932, John Philip Sousa conducted a rehearsal for a band in Reading, Pennsylvania. That night he attended a banquet given in his honor. He died the following morning in his hotel. He was seventy-seven years old.

John Philip Sousa's music lives on. Music has been in the world almost since the beginning. It is first mentioned in Genesis:

Sousa Leads the Great Lakes Navy Band

His brother's name was Jubal; he was the father of all those who play the lyre and pipe.
Genesis 4:21

Activities for Lesson 89

Thinking Biblically – Sousa worked to make sure that people who wrote music got the money for their work. Copy 1 Timothy 5:18 in your notebook.

Vocabulary – Write a definition for each of these words: conservatory (musical), score (musical), discharge (military), civilian, copyright. Look in the lesson for clues for the meaning of the words. When you are finished, look in a dictionary to check your definitions.

Literature – Read "Experiences of a Bandmaster" in *We the People*, pages 102-104.

Timeline – In *Timeline of America the Beautiful* next to 1896, write: John Philip Sousa writes "The Stars and Stripes Forever."

Family Activity – Host a Sousa Band Concert. See page 964 for instructions.

Student Workbook or Lesson Review – If you are using one of these optional books, complete the assignment for Lesson 89.

The Vanderbilts
in Their Grand Mansions

Immigrants were pouring into Ellis Island and then moving into crowded apartments in New York City or boarding trains to head west to humble homesteads. American families who had been in the country for generations were working in factories and starting new businesses in small towns. Meanwhile, a tiny number of Americans were living like royalty in grand mansions. The extravagant lifestyles of these wealthy few Americans has caused this time period to be called the Gilded Age. Homes of members of the Vanderbilt family are open today for visitors to see how the wealthy lived then. In this lesson we will learn about the Biltmore Mansion in Asheville, North Carolina; The Breakers in Newport, Rhode Island; and the Hyde Park estate in Hyde Park, New York.

Cornelius "Commodore" Vanderbilt and His Son William Henry Vanderbilt

Jan Aertsen van der Bilt came to America from the Netherlands around 1650. His descendants lived on Staten Island in New York. Cornelius Vanderbilt was born into this family in 1794. He and his wife Sophia were married fifty-three years. They had thirteen children, thirty-seven grandchildren, and twenty-seven great-grandchildren.

Cornelius "Commodore" Vanderbilt

Cornelius Vanderbilt began in business at age sixteen, when he established what would become the Staten Island ferry. He later worked as an apprentice on sailing ships, steamships, and transatlantic cargo carriers to learn all he could about shipping. He then built a shipping empire, becoming a millionaire by the time he was fifty years old. When he was seventy years old, he sold his shipping business and began to buy railroads. At right is a *Harper's Weekly* magazine cover from 1877 with his picture.

Cornelius Vanderbilt began a family tradition of living in grand mansions. He also began a family tradition of philanthropy. Because of his involvement with shipping, Cornelius was known as "Commodore," the name of a naval officer. Commodore Vanderbilt gave one million dollars to a Methodist university in Nashville, Tennessee. It became Vanderbilt University; its sports teams are called the Commodores.

Harper's Weekly Illustration of
William Henry Vanderbilt

When Cornelius Vanderbilt died, he left most of his $100 million estate to his oldest son, William Henry Vanderbilt, pictured at left. In his lifetime, William Henry doubled the money his father had left him. He was also a philanthropist, giving large sums to the Metropolitan Opera and the Medical School of Columbia University. William Henry built a mansion on Fifth Avenue in New York City. In its fifty-nine rooms, he displayed the more than two hundred paintings he collected. William Henry and his wife Maria Louisa had eight children. In time, each of his children had mansions on Fifth Avenue, plus vacation mansions by the sea or in the countryside. Let's look at vacation mansions owned by three of his children—Cornelius, George, and Frederick.

Cornelius Vanderbilt II

Cornelius Vanderbilt II, grandson of Commodore Vanderbilt, was born in 1843. He became president and chairman of the New York Central Railroad and served on the boards of directors of forty-nine other railroads. Cornelius II also served on the board of a theological seminary, a hospital, and the New York YMCA. He was known as a pious man. He gave generously to charities. Cornelius II and his wife Alice had six children.

The Breakers

Cornelius Vanderbilt II bought thirteen acres of ocean-front property in Newport, Rhode Island. A wood and brick home on the property was called The Breakers because Atlantic Ocean waves broke onto the rocks on the property. This home burned in 1892.

The Breakers

The following year, Vanderbilt hired architect Richard Morris Hunt to design a seventy-room home. Hunt designed a five-story fireproof home of Indiana limestone built on a framework of steel trusses. See photo above. The new home, also called The Breakers, was completed in two years. To make this possible, many of the rooms were constructed in Europe, taken apart, and then reassembled in Newport.

In the center was a Great Hall with a forty-five foot ceiling and a grand spiral staircase. The interior was decorated with marble from Italy and Africa. Library walls were walnut paneling and gold-embossed leather. Dining room columns were made of alabaster. Hunt hired Paris designers to create furniture and fixtures.

Floor Lamp

The home boasted these two modern inventions: an elevator and electric lights. See a floor lamp at left. Bedrooms were on the second floor. Each bedroom had an adjoining bathroom equipped with hot and cold fresh water as well as hot and cold saltwater from the ocean. Mrs. Vanderbilt's

Lavish Rooms Inside The Breakers

bathroom had a marble bathtub that weighed one ton. Rooms from the mansion are pictured above.

Cornelius and his wife Alice used The Breakers as a vacation home, where they gave lavish parties. Three hundred guests attended their housewarming party in 1895.

Visitors entered a thirty-foot gate decorated with the initials CV and with the acorns and oak leaf seal used by the Vanderbilt family. The grounds were designed by Ernest Bowditch, a student of Frederick Law Olmsted, known as the father of American landscape architecture. A gardener and his staff cared for indoor plants and outdoor flowers used in arrangements. Notice the indoor plants in the lower right photograph above.

The Vanderbilts' daughter Gladys inherited The Breakers from her parents. She and the Preservation Society of Newport County preserved the home and opened it as a museum.

George Washington Vanderbilt III

Cornelius II's brother George was born in 1862. He was quiet and intellectual. He was educated at home by private tutors and also attended private schools. He loved books and began collecting books as a child. During his lifetime, he collected twenty-three thousand. They are in the library at the Biltmore Estate. At age twelve, he began to write down the books he read and each author's name. He numbered these entries. He continued the practice the rest of his life. The last entry was number 3,159, which made an average of eighty-one books a year.

George Washington Vanderbilt III did not go to college, but he was an avid learner who helped others learn. He gave generously to the Columbia University Teacher's College in New York City and helped begin one of the first public lending libraries in America. It eventually became part of the New York Public Library system.

George Vanderbilt enjoyed traveling. He made his first trip to Europe at age ten. As an adult, he went to either Europe, Asia, or Africa almost every year. While on a vacation in the Blue Ridge Mountains of North Carolina in 1888, he saw for the first time the site of his future home, which would become the largest residence in America.

The Biltmore Estate

When George was twenty-six years old, he dreamed of creating a country estate where he could welcome his family and friends for weeks or months at a time. He envisioned a place where he could enjoy art, great books, and horticulture.

Frederick Law Olmsted designed the grounds of the 125,000-acre estate. As he developed acres of gardens and parks, he worked to protect the environment and manage the forests. He sought to reclaim land that had been over-farmed. A later Biltmore forest manager began America's first forestry school here. Look at the grounds of the Biltmore Estate below.

Building the Biltmore home was a massive undertaking. For six years, craftsmen worked to create a masterpiece. The estate had its own woodworking shop and brick factory. A three-mile railroad track was built to bring materials to the work site.

The Biltmore Estate

Richard Morris Hunt, who was also the architect of The Breakers, designed four acres of floor space for the Biltmore. The two hundred and fifty rooms included thirty-four bedrooms, forty-three bathrooms, and sixty-five fireplaces. The basement had a gymnasium and swimming pool with changing rooms, a bowling alley, kitchens, and housing for servants. When completed, the home had more than eleven million bricks, a four-story stone spiral staircase with one hundred two steps, and a chandelier with seventy-two electric light bulbs.

George Washington Vanderbilt welcomed his friends and family to the Biltmore on Christmas Eve in 1895. Three years later, George traveled to Paris. There he met Edith Stuyvesant Dresser, a relative of Peter Stuyvesant (see pages 95-96). Edith was orphaned as a child. She and her siblings grew up with their grandparents in Newport, Rhode Island. After the grandparents died, Edith and her siblings moved to Paris. They lived there four years before she met and married George Vanderbilt.

George brought his new bride to the Biltmore. See the mansion below. They spent their lives here and in their other homes in Paris and Washington, D.C. Their only daughter, Cornelia Stuyvesant Vanderbilt, was born at the home. The happy parents planted a "baby tree," a cucumber magnolia that still grows at the Biltmore.

George and Edith enjoyed entertaining at the mansion. On page 521 is a picture of Theodore Roosevelt and other guests there in 1902. Both George and Edith were committed to serving the people of western North Carolina. They began programs, industries, and schools. They were generous to their neighbors and to their many employees and their families. They believed in helping people in ways that would help those people help themselves. Edith regularly visited the families of their employees when someone was sick or when they had a new baby. She often took along Cornelia.

The Biltmore Mansion in 2005

George died suddenly in 1914 from complications after having his appendix removed. Cornelia was only thirteen years old. Edith was heartbroken. She worked hard to continue what she and her husband had begun on the estate. She worked to be a good mother and to operate the estate so that it would continue to bless the people who depended on it for employment. Edith sold 80,000 acres, including Pisgah Forest, so she could keep the estate in good financial condition. Pisgah Forest became America's first national forest. Edith lived until 1958.

View from the Biltmore

Cornelia married John Cecil and lived until 1979. Cornelia and John Cecil's son and grandchildren formed a family-owned company that continues to operate the Biltmore Estate. They sometimes use it for family gatherings. Each year their 1,700 employees welcome thousands of visitors, who tour this National Historic Landmark. See photo above. The Biltmore estate receives no government funding. The family is committed to preserving the land and managing the estate in a profitable way.

Theodore Roosevelt and Other Biltmore Guests, 1902

Frederick William Vanderbilt

Frederick William Vanderbilt, born in 1856, worked in his father's railroad businesses. He and his wife Louise purchased the six-hundred-acre Hyde Park estate in New York in 1895. The estate was famous for its beautiful landscape and its variety of native and exotic trees.

Frederick and Louise used this vacation home for a few weeks in the spring and fall, plus occasional weekends in the winter. Here they entertained guests who arrived by train or by boat on the Hudson River. After a formal dinner, guests might enjoy games of bridge or a dance. Dancing ended precisely at midnight on Saturday, in respect for Sunday. The home had thirteen rooms on the third floor just to house their visitors' maids. The Vanderbilts hired a staff of about sixty people to maintain the estate year-round.

In addition to Hyde Park, Frederick and Louise owned automobiles, yachts, their own private railroad car, and homes in Bar Harbor, Maine; Newport, Rhode Island; and the Adirondack Mountains. After Louise died, Frederick spent the last twelve years of his life at Hyde Park. Louise's niece inherited the estate. In 1939 she gave the home and part of the estate to America. She told President Franklin Roosevelt to "keep my place as it is—a memorial to Uncle Fred and a national monument." It became part of the National Park Service in 1940. It is now called the Vanderbilt Mansion National Historic Site. See the photos on the next page.

Exterior and Interior Views of the Former Hyde Park,
Now Vanderbilt Mansion National Historic Site

Honor the Lord from your wealth
And from the first of all your produce;
So your barns will be filled with plenty
And your vats will overflow with new wine.
Proverbs 3:9-10

Activities for Lesson 90

Thinking Biblically – Read Matthew 19:16-26. Why do you think it is hard for a rich man to enter the kingdom of heaven? What is the godly way to handle wealth?

Vocabulary – Write five sentences in your notebook, using one of these words in each: transatlantic, pious, theological, truss, horticulture. Check in a dictionary if you need help with their definitions.

Creative Writing – Using at least one page in your notebook, describe your dream house. Would it have an indoor swimming pool? A two-story climbing wall? What would your bedroom look like? What would you include for other members of your family? Would you provide accommodations for any special pets?

Timeline – In *Timeline of America the Beautiful* next to 1895, write: George Vanderbilt hosts a Christmas party at the Biltmore.

Student Workbook or Lesson Review – If you are using one of these optional books, complete the assignment for Lesson 90. If you are using the Lesson Review, take the quiz for Unit 18.

America Takes a New Role in the World

19

The first two Presidents elected in the 20th century were Theodore Roosevelt and William Howard Taft. Both led America as it became more involved in other parts of the world. In the early 1900s, America's leaders finally began to carry out original plans for Washington, D.C. that called for a National Mall and a National Cathedral. Also during these years, the Wright brothers taught people how to fly and brave workers carved a road through beautiful scenery God created in Glacier National Park. Many Native Alaskans of the Arctic and Subarctic continued to live their traditional lifestyles in 1912 when Alaska became an official U.S. territory.

Native Alaskan Boys in a Kayak

Lessons in Unit 19

Lesson 91 – Our American Story: Roosevelt and Taft, Presidents and Friends
Lesson 92 – An American Landmark: The National Mall and the National Cathedral
Lesson 93 – An American Biography: The Wright Brothers, Who Taught Us to Fly
Lesson 94 – God's Wonders: God Created the Magnificent Landscapes of
    Glacier National Park
Lesson 95 – Daily Life: The Arctic and Subarctic Natives of Alaska

Books Used in Unit 19

- *Maps of America the Beautiful*

- *Timeline of America the Beautiful*

- *We the People*

- *All-of-a-Kind Family* by Sydney Taylor

Roosevelt and Taft, Presidents and Friends

When America entered the 1900s, it became more involved in events beyond its borders. This involvement in international affairs has continued to the present day. Two men who served as President in the first decade of the 20th century were leaders not only in their own country but also in the larger world.

Young President Roosevelt

When President William McKinley was shot in Buffalo, New York, Vice President Theodore Roosevelt was on a speaking tour in Vermont. He rushed to Buffalo where he stayed with a close friend. When President McKinley began to improve, Roosevelt went on a vacation in the Adirondacks with his family. When President

Theodore Roosevelt (left) Walks with Two Others to the Home Where President McKinley Died

McKinley took a turn for the worse three days later, Roosevelt returned to Buffalo. He arrived a few hours after McKinley died. In the photograph above, Roosevelt and others are on their way to the home where McKinley died. Theodore Roosevelt was given the oath of office at the home of his friend. At age forty-two, he became America's twenty-sixth President and the youngest man who had ever served in that office.

Roosevelt saw his new position as an opportunity to accomplish good for others. He worked hard for causes he believed in. He easily won election to a second term in 1904, defeating Democratic candidate Judge Alton B. Parker from New York. See Roosevelt's campaign poster at left.

President Roosevelt Helps Americans

In the late 1800s, people who worked in many industries began to join together in labor unions so they could work together for higher pay and better working conditions. Most business leaders opposed labor unions. President Roosevelt

1904 Campaign Poster

Energetic Theodore Roosevelt

felt sympathy for the workers. When the United Mine Workers went on strike in 1902, Americans wondered if they would have enough coal for the winter. Roosevelt called owners of coal mines and leaders of the union to the White House. He helped the two sides work out a compromise so the miners would go back to work. The miners received a small pay increase and a shorter work day.

Some business leaders were hurting other businesses with unfair practices and were keeping prices high for customers. They made legal arrangements called trusts which helped them do this. President Roosevelt worked to end trusts. In addition to his nicknames "Teddy" and "TR," he was also called "Trust-Buster."

Roosevelt worked to make sure companies kept food safe for the American people. He loved the outdoors and sought to protect the wonders God had created in America. Roosevelt encouraged Congress to establish more national parks so that future generations would be able to enjoy them. America added several new national parks and national monuments during his presidency, including Mesa Verde in Colorado and Crater Lake in Oregon.

President Roosevelt talked directly to the American people about what the government needed to do. He called this role of the President his "bully pulpit." The photographs of Roosevelt above depict characteristics of his personality. He was a happy man who felt intense emotions about the causes dear to him. When Roosevelt spoke, he leaned forward toward his audience and spoke with great emotion.

The Panama Canal and Other Issues

President James Monroe had warned European nations in 1823 to stay out of the affairs of North, Central, and South America. In 1904 President Roosevelt announced that if a foreign government needed to get involved in Central or South America, the United States would take care of it; Europe should stay out.

525

The most important way that Roosevelt got involved in Central America was the building of the Panama Canal. During the Spanish-American War, Americans had been reminded of the need for a canal across the Isthmus of Panama so that ships did not have to go around South America to travel between the Atlantic and Pacific Oceans. The United States agreed to pay Panama for the right to build a canal.

The project began during Roosevelt's first term and was completed ten years later in 1914. President Roosevelt visited the work site, thus becoming the first President of the United States to leave the country while serving as President. In the photograph below, Roosevelt, in white, speaks to men working on the canal. After the Panama Canal was completed, the trip from New York to San Francisco was six thousand miles instead of fourteen thousand. In 1977 the U.S. signed a treaty with Panama to gradually turn control of the canal over to Panama. The first full day of Panama's official control of the canal was January 1, 2000.

Roosevelt also got involved in a conflict between Russia and Japan. The two countries both wanted to expand their power and influence in northeast Asia, and they began to fight the Russo-Japanese War in 1904. In 1905 President Roosevelt got the two sides to meet together, and he helped them negotiate an end to the war. As a result he was awarded the 1906 Nobel Peace Prize.

While Roosevelt was President, San Francisco suffered a devastating earthquake in 1906. Oklahoma became the 46th state in 1907.

Roosevelt Speaks to Men Working on the Panama Canal

The Election and Presidency of William Howard Taft

As soon as Theodore Roosevelt won the election of 1904, he announced that he would not run for a second term. In 1908 he helped his good friend William Howard Taft win the Republican nomination. Roosevelt believed that Taft would continue doing what he had begun. TR campaigned hard for Taft, who won easily over the Democratic candidate, William Jennings Bryan.

New States Admitted

1907 Oklahoma
1912 New Mexico
1912 Arizona

Taft was an honest and talented man. Both President McKinley and President Roosevelt had depended on him to do important jobs. He was dedicated to serving his fellow man. Taft was more conservative than Roosevelt. He supported some changes in the way things worked in America, but he did not want to make changes as fast as Roosevelt did. Taft was especially concerned that what he did as President was true to the Constitution and to the laws of the United States. During Taft's presidency, New Mexico became the 47th state and Arizona the 48th.

Theodore Roosevelt became disappointed with his friend and did not want Taft to win a second term as President. When the Republicans nominated Taft in 1912, former President Roosevelt helped form a third political party. This split the Republican vote and the Democratic candidate won. Learn about the lives of President Theodore Roosevelt and President William Howard Taft below and on pages 528-529.

Theodore Roosevelt
America's Twenty-Sixth President
September 14, 1901 - March 4, 1909

Theodore Roosevelt was born in 1858. He grew up in New York City. His father was Theodore Sr., a wealthy businessman and philanthropist. His mother was called Mittie. She grew up on a Georgia plantation. Theodore, known as Teedie to his family, had asthma and was often sick as a child. When he became a teenager, he worked hard to build up his health. He began lifting weights and doing gymnastics, and he became a strong man. All his life he encouraged people to exercise. Some of his favorite activities were horseback riding, swimming, and hiking.

Theodore learned at home from tutors. He and his family traveled in Europe and the Middle East. As a teenager he spent five months in Germany with a host family. When he was eighteen, he entered Harvard College, where he studied composition, German, natural history, and zoology. He also pursued boxing and wrestling.

In college Theodore began courting Alice Hathaway Lee. They married in 1880. He was soon elected to the New York legislature. On February 12, 1884, Alice gave birth to a baby girl, Alice Lee. Just two days later, Roosevelt's wife and mother both died a few hours apart at his parents' home. Alice died of kidney disease at just twenty-three years of age. Roosevelt's mother died of typhoid fever.

At first Roosevelt handled his grief by working very hard. He left baby Alice with his sister and went west to the Dakota Badlands. He bought two cattle ranches and for two years, Roosevelt rode horses, hunted grizzly bears, and chased outlaws. An emotionally-healthier Roosevelt returned to the East in 1886. He had reconnected with his childhood sweetheart Edith Kermit Carow, and they were married later that year in England. Theodore and Edith moved to Sagamore Hill at Oyster Bay, New York, where they raised his daugher Alice and the five children born to them: Theodore, Kermit, Ethel, Archibald, and Quentin. See the family photograph above.

Back in New York, Roosevelt wrote several books, including one called *The Winning of the West*. Both President Harrison and President Cleveland chose Roosevelt to help them make the giving of goverment jobs more fair. He later served as the president of the New York City Police Board. He proved himself to be an honest and fair politician.

Roosevelt was Secretary of the Navy under President McKinley. He helped prepare the Navy for the Spanish-American War. When the war began, he served with the Rough Riders in Cuba as described on page 498. Roosevelt's Rough Riders were an unusual combination of cowboys, prospectors, Native Americans, police officers, and gentlemen who had gone to Ivy League universities. TR and the Rough Riders returned to America as heroes.

After the Spanish-American War, Theodore Roosevelt was elected Governor of New York. He irritated corrupt politicians by refusing to participate in dishonest practices. In 1900 the Republican Party nominated TR to be its vice-presidential candidate. Roosevelt worked hard in the campaign. He traveled twenty-one thousand miles on a special train.

When McKinley died and Roosevelt became the youngest man to serve as President, he and his wife moved their rambunctious children into the White House. Edith Roosevelt told her closest friends that her husband was just an "ornery little boy at heart." "Teddy" Roosevelt loved to have fun with his children. He praised them and was affectionate. Once they took their pony, Algonquin, into the White House elevator. When they were at home at Sagamore Hill, he led them on obstacle hikes and swims in the ocean. He loved to tell stories about the cowboys he had met in the West.

President Roosevelt conducted his 1904 campaign in the tradition of those before him. He ran a front porch campaign from Sagamore Hill and won easily. When TR left the presidency in 1909, he and his son Kermit went on a safari to Africa. Roosevelt also toured Europe with Edith.

After losing the presidential election of 1912, Roosevelt and his son Kermit traveled for seven months on a 15,000-mile expedition in the jungles of Brazil. When he returned home, he wrote history books and scientific essays. When the United States entered World War I, he wanted to organize a volunteer division, but the War Department did not permit him to do so. All of his sons volunteered. Quentin, the youngest, was killed in action. Roosevelt toured the country giving speeeches, but he could not hide his deep sadness about Quentin. Theodore Roosevelt died in his sleep at Sagamore Hill on January 6, 1919. He was sixty years old.

William Howard Taft
America's Twenty-Seventh President
March 4, 1909 - March 4, 1913

William Howard Taft was born in Cincinnati, Ohio, in 1857. He grew up in a large family. He had two brothers, one sister, and two half-brothers from his father's first marriage. His father, Alphonso Taft, served as Secretary of War and later Attorney General under President Grant and as Ambassador to Austria-Hungary and to Russia under President Chester A. Arthur. Taft looked up to his father, who was kind and gentle. Alphonso believed in women's rights and encouraged William Howard's mother to be active in a variety of interests. She organized an art association, book clubs, German clubs, and French clubs. She often traveled with her husband while he was serving as ambassador.

As a child, William Howard loved to play baseball. He was a powerful hitter and a good second baseman. He also took dancing lessons. Taft graduated from a private high school in Cincinnati. After high school, he went to Yale University and then to the University of Cincinnati Law School. He became an attorney in 1880. Six years later he married Helen "Nellie" Herron. They had three children: Robert, Helen, and Charles Phelps.

When Nellie was a young girl, she had dreamed of becoming First Lady someday. Her father had been a law partner of Rutherford B. Hayes, and he had taken Nellie to the White House when President and Mrs. Hayes celebrated their twenty-fifth anniversary. In 1911 President and Mrs. Taft celebrated their twenty-fifth wedding anniversary at the White House, just as she had seen President and Mrs. Hayes do when she was a girl. About 5,000 guests joined them for their anniversary celebration.

William Howard Taft worked in the court system of Hamilton County, Ohio, and also as a lawyer. In 1887 he became a judge. He dreamed of one day serving on the Supreme Court. In 1890 he began working for the Department of Justice in Washington, D.C. Here he became friends with Theodore Roosevelt. Taft later served as a Federal judge on the Sixth Circuit Court of Appeals. He also became a professor at the University of Cincinnati Law School. While the Tafts lived in Cincinnati, Nellie helped to found the Cincinnati Symphony Orchestra.

Taft left his position as a Federal judge when President McKinley asked him to become Governor of the Philippines. Taft accepted the position, knowing it would be a difficult job. U.S. soldiers and Filipino soldiers were fighting against each other in a brutal war. Mr. and Mrs. Taft and their three children moved to the Philippine Islands. In the photo at left, Mr. and Mrs. Taft and two men play cards on the deck of a ship headed for the Philippines.

Taft believed that the U.S. military was being too harsh with the islanders. He got American General Arthur MacArthur removed as commander of the American forces in the Philippines (his son, General Douglas MacArthur, is mentioned in Lesson 116). Governor Taft quickly worked to set up a new government for the Philippines. Taft helped to establish a court system, public schools taught in English, and a system for hiring capable workers for government jobs. He negotiated with the Vatican (headquarters of the Roman Catholic Church) for the United States to purchase 390,000 acres of church property in the Philippines. He helped tens of thousands of Filipino peasants purchase this land by offering them low-cost mortgages.

While Taft served in the Philippines, President Roosevelt offered him a position on the Supreme Court on two ocassions. Though he had long desired that position, Taft refused so that he could finish his job in the Philippines. However, when Roosevelt offered Taft the position of Secretary of War, Taft accepted, believing he could continue to help the islands in that role.

Roosevelt depended on the counsel of his friend while Taft served in his new position. Taft supervised the construction of the Panama Canal, continued oversight of the Philippines, and served briefly as Governor of Cuba.

When the Tafts moved into the White House, Robert and Helen were in college. Charles was eleven years old. Robert graduated from Yale in 1910 and Harvard Law School in 1913. Helen earned her doctorate in history at Yale. Charles also graduated from Yale after serving in World War I.

Continuing his love of sports while in the White House, Taft started playing golf. See the photo at right above. Mrs. Taft left a lasting impact on Washington, D.C., because she was

involved in the planting of its famous cherry trees that brighten the city when they bloom each spring. The trees were a gift from Japan.

After the presidency, Taft taught at Yale University Law School until 1921 when he was appointed Chief Justice of the U.S. Supreme Court by President Warren G. Harding. He is seated in the center in the photo at left. Taft served until his death in 1930. Nellie lived for another thirteen years.

Both the Roosevelt and Taft families continued to serve in American politics. Taft's son Robert became one of the most powerful U.S. Senators of the 1900s. Robert's grandson, who was also named Robert, served as Governor of Ohio from 1999 to 2007. While her father was President, Alice Roosevelt married Nicholas Longworth, who later became Speaker of the House of Representatives. In the photograph from 1940 below, Alice Roosevelt Longworth speaks with Senator Robert Taft and his wife at a party the Tafts gave for a group of Republicans. Look at Alice's expression. Do you think Alice may have had a personality similar to her father's?

Alice Roosevelt Longworth (left)
with Senator Robert Taft and His Wife

When parents train their children well, the children often choose to continue to work for things that were important to their parents. Psalm 127 teaches:

> Like arrows in the hand of a warrior,
> So are the children of one's youth.
> How blessed is the man whose quiver is full of them;
> They will not be ashamed
> When they speak with their enemies in the gate.
> Psalm 127:4-5

Activities for Lesson 91

Map Study – Complete the assignments for Lesson 91 on Map 20 "The Lower 48" in *Maps of America the Beautiful*.

Vocabulary – Look up each of these words in a dictionary and read their definitions: union, sympathy, conservative, composition, ornery.

Literature – Read "Letters to His Children" and "Miss Delia Torrey Consents to Come" in *We the People*, pages 105-109, and "The Library Lady" in *All-of-a-Kind Family*.

Creative Writing – Why do you think no Presidents before Theodore Roosevelt traveled out of the country during their term in office? How did America's role in the world change during the 1900s? Answer this question in two or three paragraphs in your notebook.

Timeline – In *Timeline of America the Beautiful* next to 1914, write: The Panama Canal opens.

Student Workbook or Lesson Review – If you are using one of these optional books, complete the assignment for Lesson 91.

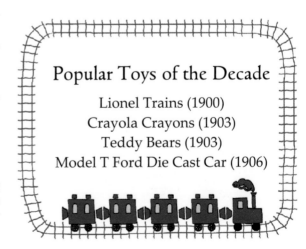

Popular Toys of the Decade

Lionel Trains (1900)
Crayola Crayons (1903)
Teddy Bears (1903)
Model T Ford Die Cast Car (1906)

Beginning with this unit, we will add a feature entitled Popular Toys of the Decade. Notice at right toys that were popular from 1900 to 1909. The year in parentheses is the year the toy was introduced.

The National Mall
and the National Cathedral

Today the Washington Monument stands as an appropriate centerpiece to the National Mall in Washington, D.C. Along the Mall are grand government buildings and monuments to people who have sacrificed to serve their country. Every year millions of people from around the world, like those pictured at right, come to visit the symbols of democracy on America's National Mall.

L'Enfant's Plan

In January 1791, President George Washington chose a site along the Potomac River for America's capital city. Later that year he commissioned Peter L'Enfant to plan the city. L'Enfant was a French artist and engineer. He and George Washington had become friends during the Revolutionary War. After the war, L'Enfant remodeled New York's old City Hall, where the first United States Congress met. He later helped design Federal Hall in Philadelphia.

Tourists walk toward the Washington Monument.

L'Enfant believed that creating a city where none had existed before was in keeping with the new American form of government. He also believed that building a new capital city was better than placing the capital in a city founded during the time of the colonies. When L'Enfant created his plan for Washington, D.C., he envisioned a city with wide avenues lined with trees. He dreamed of large open spaces and parks scattered throughout the city. L'Enfant imagined a Grand Avenue about four hundred feet wide and about a mile long, bordered with gardens. This area is now called the National Mall.

Early History of the Grand Avenue

In 1800 the United States capital moved from Philadelphia to the District of Columbia. The city was still under construction as the government established its operations there. Though city streets were built according to L'Enfant's plan, his ideas for the Grand Avenue were largely ignored during the 1800s. Both individuals and organizations used the area for raising vegetables and grazing livestock and for ornamental gardens. They also held fairs and public markets. Congress did fund a botanical garden, which was placed near the United States Capitol.

L'Enfant's original plan included a monument to George Washington. Some Americans thought it shameful that the Federal government had never funded the project. In 1833 a private group formed the Washington National Monument Society. Congress allowed the society to choose the location for a monument. President James K. Polk laid the cornerstone on July 4, 1848, but a lack of funding caused long delays in construction.

President Fillmore hired an architect in 1851 to make a landscape plan for the Mall. However, construction on the Mall continued in a disorganized way. The B&O Railroad laid tracks near the Capitol in 1854. In 1855 both the Smithsonian Institution Castle and a national armory were constructed on the Mall. During the Civil War, troops camped and paraded on the Mall. The B&O Railroad built a train depot on the Mall in 1872. Dredging work in the Potomac River in 1880 created more land at one end of the Mall. In the late 1800s the Smithsonian began a small zoo on the Mall. The Washington Monument was finally completed and officially opened to the public in 1888.

The Centennial of Washington, D.C.

By 1900 several government buildings had been built along the Mall and a few gardens had been planted, but further improvements were badly needed. United States Senator Joseph McMillan decided to take action. Washington, D.C., had served as the United States capital for one hundred years. It was time for improvements. McMillian appointed a commission to make plans for improvements. The commission included landscape architect Frederick Law Olmstead Jr., sculptor Augustus St. Gaudens, and two architects, Daniel Burnham and Charles McKim. They came up with the McMillan Plan, which proposed a return to L'Enfant's original vision.

Members of McMillan's commission went to Europe to see Paris and Vienna. Some members had been involved in planning the White City of the World's Columbian Exposition. They envisioned a geometric design with grand architecture and a ceremonial feeling. Their plan included the construction of a memorial to Abraham Lincoln and a bridge to connect Washington with Arlington National Cemetery. This bridge would symbolically reconnect the North and South. The McMillan Commission proposed that buildings match each other. In addition to removing the B&O railroad depot, the committee wanted to tear down the Smithsonian Institution and the Library of Congress. Though much of the plan was put into place, these two historic structures were left standing. Slowly, the National Mall we know today began to take shape.

Construction of the Lincoln Memorial began in 1914. See photo at right. It was formally dedicated in May of 1922. Chief Justice William Howard Taft presided over the ceremony with fifty thousand people in attendance, including Lincoln's son, Robert Todd Lincoln, as the guest of honor.

Lincoln Memorial Under Construction, 1914

A Walk on the National Mall

Before we take you on an imaginary walk around the National Mall, look at this photograph which gives you a bird's-eye view. The large building in the foreground is the United States Capitol. The tall obelisk monument in the center of the Mall is the Washington Monument. The farthest monument that you can see in the photo is the Lincoln Memorial. The photo also shows the Arlington Memorial Bridge across the Potomac. It leads to Arlington National Cemetery and Arlington, Virginia.

The National Mall

We begin at the United States Capitol. George Washington laid its cornerstone in 1793. Part of the Capitol was completed in time for Congress, the Supreme Court, and the Library of Congress to move into the building in 1800. Construction continued for several years. The Capitol received terrible damage when the British burned it in 1814. A rainstorm helped prevent it from being totally destroyed.

Since it was built, the Capitol has been renovated frequently. As America gained new states, it was expanded to make room for more Senators and Representatives. The current Capitol dome was completed during the Civil War. As new technologies were invented, Congress installed running water, electricity, telephones, and other innovations. To keep the Capitol up-to-date and in good repair, Congress employs an Architect of the Capitol.

As you walk out of the western side of the Capitol, you can look down the Mall and see the Washington Monument in the distance. In front of you is a reflecting pool, where you can see the Capitol reflected on the water. Now we will lead you on a walk around the National Mall. Look at the diagram on page 534 and find your starting place marked with an X. You will travel along the dotted line in the direction of the arrows.

Diagram of the National Mall in Washington, D.C.

Legend

▮ Lincoln Memorial

▭ White House

● Jefferson Memorial

★ Washington Monument

▦ United States Capitol

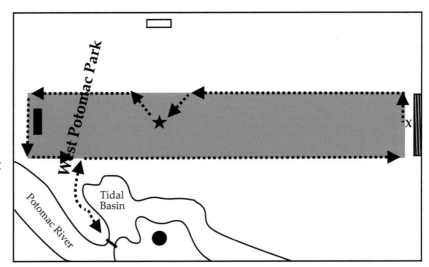

Walk north a short distance and then turn left to head toward the Washington Monument (marked by a star on the diagram). On your right is the National Gallery of Art. Next is the National Archives, which houses important American documents. The following two buildings are two of the Smithsonian museums: the National Museum of Natural History and the National Museum of American History.

White House

When you get to the Washington Monument, you will see that it is circled with American flags. Unless you have arrived very early in the morning, you will have to wait in a long line to go to the top of the monument.

From the top, look to the east to see a nice view of the U.S. Capitol. Now go to the north window. Far in front of you is the White House, home of every U.S. President since John Adams. See picture above. The home was built between 1792 and 1800. It has undergone two major reconstructions: one after the British burned it in 1814 and another from 1948 to 1952 during the administration of President Truman.

Look out the west window. Your view will be like the picture at the top of page 535. In the distance is the Lincoln Memorial. Close by is the World War II Memorial. In between is a large reflecting pool. The picture at right shows a ground level view of the World War II Memorial. Construction on it began in 2001 and was completed in 2004.

When you look out the south window, you will see the Tidal Basin. On its shore is the Jefferson Memorial.

World War II Memorial

From top to bottom in the middle are the Lincoln Memorial, Reflecting Pool, and World War II Memorial. Constitution Gardens is on the right. Find the shadow of the Washington Monument.

Take the 896 stairs as you come down from the top of the Washington Monument, so you can see the commemorative stones along the way. Nevada and Idaho gave the ones below. Many stones are gifts from states, while others are from organizations.

As you leave the Washington Monument, walk west toward the Lincoln Memorial. This portion of the National Mall cuts through the center of West Potomac Park. The picture above shows most of the park. As you head west, you will pass the World War II Memorial on your left. On your right will be Constitution Gardens and Constitution Garden Lake, seen in the right of the photograph above. Just before you reach the Lincoln Memorial, you will pass the Vietnam Veterans Memorial. You can't see it in the photo above because of the trees. The Vietnam Veterans Memorial Wall is two long pieces of marble in a wide V-shape that cuts into the ground. It is often referred to simply

Vietnam Veterans Memorial

Lincoln Memorial

as The Wall. On it are etched the names of over 58,000 people who were killed or missing in action during the Vietnam War of the 1960s and 1970s. A portion of the memorial is pictured in the second photo above. The objects below the wall were placed there by visitors.

Nevada and Idaho Monument Stones on the Interior Walls of the Washington Monument

When you reach the western end of the National Mall, you can enter the Lincoln Memorial, pictured above. Its thirty-six columns represent the states that were in the Union when Lincoln died. Inside is a sculpture of President Lincoln designed by Daniel Chester French. The statue is nineteen feet tall and weighs 175 tons; it is pictured at right. Lincoln's Gettysburg Address and his Second Inaugural Address are chiseled on the inside walls.

Let's head back east after visiting the Lincoln Memorial. You will soon pass by the Korean War Veterans Memorial on your right. This memorial has individual statues of soldiers in action. The photograph below was taken in winter.

Now you can leave the Mall briefly and stroll southward along the Tidal Basin toward the Jefferson Memorial. You will pass the cherry trees Mrs. Taft received from Japan, which circle the Tidal Basin. President Franklin D. Roosevelt laid the cornerstone for the Jefferson Memorial in 1939. See the photograph at bottom left. The circular colonnade reflects Jefferson's own tastes in architecture. It contains a nineteen-foot bronze statue of Thomas Jefferson, with Jefferson

Statue of Lincoln in Lincoln Memorial

facing toward the White House. Five quotes from Jefferson adorn the inside of the monument. The first Jefferson statue in the memorial was a plaster model. The bronze statue could not be completed until after World War II was over. The use of metal was restricted during the war so it could be saved for military uses. The bottom right photo is a view of the Washington Monument from the Jefferson Memorial. Notice the cherry trees in bloom.

Korean Veterans Memorial in Winter

Now let's return to the Mall and go back toward the Capitol. Once you pass the Washington Monument, you will pass several Smithsonian Museums including the famous Smithsonian Castle, the National Air and Space Museum, and the Museum of the American Indian. Returning to the Capitol completes your tour.

The Jefferson Memorial

Cherry Trees Along the Tidal Basin

The National Cathedral

The original plan for Washington, D.C., proposed a National Cathedral to be built on the Grand Avenue. It was about one hundred years before actual plans were made to construct the proposed cathedral. Congress gave the Protestant Episcopal Cathedral Foundation a charter to establish a national cathedral. The site chosen was Mount St. Albans in northwest Washington, D.C. President Theodore Roosevelt gave an address when building began in 1907. The photograph from 1925 below shows the cathedral while under construction. The main material used was gray Indiana limestone.

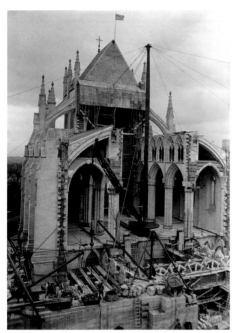

National Cathedral Under Construction, 1925

The National Cathedral was finally completed in 1990. A few features of the cathedral include the Gloria in Excelsis Tower, which is the highest point in Washington, D.C.; and over two hundred stained glass windows with Christian symbols or tributes to famous people or events.

The monuments in our nation's capital were placed there to help people remember and show honor. In Romans 13, God taught us to give honor to whom honor is due. Just a short time before Jesus died for us on the cross, He spoke about remembering. He told us how to remember Him:

And when He had taken some bread and
given thanks, He broke it and gave it to them, saying,
"This is My body which is given for you;
do this in remembrance of Me."
Luke 22:19

Activities for Lesson 92

Thinking Biblically – Read Joshua 4, in which God commands the nation of Israel to set up a memorial. Write one or two paragraphs in your notebook about how monuments and memorials help people to remember important people and events and to be thankful.

Map Study – Complete the assignments for Lesson 92 on Map 3 "American Landmarks" and Map 22 "The National Mall" in *Maps of America the Beautiful*.

Literature – Read "Dusting is Fun" and "Rainy Day Surprise" in *All-of-a-Kind Family*.

Timeline – In *Timeline of America the Beautiful* next to 1922, write: The Lincoln Memorial is dedicated.

Student Workbook or Lesson Review – If you are using one of these optional books, complete the assignment for Lesson 92.

The Wright Brothers,
Who Taught Us to Fly

Milton and Susan Wright grew up on the frontier in Indiana. Both came from families who encouraged their children to pursue knowledge. Their family heritage and their own commitment to hard work and the pursuit of learning helped their sons Wilbur and Orville create one of the most amazing inventions in the history of the world—a machine that could fly.

Orville Wright as a Child

As a young man, Milton Wright joined the Church of the United Brethren in Christ. Susan joined as a teenager. The two met while Susan was studying literature at Hartsville College in Indiana. When they married in 1859, they were both dedicated to a life of serving in their church. Milton was deeply committed to sharing Jesus with people. He was also committed to abolition and the temperance movement, which worked to help people avoid the problems associated with drinking alcohol. Milton became a minister with his church. The Wrights had a son, Reuchlin, in 1861 and another son, Lorin, in 1862.

In 1867 Milton and Susan had their third son, Wilbur. When Milton became editor of the weekly United Brethren newspaper, the *Religious Telescope,* in 1869, he moved his family to Dayton, Ohio. Orville was born in Dayton in 1871. He is pictured above. Three years later the Wrights had a daughter, Katharine. Milton's ministerial responsibilities required that the family move around, but they settled permanently in Dayton in 1884.

Wright Home in Dayton, Ohio

Learning from Loving Parents

As a child, Milton Wright studied many subjects and developed his mental abilities. Susan spent hours with her father working in his carriage shop, where she learned how to use tools. While Wilbur, Orville, and their siblings were growing up, their mother made simple appliances to use in their home as well as toys for her children. Wilbur and Orville were good students, but neither graduated from high school. Both enjoyed math and science.

In 1878 Milton Wright brought a present home for his children: a toy helicopter powered by a rubber band. A Frenchman who had experimented with aviation was the toy's designer. The toy soon broke, but Wilbur and Orville showed their interest in flight by making their own copies of it. Whenever they needed help with a project like this, they asked their mother for advice and answers to mechanical questions.

The Wright home was a happy one. Katharine said, "No family ever had a happier childhood than ours. I was always in a hurry to get home after I had been away half a day."

Susan Wright died of tuberculosis in 1889. Katharine, at age fifteen, became the household manager. She is pictured at right when she was a grown woman. Milton, Wilbur, Orville, and Katharine continued to live together until 1912.

Katharine Wright

From Bicycles to Airplanes

In the late 1800s, bicycling became popular. In 1892 Wilbur and Orville formed the Wright Cycle Company to sell bicycles. They later opened a bicycle repair shop and became bicycle manufacturers.

At the same time, they began to read about flight. Wilbur wrote a letter to the Smithsonian in 1899, asking for literature about it. People in various places were experimenting with flight. They had built successful gliders, in which people could leave a high place and glide down on the air; but no one had been successful building a flying machine that could be controlled by the pilot and powered by a power source like gasoline or steam. The brothers were discouraged to see that little progress had been made.

However, Wilbur and Orville realized that they had a good chance of creating the first flying machine. They used money they earned in their bicycle business to pay for experiments with flight. They observed birds and experimented with kites. Their work experience with bicycles improved their mechanical skills. Using these skills, they began to build flying machines in their shop.

Kitty Hawk, A Place to Experiment

Wilbur and Orville needed a place to test their theories. Weather conditions in Dayton were not the best for long-term flying experiments. They wanted a private, open place where the winds were steady and there was little vegetation. They needed a hill from which they could launch a glider. Another essential was a soft place to land.

The Wright brothers wrote to the National Weather Bureau in Washington, D.C., to find out where winds were constant. With this information in hand, they wrote to J. J. Dosher, who worked for the United States Weather Bureau at the Kitty Hawk Weather Station in the Outer Banks of North Carolina (we learned about the Outer Banks on page 265 in the lesson on America's Islands). The Wright brothers told Dosher that they needed a place for

Life-Saving Station at Kill Devil Hills

"the purpose of making some experiments with a flying machine."

Dosher replied that the sandy beaches there were wide and free of obstructions. He said that the winds blew from the north and northeast in September and October. Dosher also told Captain William Tate about the Wright brothers. Tate was a leading citizen of Kitty Hawk. He was the postmaster and served in local government. Tate told the Wrights that near Kitty Hawk was a stretch of bare beach that was one mile wide and five miles long. The postmaster also told them that the people of Kitty Hawk would be hospitable when the Wright brothers came among them.

The massive dunes of Kitty Hawk in the Outer Banks proved to be an ideal location. Each fall from 1900 to 1903, the Wright brothers traveled to Kitty Hawk to test their gliding machines. Back in their bicycle shop in Ohio, they continued to improve the aircraft.

Few people lived at Kitty Hawk, but after the two experimenters from Ohio started going there, islanders became interested in what they were doing. Dan Tate, his son Tom Tate, and lifesavers from the nearby Kill Devil Hills Life-Saving Station all helped the Wright brothers with their experiments. See the life-saving station above.

On their first trip in 1900, Wilbur and Orville stayed briefly with the Tate family before setting up a tent. That year they experimented mostly at Lookout Hill, south of Kitty Hawk. For two days, they experimented in the Kill Devil Hills.

When Wilbur and Orville returned in 1901, they set up a camp at Kill Devil Hills and built a rough workshop. In 1902 they improved it. In 1903 they built another shed where they kept their Wright Flyer.

Learning from the Experiments

The experiments at Kitty Hawk gave the Wright brothers information they needed to design a flying machine that would work. The first year they were only able to achieve a ten-second flight. Each year they learned new things and had greater success. They increased the wing length from 17 feet in 1900 to 22 feet in 1901 to 32 feet in 1902. One of the most important lessons they learned at Kitty Hawk was how to be pilots. Their experiments taught them what to do with their machine while they were in the air.

When they left Kitty Hawk in 1902, they were convinced they had a powered flying machine design that would work. They were ready to prove it in 1903.

December 17, 1903

The Wright brothers experimented with a gasoline-powered motor in 1903. When they couldn't find one that would work, they built their own. They attached it to their 605-pound Wright Flyer.

The First Flight on December 17, 1903

After an unsuccessful attempt on December 14, Wilbur and Orville Wright hoped that their long-awaited day had arrived on December 17, 1903. Dressed in coats and ties, the brothers walked over to the Wright Flyer and shook hands. Orville climbed onto the Flyer. He left the ground with the power of the Flyer's motor. For twelve seconds, he flew without losing speed. Wilbur ran alongside him. He landed on a point that was as high as the place where he had taken off. John Daniels, an employee of the Kill Devil Hills Life-Saving Station, took a photograph of the flight. Until that morning, he had never used a camera. See his famous photograph above.

Orville Wright flew for 120 feet. It was the first time in the history of the world that a man had flown a heavier-than-air machine successfully. Each brother flew twice that day. At day's end, they sent their father a telegram, telling him the figures for that day's work. Then they went back to Dayton, for the testing season was over for the year. Wilbur was thirty-six years old, and Orville was thirty-two.

After the Wright Flyer

In 1904 Wilbur and Orville Wright stopped making bicycles and devoted their efforts to flying. They formed airplane companies in America and in Europe and continued to improve their invention. The brothers sometimes returned to Kitty Hawk to experiment with further improvements. On page 542 are photos of Orville and Wilbur in 1910 and one of Orville in 1911.

At Top: The Wright Brothers at the International Aviation Tournament on Long Island in New York, 1910; At Bottom: Orville Wright, 1911

Neither Wilbur nor Orville ever married. They made an excellent income from aviation and began building a grand home together in Ohio. In 1912, before the house was completed, Wilbur died of typhoid fever at the age of 45.

Orville continued to work in aviation and to invent. He served on the National Advisory Committee for Aeronautics for twenty-eight years; it later became the National Aeronautics and Space Administration (NASA). Orville lived in the home he and Wilbur had designed together until his death in 1948 at age 77.

Perhaps since the creation of man, people have looked at birds and longed to be able to do what they do. When David was longing for relief in Psalm 55, he thought of flight:

> I said, "Oh, that I had wings like a dove!
> I would fly away and be at rest."
> Psalm 55:6

Activities for Lesson 93

Vocabulary – Find each of these words in a dictionary: temperance, mechanical, theory, vegetation, hospitable. Choose the definition that corresponds to the way the word is used in the lesson. Copy the words and definitions into your notebook.

Literature – Read "The Subject of Flying" in *We the People*, page 110, and "Who Cares If It's Bedtime?" in *All-of-a-Kind Family*.

Creative Writing – Write one page in your notebook about how the Wright brothers' invention has changed the world.

Timeline – In *Timeline of America the Beautiful* next to 1903, write: The Wright brothers fly the first airplane.

Family Activity – Make paper airplanes. See page 965 for ideas.

Student Workbook or Lesson Review – If you are using one of these optional books, complete the assignment for Lesson 93.

God Created the Magnificent Landscapes of Glacier National Park

President William Howard Taft signed a bill in 1910 setting aside a portion of northwestern Montana as Glacier National Park. Here God carved out rugged peaks and deep valleys. He has decorated them with beautiful glaciers and with over 2,000 varieties of plants. Look at the photos below.

Some of the Beauties God Placed in Glacier National Park
Clockwise from the top left: Beargrass, McDonald Lake, Bighorn Sheep, Heaven's Peak, and Arnica.

Today Glacier National Park covers over one million acres. This area contains 175 mountains, 762 lakes, and 2,865 miles of streams. The tallest peak is Mount Cleveland at 10,448 feet. The mountains of Glacier are part of the Rocky Mountains. Glacier's largest lake is Lake McDonald, which is pictured on page 543; the longest stream is Upper McDonald Creek, at almost twenty-six miles long. Look at the photos of the park at right.

Glaciers

A glacier is a mass of ice that begins on land. There are two types of glaciers: continental glaciers and alpine glaciers. A continental glacier, also called an ice sheet, is a dome of ice that covers a very large area of land. Continental glaciers are found on both Greenland and Antarctica. The glaciers in America are called alpine glaciers. Alpine glaciers are found in mountains and often flow down valleys.

Glaciers are found in places with cool temperatures in the summer and large amounts of snow and freezing rain in the winter. Most glaciers are near the north or south pole or in high mountains. Some scientists define an area of ice as a glacier only if it is currently moving. Other scientists call an area of ice a glacier if it shows evidence of having moved in the past. Generally, to be considered a glacier, an ice mass must cover at least 25 acres.

Glaciers exist in the United States in Alaska, California, Colorado, Idaho, Montana, Nevada, Oregon, Utah, Washington, and Wyoming. As of 2010, Glacier National Park had twenty-five named glaciers. The largest is Blackfoot Glacier.

From Top to Bottom: Hidden Lake, Iceberg Lake, Glenns Lake, and Thunderbird Mountain

The Wildflowers of Glacier National Park

Of the 2,000 plants in Glacier National Park, almost one thousand are wildflowers. In just one landscape, visitors can see fields aglow with colorful wildflowers and towering mountains in the background. The highest places in the park are the alpine regions. Here the wildflower season is very short because of cold temperatures.

Glacier Lily

God has created the wildflowers here so that they can withstand very high winds, cold nights, and intense ultraviolet light. Some are very close to the ground where they can soak up heat from the earth. Some have special shapes so that the strong winds don't hurt them. The glacier lily, at right, comes up in the snow. The butterwort consumes insects which stick to its gummy leaves.

Bicknell's Geranium

Almost all of the plants in the alpine region are perennials; that is, they stay alive year after year. Some alpine plants can live to be more than one hundred years old. Because of the short growing season, God put many plants here that produce new plants through their roots instead of through seeds. Two plants that do bear seeds are the rock harlequin and Bicknell's geranium, pictured at right. Their seeds wait for decades until there is a fire. After the land where the seeds are is burned, the plants make many flowers and seeds for a season or two and then the seeds wait until the next fire.

Native Americans in the Region that Became Glacier National Park

When Europeans first discovered the area that is now Glacier National Park, several Native American tribes made their homes there. The Blackfeet lived east of the mountains, while the Salish and Kootenai lived in the valleys of the West. We learned about the Blackfeet of the Great Plains region beginning on page 215 and about the Salish (also called Flathead) and Kootenai tribes of the Plateau region beginning on page 14. Native Americans called the area Shining Mountains or the Backbone of the World.

Fur Trappers, Miners, Homesteaders, and Conservationists

The first Europeans who came to the area were fur trappers. Miners came next. The Great Northern Railway was completed in 1891, allowing homesteaders to settle in northwest Montana. Soon small towns were built. George Bird Grinnell and others began working in the mid-1890s to preserve the beauty of this area for future generations. Grinnell called the Glacier area the "Crown of the Continent."

Grinnell had loved nature since he was a child. He attended school at the home of John James Audubon. After college he became a naturalist, often exploring in the West. Grinnell always tried to learn from Indian tribes. The Pawnee called him White Wolf. The Blackfeet

Twin Lakes

Sinopah and Painted Teepee

Grizzly and Her Cubs

Trumpeter Swan

called him Fisher Hat. The Cheyenne called him Wikis, which means bird. They observed that he came and went with the seasons. He worked for Indian rights all his life.

Grinnell edited a natural history magazine called *Forest and Stream* and founded the Audubon Society. Grinnell and fellow conservationists worked hard for fifteen years before Glacier National Park was established in 1910. The National Park Service celebrated the one hundredth anniversary of the park in 2010.

Railroads and National Parks

Before many Americans drove cars, railroad companies realized that they could make money by taking people to national parks. They not only provided transportation, but also built hotels. Glacier already had one hotel and a few guest cottages when the Great Northern Railway opened their first chalet in 1910. In 1914 the Great Northern Railway adopted this slogan to promote travel to Glacier National Park: "See America First." The Great Northern Railway continued to be involved in Glacier National Park until 1960.

As the photos at left show, Glacier is certainly something spectacular to see. In addition to grizzly bears and swans, visitors might see bighorn sheep and mountain goats.

Going-to-the-Sun Road

Soon after Glacier National Park was established, automobiles became popular. Roads were built so that visitors could drive through the park. Tour bus service began within the park in 1914. For many years, men worked on what was first called the Transmountain Highway. The road took fifteen years to plan and ten years to complete. The result was an engineering marvel.

Today the fifty-mile road is called Going-to-the-Sun Road, and a drive on it is one of the highlights of a trip to Glacier National Park. This road connects the east entrance of the park with the west entrance. The road is named for nearby Going-to-the-Sun Mountain, which is pictured at right. The road crosses the Continental Divide at Logan Pass.

Building the road was difficult and dangerous. Much of the road was built on a cliff. Sometimes workers had to hang suspended from ropes. Because of snow, work could only be done about two hundred days each year. When crews returned in the spring, they had to remove by hand the snow that had accumulated on the road and in their camp. Snow removal is still a big job today, but it is no longer done by hand. See the photograph below.

Rock that was dynamited away from roadbeds was used to build walls, so the road blends in beautifully with the surroundings. See the photograph at right.

Construction crews on the Going-to-the-Sun Road were strong men. Those who built the 408-foot tunnel

Going-to-the-Sun Mountain

Stone Wall and Guardrail

near Logan Pass had to be able to carry fifty pounds of dynamite down a one-hundred-foot trail and a ladder in just half an hour. While constructing the tunnel, three crews worked twenty-four hours a day. The job was just too scary for some men, who stood at the top of the ladder, looked down the cliff, and resigned.

The workers stayed in their camps for two or three weeks with no shower. To help keep them happy, supervisors made sure they always had a good cook. The cooks had to contend with bears who were also attracted by the good food, so the job required brave men and women.

The road was finished on July 7, 1933. It cost $1,700,000 and was the most difficult road project America had undertaken until that time. Opening ceremonies took place six days later. One cook and his assistant cooked chili for 2,500 people, but ended up serving over four thousand. He used 125 pounds of ground beef, five hundred pounds of chili beans, one hundred pounds of onions, thirty-six gallons of tomatoes, and fifteen pounds of chili powder. The chili was cooked in nine copper-bottom wash basins.

The crowning touch that day was when Blackfeet, Salish (Flathead), and Kootenai

Removing Snow in May on the Going-to-the-Sun Road

Left: A boy named Eagle Aims Back carves a toy canoe.
Right: Women play a stick game at a midsummer celebration near Glacier National Park.

Indians came and passed the peace pipe. Natives from the area near Glacier National Park are pictured above. The photographs were made before 1940.

In 1985 the American Society of Civil Engineers identified the Going-to-the-Sun Road as a National Historic Civil Engineering Landmark. Crews worked hard to construct a way for visitors to see Glacier National Park. Jesus gave His all to make a way for us to come to Him. He told us:

> I am the way, and the truth, and the life;
> no one comes to the Father but through Me.
> John 14:6

Activities for Lesson 94

Thinking Biblically – Read Job 38:1-30. As you read, think about the majestic region God created that is preserved in Glacier National Park.

Map Study – Complete the assignment for Lesson 94 on Map 2 "God's Wonders" in *Maps of America the Beautiful*.

Literature – Read "The Sabbath" in *All-of-a-Kind Family*.

Timeline – In *Timeline of America the Beautiful* next to 1933, write: The Going-to-the-Sun Road is completed.

Student Workbook or Lesson Review – If you are using one of these optional books, complete the assignment for Lesson 94.

The Arctic and Subarctic
Natives of Alaska

Far to the north of the rest of the United States is a state twice as large as Texas. Here Native Alaskans developed a way of life which they passed down from generation to generation. The name "Alaska" is a native word. It means "place the sea crashes against." Native Alaskans used the abundant resources God created in this region to take care of themselves,

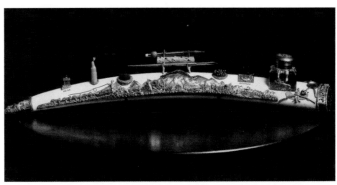

Elaborately Carved Walrus Tusk Given to President Taft

their children, and their neighbors. Here they lived lifestyles similar to those lived by native peoples in northern Canada, Greenland, and Siberia.

White explorers began coming to Alaska in 1728. The first were Russian. Russians settled on Kodiak Island in 1784 and Russian Czar Paul claimed Alaska in 1799. In 1867 Russia sold it to the United States.

While William Howard Taft was President, Alaska became an official U.S. territory. Above is an ivory walrus tusk carved by a Native Alaskan and given to President Taft.

Native Alaskan Child

When people think about Native Alaskans, they often think of Eskimos. Actually several native groups live in Alaska. Look at the map of Native American regions on page 8. We have already learned about Native Americans who lived in the eight southernmost regions; in this lesson we will learn about the natives of the Arctic and Subarctic. There actually is no one group of people in Alaska who are called Eskimos, but the term has been used to refer to both the Inuit and Yup'ik people of the Arctic region.

The Eyak, Tlingit, Haida, and Tsimshian people who live in Alaska are part of the Northwest Coast region. You learned about their lifestyles in Lesson 2.

Native Alaskans of the Subarctic

The natives living in the Subarctic are the Athabascans. For Athabascans the most important responsibility they have toward their fellow man is sharing.

Life Together

Traditionally the Athabascans lived along rivers. They migrated in small groups of twenty to forty people. Together they fished,

Alaskan Natives

hunted, and trapped. In summer they lived in fish camps and in winter they lived in villages. During the winter, they hunted small animals that lived close by. In winter they gathered to celebrate potlatches. A potlatch is a ceremony with dancing, feasting, and speechmaking. During the potlatch, the host gives gifts to his guests.

Often a woman and her brother and their two families shared a special relationship. The two brothers-in-law sometimes became hunting partners. The woman's brother was responsible for training her children to know their family's history and customs.

The Athabascans described different times of the year by telling what happened then. Some of these descriptions were "when the first king salmon comes," "when the moose lose their antlers," and "little crust comes on snow." Winter was called "the time we gathered together."

Woman Making Snowshoes

Tools

The Athabascans made tools from stone, antlers, bones, and birch wood. They used these tools to build houses and to make boats, cooking utensils, clothing, and snowshoes. Notice the woman making snowshoes in the photo at left.

Clothing

Most Athabascan clothing, moccasins, and boots were made from the hides of caribou and moose. Both men and women were good at sewing. For special ceremonies, the men wore beaded jackets. Women wore beaded dancing boots. Both men and women wore beaded tunics. See the beaded tunic above. An Athabascan chief wore a shell necklace called a dentalium.

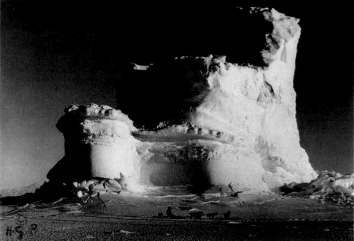

Traveling by Dogsled

Transportation and Trade

The Athabascans traveled in canoes made from birch bark, moose hide, and cottonwood trees. They also traveled by sled. Some sleds were pulled by people and others by dogs. See photos above. Athabascans also traveled on the snow in snowshoes. The men actively traded with Athabascans from other communities and with other native groups.

Native Alaskans of the Arctic

Native Alaskans of the Arctic region include the Inuit, Yup'ik, Unangax, and Aluutiq (or Sugpiaq). The Unangax and Aluutiq people are sometimes called Aleut, but many members of these groups do not like that term. The Inuit live in the northernmost regions of Alaska. The Yup'ik live in the southwest. Some Yup'ik also live on St. Lawrence Island. The Unangax and Aluutiq live in the Aleutian Islands.

Arctic Natives who lived on the mainland of Alaska depended mainly on polar bears, caribou, and sea mammals such as whales, walruses, and seals. They used a variety of other mammals as well as birds and their eggs. They also ate salmon, cod, whitefish, herring, and halibut.

Those living on the Aleutian Islands depended mainly on the North Pacific Sea, the Bering Sea, and the creeks and rivers near their villages. Traditionally a certain territory around each settlement belonged to the members of that settlement. Villagers hunted seals and sea lions; caught halibut, cod, and birds; and gathered plants and driftwood in that territory. See natives picking berries on the next page. Though some Arctic Natives now have modern jobs, all of these native groups continue to depend to some extent on a hunting and gathering lifestyle.

Life Together

Perhaps when you think of where natives of the Arctic lived, you think first of an igloo. Igloos are temporary homes made of blocks of ice. Igloos were more common among the native peoples of Greenland and Canada.

Berry Picking

Most winter homes of Arctic Natives were built underground to take advantage of natural insulation. The Inuit usually built their homes out of blocks of sod. Sometimes a framework of driftwood, whalebone, or walrus bones was built first. The entrances to their homes were usually underground tunnels.

Most Inuit homes were rectangular, measuring about twelve to fifteen feet by eight to ten feet. Eight to twelve people lived together in each home. A seal-oil lamp made from soapstone or pottery was used for light and heat. The oil also provided fuel for cooking. Many Inuit homes flooded in the summer, but by then the families had usually gone to summer camps, where they set up tent homes. See photos of Arctic homes below.

The Yup'ik living on St. Lawrence Island built circular houses. The underground homes of the Aluutiq had one room. To enter them, the Aluutiq climbed through the ceiling and down a pole ladder. The Unangax house was an oblong pit. Frames and rafters were made of whalebone or wood. Roofs were grass and sod. The homes blended in with the environment.

Inside of an Arctic Home

The Inuit also constructed community buildings called qargis. These were used as work areas. Yup'ik males lived together in a men's house called a qasgiq. There boys learned how to be men. Women brought the men's food to the qasgiq. The building also served as a community center, where the people sang, danced, and held ceremonies.

Yup'ik women and children lived in a house called an ena. The ena was half the size of the qargis. Yup'ik men and women both used the same underground tunnel entrance. The Yup'ik used the intestines of either bearded seals or walruses to make skylight windows for their homes.

Inuit Summer Camp

Villages of the Unangax and Aluutiq were usually built at the mouths of streams to provide access to fresh water. They could also take advantage of salmon migration.

Native Man Drilling Ivory

Since Arctic Natives depended on the animals that are available at certain times of year, seasons were important to them. After the work of gathering food was completed, winter was a special time to celebrate.

Among the Yup'ik and other groups, elders tell stories to younger generations so they will know their traditions and history and how to survive in their environment.

Tools and Utensils

Arctic Natives made ingenious tools from things God provided around them. In the photo at left, a native drills walrus ivory. The next picture shows halibut hooks. Below them are seal hunting tools. At bottom are many objects made from ivory.

Halibut Hooks

Unangax and Aluutiq men made elaborately-decorated tools. A traditional Inuit tool kit included stone, wood, bone, and ivory tools. They made tools to butcher meat, to tan leather, and to inscribe and carve. The Inuit made bows, arrows, spears, spear throwers, and snares to use in hunting; nets, hooks, and branch and root traps to catch fish; and the tools they needed to hunt bowhead whales, including harpoons, lances, lines, and floats made of seal bladders and seal skins.

Seal Hunting Tools

Yup'ik women used a fan-shaped knife made of slate and sewing implements made of stone, bone, or walrus ivory. Unangax and Aluutiq women wove cords, cables, and fish lines from animal tissue or kelp.

Hand Carved Ivory

Baskets Made in Southwest Alaska

The Unangax and Aluutiq wove beautiful baskets from spruce roots and grass. Women sometimes grew their fingernails long so that they could split the grass. Some baskets are as soft as cloth. Many are decorated with geometric designs. Today some women make these designs using silk thread. Some baskets are sewn so intricately that there are as many as 2,500 stitches per square inch. See native baskets above and a basket weaver below.

Clothing

Look at the faces and clothing of the Arctic Natives on page 555. These Native Alaskans are wearing traditional clothing. The photographs were taken in the late 1800s or early 1900s. Notice the variations in skin color. Look at the hairstyles. See that two women are wearing braids; the men all have bangs.

Among the Inuit, men and women wore similar clothing. They wore socks and boots, called kamiks, and two layers of clothing made of caribou skin. The inner layer included pants and a pullover top, called a parka or a kuspuk. The fur on inner clothing faced inward.

Basket Weaver

Outer clothing included pants and a pullover top called a qiipaghaq. The fur on outer clothing faced outward. A woman's top had a larger hood, so she could carry a baby inside it. Notice the women at top center and at bottom right on page 555. Men and women also wore skin gloves. The fur in gloves was turned toward the skin. Most gloves had a leather strap, worn around the neck, which kept the gloves connected. The Unangax and Aluutiq also had snow goggles.

The Alaskans also wore waterproof jackets like the one below. The jackets were made from the bladders and intestines of sea mammals. See the man at top left on page 555. He

Outer Jacket Made of a Sea Mammal Bladder

is wearing a waterproof jacket and is holding a toy boat he made for his son.

Unangax and Aluutiq natives wore clothing made from sea mammals, sea otters, bears, birds, squirrels, and marmots. They made hats from spruce roots and grass. Because of the wet climate in the Aleutian Islands, the Unangax and Aluutiq needed waterproof clothing. They developed very good sewing skills, which enabled them to make exceptionally waterproof garments. These natives made colorful dyes which they used to decorate their clothing. They also decorated clothing with feathers and puffin beaks. Some of the Unangax and Aluutiq people added decorations of carved ivory or bone, and some attached wooden figurines. The Unangax and Aluutiq wore elaborate costumes when participating in a ceremony, including carved wooden masks.

The Yup'ik peoples used fish skin and marine mammal intestines to make waterproof boots. They made insulated socks out of grass. They also used grass to make waterproof thread. When the Unangax and Aluutiq hunted in their kayaks, they wore visors made of bent wood and decorated with sea lion whiskers. These protected the hunters' eyes from glare. They were also symbols of status. Hunting success was shown by the number of sea lion whiskers on a man's visor.

Native Alaskan Clothing and Hairstyles

Transportation

The Inuit natives used two types of boats: the kayak and the umiaq (or angyaq). The kayak was a closed boat made of skin. It usually held one person. The man shown in the

Hunter in a Kayak

Men in Kayaks

picture above and the people shown at right are riding in kayaks.

The umiaq was a large, open boat made of skin. See the umiaq at bottom right and the interior frame of an umiaq at bottom left. The umiaq was usually fifteen to twenty-five feet long, though some were almost fifty feet in length. The Inuit traveled in these boats and used them to hunt whales and walruses. A large umiaq could carry fifteen people plus a ton of cargo.

The Unangax and Aluutiq also made kayaks and large skin boats, some with skin roofs. See family with toy boat at right.

Though boats were their main form of transportation, they also walked long distances on foot trails. The Inuit used a basket sled when traveling on land. They also constructed flat sleds on which they placed their umiaq when needing to carry it across ice. Those living away from the coast used snowshoes. See the man with snowshoes on on page 557.

Family with Toy Boat

Trade

Arctic Natives were active in trading. Trade helped them have a more balanced diet. It also helped them to

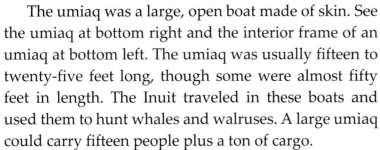

Umiaq Frame

Umiaq

take advantage of objects invented by their neighbors. Inland villagers traded moose meat and caribou meat, as well as furs from beaver, marten, mink, and muskrat. Coastal villagers traded seal oil, herring, and herring eggs. Trading became even more important for natives of the Arctic after whites arrived. Notice the Native Alaskan in the middle photo below. He is trading with a white man.

Russians have had a major influence on the Unangax and Aluutiq people. The Russian Orthodox Church is still an influential part of their communities. The people prepare Russian dishes made with ingredients found locally. Their languages include Russian words.

Native Alaskan with Snowshoes

World Eskimo-Indian Olympics

Native Alaskans continue to keep many of their traditions. The Inuit still enjoy competitive games that test strength and stamina. They also have song duels. One way traditions are kept alive is through the World Eskimo-Indian Olympics (WEIO) held in Fairbanks, Alaska, each summer.

Traditional sports at these games include the one-foot high kick, kneel jump, one hand reach, stick pull, knuckle hop, two-foot high kick, arm pull, wrist carry, scissor broad jump, and Alaskan high kick. The WEIO also has competitions in Eskimo and Indian dance, greased pole walk, fish cutting, blanket toss, ear pulling, four-man carry, Indian stick pull, drop the bomb, Eskimo stick pull, toe kick, parka and Indian dress, and a white men versus native women tug-of-war. The blanket toss below is an Inuit game. The "blanket" is usually walrus skin or seal

Native Alaskan Trades White Fox Furs with a White Trader

skin. The object is to see who can bounce the highest.

The World Eskimo-Indian Olympics includes a queen competition. The queen's crown is made of black baleen and white ivory. The winner must have a good knowledge of traditional native culture.

Blanket Toss

Man in a Canoe in Front of Muir Glacier

The natives of the Arctic and Subarctic have learned how to live in an environment that many people on earth would think was too harsh. Like the worthy woman of Proverbs 31, they have learned to think ahead, make plans, and carry them out:

> She is not afraid of the snow for her household,
> For all her household are clothed with scarlet.
> Proverbs 31:21

Activities for Lesson 95

Map Study – Complete the assignment for Lesson 95 on Map 4 "Native Peoples of North America" in *Maps of America the Beautiful*.

Vocabulary – Write a paragraph using all of these words: insulation, driftwood, oblong, stamina, ingenious. Consult a dictionary if you need help with their definitions.

Literature – Read "Alaska Days with John Muir" in *We the People*, pages 111-112, and "Papa's Birthday" and "Purim Play" in *All-of-a-Kind Family*.

Timeline – In *Timeline of America the Beautiful* next to 1784, write: Russians settle on Kodiak Island, Alaska.

Student Workbook or Lesson Review – If you are using one of these optional books, complete the assignment for Lesson 95. If you are using the Lesson Review, take the quiz for Unit 19.

Americans Go "Over There"

Americans got even more involved with other nations during the presidency of former college professor Woodrow Wilson. Many young American men like Alvin York from tiny Pall Mall, Tennessee, went to Europe and fought in the Great War. Many immigrants had arrived in America during this period, seeking freedom and prosperity. One of those immigrants began a home for boys called Boys Town on the plains of Nebraska. During Wilson's presidency, Grand Canyon National Park was established.

View of the Grand Canyon from Desert View Point

Lessons in Unit 20

Lesson 96 – Our American Story: President Wilson and the Great War
Lesson 97 – An American Biography: Alvin C. York, Hero of World War I
Lesson 98 – Daily Life: Polish, Jewish, and Italian Immigrants in America
Lesson 99 – An American Landmark: Boys Town, Nebraska
Lesson 100 – God's Wonders: God Created the Grand Canyon

Books Used in Unit 20

- *Maps of America the Beautiful*

- *Timeline of America the Beautiful*

- *We the People*

- *All-of-a-Kind Family* by Sydney Taylor

President Wilson and the Great War

America's role in the world expanded even more in the second decade of the twentieth century (1900s), when it became involved in a war in Europe. Because it was so terrible, many people hoped that it would be the war to end war. Sadly, that was not true.

The Progressive Movement

As discussed on page 470, some farmers in the late 1800s wanted to bring about reforms in American government. They were called Populists. By 1900 a new reform movement had begun. Members of this new group were called Progressives. People involved in the Progressive Movement were not from farms, but from cities.

Progressives worked to make changes in the election process. They wanted people to be able to use secret ballots so that others would not know who they voted for. They wanted U.S. Senators to be elected by the people instead of by state legislatures, which was the original way described in the Constitution. Progressives also wanted to see women gain the right to vote.

These reformers also wanted changes in business and industry. They wanted to make it illegal for companies to hire children and wanted working conditions to be safer for all employees. Progressives wanted laws that would require city apartment houses to be clean and safe. Many Progressives also worked against the sale of alcoholic beverages. Progressives were members of both the Republican and Democratic parties.

Delegates at the Progressive (or Bull Moose) Party Convention in Syracuse, New York, 1912

The 1912 Election

Theodore Roosevelt was a progressive Republican. He didn't think Taft was progressive enough and began to criticize his old friend in public. Roosevelt was sorry that he had not run for election himself in 1908. When Taft was nominated as the Republican presidential candidate in 1912, a group of Republicans broke off from their party and formed a new party they called the Progressive Party. They had a convention in Syracuse, New York. See convention delegates above.

The Progressive Party nominated Roosevelt as their presidential candidate. When the party talked to Theodore Roosevelt about running, he said he was "as strong as a bull moose." Afterwards, the party was sometimes called the Bull Moose Party. The Democrats nominated New Jersey Governor Woodrow Wilson.

This 1912 Wilson campaign poster shows Roosevelt, Wilson, and Taft with a map of the United States behind them. The map is made up of photographs of crowds.

The campaign was bitter. Theodore Roosevelt sharply criticized his former friend, hurting Taft deeply. Taft eventually made some negative comments himself. Wilson worked hard in his campaign but was also critical. Above is a Wilson campaign poster.

Though Wilson only won forty-two percent of the vote, the Republican vote was split between Taft and Roosevelt; Woodrow Wilson won the election. Roosevelt came in second and Taft only won the electoral votes of two states.

President Wilson Signs Child Labor Law

Reforms Under President Wilson

During Wilson's presidency, the majority of Senators and Representatives were Democrats. They worked together to bring about some of the reforms that Progressives desired. In the photograph at left, Wilson is signing a law limiting child labor. The 19th amendment to the Constitution, passed by Congress in 1919 and ratified by the states in 1920, gave women the right to vote.

The Great War

Some European countries wanted to expand their empires. Germany, Austria-Hungary, and Italy made an alliance, and then Great Britain, France, and Russia made an alliance. Members of each of these alliances agreed that if one of their members were attacked, the others would defend them.

Austria-Hungary claimed control of an area known as the Balkans, which lies south of Austria. In 1914 Archduke Franz Ferdinand, a member of royalty from Austria, visited the Balkans with his wife. A man who did not like Austria-Hungary's control of his country killed the couple. When Austria-Hungary moved troops to the Balkans, Russia began moving troops to defend the region. Germany declared war on Russia and then on France. When German troops went through Belgium on their way to France, Great Britain responded by declaring war on Germany. The terrible conflict dragged on for four years.

Most of the fighting in the war was done by Germany on one side and France and Great Britain on the other. The fighting took place primarily along a line called the Western Front that ran for six hundred miles through eastern France. France and Great Britain were on the western side of the line, while Germany was on the eastern side. Germany and Austria-Hungary also fought against Russia along the Germany-Poland border and along the border between Austria-Hungary and Russia. Later this fighting on the Eastern Front went deep into Russia.

American Neutrality

When the two sides began fighting, President Wilson declared that the United States was neutral; it did not officially support either side. Most Americans supported Great Britain and France, but millions of German immigrants favored Germany. German submarines attacked many ships in the Atlantic Ocean. In 1915 the German navy sank the *Lusitania*, a British passenger ship. Almost 1,200 people died; over one hundred of them were Americans. Wilson sent strong warnings to Germany, but America did not go to war.

America Enters the War.

For a time Germany stopped its attacks in the Atlantic. When Wilson ran for re-election in 1916, his slogan was "He Kept Us Out of War." However, early in 1917, Germany announced that it would start attacking ships again. Germany also tried to get Mexico to form a secret alliance with them against the United States. On April 2, 1917, President Wilson asked the U.S. Congress to declare that America and Germany were in a state of war. Wilson said, "The world must be made safe for democracy."

Four days later Congress voted overwhelmingly to declare war. Americans started sending supplies to Great Britain, training troops to send to Europe, and buying food for the soldiers. Factories started making airplanes, guns, and ships. Daylight saving time was begun for the first time, so that America could save fuel needed for the war effort. Popular songwriter George M. Cohan wrote the song "Over There," about what American troops were going to do "over there" in Europe. The song became a hit.

You may have heard of United States savings bonds. Notice the World War I posters on this page. They encouraged Americans to buy two kinds of savings bonds: liberty bonds and savings stamps. In this way American citizens could loan the Federal government money so that it could pay for the war.

On page 563 are more World War I posters. These encouraged people to conserve food. The top poster reminded people that food is a gift from God. The middle poster reminded immigrants that they came to America seeking freedom and that now they must help preserve it. The lower right poster encouraged people to save wheat for the soldiers while eating other grains themselves.

By the end of the war thirty-two countries were involved. Japan joined in the fight against Germany and Austria-Hungary. Italy was initially allied with Germany and Austria-Hungary, but during the war it came over to the side of Great Britain, France, and Russia. Worldwide over sixty million people served in the military. More than eight million soldiers died during the conflict, which came to be called the Great War. Several million civilians were also killed or died of disease or famine.

Over a year after American soldiers joined the Allies, Germany realized they could not win and asked for the fighting to stop. An agreement to stop the fighting went into effect on November 11, 1918. This agreement was called an armistice.

President Wilson wanted an international organization that could help countries work out their differences without going to war. He called the organization the League of Nations. Wilson traveled to Europe to meet with the leaders of Great Britain, France, and Italy in early 1919. Many in Europe welcomed Wilson as a hero. He was the first American President to travel to Europe while in office.

The leaders met at Versailles (pronounced *ver-sigh*), near Paris, France, to work out a peace treaty. Germany's enemies insisted that Germany make payments to the countries it had hurt during the war. They also required Germany to reduce its army. Wilson compromised his belief that Germany should not have to pay penalties so that the other countries would agree to a League of Nations. Finally, the leaders agreed on the Treaty of Versailles.

According to the Constitution, treaties must be approved by the Senate. Senators were sharply divided about the Treaty of Versailles. Though most Americans were glad that the United States and its allies had won the war, German Americans did not like the penalties that Germany would have to pay.

President Wilson wanted Congress to agree to the treaty. He traveled across America making speeches about the treaty and the League of Nations, hoping that the American people would tell their Senators to vote for the

treaty. He traveled almost ten thousand miles. Wilson collapsed while in Colorado. A few days later, he suffered a severe stroke and became paralyzed on one side.

Wilson was awarded the 1919 Nobel Peace Prize for his work, but the United States Senate did not approve the Treaty of Versailles. Other countries formed a League of Nations, but the United States never joined. A few years later, the U.S. made separate treaties with Germany and with Austria-Hungary.

President Wilson spent his last months in the White House very ill. He saw almost no one except his doctors and his wife, Edith. When Wilson needed to communicate things related to the presidency, he spoke through his wife. Read about Wilson's life below.

Thomas Woodrow Wilson
America's Twenty-Eighth President
March 4, 1913 - March 4, 1921

Woodrow Wilson was born in Virginia in 1856. He had two older sisters and a younger brother. His father was from Ohio. His mother, though born in England, had grown up in America. Wilson was raised in the South, where his father served as a Presbyterian minister. Wilson's father became a staunch supporter of Southern secession from the Union. Among Woodrow Wilson's earliest memories were watching Yankee soldiers marching into his hometown of Augusta, Georgia; watching his mother take care of wounded Confederate soldiers; and seeing Robert E. Lee go through town under Union guard after he surrendered to Grant at Appomattox Court House. In 1870 Wilson's family moved to South Carolina and four years later to North Carolina.

As a child, Wilson studied at home, learning religion, British history, and British literature from his father. He studied for one year at a school in North Carolina. He entered Princeton at nineteen. At Princeton Wilson edited the school newspaper, acted in school plays, and served as an officer in the baseball and football associations. After graduation Wilson briefly studied law at the University of Virginia. There he participated in debate and sang in the glee club and in a quartet. After leaving the university, he studied law on his own. Wilson became an attorney,

but he soon decided to go back to school at Johns Hopkins University. There he earned a Ph.D. in history and political science. During his last year at Johns Hopkins, Wilson married Ellen Louise Axson from Georgia. They are pictured above. Ellen was an artist who enjoyed music and literature. Woodrow and Ellen had three daughters, Margaret, Jessie, and Eleanor. The daughters are pictured at left with their mother.

Wilson became a university professor. He wrote several books, including a biography of George Washington and a five-volume history of the United States. In 1902 he became president of Princeton University. Eight years later he ran for Governor of New Jersey and won. As Governor, Wilson worked to bring about reforms that the Progressives desired. Two years later the national Democratic Party nominated Wilson to run for President of the United States, and he won. Wilson is the only U.S. President to hold a doctorate.

While in the White House, Wilson enjoyed riding horses and cruising on the Chesapeake Bay on the *Mayflower*, the presidential yacht. Wilson enjoyed baseball games and vaudeville performances. He read aloud from English poets. When his daughters were at home, the whole family gathered around the piano to sing hymns and popular songs. Margaret was twenty-

seven years old when Wilson became President. During World War I, she sang at Army camps. The two younger daughters were both married at the White House.

Wilson's beloved wife Ellen died the year after he became President. Ellen Wilson Lake in Glacier National Park is named for her. Sixteen months later, the President married a Washington widow, Edith Bolling Galt. See their photograph at left.

On March 4, 1921, a very ill Wilson left the White House. He rode to the Capitol with Warren Harding who had been elected as the new President. Wilson did not stay to hear the inaugural address. He retired from public life, living at a home he had purchased in Washington, D.C. Wilson afterwards rarely appeared in public. In 1923 he published a brief essay entitled "The Road Away from Revolution," encouraging an approach to relations with other countries different from the one that Harding was pursuing. On November 11 of that year, Wilson gave a short Armistice Day speech on nationwide radio. Almost three years after leaving the presidency, Wilson died quietly at his home in February of 1924. He is buried in the National Cathedral. Edith Wilson continued to live in their home. She died in 1961.

After the war, returning soldiers had a hard time finding work. Communists had taken over the government of Russia and Americans were worried that they would take over in the U.S., too. Many Americans wanted simply to live their lives in peace and not get involved again with Europe.

Woodrow Wilson worked hard and made great sacrifices to be a peacemaker.

Blessed are the peacemakers, for they shall be called sons of God.
Matthew 5:9

Activities for Lesson 96

Thinking Biblically – Copy Psalm 37:37 into your notebook. Write a paragraph about what you think it means to be a person of peace.

Map Study – Complete the assignments for Lesson 96 on Map 23 "The Great War" in *Maps of America the Beautiful*.

Literature – Read "Poetry of the Great War" and "Save and Serve" in *We the People*, pages 113-116, and "Sarah In Trouble" and "Mama Has Her Hands Full" in *All-of-a-Kind Family*.

Timeline – In *Timeline of America the Beautiful* next to 1918, write: An armistice ends the fighting in the Great War.

Student Workbook or Lesson Review – If you are using one of these optional books, complete the assignment for Lesson 96.

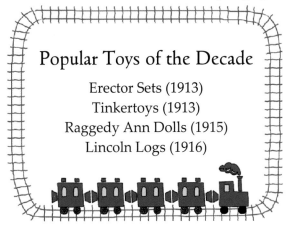

Popular Toys of the Decade

Erector Sets (1913)
Tinkertoys (1913)
Raggedy Ann Dolls (1915)
Lincoln Logs (1916)

Alvin C. York,
Hero of World War I

Alvin Cullum York was born on December 13, 1887, in a two-room log cabin in Pall Mall, Tennessee. Like many homes on Tennessee's Cumberland Plateau, it was a dog-trot cabin. These structures had two rooms with a breezeway between them. One roof covered the whole structure. Alvin was the third of eleven children. Both of his grandfathers fought in the Civil War. Like many others in East Tennessee, they fought for the Union.

Alvin's parents were William and Mary York. They earned a living by farming and hunting. William was an excellent shot and often took his sons hunting. He also earned extra income as a part-time blacksmith.

Alvin only went to school for nine months. When he grew up, he became a day laborer for a railroad in a nearby town. York learned how to shoot from his father and became a good marksman at an early age. In his twenties, he earned a reputation as a wild rabble-rouser. Alvin drank and gambled in bars near the Kentucky-Tennessee state line. His father died when Alvin was twenty-four years old, which forced Alvin to carry a great deal of responsibility for his family.

Life-Changing Events

York had a life-changing experience in 1914. After his best friend was killed in a bar fight, he thought about where his life was heading. He decided to attend a revival at an area Church of Christ in Christian Union. York was converted and became a member of the church. See photo at right.

Church in Pall Mall

This small group only had congregations in Ohio, Kentucky, and Tennessee. The church had strict rules of morality and opposed violence and war. York convinced his close friend, Rosier Pile, to join the church also. York had a good singing voice. He became a song leader and also taught Sunday School. Pile became the church's minister.

York's Commitment is Challenged

When the Great War began, Alvin York had never traveled more than fifty miles from home. He was living a frontier lifestyle, hunting deer, quail, raccoon, squirrel, and wild

82nd Airborne Division Insignia

boar with an old-fashioned muzzle-loader gun. Two months after Congress declared war on Germany in April of 1917, Rosier Pile, who was also the local postmaster, handed his friend Alvin a draft notice. Because of their church's beliefs about war, Pile encouraged York to be a conscientious objector. York wrote on his draft registration card, "Don't want to fight." Both the state of Tennessee and the Federal government refused York's request for conscientious objector status because the Church of Christ in Christian Union was not a recognized denomination.

York reluctantly left Pall Mall and headed for Camp Gordon in Georgia. He was assigned to the 82nd Airborne Division. See the division insignia at left. While in training, York studied the Bible faithfully, looking to it for guidance for his life and situation. At Camp Gordon, he proved himself an excellent shot, but he also let his superiors know how he felt about fighting. Once after participating in target practice where he shot at human silhouettes, he told an officer: "Sir, I am doing wrong. Practicing to kill people is against my religion." While at Camp Gordon, his company commander told York that sometimes war is moral and that it is sometimes ordained by God. After serious thought, York agreed to go to Europe and fight. He arrived in England in May of 1918 and was sent to France.

York Becomes a Hero

During an American assault on October 8, 1918, Sergeant Bernard Early and sixteen soldiers, including York, were sent to attack a group of German soldiers. Their map was in French. They misread it and ended up behind the German lines. A brief fight began between the Americans and a larger German force. The surprised Germans quickly surrendered. However, German machine gunners told the captured Germans to lie down. The gunners fired their machine guns at the Americans, killing nine of them. Sergeant Early was injured, so he gave command to two corporals. One of them told York to silence the machine guns, which he did.

In the end, York and seven other Americans captured 132 German prisoners. Twenty-five Germans had been killed. York believed that he was responsible for shooting at least nine of them, but he was not proud of what he had done. In the photo at right, York is revisiting the scene of the battle.

For his action, York was promoted to the rank of Sergeant. He received the Distinguished Service Cross from the United States, plus medals from France, Italy, and Montenegro (a country in the Balkans). A

After the war, York revisited the location of the battle.

Saturday Evening Post reporter heard about the incident and wrote an article about York's service in France. York returned to the United States with other "doughboys" who had served in the war. Read the box below for an explanation of doughboys.

Doughboys

A popular nickname for a World War I soldier was doughboy. Newspapers used the word and soldiers used it in their letters and diaries. No one seems to know for sure how the nickname started, but foot soldiers had been called doughboys since at least the time of the Mexican War. During World War I, the term was used for all American soldiers.

In the photo at left, wounded doughboys and their Red Cross nurses enjoy lollipops while they watch a parade in New York City in September of 1919.

York was singled out as a hero and received a hero's welcome in New York City. He received the Congressional Medal of Honor, the highest military honor given in the United States. See York wearing his medals on page 569.

Alvin York Helps His Neighbors

Because of his fame, companies wanted York to endorse their products. York said, "This uniform ain't for sale." The war was over, and he wanted to forget about it. York also wanted to go home; marry Gracie Williams, his sweetheart whom he had met in church; and return to the lifestyle he had lived before the war. Tennessee Congressman Cordell Hull helped York return to Tennessee quickly. In the photo below, York is pictured with his mother.

Gracie and Alvin were married on June 7, 1919.

Alvin and Gracie were married a few weeks after he returned to Pall Mall. See their photo at right above. They were married for fifty-five years. The Yorks had five sons, Alvin Cullum Jr., Edward Buxton, Woodrow Wilson, Andrew Jackson, and Thomas Jefferson; and two daughters, Betsy Ross and Mary Alice.

York with His Mother

Rotary Clubs in Tennessee wanted to give York a home and a farm. When they did not receive enough donations, they gave him instead an unfinished home and a mortgaged farm.

Back in the mountains, York pursued a new dream. He wanted to provide the children of his neighbors with a practical education. During the 1920s, he traveled around the country speaking to groups and raising money for a York Institute where boys and girls could be educated. He got involved in politics. His fame gave him influence with government officials, and he was able to help his home county get better roads and jobs. In 1926 the Alvin C. York Institute was founded. During the Great Depression, York worked in a government program designed to help his area.

In 1935 York was concerned that events in Europe were leading to another world war. He preached a sermon entitled "Christian Cure for Strife." He said that the church and home were cornerstones of world peace and that Christians should ignore current events. He criticized America's involvement in the Great War.

York and other American Christians were struggling over whether America should get involved in another war in Europe. York joined the Emergency Peace Campaign, which tried to keep America out of the conflict.

Sergeant York, the Movie

When New York City welcomed Alvin C. York home in 1919, Jesse L. Lasky watched the homecoming from his office building. Lasky wanted to tell York's story in a movie and tried for many years to get York's permission. Lasky had a hard time convincing York because York's church did not approve of movies. York finally said yes because he wanted to use money earned from the film to build an interdenominational Bible school.

York wanted the movie to be a true picture of his life, including what he had done after the war. He said it would not be a war movie because, "I don't like war pictures." The original screenplay was written according to York's wishes, but the final version of the movie concentrated on his role in World War I. The movie starred Gary Cooper as Sergeant York. It was a huge success. Cooper earned the Academy Award for best actor in 1942. York did build his Bible school, but it was only open from 1942 to 1943.

Life After the Movie

While the movie was being filmed, York came to believe that Germany's leader, Adolf Hitler, was evil and should be stopped. He agreed that the United States should draft men to serve in the military, the first time this had ever been done in America during peacetime. He even became the chief executive of his home county's draft board. York tried to re-enlist himself but was turned down because of his age and weight. Instead, he traveled

Portrait of Sergeant York with Medals

around the country recruiting soldiers, selling war bonds, and inspecting Army camps.

Alvin York's health began to fail after World War II. He had a stroke in 1954 and spent the last ten years of his life in bed. He died in 1964 and was buried in the Pall Mall cemetery with full military honors. Gracie died in 1984 and was buried beside him.

A statue of York stands in front of the Tennessee State Capitol in Nashville. His home, farm, and grist mill are now part of Sergeant Alvin C. York State Historic Park. In his home county are a high school called Alvin C. York Institute, York Elementary School, and York Highway. The state of Tennessee has a National Guard Armory and a Veterans Administration hospital named in his honor. In 2000 the United States Postal Service issued a Sergeant York stamp.

York wished to be remembered not as a war hero but as someone who improved education in Tennessee, brought better roads, and helped his fellow man. York was an example of what Paul wrote to the Colossians:

> Whatever you do in word or deed, do all in the name of the Lord Jesus,
> giving thanks through Him to God the Father.
> Colossians 3:17

Activities for Lesson 97

Thinking Biblically – What is a Bible verse someone could use to support fighting in a war? What is a Bible verse someone could use to support the position that war is wrong? Write down these examples in your notebook, then write a few paragraphs about your perspective on what the right choice is.

Map Study – Complete the assignment for Lesson 97 on Map 23 "The Great War" in *Maps of America the Beautiful*.

Vocabulary – Copy these words in your notebook, each on a separate line: revival, draft, denomination, silhouette, endorse. Look up each word in the dictionary. Next to each word, write what part of speech it is according to the way the word is used in this lesson.

Literature – Read "Sergeant York and His People" in *We the People*, pages 117-119, and "Fourth of July" in *All-of-a-Kind Family*.

Timeline – In *Timeline of America the Beautiful* next to 1926, write: Alvin C. York Institute is founded.

Student Workbook or Lesson Review – If you are using one of these optional books, complete the assignment for Lesson 97.

Polish, Jewish, and Italian Immigrants in America

America is a nation of immigrants. Native Americans came to America first; Europeans began coming after 1492. After Europeans began colonies in the New World, they started bringing Africans against their will. On this page are photographs of immigrants from Ireland, Germany, Estonia, Poland, and Czechoslovakia who came to America in the first half of the twentieth century. Immigration to America continues to this day.

Irish Immigrants Leaving Ireland

Daughter of a German Immigrant

Immigrants from Estonia

Immigrant from Poland

Immigrants from Czechoslovakia

Immigrant from Germany

571

Numbers of Immigrants
1821 - 1830 143,439
1831 - 1840 599,125
1841 - 1850 1,713,251
1851 - 1860 2,598,214
1861 - 1870 2,314,825
1871 - 1880 2,812,191
1881 - 1890 5,246,613
1891 - 1900 3,687,564
1901 - 1910 8,795,386
1911 - 1920 5,735,811
1921 - 1930 4,107,209

Congress passed the first U.S. law about immigration in 1790. It stated that immigrants who were white and of good moral character could become citizens of the United States after living here for two years.

During the 1840s, crops failed in Germany and Ireland experienced a potato famine. In addition, several countries had political problems and difficulties related to the growth of factories. Many immigrants came to the United States during that decade. Notice the numbers of immigrants in the 1820s, 1830s, and 1840s in the box at left.

Beginning in 1850, the U.S. Census began recording where people were born, whether inside the United States or outside of it. Immigration continued to rise in the 1850s. It slowed slightly in the 1860s because of the Civil War, but was still high because many Europeans took advantage of the Homestead Act. Notice the 1850s and 1860s immigration numbers.

The Naturalization Act of 1870 gave citizenship to African Americans, but Asians still could not become citizens. In 1882 Congress passed a law banning all Chinese immigration. After 1890 immigration from Northern and Western Europe decreased, while Southern and Eastern European immigration increased. Many of those immigrants were Jews. Ellis Island was opened in 1892 (see Lesson 88). Look at the numbers of immigrants in the 1870s, 1880s and 1890s.

In 1906 America began requiring that an immigrant know some English before becoming a citizen. A 1917 law required that immigrants be able to read at least forty words in some language. In the 1920s European immigration was limited to two percent of the number of people from that country who were living in America in 1890. This slowed the rate of immigration from Southern and Eastern Europe, since relatively fewer people from those areas were living in America in 1890. Notice the immigration figures for the decades from 1901 to 1930.

In this lesson we will learn about Polish and Jewish immigrants from Eastern Europe and Italian immigrants from Southern Europe.

Polish Americans

During the American Revolution, more than one hundred Poles came to help America in the war. Benjamin Franklin recruited two Poles, Count Kazimierz Pulawski and Tadeusz Kościuszko, to assist in the Revolution. Both became American heroes; towns and counties were named after them. The World War I poster at right is in Polish. It reminds Poles of Pulaski and Kosciuszko and encourages them to eat less wheat, meat, fats, and sugar to help bring freedom to Poland.

World War I Poster

572

Polish Farmer and Wife in Connecticut

Polish Family in Pennsylvania

Political difficulties in Poland in the 1800s caused many Poles to immigrate to America. The first permanent Polish settlement in America was in Texas. A few hundred men, women, and children emigrated from Silesia and founded the town of Panna Maria, Texas, in 1854.

Polish immigration continued, first by the thousands and then by the tens of thousands. In 1910 the U.S. Census recorded 900,000 new immigrants who spoke Polish. The rate of Polish immigration slowed after Poland gained its independence after World War I, but a total of more than two million Poles immigrated to America between the time of the American Revolution and the 1920s.

Many Polish immigrants intended to live in America for a while, earn money, and then go back to Poland. Most of them ended up staying, but their Polish heritage was important to them. Many settled near other Poles. The area around the Great Lakes reminded many of Poland, so some settled there. Many towns in Michigan, Minnesota, and Wisconsin have Polish names. Other Poles founded towns in New England and in the mid-Atlantic states. At top is a Polish farmer and his wife who lived in Connecticut. At left is a Polish family in Pennsylvania.

Look at the photographs below. At left a Polish man sews in a clothing factory. At right is a steel mill worker. Most Polish immigrants

Polish Man Working in Connecticut Clothing Factory

Polish Man Who Worked in a Steel Mill in Pennsylvania

Polish Miner in West Virginia

went to cities such as Chicago, Illinois; Pittsburgh, Pennsylvania; Detroit, Michigan; Milwaukee, Wisconsin; Cleveland, Ohio; and New York City and Buffalo, New York. They went there to work in factories, steel mills, and foundries. Others moved to the Appalachian Mountains to work in the mines. Notice the miner at left.

Wherever Polish immigrants went, they preserved their culture. They started Polish-language newspapers, social clubs, and markets. Poles founded more than nine hundred Polish Catholic churches and many Catholic schools. Notice the Polish woman preparing an Easter feast at left. At bottom left are Polish nuns and children. Children enjoy a Polish dance in the photograph below.

Polish Woman Prepares Easter Feast

Polish Dance by School Children in New York

Jewish Americans

Many Jews from Eastern Europe immigrated to the United States in the early 1900s. Look at the photograph of a Jewish man and some boys at top left on page 575. They are Russian Jews.

Jewish immigrants from Eastern Europe spoke Yiddish, a language that combines German and Hebrew elements using Hebrew letters. In 1902 a Jew from Lithuania began America's first daily newspaper in Yiddish. It reported news from Europe and New York and published advice for new immigrants. The

Polish Nuns and Children

Jewish Man and Boys from Russia

Liberty Bond Poster Printed in Yiddish

Jewish School Children Wave Flags and Repeat the Pledge of Allegiance, from a 1906 Harper's Weekly

poster above is written in Yiddish. It encouraged Jews to buy Liberty Bonds to help America during World War I.

Like other immigrants, Jews became Americans. Notice the drawing at left. It is from a 1906 issue of *Harper's Weekly*. Jewish school children are saying the Pledge of Allegiance and waving American flags.

Jewish immigrants kept traditions they brought with them from Europe and created new ones. In the image at left below, a man and boy sing on Jewish New Year in 1907 in New York City. The boy in the middle photo wears a prayer shawl on Jewish New Year in 1911. In the right picture, worshippers pray on a bridge in 1919.

Singing on Jewish New Year, 1907

Boy in Prayer Shawl, Jewish New Year, 1911

Jews Pray on New Years Day, 1919

It took time for some immigrants to figure out a way to make a living after they arrived. At right is a photo of a man selling New Year's cards. In the next photo, a Jewish man works as a peddler. Sometimes immigrants needed help. The Jewish women pictured at bottom left are receiving free food in New York City.

Jewish authors in America began to write Yiddish fiction. Jews in Chicago and New York began Yiddish theaters. The playbill at lower right is from 1940. Some Jews became involved in the new filmmaking industry. Jewish immigrants Samuel Goldwyn, Louis B. Mayer, the Warner brothers, and William Fox became household names when they started movie production companies. Movies made by Jewish producers have greatly influenced American culture. A Jewish-Polish immigrant developed makeup used in Hollywood films. Ask your mother or grandmother if she recognizes the name of this immigrant: Max Factor.

Young Jewish men created comic books that became popular in America. Jerry Siegel and Joe Shuster invented Superman; Bob Kane and Bill Finger developed Batman.

Jews served their new country by fighting in World War I. By 1917 six members of the House of Representatives were Jewish.

Jewish Man Sells New Year's Cards

Jewish Peddler, New York City

Poor Jewish Women Receive Free Food

Playbill for Yiddish Theatre

Italian Immigrants

Three of the first explorers in the New World had roots in Italy: Cristoforo Colombo (Christopher Columbus), Giovanni Caboto (John Cabot), and Amerigo Vespucci. During the colonial period and the early days of the United States, Italian craftsmen came to America. An Italian started the first opera house in the United States. Many of the paintings in the U.S. Capitol were painted by Italian artist Constantino Brumidi. Thomas Jefferson appreciated Italian culture. He hired Italian stonemasons to work on Monticello, brought Italian musicians to America to play in the Marine Band, and enjoyed meals that included pasta. He even invented a pasta machine.

Harper's Weekly Illustration from 1890:
"In the Italian Quarter—Mulberry Stret on a Winter Evening"

Beginning in the 1880s, large numbers of Italian peasants began immigrating to America. Some stayed a few years and then returned to Italy. Those who remained in America often sent money to their loved ones in Italy.

About one-third of these immigrants stayed in New York City, especially in Brooklyn, the Bronx, and Manhattan. Streets in Manhattan, particularly Mulberry Street, became a sort of "Little Italy." See the illustration of Mulberry Street in 1890 above. In these Italian neighborhoods, street vendors, store owners, and residents spoke Italian. Notice New York Italians in the street scenes below.

Italian Americans on the Streets of New York

Though many continued to speak Italian, they also learned English. Below is a photo of a class where Italians are learning English and citizenship.

Government-Sponsored English and Citzenship Class for Italians

Immigrants from some Italian villages settled near one another when they came to America. These immigrants continued to celebrate the festivals they celebrated in their home villages. Both of the photographs below were taken during a *festa*. In the top photo, a street vendor is selling buttons.

Like other immigrants, some Italian women and children did piece work in their homes. They might sew clothes or put machinery together by hand. Many Italian men worked for the New York Department of Public Works. In 1890 almost ninety percent of workers in this department were Italian immigrants. They dug canals, built bridges, and tunneled out the New York subway. Other Italians became shoemakers, masons, or barbers.

Italians were entrepreneurs, too. Italians formed the Contadina food company in 1918. The company continues to make canned tomato products. The modern Bank of America was once an Italian bank called Giannini's Banda D'Italia. Many of New York City's fruit vendors were Italian. Most of the early banana importers were Italian immigrants. See Italian banana vendor at top left on page 579.

Notice the woman in the photo at top right on page 579. She is carrying a large wooden crate to use for kindling. Making a living in a new country could be difficult, so Italians joined together to help one another. The Order of the Sons of Italy, founded in 1905, provided housing for new immigrants, supported them financially, and helped them get an education. The group is still active today.

Italians moved to other cities as well. In San Francisco they became fishermen and stevedores. A stevedore works on a dock and is often involved in loading and unloading ships. Some Italian immigrants became miners in Appalachia and in mines out West. Some worked in the rock quarries of New England and Indiana. In the center photos on page 579 are a fruit vendor and an ironworker.

Like other Americans, Italians were called upon to help during World War I. At the bottom of page 579 is a poster in Italian advertising Liberty Bonds.

Throughout American history, people have had a difficult time relating to the newest people among us. God wants us to be kind to immigrants. He told the Israelites to be kind to the strangers who lived among them.

Italians Photographed During a Festa

Italian Banana Vendor

Italian Woman Carrying a Large Box to Use for Kindling

The stranger who resides with you shall be to you
as the native among you, and you shall love him as yourself,
for you were aliens in the land of Egypt;
I am the Lord your God.
Leviticus 19:34

Activities for Lesson 98

Italian Fruit Vendor in Indianapolis

Thinking Biblically – Copy Leviticus 19:33-34 into your notebook.

Map Study – Complete the assignments for Lesson 98 on Map 6 "Europe" in *Maps of America the Beautiful*.

Literature – Read "The Cat Took the Kosher Meat" in *We the People*, pages 120-121, and "Family Outing" in *All-of-a-Kind Family*.

Italian Iron Worker in Massachusetts

Creative Writing – Imagine that it is 1918 and you are the director of a center in New York City that exists to help new immigrants get a good start in America. In your notebook, make a list of at least ten ideas for programs, classes, and activities your center could offer. Include a description of one or two sentences with each item.

Timeline – In *Timeline of America the Beautiful* next to 1902, write: The first daily Yiddish newspaper in America begins.

Family Activity – Make Hamentaschen. See page s 966-967.

Student Workbook or Lesson Review – If you are using one of these optional books, complete the assignment for Lesson 98.

Italian Poster Advertising Liberty Bonds

Boys Town, Nebraska

Edward Flanagan was born in 1886 in County Roscommon, Ireland. His parents were John and Nora Flanagan. Edward had ten brothers and sisters. Edward was a frail baby, so his grandfather kept him warm by the fire. The Flanagan home was happy. As an adult, Edward said that as a child he learned to pray and work.

Edward helped his family by taking complete care of their cattle and sheep. He watched his father pray while he worked, so he began to do the same. While still a boy, Edward decided he wanted to become a priest. He later said that he probably became a priest because he wanted to help people and teach people. Edward studied at the local public school and spent his high school years at a Catholic school in Dublin, Ireland.

By the time Edward was ready to go to college, his sister Nellie and his brother Patrick, a priest, had already emigrated to America. Nellie convinced her parents that Edward should also come to America. He arrived in America in August of 1904.

For a while, Edward lived with his mother's family in the Yonkers section of New York City. Soon he enrolled in a Catholic college in Maryland. Later, he was admitted into St. Joseph's Seminary in New York City with the help of a cousin who was president of the Emigrant Industrial Savings Bank in New York City. Just a few months before Edward entered St. Joseph's, his parents immigrated to America, too. Edward had been sickly since he was a baby. His health suffered in New York City, so the Catholic Church sent him to Omaha, Nebraska, where his brother Patrick was already serving as a priest. Edward's parents accompanied him so they could take care of him.

Edward worked as a bookkeeper in a meat packing house. He then traveled in Europe, studying in both Rome and Austria. During this time, he had periods of sickness and periods of good health. After completing his studies in Europe, Edward Flanagan became a Catholic priest in 1912.

Flanagan came home to America and was soon working as a priest in Omaha. Noticing many homeless men, he opened the Workingmen's Hotel, where men could find a bed and food. Here he talked to the men about their childhoods. He found that many of these wanderers were orphans. Some were children of divorced parents, and others came from poor families that did not meet the child's physical needs. Flanagan found out that ninety percent of criminals began breaking the law as children. He realized that he could accomplish more by ministering to boys rather than men. He believed that neglected boys become neglected men.

Flanagan began caring for boys. The juvenile court sent him two boys to care for, and he befriended three others on the streets of Omaha. In 1917, when Flanagan was thirty-one years old, he opened his first boys' home in a Victorian mansion. Boys from Omaha and from elsewhere began showing up at the doorstep. He took in boys of any race or religion who were homeless or delinquent. A delinquent young person is one who breaks rules, causes trouble, does not fulfill his duties, or disobeys the law. The home quickly filled with fifty boys. As Flanagan cared for the boys, he realized how blessed he was during his happy childhood in Ireland.

The Catholic Church assigned several nuns to help Flanagan. In 1918 he moved the home to another location, the German American Home, where he could help 150 boys. Here Flanagan and the nuns educated the boys in the home's parlors.

Flanagan began to publish a paper called *Father Flanagan's Boy's Home Journal*. It had recipes, jokes, and home remedies and also told about the boys' activities. Flanagan's grandfather had been respected as someone who could help people with home remedies, so Flanagan might have remembered the remedies from his youth.

While caring for his boys, Flanagan studied to become a U.S. citizen. He accomplished his goal in 1919. Flanagan decided to try to move his boys out of Omaha. He found Overlook Farm with 160 acres. In 1921 Flanagan moved his boys to the farm that became the Village of Boys Town. Here they planted corn, alfalfa, and potatoes. They tended a fruit orchard and a vegetable garden. They also milked cows. The farm had room for a baseball diamond, a track, and a football field.

Many people believed in what Flanagan was doing and began to contribute. Catholics and Protestants, business leaders and Omaha residents all helped. By 1922 they had raised enough money to build a five-story brick building. Inside were the classrooms, chapel, dining hall, dormitory, gym, and infirmary, where sick boys could recover. By 1930 Boys Town had 280 boys and construction was underway for a new trade school, offices for faculty, and a new gym.

The boys of Boys Town came from every state, and Flanagan made life as normal as possible for them. They were given academic and vocational training during the day. At night they participated in hobbies and did what so many other Americans did during the evenings of the 1930s—listened to the radio.

Boys Town grew into a community where boys between the ages of ten and sixteen received loving care. It became an official village of the state of Nebraska. The boys elected their own mayor, council, and commissioners. The town became famous. The Boys Town choir performed in New York City at Carnegie Hall. They also

Flanagan visited the White House in 1938. Here he visits with Joseph Keenan, Assistant to the Attorney General.

traveled to Canada, Cuba, and Japan. The Boys Town football team toured in more than twenty states. Crowds as large as 35,000 came to see them play. Flanagan had a radio show, in which he talked about his boys. More people learned about Flanagan's work when the 1938 movie *Boys Town* was released. Spencer Tracy starred as "Father Flanagan." Another star was child actor Mickey Rooney. Spencer Tracy won an Academy Award for his performance. In 1941 another movie called *Men of Boys Town* was released.

Flanagan became well-known for his work. He helped other people learn how to care for troubled children and wrote articles about the subject. After World War II, President Harry Truman asked him to travel to other parts of the world to help people learn how to care for children. Flanagan traveled to Japan, Korea, Austria, and Germany. He died in Germany in 1948 at the age of sixty-one. By the time he died, he had helped care for about 5,500 boys. The campus of Boys Town had grown to nine hundred acres.

Flanagan's body was flown back to Nebraska. He is buried in the chapel at Boys Town. In 1965 he was inducted into the Nebraska Hall of Fame. The work of Boys Town has continued and expanded to help both boys and girls. The national headquarters is still in Nebraska, but Boys Town also has programs in California, Florida, Illinois, Louisiana, Nevada, New York, Rhode Island, Texas, and Washington, D.C.

Edward Flanagan knew that boys need a purpose for their lives. He knew they need to know God. Flanagan said, "The fact is that nothing earthly can fill the void in the human heart." When this Catholic priest cared for homeless boys, he did something that is dear to God's heart:

> And [Jesus] said to them, "Whoever receives this child in My name receives Me,
> and whoever receives Me receives Him who sent Me;
> for the one who is least among all of you, this is the one who is great."
> Luke 9:48

Activities for Lesson 99

Map Study – Complete the assignment for Lesson 99 on Map 3 "American Landmarks" in *Maps of America the Beautiful*.

Vocabulary – Find each of these words in a dictionary, then find the definition that corresponds to the way the word is used in this lesson: seminary, delinquent, remedy, infirmary, vocational. Copy the words and definitions into your notebook.

Literature – Read "Succos" in *All-of-a-Kind Family*.

Creative Writing – In your notebook, write a one-page letter to your parents thanking them for their love and service to you.

Timeline – In *Timeline of America the Beautiful* next to 1917, write: Edward Flanagan opens a home for boys in Omaha.

Student Workbook or Lesson Review – If you are using one of these optional books, complete the assignment for Lesson 99.

God Created the Grand Canyon

In northwest Arizona, God created the Grand Canyon. This immense and majestic canyon is known around the world. President Woodrow Wilson and the U.S. Congress made it a national park in 1919. Today almost five million people visit each year.

Colorado River from Toroweap Overlook

The Colorado River

The Colorado River, pictured at left, is 1,450 miles long. It begins in the Rocky Mountains of Colorado and continues to the Gulf of California in Mexico. It enters the Grand Canyon at Lees Ferry and exits it 277 miles downstream at Grand Wash Cliffs. Besides this river, water is scarce in many parts of the area around the Grand Canyon. Some large springs and a few streams such as Havasu Creek, mentioned on page 46, flow into the Colorado River.

Grand Canyon Vistas

Many adventurous visitors hike to the bottom of the Grand Canyon. A few dare to raft the Colorado River on

583

Scene from South Rim Village in Winter *Winter Sunset*

the canyon floor. Most simply look at the canyon from the southern edge, called the South Rim. A smaller number gaze at the canyon from the North Rim. All of these visitors try to take in the awesome grandeur. From the rising of the sun to its setting, canyon views are in constant change. When clouds from on high cast their shadows on the canyon or a thunderstorm gathers overhead, more breathtaking vistas appear. See photos above.

Deep and Wide

The Grand Canyon is deep and wide. Two popular places to look at the canyon on the South Rim are Grand Canyon Village, an area with hotels, restaurants, and shops, and Desert View. Three historic structures on the South Rim built in the 20th century are pictured at right. The distance from Grand Canyon Village to the Colorado River on the canyon floor is about 5,000 feet—almost one mile. The distance across the canyon from the village to the North Rim is ten miles. Other parts of the Grand Canyon are even deeper and wider. At its deepest, the Grand Canyon is 6,000 feet from rim to river; the widest section is eighteen miles across from rim to rim.

Hopi House, 1905

Hiking the Grand Canyon

Grand Canyon National Park has many trails. Some follow along the rim and others lead into the canyon. Look at the pictures on page 585. A seven-mile trail runs from Grand Canyon Village to the Colorado River. A hike down this trail takes one day going and another day coming back. Hikers can stay at Phantom Ranch resort village at the bottom of the canyon or they can camp with a permit. Hikers can take the North and South Kaibab Trails to hike from rim to rim. The trek takes three days.

Lookout Studio, 1914

Indian Watchtower, 1932

On this hike they cross over the Colorado River on a narrow suspension footbridge that is seventy feet above the water. See trail and footbridge photos below.

Even experienced hikers find the Grand Canyon challenging because of the high altitude and the dangerous terrain. Over 250 people are rescued in the Grand Canyon each year. Most are healthy young males who try to cover more ground than they should in the difficult hiking conditions in the park.

South Kaibab Trail *Suspension Footbridge Across the Colorado* *Entrance to the Footbridge*

A Canyon Mule Ride

Visitors can take mule rides into the canyon from the North Rim in the summer and from the South Rim year round. Riders must weigh less than two hundred pounds and be over four feet seven inches tall. They have to understand English. Reservations for some mule rides must be made as many as thirteen months in advance. Short trips are available, as well as trips all the way to the canyon floor. Trips to the canyon

Hiking into the Grand Canyon

floor take one day going and another day coming back. Those taking the two-day trip can eat and stay overnight at Phantom Ranch. Notice the mule party at left. If you think you may like to take this ride one day, start saving your pennies. Prices in 2010 began at over $840 for two people!

A Trip Down the Colorado River

Many boating opportunities await tourists at the Grand Canyon. Adventurous travelers can take two weeks or more to experience the dangers and thrills of the Colorado River as it flows through the canyon. Those who want a shorter ride enjoy half- or full-day trips on either smooth or whitewater. Imagine gliding on the Colorado like the rafters pictured on page 586.

A Mule Party on South Kaibab Trail

The Geology of the Grand Canyon

In the beginning God created the heavens and the earth. Since then He has continued to carve, mold, and shape it. He sends water to move earth and stone. He uses volcanoes and earthquakes to shift the land. Creation is in constant change. The scientist and the casual observer alike see evidence of change in the Grand Canyon.

Rafting the Colorado River Near Havasu Creek

The canyon displays a mile of the earth's crust. Almost forty layers of rock are stacked together, mostly granite, sandstone, shale, limestone, and schist. Some rocks are harder than others. As seen above and at left, some rocks form slopes when they erode and others form cliffs. Some erode quickly while others erode more slowly. The Grand Canyon shows evidence that volcanoes were once active here. Some of the rocks in the canyon are metamorphic, meaning that they experienced heat and pressure at some time in the past. The canyon also shows evidence that water has caused some of the changes here. The rocks of the Grand Canyon contain many kinds of minerals, which give the geological formations the beautiful colors of red, yellow, and green.

*The Colorado River with
Slopes and Cliffs of the Grand Canyon*

For centuries the Havasupai people have lived in the Grand Canyon by the beautiful waters of the Havasu Creek. See Havasupai Falls below. Today they have a reservation that adjoins the national park. The Havasupai tell a tribal legend about how the Grand Canyon formed. They say it was created by a worldwide flood. Though Christians don't believe other details of the Havasupai legend, many do believe that one of the major events God used to create the Grand Canyon was the worldwide flood experienced by Noah and his family and described in Genesis 6-8.

Anyone who has experienced a flood, even a flash flood that only lasted a short time, knows that water is a powerful force. We can only imagine what happened with non-stop rain for forty days and forty nights, especially when water was also coming up from underground. God has not told us exactly how He made the Grand Canyon, but one thing is sure: He made it, and it is a place of beauty.

Havasupai Falls

586

Caves of the Grand Canyon

Spelunkers have charted over three hundred of the Grand Canyon's one thousand caves. One of the best known is Cave of the Domes. Most of the caves in the Grand Canyon are limestone. Caves of the Grand Canyon have unique cave formations called speleothems. These are mummified remains of ancient plants. The caves also have formations called split-twig figurines. Many of the Grand Canyon caves are sources of water. Examples are Vasey's Paradise, Cheyava Falls, Roaring Spring, Thunder Spring, and Tapeats Spring.

Habitats of the Grand Canyon

At first glance, the Grand Canyon appears to be a barren place, but God has created many plants and animals that thrive in the canyon environment. Grand Canyon National Park has 1,500 plant, 355 bird, 89 mammal, 47 reptile, 17 fish, and 9 amphibian species. The Grand Canyon itself has such great changes in elevation that it has distinct habitats. These are discussed below.

The antelope squirrel lives in the riparian habitat.

Riparian. A habitat where water and land meet is called riparian. The floor of the Grand Canyon is a riparian habitat with sandy beaches, lush vegetation, and many species of plants. Mammals in the riparian habitat include bats, beavers, antelope squirrels, pocket mice, spotted skunks, mountain lions, and desert bighorn sheep. The antelope squirrel is pictured above. Notice the sure-footed desert bighorn sheep below.

Common amphibians in this habitat are the canyon tree frog, red-spotted toad, and the Woodhouse's Rocky Mountain toad. Among the reptiles are the desert banded gecko. The canyon has six species of rattlesnakes, including the Hopi, southwestern speckled, northern black-tailed, Great Basin, Mojave green, and Grand Canyon pink. The Grand Canyon pink is the most common. The two largest lizards in the riparian habitat of the Grand Canyon are Gila monsters and chuckwallas. A chuckwalla, desert banded gecko, and Gila monster are pictured on page 588.

Two hundred and fifty species of birds are found here. Forty-eight bird species nest along the river. Others migrate along the Colorado River or use the canyon

Desert Bighorn Sheep in the Grand Canyon

Chuckwalla

Desert Banded Gecko

Gila Monster

as their winter home. The Colorado River is rich with trout, so one winter resident is the bald eagle.

Desert Scrub. As you travel up the side of the Grand Canyon, the next habitat is the desert scrub, which has many varieties of scrub and cacti. Scrub plants often have small

Beaver Cactus in Bloom in the Desert Scrub Habitat

leaves and thorns. See a beaver cactus from the Grand Canyon at left. Fifty species of mammals live in the desert scrub. Most are rodents and bats. Bats gather in maternity colonies in the caves of the desert scrub. Many reptiles of the riparian habitat also live in the desert scrub. The desert gopher tortoise lives in one area of the canyon's desert scrub. Thirty species of birds nest here, including California condors.

Coniferous Forests. Above the desert scrub are three coniferous forest habitats: piñon pine and juniper; ponderosa; and spruce and fir. Piñon pine and juniper grow between the desert scrub and 6,200 feet in elevation above sea level. Ponderosa pine grows between 6,200 and 8,200 feet. Spruce and fir grow on the North Rim where the elevation is above 8,200 feet.

Mammals in this habitat include mule deer, elk, black bear, porcupines, shrews, Abert squirrels, and red squirrels. See the squirrel at the top of page 589. Common amphibians that live near the rim are Utah tiger salamanders and Great Basin spadefoot toads. Many mountain short-horned lizards live here, as do other reptiles. About ninety species of birds breed in these coniferous forests, including goshawks and spotted owls.

Weather at the Grand Canyon

Though God placed the Grand Canyon in a semi-arid desert, summer temperatures on the South Rim are pleasant, ranging from the 50°s to the 80°s. Temperatures on the North Rim are even cooler

Grand Canyon Painting by Thoams Moran, 1912

because it is at a higher elevation. However, the temperature on the canyon floor may rise to 100° during the summer. Snow falls at the Grand Canyon in winter. The South Rim often has snow and the North Rim is closed all winter due to snow. See photo on page 589.

Natives, Explorers, and Miners

In addition to the Havasupai, Hualapai and Navajo tribes have lived in the canyon region for centuries. Ancient cliff dwellers once lived there. See photo below.

White Americans knew little about the Grand Canyon until natural history professor John Wesley Powell, pictured below, made a journey through the Grand Canyon in 1869. The feat was especially

Red squirrels live in coniferous forests.

impressive considering that Powell only had one arm. He had lost an arm because of wounds he received in a battle during the Civil War. Powell later became the director of the U.S. Geological Survey. In 1869 Powell, his brother Walter, and eight other explorers set out in four small wooden boats on the Colorado River. One man quit early on. Three others made most of the journey; but they became afraid and left just two days before the trip was completed. Those three were not heard from again.

Winter Snow at the Grand Canyon in 1900   *John Wesley Powell*   *Grand Canyon Cliff Dwellings*

Powell and the other five expedition members were the first people in history known to have accomplished this challenging journey. It took them three months. After the historic trip, Powell traveled and lectured about his explorations. He repeated the journey in 1871-1872 with ten others. The photographs below were taken during the second voyage. The boat on the right is the boat used by Powell. Notice that he had a chair strapped onto the boat.

Photographs from John Wesley Powell's Grand Canyon Expedition of 1871-1872

The state of Arizona has over 850 identified minerals. Varying amounts of many minerals are found in the Grand Canyon. In the late 1800s, Americans became interested in mining copper and asbestos in the canyon. A few settlers built homes along the rim in the 1880s.

The 1908 stereoscopic photograph at right shows American landscape artist Thomas Moran sketching a scene at Bright Angel Cove in the Grand Canyon. In 1912 Moran painted the beautiful image of the Grand Canyon at lower right on page 588.

Thomas Moran Sketching at the Grand Canyon

Tourists Come to the Canyon

As news about the grandeur of the Grand Canyon spread, tourists began to visit. Many made the difficult trip to the South Rim by stagecoach. They used mining trails to explore the canyon. See early tourists below. In 1901 a railroad was constructed from Williams, Arizona, to the South Rim. Soon hotels replaced the crude camps earlier tourists had used.

The El Tovar Hotel was designed by architect Charles Whittlessey. Built in 1905, it is still in use today. The photograph at the top of page 591 was taken in 1908. Notice the horse and carriage in front of the hotel.

Architect Mary Colter designed several historic structures at Grand Canyon National Park. She designed Phantom Ranch, which was built in 1922. One of its buildings is pictured on page 591. Colter also designed the structures pictured on page 584.

Colter got inspiration for her designs from Southwest natives, especially the Hopi, Zuni, and Navajo. She built with stone from the area and tried to make the structures fit into the surroundings. Colter not only designed the buildings, she also decorated the interiors. She collected antiques to use in decorating and also hired native artists to add artwork to both interiors and exteriors. At bottom of page 591 is the fireplace Colter designed for another of her Grand Canyon structures, Hermit's Rest.

Stereoscopic Photographs from the Grand Canyon, 1903 and 1906

*Horse and Carriage in Front
of the El Tovar Hotel, 1908*

Both Whittlessey and Colter worked for the Atchison, Topeka, and Santa Fe Railway. These architects also worked for the Fred Harvey Company. The Fred Harvey Company provided food on railway dining cars and also ran restaurants and hotels near the railway. The Fred Harvey Company became famous in the West for providing excellent food and service for travelers. The company hired wholesome young women to serve as their waitresses. The company provided these "Harvey Girls" with dormitories and took good care of them.

Protecting the Grand Canyon

Conservationists, including avid outdoorsman Theodore Roosevelt, encouraged the preservation of the

A Building in Phantom Ranch

Fireplace in Hermit's Rest

Grand Canyon. By the time it became a national park in 1919, annual visitation was already over 44,000 per year.

President Theodore Roosevelt said this about the Grand Canyon: "Leave it as it is. The ages have been at work on it, and man can only mar it. What you can do is to keep it for your children, your children's children, and for all who come after you, as one of the great sights which every American should see."

Through the ages, God has created a beautiful masterpiece at the Grand Canyon. We should keep this wonder for our children, our children's children, and for all who come after us to enjoy. It is a magnificent tribute to the powerful work God does each day as He continues to shape the world—east and west and north and south:

The north and the south, You have created them.
Psalm 89:12

Activities for Lesson 100

Map Study – Complete the assignment for Lesson 100 on Map 2 "God's Wonders" in *Maps of America the Beautiful*.

Vocabulary – In your notebook, make a drawing for each of these words that illustrates what it means: majestic, vista, erode, maternity, wholesome. Write the word under the drawing. Check in a dictionary if you need help with their definitions.

Literature – Read "Canyons of the Colorado" in *We the People*, pages 122-123, and "A New Charlie" in *All-of-a-Kind Family*.

Creative Writing – If you had two days to spend at the Grand Canyon with your family, what would you like to do? In your notebook, write two or three paragraphs answering this question.

Timeline – In *Timeline of America the Beautiful* next to 1919, write: Grand Canyon National Park is established.

Student Workbook or Lesson Review – If you are using one of these optional books, complete the assignment for Lesson 100. If you are using the Lesson Review, answer the questions on *All-of-a-Kind Family* and take the quiz for Unit 20.

The Roaring Twenties

At the beginning of the 1920s, Warren G. Harding served as America's President. He was followed by Calvin Coolidge, a man of integrity who stood strong for what he believed was right. Herbert Hoover was elected in 1928 and was President when America and much of the world entered the Great Depression in 1929. A growing number of Americans worked in factories during the 1920s. By the end of the decade, workers at Ford Motor Company, which was the largest factory complex in the world, were building 1.5 million vehicles a year. The complex was just outside of Detroit, which became known as Motor City, USA. Late in the decade, Gutzon Borglum began carving the faces of four Presidents on the side of Mount Rushmore in the Black Hills. In 1925 Christian statesman William Jennings Bryan stood up for his faith in a highly-publicized trial concerning a new Tennessee law that made the teaching of evolution illegal in public schools.

Lessons in Unit 21

Lesson 101 – Our American Story: Republicans in the White House
Lesson 102 – Daily Life: Working in an American Factory
Lesson 103 – An American Landmark: Motor City, USA
Lesson 104 – God's Wonders: God Created the Black Hills
Lesson 105 – An American Biography: William Jennings Bryan, Christian Statesman

Books Used in Unit 21

- *Maps of America the Beautiful*

- *Timeline of America the Beautiful*

- *We the People*

- *Blue Willow* by Doris Gates

President Hoover presses a button to start the machinery at the new Detroit News *building on December 6, 1929.*

Republicans in the White House

With the Great War behind them, Americans wanted their lives to return to normal. Many were tired of the controversy surrounding the League of Nations. They were weary of America's involvement with foreign nations. They missed the way things were before the war. Republican presidential candidate Senator Warren G. Harding from Ohio invented the word "normalcy." He told Americans that the Republicans could help them return to normalcy. Harding and vice-presidential candidate Calvin Coolidge won the election by a large margin, receiving sixty percent of the vote. Harding won every state except the staunchly-Democratic southern states. He was inaugurated in 1921. See the Hardings and Coolidges in the photo at right.

President and Mrs. Harding and Vice President and Mrs. Coolidge

The Administration of Warren G. Harding

Once in office, Harding selected many well-qualified men of good character to serve with him. In his first year in office, he appointed William Howard Taft as chief justice of the Supreme Court. With this appointment, Taft realized a long-time desire. This office meant more to Taft than being elected President in 1908. Harding also nominated future President Herbert Hoover as his Secretary of Commerce. However, Harding filled some positions with men who were corrupt.

Under Harding's leadership, the war with Germany was officially ended. In addition, treaties designed to insure peaceful relations between the world's strongest nations were signed by the U.S. and other countries.

President Harding with School Children

Like other Presidents, Harding met with people who visited the White House. In the photo at left, he meets with school children he invited to see an owl's nest found on the White House grounds. In the top left photo on page 595, Harding meets with Sioux and Crow chiefs who came to Washington.

President Harding with Sioux and Crow Chiefs

Chief Justice William Howard Taft,
President Warren G. Harding, and Robert Todd Lincoln

Harding also gave speeches at events such as the dedication of the Lincoln Memorial in 1922. In the photo above, Harding talks with Abraham Lincoln's son Robert Todd Lincoln on the day of the dedication. Chief Justice William Howard Taft was also involved in the ceremony.

A political system called Communism was growing in Europe. Americans were afraid that new immigrants might be Communists who wanted to overthrow the United States government. They were also afraid that immigrants would take jobs away from Americans. Congress severely limited immigration into the U.S.

President Harding and Others Visit a Totem Pole in Sitka, Alaska

Harding and Party in Alaska

As the corruption of some of Harding's associates became known, he was saddened. He confided to friends about how much it hurt to have friends betray him. Harding decided to travel across the country on a "voyage of understanding." He went all the way to Alaska. Along the way, he made eighty-five speeches.

The President became ill after visiting Alaska. His doctor insisted that he rest, so the presidential party stopped in San Francisco. There on August 2, 1923, President Harding died. Look at the photos above and at right and read about Harding's life on page 596.

President and Mrs. Coolidge leave the funeral of President Harding.

Warren Gamaliel Harding
America's Twenty-Ninth President
March 4, 1921 - August 2, 1923

Warren Gamaliel Harding was born in Ohio in 1865. Both of his parents were doctors. He was the eldest of six children and known as Winnie. He grew up swimming in the creek, doing farm chores, and attending a one-room school with his siblings. There he learned to read from the McGuffey Readers. When Winnie grew older, he joined a village band. He went to Ohio Central College at age fourteen, graduating in 1882. In college he was the editor of the campus newspaper.

After college Harding taught school, studied law, sold insurance, and worked for a local newspaper. In 1884, he and two friends purchased a small-town newspaper. Harding was well-respected by his employees and his readers. He reported fairly and avoided critical stories. At age twenty-five he maried thirty-year-old divorcee Florence Kling DeWolfe, who had a ten-year-old son. After their marriage, her son went to live with his grandmother.

Harding entered politics in 1899. He served first in the Ohio State Senate and later as Lieutenant Governor, before returning to his newspaper business. Harding was a favorite of the Ohio state Republican Party, so he was given the privilege of nominating William Howard Taft at the Republican convention of 1912. In 1914 Harding was elected as a U.S. Senator.

In 1920 Harding received the nomination as the Republican candidate for President. Though Harding had campaigned hard for William Howard Taft in 1916, he decided to run the same style of campaign that presidential candidates had used before the energetic campaigning of Theodore Roosevelt. Harding ran a front-porch campaign from his home in Marion, Ohio, making speeches to small groups rather than traveling to speak to large crowds. Popular American entertainer Al Jolson traveled the country singing songs in support of Harding. Harding's opponent, James Cox, another newspaperman from Ohio, traveled 22,000 miles giving speeches. At the end of the campaign, Harding won 404 electoral votes and Cox won 127.

After President Harding's death, more facts about the corruption among his appointees were made public. Florence Harding lived just over a year after the death of her husband.

John Calvin Coolidge Sr. Administers the Oath of Office to His Son

In August of 1923, Vice President Calvin Coolidge was vacationing at his father's home in their hometown of Plymouth Notch, Vermont. Early in the morning of August 3, the elder Coolidge received word of Harding's death. He awoke his son to tell him the news. Before leaving his bedroom, Calvin Coolidge knelt with his wife and asked God to bless the American people and give him the power to serve them.

Coolidge then walked to a local store and called the Secretary of State, who encouraged him to take the oath of office immediately. Coolidge went back home and his father, a local justice of the peace, administered the oath in the parlor by the light of kerosene lamps. After taking the oath of office using the family Bible, President Coolidge went back to bed.

While Coolidge was President, Congress passed the Indian Citizenship Act, which gave U.S. citizenship to all Native Americans. Coolidge supported the growth of business. Americans were pleased with his policies. In the presidential campaign of 1924, Americans were encouraged to "Keep Cool with Coolidge." Coolidge was re-elected and in 1925

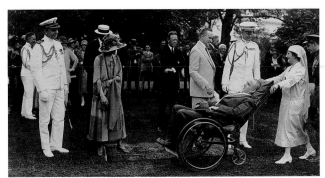

The Coolidges Meet with a Wounded Soldier

President and Mrs. Coolidge Attend Church

President Coolidge Meets Helen Keller

began to serve a full term as President. He did not seek another term in 1928.

Calvin Coolidge found comfort and strength in God, and his wife Grace was also a woman of faith. In the middle photo above, he and Mrs. Coolidge are attending church. Serving as President reminded Coolidge how much we depend on God's guidance.

Presidents meet many famous people. In the photo at right above, Coolidge is visiting with Helen Keller, who accomplished much in her life, even though she was both deaf and blind. Presidents also reach out to hurting people. In the photo at left above, President and Mrs. Coolidge meet with a wounded soldier. Read about Coolidge's life below.

John Calvin Coolidge
America's Thirtieth President
August 3, 1923 - March 4, 1929

John Calvin Coolidge Jr. was born on the Fourth of July in 1872 in Plymouth Notch, Vermont. He grew up wanting to be a good, honest, small-town storekeeper like his father. As a boy, he sold apples, did chores around his father's farm and store, helped his father keep accounts, and went to school. Calvin's mother died when he was twelve. A few years later, his younger sister and only sibling Abigail also died. His father later married again, and Calvin became close to his stepmother.

Calvin Coolidge graduated with honors from prestigious Amherst College in Massachusetts. Though his was the fifth generation of Coolidges to live in Plymouth Notch, Calvin moved to Northampton, Massachusetts, studied law, and passed the bar exam.

John Calvin Coolidge Sr. was well-respected, quiet, and careful with money. He also held several local offices and served in the Vermont legislature. His son followed in his footsteps. Calvin Coolidge worked in the local Republican Club in Northampton. He served on the city council, as city solicitor, and as county clerk. In his entire political career, Coolidge lost only one election. He ran unsuccessfully for a seat on the Northampton school board in 1905.

That same year thirty-three-year-old Calvin Coolidge married Grace Anna Goodhue, a twenty-six-year-old teacher of hearing-impaired students. The first time Grace saw Calvin he was shaving by an open window at his boardinghouse. When she saw that he was wearing a hat, she laughed out loud. Coolidge later said he wore the hat to keep his uncombed hair out of his way. The two began courting later that spring. A few months after they met, this quiet man told Grace: "I am going to be married to you." Grace loved him and quickly agreed. They were

married at her parents' home in Burlington, Vermont, that fall. The couple had two sons, John and Calvin. The family is pictured at left.

Coolidge continued to be elected to more offices. He became a Massachusetts state representative, then mayor of Northampton, a Massachusetts state senator, and then Lieutenant Governor of Massachusetts. In 1918 he narrowly beat his Democratic rival to become Governor of Massachuestts.

Governor Coolidge became well-known around the country when he called out the Massachusetts National Guard to break a Boston police strike. He said, "There is no right to strike against the public safety by anybody, anywhere, any time." When the Republicans held their national convention in 1920, Massachusetts Republicans tried unsuccessfully to get Coolidge selected as the party's presidential nominee. Coolidge instead became the vice-presidential nominee.

Vice President Coolidge took part in the Harding administration, mostly as a quiet onlooker. Though he was nicknamed "Silent Cal," Coolidge made many public appearances as President, gave monthly radio addresses, and held 520 press conferences. He and Grace entertained a great deal and made many appearances. In the lower right photograph on page 597, Grace is receiving children on May Day.

While the Coolidges were in the White House, they experienced a deep personal tragedy when their youngest son Calvin died at age sixteen of an infection. After leaving the presidency, Calvin and Grace Coolidge returned to Northampton. He wrote articles for magazines and wrote an autobiography. He also wrote a syndicated column called "Thinking Things Over with Calvin Coolidge." He died unexpectedly of heart failure in 1933. After his death, Mrs. Coolidge began to write magazine articles. She also wrote an autobiography. She enjoyed her grandchildren and listening to Boston Red Sox baseball games on the radio. She lived as a widow for twenty-four years. Grace Coolidge died in 1957.

Roaring Twenties Trends

The decade of the 1920s was called the Roaring Twenties. Technology was advancing rapidly. The photo at right shows a telegraph operator transmitting a speech that Harding is giving to a joint session of the Senate and House of Representatives. See the telegraph operator in the corner.

During the 1920s, many Americans bought radios. Harding was the first U.S. President to speak on the radio. Notice the drawing in the box on page 599 of a couple listening to the radio. At the top of the page, see Harding recording his voice for the government archives.

Telegraph Operator (Inset) Transmits Harding Speech

Many Americans went to see motion pictures. In the photo at far right, Mrs. Harding uses a movie camera. In the photograph below it is the Evangeline Theater, built in 1930 in New Iberia, Louisiana. The theater is in the art deco style popular during the 1920s.

Harding's voice is recorded for the government archives.

Florence Harding operates a movie camera on the White House lawn.

Lindbergh and his airplane, the Spirit of St. Louis

Thousands of African Americans moved north between 1916 and 1930, a period of American history called the Great Migration.

American aviation improved rapidly. In 1923 two U.S. Army lieutenants made the first non-stop flight across America. They flew from

Evangeline, an Art Deco Movie Theater in New Iberia, Louisiana

Long Island, New York, to San Diego, California. The next year airplanes began taking paying passengers from coast to coast. Charles Lindbergh, pictured above, made the first solo flight across the Atlantic in 1927. His plane, *Spirit of St. Louis*, is now on display at the Smithsonian Institution. In 1930 large commercial airlines were forming. In 1932 Amelia Earhart became the first woman to fly solo over the Atlantic. Read about more trends in the 1920s below.

In the 1920s . . .

- The dance called the Charleston began in Charleston, South Carolina, and spread across the country.
- Professional and college sports became popular.
- The Harlem Globetrotters began in Chicago. They played their first game in 1927. They added clever ball-handling tricks and on-court comedy to their game in 1939. The team has now played in more than 115 countries. The Smithsonian Institution has a permanent Globetrotters exhibit.
- The Children's Museum of Indianapolis was founded in 1925. It became the world's largest children's museum.
- Knute Rockne, immigrant from Norway, was football coach at the University of Notre Dame. He coined the phrase "win one for the Gipper" when he asked his players to win a game for team member George "Gipper" Gipp, who was ill.

Herbert Hoover Becomes President

Businesses grew rapidly during the presidencies of Harding and Coolidge, but prices of farm products fell. Still, most Americans were content with the work being done by their Republican Presidents. They thought that the prosperity of the 1920s would be permanent. In 1928 the American people elected the third Republican President in a row, Herbert Hoover.

During his first months in office, Hoover began to improve conditions on

Indian reservations. He worked to get Boulder Canyon Dam built to increase electricity production in California. It was later named Hoover Dam. Because he believed in conservation of natural resources, he increased the amount of Federal land set aside as national forests. His administration also attempted to help American farmers by establishing a Federal Farm Board.

President Hoover with Spelling Bee Winners

Hoover welcomed guests to the White House. At top right, he is pictured with winners of the 1929 National Spelling Bee. At right, Mrs. Hoover enjoys a cowboy band that visited the White House.

The Stock Market Crash of 1929

Many Americans invested in the stock market during the 1920s. When a person buys a stock, he purchases a share of ownership in a company. The company takes the money the

Mrs. Hoover with a Cowboy Band

person invested and uses it to make the company grow. When a company makes a profit, the stock owners receive income. Many Americans were so sure that business in America would continue to grow that they borrowed money to buy stocks.

In the late 1920s, people began spending less money buying what companies were selling. This meant that companies made less profit. The value of stock went down. People who had borrowed money to buy stock couldn't pay back the money they had borrowed. In the autumn of 1929, stock values fell more. They fell sharply on October 29, 1929, a day called "Black Thursday."

People began to take cash out of their bank accounts in order to buy what they needed. Some banks did not have enough cash on hand to meet the demand. If a bank was low on cash, many more people tried to withdraw their money from the bank. This is called a bank run. Banks began to close. Factories closed because people were not buying as many products, so workers lost their jobs.

President Hoover and Congress struggled to find a solution to a mammoth problem that had been caused by a lack of planning on the part of business, by the slow world-wide economy that developed as a result of the Great War, and by greed.

When Hoover became President, only five percent of Americans who wanted to work did not have jobs. The percentage of unemployed people had risen to about twenty-five percent by 1933. This means that for every four people who wanted to work, one did not have a job. Americans became upset with the Republican-led government and wanted a change. Read about Hoover's life on page 601.

Herbert Clark Hoover
America's Thirty-First President
March 4, 1929 - March 4, 1933

Herbert Clark Hoover was born in tiny West Branch, Iowa, in 1874. The Quaker meetinghouse his family attended was in sight of his home. His father was a blacksmith who also sold farm equipment. His father died when Herbert was only six and his mother died three years later, leaving Herbert and his older brother and younger sister orphans. Herbert was passed among relatives before moving to Oregon to live with an uncle who was a physician.

Herbert struggled in most subjects at the Quaker academy he attended in Oregon, but he did well in math. He was determined to enter the new Stanford University in California, so he studied hard and passed the entrance exams. At Stanford he majored in geology and was involved in many extracurricular activities. To pay for college, he worked in a university office and began a business which did laundry for other students. During summer breaks he worked with geologists in California, Nevada, and Arkansas. At Stanford he courted Lou Henry, the only female geology major in the school.

After graduation, Hoover labored in a gold mine, but soon found work as a mining engineer. His work took him to many countries. From Australia he cabled Lou and asked her to marry him. She cabled back her consent. They were married in 1899 and Lou began to travel with her husband all over the world. The Hoovers were in China in 1900 when violence broke out against foreign residents. The conflict was called the Boxer Rebellion. Herbert was involved with defending their settlement, and Lou helped to nurse wounded diplomats.

Hoover began his own business as a mine consultant, purchased silver mines in Burma, and wrote a leading textbook on mining engineering. He worked hard and became wealthy.

When the Great War began, the U.S. consulate in London asked Hoover to help evacuate 120,000 Americans who were trapped in Europe. When Germany invaded Belgium, Hoover and wealthy friends raised millions of dollars to provide food and medicine for hurting Belgians. Though Hoover was a Republican, he won the respect of Woodrow Wilson. During the war, Wilson asked him to run the U.S. Food Administration. Hoover was responsible for conserving food and other resources so that American soldiers and allies in Europe could have what they needed. America had to ration food and household goods. Americans began to use the word "Hooverize" when they spoke of rationing. After World War I, Wilson asked Hoover to help again when he appointed him head of the European Relief and Rehabilitation Administration. He was responsible for sending food, clothing, and supplies to help twenty European countries that had suffered during the Great War.

Hoover had a heart of compassion for people. His travels had given him knowledge of people from around the world. He helped President Wilson during the peace talks at Versailles, and he supported the League of Nations. After the war Hoover founded a research library at Stanford University to house information related to the Great War and the revolutions that followed it. Now called the Hoover Institution, this organization promotes peace, personal freedom, and limited government.

Herbert Hoover served as Secretary of Commerce under Harding and Coolidge. He worked to make industries run more efficiently and to help American businesses increase sales in other countries. He encouraged business leaders to work together. Hoover did not believe that the Federal government should control businesses, but that it should help them.

In 1927 Americans living along the Mississippi River experienced terrible flooding. Hoover took charge of the efforts to help them. He had nationwide respect when he ran for the presidency in 1928.

Herbert Hoover left the presidency at age 57 after one term. He and his wife continued to be generous, and Hoover continued to be active in politics. During World War II, Franklin Roosevelt appointed Hoover to be chairman of a relief organization to help Belgium, Finland, and Poland. In 1946 President Truman asked him to be coordinator of the Food Supply for World Famine. In 1947 he chaired the Hoover Commission, which proposed ways to reorganize the executive branch of the Federal government.

Lou Hoover died in 1944. Herbert Hoover continued to voice opinions on political matters until his death in 1964 at age ninety. Both Herbert and Lou Hoover are buried in West Branch, Iowa, at the site of his childhood home and the Hoover Presidential Library. Herbert and Lou Hoover's two sons honored their parents with their careers in business and public service.

Herbert and Lou Hoover are examples of being generous and willing to share. Mrs. Hoover assists at a mission at right. Jesus said:

Mrs. Hoover Assists at a Mission

> Give, and it will be given to you.
> They will pour into your lap a good measure,
> pressed down, shaken together, and
> running over. For by your standard of measure
> it will be measured to you in return.
> Luke 6:38

Activities for Lesson 101

Thinking Biblically – Copy Hebrews 13:5 into your notebook. Write two paragraphs about how the love of money contributed to the stock market crash of 1929 and how Christians should view money.

Vocabulary – In your notebook, write each of these vocabulary words: normalcy, Communism, divorcee, kerosene, commercial. Beside each word, write the letter of the correct definition and also copy the definition.

    a. a woman who has been divorced

    b. related to commerce (the business of buying and selling)

    c. the state of being normal

    d. a political system in which the state owns all property

    e. a flammable oil used for fuel

Literature – Read "Harding Appoints Taft" in *We the People*, pages 124-125, and chapter 1 in *Blue Willow*.

Timeline – In *Timeline of America the Beautiful* next to 1929, write: The stock market crash begins the Great Depression.

Student Workbook or Lesson Review – If you are using one of these optional books, complete the assignment for Lesson 101.

Working in an American Factory

By the 1920s, American companies had been building factories for many decades. The development of factories greatly changed the American way of life. In colonial times, a woman making a man's shirt might do everything from spinning the thread to weaving the fabric to cutting and sewing the shirt. A woman working in a clothing factory today might spend an entire day just sewing in sleeves on dozens of shirts, while other workers perform other individual jobs needed to complete the shirts. Notice the women at right sewing teddy bears in a factory.

Teddy Bear Factory, 1915

A colonial blacksmith made nails one at a time and sold them to individuals near his home. Today one factory employee can help make many nails, while never meeting the people who use them. First, the nails are manufactured and packaged. Then they are shipped on a truck to a giant warehouse. Later they are loaded onto another truck, which takes them to a hardware store perhaps hundreds or thousands of miles away.

Working Together

What does a person who works in a factory do all day? Millions of answers are possible to this question. The answer depends on where the person works, what the factory makes, and what the person's job is in the factory. A factory worker might help make a product. He may help ship products to warehouses or stores. He may design the product itself, design one of the machines used to make it, hire employees, or do a number of other jobs.

Factories work best when everyone remembers that each worker is important and that each job is important. The company president is important and so is the person who empties the trash. If trash piled up week after week, the company president could not find his desk! The pictures on the next page show people doing many different kinds of jobs in factories in the early 1900s.

Packing Chocolates, c. 1915

Forming Hats at the Stetson Hat Company, 1915

*Expert jewelry-makers receive enough gold
for a day's work, 1915.*

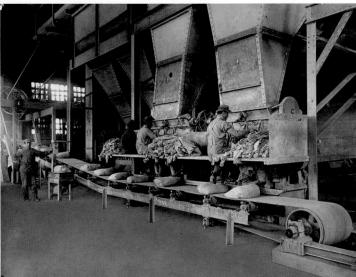

Filling Cement Bags at the Portland Cement Factory, Iowa, c. 1915

*Men and women work together
at the Express Spark Plug Company, c. 1918.*

Blind Men Making Brooms, 1920

In the left column, women wrap candy, expert jewelry-makers receive enough valuable gold and jewels for a day's work, men and women work together in the Express Spark Plug Company, and Singer Manufacturing Company workers in South Bend, Indiana, take a lunch break. In the right column, a worker forms hats at the Stetson Hat

Lunch Hour, Singer Manufacturing Company, 1908

Company, men fill cement bags at the Portland Cement Factory, and blind men make brooms. At right are workers processing sugar at the Union Sugar Company, boys who work at the Singer Manufacturing Company, and a female worker at the Caking Baking Company (that's right, Caking Baking).

Sugar Processors, Union Sugar Company, Betteravia, California

Where Americans Build Factories

Every factory needs employees to do the work, other businesses to supply needed materials, and means of transportation to bring in supplies and to carry away products. Wise businessmen don't build a water bottling factory in a desert. A company needing 5,000 employees does not build a factory in a town of five hundred. A town without a river or railway line does not attract a factory that needs large amounts of heavy products, which are difficult to transport by truck.

Boys Working at Singer Manufacturing Company

Though most factories have been built where towns or cities already existed, some business leaders have decided to build a factory and their own town, too. One example is Kannapolis, North Carolina, a company town owned by the Cannon Mills textile company. Its best known product was towels. Another example is Gary, Indiana.

Caking Baking Company, c. 1923

The Factory Town of Gary

Powerful and well-known businessmen Andrew Carnegie, J. P. Morgan, and Charles Schwab joined with Elbert H. Gary in 1901 to form the U.S. Steel Corporation. It was the largest business ever begun in American history up to that time. During its first year, the company produced more than half of all the steel made in America. The corporation built steel mills on the shores of Lake Michigan in northern Indiana. They also built a company town and named it Gary, Indiana, after Elbert H. Gary, who became U.S. Steel's first chairman. See the photograph below, taken just nine years after the formation of U.S. Steel.

Panoramic Photo of Gary, Indiana, 1910

Swiss Cheese Makers in Madison, Wisconsin

The city attracted southern African Americans and immigrants from Europe. By 1920 people from fifty-two nations made their home in Gary. Many were Croatians, Czechs, Greeks, Hungarians, Italians, Lithuanians, Poles, Russians, Serbians, Slovaks, or Turks. The population of Gary grew to 100,426 by 1930, just twenty-four years after its founding!

Cheese Factories of Wisconsin

As mentioned in Lesson 87, Wisconsin is in America's Breadbasket. God made it a good place for dairy farming. Unlike Gary, which was built as a steel town, the Wisconsin cheese industry grew because of resources already there.

Anne Pickett began Wisconsin's first cheese factory in her home in 1841. By the 1870s, cheese making had become an important industry in Wisconsin. Dairymen joined together to discover ways to sell their cheese in other states and ways to transport it cheaply by rail. By the 1880s students in Wisconsin could take college courses in making cheese and managing dairies. Wisconsin had over 2,800 cheese factories by 1922.

European immigrants who were dairy farmers or cheesemakers often chose to move to Wisconsin. Immigrants from Switzerland made Swiss cheese. The cheese makers in the Madison, Wisconsin, cheese factory above are lowering curd into a form where it will be pressed into Swiss cheese. Italians made Mozzarella, Provolone, and Gorgonzola. French immigrants made Camembert, Brie, and Bleu cheeses. Germans made Muenster. English immigrants made Cheddar, and Dutch immigrants made Gouda and Edam. Brick and Colby cheeses were invented in Wisconsin.

Mergers, International Business, Diversity, and "Yankee Ingenuity"

Every product made in a factory begins with an idea. "Yankee ingenuity" is an expression that refers to the many creative ways Americans have used the resources available to them to accomplish a variety of goals. This creativity often results in a new product made in a new factory.

The potato chip was born in Saratoga Springs, New York, at Moon's Lake House resort after a customer complained that his fried potatoes were too thick. The irritated cook sliced potatoes paper-thin, fried them, salted them, and sent them to the customer. The patron thought they were delicious. Restaurants in the region began to serve "Saratoga Chips."

George Crum, the cook at Moon's Lake, opened his own restaurant and served baskets of chips on every table. The dish spread along America's east coast. Along the way, the name changed to potato chips. In 1895 stores in Cleveland, Ohio, began to sell them. Mike-sell's Potato Chip Company began in 1910 in Dayton, Ohio. Three modern potato chip companies were born in 1921; Wise Potato Chips and Utz Potato Chips began in Pennsylvania, and Magic City Food Company began in Birmingham, Alabama. It later became Golden Flake Snack Foods. Lay's Potato Chips began in 1932 in Nashville, Tennessee.

Until 1926 potato chips were sold from cracker barrels or glass display cases. That year Laura Scudder was working in her family's potato chip business in California. She began to send her female employees home with sheets of waxed paper. At night they ironed them into bags. The next day, workers put chips inside and used a warm iron to seal the bags shut. Thus the bag of potato chips was born.

The 3M Company began as Minnesota Mining and Manufacturing. It was founded to make sandpaper and grinding wheels. When one of their scientists observed a car painter using their sandpaper, he noticed that the painter had trouble keeping paint off certain places. He decided to invent a solution. The result was masking tape. The 3M Company diversified, becoming a tape supplier, too. It has produced many kinds of tape.

Today it is hard to keep up with which company manufactures a certain brand and where that brand is manufactured. Sometimes two companies (or many companies) come together (or merge) to create a new one. Sometimes a company opens a factory in America and later opens factories in foreign countries.

Colgate Delivery Truck, c. 1920

Business leaders were already making decisions on these issues in the 1920s. The Colgate-Palmolive Company, which makes Colgate toothpaste, Softsoap, Palmolive dishwashing liquid, and many other products, is an example of mergers, international business, and diversity. William Colgate started a business in 1806 on Dutch Street in New York City. He made starch, soap, and candles.

In 1896 the Colgate Company began putting toothpaste in collapsible tubes. By its one hundredth anniversary in 1906, Colgate was offering over 800 products. In 1864 the Palmolive soap factory opened in Milwaukee, Wisconsin. In 1872 the Peet Brothers opened a soap company in Kansas City. In 1924 Palmolive became an international company when it began manufacturing soap in Paris. Colgate, Palmolive, and Peet merged in 1928 to form the Colgate-Palmolive-Peet Company. In 1953 the company was renamed Colgate-Palmolive.

The Colgate clock at right is one of the world's largest clocks. It is forty feet across. The Seth Thomas Clock Company built it for the centennial of the Colgate Company. It first adorned the Colgate-Palmolive facility in Jersey City, New Jersey, but was moved to Clarksville, Indiana, in 1924 when an even larger clock was placed on the New Jersey facility. Notice the Colgate delivery truck above.

Colgate Clock in Clarksville, Indiana

The First American Ice Cream Factory

Another example of Yankee ingenuity was the first ice cream factory in America. Nancy Johnson received the first patent for an ice cream machine with a hand crank. In 1851

Quaker milk seller Jacob Fussell opened the first large-scale ice cream factory in America. It was located in Baltimore, Maryland. Fussell used Nancy Johnson's method of making ice cream, but he invented a large industrial ice cream crank. He also opened his own icehouses. By 1909 the Fussell Ice Cream business was making and packing thirty million gallons of ice cream each year. As seen in the photo at right, by 1926 the company had become Fussell-Young Ice Cream Company. In the next photo is an ice factory around 1920. Below it is a photo of boys and men making ice cream cones in the Sanitary Ice Cream Cone Company factory in 1917.

Fussell-Young Ice Cream Company, 1926

Ice Plant, c. 1920

Famous American Brands

By the 1920s, American factories were making a wide variety of products. Here is what was happening with some famous brands during the 1920s.

Birds Eye Frozen Foods. During the 1920s, Clarence Birdseye perfected a method of freezing foods so that they could be packaged in cardboard and sold in grocery stores. The Birds Eye brand of frozen foods, first sold in 1930, is named for him. Birdseye learned about frozen food while living in Labrador. He first went to Labrador with a medical missionary in 1911 and later worked there as a fur trapper.

Sanitary Ice Cream Cone Company, 1917

Butterfinger. The Butterfinger candy bar was introduced in 1928. The Curtiss Candy Company had a contest to name it. The name comes from a popular expression of the 1920s. When an athlete dropped a ball, the sportscaster said he had "butterfingers."

Gerber Baby Food. Frank Gerber's daughter-in-law suggested that the family canning business start manufacturing strained baby foods. They researched the idea and began selling Gerber baby food in 1928.

Hershey's Chocolate. In 1907 the Hershey Chocolate Company began making Hershey's Kisses and wrapping them by hand. The company started using a machine to wrap the Kisses in 1921. The new machine could add the little white piece of paper that sticks out of the top, indicating a genuine Hershey's Kiss. In 1925 Hershey's introduced the Mr. Goodbar and in 1926 it began to sell Hershey's Syrup.

Kleenex. Celluwipes were invented in 1924. They were later called Kleenex. The Kimberly-Clark company started selling these tissues in pop-up cardboard cartons in 1928.

Madame Alexander Dolls. The parents of Beatrice Alexander Behrman were Russian immigrants. Her father operated America's first doll hospital. In 1923 when Beatrice was twenty-eight years old, she founded the Alexander Doll Company. She officially retired from the company in 1988 at age 93.

Maytag Washing Machines. On October 12, 1926, the Maytag company shipped five trainloads of washing machines. This was the world's largest single shipment of products to that time. In 1927 the company sent out an eight-trainload shipment. In the photograph at right, Maytag washers are displayed at a 1926 industrial exposition.

Maytag Washers on Display at an Industrial Exposition, 1926

Quaker Oats. In 1922 the Quaker Oats company began selling quick oats, which could be cooked faster than regular oats.

Schick Electric Razors. In 1928 retired U.S. Army Colonel Jacob Schick applied for a patent for an electric shaver he invented.

In business and in all our lives, we should remember that God is our Lord.

> Come now, you who say, "Today or tomorrow we will go to such and such a city,
> and spend a year there and engage in business and make a profit."
> Yet you do not know what your life will be like tomorrow.
> You are just a vapor that appears for a little while and then vanishes away.
> Instead, you ought to say, "If the Lord wills, we will live and also do this or that."
> James 4:13-15

Activities for Lesson 102

Vocabulary – Write five sentences in your notebook, using one of these words in each: warehouse, ingenuity, patron, merge, sanitary. Check in a dictionary if you need help with their definitions.

Literature – Read "Made in America" in *We the People*, pages 126-127, and chapter 2 in *Blue Willow*.

Creative Writing – In your notebook, write a short story of at least two pages about an immigrant that came to America and started a factory during the 1920s.

Timeline – In *Timeline of America the Beautiful* next to 1921, write: The Hershey company starts wrapping Kisses by machine.

Family Activity – Create a Cupcake Factory. See pages 968-969 for instructions.

Student Workbook or Lesson Review – If you are using one of these optional books, complete the assignment for Lesson 102.

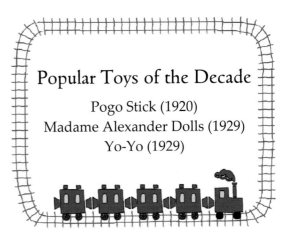

Popular Toys of the Decade

Pogo Stick (1920)
Madame Alexander Dolls (1929)
Yo-Yo (1929)

Motor City, USA

More than almost any other country in the world, America depends on cars. Driving a car was a sport in the early 1900s, but today it has become almost a necessity. In the photographs below, Herbert Hoover climbs into an automobile and Calvin Coolidge receives membership in the American Automobile Association.

Detroit, Michigan, became the premier industrial city in America during the 1920s, 1930s, and 1940s. Its most important industry was automobile manufacturing. Detroit was in an ideal location to become Motor City. Ships on the Great Lakes could bring in supplies. Copper and iron were mined in Michigan and nearby Minnesota. Coal could be brought in by rail from Pennsylvania and West Virginia. The steel mills of

General Motors in Detroit

Chicago, Illinois; Cleveland and Youngstown, Ohio; Gary, Indiana; and Pittsburgh, Pennsylvania, were all within a few hundred miles of Detroit.

From its beginning, the history of Detroit has been connected to the importance of transportation. Because of its strategic location along the Detroit River and the nearby Great Lakes, Detroit has been the site of three forts: the first built by the French, the second by the British, and the third by the U.S. Army.

The French Build Fort Pontchartrain le Détroit

The first European settlement in the Detroit region was Fort Pontchartrain le Détroit, built by the French in 1701. In 1683 Antoine de la Mothe, Sieur de Cadillac, left France and traveled to the

Herbert Hoover Before He Became President

Calvin Coolidge receives membership in the AAA.

New World. He gathered information for the French government and worked as a trader. Cadillac believed it would advance French interests in the Great Lakes area if the French built a fort along the Detroit River. Cadillac and other Frenchmen rowed up the Detroit River and selected a high bluff on the northern shore to build Fort Pontchartrain le Détroit (*le détroit* means the strait). They also built Saint Anne's Church.

Until the French and Indian War, Detroit was a tiny frontier village bordered by the modern-day streets of Fort, Griswold, Larned, and Shelby. Here lived artisans, hunters, traders, trappers, and soldiers. Cadillac had authority from the French government to grant land to settlers. He laid out "ribbon farms," which had narrow frontage on the Detroit River and ran two to three miles inland from the river. The French encouraged Native Americans to live around the village so that French and native residents could trade and help protect each other.

The Fort Changes Hands

By the time the French and Indian War began in 1754, the fort's name had been shortened to Fort Detroit. During the war, the Ottawa people lived in the area. Wanting to protect their homeland from the British, young Ottawan Chief Pontiac became an ally of the French. (Remember that the French and Indian War involved the British and the American colonists fighting against the French and their Indian allies. See page 126.) Chief Pontiac led attacks against the British. The most famous is called Pontiac's Rebellion. The British took control of Fort Detroit during the war and enlarged it.

During the American Revolution, the British built Fort Lernoult overlooking the stockaded village of Fort Detroit. An historic marker has been erected at the corner of Shelby and Fort Streets marking the location of one of Fort Lernoult's bastions. Though the Treaty of Paris which ended the American Revolution gave Michigan to America, the British and Americans continued to struggle over control of certain areas in the Northwest Territory, including Michigan. The British did not relinquish control of Fort Lernoult until 1796. The American flag which flew over the fort on July 11, 1796, was the first American flag to fly over Detroit. The fort was surrendered to the British in the first year of the War of 1812, but the Americans retook it in 1813. It was renamed Fort Shelby.

The U.S. Army Builds Fort Wayne

Fearing a war with British Canada, in 1840 the U.S. Army began to build Fort Wayne, a five-point star fort along the Detroit River. Plans included the most up-to-date cannons, which could reach Canada and ships sailing on the river. Before the cannons arrived, relations between Canada and the U.S. improved. The fort was no longer needed for defense against Canada.

1848 Barracks at Fort Wayne

The first troops did not arrive until Michigan soldiers reported for duty there during the Civil War. Michigan soldiers continued to report at the fort through the Vietnam War, which was fought in the 1960s and early 1970s. Fort Wayne was also the home of the U.S. Army chaplain school for a few years. It housed prisoners of war during World War I and World War II. In 1948 the U.S. government began giving portions of Fort Wayne to the city of Detroit. Modern tourists can visit the fort today. A Fort Wayne barracks is pictured on page 611.

Corktown Historic District

Many Irish immigrants came to Detroit from County Cork in Ireland. Beginning in the 1830s, many settled in a neighborhood that came to be called Corktown. As Irish immigrants and their descendants became more affluent, some left Corktown and spread into other areas of Detroit. Around 1900 immigrants from Malta began settling in Corktown. In the 1920s Latinos from the southwestern United States and Mexico came to Corktown to work in the Detroit auto industry.

Detroit Free Press

The *Detroit Free Press* began in 1831 and became the area's first daily newspaper in 1835. The newspaper began the first regular Sunday edition in America in 1853. In 1881 the *Free Press* began a London edition, becoming the first American newspaper to publish an edition in Europe.

Detroit and the Underground Railroad

Detroit's location near the Canadian border made it an important stop on the Underground Railroad. Seymour Finney housed fugitive slaves in his downtown hotel. Free-born African American George de Baptiste was a Detroit businessman who at various times owned a barbershop, a bakery, and a steamship. He used the steamship to transport slaves from Detroit to Canada.

De Baptiste was a member of Second Baptist Church, Detroit's first black congregation, begun by thirteen freed slaves. Their church building in Greektown housed about 5,000 fugitives over a thirty-year period. Abolitionists John Brown, Sojouner Truth, and Frederick Douglass all aided the Second Baptist Church in their efforts. The church began Detroit's first school for African American children.

Vernor's Ginger Ale

Before the Civil War, Detroit pharmacist James Vernor blended vanilla with several spices, including ginger, to calm the stomach. He placed the blend in an oak container. When Vernor returned from the war, he found a delicious beverage aged in wood. Vernor ran a soda fountain beside his pharmacy. In 1866 he began selling his ginger ale, first in his own soda fountain and later in others. Vernor eventually built a bottling plant along the Detroit River. Customers once could enjoy a five-cent Vernor's Ginger Ale while watching the drinks being made.

America's Thanksgiving Parade

In 1924 the J. L. Hudson department store began the tradition of a Thanksgiving Day parade, a tradition that continues to this day. The first parade had seven marching bands, four large heads made from papier-mâché, and a Mother Goose float pulled by horses. The parade grew to include cartoon characters, celebrities, giant balloons, and a Distinguished Clown Corps, made up of business and community leaders. The department store closed in 1983, but area corporations and the Michigan Thanksgiving Parade Foundation continue to sponsor the parade, which is now called America's Thanksgiving Day Parade.

The Big Three Automakers: Chrysler, General Motors, and Ford

In the late 1800s and early 1900s, several inventors built vehicles powered by internal combustion engines. Today the world is filled with cars, trucks, and buses numbering in the hundreds of millions. Most are still powered by internal combustion engines.

In 1900 Detroit was the thirteenth largest city in America. Its diverse industries lined the Detroit River so they could easily bring in supplies and send out completed products. By 1930 the Detroit economy was centered on automaking. The city had grown from 285,000 people in 1900 to 1.6 million, making it America's fourth largest city.

Many small factories began to make automobiles, but three companies became the Big Three Automakers. All were headquartered in Detroit and the surrounding area. The Ford Motor Company was incorporated in 1903. In 1908 William C. Durant founded the General Motors Corporation. By 1916 it included the smaller companies that made Buick, Cadillac, Oakland (later called Pontiac), and Chevrolet. See completed Cadillacs at right. Walter P. Chrysler formed the Chrysler Corporation in 1925. Chrysler began to manufacture low-priced Plymouths and mid-priced DeSotos. In 1928 *Time* magazine chose Chrysler as its Man of the Year.

Completed Cadillac Touring Cars

On July 10, 1909, Detroit was the scene of an auto parade featuring over one thousand vehicles. Below is a panoramic photograph taken of the participants.

Making automobiles required many employees, such as those sanding automobile wheels in the photo at right. Farmers suffering from low farm product prices came from the Midwest to find work. Many Detroit autoworkers

Workers Sand Auto Wheels

Participants in an Auto Parade in Detroit, July 10, 1909

emigrated from Canada, and a large number of southerners moved to Detroit to work in the auto industry.

Henry Ford recruited workers from England, Scotland, Mexico, and the Middle East. He also hired African Americans and treated them equally with other workers. For the remainder of this lesson, we will concentrate on Henry Ford because of the important contributions he made to the automotive industry and to all American industries.

Henry Ford

Henry Ford grew up on a farm in what is now Dearborn, Michigan. He attended a one-room school. When he was sixteen years old, he became a machinist apprentice. At age twenty-five, he married Clara Bryant and began to run a sawmill. In 1891 Ford began working as an engineer for the Edison Illuminating Company in Detroit. Two years later he was promoted to chief engineer. That same year Henry and Clara's only child, Edsel Bryant Ford, was born.

After work hours, Henry Ford experimented with the internal combustion engine. In 1896 he completed a vehicle he called the Quadricycle. Ford and other businessmen founded the Ford Motor Company in 1903. Henry Ford was vice president and chief engineer. The company purchased components made by other companies and produced only a few cars a day at their factory on Mack Avenue. Two or three workmen worked on each car. Early in Ford's career, he designed race cars to demonstrate the reliability of his designs.

In 1908 Henry Ford introduced the Model T, also called the Tin Lizzie. The car was easy to operate and reasonably-priced. Many people wanted to buy the Model T, so Ford built a new factory in Highland Park, Michigan. Here Ford introduced a continuously-moving assembly line. Workers stayed in one place. As an automobile moved past them, each worker added one part. With the assembly line, Ford could make cars faster and more economically.

In 1914 Ford began paying his workers $5.00 per day. His employees became more loyal, and now they could

Ford Dump Truck

Ford School Bus

Ford Touring Car

Ford Laundry Truck

Ford Lumber Truck

Ford Police Cars

Ford Tractor

Ford NuGrape Truck

Ford Bakery Truck

Ford Snowplow

afford to buy the cars they were making. In 1917 Ford began to build the largest industrial complex in the world along the banks of the Rouge River in Dearborn, Michigan. When completed the complex had the world's largest steel mill and a glass factory in addition to the assembly line buildings. Railroads and Great Lakes steamers brought in iron ore and coal from which workers produced iron and steel. Workers in rolling mills, forges, and shops made springs, axles, and car bodies from the steel. Foundries made engine blocks and cylinder heads from the iron. By September 1927, the Ford Motor Company no longer had to order parts from other suppliers. Its workers were turning raw materials into all of the parts needed to make the Model T.

That year production of the Model T ceased and was replaced with the Model A. During the construction of the Dearborn complex, Edsel Ford took over as president of Ford Motor Company. By the end of the 1920s, Ford was building 1.5 million cars each year. Thousands of visitors came from overseas to visit and photograph the massive complex. On this page and page 614, notice the different uses Americans found for Ford vehicles.

The Legacy of Henry Ford

Henry Ford worked to advance education and preserve American history. He became a good friend to Thomas Edison. Ford founded the Edison Institute, which includes the Henry Ford Museum and Greenfield Village. In 1929 Herbert Hoover dedicated the Institute in honor of Thomas Edison. The year of the celebration commemorated the fiftieth anniversary of the electric light. Orville Wright and other dignitaries attended the dedication.

Henry Ford moved historic structures to Greenfield Village. Among the buildings in the Village are Noah Webster's home, the Wright brother's bicycle shop and home, Henry Ford's birthplace, an Illinois courthouse where Abraham Lincoln practiced law, and the birthplace of William Holmes McGuffey, author of the McGuffey Readers, used by many American schoolchildren. Among the items at the Henry Ford Museum are George Washington's camp bed and the rocking chair Abraham Lincoln sat in at Ford's Theatre.

Henry Ford, pictured at right, found additional ways to give back to the American people. He built Village Industries in rural Michigan. These gave people the opportunity to work in industry during the months when they were not involved in farming. Ford tried to find ways to use agricultural products in industry. He experimented with making car parts from plastic made from soybeans. Ford also established schools in various places in America. The schools used one-room schoolhouse methods, modern teaching ideas, and activities that helped children learn by doing. Edsel Ford died in 1943 and Henry Ford died in 1949.

Henry Ford

Immigrants Take an English Class at Ford Motor Company

Henry Ford was an example of diligence. His diligence helped him provide jobs for many people, like the immigrants at left. It also gave him opportunities to give to his fellow man:

> The soul of the sluggard craves
> and gets nothing,
> But the soul of the diligent is made fat.
> Proverbs 13:4

Activities for Lesson 103

Thinking Biblically – Henry Ford was known for helping others. Read about a woman named Tabitha (also called Dorcas), who was also known for helping others, in Acts 9:36-43.

Map Study – Complete the assignment for Lesson 103 on Map 3 "American Landmarks" in *Maps of America the Beautiful*.

Literature – Read "The Only Automobile in Detroit" in *We the People*, page 128, and chapter 3 in *Blue Willow*.

Timeline – In *Timeline of America the Beautiful* next to 1927, write: The last Model T is built.

Student Workbook or Lesson Review – If you are using one of these optional books, complete the assignment for Lesson 103.

God Created the Black Hills

In the midst of the vast prairies of the Great Plains, God created the Black Hills, encompassing the southwestern corner of South Dakota and a small area in northeastern Wyoming. The Black Hills are sometimes called the "Island in the Prairie" because they appear to be an island of granite hills in the midst of a prairie sea. They are the tallest peaks between the Rockies and the Appalachians. Harney Peak is the highest. It rises to 7,242 feet. The Lakota call these hills Paha Sapa, which is translated Black Hills in English. Ninety percent of the surface of the Black Hills is covered with ponderosa pine, making them appear black from a distance.

The photograph above shows a scene in the Black Hills. Notice the dark color of the hills, the ponderosa pines, and the huge granite boulders. In the center is the Shrine of Democracy, where likenesses of George Washington, Thomas Jefferson, Theodore Roosevelt, and Abraham Lincoln have been carved into Mount Rushmore. Carving began during the presidency of Calvin Coolidge.

617

The Black Hills area is only 125 miles from north to south and sixty-five miles from east to west. God reveals an amazing variety of His creativity in this region. Here He made granite spires and mountains, prairies and meadows, deep blue lakes and bubbling brooks, massive elk and tiny cowbirds. See the photo at right.

Beneath the Black Hills are miles and miles of cave passages; underground towns filled with prairie dogs; and deposits of gold, silver, lead, copper, tin, iron, coal, petroleum, salt, mica, and gypsum. At one time the region produced $4,000,000 in gold and $3,000,000 in silver each year.

Elk in Wind Cave National Park with Cowbirds on its Back

Mount Rushmore National Memorial

The four faces pictured at left make up the Shrine of Democracy, the most famous landmark in the Black Hills and one of the most recognizable landmarks in America. Almost three million people visit it each year.

In 1885 Charles Rushmore, a young attorney from New York City, went to the Black Hills in regard to a mining claim. Mount Rushmore was named in his honor.

Shrine of Democracy on Mount Rushmore in the Black Hills

In 1923 Doane Robinson was serving as state historian of South Dakota. He came up with an idea to increase tourism to the Black Hills. He proposed that a sculptor carve likenesses of the Lakota Chief Red Cloud and of Westerners like Jim Bridger, John Colter, and Kit Carson (see pages 252-253) from rock formations in the Needles, pictured at right. Idaho-born sculptor Gutzon Borglum became involved in the project in 1924. While visiting the Black Hills, he proposed that the carving take place on Mount Rushmore instead and that the figures represent not just the West, but all of America. He chose Mount Rushmore because it is made of smooth-grained granite. At 5,725 feet Mount Rushmore rises

Needles in the Black Hills

high above the surrounding hills; and since it faces southeast, the sun shines on it for most of the day. At the top of page 619 is a photo of Mount Rushmore before carving began.

Congressman William Williamson and Senator Peter Norbeck, both of South Dakota, worked to gain financing to complete the monument. Williamson encouraged President Coolidge to come to the Black Hills for a summer vacation in 1927. While he was in the

Above: Mount Rushmore Before Carving Began

President Coolidge at Mount Rushmore Dedication

Black Hills that summer, Coolidge dedicated the Shrine of Democracy. See the second photo at left.

Borglum decided to sculpt four American Presidents. He chose George Washington to represent the struggle for independence and the birth of America. Thomas Jefferson signifies the idea of representative government. Abraham Lincoln represents the permanent union of the United States and equality for all citizens. Theodore Roosevelt signifies the United States' role in world affairs during the twentieth century.

Borglum used his artistic and engineering skills to design the monument. He created five-foot models of each figure. His models were measured and then enlarged twelve times. Workers used these measurements to know where to perform their tasks on the mountain.

Sculpting began in the fall of 1927; it was performed in four stages. First, workers used dynamite to remove rock to within three or four inches of what would become a finished face. In fact, more than ninety percent of the sculpture was carved with dynamite. This process removed about 450,000 tons of rock from the mountain. Notice powderman and the model of Washington's face at right.

The second stage was honeycombing, in which a worker used a jackhammer to make shallow holes about three inches apart. See photo below. After honeycombing, workmen used small drills, hammers, and wedging tools to remove the remaining rock. The fourth and final step was to smooth the faces with small air hammers.

Washington Model and Powderman

Honeycombing with a Jackhammer

Work continued for fourteen years. The actual carving of the monument took six and a half years, but the project was delayed several times because of weather or lack of funds. About four hundred people worked on the monument.

The work at Mount Rushmore was dangerous. Much of it was completed while men sat in swing seats which were hung from cables. However, no one died while working on the project. Notice the photos on page 620. Gutzon Borglum sits on a swing seat in the photo at left and an unidentified man hangs by Lincoln's nose in the center photo. In the photo at top right, men are operating

Winches Control Cables

Gutzon Borglum　　　*Swing Seat by Lincoln's Nose*

winches, which controlled the cables that held up the workers. Workers with many skills were needed to complete the project. Notice the blacksmith sharpening a drill at right.

A blacksmith sharpens a drill.

One by one likenesses of the Presidents' faces were completed. Borglum continued to manage the project until his death in March of 1941. His son Lincoln then directed the work through the last day of carving on October 31, 1941. The monument has had several dedication ceremonies since Coolidge first dedicated it in 1927, including one by President George H. W. Bush in 1991.

Rocky Mountain Goat

God placed Rocky Mountain goats in Canada. In 1924 Canada gave six to Custer State Park, a park near the memorial. The goats escaped and went to live on the granite peaks of the Black Hills. God made their hooves very soft, which makes them able to climb steep rocks. Today about two hundred live in the Black Hills. The one at left was photographed near the Mount Rushmore monument.

Early History of the Black Hills

The Lakota settled in the Black Hills in the mid-1700s. Many Native American tribes, including the Arapaho, Assiniboine, Blackfeet, Cheyenne, Crow, Dakota, Kootenai, Lakota, Salish, and Shoshone, believe the region and certain landmarks within it to be sacred places.

French explorers Francis and Louis-Joseph Verendrye were probably the first Europeans to see the Black Hills. According to Louis-Joseph's journal they were "in sight of mountains" on New Year's Day, 1743. According to one report, they did not go near the mountains because their Native American guides were afraid of the "hostile natives" who lived there.

620

Traders and trappers told Lewis and Clark about the Black Hills, but the Corps of Discovery did not see them. Jedediah Smith (see page 252) and several other traders traveled through them in 1823, but most trappers avoided them because the Lakota considered them sacred. When settlers and frontier soldiers came to South Dakota in later decades, they also avoided the Black Hills because they feared trouble with the Lakota. Sometimes Lakota warriors raided settlers living near the Black Hills and then retreated back into the Hills. In 1868 the United States made a treaty with the Lakota. The government agreed to keep settlers and miners out of the Black Hills if the Lakota would stop attacking settlers and railroad workers.

After residents of Yankton, South Dakota, heard stories about gold in the Black Hills, they asked the U.S. Army to explore the area. The Army resisted at first but finally decided to go in to find a suitable place to build a frontier fort. Lieutenant Colonel George A. Custer led one hundred wagons and about one thousand men, including soldiers, miners, and a geologist, into the Black Hills in 1874. On July 30, they found gold.

Miners in the Black Hills

Still, the Federal government forbade settlers and miners from entering the Black Hills since the area belonged to the Lakota. Miners rushed in anyway. The U.S. Army forced the whites to leave. However, after the winter of 1874-1875, the Army was unwilling to use force to keep the miners out.

Homestake Mines and the Town of Lead, South Dakota, c. 1891

By 1875 about eight hundred whites were in the Hills and in 1876 the number reached 10,000. Gold was so plentiful in the Black Hills that local citizens began calling it "the richest one hundred square miles on earth." Miners set up canvas tents. Businessmen started building clapboard shops. The newcomers built towns like Custer City, Deadwood, Lead (pronounced leed), Silver City, Spearfish, Rapid City, and Keystone. See photo of Lead above.

Laura Ingalls Wilder (see Lesson 79) had family members who moved near Keystone. Her uncle and aunt, Henry and Polly Quiner, and their daughter Ruby moved there during or soon after the gold rush. Uncle Henry was Caroline Ingalls' brother and Polly was Charles Ingalls' sister. The Quiners lived in Keystone the rest of their lives. Laura's sister Carrie moved to Keystone in 1911 when she was thirty-nine years old. There she managed a newspaper. The following year she married widower David Swanzey and retired to raise his two children, Mary, who was eight years old, and Harold, who was six. David Swanzey had accompanied attorney Charles Rushmore when he explored the Black Hills in 1885. Listed among those who worked on the monument was a Harold "Davie" Swanzey, who was likely David and Carrie's son. After the death of her parents, Laura's sister Mary went to live with Carrie in Keystone. Mary Ingalls died there in 1928 and Carrie in 1946.

Black Hills Gold Jewelry

According to tradition, a young Frenchman came to the Black Hills in the mid-1870s. While there he had a dream of the beautiful grapevines of France. He decided to buy gold from other miners and create beautiful jewelry with leaves, grape clusters, and vines. Frank L. Thorpe, a third generation goldsmith, founded a jewelry-making business in 1919. His grandfather, S. T. Butler of Deadwood, had made jewelry with grape leaf designs using pink, green, and yellow gold. Gold is naturally yellow. Pink gold is created when yellow gold is alloyed with copper; green gold is yellow gold alloyed with zinc and silver. Thorpe continued his grandfather's work. Since then other companies have formed to create Black Hills Gold jewelry. In 1980 a Federal judge ruled that all jewelry labeled Black Hills Gold must be made only in the Black Hills of South Dakota. The gold can come from other places, but the jewelry must be made there. Visitors to the Black Hills often take home a beautiful piece of Black Hills Gold jewelry as a souvenir.

Chinese Immigrants in the Black Hills

In some villages of southern China, America was called Gold Mountain. Sixty-six thousand Chinese immigrated to America during the 1850s. About half stayed. As white Americans and European immigrants headed for the Black Hills, so did some Chinese. As in many Western towns that grew up during a gold rush, these Chinese built a Chinatown in Deadwood. More than one hundred of the Chinese in Deadwood became launderers. Mining declined in the Black Hills, and the Chinese were gone by 1935.

A Stalemate Between Native Americans and the Federal Government

The U.S. government invited Native American leaders to Washington, D. C. in 1875 in an attempt to work out a compromise regarding the Black Hills region. President Grant offered to buy the Black Hills from the Lakota. Native leaders refused all offers and insisted that they retain ownership. In 1877 Congress passed a law stating that the Lakota must leave the Black Hills and go to live on reservations. Some of the Indian wars of the late 1800s resulted from this law.

Crazy Horse Monument

Ownership of the Black Hills is still debated. In 1980 the U.S. Supreme Court tried to settle the question by offering for the Federal government to pay Lakota tribes for the land. Again the Lakota refused the offer. In 2004 Gerard Baker, a Mandan-Hidatsa raised on North Dakota's Fort Berthold Reservation, was named superintendent of Mount Rushmore National Memorial, the first Native American to hold this position.

Crazy Horse

In 1939 Lakota Chief Henry Standing Bear asked sculptor Korscak Ziolkowski to carve a giant likeness of Chief Crazy Horse near Mount Rushmore. Ziolkowski began sculpting the monument. He died in 1982, and others have continued the work. The face was dedicated in 1998, but the statue is still under construction. See the photo on page 622.

Granite Needle

More Places to See in the Black Hills

Custer State Park. When Peter Norbeck was Governor of South Dakota, he wanted to set aside a place for the animals that lived in the Black Hills before the gold rush. Custer State Park was established for this purpose. It is home to scenic drives which display wonders God created in the Black Hills. Needles Highway winds through forests, meadows, and rugged mountains made of granite. The name Needles Highway refers to granite formations that rise tall and thin like needles. Peter Norbeck marked the entire course on foot and by horseback. The road was completed in 1922. The photo above was taken along Needles Highway. Tourists who travel the park's Wildlife Loop Road see some of the 1,300 buffalo that roam in the park, as well as prairie dog towns and other wildlife. Iron Mountain Road connects Custer State Park and Mount Rushmore. It has three tunnels through which travelers can see Mount Rushmore. Senator Norbeck also designed this road. The photos at left were taken in 2006 along these three roads. From top to bottom, they are a bighorn sheep, pronghorn, bison, prairie dog, and burro. The pronghorn is sometimes called an antelope or a pronghorn antelope. This animal is native only to North America. Its scientific name is *Antilocapra americana*, which means "American goat-antelope."

Devils Tower National Monument. Wyoming's Devils Tower, pictured at right, is a granite monolith rising 865 feet out of the ground. Its rocky top is about the same size as a football field. Cacti, sagebrush, and native grasses grow in the area. Sometimes chipmunks, mice, pack rats, and snakes are found on top. President Theodore Roosevelt designated Devils Tower a national monument in 1906, the first national monument in America.

Bighorn Sheep

Pronghorn

Bison

Prairie Dog

Burro

Devils Tower

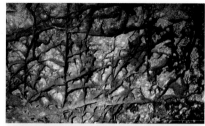

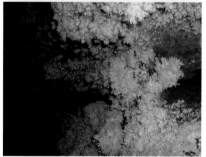

Top: Boxwork; Center: Rock Lined with Crystal; Bottom: Frostwork

Wind Cave National Park. Wind Cave National Park became America's seventh national park in 1903. Winds of 75 miles per hour have been recorded at the entrance. Native Americans knew about the cave before gold was discovered in the Black Hills. In 1881 two brothers, Jesse and Tom Bingham, heard a whistling noise. As they searched for its source, they found a small ten-by-twelve-inch hole in the ground. Wind came out so forcefully that it blew Jesse's hat off. Volunteer spelunkers have been exploring Wind Cave for many decades. By 2010 they had found more than 130 miles of complex passages. This maze of passages lies under a piece of ground that is less than 1.5 square miles. Though not common in other caves around the world, the honeycomb-like formation called boxwork is abundant in Wind Cave. Cave rocks lined with crystal and frostwork are also found there. See photos at left. Jewel Cave National Monument is also in the Black Hills. Among its special features are sparkling calcite crystals and rare formations that look like balloons.

Calvin Coolidge Statue in Rapid City

Towns of the Black Hills. Rapid City, the largest city in the Black Hills, has erected life-sized bronze statues of Presidents for several years. As you walk along its streets, you may be surprised to find a statue of your favorite President standing or sitting on a street corner, like the one of Calvin Coolidge at right. Other small towns in the area offer a variety of tourist attractions.

On the Way to the Black Hills

The Mitchell Corn Palace

Many miles before tourists reach the Black Hills from the east, they begin to see billboards for Wall Drug Store, like the one on page 625. Before reaching Wall, they pass through Mitchell, South Dakota, with its Corn Palace. See photo at left. In 1892 Mitchell residents wanted to demonstrate how fertile South Dakota soil was. They displayed corn on the outside of one of their buildings during a Corn Belt Exposition. Mitchell built its current Corn Palace in 1921. Each year the outside of the building is covered with half ears of different colors of corn arranged

Corn Mural from the Corn Palace in Mitchell, South Dakota

in designs. Inside the building are murals made of corn like the mural of Mount Rushmore pictured above.

West of Mitchell, tourists finally reach the town of Wall and its drug store. In 1932 while Mount Rushmore was under construction, Ted and Dorothy Hustead moved to tiny Wall, South Dakota, a town of 326. They had prayed about where to purchase their own drug store and were convinced Wall was the place to go.

For the first few years, business was slow. Then, in July of 1936, Dorothy had an idea. Many travelers passed on the highway near their store. In those days before air conditioned cars, she realized that people would enjoy a glass of ice water. She made up a little advertising rhyme, including the words, "Free Ice Water."

Ted and a helper built several signs and put one phrase on each. They spaced out the signs along the highway so that people could read the rhyme one sign at a time as they drove. By the time Ted returned to the store, Dorothy was running around giving out free glasses of ice water. One traveler said he was headed to Yellowstone and asked them to fill

up his jug. People began to buy ice cream cones, too. The next summer the Husteads hired eight girls to help them run the store. Wall Drug has now been expanded to a 76,000-square-foot tourist attraction. On a busy day, 20,000 people visit. See a Wall Drug scene at right.

Wall Drug Billboard

Western Character at Wall Drug

Scenes in Badlands National Park

Less than an hour east of the Black Hills is Badlands National Park, established in 1939. See photos above. The eroded buttes, pinnacles, and spires of the Badlands stand in sharp contrast to the pretty vegetation in the Black Hills.

God created the Black Hills and all that is in them. He also formed the barren yet beautiful Badlands. He made the people who had ideas such as carving faces into rock, decorating a "palace" with ears of corn, and giving away free ice water. In the words of hymnwriter Cecil F. Alexander, "the Lord God made them all."

> You have crowned the year with Your bounty, and Your paths drip with fatness.
> The pastures of the wilderness drip, and the hills gird themselves with rejoicing.
> The meadows are clothed with flocks and the valleys are covered with grain;
> They shout for joy, yes, they sing.
> Psalm 65:11-13

Activities for Lesson 104

Map Study – Complete the assignment for Lesson 104 on Map 2 "God's Wonders" in *Maps of America the Beautiful*.

Vocabulary – Look up each of these words in a dictionary and read their definitions: shrine, tourism, likeness, sacred, spelunker.

Literature – Read "Steadfast as These Ancient Hills" in *We the People*, pages 129-130, and chapter 4 in *Blue Willow*.

Creative Writing – Visualize a monument for the area where you live. It could memorialize a person, event, or period of history. Write at least one page in your notebook describing who or what the monument would feature, where it would be placed, what it would be made of, and how it would be paid for. On another page, make a sketch of the monument you have imagined.

Timeline – In *Timeline of America the Beautiful* next to 1927, write: Carving begins on Mount Rushmore in the Black Hills.

Student Workbook or Lesson Review – If you are using one of these optional books, complete the assignment for Lesson 104.

William Jennings Bryan, Christian Statesman

William Jennings Bryan

In the hot summer of 1925, reporters from across America and other parts of the world watched as William Jennings Bryan stood up for his faith at a trial in the tiny town of Dayton, Tennessee. Bryan had invested his life in public service, and he had come a long way from his 1860 birthplace of Salem, Illinois.

As a child, William Jennings Bryan enjoyed playing, reading books, and hunting rabbits. Among his chores was feeding the deer his father kept on the family farm. Bryan later said that the most pleasant memory of his childhood was his mother, who taught him until he was ten years old. Early in life he decided to be a lawyer like his father. At age fourteen, Bryan became a member of the Cumberland Presbyterian Church. His faith was always at the center of his life.

Bryan went to Illinois College. According to his parents' wishes, he studied Latin and Greek. He enjoyed mathematics, especially geometry, and believed that the discipline he learned from that study helped him later in his life. He participated in the track and field sports of foot racing and broad jumping. While at college, Bryan met Mary Baird who attended a nearby school. Bryan graduated first in his class and at graduation he gave a speech about character. In it he said, "The desire to seem, rather than to be, is one of the faults which our age, as well as other ages, must deplore." In his life, William Jennings Bryan tried to be a person of fine character rather than just seem to be so.

Bryan entered Union College of Law in Chicago. While a student there, he married Mary. William taught Mary law also. Though she never intended to practice law, Mary wanted to be closer to her husband. After William practiced law for a short time in Illinois, the couple and their little girl Ruth moved to Nebraska. There the twenty-seven-year-old Bryan became a law partner with a classmate from law school. Both William and Mary Bryan were admitted to the bar in Nebraska. The Bryans had two more children, William Jr. and Grace.

Three years after the move to Nebraska, Bryan ran for a seat in the U.S. House of Representatives. He visited every town in the district and spoke eighty times. Bryan became the first Democrat to be elected to Congress from Nebraska in the twenty years it had been a state. Two years later he was elected to a second term.

The Boy Orator of the Platte

When William Jennings Bryan began his political career, he became known as the "Boy Orator of the Platte" (the Platte is a river in Nebraska). Bryan had started giving speeches while still a boy. When his mother taught him his lessons, he memorized them and told them back to her while he stood on a little table. In college Bryan was named class orator. The first speech he gave after entering Congress was so popular with his fellow Congressmen that they gave out more than 100,000 copies of it.

Throughout his career, Bryan excelled at giving speeches. After four years in the U.S. House of Representatives, Bryan tried unsuccessfully to become a Senator. He became the editor of the *Omaha World-Herald* newspaper. He also began to travel, giving lectures that encouraged people to consider Populist ideas. (Populists are discussed on page 470.)

Some of the speeches Bryan gave during this time and also later in his life were Chautauqua speeches. The Chautauqua movement began in 1874 when a group of Sunday school teachers received training at Chautauqua Lake in New York. Other groups around the country copied the idea. Touring groups began to travel across the country. Chautauqua groups included political speakers, religious speakers, musicians, theatrical troupes, and comedians. They went from town to town educating and entertaining people, usually staying several days. The events were very popular, especially in rural areas.

In 1896, six years after he first ran for office, Bryan gave a speech at the Democratic National Convention in Chicago. The speech, called "Cross of Gold," is perhaps the most famous political speech ever given in America. When Bryan finished, men and women screamed. They waved their hats and canes and threw their coats into the air. The applause lasted thirty minutes. The following day, convention delegates nominated thirty-six-year-old Bryan as the Democratic candidate for President. Bryan was the first presidential candidate to travel widely to campaign. He traveled 18,000 miles in 1896. On some days he spoke twenty-five times. In the election, William McKinley won by a narrow margin.

Bryan Serves His Country

The Democratic Party nominated Bryan for President a second time in 1900. He lost again to William McKinley. Bryan was nominated once more in 1908, losing this time to William Howard Taft. During this campaign, he made a movie that had a recording of him talking. This was surprising because, at the time, Hollywood movies only had pictures with no sound. They were silent movies. Movie makers placed printed words between scenes so movie patrons could know what the actors were saying. The first talking movie from Hollywood was not released until 1927.

In 1912 Bryan supported Woodrow Wilson, helping him become the Democratic candidate for President. After winning the election, Wilson appointed Bryan as Secretary of State. See the photo of Wilson and Bryan on page 629. Bryan served Wilson well, negotiating many treaties with foreign nations. Bryan was a pacifist (a person who does not

Wilson and Bryan

believe in war). After serving as Secretary of State for three years, he resigned because Wilson was making decisions that would lead America into World War I.

Bryan had a major impact on American life. Many of the ideas he promoted were adopted by Congress. Among these were prohibition and women's suffrage.

The Great Commoner

Because of his defense of the common man, Bryan came to be called "The Great Commoner." In 1901 Bryan founded *The Commoner* newspaper in Lincoln, Nebraska. It was published for twenty-three years. In his lifetime, William Jennings Bryan wrote fifteen books and many pamphlets. He compiled two collections of speeches. For about thirty years, Bryan spoke about two hundred times a year. He came to be called "the silver-tongued orator." He did not shout, but he could be heard by thousands outdoors without a microphone. When he first spoke on the radio in 1922, an estimated sixty million people listened.

Bryan wrote Sunday School lessons that were published in over one hundred newspapers. After rearing their children in Nebraska, the Bryans moved to Miami, Florida, in 1920. There he taught a Sunday School class which drew crowds of 5,000 people. The class was moved to a park because of the large attendance.

"The Silver-Tongued Orator"

Bryan, the Christian

Bryan was concerned about Americans turning away from believing in Jesus and trusting in the Bible as God's inspired Word. He feared that the teaching of evolution as truth in public schools would have a negative impact on America's children. Bryan wrote a pamphlet in 1921 entitled "The Menace of Darwinism."

In 1924 William Jennings Bryan gave a speech in Nashville, the state capital of Tennessee, entitled "Is the Bible True?" A Nashville attorney sent copies to every member of the Tennessee General Assembly. In March of 1925, the Assembly passed a bill making it illegal in Tennessee public schools to teach "any theory that denies the story of Divine Creation of man as taught in the Bible, and to teach instead that man has descended from a lower order of animals." Tennessee Governor Austin Peay quickly signed the bill.

The American Civil Liberties Union (ACLU) wanted to test the Tennessee law and offered to represent a Tennessee teacher in court. Businessmen in Dayton, Tennessee, heard about the offer and decided the trial could draw attention to their town. They asked local football coach and science teacher John Scopes if he would volunteer to stand trial. He agreed. Scopes was indicted and the trial was set for the summer. Though he had not practiced law in three decades, William Jennings Bryan was asked to help prosecute Scopes.

About two hundred journalists flocked to Dayton in the summer of 1925. Sixty-five telegraph operators sent news stories to cities around America and to Europe and Australia. The trial, which was referred to as the "Monkey Trial," lasted eight days. In the end, Clarence Darrow, the lawyer defending John Scopes, asked that his client be found guilty. Darrow wished to take the case to a higher court. John Scopes was found guilty, and he was fined one hundred dollars.

Bryan traveled in the area for five days after the trial, continuing to speak. After church on Sunday, he lay down for an afternoon nap and died quietly in his sleep. He was buried in Arlington National Cemetery. Five years after his death, Bryan College, a private Christian college, was founded in his honor in Dayton. In 1937 Nebraska placed a statue of William Jennings Bryan as one of its two statues in Statuary Hall in the U.S. Capitol. It is pictured at right. Bryan's daughter Ruth followed in her father's footsteps. She was elected to the House of Representatives from Florida, became a Chautauqua lecturer, and was appointed Ambassador to Denmark.

Speaking of his belief in the resurrection, Bryan once said, "If the Father deigns to touch with divine power the cold and pulseless heart of the buried acorn, and make it burst forth from its prison walls, will He leave neglected in the earth the soul of man, who was made in the image of his Creator?"

> God created man in His own image,
> in the image of God He created him;
> male and female He created them.
> Genesis 1:27

Bryan Statue
in the U.S. Capitol

Activities for Lesson 105

Thinking Biblically – William Jennings Bryan loved and believed the Word of God. Read Psalm 119:1-24. Choose three verses to copy into your notebook.

Literature – Read "Marveling at the Mysteries" in *We the People*, pages 131-132, and chapter 5 in *Blue Willow*.

Creative Writing – In your notebook, write a two-page speech about a subject or cause that is important to you. Organize your thoughts logically, and use clear language. Give reasons for your ideas and examples that support them. Read over your speech at least twice and make changes to improve the way you make your points. Practice reading it out loud. Read your finished speech to your family.

Timeline – In *Timeline of America the Beautiful* next to 1925, write: The Scopes "Monkey Trial" is held in Dayton, Tennessee.

Student Workbook or Lesson Review – If you are using one of these optional books, complete the assignment for Lesson 105. If you are using the Lesson Review, take the quiz for Unit 21.

22 The Great Depression

In the dark times of the Great Depression, Franklin Roosevelt offered Americans a New Deal. He put many young Americans to work in the Civilian Conservation Corps. Men from San Francisco were happy to get good jobs building a bridge across the Golden Gate. The world's most famous movie star was Shirley Temple, a little girl from California. She and other movie stars helped Americans forget their troubles, if only for a little while on a Saturday afternoon. God created many ecosystems on the beautiful Olympic Peninsula. Civilian Conservation Corps workers built a cabin there in 1937, and in 1938 President Roosevelt signed legislation setting aside much of the peninsula in Olympic National Park.

Contestants in an RKO Radio Pictures Inc. "Gateway to Hollywood" Contest, 1939

Lessons in Unit 22

Lesson 106 – Our American Story: President Roosevelt and the New Deal
Lesson 107 – Daily Life: Working for the CCC
Lesson 108 – An American Landmark: The Golden Gate Bridge
Lesson 109 – An American Biography: Shirley Temple, Child Star and Ambassador
Lesson 110 – God's Wonders: God Created the Olympic Peninsula

Books Used in Unit 22

- *Maps of America the Beautiful*

- *Timeline of America the Beautiful*

- *We the People*

- *Blue Willow* by Doris Gates

President Roosevelt and the New Deal

In 1932 Americans were living through some of the worst economic conditions the country had ever known. Farmers, construction workers, miners, and those who worked in steel and automobile factories were having an especially difficult time. When the Democratic Party met that year to choose their presidential candidate, they picked Governor Franklin Roosevelt of New York. During the campaign, Roosevelt promised "a new deal for the American people." The Republican Party chose President Herbert Hoover. Though the Great Depression was not Hoover's fault, many Americans blamed him for not doing more to help. They hoped a Democrat could turn things around. A large majority of voters voted for Roosevelt. Voters also chose a Democratic majority to represent them in both the Senate and the House of Representatives.

President Hoover and President-Elect Franklin Roosevelt Ride to the Inauguration, March 4, 1933

Alphabet Soup

President Roosevelt and Congress tried many programs to help end the suffering of the Great Depression. Since many were called by their initials, people began to speak of the "alphabet soup" of New Deal programs. Two of the most remembered are the Works Progress Administration (WPA) and the Civilian Conservation Corps (CCC), which is discussed in detail in Lesson 107. Many Americans started working on WPA projects that built roads, bridges, airport runways, and public buildings. The program began in 1935.

The WPA also paid people to write books and plays and to create art. Look at the WPA posters on pages 633. They advertise a performance of Handel's *Messiah* by a community chorus, a concert performed by an African American band, a pet show, a father and son banquet, art classes for children, a performance by an orchestra, a children's theatre production, a performance of *Androcles and the Lion* by an African American theatrical troupe, and a doll and buggy parade. Find the posters that encourage people to let flowers grow, to keep clean, and to visit the zoo. Another poster invites people to go to the library and one reminds them that work by both farmers and factory workers brings prosperity.

The WPA posters above encouraged Americans to travel. The photo at right below shows a WPA office in Kentucky. Use a magnifying glass to find the words "Jesus Saves" in the photo. At left below is one of five dinosaurs constructed in Dinosaur Park in Rapid City, South Dakota, a joint project of Rapid City and the WPA.

Men in Compton, Kentucky, are trading mules and horses near the Wolfe County WPA Office.

Dinosaur Park, Rapic City, South Dakota

Construction at TVA's Douglas Dam in Tennessee

Mountain Home with New Electrical Power

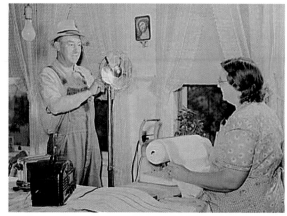

A Knoxville, Tennessee, couple uses electric appliances.

New Deal Programs Still in Operation

Tennessee Valley Authority. Another New Deal program was the Tennessee Valley Authority (TVA). The TVA built dams on the Tennessee River and on other rivers. See the photo at lower right on page 634.

These dams helped provide low-cost electricity to homes, businesses, and factories in one of the poorest regions of the country. The dams helped prevent flooding and made river transportation easier. Lakes created by the dams provided recreational opportunities.

Tugboat from Paducah, Kentucky, at a TVA Lock in Alabama

Notice the TVA photographs on this page. At top left is a home with a new electric meter. New power lines are nearby. At top right, a couple demonstrates electrical appliances families could have. Find the light bulb, the electric fan, and the radio. The woman is using an electric iron. In the photo at right is a tugboat from Paducah, Kentucky. It is using a TVA lock in Alabama. Below is a lodge built in cooperation with the Civilian Conservation Corps (CCC) and the National Park Service beside a TVA lake.

While the TVA brought improvements to many lives in the region, there were also some negative consequences. TVA lakes covered many homes and farms, so the owners

Lodge near TVA's Norris Lake

had to move. Though they were paid for their loss, the families living there did not have a choice about whether to sell or not. When TVA began producing electricity, several small private electric companies that already sold power in the region were put out of business.

Social Security. Most Americans are still affected by the Social Security program which began while Franklin Roosevelt was President. Its purpose is to provide income for people who have reached retirement age, for people who can no longer work because they are disabled, and for children who have lost a parent. To fund the program the Federal government requires employers to deduct a percentage of their employees' income from each paycheck and to send it to the Social Security Administration. Each employer is also required to send in an amount equal to what their employees pay. People who are self-employed also make Social Security payments. The amount of money individuals receive is based on the amount they have paid into the program. Almost all working Americans must make Social Security payments. Two exceptions are members of certain religious organizations and people employed by the Federal government. Federal employees do not pay into Social Security or receive payments from it because they have a different retirement and disability program.

Pros and Cons of the New Deal

The New Deal accomplished much good. Some programs helped people start working again. Congress passed laws which changed how the stock market works and set up the Federal Depositors Insurance Corporation (FDIC). The FDIC guaranteed people's money in banks. This means that individuals who deposited money in an FDIC-member bank would not lose their money, even if the bank failed.

On the other hand, Roosevelt began some programs that the Constitution did not give him authority to do. The U.S. Supreme Court declared these unconstitutional. Americans had traditionally tried to find personal solutions to problems; but during the New Deal, some came to depend on the government to help them. Through New Deal programs, the Federal government got more involved in the lives of individuals and in the affairs of businesses than in the past. This made Americans lose some of their freedoms. The Federal government spent much more money than it received in taxes, a practice that has continued most of the years since.

While it is true that many individuals were helped, unemployment remained high until the start of World War II. Some believe the Depression would not have lasted as long if the Federal government had not regulated business as much and if it had kept more money in circulation.

Hobos Walk Along Railroad Tracks After Being Put Off a Train

Still, many saw Franklin Roosevelt as a hero. He was elected to a second term in 1936. President George Washington had refused to run for a third term as President and all other American Presidents had also left the presidency after two terms. However, Franklin Roosevelt broke with this tradition when he ran for a third term and won the presidential election of 1940.

Hobos, Breadlines, and the Dust Bowl

Many Americans did not have enough to eat during the Great Depression. Homeless men wandered from place to place looking for work. Some sneaked onto trains, cooked meager meals over fires near railroad tracks, and slept wherever they could find shelter. Some knocked on people's doors and asked for food.

Men who were traveling and looking for a job were called hobos, those who worked only when they had to were called tramps, and those who never worked were called bums. Sometimes whole families traveled around while the father looked for a job. See the photo of hobos on page 636. In big cities, people stood in breadlines waiting for free bread or bowls of soup given out by churches and charitable organizations. See the photo at right.

Breadline in New York City

During the 1930s, Kansas and Oklahoma suffered from droughts. High winds created dust storms. The area came to be called the "Dust Bowl." Thousands of families from these states headed west to California looking for work.

Vermonter Takes Butter to Town, 1939

Everyday Life

Another New Deal program was the Farm Security Administration (FSA), which assisted poor farmers. FSA photographers took photos of people living their everyday lives. In the FSA photo at right, a seventy-one-year-old man is taking butter to sell in Woodstock, Vermont.

Many people went to see movies during the 1930s. Radio shows continued to be popular. By 1940 eighty percent of American homes had radios. Families could hear news, farming advice, radio plays, and comedians. Radios also brought them messages from their President. At right Roosevelt talks to Americans on the radio. He called these talks "fireside chats."

Roosevelt Presents a Fireside Chat

Examples of some buildings built in the 1930s are found below and on page 638.

City Hall, Beverly Hills, California, 1932

Coca-Cola Bottling Plant in Los Angeles, California, 1932

Monopoly

George S. Parker of Salem, Massachusetts started publishing games in 1883 when he was sixteen years old. Within five years his company was doing so well that his brother Charles joined him. They called their business Parker Brothers. Another brother, Edward, joined the team in 1898. In 1906 the Parkers started selling the card game Rook, which became very popular.

In 1933 Charles B. Darrow showed executives of Parker Brothers a game he had developed called Monopoly. They rejected his idea, saying it had too many errors. Mr. Darrow got help from a friend who was a printer. Even though the Depression was going on and people were pinching their pennies, Darrow sold 5,000 handmade Monopoly games in 1934 at a Philadelphia department store. People loved his new game. Soon, he couldn't make enough, so he went back to Parker Brothers. This time they agreed to publish it.

Coffee Shop in Los Angeles, California, 1932

The game became very popular after Christmas of 1935. Orders in the form of letters and telegrams started pouring in. There were so many orders that Parker Brothers kept them in laundry baskets in halls. The company began working three shifts six days a week. Soon they got permission from the state of Massachusetts to work on Sundays (even into the 1970s many places had laws about what businesses could be open on Sundays). By the end of 1936, the company had sold 1,810,000 games and earned $1,000,000 profit.

Gas Station in North Carolina, 1930

In the 1930s . . .

- Grant Wood's painting "American Gothic" was first unveiled at the Art Institute of Chicago in 1930. It depicts a farm woman and a farmer with a pitchfork, standing in front of a house. It has become one of the most recognized paintings in American history.
- Mickey Mouse first appeared in a comic strip in 1930.
- A company begun in 1896 by an immigrant from Austria began selling Tootsie Pops in 1931.
- Los Angeles hosted the Summer Olympics in 1932.
- Chicago hosted a World's Fair in 1933.
- German scientist Albert Einstein immigrated to America in 1933 and became a professor at Princeton University.
- New York City hosted a World's Fair in 1939.

Read the "In the 1930s . . ." box on page 638 and see the list of popular toys of the decade below. The little girl shown at right is holding dolls repaired by the WPA.

Many churches grew during the 1930s. The difficulties of the Great Depression made some people realize their need for God's comfort, strength, and help. Like David, they learned to say:

In the day of my trouble I shall call upon You,
For You will answer me.
Psalm 86:7

Girl with Dolls Repaired by the WPA

Activities for Lesson 106

Thinking Biblically – Many people faced poverty during the Great Depression. Read Deuteronomy 15:7-11 to learn about what attitude God desires that we have toward the poor.

Vocabulary – In your notebook, make a drawing for each of these words that illustrates what it means: troupe, prosperity, recreational, consequence, circulation. Write the word under the drawing. Check in a dictionary if you need help with their definitions.

Literature – Read "Fireside Chat: On Drought Conditions" in *We the People*, pages 133-134, and chapter 6 in *Blue Willow*.

Timeline – In *Timeline of America the Beautiful* next to 1935, write: The Works Progress Administration begins operating.

Family Activity – Have a 1930s Family Game and Treat Night. See page 970 for instructions.

Student Workbook or Lesson Review – If you are using one of these optional books, complete the assignment for Lesson 106.

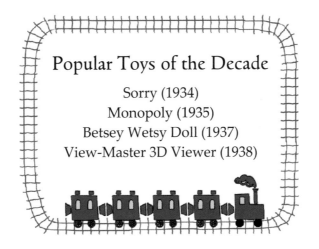

Popular Toys of the Decade

Sorry (1934)
Monopoly (1935)
Betsey Wetsy Doll (1937)
View-Master 3D Viewer (1938)

Working for the CCC

Franklin Roosevelt believed in taking care of the resources God created. As a young man, he had managed his family's Hyde Park estate in New York and had arranged for the planting of thousands of trees there. He worked to protect New York's resources while serving as Governor of that state. By the time Roosevelt became President, the quality of the soil on many of America's farms had become poor.

The main farming methods used had taken nutrients out of the soil without putting them back. When farmers left soil bare for part of the year without a cover crop, wind and water caused the soil to erode, taking away valuable topsoil. Timber companies had cut down trees from many forests and not replanted them as they should have. This also caused soil erosion and flooding. Not only did these problems make America less beautiful, they caused economic troubles. Food grown on farms and wood grown in forests are both necessary for a healthy American economy.

Roosevelt took the oath of office on March 4, 1933. In less than a week, he was actively working to establish a program that would put unemployed men to work improving

CCC Recruiting Poster

forests and helping to prevent soil erosion and flooding. The program was called the Civilian Conservation Corps (CCC). Under Roosevelt's leadership, people from many departments of the Federal government worked together to get the program going. The first recruit was Henry Rich from Alexandria, Virginia. He enrolled on April 7, 1933, just over a month after Roosevelt took office. Within three months, 250,000 men had enrolled. By the time the program ended in 1942, about three million people had participated.

CCC Recruits

The main purpose of the Civilian Conservation Corps was to employ young, unmarried men between the ages of eighteen and twenty-five (the age requirement was later expanded to include seventeen to twenty-eight-year-olds). They came to be called

CCC boys. Notice the recruiting poster on page 640 encouraging men to join. The poster was created by the Works Progress Administration.

To become part of the Civilian Conservation Corps, a young man first filled out an application. Then he waited up to two months to find out if he had been accepted. After approval of his application, the recruit went to a conditioning camp for two weeks. Most of these camps were at Army posts. He was examined by a doctor and given vaccinations. Conditioning camps introduced the recruit to Army discipline and hard labor. If the recruit was found capable of the duties required of him, he was formally enrolled and took the required oath of obedience.

CCC Uniforms

After conditioning camp, recruits went to a Civilian Conservation Corps camp, where they were given two sets of uniforms, one for work and one for dress. Work shirts and

pants were made of blue denim or khaki cotton. The first dress uniforms were olive drab Army uniforms. Once when President Roosevelt visited a CCC camp near his vacation home in Warm Springs, Georgia, he noticed the poor quality of the dress uniforms. He believed that shoddy clothing weakened morale, so he ordered the Department of the Navy to design a special uniform. In the photo at right, Robert Fechner, Director of the Civilian Conservation Corps, inspects the new spruce-green uniform worn by CCC boy Frank Papuga.

CCC Director Robert Fechner, Enrollee Frank Papuga, and District Commander Lieutenant Colonel Thomson Lawrence

CCC Camps

CCC boys lived together in a camp built near their work site. Organizers tried to have two hundred men in each camp. The first CCC camp was Camp Roosevelt in George Washington National Forest at Luray, Virginia. By 1937 there were 2,635 camps. Many early camps were run by U.S. Army officers. Some of the earliest enrollees slept in canvas tents lined up in neat rows. Notice the camp at Rocky Mountain National Park below. This photograph was taken less than two months after the first CCC recruit was enrolled.

CCC Camp at Rocky Mountain National Park, May 26, 1933

Later camps had wooden barracks, a mess hall, bath houses, officers' quarters, and other buildings. Many had a schoolhouse and a recreation hall. Corps members sometimes improved their camps. They laid gravel paths between buildings and built brick or stone fireplaces inside them. They built gates and railings and planted trees. At various camps, CCC boys built outdoor amphitheaters,

*CCC House Used from 1936 to 1941
at White River National Wildlife Refuge in Arkansas*

flower gardens, swimming pools, and fishponds. Notice the camps in Wyoming, California, and New Mexico at right and a barracks in Arkansas above.

Some early camps were integrated, but later camps were divided by race. One example of an all African American camp was the one at Gettysburg National Military Park.

A Typical Work Day

Enrollees were awakened at 6:00 a.m. They were required to be bathed and dressed in their work clothes by 6:30 a.m. The first activity of the day was physical training. Afterwards, they went to the mess hall where six to twelve men sat together at long tables. A typical breakfast was cereal, coffee, eggs, ham, milk, and stewed prunes. After breakfast CCC boys tidied up the grounds and their sleeping quarters before lining up for inspection.

About 7:45 a.m., enrollees walked or rode to the place where they would be working that day. Notice the photo at top right on page 643. The men worked until lunchtime. Lunch was usually brought to the work site. Sometimes they had a hot

CCC Camp at Grand Teton National Park, 1933

*CCC Camp called Funeral Range
in Death Valley National Park, California, 1935*

CCC Camp at Lava Beds, New Mexico, 1941

meal, but usually they ate sandwiches and pie with coffee. See the photo at top left on page 643. After an hour lunch break, enrollees went back to work until 4:00 p.m.

When they returned to camp, free time began. They played pool or table tennis, read books from the camp library, or played team sports. Some CCC camps had sports teams

CCC workers break for lunch at Many Glacier Camp in Glacier National Park in 1933.

Buses are loaded to take CCC workers to their worksites in Rocky Mountain National Park on May 26, 1933.

who played against teams from other camps or teams from nearby communities. Some CCC sportsmen got football scholarships to colleges and other young men were recruited by major league baseball scouts who traveled to CCC camps looking for potential players.

CCC boys, attired in their dress uniforms, went to the mess hall at 5:30 p.m. to eat their evening meal. They had meat, fresh vegetables, fruit, and dessert. After-dinner activities varied. The young men could attend evening classes, play table tennis or pool, or go to nearby towns for a movie or a stroll. At 9:45 p.m. camp lights were flashed to warn the boys that it was time to prepare for bed. Lights out was strictly enforced beginning at 10:00 p.m. Taps was played at 10:15. Those who were tardy often lost privileges. CCC labor was so tiring that many men went to bed long before taps. At 11:00 p.m. the camp commander walked through the barracks performing a bed check to make sure all men were there.

Weekends at a CCC Camp

The CCC boys did not work on weekends, unless bad weather had slowed down their work during the week. They might have to take care of necessary tasks like doing their laundry, as shown below, but Saturdays were set aside for recreation. They played sports, hunted, fished, wrote and performed plays, or sang in choruses. Most camps had about four dances each year. Local girls were invited. Music was usually performed by a camp swing band.

The CCC published a national newspaper called *Happy Days*. Camps sent in articles describing camp activities. By August of 1935, 1,112 camps were also producing their own

CCC boys wash and dry laundry at Glacier National Park in 1933.

camp newspapers. Enrollees did most of the work on these, working on Saturdays and during journalism classes held on weeknights.

Religious services were held on Sundays. The Federal CCC office paid 154 full-time chaplains and 189 part-time clergymen. In addition, many preachers from towns near camps volunteered their services to the CCC boys. Some boys also attended local churches.

643

CCC Benefits

Members of the Civilian Conservation Corps received free lodging, food, clothing, transportation, and medical care during their six-month enrollment period. For boys from poor families, simply getting to eat three meals a day was a great benefit. Each man earned $30 per month and was expected to send $25 home to his family. CCC boys chosen to be camp leaders received $45 per month; assistant leaders earned $36.

CCC Boys in Glacier National Park in Montana, 1933

In the beginning, those who oversaw the CCC tried to place enrollees about two hundred miles away from their homes, far enough away that they could not go home weekly, but close enough to go home once a month. Not all recruits could be placed close to home. Some traveled across the country. Notice the CCC boys above. Most are from New York, and they are working at Glacier National Park in Montana. If a recruit re-enlisted for another six months, he was given a six-day leave of absence with full pay between his tours of duty. Notice the CCC enrollee from Georgia in the photo below. He is at home with his mother.

CCC boys were off-duty on New Year's Day, Lincoln's Birthday, Memorial Day, Independence Day, Labor Day, Thanksgiving, and Christmas. They also got vacation days for their personal religious holidays, whether they were Catholic, Protestant, Greek Orthodox, or Jewish. Enrollees were given days off with pay so they could vote in the local elections where their camp was located, as well as in state and national elections.

CCC Enrollee at Home with His Mother in Georgia, 1941

The CCC boys received training in various occupations as well as a basic education. During the nine years the Corps existed, about 40,000 illiterate enrollees learned to read and write. The Corps gave young men from large cities the opportunity to experience the joys of creation. Their time working in the outdoors also improved their health. The CCC experience taught members how to work hard and work together. They learned self-discipline and respect for authority.

Economic Benefits from the CCC

Towns located near CCC camps received economic benefits. CCC boys spent some of their money there, local residents sometimes found jobs at the camps, and local residents were able to sell supplies to the camps. See the top photo on page 645. Industries also benefited from the program, since they were able to sell supplies for running the camps

Men discuss a cooperative dairy in California, which supplied milk to nearby CCC camps, 1935.

New Chevrolet Trucks Purchased for CCC Work, 1933

and completing work projects. See at left new Chevrolet trucks purchased for the CCC. Industry also benefited from a better-trained workforce.

Additional Members of the CCC

CCC publications described the average CCC boy as twenty years old and from a family of six children. His father was unemployed and the recruit himself had not worked in nine months. He had an eighth grade education, was five feet eight and a quarter inches tall, and weighed 147 pounds. About eighty-five percent of the members of the Civilian Conservation Corps were unmarried men in their late teens and early twenties.

Older and married men were allowed to join if they were veterans of the Spanish-American War or World War I, Native Americans, or residents of U.S. territories in Alaska, Hawaii, Puerto Rico, and the U.S. Virgin Islands. Veterans had separate CCC camps with more lenient rules. Others lived at home and worked on projects nearby.

Another group of CCC workers were called Local Experienced Men. These were residents who lived near a camp and had skills needed to accomplish the work at that camp. They worked as project leaders. They could be married or single and there were no age restrictions. They did not have to live at the camp. The blacksmith pictured at right worked for the CCC in Maryland.

About 8,500 women lived in CCC camps set up for women only, mainly in the Northeast. The women's program was eliminated in 1937.

CCC Blacksmith, Prince Georges County, Maryland, 1935

Work Accomplished by the CCC

The CCC motto was "We Can Take It." They lived up to their motto. The Civilian Conservation Corps set up camps and worked on projects in all forty-eight states and in the U.S. territories mentioned above. The CCC was nicknamed "Roosevelt's Tree Army" because it was involved in so many forestry projects. Enrollees cleared land for firebreaks, built fire towers in national forests, and fought forest fires. They also planted over 2.5 billion trees! The CCC enrollee pictured at the top of page 646 is weeding around loblolly pine trees in a TVA nursery near Wilson Dam in Alabama.

CCC enrollees were involved in many other projects as well, especially in national and state parks. They helped build a total of about eight hundred state parks across the country. They built guest cabins, picnic sites, and rustic furniture. They cleared hiking trails and

Weeding in Alabama

built campgrounds. They built a dam that created a lake in Savoy Mountain State Park in Massachusetts. See photo at left below. Their work in forests and parks protected many of the beauties God created in America and made it easier for Americans to visit them. Visitation at national and state parks increased greatly during the Depression.

The CCC worked on bridges and roads. See the photo at right below where members of an African American camp in Arkansas are building a road in White River Wildlife Refuge. In the bottom left photo, CCC workers dig post holes for a fence in Greene County, Georgia. In the bottom right photo, the men build a terrace to keep soil from forming gullies in Vernon County, Wisconsin. CCC boys repaired the covered bridge in Connecticut that is pictured on page 647.

Lake in Savoy Mountain State Park, Massachusetts

African American CCC workers build a road in Arkansas.

CCC boys also strung 89,000 miles of telephone lines and stocked rivers and streams with fish. They assisted victims of floods and tornados. CCC enrollees installed the first lighting system in Wind Cave National Park in South Dakota. They built the mule corral at the Grand Canyon. They cut ski trails at Stowe, Vermont.

In Alaska they built air strips, housing, shooting ranges, and fish hatcheries. They dug wells. They even restored totem poles and conducted archaeological research.

CCC workers dig post holes in Greene County, Georgia.

CCC workers build a terrace in Vernon County, Wisconsin.

When America became involved in World War II, the work of the Civilian Conservation Corps ended. Through their hard work, the CCC boys blessed their families and fellow Americans. Their work continues to bless Americans today. We can also bless others by working hard; in all our work, we should work first and foremost for the Lord Christ:

Covered Bridge near Colchester, Connecticut, Repaired by CCC Workers

Whatever you do, do your work heartily,
as for the Lord rather than for men,
knowing that from the Lord you will receive
the reward of the inheritance.
It is the Lord Christ whom you serve.
Colossians 3:23-24

Activities for Lesson 107

Thinking Biblically – Copy these words of wisdom about work into your notebook: Proverbs 14:23, 18:9, and 22:29.

Literature – Read "A Nation-Wide System of Parks" in *We the People*, pages 135-136, and chapter 7 in *Blue Willow*.

Creative Writing – In your notebook, write an article of at least one page as if it would be published in the CCC camp newspaper *Happy Days*. Make the subject of your article reasons CCC boys should use their free time profitably. Give specific suggestions of activities and create a catchy title for your article.

Timeline – In *Timeline of America the Beautiful* next to 1933, write: The Civilian Conservation Corps begins operating.

Student Workbook or Lesson Review – If you are using one of these optional books, complete the assignment for Lesson 107.

The Golden Gate Bridge

San Francisco, California, is known for Fisherman's Wharf, Chinatown, steep hills, Victorian architecture, cable cars, sourdough bread, and the beautiful Golden Gate Bridge. See illustrations at right and below. Spanish settlers founded the mission of St. Francis of Assisi in this area on June 29, 1776, five days before the signing of the Declaration of Independence. Englishman William Richardson established the small village of Yerba Buena there in 1835. It was renamed San Francisco after the Mexican War.

San Francisco remained a small town until the California Gold Rush of 1849. That year it grew to a city of 35,000! Early businesses included Wells Fargo, Levi Strauss, and Ghirardelli chocolate. The world's first cable cars began operating there in 1873. They were invented by Andrew

In San Francisco's Chinatown

Smith Hallidea, a San Franciscan who had emigrated from England during the Gold Rush. By 1906 San Francisco had about 400,000 people. That year the city experienced a major earthquake, losing 28,000 buildings. The city rebuilt and by 1915 was ready to host the Panama Exhibition to celebrate the completion of the Panama Canal.

Golden Gate

A strait is a narrow channel connecting two bodies of water. The Golden Gate Strait connects San Francisco Bay and the Pacific Ocean. San Francisco was built on the shore of San Francisco Bay. See the map at right.

The Golden Gate and the land around it are beautiful, as seen in the top photo on page 649. Most historians agree that John C. Fremont, topographical engineer, explorer, and 1856 Republican candidate for President, named

San Francisco Cable Car

this strait around 1846. It reminded him of a harbor in Istanbul which was called the Golden Horn.

God created San Francisco Bay as the perfect habitat for many animal species. Over 130 species of fish swim there. Chinook salmon migrate through the bay to and from the rivers and streams of northern California. Look at the photos below to see some of God's creations that live near the Golden Gate.

The Golden Gate Strait and the Golden Gate Bridge

Plans for a Bridge

San Franciscans had been crossing the Golden Gate by ferry for many years, but with more and more of Henry Ford's Model Ts and other automobiles traveling the highways, people began wanting another way to cross from one side of the strait to the other. Though the idea of building a bridge had circulated for many years, in 1916 James H. Wilkins, a structural engineer and local newspaper editor, began seriously to encourage construction of a bridge. Three years later city engineer Michael O'Shaughnessy began preparatory work.

Top Row: Great Egret, Sea Stars, Long-Billed Curlew; Middle Row: Phalarope, Frost on a Cranesbill Leaf, Allen's Hummingbird; Bottom Row: Forster's Terns, Ruby-Crowned Kinglet, Seagull

U.S. Navy Blue Angel plane flies near one of the tall towers, built with an Art Deco design.

The counties in the San Francisco area began cooperating in 1923 to make the bridge a reality. The United States Department of War owned the land on both sides of the strait. In 1930 the War Department gave final approval for construction of a bridge.

For several years Joseph Strauss, a nationally-known engineer from Chicago, had been encouraging officials to construct a bridge across the Golden Gate. He became chief engineer for the project. Strauss decided to build a suspension bridge. When completed it was the longest suspension bridge in the world. The Golden Gate Bridge is completely supported by two cables which run parallel to each other high above the bridge's roadway. These cables are attached to concrete anchorages built on shore at each end of the bridge. Between the anchorages, the cables pass through two tall towers. See towers and cables on page 651.

The Golden Gate Bridge is not only an engineering marvel; it is also beautiful. Strauss hired San Francisco architect Irving Morrow to determine the bridge's architectural design. Morrow is responsible for the bridge's Art Deco style, its red-orange paint (which is called International Orange), and its beautiful lighting. Morrow chose the International Orange color because it complements the surrounding landscape. A U.S. Navy Blue Angel flies near one of the Art Deco towers in the photo above.

Strauss depended on the work of Charles Ellis, professor of structural and bridge engineering at the University of Illinois. Ellis made painstaking mathematical calculations to create a bridge flexible enough to withstand earthquakes and the high winds of the Golden Gate. Ellis consulted often via telegram with respected New York bridge engineer Leon S. Moisseiff, an immigrant from Latvia.

Arrangements were made to get the steel needed for the bridge. It was fabricated in Trenton, New Jersey; Sparrows Point, Maryland; and Bethlehem, Pottstown, and Steelton in Pennsylvania. The steel was transported to Philadelphia on rail cars. From there it was loaded onto ships, which took the steel through the Panama Canal and then north to San Francisco. Individual shipments were timed so that they would arrive at the site when they were needed by construction crews.

Concrete Anchorages and Steel Towers

Workers removed three and a quarter million cubic feet of dirt to make pits on both ends of the bridge. They placed wooden forms inside the pits. Concrete flowed through long hoses known as "elephant trunks." Workers mixed the concrete to remove air pockets and leveled it inside the wooden forms. When finished they had built

Sightseers Sailing at the Golden Gate

two anchorages, each twelve stories high. Refer to the photo at right to identify an anchorage and the other bridge structures described in this section.

Construction crews built a pier on the northern shore of the strait and then built the north tower on top of the pier. When completed, it rose 745 feet in the air. While the north tower was going up, the south tower was begun. It was built in the strait 1,100 feet from shore, the first bridge support ever built in ocean waters. Work crews worked from a barge. They dropped small bombs through a pipe to dig into the rock on the ocean floor. They then dropped larger bombs. Divers went down and found wires attached to these bombs and brought them to the surface, where other crew members connected them to firing mechanisms. The crew then moved the barge away and detonated the bombs.

A crane lifted the rocks broken up by the bombs out of the water and placed them on another barge so they could be carried away. Workers repeated this process again and again until the pit was as big as a football stadium and 110 feet deep at its deepest point. Divers helped pour concrete into wooden forms in the pit until they had a foundation and a concrete ring around it, called a fender. This fender gave some protection from the ocean currents and later kept ships from hitting the tower. A second pier was built on the foundation, and then the second tower was built on top of this pier.

Much of the work on the south tower and its pier was done by divers. While fighting to keep from being swept away by the current, divers had to guide materials, including steel forms weighing forty tons, into position and make them secure. See the choppy waters of the Golden Gate in the lower photo on page 650. The divers had to feel their way around because the waters were so murky. Divers could only go down four times a day for twenty minutes each time because of the ocean tides. Though the work was dangerous, finding divers was easy because the job paid well.

The towers of the Golden Gate Bridge were made of steel that had been shaped into prefabricated sections. These were joined by rivet gangs of four members each. The boss of each gang was called a heater. He heated rivets to the right temperature on a small forge and threw them to catchers, who caught them in metal containers. Riveters hurried to put them in place while the rivets were still hot so they would make a good seal. Each tower has approximately 600,000 rivets.

Spinning Cables for the Golden Gate Bridge

The bridge design required two massive cables that were flexible enough to bend in the strong winds that go through the strait. The Golden Gate Bridge can bend up to twenty-seven feet from side to side and up to sixteen feet up and down. Since the cables had to be

Main Cables

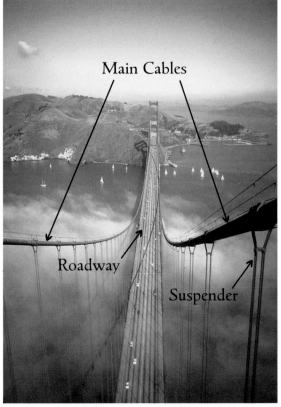

Main Cables

Roadway

Suspender

so long and strong, they were made at the work site. Strauss hired the John Roebling and Sons engineering firm to oversee their construction. John Roebling had been the chief engineer of New York's famous Brooklyn Bridge fifty-two years before.

The Roebling crew hung wire ropes from one anchorage to the top of the first tower, then strung them over the top of the second tower, and then took the wire ropes over to the other anchorage. They then attached a wooden walkway to these wires. They added handrails. Cable spinners used this walkway to make the bridge's cables.

To make a cable, workers bound many wires together into strands. They used 80,000 miles of steel wire. The wire's diameter was about the size of a pencil. Beginning on one shore of the Golden Gate, workers put wire on spinning wheels. A type of carriage took the spinning wheels from one anchorage to the other, which was over a mile away. Workers secured the wire on the other anchorage and then sent the wire back to the first one and secured it there. This process was repeated hundreds of times, making the strand larger and larger. The walkway swayed in the wind as workers maneuvered the carriages and spinning wheels back and forth across their wooden walkway.

To make the two main cables, workers bundled and compressed the strands they had made. Each main cable had sixty-one strands each, which made the cable

Views of the Golden Gate Bridge Roadway from the Side, from Underneath, and from the Air

652

over three feet in diameter. Each cable was 7,659 feet long and was made up of 27,572 wires. These two cables were the largest bridge cables ever made. Notice the cables in the photos on page 652.

To make their deadline, Roebling and Sons designed a way to speed up the process until they were able to send six wires at a time across the bridge. When weather was good, they could guide one thousand miles of wire across the bridge span in one eight-hour shift. They finished the cables ahead of schedule!

Creating the Roadway

Workers hung wire rope suspenders from the cables at intervals. They attached box-shaped beams to the suspenders. See arrow pointing to a suspender at top right on page 652. These beams formed the outer edge of the ninety-foot-wide roadway. Workers attached a variety of steel shapes to create the strong roadway. Joseph Strauss himself lowered the last beam into place. Workers built wooden forms atop the steel framework and then poured concrete inside them to form the road surface for vehicles and sidewalks for pedestrians. See photos at the bottom of page 652.

Golden Gate Bridge Builders

Building a bridge is dangerous work. This was especially true at the Golden Gate, which is one of the world's most violent bodies of water. Besides the strong winds, ocean tides come in and go out twice a day. An average of 390 billion gallons of water is moving in the strait between high and low tides each day. Powerful ocean currents flow into San Francisco Bay from the Pacific Ocean and powerful fresh water currents flow into the bay from the rivers and streams of northern California. These collide in the strait creating strong currents. Water depth in the strait is up to 335 feet.

Despite the danger, men were anxious to work on the bridge since such high-paying jobs were scarce during the Great Depression. Workers were paid from $4.00 to $11.00 per day. Their work hours began when they reached their work site. If it took a man thirty or forty minutes to reach his spot high on a steel beam on the bridge, he did the climbing on his own time.

Ironworkers were needed to build the bridge, but not enough men with this skill were available in San Francisco. Men from many different occupations became ironworkers. A work crew at one job site could include a clerk, a farmer, a taxi driver, and a cowboy.

"Hard-Boiled Hats" and a Safety Net

When work on the Golden Gate Bridge began, workers had a saying that most large construction projects averaged one loss of life for every million dollars spent on a project. Strauss wanted the Golden Gate Bridge to be an exception to this pattern. Resident

engineer Russell Cone was in charge of safety for the bridge construction. If anyone horsed around, he risked being fired immediately.

Construction workers building the Golden Gate Bridge wore a new invention—hard hats. Edward W. Bullard, a veteran who knew about the "Doughboy" Army helmets worn in World War I, designed the "Hard-Boiled Hat" in 1919. It was made out of steamed canvas and glue and was painted black. The hat had straps inside so the hard surface did not touch the wearer's head. This made it able to cushion blows to the head. In 1898 Edward's father had founded the E. D. Bullard Company in San Francisco. It made mining equipment. Miners and construction workers began wearing Bullard hard hats. While workers were constructing the Golden Gate Bridge, Edward adapted his design specifically for bridge workers. Russell Cone made sure that all men wore hard hats all the time, since flying objects were a common cause of construction injuries.

Weather posed problems for the bridge construction crew. San Francisco fog is legendary. See photos on this page and on page 652. During the day, fog can come in and go out many times. Fog made the steel wet, which made it feel like ice. Walking around on the cold, wet steel was difficult. Workers had to be careful not to be blown off by the wind, too. In an effort to make workers safer, a large safety net, similar to a circus net, was placed under the bridge during construction of the roadway. The safety net saved the lives of nineteen men who fell off the bridge during construction. The net attracted the attention of tourists on showboats, and many workers had to be warned not to jump on the net just for fun.

After construction work had gone on for over four years, only one worker had died. However, a section of scaffolding with fourteen men on it fell on February 17, 1937. Two grabbed onto parts of the bridge and hung on until they were rescued. The safety net caught the scaffolding briefly but then it fell through. Only two of the twelve who fell into the water below survived.

Finishing Touches and a Grand Opening

While the bridge was under construction, painters began to paint it so that it would not corrode before it was finished. As the finishing touches were being completed, crews put up handrails.

They installed lights to make the bridge beautiful at night and to help travelers see the roadway in the San Francisco fog.

Work on the Golden Gate Bridge began on January 5, 1933. It was completed in May of 1937, at a cost of $35 million. A Pedestrian Day was held on May 27, 1937. About 200,000 San Franciscans and their visitors gathered to celebrate the completion of this new American landmark. Thousands walked or ran across the bridge. Police motorcycles led vehicles across the bridge when it opened to traffic the next day. Chief Engineer Strauss wrote a poem for the occasion, entitled "The Mighty Task Is Done." The crew had completed the world's longest suspension bridge. Though a few longer bridges have been built since then, the Golden Gate Bridge continues to be one of the longest, most famous, and most beautiful bridges in the world.

In building the Golden Gate Bridge, people made a plan and followed it through to a successful completion.

> For which one of you, when he wants to build a tower,
> does not first sit down and calculate the cost
> to see if he has enough to complete it?
> Luke 14:28

Activities for Lesson 108

Map Study – Complete the assignment for Lesson 108 on Map 3 "American Landmarks" in *Maps of America the Beautiful*.

Vocabulary – In your notebook, copy these sentences and fill in each blank with one of these words: wharf, topographical, marvel, cubic, detonate.

1. The boys argued over who would get to _____ the enormous firecracker.
2. The fishing dory floated placidly beside the wooden _____.
3. The town hired a _____ engineer to enhance the naturally beautiful landscape.
4. When I tried to make my own box out of pieces of cardboard, I discovered the challenge of making perfect _____ forms.
5. To my friends, the sight of my grandmother doing a cartwheel is a _____.

Literature – Read "The Fog in San Francisco" in *We the People*, page 137, and chapter 8 in *Blue Willow*.

Timeline – In *Timeline of America the Beautiful* next to 1937, write: Golden Gate Bridge opens in San Francisco.

Student Workbook or Lesson Review – If you are using one of these optional books, complete the assignment for Lesson 108.

Shirley Temple,
Child Star and Ambassador

*The Ritz Theater in Greenville, Alabama,
Built in 1935*

The 1930s and 1940s are called the Golden Age of Hollywood. The age of silent movies had started to wind down after *The Jazz Singer*, the first feature-length movie with speech, appeared in 1927. Movie studios hurried to figure out how to make talking movies. Theaters switched from hiring an organist to play during silent films to installing equipment that would play sound as well as moving pictures.

During the 1930s, the first drive-in theater opened in Camden, New Jersey; Spencer Tracy starred in *Boys Town*; Judy Garland starred in *The Wizard of Oz*; Jimmy Stewart and Jean Arthur starred in Frank Capra's *Mr. Smith Goes to Washington*; and Walt Disney released the first full-length animated movie, *Snow White and the Seven Dwarfs*. Notice the restored Ritz theater above. It was built in 1935 in Greenville, Alabama. Hollywood's most famous theatre is Grauman's Chinese Theatre, built in 1927, where stars leave their handprints and footprints in the sidewalk. See right.

Forgetting Their Troubles

In the 1930s, movies began to have more heroes such as detectives and Western lawmen. These movies made people feel better during a hard economic time. They

Grauman's Theatre, Hollywood

could also enjoy the elaborate decor at movie theaters like the Regal Theater in Chicago, pictured at left. Americans all over the country flocked to the movies during the Great Depression. Look at the photographs on page 657 and notice all the different places the photos were taken.

Presidents and other Washington officials still welcome movie makers to Washington, as they did in the

Regal Theater, Chicago, 1941

656

Movie-goers line up on a Saturday morning in North Platte, Nebraska, in 1938.

Ladies buy tickets at an Air-conditioned theater in Chicago in 1940.

Naval Academy Midshipmen line up at a theater in Annapolis, Maryland, in 1942.

Children look at movie posters in Steele, Missouri, on a Saturday in 1939.

Patrons wait for the movie to open on a Sunday afternoon in 1939 in Pharr, Texas.

Children at a Theater in Littleton, New Hampshire, on a Saturday Afternoon

Movie Theater in Escalante, Utah, 1936

A child carries a sign advertising a Popeye movie in San Juan, Puerto Rico, in 1938.

A man shovels snow in front of a Chillicothe, Ohio, movie theater in 1940.

You Can't Take It with You *is playing in 1940 in Central City, California.*

Looking at posters at a theater on Beale Street in Memphis, Tennessee, 1939.

A theater advertises a Western movie with Gary Cooper in 1939 in Alpine, Texas.

1930s. Pictured at the top of page 658 are movie industry leaders who met with President Roosevelt in 1938. Included are executives from Paramount Pictures, Columbia Pictures, RKO Pictures, Twentieth Century-Fox, Universal Studios, Warner Brothers Studios, and Lowe's Theaters. The wife of Secretary of State Cordell Hull visits with actress Mary Pickford in the second photo at left. Edith and Irene Mayer, daughters of Louis Mayer,

Movie Executives, June, 1938

Supreme Court Nominee with Newsreel Cameramen, 1937

Mrs. Cordell Hull with Mary Pickford, 1938

Daughters of Louis Mayer Go to Visit President Coolidge, 1927

head of Metro Goldwyn Mayer, are pictured at lower left. They are about to call on President Coolidge.

Americans were not only entertained at the movies; they also kept up with current events in Washington and elsewhere as they watched short newsreels, which were shown before movies. In 1937 Hugo Black of Alabama was nominated to a seat on the Supreme Court. In the photo at right above, Black is being filmed for a newsreel.

President Roosevelt voiced this view of movies: "During the Depression, when the spirit of the people is lower than at any other time, it is a splendid thing that for just fifteen cents an American can go to a movie and look at the smiling face of a baby and forget his troubles." The smiling face of which he spoke was that of child actress Shirley Temple.

A Star is Born

George and Gertrude Temple of Santa Monica, California, had a baby girl on April 23, 1928, just six months after the first "talkie" was released. George was a banker and Gertrude a homemaker. They named their daughter Shirley Jane. She was welcomed by two older brothers, Jack and George Junior. By age three, Shirley was taking dancing lessons. Before long, she started acting in short movies for $10 per day.

In 1934 Shirley Temple appeared in *Stand Up and Cheer*, produced by Fox Film Corporation. It was her first full-length film and her first film for a major studio. Americans loved the cute and happy little girl with curly locks. Six-year-old Shirley Temple became a star in America. Fox Studios gave Shirley a contract and soon loaned her to Paramount

Pictures, where she made *Little Miss Marker*. That film made her an international star. Next she went back to Fox, where she made *Baby Take a Bow*. People were amazed at Shirley's singing and dancing in these films.

Singer, Dancer, and Actress

Shirley's first real dramatic role was in *Bright Eyes*. In *Bright Eyes*, Shirley sang what became her best-known song, "On the Good Ship Lollipop." The song sold a half million copies on records. Shirley received a special Academy Award, a smaller version of the ones given to adult actors.

In 1935 Fox Film Corporation merged with Twentieth Century Pictures, becoming Twentieth Century-Fox. That year the studio released four films starring Shirley: *The Little Colonel*, *Our Little Girl*, *Curly Top*, and *The Littlest Rebel*. In *Curly Top*, Shirley sang another of her famous songs, "Animal Crackers." In *The Little Colonel* and *The Littlest Rebel*, Shirley Temple danced with the great African American tap dancer Bill "Bojangles" Robinson. Some fans were shocked to see a white child and a black man dance together at a time when blacks and whites were separated, even in movie theaters. See the photo at right. Robinson and Temple danced beautifully together and became friends.

African American man climbs the stairs to the "colored" section of a movie house in Biloxi, Mississippi, 1939.

A Young Celebrity

Shirley Temple became the most popular movie star in the world. Like other famous actors, she put her footprints in wet cement in front of Grauman's Chinese Theatre, but Shirley was only six years old. Shirley made millions of dollars for her studio. To keep people thinking about her, the studio put her pictures in magazines and newspapers, had her perform on radio, and arranged for her to make appearances at events. Fans loved to catch a glimpse of their favorite star. Once when Shirley and her parents took a cross-country vacation, five thousand people watched her ride a swan boat in Boston. Before Shirley was eight years old, fans were buying 1.5 million Shirley Temple dolls each year, plus Shirley Temple dresses, hats, coats, gloves, and more.

Shirley's Handprints and Footprints at Grauman's Chinese Theatre

On and Off the Set

When Shirley was on a set making a movie, her mother was always there encouraging her, protecting her, and reminding her to sparkle. At bedtime, her mother rolled up her fifty-five curls and helped Shirley memorize her lines for the next day. Shirley worked hard at making movies, promoting her products, and making appearances; but when she was not in front of a camera, she played like a tomboy and enjoyed writing, drawing, and painting. Since she was too famous to go to the beach or a park like other children, her parents invited Shirley's friends to their home.

In the elementary grades, Shirley Temple studied with tutors in a special bungalow the movie studio provided for her. She was especially fond of her teacher Frances Klapt whom she called "Klammy." When people from other countries came to visit Shirley, Klammy taught her about their homelands.

Shirley Temple in Washington, D.C., 1938

Shirley Temple at the White House, 1938

A Famous Person Meets Other Famous People

Shirley Temple continued acting into her teens and young adulthood. During her career, she performed with many famous actors such as Gary Cooper, John Wayne, Henry Fonda, Cesar Romero, Cary Grant, Lionel Barrymore, and future President Ronald Reagan. She met dignitaries from other countries as well as many famous Americans such as comedian Will Rogers, aviator Amelia Earhart, FBI director J. Edgar Hoover, and President Franklin Roosevelt and his wife Eleanor. President Roosevelt said about Shirley, "As long as our country has Shirley Temple, we will be all right." He said she had "infectious optimism." The photos of Shirley on this page were taken when she visited President Roosevelt in Washington, D.C.

Shirley Temple Grows Up

When Shirley Temple reached her high school years, she went to a private school. She made a few films as a teenager and young adult. The most famous are *Since You Went Away* and *The Bachelor and the Bobby Soxer*. At age seventeen, Shirley married Jack Agar. They had one daughter, Linda Susan. Mr. Agar had many personal problems. They divorced in 1949 when Shirley was twenty-one years old.

In 1950 Shirley Temple Agar went on a vacation to Hawaii. There she met Charles Black, who became her second husband. They were married for fifty-five years. During the 1950s, Shirley gave birth to two more children, Charles Jr. and Lori. Shirley acted on television from 1958 to 1961 and then retired from show business to enjoy being a wife and mother. Shirley had made fourteen short films, 43 feature films, and over twenty-five storybook movies made for television.

Shirley Temple, the Public Servant

After she and Charles reared their children, Shirley Temple Black became a public servant. She ran for a seat in Congress, but lost the election. She became a representative for the United States at the United Nations in 1969 while Richard Nixon was President. While President Gerald Ford was in the White House, Shirley Temple Black was named Ambassador to Ghana and later White House Chief of Protocol, the first woman to serve in that position.

During the presidency of Ronald Reagan, Shirley was a foreign affairs officer in the Department of State. President George H. W. Bush appointed her as Ambassador to Czechoslovakia. An ambassador helps the government of one country communicate and work with the government of another country. After Shirley's retirement from public life, she and her husband lived in northern California. Charles died in 2005.

Throughout her life, Shirley Temple Black has remained a member of the Screen Actors Guild, and the Guild honored her in 2006 with its Life Achievement Award. Accompanying her at the award presentation were her three children and her granddaughter. During her acceptance speech, she said that she had been blessed with three careers: actress; wife, mother, and grandmother; and diplomat.

Shirley Temple was an ambassador for her country. Each of us has the opportunity to be an ambassador for Christ:

> Therefore we are ambassadors for Christ,
> as though God were making an appeal through us;
> we beg you on behalf of Christ, be reconciled to God.
> 2 Corinthians 5:20

Activities for Lesson 109

Thinking Biblically – Copy 2 Corinthians 5:20 in your notebook. Write one or two paragraphs about how you can be an ambassador for Christ.

Vocabulary – In your notebook, write a paragraph using all of these words: contract, dramatic, bungalow, dignitary, optimism. Consult a dictionary if you need help with their definitions.

Literature – Read chapter 9 in *Blue Willow*.

Creative Writing – Write three or four paragraphs in your notebook about the positive opportunities available to a celebrity and about the temptations they face.

Timeline – In *Timeline of America the Beautiful* next to 1928, write: Shirley Temple is born in Santa Monica, California.

Student Workbook or Lesson Review – If you are using one of these optional books, complete the assignment for Lesson 109.

God Created the Olympic Peninsula

God created the Olympic Peninsula on the northwest tip of the continental United States. It is part of the state of Washington. Like all peninsulas, it is surrounded by water on three sides. To the west is the Pacific Ocean, to the east is Puget Sound, and to the north is the Strait of Juan de Fuca, which separates Washington from Vancouver Island in British Columbia, Canada.

Every year God gathers waters from the Pacific Ocean and creates clouds that drop from 140 to 167 inches of rain on the western side of the Olympic Peninsula—that's twelve to fourteen feet! All this water makes lush vegetation grow in dense forests with some of the biggest trees in North America. Though the western side of the peninsula is very wet, the eastern side is much drier, with some areas receiving twenty-two or fewer inches of rain per year.

Elevations change quickly on the Olympic Peninsula, home not only to ocean beaches, but also to the Olympic Mountains and their more than 250 glaciers. Less than thirty-three miles from the Pacific coast, Mount Olympus, the tallest of the Olympics, rises 7,980 feet above sea level. Mount Olympus is like the hub of a wheel with mountains, valleys, and rivers forming spokes that spread out in all directions across the peninsula. Scattered within the mountains and valleys are meadows and lakes. Notice the variety of Olympic Peninsula scenes on page 663.

Modern names of the Native American peoples that have lived, hunted, fished, and traveled in the region include the Chehalis, Jamestown S'Klallam, Hoh, Lower Elwha Klallam, Nisqually, Makah, Port Gamble S'Klallam, Quileute, Quinault, Shoalwater Bay, Skokomish, Squaxin Island, and Suquamish.

European and American Explorers

When Greek navigator Juan de Fuca explored the waters off the northwest coast for Spain in 1592, he discovered the strait that now bears his name. In 1778 English explorer Captain James Cook tried to find the strait but could not. Another English explorer, Captain William Barkley, was able to find the strait nine years later; he named it for Juan de Fuca. Captain John Meares explored in the area in 1788; it was he who named Mount

Rialto Beach Along the Pacific Coast

Elwha River

Sitka Spruce Trees in the Olympic Rainforest

Mount Olympus in Winter

A Mountain Lake in the Buckhorn Wilderness

Olympus. Captain George Vancouver did extensive explorations in the region in 1792. He named Puget Sound and Mount Rainier, which is east of the Olympic Peninsula and south of Seattle. Mount Rainier is the tallest mountain in Washington state and the tallest volcano in the contiguous United States.

A few homesteaders moved onto the peninsula in the mid-1800s, mostly along the coast. Since so much of the area has dense forests, settlers found clearing land for farms difficult. However, those who stayed often wrote letters to family members in the East, telling of the beauties and natural resources surrounding their new homes.

Though local Native American groups had traveled in the Olympic Mountains for many years, it wasn't until the late 1800s that white men made extensive explorations there. Lieutenant Joseph P. O'Neil led a group in 1885. The *Seattle Press* financed the first expedition to cross all the way through the mountains in 1889-90. The party was gone for six months, exploring during one of the worst winters in American history. Lieutenant O'Neil led an expedition again in 1890. He recommended that the Olympics be included in a national park.

Preserving the Peninsula

President Grover Cleveland set aside most of the peninsula's forests as the Olympic Forest Reserve in 1897. The name was changed to the Olympic National Forest in 1907. Today the national forest covers 633,677 acres. Since the region's elk population was declining and national forest status did not protect them, President Theodore Roosevelt declared a portion of the national forest to be the Mount Olympus National Monument in 1909.

In 1937 the Civilian Conservation Corps completed the Hamma Hamma cabin, pictured on page 664. That same year President Franklin Roosevelt visited the peninsula and became passionate about preserving it. While there he visited Lake Quinault Lodge, also pictured on page 664. The lodge was built in the mid-1920s. Visitors from all over the world have stayed there, enjoying the pretty views and recreational opportunities. Attached to the chimney on the front of the lodge is a totem pole rain gauge. It measures yearly rainfall, not in inches, but in feet! The dining room where President Roosevelt had lunch at the lodge is now called the Roosevelt Dining Room. The year after his visit to the area, President Roosevelt signed legislation establishing Olympic National Park. The Olympic National Park protects 922,641 acres of the peninsula.

Hamma Hamma Cabin Built by the CCC

Lake Quinault Lodge

The Olympic Coastline

Along the coast of the Olympic Peninsula are sandy and rocky beaches where tidepools brim with life; coastal prairies with plants like cranberry, crowberry, Labrador-tea, sundew, and sphagnum moss; and dense coastal forests that reach all the way to the ocean. See Olympic peninsula tidepool life below.

Red Sea Urchin

Bloodstar

Purple Sea Urchin and Other Creatures

Strong winds pound the coastal forests so hard with sand that many trees near the beach only have branches on the side that does not face the ocean. Eagles perch in the tops of these battered trees. Logs that have drifted down the peninsula's rivers pile up on the shoreline. On the coastal forest floors, shrubs like salmonberry and evergreen huckleberry grow shoulder high. In the undergrowth are ferns, beadruby, and yellow skunk cabbage.

One hundred and thirty-five miles of the coastline is in the Olympic Coast National Marine Sanctuary, established in 1994. The Makah, Quileute, Hoh, and Quinault Native American tribes still practice traditional fishing along the Olympic coast. Birds such as

Tufted Puffin

Common Murres

rhinoceros auklets, peregrine falcons, tufted puffins, and common murres, nest here. See the bird photos at left. Rocks, sea stacks, and islands are located offshore. Also near the shore are kelp beds, subtidal reefs, and undersea canyons. Twenty-nine species of marine mammals live in the waters along the coast.

The Olympic Rainforest

A Douglas fir stands tall above fallen logs and undergrowth.

Autumn sunlight shines through fern in front of nurse log.

Temperate rainforests lie just inland from the coastal forests. Here temperatures rarely go below freezing or rise above eighty degrees, an ideal climate for a temperate rainforest ecosystem. God planted large conifers here, like Sitka spruce, Douglas fir, western hemlock, and western red cedar. Sitka spruce are pictured on page 663; see a giant Douglas fir at left. Many rainforest trees have been growing for hundreds of years. Some extend 250 feet toward the sky. If you wanted to wrap a string around the largest trees, you would need a string sixty feet long!

When these big old trees die, they can stand for years before falling. When they do fall, they slowly decay into soil, but this can take centuries. While decaying they provide homes for amphibians, insects, and small mammals, as well as fungi, mosses, and baby trees. Fallen trees are called nurse logs. A nurse log covered with mosses is pictured above. Many tree seeds germinate on fallen tree trunks and fallen branches. As the seedlings grow, their roots reach for the ground. When their nurse log finally decays, a row of trees with roots that look like stilts remains where the nurse log once lay.

The rainforest also has deciduous trees such as big leaf maples, red alders, and black cottonwoods. Epiphytes grow in the Olympic rainforest, too. An epiphyte is a plant that obtains moisture and nutrients from rain and from the air. Epiphytic ferns, lichens, mosses, and spike mosses decorate tree trunks and branches in the rainforest. A licorice fern is an epiphyte that grows on moss-covered tree trunks. See photo at right above.

Licorice Fern

Oak Fern and Oregon Oxalis

Hundreds of species of mosses, liverwort, ferns, and lichens grow in the temperate rainforest. Oregon oxalis and the small oak fern grow on the forest floor. See photo above. The rainforest has many rivers, streams, and waterfalls. See the photo of Wynoochee Falls at left.

Wynoochee Falls

The rainforest is ideal for the Roosevelt elk. The Olympic Peninsula has the largest wild Roosevelt elk population in the United States. Their grazing keeps some plants from growing too tall and dense, thereby helping low-growing plants get more sunlight.

Bunchberry

The Lowland Forests

The largest trees of the Olympic Peninsula grow in the lowland forests. They send roots down into the deeper soils and grow straight and tall for many years. The mild climate, deep soils, and heavy rainfall cause them to grow to record-breaking heights and widths. Among the tall trees of the lowland forests are Douglas fir, western hemlock, western red cedar, grand fir, and Sitka spruce.

The old growth forests of the northwestern United States are mainly in the lowland forests. An old growth forest has these characteristics: trees that are over two hundred years old, standing dead trees, many decaying trees lying on the ground, and a multi-layered canopy. The canopy of a forest is its "roof." A multi-layered canopy has trees of varying heights. Along the forest floor are small plants like the bunchberry pictured above. Many animals depend on old growth forests. Among these are Cope's giant salamanders, fishers, marbled murrelets, northern goshawks, spotted owls, and Vaux's swifts. A marbled murrelet and a Cope's salamander are pictured at right.

Marbled Murrelet

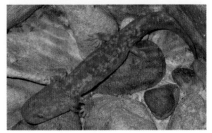
Cope's Giant Salamander

The Montane Forests

Elevations from about 1,500 feet to about 4,000 feet are home to the montane forests. Growing conditions are more difficult, so trees grow more slowly here. Still, many montane forest trees live hundreds of years, including a record-breaking Alaska yellow cedar that has reached twelve feet in diameter.

Pacific Rhododendron

Types of trees vary, depending on whether they are on the wetter western side of the park or the drier east side and whether they are on a cool north-facing slope or a sunny south-facing slope. The state flower of Washington, the Pacific rhododendron, grows from the coastal region up into the montane forests. See photo at left.

The Subalpine Forests

The subalpine forests are in a transition zone between the peninsula's dense forests and the alpine tundra. Subalpine forests are thinner. Trees get smaller and smaller as the

Alpine Tundra
Treeline

Subalpine Forest

Subalpine Meadow

elevation rises. The treeline separates the subalpine and alpine ecosystems. Above the treeline, no trees can grow. Subalpine forests are divided by rocky slopes and open meadows where deer graze. See photo at left.

Plants in the subalpine endure hurricane-force winds up to eighty miles per hour. The Pacific storms that drop so many feet of rain onto other parts of the peninsula drop snow on the mountains. Up to fifty feet of snow may fall in one winter. Sometimes the snow is so heavy that it causes avalanches. However, this snow gives moisture for the beautiful wildflowers that grow in the subalpine meadows; and it melts into little streams that flow into the powerful rivers that cut through the lowlands and rainforests to the ocean. The Piper's harebell and Jeffrey's shooting star, pictured at right, live in the subalpine region. The Piper's harebell is endemic, meaning the species is found nowhere else.

Though precipitation is heavy in the Olympics, very

Piper's Harebell

Jeffrey's Shooting Star

little of it falls in summer. When a rare storm does come, lightning may catch part of a subalpine forest on fire. However, the fires burn out when they reach a rocky slope or a meadow, so fires are usually small and don't last long.

Animals living in the subalpine region include the black bear and snowshoe hare as well as the endemic Olympic marmot and Olympic torrent salamander, both pictured at left. The Olympic torrent salamander lives at the edge of cold mountain streams.

The Olympic marmot is a very social rodent with a sharp, piercing whistle. A typical colony has one adult male, two adult females, and the offspring born in the previous two or three years. In summers they move from one subalpine meadow to another, so they can eat different plants as they bloom. In winter the marmots hibernate under several feet of snow.

Olympic Marmot

Olympic Torrent Salamander

The Alpine Tundra

Hikers, such as the one pictured at right, see beautiful scenes when they climb past the treeline and into the alpine tundra on the tallest Olympic mountains. As they stand on these rocky snow-capped peaks amidst flowing glaciers, no trees block their views. Pretty wildflowers, grasses, sedges, and tiny ferns grow in the thin soils.

The meadows, wildflowers, ferns, trees, and wildlife of the Olympic Peninsula grow strong in the environment God created for them. May we do the same.

*A hiker on Mount Elinor looks out
at Mount Pershing and other Olympic peaks.*

> How blessed is the man who does not walk in the counsel of the wicked,
> Nor stand in the path of sinners,
> Nor sit in the seat of scoffers!
> But his delight is in the law of the Lord,
> And in His law he meditates day and night.
> He will be like a tree firmly planted by streams of water,
> Which yields its fruit in its season
> And its leaf does not wither;
> And in whatever he does, he prospers.
> Psalm 1:1-3

Activities for Lesson 110

Map Study – Complete the assignment for Lesson 110 on Map 2 "God's Wonders" in *Maps of America the Beautiful.*

Literature – Read "The Beauties of the State of Washington" in *We the People*, page 138, and chapter 10 in *Blue Willow.*

Creative Writing – Write a short story of at least two pages that takes place on the Olympic Peninsula. Include the names of places, plants, and animals that you read about in this lesson.

Timeline – In *Timeline of America the Beautiful* next to 1938, write: Olympic National Park is established.

Student Workbook or Lesson Review – If you are using one of these optional books, complete the assignment for Lesson 110. If you are using the Lesson Review, answer the questions on *Blue Willow* and take the quiz for Unit 22.

Every Citizen a Soldier

23

Americans wanted to stay far away from wars overseas, but all that changed when the Japanese attacked Pearl Harbor on December 7, 1941. America declared war on Japan the next day and then Germany and Italy declared war on the United States. Millions of people entered the military, fighting a war in Europe and in the Pacific. Meanwhile the folks back home worked hard to keep the soldiers fed and equipped with everything they needed to win the war. First Lady Eleanor Roosevelt encouraged and visited the troops during the war and continued to work for causes she believed in for the rest of her life. The first Japanese attack on America happened in Hawaii, considered by many to be one of the most beautiful places on earth. New York City played a key role in the war, serving as the place many Americans left to fight and the first place they saw in America when they returned home.

Lessons in Unit 23

Lesson 111 – Our American Story: Fighting for Freedom
Lesson 112 – Daily Life: World War II on the Home Front
Lesson 113 – An American Biography: Eleanor Roosevelt, First Lady and
                      Social Activist
Lesson 114 – God's Wonders: God Created Hawaii
Lesson 115 – An American Landmark: New York, the City That Never Sleeps

Books Used in Unit 23

- *Maps of America the Beautiful*

- *Timeline of America the Beautiful*

- *We the People*

Fighting for Freedom

Though President Wilson had hoped that the Great War would be "the war to end all wars," sadly it was not. Most historians believe that World War II happened because of the

Annual Army Day Parade, 1939

many mistakes world leaders made after the first world war. Neither the Treaty of Versailles, signed after World War I, nor the weapons reduction treaties, signed during the 1920s, were enough to end the conflicts between nations.

At left a tank rolls past the U.S. Capitol in the annual Army Day Parade in April of 1939. Though the United States had an army and a navy, it was not ready to fight another war. Memories of World War I made Americans want to stay far away from conflicts overseas.

The Axis Powers Conquer Other Countries

After World War I, dictators rose to power in Germany, Italy, and Japan. Benito Mussolini gained power in Italy in 1922, the military gained power in Japan in the late 1920s, and Adolph Hitler became dictator of Germany in 1933. They ruled their own people harshly and tried to gain control of other nations, saying their people needed what other countries had. It began like this:

1931 — Japan invaded China.

1935 — Italy invaded Ethiopia in northern Africa.

1936 — Germany moved military forces close to its border with France, which was something prohibited by the Treaty of Versailles. Later that year, Hitler and Mussolini committed their countries to helping each other. Mussolini declared that Berlin, Germany, and Rome, Italy, were the new axis around which the whole world turned. Thus the two nations came to be called the Axis Powers.

1937 — Japan joined the Axis. World War II began in the Pacific when Japanese and Chinese troops began fighting each other.

1938 — Germany took control of Austria, a German-speaking country, and Czechoslovakia, where many German-speakers lived. Hitler's excuse was that he wanted

670

to bring all German-speaking people together. (The German takeover of Austria is portrayed in the movie *The Sound of Music*.) That year Italy took control of Albania.

1939 — Germany wanted to take control of Poland. Knowing this, Great Britain and France announced that if Germany attacked Poland, they would declare war on Germany. Great Britain and France had been confident that the Union of Soviet Socialist Republics (U.S.S.R.) would support them against Germany. The world was shocked in August when Germany and the U.S.S.R. announced that the two countries had signed a treaty promising not to attack each other. Actually Germany and the U.S.S.R. had made a secret deal to divide Poland. When Germany attacked Poland from the west on September 1, the U.S.S.R. prepared to capture eastern Poland. Two days later Great Britain and France declared war on Germany. The war in Europe had begun.

The American Response

At first only a few countries had seriously condemned what the Axis powers were doing. Among them were Great Britain and France. President Roosevelt announced that the United States would remain neutral. However, when Germany invaded Poland, the United States began to sell weapons to Great Britain.

Axis Powers Continue Their Aggression

1940 — Germany conquered Denmark, Norway, and France. Italy declared war on Great Britain and France. The Axis seemed unstoppable. Germany began to bomb Great Britain in the summer of 1940. German planes bombed targets in Britain almost constantly. Night after night British citizens hid in bomb shelters. Buildings in many cities were destroyed. German bombers damaged or destroyed one-third of the homes in London. Thousands of people died.

Germany intended to weaken Great Britain and follow the bombing with an invasion. However, the British Royal Air Force fought well. The leaders and citizens of Great Britain refused to surrender. They decided to stand firm, no matter the cost. Great Britain was victorious in this Battle of Britain. They showed the world that Germany could be stopped. Later in 1940, Germany, Italy, and Japan signed an agreement, stating that they would come to one another's aid and declare war on any country that declared war on any of them.

Because of the possibility that America might be drawn into the war, the U.S. government began drafting soldiers in 1940. Those drafted first were men between ages twenty-one and thirty-five. In 1941 the age range was changed to twenty to forty-five. The minimum age was lowered to eighteen in 1942.

1941 — President Franklin Roosevelt was inaugurated to serve a third term as President of the United States. See Roosevelt with his wife Eleanor at right. Germany and Italy conquered

President and Mrs. Franklin Roosevelt, 1941

Above: Barrels of Powdered Eggs
At Right: Workers at the Kroger and Baking Company can pork for the U.S.S.R.

southeastern Europe and northern Africa. Hitler changed his mind about the Soviets, and Germany invaded the U.S.S.R. in June. Japan took over more and more of Asia. The United States began a lend-lease program which supplied ammunition, tanks, airplanes, trucks, and food to Great Britain and also to the U.S.S.R. and China. Food prepared for America's allies through the lend-lease program is pictured above.

August 19, 1941 — British Prime Minister Winston Churchill met secretly with President Roosevelt on a ship in the Atlantic Ocean, asking him for more help in the war. See picture at far right.

British Prime Minister Winston Churchill walks on the deck of the HMS Prince of Wales during his Atlantic conference with President Roosevelt.

"A Date Which Will Live in Infamy"

December 7, 1941 — Japan sent military planes to attack U.S. naval and air bases at Pearl Harbor in the U.S. territory of Hawaii. Over 2,000 people died in the attack. Japan also bombed other American military bases and British bases on islands in the Pacific that day. At right are photographs of American ships following the attack. The next day President Roosevelt called December 7 "a date which will live in infamy," and the U.S. Congress declared war on Japan. A few days after that, Germany and Italy declared war on the United States. See a photo of Roosevelt and his war cabinet on page 673.

U.S. sailors risk their lives to put out flames on the USS West Virginia.

The USS West Virginia, the USS Tennessee, and the USS Arizona (pictured from left to right) were all damaged by Japanese torpedoes and bombs. The USS Arizona later sank.

Many young American men volunteered for the military and others were drafted. At right are two photographs of soldiers at Fort Knox. Soon young women were encouraged to join a special branch of the military, as seen in the recruiting poster below.

Soldiers Training at Fort Knox, Kentucky

President Roosevelt and his War Cabinet in December of 1941.

World War II Recruiting Poster

Soldier Serving as a Mechanic and Truck Driver at Fort Knox

The Allies Win Victories

1942 — For most of 1942, Japan continued to gain control of areas in Asia and the Pacific Ocean, while Germany and Italy continued to control Europe and northern Africa. Germany kept trying to conquer the U.S.S.R. However, late in 1942, the Soviet army started pushing Germany back. At the same time, troops from Great Britain, the Soviet Union, and the United States (these countries were called the Allies) started winning battles in northern Africa. American forces also attacked Japanese forces on Guadalcanal Island near Australia. Slowly the Allies began to push Japanese forces back toward Japan.

General Marshall, President Roosevelt, Brigadier General Wilbur, and General Patton (from left to right) in Casablanca

1943 and Early 1944 — In January of 1943, President Roosevelt met with British Prime Minister Winston Churchill in Casablanca, Morocco, to make plans for the war. At left, President Roosevelt pins the Congressional Medal of Honor on Brigadier General William Wilbur. Also present are General George Patton and General George Marshall.

In May of 1943 Allied troops defeated the last German forces in northern Africa. In July the Allies invaded the Italian island of Sicily. After this, Mussolini lost power. The new Italian government wanted to surrender to the Allies, but German troops moved in to keep Italy under Axis control. The Allies invaded Italy in September. Meanwhile, American and British planes bombed Germany, which seriously limited its ability to manufacture weapons. In late 1943 and early 1944, the United States sent over one million more American troops to Europe. They went to Great Britain where they made preparations to bring freedom to the areas taken over by the Nazis.

American General Dwight Eisenhower, Commander of all Allied military forces, encourages paratroopers in England on D-Day.

D-Day, June 6, 1944

Allied military leaders developed a plan to conquer Germany. First they would invade German-occupied France, then liberate Paris, and

This sketch by Victor Alfred Lundy was drawn at Fort Jackson, South Carolina, on June 6, 1944.

finally push toward Germany. The Germans knew an invasion was coming, but the date was top secret. In the photograph at left above, General Eisenhower is encouraging soldiers before they go to France. Other soldiers were still training in America at this time. At top right is a sketch by a soldier at Fort Jackson, South Carolina.

On June 6, 1944, known as D-Day, the first Allied troops crossed the English Channel and landed on Normandy Beach on the coast of France. Many soldiers lost their lives in the fierce fighting on D-Day and the days after, but the Allies were able to push the German troops back. The Americans and British continued to push forward through France. They freed Paris from German control on August 25. The conflict continued in Belgium and the Netherlands in the following weeks.

A Fourth Term for Roosevelt and the End of the War in Europe

The Allies continued moving toward Germany during the fall of 1944. That November Franklin Roosevelt was elected to a fourth term as President.

In December the German army fought back and created a bulge in the Allied lines. This Battle of the Bulge only slowed the Allies down; it did not stop them. The Allies reached Germany on March 7, 1945.

For many months President Roosevelt had been very ill. As the Allies pushed toward

Mrs. Roosevelt, French President Charles DeGaulle, and Others at the Grave of President Roosevelt

Berlin, he died on April 12 while vacationing in Warm Springs, Georgia. Vice President Harry S. Truman became President in his place. Just over two weeks later, German Fuhrer Adolph Hitler died. On May 7, 1945, German commanders surrendered to the Allied forces. The following day was declared Victory in Europe Day, or V-E Day.

Marines on the Pacific Island of Iwo Jima

Fighting in the Pacific Until V-J Day, August 14, 1945

Meanwhile, the war in the Pacific continued as the Allies kept slowly pushing Japanese troops back toward Japan. Look at the photograph at left of U.S. Marines on the Pacific island of Iwo Jima. Below are photographs taken aboard the USS *Cebu*, whose crew was responsible for making repairs that other ships needed while they were fighting in the Pacific. In the lower right photograph, a sailor is receiving a Purple Heart. This is a medal given to soldiers who are wounded in combat.

In the summer of 1945, American scientists told President Truman about a weapon they had developed. They told him that it had enormous power and could be used against Japan. President Truman believed that using this weapon would stop the war by forcing Japan to surrender. He believed that it would save the lives of many American soldiers.

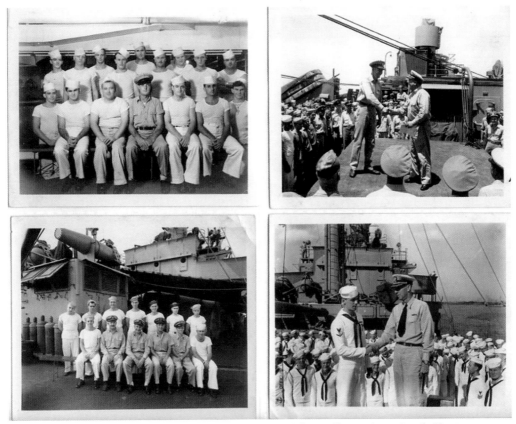
Photographs Taken on the USS Cebu. *At lower right, a sailor receives a Purple Heart.*

675

President Truman decided to use the weapon. On August 6, 1945, an American plane dropped an atomic bomb on Hiroshima, Japan. Three days later, another atomic bomb was dropped on Nagasaki, Japan. Tens of thousands of people died in both cities, and Japan surrendered on August 14. People in Allied countries celebrated Victory in Japan Day, or V-J Day.

A Devastating War

War is a horrible thing. Fifteen million men and several hundred thousand women served in the armed forces of the United States. Of these, one in forty died. As the war ended, people learned of the terrible concentration camps run by the German government. Millions of Jews, Gypsies, and others were tortured and killed in the camps. This is known as the Holocaust. As many as fifty million people around the world lost their lives during World War II.

Leaders and citizens in the Allied countries pulled together to fight in a cause in which almost everyone believed. Americans believed it was their duty to defend their country and work to free others from oppression. Their beloved President Franklin Roosevelt had voiced it well on January 6, 1941, when he told the U.S. Congress:

> We look forward to a world founded upon four essential human freedoms. The first is freedom of speech and expression—everywhere in the world. The second is freedom of every person to worship God in his own way—everywhere in the world. The third is freedom from want . . . everywhere in the world. The fourth is freedom from fear . . . anywhere in the world.

Read about Roosevelt's life below.

Franklin Delano Roosevelt
America's Thirty-Second President
March 4, 1933 - April 12, 1945

Franklin Roosevelt's father James made his fortune in railroads and coal. He was a widower with one adult child, also named James, when he married Sara Delano. Sara Delano had grown up in Hong Kong and on an estate near the Hudson River in New York. Her father had made his fortune in China. Except for a brief time in 1867, when she went to school in Dresden, Germany, Sara Delano was educated at home. She was twenty-six when she married James; he was fifty-two. Sara and James lived happily at Hyde Park, his estate along the Hudson River.

James and Sara had one child, Franklin, born at Hyde Park in 1882. Sara devoted herself to her son. While many wealthy mothers had servants to care for their children, Sara took care of Franklin herself.

Franklin Delano Roosevelt (FDR) was educated at home by tutors until he was fourteen years old. He then entered the elite, private Groton School in Massachusetts. While Franklin was at Groton, Endicott Peabody, the head of the school, encouraged him and other students to be public servants. Franklin's distant cousin Theodore Roosevelt once gave a talk at the school, and Franklin came to admire him. Both TR and Peabody had a great impact on Franklin's life.

After attending Groton, Franklin entered Harvard. His father died a few months later. At left is a photograph of James, Sara, and Franklin Roosevelt, taken in 1899, about a year before James' death.

At Harvard Franklin became the president of the *Harvard Crimson*, the college newspaper. He also met and courted Theodore Roosevelt's niece, Eleanor, who was also his own distant cousin. Sara Roosevelt objected when they became engaged in 1903 and insisted they wait a year before marrying. Franklin entered Columbia University Law School in the fall of 1904. The couple married the following spring.

Franklin continued in law school. Though he never graduated from Columbia, he passed the bar and began to practice law. Between 1906 and 1916, Franklin and Eleanor had six children, five of whom survived infancy: Anna, James, Elliott, Franklin Jr., and John.

In 1910 Franklin Roosevelt was elected to the New York state senate. In the senate he headed the Forest, Fish and Game Committee. For the rest of his life, he supported conservation of natural resources. While Woodrow Wilson was President, FDR served as his Assistant Secretary of the Navy for seven years. In 1920 Democrat James Cox ran unsuccessfully for President against Warren Harding. Franklin Roosevelt was his running mate.

Besides their home in New York City, the Roosevelt family had homes at Hyde Park and at Campobello along the Atlantic coast in southern Canada, just north of Maine. In 1921 FDR contracted polio while at Campobello. The disease was much feared because it sometimes killed or paralyzed its victims. FDR became paralyzed from his waist down. He worked hard to regain the use of his legs, trying various treatments. Beginning in 1924, he exercised in warm mineral waters at Warm Springs, Georgia. The treatments at Warm Springs helped Roosevelt regain some feeling and strengthened his muscles, though he never walked again without help. FDR bought an old resort hotel there and established a rehabilitation center for polio patients. For the rest of his life, he stayed involved with the center, returning almost every year to celebrate Thanksgiving with other polio patients.

While Roosevelt recuperated, he stayed in contact with the Democratic Party. Eleanor became very involved with Democratic women. In 1928 FDR ran for Governor of New York and won. The following year the stock market crashed. Governor Roosevelt began a program that put 10,000 men to work planting trees and building roads and buildings in New York's state forests and state parks. The program was similar to the CCC that he later helped to establish across the whole country.

In 1932 Roosevelt ran for the presidency of the United States against incumbent Herbert Hoover. Roosevelt won easily. Though FDR was President during the hard times of the Great Depression and World War II, he continued his hobbies of collecting stamps and bird-watching. He enjoyed playing cards. He had a pool built in the White House and enjoyed swimming in it. In addition to official functions, Franklin Roosevelt hosted small parties and spent time with close friends. He was an outgoing man who loved to be around other people.

The Roosevelt's daughter Anna served as an assistant to her father during World War II and as hostess at the White House. James worked in Roosevelt's 1932 presidential campaign and later as FDR's secretary. He was in the Marines during World War II. Roosevelt sons John and Franklin served in the Navy, and Elliott joined the Army Air Force.

Roosevelt is the only President in American history to be elected more than twice. FDR's mother Sara died a few months after he was elected to a third term. You will read more about Eleanor Roosevelt in Lesson 113.

First of all, then, I urge that entreaties and prayers, petitions and thanksgivings,
be made on behalf of all men, for kings and all who are in authority,
so that we may lead a tranquil and quiet life in all godliness and dignity.
This is good and acceptable in the sight of God our Savior.
1 Timothy 2:1-3

Activities for Lesson 111

Thinking Biblically – In your notebook, compose a one-page prayer for "kings and all those in authority," according to the command in 1 Timothy 2:1-3.

Map Study – Complete the assignments for Lesson 111 on Map 24 "World War II in the Pacific" and Map 25 "World War II in Europe" in *Maps of America the Beautiful*.

Literature – Read "D-Day Message" in *We the People*, page 139.

Timeline – In *Timeline of America the Beautiful* next to 1941, write: Japanese planes attack Pearl Harbor.

Student Workbook or Lesson Review – If you are using one of these optional books, complete the assignment for Lesson 111.

Wesley Notgrass with Two New Friends in Europe

World War II on the Home Front

We are all in it—all the way. Every single man, woman, and child is a partner
in the most tremendous undertaking of our American history.

President Franklin Roosevelt spoke those words on the radio two days after the United
States entered World War II. Though millions were called upon to go "over there" to fight,
many more millions stayed behind and became a civilian army. While the folks back home
loved, encouraged, and prayed for the soldiers in their own families and for others, they
kept busy supplying them with what they needed to fight.

*Ford employees attend an early morning meeting
of the Automobile Council for War Production
in Detroit, Michigan, in 1941.*

The Arsenal of Democracy

When the war began, American industries
were manufacturing ammunition, guns, planes,
ships, tanks, and trucks for the Allies. By
producing these supplies, America had become
what Franklin Roosevelt called an "Arsenal of
Democracy" (an arsenal is a place where military
supplies are stored). As the war got bigger and
American soldiers went into battle, demand for
military supplies and equipment increased
dramatically.

At first the task seemed too hard. Imagine the challenge of figuring out what was
needed to fight a huge war, getting all those things made, and then transporting them to
where they were needed. Think first about just providing clothing for the Army. When
America declared war on the Axis powers, the Army ordered 250,000,000 pairs of pants
and 500,000,000 socks right away!

American industries and the American people, like the Ford workers in the photograph
above, were ready for the challenge. Though America had experienced hard times during
the Great Depression, it was still in much better financial condition than Germany, Italy,
and Japan. In 1938 the total income of the United States was twice the income of those three
countries combined. Japanese companies had built 26,000 automobiles in 1937. By contrast,
American companies had built five million and could build five million more.

Ambassador Joseph Grew and Edsel Ford stand beside a new B-24E Liberator after inspecting Ford's Willow Run plant.

To the Axis powers, the Allies seemed to have an endless supply of whatever they needed. By the end of the war, Americans had produced 324,000 aircraft, 88,000 tanks, 8,800 warships, 5,600 merchant ships, 2,382,000 trucks, and 79,000 landing craft, plus 15,000,000 guns, 224,000 pieces of artillery, 2,600,000 machine guns, 41,000,000,000 rounds of ammunition, and 20,800,000 helmets! Without this steady stream of supplies, World War II might have lasted much longer with more loss of life and more destruction, and the outcome could have been different.

Factories Switch from Peacetime Products to Wartime Supplies

Factories that produced military equipment could not keep up with all that the troops needed, so more factories were constructed. Companies that had been making other products had to pitch in, too. For instance, factories that made women's stockings started making parachutes instead. The Schick company, which normally made electric shavers, made equipment for the Navy.

With their past experience of providing milk chocolate bars to American soldiers during World War I, the Hershey Chocolate Corporation produced more than a billion Ration D bars for soldiers. These were designed to keep a soldier alive when he was unable to get regular food. The Hershey machine shop made parts for anti-aircraft guns.

Harley Davidson had made about 20,000 military motorcycles during the Great War, so the U.S. Army turned to them again. The company produced 88,000 motorcycles for American troops and the Allies. This number included 1,011 designed especially for use in the deserts of North Africa.

The automobile industry was extremely important during the war. Many factories switched from building cars to building jeeps, bombers, and tanks. In the photograph above, Henry Ford's son Edsel speaks with Joseph Grew, who had been U.S. Ambassador to Japan when Pearl Harbor was attacked.

American Workers Get the Job Done

When America entered World War II, three million men were unemployed. The country soon went from high unemployment to a labor shortage. Industry needed over seven million more employees. A few of these jobs went to older men, like those at right. Many went to teenagers, some of whom dropped out of school to work. Many more were filled by women, like those pictured on page 681. African American workers moved into the highest paying jobs they had ever received, though they still were not treated as

Elderly men perform inspections at a Packard Motor Company plant in Detroit.

well as white workers. See an African American worker below.

Though the District of Columbia and every state and territory in America were involved in the war effort, many of the best-paying jobs were in the North and the West. Southerners moved north, with some 350,000 moving to Detroit. Easterners moved west. Between 1940 and 1950, the population of California grew seventy-five percent. By the end of the war, one out of five Americans had moved, many to other states.

Men and women operate drill presses at the Willow Run plant.

During World War II, an American worker could produce twice as much in one hour as a worker in Germany could and five times as much as a worker in Japan. By 1944 Ford's Willow Run factory could build a bomber in an hour. In a month, they could build six hundred. The work week was lengthened to forty-eight hours. Workers, like the man and women at lower left, brought food from home so lunch breaks could take only thirty minutes.

Josef Stalin, leader of the U.S.S.R., said, "The most important things in this war are machines, and the United States is a country of machines."

Woman at Ford's Willow Run plant inspects tubes used in bombers.

African American worker adds screws to bomber wing at the Willow Run plant.

Men Deferred from Military Service

Over the course of the war, four million men who could have been drafted were allowed to stay out of military service so they could work in essential industries. An additional two million farmers were deferred so they could continue to work in agriculture.

About 70,000 men requested deferment because they were conscientiously opposed to war. About half of the requests were granted. Many conscientious objectors were Quakers, Mennonites, or members of the Church of the Brethren. Most were given non-combat positions in the military. Some became medics, who served unarmed and faced great danger when they went onto battlefields to rescue their fellow soldiers.

A few hundred conscientious objectors volunteered for medical experiments and tests. Some worked as smoke jumpers in Oregon. The Japanese released thousands of timed incendiary balloons meant to start fires. Smoke jumpers parachuted down to fight the fires.

Workers at the Willow Run plant stop for a thirty-minute lunch break.

Recycling and Rationing

During World War II, Americans at home had to do without, so that the soldiers would have enough. Americans were encouraged to "Use it up, wear it out, make it do, or do without," and were told, "If you don't need it, don't buy it." Familiar goods such as Scotch tape were in short supply because they were needed by the Army. The 3M company advertised that when victory came, tape would be back in homes and offices.

In 1942 the Federal government began to ration goods to try to make goods available for everyone. The government issued ration books. See the photo at left. Each month a

A ration book is explained in Washington, D.C.

person was allowed a certain ration of butter, canned goods, cheese, coffee, eggs, fish, milk, sugar, and meat. Gasoline and shoes were rationed, too. See the photo below.

Most of the world's rubber comes from rubber tree plantations in Southeast Asia. The Japanese quickly seized these countries, so Americans had to conserve rubber. Rubber drives were held for people to donate rubber boots, raincoats, gloves, garden hoses, and old tires. Americans eventually found it almost impossible to replace the worn tires on their cars. A "victory" speed limit of thirty-five miles per hour was set so that tires would last longer. See photo on page 669.

Metal and paper drives were held, too. People saved grease they had used in their kitchens and donated it for the war effort. The government even gave guidelines on fashion so that less fabric would be used in clothing. Men were encouraged to wear pants without cuffs and to quit wearing vests. Women began to wear narrower skirts. Wrap-around skirts became popular, since there was a shortage of metal zippers and snaps.

A gas station attendant compares the ration book with the license number. A sign tells customers that today's quota for this gas station is sold out.

Growing and Raising Food

American farmers had to produce the food necessary for America's troops. Though two million farmers were deferred from military service, 1.8 million men and women from farm families served in the armed forces. While trying to raise more food than ever before, farmers experienced shortages of workers, gasoline, new farm equipment, and parts to repair old equipment. Sometimes farmers' wives took over farm work when their husbands left to become soldiers.

Farmers attend a Food for Victory meeting at a schoolhouse in North Dakota.

Farmers, like those pictured above, were encouraged to take part in a Food for Victory program to raise more food for the war effort. 4-H club members could win awards ranging from one dollar war stamps to $250 war bonds. Notice the 4-H member at right with food she raised. Pictured below are a load of fish caught and used in the program and a "Victory Flock."

The Federal government encouraged families to raise fruits and vegetables in victory gardens. See the poster below. Americans raised an estimated twenty million victory gardens in yards, empty lots, and even on urban rooftops. The program helped a great deal; home gardens began growing as many fruits and vegetables as commercial farms did. Look at the victory garden photographs below.

4-H Club Member with Food Canned from Her Garden in Rockbridge County, Virginia

Fish caught for the Food for Victory program, Gloucester, Massachusetts, 1942

Home canning was also encouraged so that other canned goods could be sent to the troops. As one poster stated: "Can all you can—it's a real war job!" American women responded with patriotism. Some canned at home; over four times as many home pressure canners were sold in 1943 as had been sold in 1942. Others canned at community canneries. See a photo of the

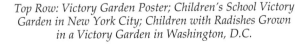

Top Row: Victory Garden Poster; Children's School Victory Garden in New York City; Children with Radishes Grown in a Victory Garden in Washington, D.C.

Bottom Row: Victory Flock in Homemade Brooder in Washington, D.C.; Garden in Escambia Farms, Florida; Victory Gardeners

Works Progress Administration (WPA) cannery in Jeffersontown, Kentucky, at right.

Community Cannery Begun by the Works Progress Administration in Jeffersontown, Kentucky, 1943

America Helps Win the War

Americans came up with many innovative ideas that helped win the war. They improved radar, invented electronic devices, and found new uses for plastics. Many scientists working together produced the atomic bomb, though many of them hoped it would never be used as a weapon.

People from many walks of life were eager to contribute to the war effort. Hollywood producers made military training films. Doctors learned better ways to treat diseases and better surgical techniques. They also improved blood transfusions. Even toy makers helped. The View Master 3-D Viewer toy that was popular in the 1930s became a military tool when the Army had special reels made to use in training soldiers.

One example of Yankee ingenuity came from a World War I veteran who had grown up on a Navajo reservation as the son of a missionary. Philip Johnston knew that the military needed a secret code to fool the Japanese. As a fluent speaker of Navajo, he came up with the idea of using native Navajo-speakers.

Since Navajo is extremely complex and is not a written language, Johnston believed they could help. He convinced the Marines to try his idea. They recruited young Navajo men. The first twenty-nine recruits developed a secret code based on their language. The Japanese never broke it. Of the 540 Navajos in the Marines, about 400 were trained to use the code. Between 1942 and 1945, Navajo code talkers participated in every attack the U.S. Marine Corps conducted during the war in the Pacific.

The Role of Women

As in other wars, women filled many new roles during World War II. They were asked to "Do the job he left behind." At the beginning of the war, one in four American workers was female. By the end of the war, the number of working women had risen to one in three. Many worked in industry. Some, like the woman below, worked at military bases.

A worker at Navy Air Base in Corpus Christi, Texas, reconditions spark plugs.

Women often saved the money they earned. After the war, they used it to make large purchases such as houses. Though some continued to work after the war, many viewed these jobs as temporary and expected to return to their homes after the war. Rosie the Riveter/World War II Home Front National Historical Park in Richmond, California, teaches about life on the home front during World War II, especially the contributions made by working women.

Posters reminding Americans how they could help the war effort.

Keeping America Safe

Americans were afraid that our enemies might attack our country directly, especially along the east and west coasts. To make sure that enemies could not see their cities at night, they turned off outside lights and covered their windows so that no light could shine out. Sometimes communities had air raid drills. When an air raid siren sounded, everyone would go to a safe place, as though bombs were about to fall on their city.

Victory Corps members learn basic first aid at Benjamin Franklin High School, New York City.

Citizens also protected America's secrets. They were careful about what they said so that Axis spies would not learn information that could be used against America. Letters to soldiers had to be worded carefully. They couldn't even mention the weather. Americans were reminded that "loose lips might sink ships."

Schools formed organizations called Victory Corps, which taught students skills like first aid and gave them opportunities to serve. Students learn first aid in the photo at left.

Soldiers Prepare in America

America had more soldiers than ever before. New military bases were needed. Many were built in rural areas where soldiers and their secrets would be safer from enemies. New soldiers had to be trained. They had to practice what they would need to do overseas. This practice was called maneuvers.

One place where maneuvers were held was Middle Tennessee, where the terrain was similar to that in Europe. See the photo at right. Some soldiers camped on people's farms. Men from big cities got their first taste of rural life. The soldiers were divided into armies that had practice battles. They learned

Second Army Maneuvers in Middle Tennessee

how to find their way in strange territory. They dropped bombs made of flour. Local citizens often invited the men for meals and found other ways to serve them.

Soldiers were treated kindly across America. National parks were opened to them so they could enjoy rest and relaxation. Churches hosted social events. Their fellow Americans were well aware of the great sacrifice they were making and were eager to help.

Prisoners on American Soil

Americans were shocked when the Japanese attacked Pearl Harbor on December 7, 1941. Many became afraid of Japanese immigrants and their descendants. They were afraid that Japanese soldiers might invade the west coast and that Japanese Americans might help them.

Girls in Sunday School Class at Manzanar Relocation Center, California

Corporal Jimmie Shohara was an American soldier who visited his parents at Manzanar.

In February of 1942, President Roosevelt ordered that 110,000 Japanese Americans living on the west coast be moved to internment camps in Arkansas, Arizona, California, Colorado, Idaho, Utah, and Wyoming. Many were American citizens. They were not released until December 17, 1944.

The vast majority of those interned were loyal Americans. The U.S. Army had an all-Japanese American combat unit that fought bravely in Italy. Famous photographer Ansel Adams took many photographs at the Manzanar Relocation Center in California, including the ones on this page. The Center is preserved as Manzanar National Historic Site. Around 5,000 German and Italian Americans were also interned, mainly in North Dakota and Montana.

Catherine Natsuko Yamaguchi was a nurse.

The U.S. military captured German, Italian, and Japanese prisoners during the war. The first prisoners of war (POWs) were German sailors, rescued after their submarine sank off the east coast. They were taken to Fort Bragg in North Carolina. By the end of the war, more than 400,000 prisoners were held on American soil. Most camps were in the South and Southwest, because these regions were more isolated and secure than other regions. They were also warmer.

However, by the end of the war, every state except Nevada, North Dakota, and Vermont had POW camps. Most prisoners were treated well. They lived in tents or barracks. Many planted and harvested crops. Some cut timber. German POWs were amazed at the amount of food they received. For recreation the prisoners planted gardens of flowers and vegetables, played soccer, and formed music bands.

War Bonds and the Income Tax

World War II cost Americans $304,000,000,000! The Federal government raised money by changing income tax laws. Before the war, a person could make $1,500 per year without paying an income tax. In 1942 the amount was changed to $624. This meant that thirteen million more Americans began to pay an income tax. The wages of people who made products used in the war rose higher and higher, so the amount of money received through income taxes rose, too. The Federal government also borrowed money from the American people by selling war bonds and war stamps. Paying income taxes and buying war bonds and stamps were considered acts of patriotism.

In 1942, children sing a hymn in Sunday School, celebrate Columbus Day at school, and do a folk dance.

Life Goes On

Not everything that happened in America between 1941 and 1945 was directly related to the war. Young adults began dancing the jitterbug. In 1941 Anna M. Moses, the famous artist who later became known as Grandma Moses, painted her "Black Horses." That same year Iowa hosted the National Tall Corn Contest. The winning entry was twenty-three feet two and one half inches tall!

Americans enjoyed spending the high salaries they were earning. They continued going to the movies and enjoyed radio shows, like *The Shadow*, which was a mystery show; *Superman*, an adventure show; *Truth or Consequences*, a game show; and *Ozzie and Harriet* and *Abbott and Costello*, which were comedies.

Children continued to go to Sunday School, as pictured at left above. They enjoyed holidays. The children in the center above are celebrating Columbus Day. The children at right above are doing a folk dance. The photo at right shows the daughter of Czech immigrants at a twice-weekly class to help children retain the Czech language.

Student and Teacher at a Czech School

The National World War II Memorial

In 2004 the U.S. National World War II Memorial was dedicated on the National Mall in Washington, D.C. It stands between the Lincoln Memorial and the Washington Monument. Former Senator and World War II veteran Robert "Bob" Dole along with Academy Award-winning actor Tom Hanks led the fundraising effort to build it. The memorial honors the Americans—both military and civilian—who worked together to win the war. The Rainbow Pool, which has long lain at the foot of the Washington Monument, was refurbished for use in the memorial. During World War II, the United States of America included forty-eight states, seven territories, and the District of Columbia. Since they all worked in unity to win the war, the memorial includes fifty-six pillars. These surround the pool. On each pillar is a bronze oak wreath, representing industry, and a bronze wheat wreath, representing agriculture. Another

A woman stands in her 1943 victory garden in Washington, D.C. Two blue stars hang in the window.

feature of the memorial are twenty-four bronze bas relief panels. These panels illustrate scenes from the war on the battlefield and on the home front.

When a soldier went to war, his family often placed a flag with a blue star in a window of their home. Notice the two stars in the photo above, indicating two family members in the service. If a soldier died, the blue star was replaced with a gold star. The National World War II Memorial includes 4,048 stainless steel stars coated with gold. Each star represents one hundred military personnel who lost their lives during the war.

Because of their great sacrifices for others, Americans of the World War II era have been called the greatest generation. May we give them the honor they are due.

Render to all what is due them: tax to whom tax is due; custom to whom custom;
fear to whom fear; honor to whom honor.
Romans 13:7

Activities for Lesson 112

Thinking Biblically – In your notebook, write one or two paragraphs about the ways the WWII generation, those in combat and on the home front, served one another.

Vocabulary – Look up each of these words in a dictionary and read their definitions: arsenal, artillery, conscientious, incendiary, ration.

Literature – Read "Fireside Chat: On the Declaration of War with Japan" and "Code-Talkers" in *We the People*, page 140-144.

Timeline – In *Timeline of America the Beautiful* next to 1942, write: Rationing begins in the United States.

Family Activity – Make WWII Home Front Posters. See page 971 for instructions.

Student Workbook or Lesson Review – If you are using one of these optional books, complete the assignment for Lesson 112.

Eleanor Roosevelt, First Lady and Social Activist

Eleanor Roosevelt, Age Fourteen

Eleanor Roosevelt was born in 1884 in New York City. Her parents were Elliott and Anna Hall Roosevelt. Her family was wealthy, but her father suffered from depression and alcoholism and was often away from home. Eleanor's mother was distraught about her husband's behavior. Eleanor would often sit by her mother's bed, stroking her head to comfort her when she had bad headaches. When Eleanor was eight, her mother died.

Her father still stayed away from home a great deal, but Eleanor adored him. When he was home, he was playful with her. She was confident of the love he had for his "own darling little Nell." Her heart was broken when he died, too, just nineteen months after her mother. When Eleanor was ten, her maternal grandmother became her guardian. Life with her grandmother was lonely for Eleanor.

Above is a photograph of Eleanor when she was fourteen years old. Her grandmother sent her at age fifteen to Allenswood School in London, pictured below. For three years Eleanor studied language, literature, and history. At Allenswood she developed a good relationship with the school's headmistress, Mademoiselle Marie Souvestre. In the summers Eleanor and Marie traveled together in Europe. They visited both grand tourist attractions and places where people lived in poverty.

In the aristocratic society to which Eleanor belonged, girls were expected to make a debut into society. Eleanor returned to America for her debut, or "coming out," in 1902. See her coming out portrait on page 690. Eleanor participated in the social obligations expected of a young woman of her social class, but she also became involved in helping the poor.

Eleanor Roosevelt and Schoolmates at Allenswood School in London

Eleanor Roosevelt: The Bride

In 1902, when Eleanor was taking a train to visit her grandmother, she ran into her distant cousin Franklin Delano Roosevelt. They had seen each other before, but soon they grew to like each other and began to court secretly. In November of 1903, they were engaged. They waited over a year, according to the wishes of Franklin's mother, before they were married in March of 1905. Eleanor's uncle Theodore Roosevelt, then President of the United States, gave her away at the wedding.

Eleanor Roosevelt's Coming Out Portrait, 1902

Below are a portrait of Eleanor in her wedding gown and a photo of Franklin and Eleanor taken soon after their wedding.

Left: Eleanor Roosevelt in Her Wedding Gown; Center: Franklin and Eleanor Roosevelt About Two Months After Their Marriage; Right: Franklin, Eleanor, Anna, and James Roosevelt in 1908

Eleanor Roosevelt: Mother, Servant, and Politician

During the first eleven years of their marriage, Franklin and Eleanor had six children, Anna Eleanor (1906-1975), James (1907-1991), Franklin Jr. (eight months, 1909), Elliott (1910-1990), Franklin Jr. (1914-1988), and John Aspinwall (1916-1981). Above at right, see the photo of the Roosevelts in 1908 with their first two children. Below is a family portrait with Franklin's mother in 1919.

The Roosevelts lived first in New York City; then in Albany, New York, where Franklin served as a state senator. Later they moved to Washington, D.C., while Franklin served as Assistant Secretary of the Navy during World War I. In Washington Eleanor became involved with helping people, first through the Navy Relief organization and then through the Red Cross.

When the Roosevelts left Washington, they returned to New York City. In 1920 FDR was nominated as the Democratic candidate for Vice President. Eleanor became involved in politics, too. Eleanor was active in the

Franklin and Eleanor Roosevelt with Sara Roosevelt and the Roosevelt Children, 1919

Democratic Party. She began to write articles for political, scholarly, and popular magazines and to speak at political events. By the time her husband ran successfully for Governor of New York in 1928, Eleanor was a major influence in Democratic politics.

See a photograph of Eleanor and four of her children at right. It was taken in 1920 during a vacation at their Canadian retreat, Campobello.

Eleanor and Four of Her Children at Campobello, 1920

Eleanor Roosevelt: Teacher

A year before becoming First Lady of New York, Eleanor had learned that Todhunter School, a private school for upper-class girls in New York City, might be for sale. She suggested that she and two friends purchase the school. Eleanor became a teacher there. She wanted to give girls the kind of experience she had at Allenswood School. She taught American history, current events, American literature, and English to juniors and seniors. She took students on field trips to markets, tenement houses, and New York Children's Court so they could see the problems poor people faced in New York City. Though she moved with her husband to Albany when he became Governor, she continued to teach three days a week. She said, "I teach because I love it. I cannot give it up."

After her husband was elected President of the United States, Eleanor Roosevelt gave up her teaching job with a great deal of sadness. Until the school merged with another school in 1939, she continued to attend school events, give lectures to alumnae, teach an occasional class in current events, and deliver graduation addresses. She also invited Todhunter girls to the White House.

Eleanor Roosevelt: First Lady of the United States

By the time Franklin Roosevelt was elected President in 1932, his wife was chairman of the Women's Division of the National Democratic Party. Americans were not sure what to think about a First Lady who was such an active politician and a professional magazine writer. Though Eleanor believed in and respected her husband, she was not happy about the changes the new role would mean to her personally.

Two days after FDR was inaugurated, the First Lady let Americans know that she would be an active President's wife. She held her own press conference and announced that she would meet with female reporters once a week. Eleanor began writing a monthly column in *Woman's Home Companion* magazine, giving the $1,000 per month she earned to charity. She titled her first article, "I Want You to Write Me." By the following January, 300,000 Americans had done so.

When guests came to the door of the White House, Eleanor often greeted them herself. Though she had grown up in a privileged family, she was comfortable with poor, hurting people and reached out to them while she served as First Lady. She traveled widely and

Eleanor Roosevelt at a WPA Work Site in Iowa, 1936

Eleanor Roosevelt at a Nursery School for African American Children in Des Moine, Iowa, 1936

became involved in New Deal projects. At right above, she is visiting a WPA site in Iowa.

Eleanor Roosevelt encouraged fair treatment of African Americans and supported their efforts to be treated equally. In the photo at left above, she is visiting a WPA nursery school in Des Moines, Iowa. She began to write a daily newspaper column called "My Day" in 1935. Eleanor went on national speaking tours and represented America overseas.

Like other First Ladies, Mrs. Roosevelt spent time with other famous people. She is pictured below with Shirley Temple; Mrs. Winston Churchill, wife of the British Prime Minister, and Princess Alice, a member of the British royal family; Ruth Bryan Owen, daughter of William Jennings Bryan; King George VI and his wife Elizabeth; and famous Hollywood actors.

Mrs. Roosevelt with Shirley Temple, 1938

Mrs. Roosevelt, Princess Alice, and Mrs. Winston Churchill in Canada, 1944

Above: An Autographed Photo of Mrs. Roosevelt and Ruth Bryan Owen, 1934

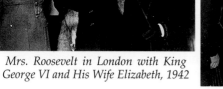

Mrs. Roosevelt in London with King George VI and His Wife Elizabeth, 1942

At Left: Eleanor Roosevelt cuts a cake at a birthday party in 1944. Behind the cake are Red Skelton and Lucille Ball, popular comedians of the day.

Before and during World War II, Eleanor personally helped European refugees find safety in the U.S. She traveled widely during the war, encouraging and serving soldiers and civilians. In the photos below, she visits Honolulu, Hawaii; encourages a wounded soldier at a naval hospital in Seattle, Washington; pins a Purple Heart on a soldier in New Caledonia, a French colony near Australia; spends time with soldiers on the Galapagos Islands off the coast of South America; visits with sailors on the Pacific island of Bora Bora; and visits the Japanese American internment center at Gila River, Arizona.

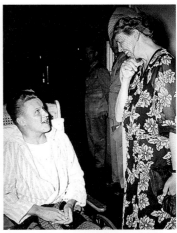

Eleanor Roosevelt in Honolulu　　　*Eleanor Roosevelt at Naval Hospital*

Eleanor Roosevelt Awards a Purple Heart in New Caledonia

Eleanor Roosevelt in the Galapagos Islands

Eleanor Roosevelt in the Galapagos Islands

Eleanor Roosevelt on Bora Bora

Eleanor Roosevelt at the Gila River Internment Center

Eleanor Roosevelt: Author, Activist, Public Servant

Eleanor Roosevelt with a Spanish Version of the Universal Declaration of Human Rights

When her husband died, Eleanor Roosevelt grieved her great loss and helped to plan his funeral. She said goodbye to people she had worked with for twelve years, moved out of the White House, and wondered what she would do in the future. She wanted to be useful and to honor her husband's work.

President Truman appointed Eleanor Roosevelt as a delegate to the United Nations, where she worked for human rights and helped refugees. In the photo at top left, Mrs. Roosevelt is holding a copy of the Universal Declaration of Human Rights, passed by the U.N. in 1948.

In the last seventeen years of her life, Eleanor Roosevelt published sixteen books, including four biographies, one book about Christmas, one about etiquette, and several about current events and politics.

1949 — Mrs. Roosevelt and Dignitaries from India: Mrs. Ghandi, Mrs. Pandit, and Prime Minister Nehru at Mrs. Roosevelt's Home in Hyde Park

1949 — Eleanor Roosevelt with West Point Cadets

During the 1950s, Eleanor Roosevelt continued to speak out for equal treatment of African Americans. She hosted events that honored her late husband and continued to be involved in the Democratic Party. When John F. Kennedy ran for President in 1960, she campaigned for him.

The pictures on these two pages are arranged in chronological order. Look at them and read about some of her many activities. For the last two years of her life, Eleanor Roosevelt struggled with anemia and tuberculosis. Still she continued to be active. In the fall of 1962, she worked to finish her last book and then died on November 7.

1950 — Eleanor Roosevelt with Some of her Children and Grandchildren

For twenty-seven years Eleanor Roosevelt wrote her column "My Day," six days a week. She missed only four days when her husband died. Remember that it is God who gives us each day.

God called the light day, and the darkness He called night, and there was evening and there was morning, one day.
Genesis 1:5

1950 — Eleanor Roosevelt at an Event at the Franklin D. Roosevelt Library, Hyde Park

1953 — Eleanor Roosevelt in Hiroshima, Japan

Activities for Lesson 113

Vocabulary – Write five sentences in your notebook, using one of these words in each: aristocratic, debut, retreat, alumnae, etiquette. Check in a dictionary if you need help with their definitions. Look in the lesson for clues to the word meanings.

1955 — Eleanor Roosevelt in France, Visiting with Jewish Refugees Headed for Israel

1959 — Eleanor Roosevelt with President Harry Truman

Literature – Read "Press Release" in *We the People*, page 145.

Creative Writing – Look closely at the photographs in this lesson, especially at the faces and posture of the people pictured alongside Eleanor Roosevelt. Write one or two paragraphs in your notebook about what the photographs communicate about how people felt about her.

Timeline – In *Timeline of America the Beautiful* next to 1884, write: Eleanor Roosevelt is born in New York City.

Student Workbook or Lesson Review – If you are using one of these optional books, complete the assignment for Lesson 113.

1959 — Eleanor Roosevelt in Israel

1962 — Eleanor Roosevelt with Son Franklin Jr. and Grandson, Franklin III

1962 — Presidents Kennedy, Truman, and Eisenhower and Future President Lyndon Johnson at Eleanor Roosevelt's Funeral

God Created Hawaii

God created thousands of islands in the Pacific Ocean. Among them are the Hawaiian Islands, well known for their beautiful landscapes. American author Mark Twain visited the islands in 1866. He said, "They are the loveliest fleet of islands that lies anchored in any ocean." Hawaii, like Niagara Falls, is a place many couples visit on their honeymoon. At left is an 1893 photo of Princess Kaiulani, a member of the Hawaiian royal family.

Princess Kaiulani

Where Is Hawaii?

The Hawaiian Island chain stretches out in a 1,500 mile-long crescent. It includes eight main islands and 124 islets. As seen in the map below, Hawaii is far from the rest of the United States. To get to the state capital of Honolulu from San Francisco, you must travel 2,397 miles. From Anchorage, Alaska, the distance is 2,780 miles. Coming from the east, the first island is Hawaii, often called the Big Island because it is the largest. The next largest island is Maui, followed by Kahoolawe, Lanai, Molokai, Oahu, Kauai, and Niihau. On page 697 is a picture of the islands from space.

The Volcanoes and Mountains of Hawaii

The Hawaiian Islands are actually the tops of volcanoes that rise from the ocean floor. Though most are dormant, God has not yet finished carving

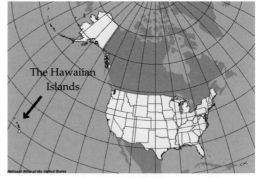

Map of the United States

the Big Island of Hawaii. It has two active volcanoes: Mauna Loa and Kilauea. Both are in Hawaii Volcanoes National Park. Three scenes from the park are pictured on page 697.

At 13,678 feet, Mauna Loa is also the second highest mountain in Hawaii. Kilauea is one of the most active volcanoes on earth. It has erupted many times since Europeans first visited the island, and it began to erupt almost continuously in 1983. In Hawaiian its name means "spewing" or "much spreading." The highest mountain in Hawaii is Mauna Kea, also on the Big Island. It rises 13,796 feet above sea level. It is the tallest island mountain in

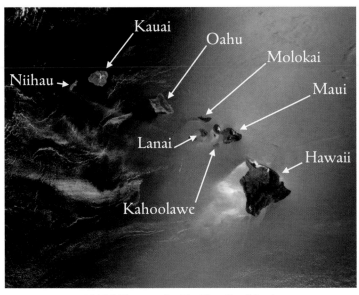

NASA Photograph of the Hawaiian Islands

the world. Local residents and tourists hunt, hike, and birdwatch on its lower slopes, but its summit is a plateau of lava with cinder cones.

At the summit are the Mauna Kea Observatories, the most powerful collection of telescopes in the world. Astronomers from eleven countries, including Argentina, Australia, Brazil, Canada, Chile, France, Japan, the Netherlands, Taiwan, the United Kingdom, and the United States, scan the universe through several different telescopes. The air there is dry, and many nights the sky is free of clouds. Below the summit, God has placed a cloud layer called a tropical inversion. The cloud layer, about 2,000 feet thick, traps moist sea air and keeps the atmosphere above them pure. Mauna Kea is an ideal location for observing the heavens.

Steam Vents at Hawaii Volcanoes National Park

Arching Lava Fountain at Hawaii Volcanoes National Park

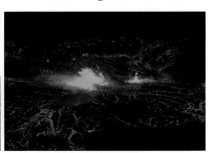

Lava at Hawaii Volcanoes National Park

Hawaiian Climate and Agriculture

Hawaii has only two seasons. In winter the average temperature is in the low seventies and in summer the average is in the high seventies. Hawaiian mountains have cooler temperatures. The tops of Mauna Kea and Mauna Loa often have snow during the winter. Though much of Hawaii is humid, winds blowing in from the Pacific Ocean make the weather comfortable. The winds also bring moisture, which makes native plants grow lush, as seen in the photo of Hawaiian mountains at right. Can you find the thin ribbon of a waterfall deep in the mountains?

Hawaiian Mountains with Waterfall

With a tropical climate and rich soils, Hawaii is an ideal place to grow foods such as pineapples, sugarcane, bananas, coconuts, limes, and avocados.

Rainfall in Hawaii varies greatly. God sends about 450 inches per year on Mount Waialeale on the island of Kauai, which is known as the wettest place in the world. However, at Kawaihae on the Big Island, rainfall averages only nine inches each year.

Plants and Animals of Hawaii

God created habitats that support a wide variety of life in Hawaii: ocean waters, lagoons, and streams, plus mountains, cliffs, caves, valleys, coastal plains, calderas (volcano craters that have collapsed), and beaches. The Hawaiian Islands are home to 17,000 species of land plants and animals, five hundred species that live in freshwater, and 5,500 species that live in saltwater.

The Hawaiian Islands have many endemic species, types of plants and animals found only in Hawaii. Of the 10,000 insects that live in Hawaii, ninety percent are endemic. Though immigrants have brought many mammals to Hawaii, the only native land mammal is the 'ōpe'a pe'a (Hawaiian hoary bat in English). The Hawaiian nene goose and the Hawaiian stilt are endemic water birds. Several species of honeycreepers live in Hawaiian forests. Look at the photos of some of God's creatures in Hawaii on page 699.

Two of the many marine mammals that live in Hawaiian waters are the spinner dolphin, pictured below, and the endemic Hawaiian monk seal, pictured on page 699. In the daytime, Hawaiian spinner dolphins rest, play, and socialize with each other in some of Hawaii's lagoons. As their name implies, they like to spin, sometimes as many as fourteen times in a row! They spin both vertically and horizontally. They also leap and make back and head slaps. An especially impressive move is its tail over head leap, in which it shoots head first out of the water and then flips its tail over its head before re-entering the water head first.

Female spinner dolphins give birth to one calf, which is watched closely by its mother and other adults. Sometimes the mother leaves her calf with a babysitter. Even the pinkish newborn calves sometimes try to spin. At night dolphins move as a group to feed on small fish, squid, and shrimp. By traveling together, they avoid their main predators— tiger and cookie-cutter sharks.

Once each year Hawaiian monk seals come ashore to rest and to molt their hair and a

Spinner Dolphins

layer of skin. This takes seven to ten days. The seal in the photo at right is resting on shore. These seals are about six feet long and weigh around 440 pounds. They give birth to twenty-five pound babies, which nurse their mother's rich milk for five to six weeks. By six weeks of age, the baby seals weigh over one hundred pounds! Most Hawaiian monk seals live their entire lives near where they were born.

Akepa Honeycreeper

Flying Laysan Albatross

Laysan Albatross

Hawaiian Monk Seal on Beach

Flying Earwig Hawaiian Damselfly

Hawaiian Nene Gosling

Pacific Hawaiian Damselfly

Hawaiian Nene Geese

Hawaiian Stilt Chick

Hawaiian Stilt Adult

Holai Sea Arch in Hawaii Volcanoes National Park

Hawaii is home to a complex coral reef ecosystem, with many species of seaweeds, corals, snails, and seashells. Echinoderms like the slate pencil urchin, crown-of-thorns sea star, and white speckled cucumber live here. Among the crustaceans in Hawaii are snapping shrimp, slipper lobsters, and hermit crabs.

People are not the only Hawaiian visitors. Each year the golden plover flies 3,000 miles non-stop from Alaska to Hawaii. Humpback whales also migrate here from Alaska.

Hawaii has many national and state parks and historical sites. Three are pictured on this page. These provide places people can see Hawaii's beautiful plants and animals and places where wildlife can grow freely. The Midway Atoll National Wildlife Refuge is on the three Midway islands of Hawaii. Midway was home to military facilities for many years and was important during World War II. The U.S. Navy turned the islands over to the U.S. Fish and Wildlife Service in 1993. These are the only islands in the Hawaiian Island chain that are not part of the state of Hawaii. Midway Atoll is less than 150 miles east of the International Dateline. It was named Midway because it is approximately midway around the earth from the Greenwich meridian of longitude in England.

Pu`uhonua o Honaunau National Historical Park

The People of Hawaii

The first people on the Hawaiian Islands were probably Polynesians who came in boats from the Marquesas Islands about three hundred years after the birth of Christ. They likely continued to migrate to Hawaii over the next three centuries. More immigrants probably came from Tahiti around 800 A.D.

English explorer Captain James Cook landed on Hawaii's Kauai Island in 1778. He named the group the Sandwich Islands in honor of his supporter John Montagu, Earl of Sandwich. When Cook arrived, the islanders were led by chiefs and priests. The people believed in gods and goddesses and had many myths and legends. The wealthiest Hawaiians had been enjoying the sport of surfing for at least three or four hundred years before Europeans arrived. The Hawaiians practiced religious rituals along with the sport.

Kaloko-Honokohau National Historical Park

The Hawaiian people had great knowledge of plant and animal life and were master boat-builders and navigators. They made no pottery and did not have metal tools; but they made useful objects from wood, shells, stones, and bones. See photos illustrating Hawaiians and their culture on page 701.

In the early 1800s, American whalers began to spend winters in Hawaii. Missionaries from New England first arrived in 1820. Over the next thirty years, many islanders became believers in God. Christianity is the main religion in Hawaii. The islanders had no written language and were

Traditional Temple at Kaloko-Honokohau National Historical Park

also eager for the missionaries to teach them how to read and write.

Native Hawaiians were fishermen and farmers. English Captain George Vancouver brought livestock to the island in 1792. In the 1830s, some Hawaiians became *paniolos* when *vaqueros*, who emigrated from Mexico, taught them how to manage herds of cattle. *Paniolos* are Hawaiian cowboys and *vaqueros* are Mexican cowboys. Most of the Hawaiian Islands have ranches.

Europeans living in Hawaii began to establish agricultural plantations. Laborers from China, the Azores, Japan, Korea, the Philippines, and Puerto Rico came to work on them. Since English explorer Captain James Cook came to Hawaii in 1788, immigrants from all over the world have moved there.

Wagon Carrying Traditional Hawaiian Grass House in a Parade in Honolulu, 1910

Native Hawaiian, 1927

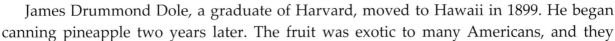

Hawaiian Couple Making Poi, a Traditional Food Made from Taro Root, c. 1915

James Drummond Dole, a graduate of Harvard, moved to Hawaii in 1899. He began canning pineapple two years later. The fruit was exotic to many Americans, and they didn't know what to do with it. Dole and other pineapple suppliers in Hawaii advertised recipes for pineapple pie and salad. When the Dole company sponsored a recipe contest in 1925, it had 60,000 entries. The pineapple-upside-down cake became popular as a result of this contest. See the pineapple plantation at right.

Hawaiian Pineapple Plantation, c. 1915

From King Kamehameha's Reign to Statehood

Around 1800 Kamehameha I united the Hawaiian Islands under his rule. Hawaii was ruled by monarchs until a group of American and European businessmen overthrew the monarchy in 1893. Hawaii became a U.S. territory in 1900. All Hawaiians became American citizens at that time, and many worked to get Hawaii admitted to the Union as a state. Hawaii became the fiftieth state in 1959.

See a statue of Kamehameha at right. An identical statue stands in the U.S. Capitol, where a ceremony is held in his honor each year on Kamehameha Day, June 11.

Pearl Harbor

Kamehameha Statue

When the Japanese decided to attack America in 1941, they did not come all the way to the forty-eight continental states. They went instead to a place much nearer to Japan—Pearl Harbor on the island of Oahu in Hawaii. Pearl Harbor was once rich with pearl-producing oysters, so the ancient Hawaiians called the harbor Wai Momi, meaning "Waters of Pearl." Twenty five years before Hawaii became a U.S. territory, the United States and Hawaii signed a treaty giving the U.S. authority to use Pearl Harbor. The harbor was blocked by a reef, and only in 1902 was the entrance dredged to provide a good entrance for ships. Congress officially made Pearl Harbor a naval station in 1908. When it became obvious that Japan would probably be a threat to the United States, the U.S. Navy made Pearl Harbor the main port for its Pacific fleet. Ships put there to protect America became targets for the Japanese.

The creatures, mountains, beaches, forests, and volcanoes of Hawaii display the creative power of God.

He looks at the earth, and it trembles; He touches the mountains, and they smoke.
Psalm 104:32

Activities for Lesson 114

Thinking Biblically – If you were one of the early Christian missionaries to the native peoples of Hawaii, how would you present the gospel message to a people whose belief system included many gods and superstitions? Write at least two paragraphs in your notebooks answering this question.

Map Study – Complete the assignments for Lesson 114 on Map 26 "Hawaii" in *Maps of America the Beautiful*.

Literature – Read "Great Our Joint Rejoicings Here" in *We the People*, pages 146-149.

Timeline – In *Timeline of America the Beautiful* next to 1900, write: Hawaii becomes a U.S. territory.

Student Workbook or Lesson Review – If you are using one of these optional books, complete the assignment for Lesson 114.

New York, the City That Never Sleeps

New York City is located at the mouth of the Hudson River. The city spreads across Manhattan Island, Staten Island, western Long Island, and a small area on the New York state mainland. The city contains five sections called boroughs: Manhattan, Brooklyn, the Bronx, Queens, and Staten Island. Its metropolitan area extends into New Jersey to the south, Connecticut to the east, and the state of New York to the north.

When World War II began, New York City was the largest city in America. It still is. Here the Hudson and East Rivers empty into an excellent harbor, which has long been a gateway to and from America. During World War II, refugees escaping from their war-torn homelands found refuge here.

Soldiers from military bases around the U.S. arrived on trains at Grand Central Station, pictured above at right. The terminal was guarded carefully during World War II, since it was an important part of moving American troops headed overseas. More than 3.2 million members of the United States military left from New York City to go to Europe and North Africa.

Before leaving for the war, many American soldiers saw New York City's famous landmarks. The Chrysler Building, completed in 1930, is shown above. It was the tallest building in the world until the Empire State Building was completed in 1931. See Empire State Building at left. Soldiers also visited the Statue of Liberty, the Bronx Zoo, Yankee Stadium, and Times Square.

Interior of Grand Central Station in New York City with Mural Encouraging People to Buy War Bonds and Stamps

Skyline with Chrysler Building as Seen from the Empire State Building

Empire State Building

African American Marines in Harlem

Brooklyn Bridge with New York Skyline

They visited Harlem, above left; saw the Brooklyn Bridge, above right; rode the Staten Island ferry; and relaxed in Central Park, at right. Awed by the sights their eyes beheld, rural soldiers felt far away from Kansas or Wisconsin or Iowa, while realizing that they would soon be much farther away from home.

Sailors in Central Park

Paper Drives, War Bonds, and War Industries

The people of New York City were part of the World War II experience shared by Americans across the country. People had paper drives and purchased war bonds. At left men work on a war bond mural at Grand Central Station. As was true in other cities, many of its sons, husbands, and brothers went to war, along with some of its daughters and sisters. About 800,000 New Yorkers entered the military during World War II. New York also had 341 war factories. New Yorkers could thank God that the devastation of war did not directly affect them while at home. As seen below, they were able to enjoy many aspects of their lives as they had before the war.

Workers prepare mural for Grand Central Station

1942 — A mother and daughter visit Macy's at Christmas. A police officer and a little girl enjoy a day at Central Park.

WACs, WAVES, SPARs, and the USMCWR in New York

During World War II, women performed a variety of jobs in the military. Those serving in the U.S. Army were called WACs because they were part of the Women's Army Corps. Women in the U.S. Navy were WAVES (Women Accepted for Volunteer Emergency Service). Ladies in the Coast Guard were known as SPARs ("*Semper Paratus* Always Ready," *Semper Paratus* means "always ready" in Latin). Women in the Marine Corps were

WAVES and SPARs take the oath of enlistment in front of New York City Hall, Feburary 8, 1943

part of the United States Marine Corps Women's Reserve. Hunter College in the Bronx became a training center for 80,000 WAVES, plus many SPARs and female Marines. In the photo at left, WAVES and SPARs take the oath of enlistment in front of New York City Hall.

New York Entertainment

New York has long been a center for art, music, and athletics. During World War II, soldiers on duty in New York received free tickets to plays on Broadway, a street in New York with many theaters; the latest movies from Hollywood; and sporting events. Soldiers enjoyed the sounds of Big Bands and popular singers. Broadway actors were among the many celebrities who entertained troops in shows put on by the United Service Organizations (USO). An executive who worked for a top New York talent agency oversaw the shows.

A plane carrying USO actors and singers crashed near Lisbon, Portugal, in 1943. Broadway singer Jane Froman was badly injured. Just a few months later she returned to the Broadway stage in a wheelchair. Long gloves and an evening gown covered her scars and cast. In 1945, still on crutches, she entertained troops in Europe. Miss Froman later married the co-pilot of the plane that crashed. It was he who saved her life in the crash.

Irving Berlin's Broadway musical *This Is the Army* raised $10 million for service members and their families. A movie version was made, and Berlin and a cast of soldier-actors took the musical on a tour to perform for soldiers around the world.

New York Harbor and the East River

New York's harbor and the East River were busy during the war. American troops were stationed on Governor's Island in the harbor. The Brooklyn Navy Yard along the East River repaired five thousand Allied ships damaged by bombs and torpedoes. Three battleships and four aircraft carriers were launched from the Brooklyn Navy Yard, including the USS *Missouri*, the ship on which Japan surrendered. During the war, the Brooklyn Navy Yard had a workforce of 75,000 men and women. See right.

Italian American Frank Romano with His Wife and Baby. Mr. Romano worked at the Brooklyn Naval Yard.

Protecting the Home Front

By 1943 New York City and the surrounding area was protected by New York National Guard units. Federal troops were also stationed in New York City with artillery ready to defend the city from the threat of Axis attack.

During the war, four hundred thousand New York citizens served as volunteer air raid wardens. They were responsible for making sure that people turned out their lights and went to shelters during air raid drills. They had little official equipment at first, but were later issued armbands, helmets, and gas masks. Other volunteers scanned the skies for enemy planes.

Times Square Advertisements, c. 1940

Because New York is such a busy town, it is known as "The City That Never Sleeps." However, during World War II, New Yorkers had to make adjustments to their normal activities. The city often practiced blackouts during air-raid drills, but it did not have to conduct real blackouts for long periods. However, New York City had so many lights shining at night that the city's glow made the silhouettes of ships offshore visible. Since German submarines sank many U.S. ships carrying oil and freight to Great Britain, the U.S. military feared that these offshore ships would also become targets.

To eliminate the lighted silhouettes, the Army ordered a dimout. Streetlights and traffic lights used lower wattage. Windows in offices and apartment buildings above fifteen stories high were covered. The bright neon signs on Times Square, pictured above before the dimouts, were turned off. Stores and restaurants used fewer outside lights. Drivers placed hoods over their automobile lights. Baseball teams played no night games. The feared attacks on the ships never happened.

German Spies in New York

Though New York City was never actually attacked by the Axis, German spies did try to harm the city. Before dawn on June 13, 1942, a German submarine (known as a U-boat) dropped off four German spies along the coast of Long Island. All had lived in America before the war and spoke English. Once ashore, they encountered John Cullen, a member of the Coast Guard, who was patrolling the beach. The spies told him they were lost fishermen. He became suspicious when one of them spoke a few words in German.

Cullen was not armed and could not capture them, so he went to his station and set off an alarm. The spies ran away and took the Long Island Railroad into Manhattan. The leader got scared and turned himself in to the Federal Bureau of Investigation (FBI). All four were captured, as were four German spies carrying out a similar plan in Florida. Coast Guardsman Cullen became a hero and made many appearances at parades and ship launchings in New York.

Two Staten Island air raid wardens, Ernest Lehmitz and Erwin De Spretter, also acted as spies for Germany. Lehmitz had received training as a spy in Germany. He pretended to be a patriotic American, planting a Victory Garden and fulfilling his duties as an air raid

Crowd reads news of D-Day on the newsline of the Times Building at Times Sqauare.

Soldiers in Times Square on D-Day

Sailors read D-Day news on newsline of the Times Building at Times Sauare.

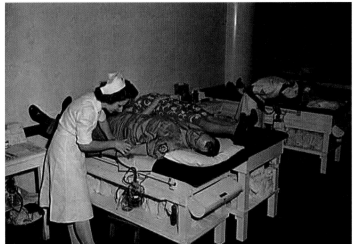

New Yorkers read "Invasion News" on D-Day.

People donate blood on D-Day.

Crowd in Madison Square listen to Mayor LaGuardia on D-Day.

warden. However, he spied on American military activity from his attic and sent letters to the enemy using invisible ink. Both Lehmitz and De Spretter were captured and pled guilty. Each received a thirty-year sentence in Federal prison.

Unlike these examples, the majority of German Americans were loyal to the United States, and many joined the military.

The Manhattan Project

Physicists at New York City's Columbia University were the first to split uranium atoms. In 1939, when Albert Einstein informed President Roosevelt that it was possible to create deadly bombs using nuclear energy, Einstein based his opinions partly on the research of these physicists. Einstein also let Roosevelt know that the Germans were working on such bombs. President Roosevelt encouraged American scientists to work on nuclear weapons in what became known as the Manhattan Project. Columbia University football players were paid to carry the heavy graphite and uranium needed for the project. Uranium was stored in Manhattan and Staten Island warehouses.

New Yorkers Celebrate the End of WWII

As seen in the photos on page 707, D-Day captured the attention of New Yorkers. As they went about their daily activities, they sought news about the invasion, gave blood, gathered in Times Square, and listened to a speech by Mayor Fiorello LaGuardia at Madison Square.

Millions of New Yorkers celebrated in Times Square on V-E Day and V-J Day. They were eager to welcome back soldiers as they returned from the war victorious. Millions of soldiers came back to their home country through New York harbor, rejoicing to see the Statue of Liberty and be on American soil again.

Rejoice always; pray without ceasing; in everything give thanks;
for this is God's will for you in Christ Jesus.
1 Thessalonians 5:16-18

Activities for Lesson 115

Map Study – Complete the assignment for Lesson 115 on Map 3 "American Landmarks" in *Maps of America the Beautiful*.

Vocabulary – Copy these words in your notebook, each on a separate line: rural, warden, wattage, Federal, nuclear. Look up each word in the dictionary. Next to each word, write what part of speech it is according to the way the word is used in the lesson.

Creative Writing – In your notebook, write a war-time short story that takes place in New York City. Use places and facts from this lesson in your story.

Timeline – In *Timeline of America the Beautiful* next to 1931, write: Empire State Building opens.

Student Workbook or Lesson Review – If you are using one of these optional books, complete the assignment for Lesson 115. If you are using the Lesson Review, take the quiz for Unit 23.

French Sailors in Central Park on a Sunday in 1943

America Recovers and Moves Forward

24

Americans were ready to enjoy themselves after four long, hard years at war. President Truman led them with determination and skill and then surprised political experts when he won election to a second term in 1948. During Truman's second term, the United States became involved in a war in Korea.

Americans, including their President, were fascinated with automobiles and where they could go in them. Route 66 carried them to Western wonders like the Petrified Forest. At home they enjoyed watching and playing baseball, their favorite sport. Jackie Robinson made a giant step in the struggle for civil rights when he ran onto the playing field with his fellow Brooklyn Dodgers in 1947.

Korean War Memorial on the National Mall:
Aerial View and Under a Blanket of Snow

Lessons in Unit 24

Lesson 116 – Our American Story: The President from Independence
Lesson 117 – An American Landmark: Route 66, Main Street of America
Lesson 118 – God's Wonders: God Created the Petrified Forest
Lesson 119 – Daily Life: Baseball, America's Pastime
Lesson 120 – An American Biography: Jackie Robinson, Athlete Who Broke the Color Barrier

Books Used in Unit 24

- *Maps of America the Beautiful*

- *Timeline of America the Beautiful*

- *We the People*

The President from Independence

President Harry S. Truman, April 19, 1945

Harry Truman had become Vice President less than three months before President Franklin Roosevelt died. Truman had spent very little time with the President. When Truman was sworn in, the tasks before him required a man willing to gather information quickly, work hard, and make difficult decisions. Truman lived up to this task. The photo at left was taken just one week after he took office.

When the war was over in 1945, Americans were again ready for life to return to normal. Former soldiers wanted to get jobs and enjoy their lives as civilians. Those who had worked hard on the home front were happy that wartime sacrifices were coming to an end.

The G.I. Bill, the Baby Boom, and Civil Rights

While American soldiers served in the war, their clothes, food, and weapons were provided by the Federal government. These supplies were described as "government issue" (or G.I.). Soldiers came to be called G.I.s. In 1944, to show appreciation to the men who had served their country, Congress had passed the G.I. Bill, which provided veterans with low-cost medical care, loans to buy houses, and financial help to go to college or a trade school. The G.I. Bill helped returning soldiers adjust to civilian life.

Married soldiers happily returned to their wives and children after the war and most single soldiers got married. As these couples began to have babies, the population of America grew rapidly. Twice as many children were born in the decade of the forties as had been born in the thirties. The period from 1946 to 1964 is called the Baby Boom. Forty million babies were born during those years. They are called Baby Boomers.

When black soldiers returned home, they wanted to be treated equally with whites. As a step in that direction, President Harry Truman ordered the military to stop

Truman Addresses the NAACP on the National Mall in 1947

710

practicing segregation. In the photo at the bottom of page 710, President Truman addresses the National Association for the Advancement of Colored People (NAACP) on the National Mall in Washington, D.C. in 1947.

Fear of Communism and the Cold War

Soldiers Celebrate Christmas in Italy, 1943

Americans were seriously worried about Communism, a philosophy and form of government that took away many personal freedoms. Some people who believed in Communism had declared that they wanted to take over the world. Many Americans worried about the dangers of war with nations like the Soviet Union that had become Communist. They also worried about fellow citizens who might be Communists. A few Federal employees had been found to be secret Communists. Some acted as spies and sent government secrets to the U.S.S.R. (Soviet Union). It was easy to accuse someone, but it was often hard to prove that someone was a Communist or had done anything to endanger the United States. Fear of Communism caused some people to be falsely accused. Once someone was accused it was hard for him to get his good reputation back.

Allied armies had entered European countries during the war. For example, the U.S. Army had moved into Austria, Belgium, France, Italy, the Netherlands, and western Germany to free them from Axis control. In the photo above four soldiers celebrate Christmas in Italy in 1943. After the war, the United States helped these Western European countries reorganize their governments and become free again.

During World War II, the Soviet Union was one of the Allies. Its army had entered Eastern European countries. At the end of the war, the Soviet Union (Soviets) took advantage of the situation and expanded Communism into Eastern Europe. It seized control of Bulgaria, Czechoslovakia, Hungary, Poland, Yugoslavia, and eastern Germany and organized Communist governments in those countries.

After trying to take over the world, Germany itself was now divided. West Germany was called the Federal Republic of Germany and East Germany was called the German Democratic Republic (this is confusing because East Germany was certainly not democratic). Even the city of Berlin was divided. Though the entire city was inside of East Germany, Berlin was divided into West Berlin which was free and East Berlin which was Communist. In a 1946 speech in Fulton, Missouri, Winston Churchill said that an "Iron Curtain" had descended across Europe, dividing free countries from those controlled by Communists.

People living in free European countries were afraid that the Soviet Union would try to take over their homelands, too. Communists did try to take over Greece, and many worked hard to make Italy a Communist nation also. In 1949 Communists took control in China. The conflict between democratic and Communist countries never caused another world war, but the conflict between them came to be called the Cold War.

America Joins the United Nations and NATO

The United States had long tried to remain neutral and not take sides in disputes between other countries. Fear of Communists and the horrors of two world wars in just over thirty years made Americans think differently. They wanted to work with other countries to try to stop the spread of Communism and to prevent another war. America helped create two new organizations, the United Nations (U.N.) and the North Atlantic Treaty Organization (NATO).

While President Roosevelt and British Prime Minister Churchill met on a ship in the Atlantic in August of 1941 (see page 672), they wrote goals for the war against Germany, Italy, and Japan. The document was called the Atlantic Charter. A few months later, Japan attacked Pearl Harbor. Less than a month after that, representatives from twenty-six Allied nations met together in Washington, D.C. and pledged to support the Atlantic Charter. The twenty-six representatives signed a "Declaration by United Nations." President Roosevelt suggested the term "United Nations."

Just thirteen days after President Truman took office, representatives from fifty countries met in San Francisco to write a charter for the United Nations. Truman gave a radio speech to open the meeting. In January of 1946, representatives from fifty-one countries met in London for the first General Assembly of the U.N. In 1949 the cornerstone was laid for the current United Nations building in New York City.

The U.N. was similar to the League of Nations, but it worked better. The United States, the Soviet Union, Great Britain, France, and Taiwan became permanent members of the United Nations Security Council, giving them the final say in U.N. decisions. The countries of the world were asked to bring their conflicts to the U.N. before they started fighting.

Today the United Nations is controversial because many Americans fear that our country is letting the organization have too much control over America. While recognizing its failures, we can honor those who began it with good intentions in an effort to halt the suffering of war.

Fearing Communism, the United States and other countries in North America and Europe formed NATO, agreeing to help each other if any of them were attacked.

The Marshall Plan and the Berlin Airlift

Many countries were devastated by World War II. Though Americans had sacrificed greatly, they were much better off than others. World War II General George Marshall,

Loading Milk onto a Plane During the Berlin Airlift

who served as Truman's Secretary of State, came up with the Marshall Plan to help the hurting people of Europe. Even though Germany had been their enemy, America helped that country, too. Truman, Marshall, and other U.S. leaders believed this aid would serve two purposes: helping needy people and helping to prevent another war.

The Soviets allowed West Berliners to travel through East Germany to West Germany by a certain travel corridor. In 1948 they closed this corridor in an effort to force West Berlin to become part of East Germany. Truman ordered that tons of food, clothes, and other supplies be sent by plane to West Berlin. For over a year, brave pilots flew over East Germany to deliver these supplies in what was called the Berlin Airlift. See photo at the bottom of page 712. The Soviets finally reopened the corridor on May 12, 1949.

The Campaign of 1948

Truman During 1948 Campaign

When President Roosevelt died, he had been President for twelve years. During that time, the Democrats had controlled Congress. The Federal election held between two presidential elections is called a mid-term election. In the 1946 mid-term election, many voters turned back to the Republican Party. When the new Congress met in 1947, most members of both the House and Senate were Republicans.

As the 1948 presidential election approached, some Democrats blamed President Truman for rising prices and other economic difficulties. They did not think Truman was a good leader. Some Democrats tried to get Truman not to run, but he decided to run anyway. The Democratic Party chose him as their candidate. Two other Democrats decided to run as independents. Many people thought that this division within the Democratic Party would make Truman lose.

Thomas Dewey was the Republican candidate. He had served as Governor of New York and had been the Republican candidate against Franklin Roosevelt in 1944. That year he came closer to beating Roosevelt than any other candidate who had run against him. Many thought he would easily defeat Truman.

Harry Truman set out to prove them wrong. He worked hard to be elected. He boarded a train and traveled around the country on a "whistle-stop" campaign. See photo above. He criticized the Republican-led Congress, calling them a "do-nothing" Congress. Evidently Americans were behind their President because he accomplished what many believe is the most amazing electoral victory in American history. Not only did Truman defeat Dewey, but Democrats also added nine Senators and seventy-five members of the House of Representatives. The Democrats again controlled Congress.

The Korean War

At the end of World War II, Soviet forces controlled northern Korea, while American forces controlled the southern half of the peninsula. In June of 1950, the Cold War exploded into a real war when Communist forces in the north invaded southern Korea. The United Nations Security Council condemned the invasion. The United Nations formed a military force of 800,000 soldiers, about half from South Korea and the rest from the United States and other countries. President Truman committed about 350,000 American troops to the effort. American General Douglas MacArthur was appointed commander of the U.N. forces. Fighting in Korea was fierce. Troops from Communist China started helping North Korea. Finally, on July 27, 1953, the opposing sides agreed to a cease-fire. The Communists

Navy Lieutenant Thomas Hudner Receives Medal of Honor, 1951

controlled above the 38th parallel of latitude and U.N. troops held the south. Korea officially divided into North Korea and South Korea. Though the fighting stopped, a peace treaty between the two countries has never been signed. See President Truman with a Korean War hero at left.

Read the box on page 715 to see that not all of the news in the 1940s was about war and conflict. Read about the life of President Truman below.

Harry S. Truman
America's Thirty-Third President
April 12, 1945 - January 20, 1953

Harry S. Truman was born in 1884 in Lamar, Missouri. He was the eldest child of John and Martha Truman. Harry soon had a younger brother and sister. The family lived on a farm in Grandview and then moved to Independence. After graduating from high school in Independence in 1901, Harry worked as a timekeeper in railroad construction and as a bank clerk before returning to Grandview to spend the next ten years helping his father run the family farm.

During his time on the farm, Truman joined the Missouri National Guard. When the U.S. became involved in World War I, he helped organize an artillery unit and served in France, rising to the rank of Captain. After the war, he joined the reserves and rose to the rank of Colonel.

After a long courtship, Harry Truman married Bess Wallace in June of 1919. Their only child, Mary Margaret, was born in 1924. Harry and Bess were always deeply devoted to their daughter.

For the first three years after his marriage, Truman and an Army friend ran a men's clothing store in Kansas City. The store failed in the hard economic times after the Great War. After his business failure, Truman became a public servant. Beginning in 1922, he spent most of the twenties serving as a judge for Jackson County, Missouri. In 1934 Truman was elected to the United States Senate. He became known nationally in 1940 when he investigated war-related industries to be sure they were making quality goods at fair prices.

In 1944 Senator Truman was nominated to run for Vice President with President Roosevelt. He served as Vice President for eighty-two days before President Roosevelt died. At that point he became the thirty-third President. His mother lived to see her son become President of the

United States. She died in 1947. After his second term in office, the Trumans returned to their home in Independence, a place they loved and had missed. In retirement he and Bess enjoyed their daughter, pictured at left, her husband, and their four grandchildren. Harry Truman read, wrote, gave lectures, and took long walks. In his memoirs he called himself "Mr. Citizen." In 1955 he said, "I hope to be remembered as the people's president." Harry Truman died the day after Christmas in 1972. Bess lived for almost ten more years. Both are buried at the Harry Truman Presidential Library, which Truman opened during his retirement.

In his farewell address in 1953, President Truman said, "When Franklin Roosevelt died, I felt there must be a million men better qualified than I to take up the Presidential task. But the work was mine to do and I had to do it. And I have tried to give it everything that was in me."

When President Truman lit the National Christmas Tree for the first time as President in 1948, he said: "The message of Bethlehem best sums up our hopes tonight. If we as a nation, and the other nations of the world, will accept it, the star of faith will guide us into the place of peace as it did the shepherds on that day of Christ's birth long ago."

> Glory to God in the highest,
> and on earth peace among men
> with whom He is pleased.
> Luke 2:14

Activities for Lesson 116

Thinking Biblically – Many of Truman's priorities after WWII were related to working for peace in the world. Read Leviticus 26:3-13. God promised peace to the Israelites, along with other blessings, if they followed His decrees. Write two or three paragraphs in your notebook about why peace is a blessing to a person and to a nation.

Literature – Read "Time for Action," "Letter to Bess," and "Letter to Eleanor Roosevelt," in *We the People*, pages 150-153.

Timeline – In *Timeline of America the Beautiful* next to 1945, write: World War II ends.

Student Workbook or Lesson Review – If you are using one of these optional books, complete the assignment for Lesson 116.

In the 1940s . . .

- Gary Cooper starred in *Sergeant York*.
- Elizabeth Taylor starred in *Little Women*.
- *Young Tom Edison*, starring Mickey Rooney, and *Edison, the Man*, starring Spencer Tracy, portrayed the life of Thomas Edison.
- Jimmy Stewart and Donna Reed starred in *It's a Wonderful Life*.
- New cartoon characters included Bugs Bunny, Tom and Jerry, Woody Woodpecker, and Mighty Mouse.
- Disney Studios released *Pinocchio*, *Dumbo*, and *Bambi*.
- New food products included Kellogg's Raisin Bran, Nestlé's Quik, and Almond Joy candy bars.
- American soldiers were the first to enjoy M&Ms. At first they were sold in tubes. They have been sold in brown packages since 1948.
- The Dannon yogurt company began in 1942. Its product was sold as a health food.
- The University of Florida's Citrus Research and Education Center invented frozen orange juice concentrate, patented in 1948.
- Presper Eckert and John Mauchly invented the ENIAC computer.

The **40s**

Route 66, Main Street of America

America is a country founded on freedom. When Henry Ford made the Model T affordable in the early 1900s, he opened up a new way for people to feel free. Americans wanted to hit the road. The problem was that they needed roads for their new automobiles.

The first trails in America were suitable for walking and horseback riding. Later they were widened into roads big enough for wagons and carriages. When people headed west on trails such as the Oregon Trail and the Santa Fe Trail, they often spread out over a wide area and only came close together when the geography of the land made them go through narrow places. Roads needed for automobiles were very different from those trails and from roads that horses and wagons could use.

By the time automobiles became popular, most Americans who wanted to travel long distances over land were traveling by train. Trains carried freight, too. Cities had streets and counties had market roads to carry agricultural products to town, but there was no well-organized system of roads across states and from one state to another as we have today. In 1910 the United States had about 2,200,000 miles of rural roads. More than ninety percent were dirt. Other common surfaces were brick, gravel, stone, shells, oiled earth, a combination of sand and clay, and bituminous pavement (a combination of tar and gravel).

Auto Trails

Automobiles could travel on streets in large cities, but when they got into the countryside they were likely to end up stuck in mud. Individuals and automobile clubs marked roads that were somewhat suitable for cars. They put signs on telephone poles to mark routes they called auto trails. When people began to talk about the need for better roads, some Americans thought highways that went across states were just for wealthy people who had time to spend weeks riding around the country.

The Lincoln Highway

Carl Fisher of Indianapolis was a man who had big ideas. He owned a bicycle shop and made a lot of money when bicycles became popular. He was also a bicycle racer. When automobiles came on the scene, Fisher turned his bicycle shop into an automobile shop that sold and repaired automobiles.

After visiting Europe and finding out how much faster European automobiles went than those manufactured in America, Fisher came up with the idea of a place to test and race automobiles. With other investors, he formed the Indianapolis Motor Speedway Company, home to the Indianapolis 500 auto race since Memorial Day of 1911.

Lincoln Highway, Green County, Iowa, 1940

In a speech at a dinner party for automobile manufacturers the following year, Fisher spoke about a new idea he had—building a highway across America. Thirty minutes later he received a $300,000 donation from an executive at Goodyear Tire and Rubber Company. More donations followed, and by the end of a month he had $1 million. The Lincoln Highway Association was founded in 1913 with the purpose of building a road called the Lincoln Highway from Times Square in New York City to Lincoln Park in San Francisco. Donations continued, including ones from President Woodrow Wilson, former President Theodore Roosevelt, Thomas Edison, and a group of school children in Alaska, who had heard about the highway that would honor Abraham Lincoln.

Of course paving a road that long did not happen overnight. Early guidebooks suggested that the trip along the Lincoln Highway would take twenty to thirty days if the auto could average eighteen miles per hour. People were encouraged to buy gasoline anytime they could, even if it had not been long since their last purchase. They were told to wade through water first to check it out before they took their car through it. They were also reminded to take camping gear and advised not to wear new shoes. In 1919 the U.S. Army drove a convoy of trucks and tanks across the country on the Lincoln Highway. Vehicles got stuck in mud; bridges cracked and had to be rebuilt. Young Lieutenant

Lincoln Highway, Paradise, Pennsylvania, 1941

Colonel Dwight D. Eisenhower was on this trip, which he described as tiring, difficult, and fun. By the twenty-fifth anniversary of the Lincoln Highway in 1938, all but forty-two miles had a surface better than gravel. The photos above and at left were taken in the early forties, when a trip on the Lincoln Highway was much less adventurous than in the early years.

Harry Truman and the National Old Trails Road

In 1909 a group of women started identifying the old Santa Fe Trail and marking it with monuments. From this beginning came the idea of a National Old Trails Road, a cross-country road that would include several historic trails. In 1911 the Daughters of the American Revolution (DAR), a club for women whose ancestors fought in the American Revolution, got involved. The National Old Trails Road Association was formed in 1912. Its purpose was to help the DAR mark old trails and to promote the building of a modern ocean-to-ocean highway. The association's first president was Judge J. M. Lowe, who, like

Harry Truman, had been County Judge of Jackson County, Missouri. When completed, the National Old Trails Road (NOTR) extended from Baltimore, Maryland, to Los Angeles, California, with branches to New York City and San Francisco. The road included the National Road, also called the Cumberland Road (see page 242), and the Santa Fe Trail (see page 462).

Truman's father had a job repairing rural roads. After his father died in 1914, Harry briefly took over the job. That same year Harry Truman paid $650 for a used handmade 1911 Stafford. It is pictured at right.

While in France during World War I, Harry Truman wrote to Bess: "The French know how to build roads and also how to keep them up. They are just like a billiard table." When elected Jackson County Judge in

Harry Truman, Bess Wallace, and Friends in His Stafford While Harry and Bess Were Courting, c. 1915

1922, he became familiar with roads and bridges all over the county. Between his terms as judge, he had a job with the Kansas City Automobile Club.

Truman became president of the National Old Trails Road Association in 1926. On occasion he drove the road from coast to coast, encouraging members of the association to make improvements on the section of the road that went through their area. As seen in the photos below, when traveling from coast to coast, motorists encountered a variety of road conditions.

NOTR Near Alexandria, West Virginia

NOTR Near Columbia, Missouri

Truman worked with the Daughters of the American Revolution to mark the road with monuments, just as the original group of women had set out to do in 1909. The DAR decided to erect identical Madonna of the Trail statues in each of the twelve states through which the National Old Trails Road passed. Truman had the difficult job of choosing sites for the statues. He attended most of the dedications. The DAR description of the statue read: "The 'Madonna of the Trail' is a pioneer clad in homespun, clasping her babe to her breast, with her young son clinging to her skirts. The face of the mother, strong in character, beauty, and gentleness, is the face of a mother who realizes her responsibilities and trusts in God."

NOTR on a Navajo Reservation

NOTR in the Mojave Desert, California

NOTR Near Algodones, New Mexico

St. Louis sculptor August Leimbach created the statues from algonite stone, which has a warm pink color. See one of the statues at right. As you travel from east to west, you can see the statues in Bethesda, Maryland; Beallsville, Pennsylvania; Wheeling, West Virginia; Springfield, Ohio; Richmond, Indiana; Vandalia, Illinois; Lexington, Missouri; Council Grove, Kansas; Lamar, Colorado; Albuquerque, New Mexico; Springerville, Arizona; and Upland, California.

All his life, Harry Truman enjoyed cars and driving. After retiring from the presidency, he convinced Bess to take a road trip from Independence to Washington, D.C., assuring her that they would not be recognized. Since Truman refused Secret Service protection when he retired, they traveled alone. He was mistaken about not being recognized. Many along the way enjoyed catching a glimpse of the former President. Truman remained president of the National Old Trails Road Association until his death in 1972.

Madonna of the Trail

Cyrus Avery, Father of Route 66

In 1916 Congress passed the Federal Road Act, which provided the states with money for road construction. Five years later, during the presidency of Warren Harding, the Federal Highway Act became law, appropriating more funds to the states. That same year Cyrus Avery became president of the Associated Highways Association of America.

Avery was born in Pennsylvania in 1871. His family moved to Oklahoma when he was a teenager. Avery married after graduating from Jewell College in Liberty, Missouri. In 1902 he brought his new bride to Tulsa, Oklahoma, where he became involved in real estate, coal, and oil businesses. Avery wanted the barren lands around Tulsa to grow in prosperity. He became interested in roads and highways. From this early desire to help the area where he lived, he became interested in helping create national highways.

Highway Signs in Waco, Texas, 1939

In 1924 the United States Secretary of Agriculture chose Avery, who also served as the state highway commissioner for Oklahoma, to be a consulting highway specialist for the Federal government. Avery and other leaders began to organize a system of U.S. highways.

The Lincoln Highway, the Dixie Highway, and other early roads were named just as early trails had been, but organizers of the new U.S. highway system decided to give roads numbers. The new system would have twelve Federal highways running generally north and south; these would be given odd numbers. Ten more highways would run generally east and west and would have even numbers. These roads would be marked with a shield-shaped sign. See photo at left. Main highways would have numbers under 100 and the numbers for the most important roads would end in zero (40, 50, 60, etc.). States across the country began to put up the new signs. Federal and state highways are still marked this way today.

By November of 1926, the Federal highway which would run from Chicago to Los Angeles was given the number 66. Cyrus Avery soon co-founded the National U.S. 66 Highway Association. Because of his efforts to promote the road, Avery has become known as the Father of Route 66.

Route 66 Sign in Arizona

The National U.S. 66 Highway Association started advertising to get people to travel on the new highway. Avery had the idea of calling it the "Main Street of America." Brochures, maps, and postcards used that name. The highway association sponsored a 3,422-mile foot race, which went from Los Angeles to Chicago along Route 66 and then on to New York. Reporters called it the "Bunion Derby" (a bunion is a swelling of the big toe which can happen when someone runs a great deal). On March 4, 1928, 199 runners began the race. Some ran in bare feet. Some carried Bibles. One man played a ukulele and another carried a cane. After eighty-four days, fifty-five men completed the race. You can imagine the thrill for Cyrus Avery when Andrew Payne, a part-Cherokee farm boy from Oklahoma, came in first place after 573 hours, four minutes, and thirty-four seconds (the runners stopped at night to sleep). With his $25,000 in prize money, Payne paid off the mortgage on his parents' farm, built them a new house, and bought land of his own. He married his sweetheart Vivian the next year.

Route 66 Through Elkhart, Illinois, 2009

Main Street of America

Though it did not have a number ending in zero, U.S. 66 would truly become the "Main Street of America." Another of its nicknames was "The Mother Road." When completed it was America's longest paved highway. Today many highways are designed to go around cities, but the original Federal highways were very different. They went through the center of large cities and were the main street of many small towns. One of their purposes was to take motorists into towns so they would shop and provide income for town residents.

Route 66 originally began at the corner of Michigan Avenue and Jackson Boulevard in Chicago and ended at the corner of Broadway and 7th in Los Angeles. Along the way, it went through the hearts of cities such as Springfield, Illinois; St. Louis, Springfield, and Joplin, Missouri; Tulsa and Oklahoma City, Oklahoma; Amarillo, Texas; Tucumcari, Santa Fe, Albuquerque, and Gallup, New Mexico; Holbrook, Flagstaff, and Kingman, Arizona; and Needles, Barstow, and San Bernardino, California; and through many small towns and tiny hamlets in between. The route through Elkhart, Illinois, is pictured above. When the Great Depression hit in 1929, Route 66 became a "Main Street" to California as many poor families used it to leave the Dust Bowl and head west.

Get Your Kicks on Route 66

In 1946 African American singer Nat King Cole recorded a song written by ex-Marine Bobby Troup called "Get Your Kicks on Route 66." By the thousands, travelers did just that. American soldiers coming home from World War II and those who had been working hard on the home front wanted to hit the road. They were ready for days when gas wasn't rationed and speed limits were more than thirty-five miles per hour. A popular road to hit was Route 66. On it Americans could get in their cars, cross the Continental Divide, and see all the sights along the way. Easterners wanted to see the caves, mountains, canyons and deserts God had created in the West. They wanted to see Native American cultures for themselves. Westerners wanted to see the cities and historic sites of the East.

Business owners in the cities, towns, hamlets, and countryside along Route 66 found many ways to lure customers to stop along the way. They erected businesses out of local materials. In Illinois they used wood or brick; in Missouri, sandstone; and in the West, adobe. As travelers drove along, they got a picture of the varied lifestyles of their fellow Americans across the country.

Gasoline, of course, was a necessity. When automobiles were first invented, general stores, liveries (stables where horses were boarded), and repair shops sold gasoline in buckets. It was poured into the vehicle through a funnel. In 1905 Sylanus F. Bowser turned a water pump he had invented into a gas pump. He called his pump "The Filling Station." General stores began installing pumps out front. Gas stations began to be erected with a canopy over the pumps so attendants could pump gas rain or shine. At first the gas stations were built in the style of other buildings in a particular location; but over the years, various oil companies began to have standard designs for their stations. However, some, like the Tee Pee Curios Shop at top right, reflected the imagination of their builders.

At right is a Phillips 66 gas station in Chandler, Oklahoma. The Phillips 66 company uses a shield-shaped sign, inspired by the shape of the highway sign. In 1927 the Phillips Petroleum

Landmarks Along Route 66

Tucumcari, New Mexico — The Tee Pee Curios Shop was built in the 1940s as a gas station, grocery store, and souvenir shop.

Chandler, Oklahoma — Phillips 66 gas station, built in the cottage style with antique cars parked in front.

721

Company chose Route 66 to conduct a test drive of their new high-octane gasoline. The vehicle could go up to sixty-six miles per hour. The company named their new fuel Phillips 66. In the late 1930s, Phillips 66 began a Highway Hostesses program to attract customers.

Landmarks Along Route 66

Holbrook, Arizona — Chester Lewis once passed through Cave City, Kentucky, and noticed the "Wigwam Village" cottages built by architect Frank Redford to provide lodging for people visiting Mammoth Cave. Mr. Lewis bought copies of Mr. Redford's design and the right to use the name. The structures are actually shaped like tepees, but Mr. Redford did not like that word, so he called them wigwams instead. Mr. Lewis built fifteen "wigwams" out of steel and concrete and opened the Wigwam Motel in Holbook, Arizona, in 1950. Rooms were fitted with handmade furniture made from hickory. The village closed in the late 1970s after the construction of Interstate 40 took traffic away from Route 66, but later Mr. Lewis' widow and their children honored him by reopening and operating the village once more. It is now on the National Register of Historic Places. Antique automobiles are parked throughout the village.

Their job was to inspect Phillips restrooms to make sure they were clean. Many of the ladies hired were nurses. They came to the station dressed in a white nurse's uniform, white nurse's cap, and a blue nurse's cape. They drove cars with "Certified Clean Rest Rooms" printed on its doors.

Camping became popular in the early 1900s. At first towns roped off areas and let travelers stay for free. Then people began to build campgrounds with bathhouses, kitchens, garages, tent sites, and gas stations for the campers. Some had cabins that tourists could use in case of rain. Soon business owners began to build a series of small cabins or cottages, sometimes in imaginative shapes, like those at left. After World War II, entrepreneurs began building motor courts (or motels) with several connected rooms under one roof. Many added swimming pools and souvenir shops. By 1948 there were about 30,000 motels along Route 66.

Early 1900s travelers often brought their food along when they traveled, but through the years cafes became popular. Fred Harvey, who had supplied railroad travelers with restaurants (see page 591), saw new business opportunities on Route 66 and began to provide restaurants for motorists. Owners of motor courts realized they could make more profit by turning the kitchens they provided for their customers into cafes.

Entrepreneurs on Route 66 have used their imagination to create fun advertising. Perhaps the most famous ads were those for Burma-Shave shaving cream, as seen on page 723. When Allen Odell saw four signs in a row advertising a gas station, he thought it might be a good way to advertise his dad's Burma-Vita Company. He and his brother built the first signs out of scrap lumber and set them up in Minnesota. The signs soon spread to Route 66 and other highways across the country, entertaining motorists with their humorous jingles and getting people to buy Burma-Shave. A few

Burma-Shave Signs on Route 66

words were placed on each sign so that motorists could read them as they drove along. Here is an example from 1948 (remember that each phrase was printed on a separate sign):

"If you think" — "She likes" — "Your bristles" — "Walk bare-footed" — "Through some thistles" — "Burma-Shave."

Burma-Shave signs were not the only things that parents pointed out to their children as they drove along Route 66. Look at the giant milk bottle on top of the tiny grocery store and the large cowboy restaurant sign below.

Landmarks Along Route 66

Oklahoma City — This tiny triangular building was built in 1930, right in the middle of a street near Route 66. The giant sheet metal milk bottle was added in 1948.

Amarillo, Texas — The Big Texan Steak Ranch opened in 1960. The restaurant still offers a free 72-ounce steak to any customer who can eat the whole steak within an hour!

Route 66 was an important thoroughfare to the West, especially from 1926 to 1970. In 1985 it was taken out of the Federal highway system and the shield-shaped Route 66 markers came down. Today motorists can still travel on about eighty-five percent of what was once Route 66, though the road itself no longer exists as a Federal highway. Realizing that the road was an important part of American history, Congress has passed a law creating the Route 66 Corridor Preservation Program.

American families made wonderful memories as they traveled on this famous road. Two men mentioned in the twenty-fourth chapter of Luke had a truly unforgettable experience in Israel on a road, the road to Emmaus. They saw Jesus, who had just risen from the dead.

> And they got up that very hour and returned to Jerusalem,
> and found gathered together the eleven and those who were with them, saying,
> "The Lord has really risen and has appeared to Simon."
> They began to relate their experiences on the road
> and how He was recognized by them in the breaking of bread.
> Luke 24:33-35

Activities for Lesson 117

Map Study – Complete the assignments for Lesson 117 on Map 3 "American Landmarks" and Map 27 "Great American Highways" in *Maps of America the Beautiful*.

Vocabulary – In your notebook, write your own definition for each of these words: investor, executive, homespun, lure, curio. Look in the lesson for clues for the meaning of the words. When you are finished writing your definitions, look in a dictionary for comparison.

Literature – Read "Don'ts for Tourists" in *We the People*, pages 154-155.

Creative Writing – Write a poem of at least three stanzas about a trip on Route 66.

Timeline – In *Timeline of America the Beautiful* next to 1926, write: Route 66 opens.

Family Activity – Have a "Get Your Kicks on Route 66" party. See pages 972-973 for instructions.

Student Workbook or Lesson Review – If you are using one of these optional books, complete the assignment for Lesson 117.

God Created the Petrified Forest

Globemallow in Petrified Forest National Park

Petrified wood is found in every state in America and in many countries of the world. Petrified Forest National Park in Arizona has one of the largest and most colorful collections anywhere. See a pile of petrified wood in the Petrified Forest National Park's badlands area below.

The park includes parts of the Painted Desert, which also stretches into the nearby Navajo Nation. The scenery in the region is beautiful. On clear days you can see almost one hundred miles, especially in winter when the air is crisp and cold. The Painted Desert is actually a grassland where God shows the beauty of His creation each summer with brilliant displays of wildflowers, such as the globemallow at left.

Petrified Logs in the Badlands of Petrified Forest National Park

Petrified Wood

God's hand is in everything we see. Sometimes He takes something He has already created and makes something new. This is true of petrified wood. At one time each piece of petrified wood was part of a living, growing tree. The wood in Petrified Forest National Park comes from seven different species of trees. It is possible that the wood comes from other species, too; but scientists cannot identify them since only the trunks are left and many tree trunks have similar cell structures.

Petrified wood is mostly quartz. Many pieces sparkle in the light and look like they are covered with glitter. Each piece is like a giant crystal. Many have the colors of the rainbow. One area in the park is called Rainbow Forest.

Scientists believe that petrified wood is made when a piece of wood is covered

Petrified Logs in Petrified Forest National Park

with clay, mud, and sand, along with some volcanic ash. When trees are covered, they cannot decay because their oxygen is cut off. A chemical called silica, either within the volcanic ash or within groundwater, soaks into the porous wood. The silica crystallizes within the tree's cells. When a tree that is petrifying has a crack in it, gems of clear quartz, purple amethyst, smoky quartz, and yellow citrine form.

One problem with the above explanation is that scientists have found no evidence of volcanoes in the area. The piles of petrified logs in the Petrified Forest look like forested areas do after they have received flood damage. Some Christian scientists believe the petrified trees could have come to the area during the Great Flood described in Genesis 6.

The Petrified Forest has petrified tree stumps which are still in the ground where the tree once grew. It also has long petrified logs. Two were measured at 137 and 141 feet long. If these two trunks are the entire trunks of those two trees, the original trees were probably about two hundred feet tall. If the trunks have been broken, the trees were even taller.

The park has many log sections that look like they were cut with a saw. You could not actually cut one of these petrified logs even with a chainsaw because they are very hard. Only the gems topaz, ruby, sapphire, and diamond are

Petrified Fragments in Petrified Forest National Park

harder than petrified wood. When cylindrical quartz breaks, it makes a clean break. This is the reason logs of the Petrified Forest appear to have been cut with a chainsaw. Perhaps the logs were buried at some time in the past. After the logs turned to quartz, gradual shifts in the earth's surface could have caused them to break.

The park has no petrified branches, roots, or cones. However, it does have some fossilized leaves. Only one piece of petrified wood has been found in the park with the bark attached. Scientists believe that the roots, branches, and bark were knocked off when water brought the logs to the area.

Collard Lizard

Artists and craftsmen use petrified wood found on private land to make jewelry, bookends, paper weights, and other objects.

Plants and Animals in Petrified Forest National Park

Most of the park is a shortgrass prairie. Cliffroses, sagebrush, many wildflowers, and almost one hundred species of grasses grow in the park.

Desert Cottontail

Petrified logs provide homes for wildlife. Birds, insects, and mice live in the hollow openings in the logs. The park is home to nine species of mice. Snakes and lizards live under the logs. See the collard lizard on a piece of petrified wood above. The desert cottontail in the center picture has found shelter in a petrified log. Many other animals live in the park, including the bobcat, white-tailed antelope squirrel, mule deer, badger, many songbirds, ten species of bats, and the Gunnison prairie dog at right.

Native Americans and the Spanish in the Petrified Forest Region

More than 650 Native American sites have been found in Petrified Forest National Park. Some are one-

Gunnison Prairie Dog

room shelters. The largest is a one-hundred-room pueblo. Some native peoples used petrified wood as building materials and for making tools. The ruins of one Native

American structure in the park is called Agate House. It is made of pieces of petrified wood stacked like bricks. Archaeologists believe it was occupied around 1100 to 1150 A.D. The CCC reconstructed Agate House in the 1930s. The park has thousands of Native American artifacts, including stone tools, many fragments of pottery, and petroglyphs. The petroglyph at right is called Newspaper Rock.

Newspaper Rock in Petrified Forest National Park

The Spanish entered the region after they began to explore the Southwest in the 1500s. According to legend, a Spanish explorer named the area El Desierto Pintado, which means The Painted Desert. However, Spanish records do not mention the Petrified Forest.

Traveling by Road, Camel, and Railroad Through the Painted Desert

U.S. Army Lieutenant Amiel Whipple explored this region in 1853. When he saw the Petrified Forest, he wrote, "Quite a forest of petrified trees was discovered today. . . . They are converted into beautiful specimens of variegated jasper. One trunk was measured ten feet in diameter, and more than one hundred feet in length. . . ."

Four years later the U.S. government hired E. F. Beale, a civilian explorer, to build a wagon road near the Petrified Forest. The wagon road followed the 35th parallel of latitude along a route used by Native Americans. Portions of the wagon road are still visible today.

In addition to his road-building duties, Beale was in charge of a government experiment to see if camels could be used for transportation in the area. The camel's capacity to go for long periods without water was a benefit. However, while camel's feet do well on sand, they did not do well on the clay soils and rocks of the Painted Desert.

One of the earliest routes in the area was the Santa Fe Trail. The National Old Trails Highway passed through the Painted Desert. Today's Interstate 40 follows parts of both the National Old Trails Highway and Route 66. I-40 runs just north of Petrified Forest National Park. In the early 1880s, the Atlantic and Pacific Railroad laid lines through the Petrified Forest. More than sixty trains a day still pass through the park.

Eroded Badlands in Petrified Forest National Park

The Petrified Forest Becomes a National Park

Thousands of cattle, horses, and sheep grazed in the region during the 1800s. Cattle grazed in the Petrified Forest until the middle of the 1900s. The area around the park still has many cattle ranches today.

Visitors in the Petrified Forest, 1908

Tourists and businesses became interested in the region in the late 1800s. Residents began to worry that its treasures would be lost. In 1895 the Arizona territorial legislature asked the U.S. Congress to make it a national park, but Congress refused. However, in 1906 President Theodore Roosevelt signed the Antiquities Act, which was designed to preserve and protect places of scientific importance. The Petrified Forest was one of the first national monuments set aside through this law. See photos above and at right. The Federal government continued to buy land to make the monument larger. It became a national park in 1962. President George W. Bush signed a bill in 2004 authorizing its further expansion.

Agate Bridge in Petrified Forest National Monument, 1911

Painted Desert Inn

The CCC in the Petrified Forest

The Civilian Conservation Corps worked in the Petrified Forest National Monument from 1934 until 1942. Since 1924 the Stone Tree House, later called the Painted Desert Inn, had served as an inn and restaurant for tourists. Its owner sold it to the park after the park purchased the land all around it. National Park

Painted Desert Inn Soda Fountain

Service architect Lyle Bennett and his crew of CCC workers transformed the inn into the Pueblo-style building above. Between 1947 and 1963, the Fred Harvey Company ran the inn for the park. At left is their Painted Desert Inn soda fountain, a great stop for people traveling Route 66. The Fred Harvey company commissioned Hopi artist Fred Kabotie to paint murals for the inn. One is pictured on page 730.

The man at right is stargazing in Petrified Forest National Park. Dark skies there make it a great place to view the stars. Both day and night, you can see God's handiwork at the Petrified Forest.

The heavens are Yours, the earth also is Yours;
The world and all it contains, You have founded them.
Psalm 89:11

Stargazing in Petrified Forest National Park

Activities for Lesson 118

Thinking Biblically – In your notebook, write a prayer of praise to God for the creations you learned about in this lesson.

Map Study – Complete the assignment for Lesson 118 on Map 2 "God's Wonders" in *Maps of America the Beautiful*.

Vocabulary – In your notebook, write a paragraph using all of these words: petrified, decay, porous, petroglyph, variegated. Consult a dictionary if you need help with their definitions.

Timeline – In *Timeline of America the Beautiful* next to 1962, write: Petrified Forest National Park is established.

Student Workbook or Lesson Review – If you are using one of these optional books, complete the assignment for Lesson 118.

Mural by Hopi artist Fred Kabotie

Baseball, America's Pastime

Boys in a Baseball Stadium, 1924

Baseball is America's game. Many American boys and girls have gathered on farms, in town parks, and on vacant city lots to play baseball. Men at family reunions gather the children for a game while the ladies clean up the kitchen. Servicemen fighting wars have played baseball for recreation.

Baseball was a popular pastime after World War II. Major league teams began to play more night games, which meant that people could go to a game after work. Fans who could not make it to the game, or who lived far away from a major city, listened to baseball on the radio. Soon fans would watch games on television, too. Baseball could be enjoyed by everybody—young and old, rich and poor, men and women. When African Americans were allowed to play in the major leagues beginning in 1947, the game became even more of a truly national pastime.

An Uncertain Beginning

The history of baseball is a little mysterious. According to legend, the game was invented by Abner Doubleday in 1839 in Cooperstown, New York; but many historians don't think this is true. Though we do not know exactly how or when it started, we do have some clues.

Americans have been playing games with balls and sticks at least since the time of the American Revolution. In 1778 American soldiers at Valley Forge participated in a sport they called "playing at base." In 1787 Princeton College had a rule that students could not "play with balls and sticks" on the common (a large open space on campus).

In the early 1800s American men played versions of the British games of cricket and rounders, often calling it "town ball." *The Book of Sports*, published in America in 1834, tells about a game called base ball (or goal ball).

A young Brooklyn reporter named Walt Whitman, who later became a famous poet, wrote this in 1846: "In our sundown perambulations of late, through the outer parts of Brooklyn, we have observed several parties of youngsters playing base, a certain game of ball." A young man named Alexander Joy Cartwright and his friends played a game they called "base ball" in New York City in the 1840s. Its rules were similar to those played today. Some people believe that it was Cartwright who put together the rules of baseball. He changed the practice of hitting a runner to cause him to be "out" to the practice of tagging him. This change made it possible for baseballs to be harder, since they would not be thrown at people, and for playing fields to become bigger, because a hard ball goes farther when hit than a soft one does.

Before the Civil War, teams in the New York City area began to play games of baseball with a harder ball and with tagged-out runners. Evidently teams around Boston and Philadelphia continued to play the older game with a softer ball. The latter was called the Massachusetts game, while the hardball version was called the New York game. During the war, Union soldiers from New York and New Jersey taught other soldiers their version; and it became the more popular way to play. One of the first photographs of a baseball game was taken during the Civil War at Fort Pulaski near Savannah and Tybee Island, Georgia. Some of those in the photograph were volunteers from New York.

The Game of Baseball

Baseball is a game played by two opposing teams on a large **baseball field**. A baseball field inside a stadium is pictured below. Three **bases** and a **home plate** are laid out on the points of a square. This square is positioned like a diamond on the baseball field. Inside this **baseball diamond** is a **pitcher's mound**. The diamond and the area inside it is called the **infield**. Beyond the **diamond** is the **outfield**.

A major league baseball game has nine **innings**. During an inning, each team takes a turn in the **field** and a turn **at bat**. When a team goes out to take its turn in the field, its **pitcher** goes to the pitcher's mound, while its **catcher** squats behind home plate. The **first baseman** stands near **first base**, the **second baseman** near **second base**, and the **third baseman** near **third base** (in the photo below, the bases are marked with an x). The **shortstop** stands behind the **baseline** between second and third base. The other three players head to the **outfield**. The **left fielder** goes to **left field**, the **center fielder** to **center**

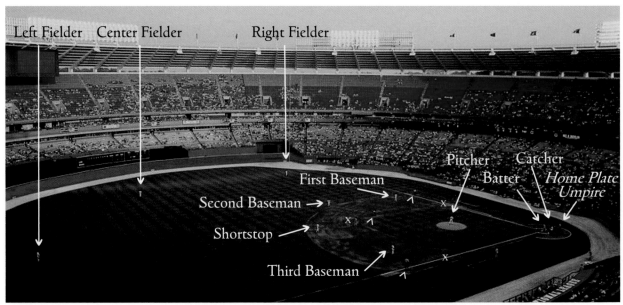

Home of the Atlanta Braves in Atlanta, Georgia, 2006

Outfielder George Harper of the Detroit Tigers, 1916

Third Baseman Chuck Wortman of the Chicago Cubs, 1918

field, and the **right fielder** to **right field**. Outfielder George Harper of the Detroit Tigers and third baseman Chuck Wortman of the Chicago Cubs are pictured at left.

Members of the team that is at bat wait in the **dugout** while one player **goes up to bat**. After the batter steps into the batter's box at home plate (or "**steps up to the plate**"), the pitcher **pitches** the ball. He may throw a **fast ball** or a **curveball** or try some other kind of pitch. Sometimes the pitch is a **strike** and sometimes it is a **ball**. The **home plate umpire** decides which it is and yells out "strike" or "ball" (in the photo on the bottom of page 732, the umpires are marked with a ^). "Strike" means that the pitch went over home plate and was neither too high nor too low. "Ball" means that the pitcher missed this **strike zone**. When the pitcher pitches the baseball, the **batter** may **swing** at it or choose not to swing. If the batter swings and misses, he has made a **strike**. If the batter hits the ball and it goes to the left or right of the diamond or behind home plate, he has hit a **foul ball**. A foul ball also counts as a strike unless the batter already has two strikes. If the batter makes a total of three strikes, the umpire will yell "**out**" and the next batter in the lineup comes up to bat.

If, on the other hand, the batter hits the ball into the infield or outfield, he will try to run as far as he can around the bases without being tagged with the ball by an opposing player. The batter is **out** if a fielder catches the ball in the air or touches first base while holding the ball before the batter touches first base. If the **runner** makes it to first base, he has made a **base hit** and he is **safe**. If the runner gets to first, second, or third base, he must wait there until another of his teammates makes a hit, at which time he can continue running around the diamond toward home. If the batter hits the ball out of the park, it is a home run. When a batter crosses home plate without getting out, he has scored a **run** for his team.

The first, second, and third base umpires and the home plate umpire decide whether a player is safe or out at their respective bases. Umpires are pictured at right.

Play continues until the team at bat get three outs and then the teams switch places. When the second team has had their turn at bat and made three outs, the inning is

The home plate umpire watches as a runner slides into home and the catcher tags him out, c. 1920.

Three Base Umpires and the Home Plate Umpire at the 1916 World Series

A base umpire stands ready to make a call during a game, c. 1920.

over and a new one begins. Play continues in this way for nine innings. The team with the most runs wins. If the score is tied after nine innings, the teams play extra innings.

Major League Baseball

Players on a professional team receive pay for playing. The first professional baseball team, the Cincinnati Red Stockings, was organized in 1869. A professional National League was organized in 1875 and an American League was founded in 1900. A baseball league is a group of teams that play against each other.

Major league teams are based in large cities, where many fans can come to watch them. Some have remained in the same city since the team was founded, while others have moved from place to place. Some have the name they had at the beginning, while others have changed their names. The chart below lists major league teams during the presidency of Harry Truman. Names given are those used in the 1952 season. See historic major league ball parks and some enthusiastic spectators below.

Each year the National League champion and the American League champion play a series of games called the World Series to determine the world champion. The Pittsburgh Pirates and the Boston Americans (later the Boston Red Sox) competed in the first World Series in 1903. A second World Series was held in 1905. These championship series have been played every year since then except in 1994, when major league players were on strike.

Fenway Park, Boston

Shibe Park, Philadelphia

Major League
Baseball Teams, 1952

National League

Boston Braves
Brooklyn Dodgers
Chicago Cubs
Cincinnati Reds
New York Giants
Philadelphia Phillies
Pittsburgh Pirates
St. Louis Cardinals

American League

Boston Red Sox
Chicago White Sox
Cleveland Indians
Detroit Tigers
New York Yankees
Philadelphia Athletics
St. Louis Browns
Washington Senators

Spectators try to see Pittsburgh and Detroit in the 1909 World Series.

Forbes Field, Pittsburgh

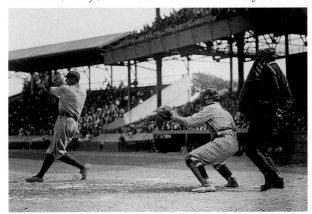

Babe Ruth, at Left, with Other Boston Red Sox Players, 1916

Babe Ruth at Bat for the New York Yankees, 1920

Babe Ruth

Babe Ruth is considered the greatest baseball player of all time. George Herman Ruth Jr. was born in Baltimore, Maryland, in 1895. He began getting into serious trouble as a boy and his parents felt that he was more than they could handle. They sent him to a Catholic school for boys and gave the school custody of him. George stayed for twelve years, rarely seeing his family.

At the school, George became close to a monk named Brother Mathias, who became a father figure to him and encouraged him in the right way. George played on the school's baseball teams. Jack Dunn, who owned a local team, noticed the boy's talent. At age nineteen, George signed a contract to play for Mr. Dunn. The other players on the team called George "Jack's newest babe." The nickname stuck. Five months later, the Boston Red Sox purchased Ruth's contract; and he became a major league baseball player at only nineteen years of age. While playing for the Red Sox, Babe Ruth became a star pitcher. In his last year with them, he hit twenty-nine home runs. See top photo.

After six years, the owner of the Boston Red Sox sold his star player's contract to the New York Yankees for $100,000. During his first season with the Yankees in 1920, Babe Ruth hit fifty-four home runs! The above photo shows Ruth during his first season with the Yankees. The Yankees shared a field with the New York Giants. When fans flocked to see Babe Ruth hit home runs, the Yankees were able to build their own stadium. It opened in 1923. People called it "The House That Ruth Built." John Philip Sousa's band played at the opening day ceremonies. Babe Ruth hit a home run the day the stadium opened!

As sportswriters followed his career, they gave Ruth other nicknames, "The Sultan of Swat" and "The Great Bambino." In 1927 Ruth hit sixty home runs. By the time he retired, Babe Ruth had hit 714 home runs. See photo at right. Ruth was among the first five players to be inducted into the Baseball Hall of Fame in 1936. In retirement he gave talks at orphanages, in hospitals, and on the radio. During World War II, he encouraged people to buy war bonds. In June of 1948, Babe Ruth was honored at the twenty-fifth anniversary of "The House That Ruth Built." He died two months later.

Babe Ruth Crossing Home Plate
After his First Home Run of the 1924 Season

American Legion Baseball

Many of America's veterans are members of the American Legion, a patriotic organization founded in 1919 that serves fellow veterans, current members of the military, and communities. In 2010 this organization had over two and half million members. Major John Griffith spoke at the South Dakota state American Legion convention in 1925. He encouraged the organization to consider helping American youth receive training through athletics. He told them that athletic competition teaches courage and respect for others. He said that it helps people become active citizens. The South Dakota convention passed a resolution urging the national organization to organize a summer baseball league for teenage boys. The following year American Legion baseball teams were organized in fifteen states. In the first American Legion Baseball World Series that year, a team from Yonkers, New York, defeated a team from Pocatello, Idaho. The winning team won a trip to watch the major league World Series.

Over the years, ten million young men have played American Legion baseball. Today almost seventy-five percent of those who play college baseball and over half of major league players played on American Legion baseball teams when they were in their teens.

Kids at the Detroit Tigers' Briggs Stadium, 1942

Little League Baseball

Carl Stotz of Williamsport, Pennsylvania, had no sons of his own, but enjoyed playing baseball with his nephews. He wanted them to be able to play on an organized team. In 1938 he gathered children from his neighborhood and tried out different sizes of baseball diamonds and various kinds of equipment to find out what would work well with young children. The next year Carl and his wife Grayce asked their friends, George and Annabelle Bebble and Bert and Eloise Bebble (George and Bert were brothers), to help start a baseball league for young boys. That summer Carl, George, and Bert managed three teams that had local sponsors. The first teams, Lycoming Dairy, Lundy Lumber, and Jumbo Pretzel, played their games on a vacant lot. A member of the Lycoming Dairy team who played in the first game that summer later signed a professional baseball contract with the Boston Braves organization.

Soon John and Peggy Lindenmuth joined the other three couples to form a board of directors. Carl got support from his community and decided on the name Little League. His dream of helping the boys of Williamsport enjoy a wholesome program where they could learn sportsmanship, fair play, and teamwork had now come true.

After Little League began in Williamsport, other communities began to organize leagues. In 1949 a popular news magazine, the *Saturday Evening Post*, had an article about Little League. That same year, moviegoers saw newsreels about the 1948 National Little League Tournament (now called the Little League World Series). After this publicity, Mr.

Stotz received hundreds of requests for more information and the program grew even more rapidly. In 1953 the Little League World Series was televised. In 1974 the Little League organization began sponsoring softball programs for girls. In 2010 over two and a half million children participated in Little League teams in all fifty states and in more than eighty foreign countries.

Today the American Legion and Little League organizations are two of many groups that provide opportunities for children and teenagers to play on baseball teams.

As American as Baseball and Apple Pie

American Presidents have enjoyed and supported baseball. Presidents Andrew Johnson, Ulysses Grant, and Chester Arthur all hosted baseball teams at the White House. President Benjamin Harrison was the first President to attend a major league game. In 1910 President Taft threw out the first pitch on opening day of the season, as many Presidents have done since then. Harry Truman was the first left-handed President to throw out the first pitch. Wilson was the first President to attend a World Series game, and Coolidge was the first President to throw out the first pitch at a World Series.

As a young man, Ronald Reagan was a sportscaster who broadcast baseball games in Iowa. He was the first President to watch a major league game from the dugout. While in the presidency, he broadcast an inning and a half as a play-by-play announcer. President George W. Bush was a managing general partner of the Texas Rangers, a major league team, prior to becoming President of the United States.

Baseball has become part of everyday life in America. When describing something that is very American, a person might say it is "as American as baseball and apple pie." Think about the baseball terms we use in our everyday conversations:

President Taft at a Major League Game, 1910

- "I just want to be sure I'm in the right **ballpark**" means that I want to be sure that my idea is pretty nearly correct.
- When a man gets a major promotion at work, his friend might say, "You're in the **big leagues** now."
- When a person does something you are not expecting, you might say, "Wow, you really threw me a **curveball**."
- If your dad is proud of you for helping out when you were not asked, he might say, "You really **stepped up to the plate**."
- If your mother wants you to check with her before you go somewhere, she might say, "I want to **touch base** with you before you go."
- When someone does something he does not feel confident about, he may say, "I'm out of my **league**."

Baseball has many traditions. "Hot dogs! Peanuts! Cracker Jacks!" yells the concessionaire at the baseball park. Cracker Jack sales soared after entertainer Jack Norworth scribbled the words to "Take Me Out to the Ball Game" on a scrap of paper in 1908 and later got his song published. In the 1970s, a popular sports announcer started singing the song during the seventh inning stretch. Now baseball fans around the country sing "Take Me Out to the Ball Game" while they are standing up for the traditional stretch in the middle of the seventh inning.

Of course, kids in the late forties and early fifties played other things, too. Look at the box below to see what else was popular.

Playing games with other people is a good way to learn about fair play and cooperation. We all know that it is "not whether you win or lose, but how you play the game." However, be sure that you always put your best effort into things that will last forever.

Everyone who competes in the games exercises self-control in all things.
They then do it to receive a perishable wreath, but we an imperishable.
1 Corinthians 9:25

Activities for Lesson 119

Vocabulary – Look up each of these words in a dictionary and read their definitions: perambulation, strike, umpire, vacant, newsreel.

Literature – Read "Casey at the Bat" and "Take Me Out to the Ball Game" in *We the People*, pages 156-158.

Creative Writing – In your notebook, write at least two or three paragraphs about the impact baseball has had on American life. If you have your own baseball memories, or currently enjoy watching or playing baseball, include this in your essay.

Timeline – In *Timeline of America the Beautiful* next to 1927, write: Babe Ruth hits 60 home runs in one season.

Student Workbook or Lesson Review – If you are using one of these optional books, complete the assignment for Lesson 119.

Popular Toys of the Decade

Tonka Trucks (1947)
Scrabble (1948)
Slinky (1948)
Clue (1949)
Candy Land (1949)

Jackie Robinson, Athlete Who Broke the Color Barrier

Jackie Robinson amazed baseball fans in the 1940s and 1950s with his great work as a first baseman, his powerful hitting, and his fast running. He was the first African American to play in the major leagues in the twentieth century. However, the first black player to play major league baseball was Moses Walker, who played briefly for the Toledo Mud Hens beginning in 1884. Walker played in only forty-six games and his younger brother later played six games for the team. From then until April 15, 1947, major league baseball was a segregated sport.

Negro League Baseball

For a while after Moses Walker's brief stay with the Toledo Mud Hens, African Americans continued to play on some minor league professional teams. However, in 1890 leaders of one of the minor leagues decided not to allow African Americans to play anymore. Within a few years, the minor leagues became completely segregated, too. Many smaller cities across America still have minor league teams. Major league teams often get their players from these minor league teams. The Toledo Mud Hens are now a minor league team.

During the late 1800s about two hundred all-black teams formed across the country. Between the first and second World Wars, all-black teams formed leagues and professional baseball became an important and successful black-owned business. During the 1930s and 1940s an all-black East-West All-Star game was played each year before a large crowd at Comiskey Park in Chicago. During this time, professional African American teams and white major league teams began to play exhibition games against one another.

Native Americans Play Ball

While blacks were excluded from major league baseball, Native Americans from many tribes were welcomed. From the 1890s to 2010 major league baseball has had at least one Native American player in every decade except the 1950s and 1990s. Native Americans from the Cahuilla, Cherokee, Chickasaw, Choctaw, Creek, Cheyenne, Sauk and Fox, Kickapoo, Lakota, Lumbee, Ojibwe, Osage, Mohawk, Muscogee, Navajo, Nomiaki Wintun, Pawnee, Penobscot, Potawatomi, Seneca, and Winnebago tribes have played in the major leagues.

The Color Barrier Comes Down

On April 15, 1947, Jackie Robinson ran onto the field with his fellow Brooklyn Dodgers to play the Boston Braves at Ebbets Field in Brooklyn. He became an inspiration to his fellow Americans and a leader in the movement to give blacks equal opportunities in American life. This movement came to be called the civil rights movement. In the beginning, Jackie Robinson faced much prejudice from members of opposing teams and from a

Jackie Robinson, First Baseman for the Brooklyn Dodgers, 1947-1956

few of his own teammates. Sometimes pitchers would even throw a "beanball" at him (a beanball is a pitch thrown purposely at the batter's head). He faced all this with dignity.

Jack Roosevelt Robinson was born in 1919 near Cairo, Georgia, just a few miles north of the Florida state line. Jerry and Mallie Robinson named their fifth child after President Theodore Roosevelt. Jerry Robinson was a sharecropper. Six months after Jackie's birth, his father deserted the family and Jackie never saw him again. Ten months later Mallie Robinson took her five children by train to Pasadena, California, where her brother lived. She soon got a job washing and ironing. She taught her children the importance of faith in God, family unity, and kindness to others. Jackie's sister Willa Mae babysat him while his mother worked. The year before he was old enough to go to school himself, Mallie asked Willa Mae's teacher if Jackie could stay in the sandbox on the school's playground while his sister was in class. The teacher agreed. When it rained, he was allowed to stay in the kindergarten classroom. Even as a child, Jackie realized how hard his mother worked to provide for them all. He thought she must have a kind of magic to be able to do everything she did.

As he grew up, Jackie's mother continued to be gone during the daytime and Jackie began getting into trouble. A mechanic who lived in the neighborhood pulled him aside and told him that he was just following the crowd and that if he did not straighten up, he would hurt his mother and himself. The man told Jackie that following the crowd is easy, but that it takes courage and intelligence to be different. Jackie took his rebuke to heart. His minister also had a positive impact on him.

Jackie excelled in sports in the Pasadena public schools. His older brother Mack was also an outstanding athlete. Mack Robinson won a silver medal in the 1936 Olympics in Berlin, Germany, finishing second behind the legendary Jesse Owens in the 200 meters race.

After high school, Jackie attended Pasadena City College, the local junior college, where he broke a record in the long jump (a record Mack had set), and was named most valuable player of the football squad and the greatest base runner on a junior college team. Jackie then went to the University of California at Los Angeles (UCLA) where he was again a star athlete. Schools often give an award called a letter to an athlete who does well in a particular sport. Robinson became the first UCLA athlete to letter in four sports in one school year. He played on the basketball team, was the national champion in the long jump, played shortstop on the baseball team, and played halfback on the football team. Jackie was also named an All-American in football.

After his time at UCLA, Jackie served in the Army. Following his military service, he played for the Kansas City Monarchs, a Negro League baseball team.

Meanwhile in New York, Branch Rickey, the general manager of the Brooklyn Dodgers, decided he wanted to try a noble experiment—to desegregate the major leagues. Rickey sent out scouts to look for talent in the Negro League. They all noticed Jackie Robinson. Rickey researched Robinson and then brought him in for an interview on August 28, 1945. Rickey explained to Jackie his plan for desegregation. Rickey told him about the prejudice he would face in the major leagues. He even acted out the role of a racist baseball fan by shouting insults at Jackie and poking at him. He watched how Jackie responded. Jackie agreed to Rickey's instructions to fight back by simply showing the crowds great baseball talent.

A few months after the interview, Jackie married Rachel Isum, a nurse whom he had met while she was a student at UCLA. The newlyweds set off across the country, headed for baseball training camp in Daytona Beach, Florida. They were discriminated against during their trip. They were bumped from airplane flights and refused service in a bus station coffee shop. The discrimination continued when they reached Florida.

In Florida Jackie trained with the Montreal Royals minor league team, which was part of the Brooklyn Dodgers organization; and then he began to travel with the Royals. When they played a series of games in Baltimore, Maryland, people threatened to boycott the games if Jackie went onto the field. Branch Rickey wanted Jackie to play anyway. As they played game after game, Jackie's talent became obvious. One day he stole home, and Royals fans gave him a standing ovation.

When major league teams began training in the spring of 1947, the Brooklyn Dodgers played a special exhibition game against their "farm team," the Montreal Royals. That day the Brooklyn Dodgers announced that Jackie would become a part of their team. He was twenty-eight years old.

When Jackie walked out onto the field five days later, he lifted his cap and the Dodger fans cheered. Though he experienced a great deal of discrimination that first year, Jackie played very well. He was first baseman in 151 of the Dodgers' 154 games. The team won the National League pennant (a baseball term meaning championship) and Jackie was named Outstanding Rookie of the Year by *The Sporting News*. In 1982 this award was renamed the Jackie Robinson Award.

Jackie Robinson played bravely and with determination, while he handled discrimination the same way. During the ten years that he played with the Brooklyn Dodgers, they won the National League Championship five more times. During the 1949 season he had the best batting average of any player in the National league and received the Most Valuable Player award. In 1955 the Dodgers won the World Series. Meanwhile Jackie and Rachel raised three children in a home they built in Stamford, Connecticut.

Jackie Robinson became popular across America. In June 1949, Woodrow "Buddy" Johnson published a song, "Did You See Jackie Robinson Hit That Ball?" In 1950 Eagle-Lion Films produced a movie, *The Jackie Robinson Story*. The *Jackie Robinson* comic book pictured on page 742 was published in 1951.

Jackie Robinson and His Son at the Civil Rights March, Washington, D.C., 1963

Jackie retired from professional baseball in 1956. In 1962 he was inducted into the Baseball Hall of Fame. In retirement he worked in business and helped found the Freedom National Bank in Harlem in New York City. He became involved in the civil rights movement, hosted radio shows, wrote a book, and also wrote newspaper columns. See photo of Jackie with his son at the 1963 Civil Rights march in Washington, D.C.

During his retirement years, Jackie suffered from bad health. He died in 1972 when he was only 53 years old. The following year, Rachel founded the Jackie Robinson Foundation, which provides four-year college scholarships to people of color who lack the advantages many other people enjoy. In addition to the scholarships, the students are helped with life skills, given opportunities to travel to other countries, and trained to be leaders. They are also given opportunities to serve their communities. Almost everyone who receives a Jackie Robinson Foundation scholarship graduates from college.

Jackie Robinson changed the course of his life when he made the decision to listen to the mechanic who warned him about hurting his mother.

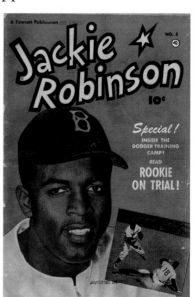

1951 Comic Book

> . . . let her rejoice who gave birth to you.
> Proverbs 23:25

Activities for Lesson 120

Thinking Biblically – In your notebook, write at least one page about why you think people discriminate against others of different backgrounds, religions, and ethnic groups and about how the transforming teachings of Christ address discrimination.

Literature – Read "Spirit of Freedom" in *We the People*, page 159.

Creative Writing – Write a letter to Jackie Robinson's widow, Rachel Robinson. You may want to write about what you admire about her and her husband and what you want to learn from Jackie Robinson's legacy.

Timeline – In *Timeline of America the Beautiful* next to 1947, write: Jackie Robinson becomes the first black player in modern major league baseball.

Student Workbook or Lesson Review – If you are using one of these optional books, complete the assignment for Lesson 120. If you are using the Lesson Review, take the quiz for Unit 24.

The 1950s

When President Harry Truman chose not to run for another term in 1952, General Dwight David Eisenhower won easily. Ike served for eight years during a time when many Americans were enjoying peace and prosperity. However, African Americans still suffered discrimination. Americans watched on their new television sets as blacks and whites came into conflict when Little Rock Central High School was required to let black students attend there. Norman Rockwell painted scenes from American life. The wondrous land God created in Alaska became the forty-ninth state in 1959, followed later that year by Hawaii.

The Eisenhower family celebrates Christmas at the White House in 1955. Notice the nativity scene at right.

Lessons in Unit 25

Lesson 121 – Our American Story: A World War II General Becomes President
Lesson 122 – Daily Life: Drive-Ins, Bobby Socks, and Poodle Skirts
Lesson 123 – An American Landmark: Little Rock Central High School
Lesson 124 – An American Biography: Norman Rockwell, Painter of American Life
Lesson 125 – God's Wonders: God Created Alaska

Books Used in Unit 25

- *Maps of America the Beautiful*

- *Timeline of America the Beautiful*

- *We the People*

- *Homer Price* by Robert McCloskey

A World War II General Becomes President

The 1950s were prosperous years for many Americans. Business grew. More people had jobs and received good salaries. Many were able to buy their own homes and the latest appliances to go in them. When it was time to elect a new President in 1952, America turned to World War II hero Dwight David Eisenhower.

Dwight Eisenhower at Washington International Airport with the Nixon Family During the 1952 Campaign

The Election of 1952

All Presidents, except Franklin Roosevelt, had followed the example of President George Washington and made the decision not to serve more than two terms. However, FDR had run and been elected four times in a row. During the two years that the Republicans had a majority in Congress from 1947 to 1949, they had passed the Twenty-Second Amendment to the U.S. Constitution. It stated that a person can only be elected as President twice. Though Harry Truman had been President for almost eight years, he had only been elected once and could have run in 1952, but he chose not to do so.

For twenty years a Democrat had been in the White House. Of course, the Democrats wanted things to stay that way, while Republicans wanted a change. Both parties looked to General Dwight David Eisenhower as a possible candidate. Eisenhower was more comfortable with Republican ideals and began to campaign as a Republican. The other

Dwight and Mamie Eisenhower in the 1952 Campaign

Republican candidate who had a good chance of being nominated was Robert Taft, son of William Howard Taft. When the Republican convention met, the party chose Eisenhower. Eisenhower picked Richard Nixon, a Senator from California, as his vice-presidential running mate. The Democratic Party nominated Adlai Stevenson, Governor of Illinois. Stevenson chose John Sparkman, a Senator from Alabama, as his running mate.

As Supreme Commander of all the Allied forces in Europe during World War II, General Eisenhower had overseen the D-Day invasion, which began the Allied push that defeated Germany. Eisenhower was greatly admired. The Republican vice-presidential nominee,

Richard Nixon, was well-known for trying to discover government officials who were secret members of the Communist party. Eisenhower and Nixon won easily. A popular campaign slogan was, "I Like Ike." Ike was Eisenhower's nickname. See the campaign photos on page 744.

The Republicans again won a majority in Congress, but that majority lasted only two years. The Democrats won a majority in the mid-term elections of 1954. The Republicans did not have a majority in both houses of Congress again until 1994, forty years later!

President-elect Eisenhower, his wife Mamie, and his staff attended services at the National Presbyterian Church on Connecticut Avenue in Washington, D.C. before the inauguration on January 20, 1952. See photo at right.

Mamie Eisenhower, President-Elect Eisenhower, and Church Pastor Edward L. R. Elson Leaving the National Presbyterian Church

President Eisenhower and Great Britain's Queen Elizabeth II at the Dedication of the St. Lawrence Seaway

The St. Lawrence Seaway

God created the St. Lawrence River, which flows between the Great Lakes and the Atlantic Ocean. The river forms part of the border between Canada and the United States. Before 1954 it was not navigable for ocean-going vessels. In 1954 the United States and Canada began construction of the St. Lawrence Seaway. This joint project created a series of locks, dams, canals, and channels. Now ocean-going vessels can bring imports to ports on the Great Lakes and take exports into the Atlantic. Dams on the Seaway provide hydroelectric power. When the project was completed in 1959, both President Eisenhower and Queen Elizabeth II of Great Britain participated in the dedication. See photo at left.

Another transportation project that began in the 1950s was the Interstate highway system. When Eisenhower was in Germany during World War II, he was impressed with the country's Autobahn highway system. He wanted America to have good highways as well. You will study the Interstate system in Lesson 128.

The Continuing Cold War

The Korean War ended during the early months of Eisenhower's presidency, but the Cold War continued throughout the fifties. In fact it continued through the 1980s. The Soviets developed an atomic bomb in 1949. In 1952 the United States developed the hydrogen bomb, an even more powerful weapon. Russian scientists did the same the next year. (The people of the Union of Soviet Socialist Republics were often called Russians because Russia was by far the largest of the Soviet states.) Many people feared that these powerful weapons would be used in a third world war.

In 1955 President Eisenhower traveled to Geneva, Switzerland, for a summit with Nikita Khrushchev, leader of the Soviet Union, and with the leaders of Great Britain and France. Though it did not result in any great decisions, the leaders did talk face to face with one another. In 1959 Vice President Nixon visited the Soviet Union. See photos at right. Khrushchev visited the United States later that year and invited President Eisenhower to visit the Soviet Union.

Nixon (center) and Reporters on Their Way to Moscow, 1959

Both the Soviet Union and the United States had spies trying to gain information about the other country's military. In 1960 the Russians shot down an American U-2 spy plane that was taking photographs of Soviet military bases. They took the American pilot prisoner. Khrushchev withdrew his invitation to President Eisenhower. The Soviets released the captured pilot in 1962.

The Space Race

On October 4, 1957, the Soviet Union launched *Sputnik*, the world's first man-made satellite. Americans were shocked that the Russians had made such technological advances. A month later,

Nikita Khrushchev and Nixon on Soviet Television, 1959

the Russians launched an even bigger satellite. The United States sent up its first small satellite in January of 1958. The Russians went even farther ahead in 1959 when they hit the moon with an unmanned spacecraft. In 1961 they sent a man into orbit around the earth.

A space race had begun and America seemed to be losing. Americans were afraid that the Soviets would use spacecraft to attack the U.S., perhaps even with nuclear weapons. America was embarrassed that the Soviet Communist system apparently had better science and technology than America did. The United States began spending more money to develop rockets and satellites. The National Aeronautics and Space Administration (NASA) was created. The U.S. also tried to improve mathematics, science, and foreign language instruction in public schools.

Kurt Debus, Wernher Von Braun, General John Medaris, and General John Barclay gather at the Launch of Pioneer IV.

On May 5, 1961, Alan Shepard became the first American in space. On February 20, 1962, John Glenn became the first American to circle the globe. In the photo at left are American scientists who worked in the space program. Second from left is Wernher Von Braun, a German who came to America in 1945 and became a U.S. citizen in 1955. Von Braun became a leader in the American space program.

The Domino Theory

The President-Elect in Korea, 1952

In the photo at left, President-elect Eisenhower visits troops in Korea in December of 1952. U.N. forces had been successful in keeping Communism out of South Korea during the Korean War. Still, much of the free world (countries who do not have Communist governments) feared that Communists would continue their attempts to conquer free people.

After his experience in World War II, President Eisenhower was very concerned about this problem. In 1954 the Communists were growing in power in the small country of Vietnam in Southeast Asia. On April 7, 1954, President Eisenhower held a press conference. He spoke about his fears that many people might soon fall under a dictatorship. He talked about the world's need for the rubber, jute, sulphur, and other products that Vietnam produced. Eisenhower told the reporters that if Vietnam became Communist, other countries in the region might also. To illustrate this, Eisenhower talked about what happens when you set up dominoes and then knock them down. He was afraid that if Vietnam became Communist, other countries would fall to Communism quickly, one after the other. He called this a "falling domino principle." For many years, the "Domino Theory" was used to explain why America needed to be involved in places like Korea and Vietnam.

Later in 1954, representatives from the United States and other countries met in Geneva, Switzerland, to discuss the problems of Vietnam. At the meeting, Vietnam was divided into North and South Vietnam, with Communists in control of the North. Many Americans feared that the dominoes were beginning to fall.

Dwight and Mamie Eisenhower During the 1956 Campaign

The Election of 1956

President Eisenhower suffered a major heart attack in 1955 and almost died. For two months he was unable to work. His health improved, however, and he announced in February of 1956 that he would run for a second term. Richard Nixon was again his running mate. The Democrats again chose Adlai Stevenson. His vice-presidential candidate was Estes Kefauver (KEY-faw-ver), a Senator from Tennessee. Eisenhower won easily. See the campaign photo above.

New States
Admitted

1959 Alaska
1959 Hawaii

During Eisenhower's second term, two more states joined the Union, bringing the total to fifty. Both were added in 1959, first Alaska and then Hawaii. Read about the life of Dwight David Eisenhower on pages 748 and 749.

Dwight David Eisenhower
America's Thirty-Fourth President
January 20, 1953 - January 20, 1961

In the second half of the nineteenth century, a group of Mennonites migrated to Kansas. There they became known as the River Brethren because they baptized in rivers. Among them were the paternal grandparents of Dwight David Eisenhower.

Dwight was the third child of David and Ida Stover Eisenhower of Abilene, Kansas. He was one of seven sons, all born in Kansas except Dwight, who was born in Denison, Texas, in 1890. The family lived there briefly before returning to Abilene.

After Dwight graduated from high school in 1909, he worked at a local creamery for two years to help support his brother Edgar who was in college at the University of Michigan. A friend suggested to Dwight that he apply to the Naval Academy at Annapolis. Eisenhower passed entrance exams to both Annapolis and West Point. He was too old to be admitted to the Naval Academy, however, so he entered West Point in 1911.

His first military assignment after graduation from West Point was at Fort Sam Houston, Texas. There he met eighteen-year-old Mary Geneva Doud, called Mamie. They were married nine months later. On their ten-day honeymoon, they went to Colorado and visited his parents in Kansas. Two years later Mamie gave birth to a son, Doud Dwight, whom they called "Icky." The couple was devasted three years later when he became ill with scarlet fever and died. Another son, John Sheldon Doud Eisenhower, was born the following year.

In their early years of marriage, Eisenhower was moved from one military post to another. Though he applied again and again for an assignment overseas in World War I, he was never granted his request. Instead, he trained troops for overseas combat. After the war, Eisenhower volunteered to participate in the transcontinental convoy across America on the Lincoln Highway (see page 717).

Dwight Eisenhower served in the Panama Canal Zone from 1922 to 1924. There he met General Fox Conner, who became a mentor to him. Conner encouraged Dwight to read history, military science, and philosophy. Conner told him that another world war would surely come. He helped Eisenhower to be accepted into the Command and General Staff School at Leavenworth, Kansas, an elite graduate school for Army officers. Eisenhower graduated in 1926, first in his class. From 1926 to 1941, Eisenhower served in the U.S., Europe, and the Philippines. His various responsibilities prepared him for the role he would take in World War II. About ten years before the war began, he was given the assignment of developing a plan to pull together soldiers and supplies for the Army, just in case there was another war.

A few months before Pearl Harbor, Eisenhower received a promotion to Brigadier General. Five days after Pearl Harbor, he was transferred to Washington, D.C. where Army Chief of Staff General George C. Marshall tested Eisenhower's abilities by giving him a variety of assignments one after the other. In March of 1942, Eisenhower was promoted to Major General. Two months later he arrived in England as Commanding General of the European Theater. In November he became Commander-in-Chief of the Allied Forces in North Africa, with responsibility to lead troops as they drove the Axis powers out of northern Africa. Afterwards, he commanded the Allied invasions of Sicily and Italy.

In December of 1943, Eisenhower became Supreme Commander of the Allied Expeditionary Forces. From then until June, 1944, he worked on the plan for Operation Overlord, which was designed to defeat Germany. The main attack began on D-Day, June 6. While Allied forces continued to work their way through Europe and into Berlin, Eisenhower was promoted to General of the Army in December of 1944, making him a five-star general.

After the war, Dwight and Mamie were joyfully reunited after seeing one another for only a few days during the previous three years. Dwight spent three years as the U.S. Army Chief of Staff. In 1948 he became president of Columbia University. In December of 1950 he became the first Supreme Allied Commander of the North Atlantic Treaty Organization (NATO).

When Americans began a "Draft Eisenhower" campaign to get him elected as President, Dwight retired from active military service and announced from Abilene that he would be a candidate. After his presidency, Ike and Mamie moved close to Gettysburg, Pennsylvania, near their son John and his family and not far from where his grandparents had left to settle in Kansas many years before. Ike and Mamie enjoyed living on their own farm, having moved more than thirty times during his career. In retirement Eisenhower enjoyed painting and golf. He raised livestock and planted a garden. When he and Mamie entertained guests, Ike often cooked the meal. He wrote letters and wrote his memoirs. Both President Kennedy and President Johnson asked him for advice.

Toward the end of his life, Eisenhower suffered from severe heart disease. On March 28, 1969, Ike said, "I want to go; God take me." He died peacefully that day. He had a full military funeral in Abilene and was buried there in a small chapel on the grounds of the Eisenhower Presidential Library near his son Icky. Mamie was later buried there also. Their son John graduated from West Point, spent twenty years in the military, and became a military historian. He served as an aide to his father during his second term as President. Modern Presidents enjoy time away at a retreat called Camp David. President Eisenhower named it after his grandson.

Eisenhower enjoyed a restful retirement. Serving as President is exhausting, and for many years Presidents have enjoyed the retreat of Camp David. Jesus told His disciples:

Come away by yourselves to a secluded place and rest a while.
Mark 6:31

Activities for Lesson 121

Thinking Biblically – During the Space Race, Soviet and American astronauts were able to see God's created universe in a new way. Copy Isaiah 40:21-26 into your notebook.

Vocabulary – Copy these words in your notebook, each on a separate line: nominee, summit, paternal, mentor, elite. Look up each word in the dictionary. Next to each word, write what part or parts of speech it is according to the way the word is used in the lesson.

Literature – Read "My Hope and My Deep Faith" in *We the People*, page 160, and chapter 1 in *Homer Price*.

Timeline – In *Timeline of America the Beautiful* next to 1958, write: The first U.S. satellite is launched.

Student Workbook or Lesson Review – If you are using one of these optional books, complete the assignment for Lesson 121.

Drive-Ins, Bobby Socks, and Poodle Skirts

Photographs from Thalhimer's Department Store: Bicycle, Doll with Accessories, and Record Player

Drive-Ins. Bobby Socks. Poodle Skirts. These words make us think of the 1950s. What was life really like then? For many children, the decade of the fifties was a fun time to grow up. Kids played outside—a lot! They rode bicycles and played cowboys and Indians. They joined the Boy Scouts and the Girl Scouts. They listened to records and played board games. Their parents read them Dr. Seuss.

Girls played with dolls and boys played with toy guns. Girls had slumber parties; boys joined Little League. Girls and boys drank Kool-Aid, ate Life

Roy Rogers, Mamie Eisenhower, Barbara and John Eisenhower, Elivera Doud (Mamie's mother), President Eisenhower, and Dale Evans with David Eisenhower

Savers, chewed Dubble Bubble, and tried to do the hula hoop. Ice cream trucks came to their neighborhoods, playing a jingle that brought the children to the truck to buy a treat.

At left are popular toys of the 1950s. At first, when children played with Mr. Potato Head, they had to get a real potato from their mothers because the toy came with accessories only. The plastic head was added in 1964. Play-Doh was born when a man who ran a company that made wallpaper cleaner realized that their product could be molded into different shapes.

Popular Toys of the Decade

Silly Putty (1950)
Mr. Potato Head (1952)
LEGO Building Sets (1953)
Matchbox Cars (1954)
Play-Doh (1956)
Frisbee (1957)
Hula Hoop (1958)

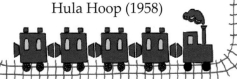

William Fox School Safety Patrol, 1957

Other products that entertained children are pictured on page 750. These were all sold in department stores.

Children went to school where they learned to read with the Dick and Jane readers. When they got older, they enjoyed the adventures of the Bobbsey Twins and the Hardy Boys. Teachers said prayers at school and taught the children Bible memory verses. In some communities, chapel was held at school once a week with local ministers serving as speakers. High school football games and many other community events began with prayer.

Look at the school scenes on this page. A school safety patrol is pictured above. At top right, a boy is looking at a filmstrip projector, which is a machine that projects strips of still photographs one at a time onto a screen. The girl in the photo is holding a box of educational filmstrips. At right is a photo of six sets of twins at a school in Richmond, Virginia. Below it are children celebrating May Day. In the lower right photo, kids are enjoying watermelon at a school fair.

Television

Television became a regular part of people's lives in the 1950s. In the photo below, students gather in the school library to watch television. Children watched *The Mickey Mouse Club*, *Captain Kangaroo*, the *Howdy Doody Show*, and *Romper Room* before or after school. They followed the adventures of Roy Rogers and his wife Dale Evans and their horses Trigger and Buttermilk. On page 750 is a photo of Roy Rogers and Dale Evans when they

Schoolchildren with Film Strips and Projector, 1958

Six sets of twins stand on the stairs at William Fox School in Richmond, Virginia in 1957. The two girls at right in front are wearing their Brownie Girl Scout uniforms.

May Day at a Virginia School, 1954

Students watch TV in the school library, Schenectady, New York, 1954.

School Fair, 1958

751

were guests at the birthday party for President Eisenhower's grandson. In the evenings, families watched *Daniel Boone*, *The Lone Ranger*, and *Davy Crockett, King of the Wild Frontier*.

Ed Sullivan was a popular variety show host who had a show on Sunday nights. He is pictured below. In the photo below Sullivan, a dad reads a newspaper while his children watch TV. In the top photos, Eleanor Roosevelt appears on two news talk shows. In the other photo below, President Eisenhower speaks to the nation in the White House broadcast room.

Eleanor Roosevelt on Meet the Press *and* Face the Nation, *1956*

Variety Show Host, Ed Sullivan

Eisenhower in White House Broadcast Room

New York City, 1954 — Children watch TV while Dad reads newspaper.

1954 — A family shops for a car at a Nash dealership.

Drive-In Movies

Going to the drive-in was a fun family outing. Dad and Mom got into the front seat of the family station wagon, or perhaps a Nash sedan, like the one at left. The kids got in the back. Dad pulled up to the ticket booth and paid the admission. On special nights the whole carload could get in for a dollar. At the drive-in pictured on page 753, the ticket booth is the small building in the front.

Then Dad pulled into the parking lot which faced the giant movie screen. In the picture, the screen is on the reverse side of the tall structure that says "66 Drive-In Theatre." Dad pulled in between the poles stuck in the ground between each parking space. He took down the speaker that was attached to the pole and hooked it onto his partly-rolled-down car window. The owner or an employee started the movie projector in a room above the concession stand at the back of the lot. The projector's light beamed above the cars and played the movie on the screen.

Drive-In Theater on Route 66 in Carthage, Missouri

Many drive-ins showed two movies, called a double feature, and had an intermission between them. During intermission theaters showed commercials advertising the concession stand. By the end of the movie, many children were curled up asleep on the back seat. Lying down was easy because most families had no car seats or seatbelts—these came along later in American history.

Kids found it fun when their family drove by movie theaters at night, even if they were not stopping for the show. They loved to stretch their necks to see if they could catch just a glimpse of the movie as the car sped past the screen. In 1959 the Remco toy company sold a drive-in theatre toy called Movieland. Children could place its toy cars on its parking lot and turn the hand crank to show a movie.

A few drive-in theaters were used as churches. People sat in their cars and listened to the service on the speakers!

Bobby Socks and Poodle Skirts

After the sacrifices of World War II, women's fashions began to use more fabric. Full skirts were popular, including the circle skirt. Though circle skirts were popular for girls and women, the poodle skirt was especially popular with teenage girls. A white poodle was appliqued (sewn) onto a circle skirt, sometimes with pom-poms where

Saddle Oxford Shoes and Other Shoe Styles from the Fifties

a groomed poodle's curls would be. The poodle had a collar and a long leash sewn in a curved line on the skirt. Girls wore their poodle skirts with white cotton blouses, bobby socks, and saddle oxford shoes.

Cheerleaders and Members of a Girls' Basketball Team

The girl holding the filmstrips on page 751 is wearing a circle skirt and saddle oxford shoes. Saddle oxford shoes and other popular shoe styles from the fifties are pictured above. The cheerleaders at left are also wearing circle skirts.

People got dressed up often. Look at the pictures on page 754. All of the girls and women are wearing dresses. Big girls and little girls wore dresses much of the time. Moms wore dresses, hats, gloves, and high-heeled shoes, not only to church but also to go shopping! Dads wore

A Gathering for Adults, 1956

suits to the office and many other places, too. Notice the fancy clothes the children are wearing at David Eisenhower's birthday party and that two of the Girl Scouts on this page are wearing white gloves.

Cadet Girl Scouts

Children at a Birthday Party for David Eisenhower

Washington, D.C., Schoolgirls in 1955

Eisenhower Grandchildren on the Steps of the White House

Anacostia High School, Washington, D.C., 1957

Parades

President Eisenhower's first inaugural parade lasted two and one-half hours. It had sixty-five musical entries, 350 horses, three elephants (the Republican symbol), and a dog team from Alaska. It was the most elaborate inaugural parade that had ever been held.

Float in a Parade in Richmond, Virginia, 1953

St. Patrick's Day Parade, New York City, 1955

The President waves from a convertible in the photo at right. Pictured at top right is a float in a parade in Richmond, Virginia. The float's theme is

President Eisenhower in His First Inaugural Parade, Washington, D.C., 1953

bees. In the photo above are girls dressed in Irish band uniforms for the 1955 New York City St. Patrick's Day parade. Notice the costumes of the ladies on the floats and the hairstyles of the little girls.

A Vaccine for Polio

Polio, the disease that crippled President Franklin Roosevelt, had been a serious health problem for many years. The virus infected 57,628 Americans in 1952, many of whom were children. Most people who got polio had mild cases and got well quickly and completely. Many children with polio spent time in a hospital. Children's hospital wards were similar to the nursery pictured below.

Some polio patients became very ill; a smaller number remained paralyzed for the rest of their lives. A few people died from the dreaded disease. After years of research, Dr. Jonas Salk and other researchers developed a vaccine against the disease in 1952. Dr.

Thomas Francis began testing the vaccine on 1.8 million children in the United States, Canada, and Finland. In 1955 Dr. Francis announced that Salk's vaccine worked and was safe. After the vaccine became available, cases in the United States dropped about eighty-five percent. By 1994 there were no reported cases of polio in North or South America.

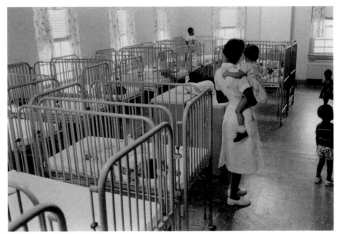

Junior Village, Washington, D.C., 1958

Home economics student practices as "mother of the week."

Chrome Dinette Set with Formica Top and Vinyl-Covered Cushions

Model Kitchen in Miami's Burdine's Department Store

A Family Home

Colorful appliances were first introduced in the fifties. The most popular color was pink! A model kitchen on display at a department store in a shopping center in Miami, Florida is pictured at top right. In the photo at top left a high school student practices in a more typical kitchen. She is "mother of the week" in a school home economics class. Furniture made of modern materials was popular. The dinette set above is made of Formica and chrome. In 1950 the Formica company made 55,000 tabletops per week.

Clothespins and Milk Bottles

During the fifties, many American mothers were homemakers. They spent their days taking care of their homes and families rather than working at a job away from home. In the evenings, families gathered around the kitchen table or in the dining room for a meal she prepared for them. A dry cleaning company picked up the family's clothes needing to be dry cleaned and brought them back a few days later. The milkman brought milk to their door step. Children used these milk bottles to play a party game. They tried to drop into the bottle one of the clothespins that their mothers used to hang laundry on an outdoor clothesline. See clothespins and milk bottles above.

Technology

New technologies changed American life during the 1950s. Though the Soviet Union was advanced in space technology, its citizens had few technological conveniences in their everyday lives. In the photo below, Soviets examine American television sets at the American Exhibition in Moscow in 1959. In an attempt to catch up with the Soviets in the space race, America began to spend more on science education. See a 1956 National Science Fair winner at right.

Soviets examine American products at American Exhibition in Moscow in 1959.

Estonian Immigrant Taimi Toffer Anderson, Winner, Girl's Physical Sciences Division, National Science Fair, 1956

In God We Trust

President Eisenhower met with evangelist Billy Graham during his 1952 campaign. Graham told him he should join a church. Eisenhower said that he would do so, but not during the campaign because he did not want to use the church politically. During his first year in office, he studied with a minister and became a member of the Presbyterian church. Eisenhower once told Graham that he believed that one of the reasons he was elected President was to lead America spiritually. He once said that the principle of equality of all people meant nothing unless we recognize "the Supreme Being, in front of whom we are all equal." When he began his first inaugural address, President Eisenhower asked his listeners to give him "the privilege of uttering a little private prayer of my own." In his autobiography, he explained that he chose to do this because he thought America was getting too secular. While he was President, cabinet meetings began with a prayer.

In 1954, President Eisenhower pushed to have the phrase "under God" added to the pledge of allegiance. Two years later he signed a law making "In God We Trust" America's official motto and requiring that the motto, which was already engraved on coins, also be printed on all American paper money.

> Blessed is the nation whose God is the Lord.
> Psalm 33:12a

Activities for Lesson 122

Literature – Read "Pledge of Allegiance" in *We the People*, page 161, and chapter 2 in *Homer Price*.

Creative Writing – Write one or two pages about how television has changed American culture. Discuss what you think are positive and negative aspects to these changes.

Timeline – In *Timeline of America the Beautiful* next to 1956, write: "In God We Trust" is adopted as America's national motto.

Family Activity – Create a 1950s Mini TV Puppet Stage. See pages 974-976 for instructions.

Student Workbook or Lesson Review – If you are using one of these optional books, complete the assignment for Lesson 122.

In the 1950s . . .

- *I Love Lucy* premiered in 1951.
- Harlan Sanders opened his first Colonel Sanders' Kentucky Fried Chicken in 1955.
- Cecil B. DeMille produced *The Ten Commandments* film in 1956.
- Dr. Seuss published *The Cat in the Hat* and *How the Grinch Stole Christmas* in 1957.
- The first Pizza Hut restaurant opened in Wichita, Kansas, in 1958.
- Charleton Heston starred in the movie *Ben Hur* in 1959.

Little Rock Central High School

Rosa Parks

During the 1950s, African Americans struggled for equal rights in many places. Two famous events occurred in Montgomery, Alabama, and in Little Rock, Arkansas. In 1955 Rosa Parks, pictured at left, refused to give up her seat to a white man, even though a local Montgomery law said she had to do so. After she was arrested, blacks in Montgomery refused to ride on city buses for almost a year. The bus system suffered from this boycott. The Little Rock incident involved school integration.

Little Rock Central High School was built in 1927. The American Institute of Architects named it "The Most Beautiful High School in America." See photo below. Thirty years later, the Little Rock school board prepared to admit the school's first black students, three boys and six girls, who had been carefully chosen by African American leaders in Little Rock. Each one was an excellent student who was committed to participating in this historic event.

Brown v. Board of Education

In 1896 the United States Supreme Court had ruled that blacks and whites could be kept separated in public facilities as long as the facilities for each were equal. Though some schools in America had both black and white students, schools in the South and many schools in the North were segregated.

On May 17, 1954, the Supreme Court announced their ruling in the case of *Brown v. Board of Education of Topeka.* The justices declared that having separate black and white

Little Rock Central High School, Little Rock, Arkansas
The four statues that stand above the entrance doors represent Ambition, Personality, Opportunity, and Preparation.

public schools was unconstitutional, meaning that the practice was illegal according to the U.S. Constitution. The following year, the Supreme Court declared that schools must be integrated "with all deliberate speed." The Little Rock school board stated that it would obey. The board decided to integrate gradually, starting with the high school. Many people in the city opposed the integration of public schools.

City Street in Little Rock, Arkansas, with State Capital in the Background, 1958

Governor Faubus and the National Guard

As the first day of the 1957-1958 school year drew near, students and parents, both black and white, were worried about whether violence would break out if blacks entered Little Rock Central High School. On Labor Day, September 2, 1957, Arkansas Governor Orval Faubus gave a speech on television, stating that he was going to send the Arkansas National Guard to Central High to keep the black students from entering the school. He said he was sending the Guard to prevent violence. See a view of Little Rock above.

On September 4, Minnijean Brown, Elizabeth Eckford, Ernest Green, Thelma Mothershed, Melba Pattillo, Gloria Ray, Terrence Roberts, Jefferson Thomas, and Carlotta Walls tried to enter the school. The Arkansas National Guardsmen turned them away.

President Eisenhower sent the Governor a telegram, saying that he would make sure the Constitution was upheld by every legal means he could use. On September 14, the President and the Governor met face to face to discuss a solution. On September 20, Federal District Judge Ronald Davies ruled that Governor Faubus had not used the National Guard to preserve law and order. He ordered that the guardsmen be removed.

Riots Break Out in Little Rock

On September 23, Little Rock police stood guard as the "Little Rock Nine" walked into Central High School amidst 1,000 angry white protestors. People began to riot. The American people watched the scene in horror that night on television news. The Little Rock police had to escort the students out through the back of the school. President Eisenhower called the riots disgraceful and made the historic decision to send in soldiers to help uphold the law in Little Rock.

The Little Rock Nine Are Escorted to School by Soldiers

On September 24, President Eisenhower sent 1,200 "Screaming Eagles" from the 101st Airborne Division at Fort Campbell, Kentucky, to keep peace in Little Rock. The Arkansas National Guard was put under the authority of the Federal government instead of Governor

Soldiers escort the Little Rock Nine into Central High School.

Faubus. After trying to keep up with their studies at home, the nine black students were allowed back into the school on September 25. As seen in the photo above, they entered the building with an Army escort. U.S. Army General Edwin Walker spoke to the white students in the school auditorium before the black students arrived. The Little Rock Nine were able to stay the whole day. Soldiers guarded them as they went to their classes. For the first month, the students were taken to school each day in military vehicles. Finally, on October 25, they went to school in civilian cars. At left are scenes inside the school.

One of the African American leaders in Little Rock was Daisy Bates. Bates was the president of the Arkansas chapter of the National Association for the Advancement of Colored People (NAACP). Her husband was the publisher of Little Rock's largest black-owned newspaper. Mrs. Bates became a personal friend and mentor to the Little Rock Nine and was influential throughout the integration process. During the crisis, she said, "Any time it takes 11,500 soldiers to assure nine Negro children their constitutional rights in a democratic society, I can't be happy."

Ernest Green, First Black Graduate of Little Rock Central High School

Guardsmen gradually took over the duties of the Screaming Eagles. By the end of November, the last of the 101st Airborne were able to leave. The black students continued in school; but some white students attacked them verbally and physically. Because of their behavior about one hundred white students were suspended for a few days that year, and four were expelled from school

Scenes Inside Little Rock Central High School

entirely. One of the Little Rock Nine received discipline

as well. When a student hit Minnijean Brown, Minnijean called the student "white trash." The principal expelled Minnijean, who moved to New York and graduated from high school there.

In May of 1958, Ernest Green, the only senior among the Little Rock Nine, became the first African American to graduate from Little Rock Central High School. Civil rights leader Martin Luther King attended the ceremony. A few days after graduation, the school board began an effort to get the courts to allow them to delay integration of Little Rock's schools. The Supreme Court ordered the board to reopen the schools on September 15, 1958.

Central High Students Have Lessons on Television

Little Rock Schools Close

Governor Faubus ordered all Little Rock high schools to close until citizens could vote on the issue. On September 27, citizens voted 19,470 against integration and 7,561 for it. The high schools remained closed for the entire school year. Both black and white high school students watched their classes on television. See photos above. Instead of being able to choose from the eighty-seven subjects they would have had at school, they were only able to take English, history, math, and science.

An African American child watches a group of protestors in 1959.

A group of women formed the Women's Emergency Committee to Open Our Schools. They joined forces with local business leaders to fight for justice from the school board and for the reopening of the schools. Even though protests continued, as seen in the photos at left and below, the schools reopened in August of 1959, allowing black and white students to be educated together.

Protests at the State Capitol

Little Rock Central High School Today

In 1977 Little Rock Central High School was listed on the National Register of Historic Places. It became a National Historic Site in 1998. Visitors can view exhibits in the Central High Museum and Visitor Center, located in a nearby service station that has been restored to look as it did in the 1950s. Each of the Little Rock Nine students received the Congressional Gold Medal in 1999.

Hundreds of people gathered at Little Rock Central High School on September 25, 2007 to remember the integration of the school fifty years earlier. Former President Bill Clinton, other dignitaries, and each of the Little Rock Nine were present for the anniversary. The photo at right was taken on the day of the celebration, which commemorated a major event in the history of the civil rights movement—the history of blacks and whites learning to live, work, and learn together.

Birds Flying Above Little Rock Central High School

> The Lord looks from heaven;
> He sees all the sons of men;
> From His dwelling place he looks out
> On all the inhabitants of the earth,
> He who fashions the hearts of them all,
> He who understands all their works.
> Psalm 33:13-15

Activities for Lesson 123

Thinking Biblically – Imagine that you are a minister in Little Rock, Arkansas, at the time of the school integration crisis. In your notebook, write a sermon of one or two pages with the intent of guiding your congregation toward godly thinking about the situation. Use some Biblical examples and verses as part of your sermon.

Map Study – Complete the assignment for Lesson 123 on Map 3 "American Landmarks" in *Maps of America the Beautiful*.

Literature – Read "The Situation in Little Rock" in *We the People*, pages 162-164, and chapter 3 in *Homer Price*.

Timeline – In *Timeline of America the Beautiful* next to 1957, write: Central High School in Little Rock, Arkansas, is desegregated.

Student Workbook or Lesson Review – If you are using one of these optional books, complete the assignment for Lesson 123.

Norman Rockwell, Painter of American Life

Norman Rockwell painted moments from American life: Thanksgiving dinner with the family gathered around the table, Boy Scouts praying at their campsite, Mother's arms outstretched when her son comes back from war. Rockwell's career began well before his twentieth birthday and continued for more than sixty years. He painted scenes that made us feel good about ourselves, that lifted us up to a better way of living. He made us see the value of each human being. Norman Rockwell said:

> Without thinking too much about it in specific terms, I was showing the America I knew and observed to others who might not have noticed.

Norman Rockwell was a storyteller, who used pictures rather than words. Look at the magazine cover below, painted when Rockwell was twenty-two years old. This illustration is called "Schoolitis." Why is the doctor winking at the viewer? Do you think the boy looks sick? What is the doctor holding? Why is the mother standing by the bed? Why is she holding a fan? What did Rockwell include in the picture to let us know that the man is a doctor? Do you think this doctor might remember what it was like to want to avoid going to school?

Cover of Leslie's Illustrated Weekly Newspaper, *1916*

Painting an Illustration

Rockwell tried to paint people in situations that his viewers would immediately recognize. His paintings make us smile, chuckle, or belly laugh. They make us feel sympathy for others. They make us think.

Norman Rockwell made art look simple, but the steps he took to create his illustrations were far from simple. First, he began with an idea. Then, he gathered models and objects that would illustrate the idea. When he put a bed, books, a chair, and a doctor bag in a painting, he did not try simply to imagine or remember what they looked like; he actually created the scene with real objects and real people, called models. He found his models among people he knew. He kept a supply of objects he found in antique stores and a supply of costumes for his models to wear. When looking for a model among his neighbors and friends, he would see how far they could raise their eyebrows. He wanted to be sure that they could make the facial expressions he wanted.

Rockwell's neighbors could recognize many of the people in his work. His fans learned to recognize some of them as well because he used the same people in many paintings. He paid his own children a dollar a day to pose for him. If you look closely at his paintings you will find Norman Rockwell himself in ninety-two of them.

Detail was very important to Norman Rockwell. When he illustrated *The Adventures of Tom Sawyer*, he went to its setting in Hannibal, Missouri, to be sure his illustrations were accurate. When he painted a scene in an auto mechanic's garage, he gathered his models and objects into a local garage.

Once he had the people and objects he needed, he put them in position, moving them again and again until they looked just right. He might send his models to change clothes. He acted out the expressions he wanted them to have.

Leslie's, *1919*

When everything was just to his liking, he made sketches of how he wanted the finished illustration to look and then painted it on a large canvas. When it was finished, he sent it to the magazine publisher, book publisher, or advertising agency who paid for the right to publish the illustration.

Becoming an Illustrator

Norman Percevel Rockwell was born in 1894 in New York City to Jarvis Waring and Ann Mary Hill Rockwell (called Nancy). His father worked at a textile company and enjoyed drawing for fun. Nancy's father was a painter.

Norman had an older brother, Jarvis Rockwell Jr., who was athletic. Norman was always skinny and never good at sports. When he was ten years old, he wanted to be a weight lifter, so he began an exercise program. He stood in front of his bedroom mirror and did pushups, deep knee bends, and jumping jacks. After a month he gave up. He decided to do what he was good at—drawing.

As a boy, Norman played with his friends in New York City. They pretended to dig holes to China and then listen for people speaking in Chinese. At night they watched the lamplighter light the gas street lamps. Norman also enjoyed trips to the country. When he was a child, farm families took in boarders for the summer. Until Norman was nine or ten years old, the Rockwells spent summers on a farm. He loved the cool green grass, swimming in the river, hunting for bullfrogs, and going on hay rides.

One sad memory from Rockwell's childhood happened when he was seven years old. The day after President William McKinley was assassinated, Norman's family went to church. He remembered his parents crying when the congregation sang McKinley's favorite hymn, "Nearer, My God, to Thee."

The Rockwell family moved to Mamaroneck, New York, by Long Island Sound, when Norman was nine. He enjoyed the more rural setting. As a teenager, Norman took classes at Chase School of Art, which had been founded in 1896. American artist Edward Hopper was a student there just a few years before Rockwell. When he was fourteen, Norman left high school and enrolled full-time at the National Academy of Design, founded in 1825 by Samuel F. B. Morse and other artists. Artist Winslow Homer had once taught at the National Academy. After a year there, Norman entered the Art Students League. All three art schools were in New York City.

The first person to pay Norman Rockwell to create art was a neighbor who asked him to draw four Christmas cards. When he was just sixteen years old, he created the illustrations for a book, *Tell Me Why Stories About Mother Nature* by Carl H. Claud. By the time he turned twenty, he had illustrated four children's books and become the art director of *Boy's Life*, a magazine published by Boy Scouts of America. He also created illustrations for several publications for young people.

Leslie's, *1917*

When Rockwell was twenty-one years old, he and his family moved to nearby New Rochelle, New York. There he set up an art studio which he shared with a cartoonist. In New Rochelle, he became acquainted with other illustrators. He began providing illustrations for magazines such as *Life, Literary Digest, Country Gentleman,* and *Leslie's Illustrated Weekly Newspaper*. The four magazine covers pictured in this lesson are all from *Leslie's*. They were created in 1916, 1917, and 1919.

Rockwell and the Boy Scouts

After serving as art director for *Boy's Life* for three years, Norman Rockwell resigned from that position; but he continued to illustrate for the Boy Scouts for the next six decades. He painted illustrations for stories in *Boy's Life* and also created covers. He illustrated several scouting books, including the *Boy Scouts Hike Book*, the *Boy's Camp Book, Scouting with Daniel Boone,* and *The Boy Scout Courageous*. In 1924 he painted "A Good Turn" for their annual calendar. To thank the Boy Scouts for helping him get his career started as an illustrator, he painted it for free. Rockwell continued to paint Boy Scout calendar covers until 1974, missing only 1928 and 1930. Forty-seven of the original paintings are in the National Scouting Museum in Irving, Texas.

Rockwell's Boy Scout paintings were designed to honor America's history, to help boys reach high standards, and to honor the boys' service. In the painting "Our Heritage," a Boy Scout helps a Cub Scout. As he does so, he looks over his shoulder and sees General George Washington praying at Valley Forge.

When Norman Rockwell was seventy-five years old, the Boy Scouts asked him to paint himself in a Boy Scout painting. In the finished work, Rockwell stands before a canvas set out in a field, holding brushes. He looks comfortable in a Scout leader's uniform. Boy Scouts stand and watch. Norman Rockwell was known to Scouts as "Mr. Scouting." He received the Silver Buffalo Award, the highest honor bestowed in Scouting.

Rockwell and *The Saturday Evening Post*

When Norman Rockwell left his job as art director of *Boy's Life*, he began to create covers for *The Saturday Evening Post*. His first cover, "Boy with Baby Carriage," published in 1916, entertained *Post* readers and made them feel sorry for the poor boy who somehow got stuck with what he felt was a very unmanly chore. For his April 29, 1922 cover, Rockwell drew from his own childhood experiences when he painted a skinny boy holding dumbbells and looking at a picture of a muscular man he had tacked to his wall.

From 1916 until 1963 Rockwell drew 323 covers for *The Saturday Evening Post*. While his work for the Boy Scouts was seen by Scouts and their families across the country, the *Post* covers were seen by millions of people from many walks of life.

Sailor and Patriot

Norman Rockwell was eight pounds underweight when he tried to enlist in the Navy during World War I. He began to consume a lot of liquid, bananas, and doughnuts to gain weight. When he tried again, he made it. He served at the Naval Reserve Base at Charleston, South Carolina, where he was made art editor of *Afloat & Ashore*, a small publication distributed on the Naval Reserve Base.

During and after World War I, Rockwell created magazine covers that honored soldiers. In 1917 he painted "They Remembered Me" for the cover of a special edition of *Leslie's Illustrated Weekly Newspaper*. In the illustration, a World War I doughboy beams a smile as he enjoys a box full of Christmas presents sent from home. The cover of a 1919 issue of *Literary Digest* was a Rockwell illustration of a young woman hugging a returning soldier, while Dad and Mom and little brother stand close by, gazing at their hero. On the little boy's head is his big brother's helmet. In another illustration, an erect soldier with medals on his chest walks down the street. Five admiring boys crowd around him.

During World War II, Rockwell created posters like the one below. The posters encouraged those on the home front to keep doing their part. A 1945 cover for *The Saturday Evening Post* had a smiling sailor in his white uniform and cap. He lies in a hammock with his dog on his lap. The title was simply, "On Leave." Another 1945 illustration was "Imperfect Fit," which depicted a young man who had just come home from the war. His Army hat and jacket are hanging on a chair while he tries on his old suit. The pants are too short and he's grown too tall for his mirror.

War Department Poster, 1942

Rockwell also created an imaginary soldier named Willie Gillis Jr. He painted several *Post* covers that showed Gillis in a variety of situations. In "Willie Gillis at the USO," he is being served food by volunteers. In "Willie Gillis at Church," he sits alone on a pew, wearing his uniform.

When President Roosevelt gave his State of the Union speech in 1941, he spoke of America looking forward to a world founded on four essential human freedoms: freedom of speech, freedom of worship, freedom from want, and freedom from fear. Rockwell illustrated each of these in a series entitled "The Four Freedoms" in 1943. *The Saturday Evening Post* sent the paintings around the country to sixteen cities. The Federal government made posters of them. These paintings inspired Americans to buy $132 million dollars worth of war bonds. These illustrations remain some of Rockwell's most recognized and beloved.

Family Life

At age twenty-two, Norman Rockwell married Irene O'Connor. They were married for twelve years before the marriage ended in divorce. In 1930 at age 34, Rockwell married a teacher named Mary Rhodes. Norman and Mary lived in New Rochelle, New York. They had three sons, Jarvis Waring, Thomas Rhodes, and Peter Barstow. Thomas grew up to be a writer, and Jarvis and Peter both became artists.

In 1939 Norman Rockwell moved his family to New England. They lived in Arlington, Vermont, until 1953, when they moved to Stockbridge, Massachusetts. The Rockwells became part of both communities, whose citizens provided many of his models.

Norman Rockwell

Mary died in 1959 after they had been married for twenty-nine years. The following year Norman and his son Thomas worked together to complete an autobiography, *My Adventures as an Illustrator*. Norman also painted a self-portrait, which appeared on the February 13, 1960 issue of *The Saturday Evening Post*. The following year Norman took a poetry reading class in Stockbridge. He met retired schoolteacher Molly Punderson. They were married in 1961.

In 1963 Rockwell painted his last cover for *The Saturday Evening Post*. The following year he began publishing illustrations for *Look* magazine. During the 1960s, Rockwell portrayed many current events in his work. He created paintings of Presidents and astronauts. He painted "The Problem We All Live With," which illustrated Ruby Bridges, a little African American girl being escorted to school by U.S. marshals as she integrated an elementary school in New Orleans, Louisiana.

In 1976 at age 82, Rockwell traveled to Rome to visit his son Peter. That year he created a painting to celebrate America's bicentennial. He painted himself putting a Happy Birthday ribbon on the Liberty Bell. Also in 1976 he published his final Boy Scouts of America calendar. His adopted hometown of Stockbridge had a parade in his honor which he and Molly attended. The next year President Gerald R. Ford presented him with the Presidential Medal of Freedom. He died peacefully at his home in 1978 at age 84. He was survived by his widow, three sons, and seven grandchildren.

Keeping On Keeping On

Norman Rockwell created a successful career as an illustrator by working hard and not giving up. Though he is perhaps best remembered for the Four Freedoms and his work with the Boys Scouts and *The Saturday Evening Post*, he also created ads for more than one hundred and fifty companies and painted portraits of famous people.

Leslie's, 1917

Sometimes Rockwell felt stuck and wondered what to do next. He felt afraid that his career was over. He did not get discouraged or give up, however, but kept trying. When he had trouble thinking of an idea, he would get ten or twelve pads of paper and a pencil and place them on his dining room table. First he drew a lamppost and then sketched a story around it. He kept drawing sketch after sketch, letting one idea lead to another until he had figured out what to do. He also kept painting when he wasn't sure what to paint. He went to his studio at eight o'clock in the morning and painted. He stopped at noon for lunch and then went back to the studio to paint until five or six o'clock in the evening. Instead of trying to think his way out or trying to escape a problem, Norman Rockwell believed he should work his way out of it.

> Do you see a man skilled in his work?
> He will stand before kings;
> He will not stand before obscure men.
> Proverbs 22:29

Activities for Lesson 124

Vocabulary – Find each of these words in a dictionary: agency, textile, boarder, enlist, editor. For each word, decide which definition corresponds to the way it is used in this lesson. Copy the words and definitions into your notebook.

Literature – Read chapters 4-5 in *Homer Price*.

Creative Writing – In your notebook, write a short story of at least two pages based on one of the Norman Rockwell paintings in Lesson 124.

Timeline – In *Timeline of America the Beautiful* next to 1943, write: Norman Rockwell paints his series of the Four Freedoms.

Student Workbook or Lesson Review – If you are using one of these optional books, complete the assignment for Lesson 124.

God Created Alaska

When God made Alaska, He put many of His creative thoughts together in one magnificent place: towering mountains, gigantic glaciers, active volcanoes, giant polar bears, camouflaged snowshoe hares, and Arctic foxes, just to name a few. See photos below.

God created a massive peninsula and surrounded it with the Arctic Ocean to the north, the Bering Sea to the west, and the Gulf of Alaska to the south. It is the largest peninsula in the Western Hemisphere with a 6,640-mile-long coastline.

Peninsulas, a Panhandle, and Two Thousand Islands

As seen on the map on page 770, the giant peninsula of Alaska has three peninsulas of its own. Just south of the Arctic Circle, Seward Peninsula reaches westward into the Bering Sea. It is home to the city of Nome. At its tip is the Bering Strait, separating Alaska from Russia. The Diomede Islands are in the Bering Strait. Little Diomede belongs to America

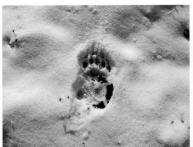

Top Row: Hiker in Denali National Park; Bear Track in Denali; Kenago Volcano on Kanago Island in the Aleutians; Bottom Row: Arctic Fox; Holgate Glacier Calving in Kenai Fjords National Park on the Kenai Peninsula

and Big Diomede belongs to Russia. They are two and a half miles apart. See NASA image at left.

The Alaska Peninsula divides the Bering Sea from the Gulf of Alaska. The state's largest lake, Iliamna Lake, is on the Alaska Peninsula. It covers 1,100 square miles. The Alaska Peninsula is home to more than fifty active volcanoes, all part of the Aleutian range. In 1912 volcanic eruptions changed the landscape of the area now called Valley of Ten Thousand Smokes. The 150 Aleutian Islands extend westward into the Pacific Ocean beyond the tip of the Alaska Peninsula. Scenes from the Alaskan Peninsula and the Aleutian Islands are pictured below.

Volcano Calder and Mount Griggs in Katmai National Park on the Alaska Peninsula

Mount Pavlof (right) and Pavlof Sister (left) at the Tip of the Alaska Peninsula

A brown bear gives her cub a ride in Katmai National Park

Valley of Ten Thousand Smokes on the Alaska Peninsula

Aghileen Pinnacles in the Aleutian Islands

Look again at the map above. The peninsula marked with a ^ is the Kenai Peninsula. Kenai Fjords National Park is here, as is the town of Seward (not to be confused with the peninsula of the same name). The city of Anchorage lies on Alaska's southern coast, just west of the Kenai. Photos from the Kenai Fjords National Park are at right. Just past the tip of the Kenai Peninsula is Kodiak Island, the largest of Alaska's 2,000 islands and home to the city of Kodiak. See a bear in Kodiak National Wildlife Refuge below.

Scenes of Kenai Fjords National Park

The thin strip of land extending southeast from the main body of the state is called the Alaska Panhandle. The waters of the Gulf of Alaska are to its west and the Canadian province of British Columbia is to its east. To the west of the panhandle

A Stellar Seal in Kenai Fjords National Park

is the Alexander Archipelago. It is home to more than half of Alaska's islands. Between these islands and the mainland is the calm Inside Passage where ships find protection from storms.

Bear in Kodiak National Wildlife Refuge

Brady Glacier in Glacier Bay National Park

Many of Alaska's thousands of glaciers are along the coast of the upper panhandle. See two of Glacier Bay National Park's glaciers at left and above.

The glaciers are a stark contrast to the rainforest in the southern panhandle. The small town of Port Walter on Baranoff Island in the Alexander Archipelago gets more than two hundred inches of rainfall per year. The towns of Skagway, Juneau,

Margerie Glacier in Glacier Bay National Park

Sitka, and Ketchikan are in the Alaska Panhandle/Alexander Archipelago region. Juneau is the capital of Alaska. It is the only state capital with no road connecting it to the rest of the state. People must use a boat or a plane to get to Juneau.

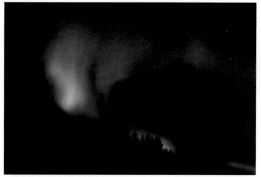

Aurora Borealis Seen from Glacier Bay National Park

The beautiful aurora borealis (or northern lights) sometimes lights up the fall, winter, and spring skies in Alaska. The aurora borealis is a glow that appears in the upper atmosphere. It is made when energetic particles enter the atmosphere from above. At left is a photo of the northern lights as seen from Glacier Bay.

In southern Alaska, the terrain changes quickly from sea level to high mountains. Near the place where the panhandle joins the main body of Alaska, Mount St. Elias rises to more than 18,000 feet, making it one of the tallest mountains in North America. To the north of St. Elias are the Wrangell Mountains. This region is in St. Elias-Wrangell National Park. The photo at right below was taken in the St. Elias region. The one at left was taken where the Copper River empties into the Gulf of Alaska west of the park.

Scene at the Mouth of the Copper River

Cliff and Waterfall in St. Elias Region

The Alaska Mountain range lies between the panhandle and the Alaska Peninsula. Much of the range is in Denali National Park, including Mount McKinley, pictured below. At 20,320 feet it is the tallest mountain in the United States and in all of North America. See more scenes from Denali below.

*Surrounding the magnificent view of Denali National Park in the center are:
a rock climber, a bull moose, Mount McKinley, and a Ptarmigan.*

The Alaskan Interior

North of the Alaska Mountain range is the Alaskan interior. See photos below. Here the highest elevations are around 4,000 feet. The interior has the coldest winter and the hottest summer temperatures in Alaska. The city of Fairbanks is in this region. Notice the Federal employee in Fairbanks pictured below. As he throws water into the air at -40°F, it freezes instantly. The city of Fairbanks is about 3,280 miles from New York City, 4,230 miles from London, and 3,520 miles from Tokyo.

The Yukon River, at far right, is one of the world's longest navigable rivers. It flows from Canada's Yukon territory across the interior region and empties into the Bering Sea south of the Seward Peninsula. More than 650 species of flowering plants live in the interior, plus algae, fungi, lichens, and mosses.

Top Row: Scene in Yukon Flats National Wildlife Refuge; Yukon River
Bottom Row: Church 190 Miles Northwest of Fairbanks;
Water Frozen in Midair in Fairbanks

The Arctic Region

North of the interior of Alaska is the Arctic region. The northernmost point in the Arctic region is Point Barrow, home of the town of Barrow, Alaska. In the Arctic much of the ground is permafrost, which is ground that is always frozen. Many rivers run through the region. Here God placed rich deposits of coal, gas, and petroleum underground. Many migratory birds nest here and hundreds of thousands of caribou come each summer to give birth to their calves. Running east and west through the Arctic Region are the mountains of the Brooks Range, pictured at left. Below are photos from Gates of the Arctic National Park. See more arctic photos on page 774.

Brooks Range

From Left to Right: Autumn Tundra; Snowshoe Hare; Arctic Wintergreen; and Arrigetch Peaks

Left to Right: Snow Bunting at Point Barrow, Polar Bear and Her Cubs on the Northern Arctic Coast, Ribbon Seal on Bering Sea, Walrus Giving a Pup a Ride

From Discovery to Statehood

On January 3, 1959, President Eisenhower signed legislation making Alaska America's forty-ninth state. In the photo below, Territorial Governor Mike Stepovich holds the *Anchorage Daily Times* with the giant headline,

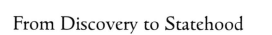

"We're In." In Lesson 95, we learned about the native peoples who lived in Alaska before Europeans discovered it. What happened between its discovery and 1959?

President Eisenhower, Territorial Governor of Alaska Mike Stepovich, and Secretary of the Interior Fred A. Seaton

Russians, Englishmen, and Americans

One of the first Russian explorers to come to Alaska was Vitus Bering. His first exploration in the area was in 1728. He returned in 1741. Bering died in Alaska that year and was buried on Bering Island. The island, the Bering Strait between Alaska and Russia, and the Bering Sea are named for him. In 1778 English explorer Captain James Cook came to the region when he explored the Arctic Ocean. The first non-natives to live in Alaska settled on Kodiak Island, moving there from Russia in 1784. Russians were attracted to Alaska because of the wealth they could acquire as fur trappers. Russian influence in Alaska continues today.

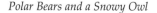

Polar Bears and a Snowy Owl

774

In 1835 the United States and England received permission from Russia to trade in Alaska. American whalers began whaling in Alaskan waters in 1848. From 1865 to 1867, surveyors mapped a route for telegraph lines through Alaska to Siberia.

In 1843 the Russian Orthodox Church set up its first mission school for Native Alaskans. Many Alaskans are still part of the Russian Orthodox Church. Notice the photo of a Russian Orthodox Church in 1912 at right. The ground is covered with volcanic ash from the eruptions in the Valley of Ten Thousand Smokes (see photo on page 770).

Russian Orthodox Church with Volcanic Ash from the 1912 Eruption of Mount Katmai

Several churches began to establish mission schools throughout Alaska in 1867. Swedish Evangelical, Roman Catholic, Congregational, Moravian, Presbyterian, and Episcopalian churches, and the Society of Friends all had mission schools here. For many years the U.S. government helped pay for the education children received at mission schools.

Alaska Becomes Part of America

On October 18, 1867, Russia sold Alaska to the United States. The U.S. established the District of Alaska in 1884. When Alaska became an official U.S. territory in 1912, it organized a territorial legislature. This was a step toward statehood.

During the late 1800s and early 1900s, salmon and gold, two of the resources that God had created in Alaska, began attracting businessmen and settlers. Businesses began to can salmon in 1878. The industry grew until Alaska became the largest salmon canning region in the world. The first gold discovery in Alaska was at the Stikine River in 1861. Gold was discovered in Juneau on Fortymile Creek in the 1880s. As you have learned in previous lessons, when gold was discovered in a particular location, people came flocking. The town of Skagway was founded when prospectors passed through Alaska on their way to the Klondike Gold Rush in 1897. Gold was discovered in Nome in 1898 and in Fairbanks in 1903.

In 1890 a Presbyterian missionary had the idea of importing reindeer to Alaska. The U.S. government helped fund the project. The first reindeer were imported from Siberia. In 1898 families from Norway and Lapland (in Finland) moved to Alaska to help with the project. Native Alaskans became their apprentices to learn how to be reindeer herders. Reindeer herding is still practiced in Alaska today. Notice Alaskan reindeer below.

The first railroad in Alaska was begun in 1898. It went from Skagway into the Yukon Territory. In 1923 the five-hundred-mile Alaska Railroad was completed. It connected Seward, Anchorage, and Fairbanks.

In the years before World War II, the U. S. military warned Congress that Alaska would be important if war began with Japan. America had many military resources in Hawaii but only one base in the giant territory of Alaska. Six months after Pearl Harbor, Japanese forces came to Alaska. They bombed Dutch Harbor on

Reindeer and Native Alaskans

Unalaska Island and occupied Attu and Kiska, two of the Aleutian Islands. They took Aleutian prisoners. Americans fought a nineteen-day battle on Attu in 1943. The Americans were finally triumphant. See photo at right. Canadian forces joined American forces to retake Kiska two months later, only to find that the Japanese had escaped through the fog and abandoned the island. During World War II, America and Canada joined together to build the Alaska Highway so that troops and equipment could get to Alaska. America also built large airfields there.

Troops carry supplies to Americans fighting Japanese on the Aleutian Island of Attu in May 1943.

Since the Soviet Union and Alaska were so close geographically, military bases in Alaska were important to the United States during the Cold War. The Cold War was very real to Alaskans, especially the Native Alaskans living on the Diomede Islands. The Soviets built a military base on Big Diomede. Sometimes the Soviets captured, questioned, and then released Yup'iks from Little Diomede when they visited relatives on Big Diomede. In 1960 the Alaska Army National Guard built an outpost on Little Diomede. Local residents served as scouts and participated in blackouts to keep Soviets from spying on them through their windows. While Americans across the country worried about the Cold War, it was very close to home for many in Alaska.

Alaska is full of magnificent wonders. May we all give glory and honor to the God who made them.

> Let them give glory to the LORD and declare His praise in the coastlands.
> Isaiah 42:12

Activities for Lesson 125

Thinking Biblically – Read Psalm 148 and reflect on what you learned about God's handiwork in Alaska.

Map Study – Complete the assignments for Lesson 125 on Map 28 "Alaska" in *Maps of America the Beautiful*.

Vocabulary – In your notebook, make a drawing that illustrates the meaning of each of these words: archipelago, panhandle, navigable, prospector, outpost. Write the word under the drawing. Check in a dictionary if you need help with their definitions.

Literature – Read "The Northern Lights" in *We the People*, pages 165-166, and chapter 6 in *Homer Price*.

Timeline – In *Timeline of America the Beautiful* next to 1897, write: The Klondike Gold Rush begins.

Student Workbook or Lesson Review – If you are using one of these optional books, complete the assignment for Lesson 125. If you are using the Lesson Review, answer the questions on *Homer Price* and take the quiz for Unit 25.

The 1960s

The 1960s have been well-described as turbulent. Conflict with Communists, war in Vietnam, riots about civil rights, and three assassinations made Americans dread turning on the nightly television news. Two very different Presidents occupied the White House for most of the decade, one youthful and sophisticated, the other down-to-earth and, by the end of his presidency, heartbroken. The complex Interstate system grew larger and larger during the decade. With that growth, American businesses and industries grew. As in the decades before and after, the Great Salt Lake continued to attract millions of visitors—visiting birds, that is. Evangelist Billy Graham gave a message of hope in this turbulent time.

President Johnson's Night Reading Placed on His Pillow in His Bedroom at the White House, October, 1966

Lessons in Unit 26

Lesson 126 – Our American Story: Civil Rights and the War in Vietnam
Lesson 127 – Daily Life: Living in the White House
Lesson 128 – An American Landmark: The Interstate System
Lesson 129 – God's Wonders: God Created the Great Salt Lake
Lesson 130 – An American Biography: Billy Graham, Missionary to the World

Books Used in Unit 26

- *Maps of America the Beautiful*

- *Timeline of America the Beautiful*

- *We the People*

Civil Rights and the War in Vietnam

While President Eisenhower served his last year in office, the Democratic and Republican parties prepared for the 1960 election. The Republicans chose Eisenhower's Vice President, Richard Nixon, as their presidential candidate. His running mate was former Senator Henry Cabot Lodge Jr. For many Americans, Minnesota Senator Hubert

Kennedy with Eleanor Roosevelt, 1960

Humphrey seemed the obvious choice to be the Democratic candidate, but he was challenged by others, including Massachusetts Senator John Fitzgerald Kennedy and Texas Senator Lyndon Johnson.

Campaigning for the presidency requires hard work and a great deal of money. Candidates need help from many people. In the photo at left, Kennedy is pictured with Eleanor Roosevelt. He went to visit her personally to obtain her help in his campaign. This is an example of the many things a candidate must do, first to get nominated by his party and then to campaign for the election.

Senator Humphrey worked very hard to secure the Democratic nomination, even taking money from the savings he planned to use for his daughter's wedding. Kennedy was from a wealthy family and was able to spend far more money than Humphrey, who finally gave up. At the Democratic Party convention, Kennedy was chosen as the

presidential candidate. He chose Lyndon Johnson to be his running mate. See a portrait of Johnson and Kennedy at right. In the photo at the top of page 779, they campaign in the Texas capital of Austin.

Kennedy was only forty-three years old, and many Americans were afraid that he was too young to lead a nation facing the danger of Communism. Some American voters were also concerned because Kennedy was Catholic. They were worried he would allow the Catholic Church to tell him what to do. Though Nixon was only forty-seven, he was well-known across the country.

Senator Lyndon Johnson and
Senator John Fitzgerald Kennedy

Kennedy challenged Nixon to four debates to be broadcast on television. Seventy million people watched the first debate, while many listened on radio. Kennedy made a better impression in front of the television camera. He was tanned and wearing makeup; but Nixon, who was recovering from recent surgery, looked pale. Many who heard the debates on radio believed Nixon had done a superior job, but the television viewers were left with a different impression.

Though the election was one of the closest in American history, John F. Kennedy won, becoming the youngest man ever elected to the presidency. Since Eisenhower was twenty-seven years older than Kennedy, Americans realized that a new generation had taken charge. See Eisenhower and Kennedy in the photo below.

Johnson and Kennedy Campaign in Austin, Texas

Kennedy called his goals for America the New Frontier. Two of his key efforts as President were space exploration and the Peace Corps. A few months after his inauguration, Kennedy gave a speech before Congress in which he encouraged America to land a man on the moon before the end of the 1960s. See photograph below.

Eisenhower and Kennedy

Once during his presidential campaign, Kennedy arrived at the University of Michigan at 2:00 a.m. after a long, hard day. Ten thousand students were waiting to hear him speak. Standing on the steps of the Student Union building, he asked the students how many of them would be willing to serve the cause of peace by volunteering in a poor country. President Kennedy established the Peace Corps, which sends Americans overseas to help train workers, to help people in other countries understand Americans, and to help Americans understand others. Countries around the world from Afghanistan to Zimbabwe have been served by America's Peace Corps volunteers.

Americans became fascinated by the young and handsome Kennedy, his beautiful wife Jacqueline, and their two young children, Caroline and John. Women across the country began to dress like "Jackie." Kennedy had an upper class Bostonian accent that was mimicked by comedians on television.

Communists in Cuba

Relations with the U.S.S.R. continued to be frightening to Americans during the Kennedy administration. Americans were alarmed when

Speaking to a joint session of Congress, Kennedy challenges America to put a man on the moon before the end of the decade.

President Kennedy Meets with Soviet Leader Nikita Khrushchev in Vienna, Austria, June 1961

Communist Fidel Castro led a revolt on the island of Cuba, just ninety miles south of Florida. Castro became Cuba's prime minister in 1959 and established a close political relationship with the U.S.S.R. When Kennedy took office, he was informed that the United States government was already training 1,500 Cubans who lived in the United States so that they could invade Cuba and overthrow Castro. Kennedy approved the plan. When the American-trained Cubans landed at the Bay of Pigs in Cuba in April, just three months after the inauguration, they failed miserably in their attempt to gain control of their country. It was a huge embarrassment to the United States.

As seen in the photo above, President Kennedy met with Soviet leader Nikita Khrushchev in Vienna, Austria, in June of 1961. In October the U.S. discovered that the Soviets were working to place missiles with nuclear bombs on them in Cuba. These missiles were close enough to hit targets in the United States. Kennedy sent ships from the U.S. Navy to blockade Cuba and keep Soviet ships from entering its harbors. After anxious and tense days, the United States and the Soviet Union came to an agreement. The Soviets agreed to remove the missiles, while Kennedy promised that the U.S. government would not sponsor any more attempts to overthrow Castro. In an effort to avoid a nuclear war, the U.S. and the U.S.S.R. installed a special telephone line, called the "hot line," so that leaders of the two countries could communicate quickly with each other.

Also in 1961, the Communist government of East Germany built a wall between East Berlin and West Berlin to keep East Berliners from leaving. The Berlin Wall became a symbol of the division between the Communist world and the free world. Kennedy visited Berlin in 1963 and expressed his sympathy for the people of East Berlin.

One way that America and the Soviet Union fought the Cold War was by spying on one another. The planes at right are U.S. spy planes called SR 71s. The pilots wore space suits because they flew so high into the stratosphere. A pilot once took an SR 71 nineteen miles above the earth!

Two U.S. SR 71 Spy Planes with Pilots

The Civil Rights Movement

Like abolitionists and workers on the Underground Railroad before the Civil War, the Little Rock Nine of the 1950s, and many others in between, black and white Americans continued to work for the equal treatment of black citizens during the 1960s. Martin Luther King Jr. and others led civil rights workers in non-violent methods. Peaceful marches and sit-ins were held in many cities. At a sit-in, a black person would enter a restaurant that

James Meredith, First Black Student at Ole Miss

served only whites and sit down. When he or she was arrested, another would come in to take his or her place.

In 1962 James Meredith, an African American U.S. Air Force veteran, tried to enroll at the all-white University of Mississippi (Ole Miss). See photo at left. Federal courts ordered the school to enroll him, but the Governor refused. Just as Eisenhower had taken control of the Arkansas National Guard during the Little Rock integration crisis, Kennedy took control of the Mississippi National Guard. The Guard forced the school to enroll Meredith. As a result, riots broke out on campus and lasted fifteen hours. Hundreds of people were injured and two died. Meredith was able to begin attending classes two days later and after three years he graduated from the university.

On August 28, 1963, about 200,000 black and white Americans gathered on the National Mall for a "March on Washington" for civil rights. The protestors asked for jobs and freedom for African Americans. Singers Bob Dylan and Joan Baez sang at the event. Actor Charleton Heston spoke. The last speaker on the program that day was Martin Luther King Jr. On the steps of the Lincoln Memorial, he delivered his famous "I Have a Dream" speech. It was broadcast on television. King told his fellow protestors many of his dreams for civil rights, including this one: "I have a dream that one day this nation will rise up and live out the true meaning of its creed: 'We hold these truths to be self-evident: that all men are created equal.'"

Governor and Mrs. John Connally and President and Mrs. Kennedy ride in a motorcade in Dallas, Texas on November 22, 1963.

A Terrible Day in Dallas

In the fall of 1963, Kennedy toured the nation. On November 22, 1963, he visited Dallas, Texas. Onlookers lined the streets to watch President and Mrs. Kennedy pass by in an open convertible, along with Texas Governor John Connally and his wife. See photo at left. Suddenly the President was shot from a building along the route. He was pronounced dead at a Dallas hospital a short time later. The assassin was later identified as Lee Harvey Oswald.

As Jacqueline Kennedy, Vice President Lyndon B. Johnson, and others prepared to accompany the President's body back to Washington, Johnson was sworn in as the thirty-sixth President. Mrs. Kennedy stood at Johnson's side in the presidential jet as it waited for take-off at Love Field in Dallas. See photo at right.

The sad news traveled across the country immediately. The nation grieved as they watched the funeral on television. They shared the grief of Mrs. Kennedy, her two young children, other family members, and dignitaries from around the world. Read about John F. Kennedy's life on page 782.

Mrs. Kennedy stands by Lyndon Johnson as he takes the oath of office aboard Air Force One.

781

John Fitzgerald Kennedy
America's Thirty-Fifth President
January 20, 1961 - November 22, 1963

John Fitzgerald "Jack" Kennedy was born in Brookline, Massachusetts, on May 29, 1917, soon after America entered World War I. He was the first President born in the twentieth century. His father Joseph was the grandson of Irish immigrants. Joseph had met his personal goal of being a millionaire by the time he was thirty-two years old. The father of John Kennedy's mother Rose had served as mayor of Boston. When Jack was ten years old, his family moved into a mansion in Riverdale, New York. As a child Jack suffered from several illnesses and spent a lot of time recuperating. He joined the Boy Scouts. While other families suffered through the Great Depression, John Kennedy and his eight brothers and sisters had servants, spent vacations at their summer homes, and went to private schools. Jack was voted most likely to succeed when he graduated from high school.

In the fall of 1935, John Kennedy enrolled at Princeton but had to leave for health reasons. He worked as a ranch hand in Arizona and spent time sailing in Massachusetts before entering Harvard the following fall. In 1938, just before World War II began, Jack inherited one million dollars. He toured Europe and researched for a paper he was writing for the honors program in which he was enrolled at Harvard. That same year his father Joseph Kennedy was appointed as Ambassador to the United Kingdom of Great Britain and Northern Ireland. While in England with his father, John Kennedy wrote his senior essay about England's unpreparedness for World War II. He published it as a book entitled *Why England Slept*; it became a bestseller.

When World War II began, Jack was rejected by the Army because of his chronic back pain. His father helped him get into the Navy. John Kennedy commanded a small motor-torpedo boat called PT 109. When the ship was attacked, Kennedy rescued a crew member and led his crew as they swam three miles to a nearby island. He received a Purple Heart for his injuries and a medal for valor. His older brother, Joseph Jr., was killed during the war in Europe.

After the war, Kennedy was elected to serve in the U.S. House of Representatives, representing a district in Massachusetts. In 1952 he was elected to the Senate. In 1953 Kennedy married Jacqueline Lee Bouvier, whom he had met at a dinner party.

Kennedy's frequent illnesses continued. He often suffered back pain and had several surgeries. In 1956, while recovering from surgery, he wrote a Pulitzer Prize-winning biography of eight U.S. Senators called *Profiles in Courage*.

The Kennedys had three children. Caroline was born in 1957, and John was born sixteen days after his father's election to the presidency. Another son, Patrick, was born in 1963 while Kennedy was President, but he only lived for two days. Jack took pain medication constantly, but still his back was so painful that he could not even lift his children. The statue at left is one of the presidential statues in Rapid City, South Dakota. It is based on a famous photo of Kennedy and his son.

Kennedy was from a powerful political family. His father Joseph had helped elect Franklin Roosevelt in 1932. As President, Jack Kennedy appointed his brother Robert as Attorney General. He appointed his brother-in-law Sargent Shriver as head of the Peace Corps. His youngest brother Edward "Teddy" Kennedy was elected as a U.S. Senator from Massachusetts in 1962. In 1964 his brother Robert Kennedy was elected as a U.S. Senator from New York.

In the photo at left, Jacqueline Kennedy and her children leave the church after John Kennedy's funeral. Americans have honored Kennedy in many ways since his assassination. A statement Kennedy made in his inaugural address has become one of the most famous quotes in American history: "Ask not what your country can do for you—ask what you can do for your country."

The Presidency of Lyndon Johnson

Five days after Kennedy's death, President Johnson spoke to a joint session of Congress telling them he would continue to support what Kennedy had begun. The following year he spoke to an audience at the University of Michigan, telling of his dreams of a Great Society "with abundance and liberty for all." Meanwhile Johnson's old friend Senator

President Johnson Signs Civil Rights Act of 1964

Hubert Humphrey was working hard to get his fellow Senators to pass a law that would guarantee equal rights for people of all races. Finally the Civil Rights Act of 1964 was passed by the U.S. House and the Senate. As seen above, President Johnson signed it into law that July in a televised ceremony. It was a giant step forward for those fighting for civil rights.

The Democratic Party chose President Johnson as their presidential candidate in 1964. Johnson chose Senator Hubert Humphrey as his running mate. Johnson easily defeated the Republican candidate, Senator Barry Goldwater of Arizona. President Johnson had served without a Vice President since he took the oath of office on November 22, 1963. Johnson was inaugurated as President and Humphrey was inaugurated as Vice President in January of 1965, and they began to work with Congress to pass Johnson's Great Society programs.

Peace and Violence for Civil Rights

On March 7, 1965, civil rights workers attempted to march from Selma, Alabama, to Montgomery to bring attention to the need for equal voting rights for all. State and local law enforcement officers tried to force them to stop. A Federal judge ruled that it was legal for them to march, even on public highways. About 3,000 people began again on Sunday, March 21. By the time they reached Montgomery on Thursday, the number of marchers had grown to 25,000. See photo on page 784.

Other African Americans began to use violence to force changes. From 1965 to 1967, several American cities experienced riots where people were hurt and property was destroyed. Congress passed and President Johnson signed the Voting Rights Act of 1965 that August. No longer could local officials keep blacks from voting. This was another great victory for civil rights activists.

In 1967 President Johnson appointed America's first African American Supreme Court Justice, Thurgood Marshall.

Selma-to-Montgomery March, March 21-25, 1965

The War in Vietnam

During the 1960s, the U.S. again became involved in a war overseas. This time it was in Vietnam. Just like Korea, Vietnam had divided into a Communist North and a free South after World War II (though in the 1960s this "free" government was corrupt). North Vietnam wanted to take over South Vietnam and make it Communist. Some South Vietnamese, called Viet Cong, supported the Communists taking over in the South. Because America wanted to help stop the spread of Communism, it began to help South Vietnam. People feared the "domino effect" that President Eisenhower had discussed (see page 747). The Soviet Union and Communist China were helping North Vietnam.

War Protesters in Front of the White House, 1968

In an effort to keep South Vietnam from being taken over by Communists, Eisenhower and then Kennedy sent military advisors to help South Vietnam. President Johnson decided to start sending American soldiers there in 1965. Eventually the number of Americans serving in Vietnam was about a half million. American soldiers were not accustomed to the jungle warfare used by the North Vietnamese and the Viet Cong. The fighting was hard and many American soldiers lost their lives.

President Johnson agonized over what to do; he suffered greatly from the stress brought on by the war. American citizens questioned whether America should be fighting a war in Vietnam. The United States did not have an all-volunteer Army. Instead, young men were drafted to serve. Many were only eighteen years old. Beginning in 1965, students on college campuses began to hold protests against the war. See protestor above. In the midst of the protests, other Americans were adamant that America must

Bob Hope Arrives in Vietnam to Entertain Troops

support her troops. America was becoming divided, not only over civil rights but also about the war in Vietnam.

In the photo at lower right on page 784, Bob Hope and other entertainers arrive in Vietnam to encourage the troops by presenting a Christmas show.

1968

At the beginning of 1968, the war in Vietnam grew worse. Many people blamed President Johnson. In March he announced that he would not run for re-election. A few days later, an assassin shot Martin Luther King Jr. while he was in Memphis, Tennessee, working for civil rights. After his death, African Americans in sixty cities began rioting.

Martin Luther King Jr. and Robert Kennedy

That spring John F. Kennedy's brother Robert decided to seek the Democratic nomination for President. Robert is pictured at right with Martin Luther King Jr. While Robert campaigned in Los Angeles, he was assassinated by a Palestinian man. The man hated Kennedy because Kennedy supported Israel.

Many young people continued to protest the war in Vietnam and to burn the draft cards issued to them by the Federal government.

Although many American families were far removed from riots, assassinations, and the war in Vietnam, these horrors came into their homes each evening on the television news. America suffered from one tragedy after another. Riots even broke out in the streets outside the Democratic convention that summer in Chicago.

Americans were divided between three candidates in the 1968 presidential election. Hubert Humphrey was the Democratic candidate, and Richard Nixon was the Republican. Segregationist Governor George Wallace of Alabama broke with the Democratic Party and ran as an independent. When the votes were counted, Nixon came out on top followed by Humphrey and then Wallace. The count was so close that Nixon waited until the day after the election to make his victory speech. He told the American people that he had been inspired during the campaign by a girl who held a sign saying, "Bring Us Together." Nixon said that was what he wanted to do. President and Mrs. Johnson retired to their Texas ranch after Nixon was inaugurated in January of 1969. Read about Johnson's life below.

Lyndon Baines Johnson
America's Thirty-Sixth President
November 22, 1963 - January 20, 1969

Lyndon Baines Johnson was born in Stonewall, Texas, in 1908. In the photo at left, he is six months old. He was the eldest of five children born to Sam and Rebekah Baines Johnson. His grandfather predicted that Lyndon would become a Senator. When he was four years old, he ran to the nearby one-room school to play with his cousins when they went out for recess. His mother convinced the teacher to let Lyndon stay and begin school. He sat in his teacher's lap and recited his lessons. In 1913 the Johnsons moved to nearby Johnson City, which had been named for his ancestors. The photo at right was taken about that time. LBJ graduated from high school, top in his class of six, when he was only fifteen years old.

After graduation Lyndon Johnson went to California where he worked as an elevator operator and at odd jobs. After a year, he came back to Texas and worked in road construction before borrowing money to enroll in a state teacher college. He dropped out for a while and taught fifth, sixth, and seventh grades and served as principal of a Mexican-American school. After graudation, he taught public speaking at Sam Houston High School in Houston.

In 1931 Johnson went to Washington to work for three years as secretary for the Representative from his district. On a visit home to Texas, he met Claudia Alta Taylor, known as Lady Bird. They were married in 1934. The photo at left was taken around the time of their marriage. At age twenty-six, Lyndon Johnson became Texas state director for one of Roosevelt's New Deal programs.

Johnson ran for a seat in the U.S. Congress in 1937. Though ten men ran, Johnson won by a good margin. He worked hard in the House of Representatives, serving until 1948. Just two days after the attack on Pearl Harbor, Johnson reported for duty in the U.S. Navy, becoming the first member of Congress to volunteer for active duty. He received a medal for gallantry. After serving just seven months, President Roosevelt ordered all members of Congress to return to their offices in Washington. Two years later, Lady Bird Johnson gave birth to their first daughter, Lynda Bird. Three years after that, Lady Bird gave birth to a second daughter, Luci Baines.

In 1948, the year that Truman defeated Dewey, Johnson ran successfully for the U.S. Senate. As pictured below, Johnson traveled around the state to campaign in a helicopter, a vehicle that

had just been invented seven years before. He became a leader in the Senate. In July of 1955 Johnson suffered a severe heart attack and spent the rest of the year recuperating at his LBJ Ranch near Stonewall. When he returned to the Senate, he worked for civil rights and helped to begin the National Aeronautics and Space Administration (NASA).

After failing to obtain the presidential nomination himself in 1960, Johnson became John F. Kennedy's running mate. He campaigned hard, helping Kennedy win the election. When Lyndon Johnson spoke to a joint session of Congress five days after John F. Kennedy's death, he said: "All I have I would have given gladly not to be standing here today."

When Lyndon and Lady Bird Johnson left the White House on January 20, 1969, after the inauguration of Richard Nixon, they went home to the LBJ ranch. In May of 1971, Johnson attended the dedication of the Lyndon Baines Johnson Library on the campus of the University of Texas at Austin. During his retirement, he wrote *The Vantage Point*, a memoir of his presidency. Lyndon and Lady Bird are pictured at right in 1972 on their ranch. Johnson died at his ranch on January 22, 1973. He is buried there in the family cemetery.

Major changes occurred in education during the 1960s. The U.S. Congress passed a bill promising Federal money to elementary schools and high schools. When Johnson signed the bill, the teacher who had taught him when he was four years old was sitting next to him. With the Federal government giving more money to public schools, it started making rules that those schools had to follow and local citizens began to lose control of what their children learned.

Since the days of the thirteen colonies, public school teachers had read the Bible to students and led them in prayer. Two rulings by the U.S. Supreme Court in the early 1960s began to change that. The Court ruled that a school could not require a prayer to be said at the start of each school day. The following year, the Court declared that a state could not require a daily reading from the Bible in public school classrooms. To make sure they did not get sued, many schools quit having any Bible reading or group prayers. This weakened the influence of Christian thinking in public schools. The opportunity to study the Bible and pray during school is a great benefit to homeschooling families.

Devote yourselves to prayer, keeping alert in it with an attitude of thanksgiving.
Colossians 4:2

Activities for Lesson 126

Thinking Biblically – Read Matthew 10:28-31 and John 16:33. In your notebook, write one page about a godly response to anxious and troubled times, when there is much to fear.

Literature – Read "The Exciting Adventure of Space" in *We the People*, pages 167-168.

Creative Writing – In your notebook, write two letters to a member of Congress, each one-half to one page long, as if they were written in the 1960s during the Vietnam War. In one letter, express the opinions of a person in favor of the war. In the other, express the opinions of a person who wants America to get out of the war.

Timeline – In *Timeline of America the Beautiful* next to 1963, write: Martin Luther King Jr. gives his "I Have a Dream" speech in Washington, D.C.

Student Workbook or Lesson Review – If you are using one of these optional books, complete the assignment for Lesson 126.

In the 1960s . . .

- The Beatles, a British rock and roll group, performed on *The Ed Sullivan Show* in 1964.

- Some young people became part of the "hippie" movement.

- In 1967 the Green Bay Packers won the first Super Bowl ever played.

- Popular attire for young people included jeans, Nehru jackets, go-go boots, and love beads.

Living in the White House

President and Mrs. Kennedy arrive at the White House on February 4, 1961 with their children, Caroline, 3, and John, 2 months.

When three-year-old Caroline and two-month-old John Kennedy arrived at the White House with their parents on February 4, 1961, they were the first young children to move into the White House since Teddy Roosevelt brought his family there in 1901. When the children arrived, the ground was covered with snow. A big snowman with outstretched arms welcomed them. Jackie Kennedy had asked the White House gardeners to build him. In the photo at left, the Kennedy family enters through the south portico.

Mrs. Kennedy had instructed remodelers to add a small kitchen, dining room, and pantry to the family living quarters of the White House. She also told them to brighten John's room with blue paint and Caroline's with pale pink. A bedroom for the children's British nanny, Miss Shaw, was prepared between the children's rooms.

Since the Kennedys were a wealthy family, they were used to having a butler, a maid, and a cook; but their new home had hundreds of servants who cared for the First Family and all the people they entertained in the 132-room mansion.

Restoring the White House

First Lady Jacqueline Bouvier Kennedy had been educated in fine arts and literature and she loved history. These interests showed when she entertained and when she chose a special project to complete as First Lady. The White House was beautiful on the outside; but when Mrs. Kennedy toured the interior with Mamie Eisenhower, she was dismayed at its condition. Mrs. Kennedy wanted the White House to tell the story of American history and she wanted it to be decorated in a grand fashion similar to palaces in Europe.

While Jacqueline Kennedy rested in Palm Beach, Florida, after the birth of her son John, she studied the decorations that had been used in the White House in the 1800s. Mrs. Kennedy wanted to copy curtains, carpets, and furniture that had been used in the past. First Ladies Grace Coolidge, Lou Hoover, and Mamie Eisenhower had tried to make similar changes before, but Jackie had the advantage of having very wealthy friends who could make generous donations.

Within a month after her husband took office, Mrs. Kennedy formed a Fine Arts Committee. She personally asked Henry du Pont, founder of the Winterthur Museum, Garden, and Library in Delaware, to be its chairman. The du Ponts are one of America's wealthiest families. Their family wealth was first earned in the manufacture of gunpowder in the 1800s. In the 1900s the du Pont industries grew to become the nation's largest chemical corporation. Henry du Pont was an antique expert and collector.

Jacqueline Kennedy's First Formal Portrait as First Lady, 1961

Mrs. Kennedy made her project known to the American people. She made it clear that her work was restoring the White House and not simply redecorating it. Citizens began to send letters that described Presidents' furniture that had been passed down in their families. Though most antiques used in the restoration were purchased through antique dealers and members of the Fine Arts Committee, a few important pieces of furniture were returned to the White House by families who had cherished them for generations.

In November of 1961, Mrs. Kennedy helped complete *The White House: An Historic Guide*. In addition to donations from wealthy patrons, sales of the guide book also brought in money to complete the project.

Though the work continued into 1963, Jacqueline Kennedy hosted a one-hour televised tour of the White House on Valentine's Day in 1962 to show the American people what had been accomplished thus far. She shared the mansion's history with viewers and told them that the White House was not only a home, but a place for Americans to visit. Fifty-six million Americans watched the First Lady's tour. See portrait of Mrs. Kennedy above.

School in the Sun Room

Jackie Kennedy turned the third floor sunroom into a preschool room for Caroline and children from the neighborhood where they had lived while her husband was a Senator. President Taft had the first White House sunroom built because he wanted a cool place for his family to sleep on hot summer nights. After the Coolidges improved the sunroom in 1927, Grace Coolidge called it the Sky Parlor. Mamie Eisenhower played bridge there; and when the Johnsons moved in, it became a hangout for their teenage daughters.

Visiting with Daddy and Mommy

The Kennedy children visited with their father before he went to his office in the morning, and the whole family went to the family quarters after lunch to take naps. John and Caroline spent much of the day with Miss Shaw, but sometimes they got to visit their father while he was working in the Oval Office. See the top left photo on page 790.

Caroline and John Kennedy visit their dad in the Oval Office.

John Kennedy plays with John Jr. on the West Wing colonnade.

Sometimes President Kennedy clapped his hands after Caroline's outdoor recess to signal that she and her friends could come and visit with him. On the day Kennedy learned of the Soviet missiles in Cuba, he took a break from his meeting and clapped for his daughter; but she did not come. A short time later she came running into his secretary's office. The secretary told her that her father was in the Cabinet Room and that she couldn't go in there. Caroline said that she had to go. She went in and told her dad that she would have come sooner, but her teacher wouldn't let her. Her daddy told her that it was okay.

The First Lady Holding John Kennedy Jr.

In the photo at top right, John plays with his father on the West Wing colonnade. Jackie took John outside for an hour each morning while Caroline was at school. See photo above. Both children often ate lunch with their mother. They ate dinner with Miss Shaw, but afterwards their mother read to them. If their parents were not hosting guests, the children spent time with them before bedtime. Sometimes Caroline and her mother went upstairs to play in the school room. If Mrs. Kennedy was preparing for a formal event, the children played in her room while she dressed. In the photo at left, John plays with her pearl necklace.

John plays with his mother's pearls.

Harry Truman plays piano in the East Room, 1961

Sometimes Caroline and John had to stay at home with Miss Shaw while their parents went overseas, but Mrs. Kennedy sent postcards every day.

Entertaining at the White House

American Presidents and their wives have enjoyed formal social gatherings since George Washington danced the minuet at his first inaugural ball. Presidents host dignitaries from America and from around the world. They have a busy social calendar full of dinners, luncheons, parties, concerts, receptions, and ceremonies.

First Ladies have their own individual tastes when it comes to entertaining at the White House. Jacqueline Kennedy carefully planned the details of official dinners, receptions, and parties. She used elegant glassware and embroidered table linens. A French chef planned the menu. After dinner, guests enjoyed entertainment such as opera songs and scenes from Broadway musicals. As seen in the photo above, the Kennedys hosted former President Harry Truman and other guests in the East Room in 1961. Truman entertained those assembled by playing the piano. In 1947 Truman had become the first President to deliver a televised address from the White House.

John, Jacqueline, and Caroline Kennedy at Glen Ora, their Country Home in Virginia

First Pets of the Kennedy Family

The Kennedy family already had four dogs, plus Caroline's cat Tom Kitten, when the President and First Lady visited with Soviet Premier Khrushchev in June 1961. After their meeting, the premier sent Mrs. Kennedy a dog named Pushinka. She was the daughter of

The Kennedys and some of the family dogs visit Joseph and Rose Kennedy's vacation home in Hyannisport on Cape Cod in Massachusetts.

Strelka, a dog that had circled the earth in a Russian spaceship. When Pushinka and the Kennedy's Welsh terrier Charlie had four puppies, Mrs. Kennedy and some of the White House staff held a contest to give two of them away. Ten thousand children wrote letters, telling why they could provide a good home for a puppy. Two winners received puppies, while relatives of the Kennedys took the other two. The Kennedys are pictured at left with some of their dogs.

Vice President Lyndon Johnson gave Caroline a pony named Macaroni. In the photo above, Caroline

On May 29, 1963, the White House staff gave President Kennedy a birthday party.

rides Macaroni at the family's country home in Virginia, while her mother gives John a ride.

A Change of Style

The First Family spends a great deal of time with the White House staff, and they often become close to one another. When President Kennedy turned forty-five years old in May of 1963, the staff gave him a party. See photo at left.

Just six months later, after President Kennedy died, the Johnson family moved into the White House at 1600 Pennsylvania Avenue. See Mrs. Johnson carrying a portrait, the Johnson's daughter Luci, and the family dogs, Him and Her, below. They are being welcomed by the chief usher of the White House.

The Kennedys had brought their sophisticated lifestyle to the White House. While Jacqueline and Caroline Kennedy rode horses on their country estate, Lyndon Johnson donned a cowboy hat and hit the dusty trails of his Texas ranch in his Cadillac convertible. As seen in the photos below, the Johnsons sometimes dressed in formal attire and attended grand parties as the Kennedys had done; but they also brought a down-home quality to the presidency.

The chief usher of the White House welcomes Lady Bird and Luci Johnson and the family dogs, Him and Her.

The photos at the top of page 793 show President Johnson at a dinner in the State Dining Room and hosting a barbecue during a Latin American ambassadors weekend at the LBJ Ranch.

Mrs. Johnson in Her 1965 Inaugural Ball Gown; the Johnsons Dancing in the White House; the Johnsons in Formal Attire

792

A Dinner in the White House State Dining Room

A Latin American Ambassadors Weekend at the LBJ Ranch

Yuki, President Johnson, and Grandson Patrick Nugent

First Pets of the Johnson Family

While the Johnsons lived in the White House, Him sired eight puppies. In the photo at right below, Johnson shows the puppies to a young visitor. Lyndon Johnson adored his dog Yuki, a stray that his daughter Luci found at a service station in Texas. The President and Yuki entertained people by singing duets. In the photo at left, taken at the Johnsons' ranch, he entertains his grandson Patrick Lyndon Nugent. In the photo at lower left, Johnson entertains David Bruce, Ambassador to the United Kingdom.

Ambassador David Bruce, Yuki, and President Johnson

A Young Visitor with President Johnson and Him's Puppies

A White House Wedding

On December 9, 1967, President Johnson gave his daughter Lynda in marriage to Marine Captain Charles S. Robb. The ceremony and the reception that followed were held in the East Room of the White House. Robb later served as Governor of Virginia from 1982

Top: The Father of the Bride Gets Dressed;
Center: Captain and Mrs. Robb;
Bottom: The Johnsons Dance at the Reception

to 1986. From 1989 to 2001, he represented Virginia in the United States Senate. See wedding photos at left.

Dolley Madison arranged the first wedding ceremony in the White House in 1812, when her widowed sister married a Supreme Court justice. Many others have married there since then, including the children of eight Presidents: James Monroe's daughter Maria in 1820; John Quincy Adams' son John in 1828; John Tyler's daughter Elizabeth in 1842; Ulysses Grant's daughter Nellie in 1874; Teddy Roosevelt's daughter Alice in 1906; both of Woodrow Wilson's daughters, Jessie in 1913 and Eleanor in 1914; Lyndon Johnson's daughter Lynda Bird in 1967; and Richard Nixon's daughter Tricia in 1971. In attendance at the Johnson-Robb wedding was Theodore Roosevelt's daughter and former White House bride, Alice Roosevelt Longworth. Notice that all of these Presidents' children were daughters, except for the son of John Quincy Adams. As discussed on page 471, the first President to be married in the White House was President Grover Cleveland, who married Frances Folsom in the Blue Room in 1886.

Family Togetherness

Like other parents and grandparents the world over, Presidents and First Ladies enjoy being with their children and grandchildren. At the top of page 795 is President Johnson with his daughter Luci Nugent and his first grandchild Patrick. In the next photo, daughter Lynda Robb holds Lucinda, the Johnson's first granddaughter.

In the photo at the bottom of page 795, the Johnsons gather with their daughters and grandchildren for a Christmas Eve photo in the Yellow Oval Room. Benjamin Harrison was the first President to bring a Christmas tree inside the White House. Now the White House has many Christmas traditions such as sending official Christmas cards and having an elaborate gingerbread house on display. In 1923 President Coolidge placed the first National Christmas Tree in Lafayette Park on the White House grounds. See the 1965 National Christmas Tree at the top right of page 795.

Left: Johnson visits his daughter Luci and grandson Patrick in the hospital.
Center: Patrick delights his grandfather. Right: The National Christmas Tree, 1965
Below: Lynda Johnson Robb holds the Johnsons' first granddaughter Lucinda.

Many who have served the American people have done so in order to bless Americans in their own day and also those who are yet unborn, especially those in their own families. The best way we can seek the good of future generations is by prayer and service to God.

But the lovingkindness of the Lord is
from everlasting to everlasting on those who fear Him,
and his righteousness to children's children,
to those who keep His covenant
and remember His precepts to do them.
Psalm 103:17-18

Activities for Lesson 127

Vocabulary – Find each of these words in a dictionary, then find the definition that corresponds to the way the word is used in this lesson. Copy the words and definitions into your notebook: portico, dismay, colonnade, minuet, linen.

Creative Writing – In your notebook, write a letter to the current First Family. You might want to ask questions, send well-wishes, or express your opinion on a topic of national importance. Include your name and return mailing address on the envelope and letter. Neatly copy your letter on stationery, and mail it to:

> The White House
> 1600 Pennsylvania Avenue NW
> Washington, DC 20500

Timeline – In *Timeline of America the Beautiful* next to 1947, write: Truman delivers the first televised address from the White House.

Family Activity – Complete the White House Family Research Project. See page 977 for instructions.

Student Workbook or Lesson Review – If you are using one of these optional books, complete the assignment for Lesson 127.

Luci, Patrick, Lady Bird, Lyndon, Lynda, and Lucinda
with Yuki on Christmas Eve, 1968

The Interstate System

What do you see when your family drives on the Interstate? Cars, vans, pickup trucks, motor homes, ambulances, tour buses, and semi trucks. Where are the people in these vehicles going? To work in a tall office building. To deliver baby chicks to a chicken farm. To see a friend in the hospital. To deliver vegetables to a warehouse. To the Grand Canyon. The answers seem almost endless.

The Interstate system on which these vehicles travel today is the largest public works project America has ever attempted. Construction began in the 1950s and continued through the sixties and into the seventies. See photo below. Today's American Interstates cover over 46,000 miles.

The massive project involved the cooperation of every state. Each state transportation department decided on the design and location of the roads within its borders. The states were responsible for buying the land and constructing the highways. The Interstate system cost $129 billion. Ninety percent of the construction cost was financed by the Federal government with money collected through gasoline taxes and fees paid by commercial trucks. The states paid the remaining ten percent. The Interstates belong to the states, not to the Federal government, and the states are responsible for keeping them in good condition.

Building I-95 in Downtown Richmond, Virginia, 1958

Dwight D. Eisenhower National System of Interstate and Defense Highways

Though Franklin Roosevelt and Harry Truman had realized a need for a better road system in America, it was Dwight D. Eisenhower who got the project moving. Roosevelt thought three toll superhighways going from north to south and three going from east to west would be enough. Eisenhower's experiences gave him a much grander vision. While in Germany during

World War II, Eisenhower was impressed with Germany's Autobahn system and the way it helped with the transportation of military vehicles. The Autobahn reminded him of the military convoy he had experienced after World War I (see page 717). In his book *At Ease*, Eisenhower said, "The old convoy had started me thinking about good, two-lane highways, but Germany had made me see the wisdom of broader ribbons across the land."

Eisenhower Signs the Federal Highway Act of 1954

When Eisenhower became President, he made a better road system for America a top priority. The threat of the Cold War made the need urgent. If America got involved in a war at home, Eisenhower wanted a good way to mobilize troops. In 1954 he began trying to gain support from Congressmen. That year Congress passed the Federal Highway Act of 1954. It was a small step, but at least it was a step in the right direction. In the photo above, Eisenhower signs that bill.

When a conference of state governors met later that year, Eisenhower was not able to attend. He sent Vice President Richard Nixon to deliver his speech. Nixon told the governors that the bill recently passed was a good start but that America needed a system that would reduce highway accidents, detours, and traffic jams, and allow better truck transportation. He said that America's roads had "appalling inadequacies to meet the demands of catastrophe or defense, should an atomic war come."

In 1955 Eisenhower had a difficult time convincing Congress of his ideas for how to pay for these new roads. In his State of the Union address in 1956, he brought up the issue again. Finally in June of 1956, the U.S. Senate and House of Representatives came to an agreement and passed the Federal Aid Highway Act of 1956. Eisenhower was in Walter Reed Hospital with a minor ailment at the time. He signed the bill in the hospital.

In 1991 the Interstate system was officially named the Dwight D. Eisenhower National System of Interstate and Defense Highways. The U.S. Secretary of Transportation worked with the Federal Highway Administration, the American Association of State Highway and Transportation Officials, and representatives of President Eisenhower's family to create an appropriate sign to be placed along Interstate highways. The sign chosen was a thirty-six by thirty-six inch square with the design pictured at left. When the design was

unveiled in 1993, President Eisenhower's son John, granddaughter Susan, and other family members were present, along with Senators and members of the House of Representatives.

Interstate 80 is one of the longest highways in the system. It begins near New York City and ends at San Francisco. After it enters Ohio, it follows the same general route that Eisenhower traveled with the Army convoy back in 1919.

Rules for the Roads

The Federal government made guidelines for Interstates. The most important difference between Interstates and other highways is that Interstates have limited access. The entire Interstate system of more than 46,000 miles has only about 16,000 entrance ramps, usually at least one mile apart in cities and three miles apart in rural areas. By spacing out entrance ramps

Overpasses and Underpasses

and exit ramps, vehicles can travel more quickly and safely. Because of their limited access, Interstates are also called expressways. When a vehicle enters an Interstate, it can keep moving as long as traffic is not backed up. It does not have to stop for stop signs or traffic lights. When another road crosses it, the Interstate route either goes under the road through an underpass or over it on an overpass. See overpasses and underpasses above.

Interstates have at least two lanes going in each direction. Lanes must be twelve feet wide. Shoulders must be ten feet wide on the right and four feet wide on the left. The design must allow vehicles to travel at seventy miles per hour, except in cities and through mountains. At first overpasses had to be fourteen feet high. This was later raised to 16.5 feet so that taller military vehicles could go under them.

Interstate 5 Through Camp Pendleton
Marine Base in California

Interstate 5 Through San Diego, California

Interstate Signs and Numbers

Interstates that run north and south have odd numbers and the main ones end in five. Notice the north-south Interstates at right. In the top photo at right, vehicles are traveling through a Marine base.

Interstates running east and west have even numbers; main east-west routes end in zero. Notice east-west Interstates on page 799. Interstate loops that go around cities have three digits, as do short Interstate spurs. The Interstate highway numbers in Alaska are preceded by an A and those in Hawaii are preceded by an H.

Interstate 65 Through Nashville, Tennessee

The shield-shaped Interstate sign, pictured at left, was chosen on August 14, 1957. Several state highway officials proposed designs for an Interstate sign. The design chosen was submitted by Texas. In 1967 the shield received a trademark registration number so that private businesses could not make signs that look the same, thereby confusing drivers.

Highway Safety

Interstates are the safest roads in America. For every one hundred miles driven, the number of fatal accidents on Interstates is half that of other roads. Since the first Interstates were built, highway construction technology has advanced and the rate of traffic accident deaths per year has dropped significantly. Shoulders are now wider. Pavement materials resist skidding. Guardrails are stronger. Signs are clearer. Sign posts and utility poles break more easily, causing less damage when they are struck. Vehicles are safer now, as well, with shatterproof glass, padded interiors, air bags, and safety belts.

I-8 Through California's Imperial Valley

I-80 Through Omaha, Nebraska

Interstate Tidbits

- Two states claim to have the first section of an Interstate highway. Both are sections of I-70. One is in Missouri and the other is in Kansas. However, limited access freeways, like the Pennsylvania Turnpike, the Hutchinson River Parkway in New York, and the Merritt Parkway in Connecticut were already in use in 1956. Though not constructed with money authorized in 1956, theses roads were made part of the Interstate system at that time.
- Many state departments of transportation have planted wildflowers along their Interstates. They provide beauty and reduce the need for mowing.
- The longest east to west Interstate is I-90, which runs from Boston, Massachusetts, to Seattle, Washington, and is over 3,000 miles long.
- The longest north-south Interstate is I-95. It goes from Maine to Miami, passing through each of the original thirteen colonies plus Maine, Florida, and the District of Columbia. It is almost 2,000 miles long.
- Interstate highways include about twenty-nine miles of tunnels. Most go through mountains or under rivers.

Impact of the Interstate System on America

In President Eisenhower's 1963 book *Mandate for Change: 1953-1956*, he said:

> More than any single action by the government since the end of the war, this one would change the face of America with straightaways, cloverleaf turns, bridges, and elongated parkways. Its impact on the American economy—the jobs it would produce in manufacturing and construction, the rural areas it would open up—was beyond calculation.

The impact of Interstates on America has been both positive and negative. Once-thriving small towns have lost business because the chosen route of the nearest Interstate does not go through them. Some of these small towns have lost population. Better road transportation has encouraged Americans to move out of cities. While many people have been able to experience country and suburban life, commuting has caused Americans to be more dependent on petroleum and has contributed to air pollution.

Interstate exits usually attract national restaurant and service station chains. This makes the travel experience less interesting than it was when people stopped in the business districts of small towns and large cities or at "Mom and Pop" stores and restaurants along the road. However, Interstates have made it easier for people to travel across the country, giving them the opportunity to experience more of America.

Interstates have greatly expanded American business and industry. They have made it easier for trucks to transport goods. Though only one percent of America's roads are part of the Interstate system, they carry nearly one-fourth of the country's passenger traffic and about forty-five percent of its freight. Interstates have made it possible for people to do business in a much larger geographic area. When a product is shipped, the item will often travel on an Interstate for at least part of the way.

> The way of the lazy is as a hedge of thorns,
> but the path of the upright is a highway.
> Proverbs 15:19

Activities for Lesson 128

Thinking Biblically – The Bible uses the idea of a road as a metaphor for life's journey. Copy Matthew 7:13-14 into your notebook.

Map Study – Complete the assignment for Lesson 128 on Map 3 "American Landmarks" in *Maps of America the Beautiful*.

Vocabulary – Write five sentences in your notebook, using one of these words in each: convoy, mobilize, appalling, trademark, suburban. Check in a dictionary if you need help with their definitions.

Timeline – In *Timeline of America the Beautiful* next to 1956, write: The Interstate highway system is created.

Student Workbook or Lesson Review – If you are using one of these optional books, complete the assignment for Lesson 128.

Popular Toys of the Decade

Etch-a-Sketch (1960)
Game of Life (1960)
Troll Dolls (1961)
Easy Bake Oven (1963)
G.I. Joe Dolls (1964)
Operation (1965)
Twister (1966)
Battleship (1967)
Lite Brite (1967)
Hot Wheels (1968)

God Created the Great Salt Lake

God created the Great Salt Lake. He filled it with salt—and with life. Millions of birds live along its shores or visit the lake during their annual migrations. People earn billions of dollars each year by harvesting valuable products from the lake.

The Great Salt Lake lies within the Great Basin Desert, which includes most of western Utah, almost all of the state of Nevada, and portions of Idaho, Oregon, and California. The lake lies entirely within the state of Utah in the eastern portion of the Great Basin. In 1986 a portion of the Great Basin near Baker, Nevada, was set aside as Great Basin National Park. Native Americans have lived in the Great Basin for centuries (see Lesson 3).

Great Salt Lake in American History

In 1776 Native Americans told Spanish missionaries about the Great Salt Lake, but the Spaniards did not see it themselves. The first white person known to have visited the lake was fur trapper Jim Bridger in 1824. Look at the photos of the lake at left. Imagine what it must have been like to discover it. John C. Fremont made scientific investigations of the lake in 1845. According to legend, Kit Carson, who accompanied Fremont, carved a cross on a rock near the highest elevation on Fremont Island in the northern part of the lake. The carving is still visible today. (Bridger, Fremont, and Carson were discussed on pages 252 and 253.)

The Great Salt Lake has eleven islands. Antelope is the largest. A ranch house on Antelope Island that was built in 1848 is considered the oldest structure in Utah still on its original foundation. Today almost one-tenth of Antelope Island is a state park. Conservationists

Views of the Great Salt Lake

Sunset Over Antelope Island

A Balloon from the Antelope Island Balloon Festival

introduced buffalo to the island in the late 1800s, and the island continues to have a thriving herd.

A judge and his family lived on Fremont Island from 1884 to 1891. Others have also lived there. People tried to homestead on Gunnison and Carrington Islands, but they were not successful. See Antelope Island photos at left.

About ten miles west of the Great Salt Lake is Promontory Point, Utah, the site where the last spike was driven for the transcontinental railroad in 1869 (see Lesson 73). To avoid trains having to climb the Promontory Mountains, the Southern Pacific Railroad built a new rail line across the Great Salt Lake in 1902. Trains crossed the lake on a twelve-mile wooden trestle.

Between 1957 and 1959, the trestle was replaced with a solid causeway made of rock, sand, and gravel. It has two fifteen-foot culverts to let water pass between the northern and southern parts of the lake. The causeway keeps water from flowing freely into the northern arm of the lake, so that part has become saltier. The types of algae and bacteria growing in the northern environment make the water look pinkish purple, while the southern part looks blue. Below are a NASA image of the Great Salt Lake and a photo of the northern arm's purple waters taken from Gunnison Island.

Great and Salty

Great Salt Lake is true to its name. It is great, and it is salty. The size of the lake is constantly changing, depending on weather conditions in the region. Its average length is seventy-five miles, its average width is thirty-five miles, and its average area is 1,700 square miles. This makes it the largest lake in America after the Great Lakes. It reached its largest size in 1986-1987 and shrank to its smallest size on record in 1963. That year it was less than half as large as it was in 1986-1987. At thirty-three feet deep, the lake is relatively shallow compared to its length and width. The Great Salt Lake is so large that it causes lake effect snow in nearby areas that are downwind.

The Great Salt Lake contains about 4.3 billion tons of salt. The Bear, Jordan, and Weber Rivers flow into it, as do smaller streams. The Ogden River is also a major contributor because it enters into the Weber River at Ogden, Utah, about ten miles east of the lake.

NASA Image of the Great Salt Lake

Photo Taken from a Peak on Gunnison Island

When God created the world, He put salt in the ground. As rivers and streams flow over rocks and soil, they pick up salt and other minerals. Each year God sends about 2.2 million tons of salt into the Great Salt Lake by way of rivers and streams. Since no rivers or streams flow out of the lake, the water sits there with no place to go. As the water evaporates, it leaves salt and other minerals behind. Just as the size of the lake varies depending on weather conditions in the area, the saltiness of the water varies, too.

Companies remove about two million tons of salt from the Great Salt Lake each year. They pay a fee to the state of Utah, which owns the lake. Among other uses, some salt is pressed into pellets used in water softeners and some into salt blocks used for livestock. It is not considered pure enough for human food, so it does not end up on your dinner table.

Avocets at the Bear River Migratory Bird Refuge

Surrounding the Lake

Salt Lake City, the state capital of Utah, is to the southeast of the Great Salt Lake. Near the lake are the Lakeside Mountains, the Wasatch Range, and the Hansel Mountains. The Promontory Mountains extend onto a peninsula jutting into the northeast part of the lake. The Great Salt Lake is a vital stop on the Pacific Flyway, a route used by migratory birds. The lake is surrounded by the Gillmor Bird Sanctuary, the Inland Sea Shorebird Preserve, the Nature Conservancy Layton Wetlands Preserve, many wildlife management areas, and the Bear River Migratory Bird Refuge, pictured at left.

Many of the beaches around the Great Salt Lake are made of oolitic sand. At the center of an oolite is a core, often a tiny piece of mineral or a fecal pellet of a brine shrimp (tiny creatures that inhabit the lake). Calcium carbonate builds up around this core in concentric layers, forming in much the same way as a pearl does. Oolites vary in color from brown to white, are shaped like a jelly bean, and have a pearl-like shine.

Tiny Creatures in the Great Salt Lake

God created all life on earth and the habitat that each kind of living being needs. Some of these habitats are extreme, but God has created creatures ideally suited to the extreme environments. Cold ocean depths have life, the hot waters of Yellowstone National Park have life, and the extremely salty Great Salt Lake has life.

About a dozen species of algae and another dozen species of bacteria have been found in the Great Salt Lake. Chemical reactions between the lake and its microorganisms help form limestone reefs at the bottom of the lake and provide nourishment for the brine fly and brine shrimp.

Two species of brine flies live at the Great Salt Lake. Females lay eggs continuously throughout the summer, and these eggs hatch quickly. As larvae, they feed on the algae and bacteria that grow on rocks, on logs, and on the lake bottom. The larvae receive all their necessary oxygen from the algae. When they reach the pupae stage, they find a floating object, attach to it, and form a chrysalis, similar to a caterpillar's cocoon. When they come out of the chrysalis, they trap air bubbles, which cause them to float to the surface. Winds blowing across the lake carry the pupae to shore. There they quickly grow into adulthood.

Brine flies swarm in such large numbers that they look like dense clouds on the lake's beaches. In summer flies may number as many as 370 million per mile! During their brief adult lives, which last only three to five days, they reproduce and the cycle begins again.

Brine shrimp, also called sea monkeys, are a popular aquarium pet. See photo on page 805. Adult brine shrimp feed on algae that live between the surface and the bottom of the Great Salt Lake. They also graze on algae that grows on the limestone reefs. God shows His creative powers in these tiny creatures, too. The brine shrimp hatches from a thick-shelled egg, called a cyst. Sometimes weather and other conditions at the lake are so good that a female brine shrimp can lay up to three hundred eggs every four days, but usually they lay eggs about three times per year. Brine shrimp cysts are so small that fifty can fit on the head of a pin.

Brine shrimp cysts float on top of the lake. The shrimp are so numerous in the Great Salt Lake that their floating cysts sometimes make brown-red streaks on the surface of the water. The eggs are so strong that they can lie dormant for years if they stay dry. When they become wet, they hatch and grow into healthy adults.

Aquarium owners can purchase cysts and watch them grow into adults. Between the time one hatches from the egg until it becomes an adult, this fascinating creature molts (sheds its skin) fifteen times. The brine shrimp industry at the Great Salt Lake began in the 1950s, when the adults were collected to be sold as aquarium food. In the 1970s, the industry began to concentrate mostly on cysts, which were used to feed shrimp, pawns, and some fish raised on fish farms overseas. The harvesting of brine shrimp cysts in the Great Salt Lake is a multi-million dollar industry.

Great Salt Lake at Ogden Bay

An aquatic insect called the corixid is also found at the Great Salt Lake. Corixids feed on brine flies and brine shrimp. These insects are also called "water boatmen." Shore birds feed on brine flies, brine shrimp, and corixids.

Though the Great Salt Lake receives waste water from nearby cities and from industry, its pollution levels are low. Evidently the habitat cleans itself.

Birds at the Great Salt Lake

Over 7.5 million birds use the Great Salt Lake annually. It is crucial for migrating birds. By creating the lake so that it is constantly changing, God provides for the needs of many different kinds of birds which arrive at various times during the year. God has also created many kinds of habitats there. Some birds need a specific habitat and others are at home in more than one. Eared grebes feed in the open salt waters of the lake. Over 2.5 million of the

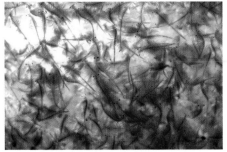

Brine Shrimp Shown at Actual Size

birds that come to the Great Salt Lake are eared grebes. See photo at lower left.

Some birds visiting the Great Salt Lake need fresh water, which is available in the rivers that flow into the lake. Some even find fresh water on the lake itself. At times, especially in winter, a layer of fresh water floats atop the salt water of the Great Salt Lake.

Some kinds of birds find what they need along saltwater shorelines and beaches. There they feast on the clouds of brine flies. Common goldeneyes and phalaropes, pictured at right, eat adult brine shrimp and brine fly pupae. The estimated population of the various species of phalaropes in the world is 1.5 million. About one-third of these rest and feed at the Great Salt Lake. Other species of birds nest in or nearby the edges of the riverbanks that empty into the lake.

The area where freshwater rivers flow into the salty waters of the lake is called the saltwater-freshwater interface. This area attracts tens of thousands of birds of various kinds. During late summer and fall, black-necked stilts and American avocets, like those pictured at right, are found there.

The Great Salt Lake and its tributaries are surrounded with wetlands; some are salt marshes and others are freshwater wetlands. Avocets and stilts nest in salt marshes. The freshwater wetlands are home to the greatest variety of birds in the Great Salt Lake region. One is the white-faced ibis. See photo at the top of page 806.

Common Goldeneye

Red-Necked Phalarope

American Avocet

Eared Grebe

Black-Necked Stilt

805

People have built hundreds of miles of levees and dikes in the Great Salt Lake area. These man-made structures provide nesting sites for some birds. Flocks of ibises will fly twenty miles or more to feed in a farmer's irrigated pasture. Sandhill cranes even nest in them.

American white pelicans and other birds nest on islands in the Great Salt Lake, as do some duck species. Notice the white pelicans pictured at right.

Some islands have rocky shores. Gunnison Island is an important feeding and resting site. As many as 20,000 pelicans nest there each year. During research completed between 1972 and 1974, 110 different species visited the island.

When thinking about the abundant life of the Great Salt Lake, remember what God said to the creatures He created on the fifth day of the creation week.

White-Faced Ibis

American White Pelicans

God blessed them, saying, "Be fruitful and multiply, and fill the waters in the seas and let birds multiply on the earth." Genesis 1:22

Activities for Lesson 129

Map Study – Complete the assignments for Lesson 129 on Map 2 "God's Wonders" and Map 29 "The Great Salt Lake" in *Maps of America the Beautiful*.

Literature – Read "Immense Flocks" in *We the People*, pages 169-170.

Creative Writing – Write a short story of two or more pages with Utah's Great Salt Lake as the setting.

Timeline – In *Timeline of America the Beautiful* next to 1986, write: Great Basin National Park is established.

Student Workbook or Lesson Review – If you are using one of these optional books, complete the assignment for Lesson 129.

Billy Graham, Missionary to the World

Whether the story of Christ is told in a huge stadium, across the desk of a powerful leader, or shared with a golfing companion, it satisfies a common hunger. All over the world, whenever I meet people face-to-face, I am made aware of this personal need among the famous and successful, as well as the lonely and obscure.

These are the thoughts of evangelist Billy Graham, who has probably preached to more people than anyone who has ever lived and who has met with every U.S. President from Harry Truman to Barack Obama.

Billy Graham's Childhood and Young Adulthood

William Franklin "Billy" Graham Jr. was born in Charlotte, North Carolina, in 1918. His parents were William Franklin "Frank"and Morrow Coffey Graham. Billy grew up on his parents' dairy farm. When he was a child, his family gathered together for prayer and Bible study. In years to come, Billy would say about his mother, "Of all the people I have ever known, she had the greatest influence on me."

When Billy was fifteen years old, he attended a revival led by evangelist Mordecai Ham. That night he made a decision to give his life to Jesus Christ. When Billy was eighteen, he left home for the summer to work as a Fuller Brush salesman. In those days, it was common for salesmen to knock on doors and try to sell household items, books, or other goods. During that summer, Billy Graham sold brushes door-to-door in North and South Carolina. That fall he attended Bob Jones College, then located in Tennessee. He left after a few months.

Billy Graham's mother had read in *Moody Monthly* magazine about Florida Bible Institute, called FBI. Billy decided to attend the school and early in 1937 the Grahams drove him there. While their son was at the institute, William and Morrow Graham went to an upstairs room each morning at 10:00 a.m. to pray for him.

FBI was dedicated to teaching students the Bible and training them in practical ministry. On Sunday night, March 28, 1937, Billy preached his first sermon. To prepare for preaching he would go outside, memorize a paragraph from another preacher's sermon, and then practice out loud. During his time at FBI, Billy continued preaching and began reaching out to hurting people.

After Graham received a bachelor of theology degree from Florida Bible Institute, he enrolled at Wheaton College in Illinois. There he continued to preach. While at Wheaton, Billy rented a room from a local resident. She remembered him coming home from school happy and recalled the day he told her that by God's grace, he was going to serve Him. In 1943 he graduated with a bachelor of arts in anthropology. That same year he married fellow student Ruth McCue Bell, the daughter of missionaries to China.

Graham's Work with Youth for Christ

After graduation, Graham became the pastor of a fifty-member Baptist church in the Chicago suburb of Western Springs. During the year and a half he served there, the church doubled in size and changed its name from Western Springs Baptist Church to Village Church, so that it would attract non-Baptists. He began to do a radio program called *Songs in the Night*. He asked well-known gospel singer George Beverly Shea to sing on the program. Shea agreed and also joined Village Church.

Shea was involved in a national movement called Youth for Christ, which held Saturday night meetings for teens and young adults. Graham began to work full-time for Youth for Christ in 1944. That fall he resigned as minister of Village Church and began to travel full-time. In 1945 he traveled 135,000 miles while he went from city to city preaching. Graham's work in Youth for Christ taught him how to speak to large crowds, how to work with a team, and how to work with an organization. The first time Graham spoke to a huge audience was when Youth for Christ held a meeting at Chicago's Soldier Field (now the stadium used by the Chicago Bears) a few days after World War II ended in Europe. Graham had a small part in this program, which drew a crowd of 65,000.

A Larger Mission

In 1946 Graham traveled with other Youth for Christ workers to conduct evangelistic meetings in the British Isles and Western Europe. The group had a combined total of 101 meetings in forty-six days. Later that year Billy took his wife Ruth and his future song leader Cliff Barrows back to the British Isles. There they held meetings and had opportunities to study about what ministers in the past had done to bring spiritual revival to large cities.

Evangelist Billy Graham

When Graham came back home, he began to implement what he had learned. Graham, Cliff Barrows, George Beverly Shea, and childhood friend Grady Wilson began to conduct evangelistic crusades in American cities. The first was in Graham's hometown of Charlotte, North Carolina. During their early years of working together, these four men made a commitment not to allow Satan to tempt them into sins that were especially tempting to well-known evangelists. They prayed and then made a commitment to be morally upright and to be honest in their finances. They agreed not to criticize local ministers and worked against becoming prideful.

Christ for Greater Los Angeles Evangelistic Campaign

By the late 1940s, the local Christian Businessmen's Committee in Los Angeles, California, had formed a branch called the Christ for Greater Los Angeles Committee. It was made up of Protestant evangelical ministers and church members. The group hosted evangelistic meetings. In 1949 the committee decided to invite Billy Graham to be their speaker at an evangelistic crusade that would last three weeks. This would be Graham's seventh campaign. However, something was very different about this one. Graham and those involved in his ministry were joining forces with a group that had long experience in organizing outreach events in Los Angeles.

Many individuals and groups worked together. Some people volunteered to be ushers, choir members, and counselors, while others worked in advertising and in organization. Local Lutheran minister Armin Gesswein, who had been leading a Los Angeles prayer ministry for ten years, encouraged thousands of believers to pray especially for the campaign planned for the fall of 1949.

The Los Angeles committee decided to host the event on a dirt lot they had used before for other outreach events. It was near the downtown shopping area. They covered the dirt with sawdust and set up a big tent. Printing on the front of the tent read:

HUNDREDS OF CHURCHES UNITING

GREATER LOS ANGELES REVIVAL

EVERY NITE 7:30   BILLY GRAHAM   SUNDAYS 3-8:45

6,000 *free* SEATS • DYNAMIC PREACHING • GLORIUS MUSIC

Yes, they misspelled glorious! For the first three weeks Graham spoke to crowds of 2,000 to 3,000. Graham's soloist George Beverly Shea flew back and forth from Chicago to Los Angeles to sing in the crusade while still fulfilling his responsibilities with a Chicago radio show. At the end of three weeks, local organizers wondered whether to continue the meeting for a longer time. They and Graham prayed about it. When local weather improved, they believed this was God's answer and announced that the meetings would continue. Immediately after the decision, the announcer on a local radio show came to see Billy Graham early one morning. The announcer told Graham that he had attended the meeting the night before and wanted to commit his life to Christ. Other well-known people made the same decision, including one man who was both an athlete and a war hero, one who was a local television star, and a criminal who had worked in organized crime.

Attendance at the meetings increased until the tent held between 6,000 and 6,500, with thousands more standing outside. Some people drove hundreds of miles to participate.

During a typical evening, a prayer service was held before the evangelistic meeting began. The actual evangelistic meetings included preaching by Billy Graham and solos by George Beverly Shea. Other activities included brief messages by local ministers, singing by choirs and other soloists, and congregational singing. During the evening, Graham offered an invitation for people in the audience to come to Christ. People who wanted to do so walked to the front of the tent. After the meeting, volunteer counselors met with them in a smaller tent. Their names and addresses were given to local churches so they could follow up with them afterwards. During the daytime on Saturdays, thousands of children came to a children's rally. The local Youth for Christ group met with the crusade on Saturday nights.

Theaters in Los Angeles began to show newsreels about the crusade. Graham became known across the country when newspapers began to report on the events in Los Angeles. Both *Time* and *Life* magazines carried stories and photographs about the crusade.

The meetings went on for eight weeks. During this time, Graham met in the daytime with various groups. He ran out of the sermons he had prepared and had to borrow some from friends. One night he used a sermon by Jonathan Edwards after telling the audience about the famous preacher (see pages 117-118).

When the meetings that had begun on September 25 ended on November 20, a tired Graham went home by train that very night to Minneapolis, where he was serving as president of a small Christian college. The Los Angeles campaign had not only blessed the people of Los Angeles and brought the thirty-one-year-old Graham national fame, it also gave him a pattern for how to conduct a crusade. Graham used the pattern again and again in cities across America and in other countries for the next fifty-six years.

Billy Graham Evangelistic Association

In 1950 Graham founded the Billy Graham Evangelistic Association (BGEA) in Minneapolis. The BGEA began a weekly radio program called *Hour of Decision*. The first broadcast was heard on 150 stations on the ABC radio network. The ministry grew in the 1950s and 1960s; by 1970 over 1,200 stations were carrying it. In 1952 Graham began to write a newspaper column called "My Answer." It was printed in newspapers across the country. The BGEA eventually began to film crusades, which were then aired on television.

Over the years the association grew until it had a team of evangelists, musicians, and a support staff. The heart of the BGEA work was evangelistic campaigns, but the organization also produced magazines in six languages, books, audio recordings, films, and radio and television programs.

1966 World Conference on Evangelism

In 1966 the BGEA and *Christianity Today* magazine sponsored a world conference on evangelism in West Berlin to give Protestant evangelicals from around the world an opportunity to fellowship and share ideas. Billy Graham spoke at the conference, as did concentration camp survivor Corrie Ten Boom, American theologian Francis Schaeffer, and many others. In attendance were two members of Ecuador's Waorani tribe who had become believers since the time ten years earlier when members of the tribe had killed five American missionaries, including Jim Elliot.

Graham and President Johnson at the LBJ Ranch, 1965

Meeting With Presidents

In 1950, when Billy Graham was in the early years of his seven-decade ministry, a U.S.

Congressman invited him to meet President Truman. During the meeting, Graham and Truman prayed together. Truman told Graham that he tried to live by the Sermon on the Mount. After Truman retired, Graham visited him at his home in Independence, Missouri.

Eisenhower and Graham had a very good relationship. Eisenhower consulted with Graham before he sent troops to Little Rock. Shortly before Eisenhower died, Graham visited him at Walter Reed Hospital. They prayed and Eisenhower asked Graham to assure him of the message of salvation.

Between John F. Kennedy's election as President and his inauguration, he invited Graham to spend a day with him. They drove around in Kennedy's convertible as JFK told him of his concerns about the moral and spiritual condition of America.

Billy Graham and Lyndon Johnson were close friends. Graham visited the White House many times during Johnson's presidency. He also visited the family ranch in Texas several times, as seen in the photo on page 810. When Graham would ask Johnson to pray with him, Johnson would get down on his knees to pray. Johnson once wrote to Graham: "My mind went back to those lonely occasions at the White House when your friendship helped to sustain a President in an hour of trial."

Richard Nixon and Billy Graham had been friends for many years when Nixon was elected President in 1968. He often asked Graham to read the Bible and pray with him.

In 1966 Jimmy Carter served as chairman of an evangelistic film crusade in Americus, Georgia. After Carter was elected Governor of Georgia in 1972, Billy and Ruth Graham visited him and his wife Rosalynn in the Governor's mansion. Graham later visited the Carters in the White House.

Graham with the Reagans, 1981

When Ronald Reagan was elected President, he and Graham had been close friends for many years. Reagan said that Billy Graham helped him pray more than just daily. Graham respected President George H. W. Bush, and Bush viewed Graham as an inspiration in his life. He said that Billy Graham helped him understand that no one can be President without faith or without understanding the power of prayer. Graham supported both Reagan and Bush during times of crisis. Graham is pictured with the Reagans at right.

When Bill Clinton was serving as Governor of Arkansas, he attended a crusade Graham held there in 1989. Graham later visited Clinton in the White House after he was elected President. Clinton complimented Billy and Ruth Graham for being friends with Presidents and for keeping those friendships private and genuine.

President Obama with Billy Graham, 2010

In George W. Bush's 1999 autobiography, he told of a talk he had with Billy Graham on the coast of Maine in 1985. He said that Graham planted a seed that later led him to recommit his heart to Jesus Christ.

In April of 2010, President Barack Obama visited Billy Graham in his home. They had a time of private prayer. See photo at left.

Later Years

Graham was diagnosed with Parkinson's Disease in 1992. In 1995 his son William Franklin Graham III became vice chairman of BGEA. It was announced that when Billy retired, Franklin would take his place as president.

In 2001 Franklin Graham took on the role of president of BGEA. Billy Graham continued to conduct crusades until 2005, when at age 86, he held his last crusade in New York City. Even in retirement, he continued to be involved in the organization he began fifty-five years earlier. Since 1955 Americans have chosen Billy Graham as one of the "Ten Most Admired Men in the World" forty-eight times.

Billy Graham's Family

After Billy Graham left Village Church in 1945, he and his wife Ruth moved to Montreat, North Carolina. It was there that they raised their five children: Virginia Leftwich (1945), Anne Morrow (1948), Ruth Bell (1950), William Franklin III (1952), and Nelson Edman (1958). Though Billy Graham himself was often away and his two sons spent part of their youth in rebellion, eventually all five children became involved in some type of public ministry. Billy's wife Ruth died in 2007. By her bedside were her husband Billy and their five children.

Billy Graham's legacy continues not only in his children but also in his grandchildren. Grandson William Franklin "Will" Graham IV is an evangelist who preaches to large audiences as part of the BGEA ministry. This faith legacy goes back to Billy's own parents. He once said: "I am sure one reason that the Lord has directed and safeguarded me, as well as Ruth and the children, through the years was the prayers of my mother and father."

Blessed be God, who has not turned away my prayer
nor His lovingkindness from me.
Psalm 66:20

Activities for Lesson 130

Thinking Biblically – Billy Graham has made it his life's mission to tell people the message of salvation in Christ. Read Romans 5.

Vocabulary – Look up each of these words in a dictionary: obscure, anthropology, evangelistic, crusade, rally. In your notebook, write each word with its definition.

Literature – Read "I Will Sing the Wondrous Story" in *We the People*, page 171.

Timeline – In *Timeline of America the Beautiful* next to 1966, write: Billy Graham helps sponsor the World Congress on Evangelism.

Student Workbook or Lesson Review – If you are using one of these optional books, complete the assignment for Lesson 130. If you are using the Lesson Review, take the quiz for Unit 26.

The 1970s

America suffered a great crisis in 1974 when President Richard Nixon came close to being impeached and later resigned. President Gerald Ford stepped in to take his place and brought healing. Ford was followed by President Jimmy Carter, who worked for peace in the Middle East and has taught Americans how to keep serving and growing in retirement. Early in Nixon's presidency, an American became the first person in history to walk on the moon. This followed many years of hard work at the Marshall Space Flight Center and other NASA facilities. Meanwhile, California farms were feeding America and the world; and Fred Rogers was teaching American youngsters and their families what it means to be a neighbor.

NASA Photo of the Surface of the Moon

Lessons in Unit 27

Lesson 131 – Our American Story: A Crisis in the Presidency
Lesson 132 – An American Landmark: Marshall Space Flight Center
Lesson 133 – Daily Life: American Astronauts
Lesson 134 – God's Wonders: God Created the Agricultural Lands of California
Lesson 135 – An American Biography: Mister Rogers, Neighbor to America's Children

Books Used in Unit 27

- *Maps of America the Beautiful*

- *Timeline of America the Beautiful*

- *We the People*

A Crisis in the Presidency

The American people learned better how to work together during the 1970s. In many ways the girl who held up a sign asking Richard Nixon to "bring us together" got what she wanted. The rioting in the streets calmed down. The country faced new challenges, but the people worked together to handle them. Though President Nixon faced some of the most difficult problems of any President, and many were of his own making, he also had good times. We will discuss the happy times first.

Between the November 1968 election and the inauguration in January, the Nixons' daughter Julie married President Eisenhower's grandson David in a small ceremony in New York. They were married by Norman Vincent Peale, a well-known minister. The two had known each other since they were children. In June of 1971, the Nixons' older daughter Tricia was married in the White House's Rose Garden. See photos below.

Tricia Nixon Cox

Tricia and Ed Cox

Left: President Eisenhower stands with his two oldest grandchildren, Susan and David. Vice President Nixon stands with his two daughters, Julie and Tricia, 1957

Right: President Nixon talks with a carpenter who is preparing the White House for Tricia's wedding, 1971.

First Lady Pat Nixon welcomes Big Bird, star of the PBS children's show, Sesame Street, *1970.*

President Nixon meets the poster child for the 1971 Easter Seal fund raising efforts.

President Nixon accompanies popular singer Pearl Bailey on the piano, 1974.

Nixon shakes hands with rock star Elvis Presley, 1970.

Mrs. Nixon welcomes Native Americans, 1974.

The Nixons hosted many guests at the White House, as seen in the photos above. Nixon enjoyed quiet moments and recreation. At lower left, he bowls in the White House bowling alley. At right he sits in formal attire in the Lincoln sitting room. In the center are the Nixons' Irish setter, King Timahoe, Julie's poodle Vicky, and Tricia's terrier Pasha.

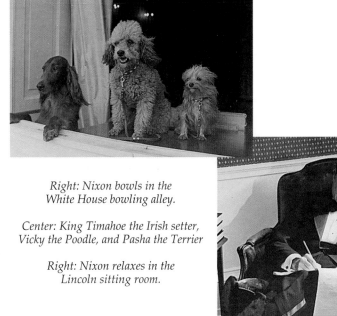

Right: Nixon bowls in the White House bowling alley.

Center: King Timahoe the Irish setter, Vicky the Poodle, and Pasha the Terrier

Right: Nixon relaxes in the Lincoln sitting room.

School Busing

The efforts to integrate black and white Americans continued in the 1970s. Many communities tried to accomplish integration by a practice called school busing. Since black families and white families often lived in different neighborhoods, school boards sometimes required children to ride buses from their own neighborhoods to schools across town. Black children were sometimes sent to schools that were mostly white and white children were taken to schools that were mostly black. Both black and white parents disliked the practice, because they wanted their children to go to school near their homes in their own neighborhoods and did not want them to spend so much time on a bus.

Relations with China and the Soviet Union

President Nixon worked to improve relations between America and the Communist countries of China and the U.S.S.R. Early in 1972, President Nixon announced that he would visit Communist China. He arrived there on February 21. See photo below. Until that time, the United States had only recognized the tiny Nationalist Chinese government on the island of Taiwan as the real Chinese government. (These Nationalists had ruled China before the Communists took over after World War II. During the fighting between Nationalists and Communists, the Nationalist government had escaped to Taiwan and set up a government there.) By visiting Communist China, Nixon was making a first step toward America officially recognizing the Communist government of China. Gradually relations between America and China improved to the point that China became a major supplier of goods sold in America. Though the quantity of Chinese goods sold in America is a controversial topic, business contacts between the Chinese people and Americans have given the Chinese

Chinese soldiers stand on the airport tarmac as President Nixon lands in China on Air Force One.

glimpses of a free society. President Nixon began to open a door into China, a door through which many have entered to share the gospel.

Also in 1972, Nixon became the first American President to visit the Soviet Union. It was a step toward making relations between the two countries friendlier and less tense. During Nixon's presidency, the two countries signed a treaty in which they each agreed to destroy some of their nuclear weapons.

An End to the War in Vietnam

President Richard Nixon worked to end U.S. involvement in the Vietnam War. His purpose was to get American soldiers out while keeping America's honor. He chose three courses of action.

- He sent U.S. representatives to Paris, France, to meet with representatives from North Vietnam, as Johnson had done during his last year in office.
- He brought some of the American troops home, gradually giving South Vietnam more and more responsibility for the fighting.
- He instructed the U.S. military to increase its bombing of Communist positions.

Communists were attacking South Vietnam and the U.S. military from the neighboring country of Cambodia, which was officially a neutral country. The U.S. responded by bombing Communists in Vietnam and also in Cambodia. When the American people learned about this action, they were angry, fearing that Nixon was not ending the war but spreading it. Students on many college campuses protested.

North and South Vietnam and the United States finally agreed to a cease-fire in January of 1973. The North Vietnamese began to release most of the American prisoners of war they had been holding in deplorable conditions. One prisoner was future Senator and presidential candidate John McCain. After the cease-fire, American troops came home.

After the Americans left, Communist forces started attacking South Vietnam again. In 1975 they began a full-scale attack, which caused the South Vietnamese army and government to collapse. The North Vietnamese completed what they had originally intended. They took over the South and united the two countries under Communism. Many Vietnamese refugees escaped at the time, and thousands have continued to do so since. Many American churches and individuals have helped them get a fresh start in America. Today almost one million first and second generation Vietnamese-Americans live in the United States.

Watergate and the Presidential Election of 1972

As President Nixon and Vice President Spiro Agnew began to prepare for the 1972 election, people who supported them formed a Committee to Re-Elect the President. Nixon was a popular President. Americans appreciated his efforts to improve relations with the Chinese and the Soviets. His efforts to remove American forces from Vietnam were underway and the nation was grateful. President Nixon had no reason to be concerned that he would not be elected to another term. However, shocking events were revealed during the campaign.

On June 17, 1972, before either the Republican or Democratic conventions had been held, five burglars broke into the headquarters of the Democratic National Committee (DNC), which was in the Watergate building, an office, apartment, and hotel complex in Washington, D.C. They were discovered and arrested while still in the DNC office. The burglars were all employees of the Committee to Re-Elect the President. Evidence showed that the men had broken in so they could install secret listening devices which would allow others to hear phone calls and conversations within the DNC office.

The burglars pleaded guilty and went to jail. President Nixon and the Committee to Re-Elect the President denied knowing anything about what had happened. The break-in was reported in newspapers and on television, but it was not a major news story. At their convention later that summer, the Republicans nominated President Nixon and Vice

President Agnew for re-election. The Democrats nominated South Dakota Senator George McGovern for their presidential candidate. Nixon won by a huge majority.

After the election, the *Washington Post* newspaper began to investigate what had happened at the Watergate complex. The break-in and the investigations that followed it came to be called simply Watergate or the Watergate scandal. The Senate formed a special committee to investigate the incident.

While the Watergate investigations were going on, President Nixon had to wrestle with three other major problems: inflation, an Arab oil embargo, and serious failings by his Vice President.

Inflation. The American economy had serious problems in the 1970s. Since the Federal government had borrowed so much money to pay for the Vietnam War and the Great Society programs, there was not enough money left for citizens to use. When an economy does not have enough money, prices increase. This is called inflation. When prices increase, people buy less and companies begin to lay off workers.

Arab Oil Embargo. To make matters worse, Arab countries got angry at the United States because it supported Israel. By 1973 the Arabs were not selling as much oil to the United States. This caused the price of gasoline to rise significantly. Americans sat in long lines to buy gasoline and they began to purchase smaller, more fuel efficient cars. The Arab oil embargo ended in 1974.

Vice President Agnew. Spiro Agnew had been Governor of Maryland before becoming Vice President of the United States in 1969. In April of 1973, Nixon was informed that Agnew had committed illegal acts while Governor of Maryland. In October Agnew resigned as Vice President. President Nixon appointed Gerald R. Ford, the leading Republican in the House of Representatives, to take Agnew's place. The Twenty-Fifth Amendment to the Constitution, ratified in 1967, had set forth what to do when the country was left without a Vice President.

In the months before Agnew resigned, the *Washington Post* and the Senate's Watergate special committee discovered that members of Nixon's staff and members of the Committee to Re-Elect the President had been involved in planning the break-in. They also found out that Nixon did not know about these things ahead of time. However, they discovered that when Nixon found out that members of his staff were involved, he decided to cover up evidence. Keeping evidence secret is a crime called obstruction of justice.

The U.S. House of Representatives began going through steps that could lead to President Nixon being impeached. The House Judiciary Committee approved three charges of impeachment against the President. This meant that the full House of Representatives was about to vote on whether to impeach Nixon. If they had done so, the U.S. Senate would have held an impeachment trial to determine whether to remove Nixon from the presidency.

Before the House of Representatives voted on the matter, President Nixon called his family together in the White House sunroom on August 8, 1974, and told them he had decided to resign as President. See the photos of Nixon and his family on page 819. After speaking with his family, the President went on television and told the American people of his decision to leave the presidency at noon the following day. The following morning he gathered with the White House staff and others for a sad goodbye and then left the White House. President and Mrs. Nixon boarded Air Force One and flew to their home in California.

Read about the life of Richard Nixon below.

Richard Milhous Nixon
America's Thirty-Seventh President
January 20, 1969 - August 9, 1974

Richard Milhous "Dick" Nixon was born in 1913 on his parents' lemon ranch in Yorba Linda, California, which is now the home of the Nixon Presidential Library and Museum. He was the second of five brothers. When the ranch failed, Nixon's father opened a grocery store/gas station in Whittier, California.

After high school, Richard Nixon lived at home and worked in the family store while attending Whittier College. After college he won a scholarship to Duke University Law School, where he excelled. In 1937 he returned to Whittier. While participating in a community play, he met Thelma Catherine "Pat" Ryan, a school teacher who was also in the play. They were married in 1940. After working briefly in Washington, D.C., Nixon joined the Navy and served in the Pacific region during World War II.

In 1946, after the war, Nixon was elected as a U.S. Congressman from his home district in California. His two daughters, Tricia and Julie, were born in 1946 and 1948. After serving two terms in the House of Representatives, he was elected to the U.S. Senate in 1950. Just two years later, he became Eisenhower's running mate. He was inaugurated as Vice President of the United States in 1953 and again in 1957. Nixon was chosen by the Republicans as their presidential nominee in 1960, but he lost to John F. Kennedy.

Nixon returned to California and began to practice law. He ran for Governor of California in 1962 but lost. The Nixons then moved to New York City where he continued to practice law. He also campaigned for other Republicans. When the Republicans again chose Nixon as their presidential candidate in 1968, Nixon was successful and became the thirty-seventh President.

When Nixon left the presidency, he and Pat moved back to their home in San Clemente, California. In 1980 they moved to New York City, and then in 1981 to New Jersey. In his retirement years, President Nixon traveled across the country and overseas. He often met with world leaders. In 1981 Presidents Nixon, Ford, and Carter all traveled to Egypt as official U.S. representatives at Anwar Sadat's funeral.

Nixon made many speeches at events around the country. He also wrote ten books. Nixon helped plan his presidential library. His wife Pat died in 1993. Billy Graham was one of the speakers at her funeral. President Nixon died the following year.

The Nixon Family in 1974: Ed and Tricia Cox, President and Mrs. Nixon, Julie and David Eisenhower

During the Nixons' flight to California on August 9, 1974, Vice President Ford took the oath of office at noon. See photo at right. Though a sad occasion, this peaceful transition at a time of such difficult circumstances demonstrated the wonderful form of government formed by America's founding fathers, the brilliance of the U.S. Constitution, and the quiet strength of the American people.

Gerald Ford takes the oath of office.

Ford announces a pardon for Nixon.

Ford chose former New York Governor Nelson Rockefeller as his Vice President and the Senate confirmed him. America had a President and a Vice President, neither of whom had been elected to serve in those positions.

In September President Ford issued a pardon for Richard Nixon for any crimes he may have committed. See photo at left. With this pardon, Nixon could not be put on trial. Many people were upset with President Ford for doing this, but he said that it was time for the country to put Watergate in the past and move forward. He did not believe that it would help America for a former President to go through a public trial.

In his role as President, Ford welcomed numerous foreign heads of state, many of whom came to America in honor of its two hundredth birthday in 1976. The photos at right illustrate some of Ford's experiences as President. Some were gravely important and some were just plain fun. See Ford with Soviet leader Leonid Brezhnev, Great Britain's Queen Elizabeth II, and two rock and roll stars.

Election of 1976

President Ford provided America with calm, positive, and trustworthy leadership. He helped America heal from the pain of Watergate. The Republican Party chose him as their candidate for President in 1976. Robert "Bob" Dole, a Kansas Senator, was his running mate.

Few people in America had ever heard of former Governor Jimmy Carter of Georgia when he announced that he would seek the 1976 Democratic nomination. One newspaper headline in his home state read, "Jimmy Who is Running for What?" However, with his many volunteers and excellent organization, Carter won the nomination. He chose Minnesota Senator Walter Mondale to be the vice-presidential candidate. The Carter family spread out across the country to get Jimmy elected. His mother "Miss Lillian" gave six hundred speeches. With the Watergate

Presdient Ford meets Russian Premier Leonid Brezhnev when Ford visited Russia in November of 1974.

Singers Billy Preston and George Harrison visit President Ford at the White House, 1974.

President Ford dances with Queen Elizabeth II after a state dinner in 1976.

scandal still fresh in their memories, the American voters elected Carter and Mondale, though the election was one of the closest in American history. Read about President Ford's life below.

Gerald Rudolph Ford
America's Thirty-Eighth President
August 9, 1974 - January 20, 1977

Gerald R. Ford was born in Omaha, Nebraska, on July 14, 1913. At birth he was named Leslie Lynch King Jr. Two weeks after he was born, his parents separated. Baby Leslie and his mother Dorothy went to Grand Rapids, Michigan, to live with her parents. Two years after the divorce was finalized, Dorothy married Gerald R. Ford Sr. of Grand Rapids. Gerald and Dorothy began to call her son Gerald Jr. The photo at right shows Gerald about age three with his pet dog.

Gerald Jr. grew up in a close family with three younger half-brothers. When Gerald Jr. was thirteen years old, he learned that Gerald Sr. was not his biological father. Near the end of his high school years, Gerald Jr. finally met his biological father.

Ford excelled at both academics and athletics while in high school and achieved the rank of Eagle Scout. In 1935, at the age of twenty-two, he legally changed his named to Gerald R. Ford Jr.

In college at the University of Michigan in Ann Arbor, Ford majored in economics and political science. While there, he played on U of M's national championship football team. Ford received offers to play for two professional football teams, but he chose to coach boxing and serve as assistant football coach at Yale while attending law school there. After law school, he began to practice law in Grand Rapids, while also teaching business law and serving on the coaching staff at the University of Grand Rapids. During World War II, Ford joined the Navy and served in the South Pacific.

Ford returned to law practice after the war. In 1948 he ran for a seat in the U.S. House of Representatives and won. During the campaign, he married Elizabeth Anne "Betty" Bloomer Warren. Their children were Michael, born in 1950; John, born in 1952; Steven, born in 1956; and Susan, born in 1957. Ford continued to serve in the House of Representatives until 1973. He was re-elected twelve times, always with more than sixty percent of the vote. In the House of Representatives, Gerald Ford led the Republicans as they opposed many of Johnson's Great Society programs. He also opposed Johnson as the President sent more and more Americans to Vietnam. Late in 1973, President Nixon appointed Ford to replace Spiro Agnew as Vice President. The Federal Bureau of Investigation (FBI) conducted the most thorough background check in FBI history before the Senate confirmed Ford as Vice President.

Ford believed in a limited role for the Federal government. As President he followed his long-held philosophy, "A government big enough to give us everything we want is a government big enough to take from us everything we have."

When the Fords left the White House, they built a new home in California. He published *A Time to Heal: The Autobiography of Gerald R. Ford* in 1979. Ford spoke out about policial issues. He lectured at colleges, participated in conferences, and received many awards. Ford died in 2006 and was buried at his presidential library in Grand Rapids.

Jimmy Carter did not like pomp and ceremony. After his inauguration, instead of riding to the White House in a limousine, he walked with his wife Rosalynn and their nine-year-old daughter Amy. See Amy at right. Jimmy and Rosalynn Carter had been partners in business before he became Governor of Georgia, and she had worked hard to get him elected to the presidency. She continued to be a valued advisor to the President. See a photo of the Carters below.

Amy Carter holds her Siamese cat, Misty Malarky Ying Yang.

Carter showed himself to be a man of integrity. He worked hard to lead well. However, inflation grew worse. The entire economy struggled. When individuals and businesses borrowed money, the interest rates were very high. Carter's major success as President involved the struggle for peace in the Middle East.

Camp David Accords

The nations of Israel and Egypt had been enemies for many years. In November of 1977 Egyptian President Anwar Sadat visited Jerusalem, Israel, to start peace talks between the two countries. A short time later, President Carter invited Sadat and Israeli Prime Minister Menachem Begin and their chief aides to meet together at Camp David. The three leaders spent thirteen days together. In the end they made two agreements, called the Camp David Accords. Though peace did not come to the entire Middle East, this was an important accomplishment. Begin and Sadat were awarded the Nobel Peace Prize in 1978. Sadat, Carter, and Begin are pictured at right.

President and Mrs. Carter have lunch in the Oval Office under a painting of George Washington.

Sadat, Carter, and Begin

President Truman with the Shah, 1949

American Hostages in Iran

A problem in Iran caused great difficulties for President Carter. The king of Iran (called the Shah) had long been an ally of America. As seen in the photos at left and below, he had visited the United States many times. In 1979 militant Muslims removed him from power. On November 4,

The Shah with Eleanor Roosevelt, 1959

The Shah with the Nixons, 1973

President Carter and the Shah, 1977

a mob took over the American embassy in Iran and took Americans hostage. After five months, Carter sent in rescuers; but their mission failed before they reached Tehran and eight servicemen died. The hostages remained captive for the remainder of Carter's presidency. In the election of 1981, American voters were again ready for a change.

Read about Carter's life below.

James Earl Carter Jr.
America's Thirty-Ninth President
January 20, 1977 - January 20, 1981

James Earl "Jimmy" Carter Jr. was born in 1924 in Plains, Georgia, the eldest of four. His siblings were Gloria, Ruth, and Billy. Jimmy grew up on a farm in nearby Archery. James Earl Sr. was a farmer and businessman. Jimmy's mother, Lillian Gordy Carter, was a registered nurse. Jimmy attended public schools in Plains.

In 1946 Carter graduated from the United States Naval Academy and began what he expected to be a long career in the Navy, serving on a nuclear submarine. In July of 1946, he married Rosalynn Smith, also from Plains. When Carter's father died in 1953, they came home to Plains for the funeral. Hearing from townspeople what a profound impact his father had had on his community, Carter decided to give up his promising career in the Navy to make a difference at home as his father had done. Jimmy and Rosalynn struggled financially at first, as they managed a peanut farm and a seed and farm supply business. They lived for one year in a government housing project for low income families in Plains.

Carter learned about public service from both his parents. His mother often cared for the sick without pay. Later, when she was in her late sixties, she spent two years serving with the Peace Corps in India. After serving in local offices, Jimmy Carter was elected to the Georgia Senate in 1962. He lost the first time he ran for Governor; but he won the second time, becoming Georgia's Governor in 1971.

Jimmy Carter's greatest accomplishments have come since he returned to private life after his presidency. He has written more than twenty-five books, including books about faith, aging, government, and world peace. He has written a novel, a book of poetry, a children's book which his daughter Amy illustrated, and a biography of his mother called *A Remarkable Mother*. Carter is an accomplished woodworker and an artist. Along with Rosalynn, he is an avid fly-fisherman and bird watcher. For several years after leaving the presidency, he was a mountain climber. He climbed partway up Mt. Everest at age sixty, to the top of Mt. Kilimanjaro in Africa when he was sixty-four, and to the top of Mt. Fuji in Japan when he was seventy.

Jimmy Carter is openly Christian. He once went on an evangelistic campaign, going door to door sharing his faith. He and Rosalynn are members of Maranatha Baptist Church in Plains, where he has taught Sunday School for decades. The Carters lead a Habitat for Humanity team for one week each year. Jimmy and Rosalynn have three sons, Jack, Chip, and Jeff; a daughter, Amy; and several grandchildren and great-grandchildren.

In 1982 Carter founded the Carter Center, a nonprofit organization without connection to any political party. The center works to increase agricultural production in Africa, to promote fair treatment of people, to resolve conflicts between nations, and to make sure elections around the world are honest and fair. He and Rosalynn have traveled the world to carry out the center's work. In 2002 President Carter won the Nobel Peace Prize. The title of the book Carter published in 2006 is a good description of what he has tried to do in his post-presidential years: *Beyond the White House: Waging Peace, Fighting Disease, Building Hope.*

On the day that President Nixon left Washington and President Ford took the oath of office to become President in his place, Ford said, "The long national nightmare is over. Our Constitution works." President Nixon disappointed those who had voted for him and all the Americans he should have served with honesty. Their political ideas differed greatly from each other, but both Ford and Carter brought a return of integrity to the presidency.

He who walks in integrity walks securely,
But he who perverts his ways
will be found out.
Proverbs 10:9

Activities for Lesson 131

Thinking Biblically – Copy these verses into your notebook: Proverbs 10:9; 11:3; and 13:6. Write one or two paragraphs about what it means to be a person of integrity.

Vocabulary – In your notebook, write each of the sentences below, inserting one of these words: nationalist, scandal, inflation, obstruction, impeach.

1. The U.S. House of Representatives has the duty to _____ the President when he is guilty of serious misconduct.
2. The local _____ involving bribes given to judges was first exposed in the newspaper.
3. My dad can't do anything about _____ , but his customers in the grocery store complain about it anyway.
4. The small _____ band slowly collected arms in preparation for the revolution.
5. Mom had to call a plumber to remove an _____ from the pipes. It turned out to be my brother's lost jacks.

Literature – Read "Unchanging Principles" in *We the People*, pages 172-174.

Timeline – In *Timeline of America the Beautiful* next to 1974, write: Richard Nixon resigns as President.

Student Workbook or Lesson Review – If you are using one of these optional books, complete the assignment for Lesson 131.

In the 1970s . . .

- In 1971 eighteen-year-olds were given the right to vote in Federal elections.
- The Louisiana Superdome was completed in 1971.
- The World Trade Center in New York City opened its first office in 1971.
- In 1971 Federal Express began operating as the world's first overnight delivery service.
- The U.S. Supreme Court declared abortion legal when it decided the *Roe v. Wade* case in 1973.
- During the Vietnam War, many young men fled to Canada to avoid being drafted. President Carter pardoned them in 1977 so they could return home.
- The music craze of the seventies was disco.
- The hairstyle at right was popular with many men and some women. It was called an Afro or fro.

Marshall Space Flight Center

And the rocket's red glare, the bombs bursting in air . . . .

When Francis Scott Key penned the words of "The Star-Spangled Banner," he was speaking of rockets the British military used during the War of 1812. A century and a half later, rockets were blasting off from Cape Kennedy to take astronauts to the moon.

The first recorded rocket-like device was designed around 400 B.C. by a Greek man named Archytas. He entertained people by propelling a wooden pigeon with steam. Many cultures have stories about rockets. The first known true rockets were used by the Chinese

Robert H. Goddard transports one of his rockets in the early 1930s.

against the Mongols in 1232. They were described as "arrows of flying fire." The Mongols soon produced rockets, too, and the weapon also spread to Europe.

In the 1500s rockets were used as a type of fireworks. Johann Schmidlap, a German fireworks manufacturer, invented a step rocket, which consisted of a large rocket that carried a smaller rocket. This basic concept is the one still used in all modern rockets that go into outer space. For many years, including during the War of 1812, rockets could not be launched with accuracy; but in the mid-1800s, Englishman William Hale invented spin stabilization by using small tail fins at the bottom of rockets. This technique is still used today.

Goddard with 1926 Rocket

In 1898 Russian schoolteacher Konstantin Tsiolkovsky proposed that rockets be used to explore in space. He suggested using liquid propellants to make them go farther. Tsiolkovsky is called the father of modern astronautics.

In the early 1900s, American physics professor Robert H. Goddard conducted rocketry experiments. In the photo above, he drives a Model T truck pulling a rocket on a wagon. His wife took the photo at left of Goddard with a liquid-propellant rocket in 1926. The rocket flew for two and half seconds, went forty-one feet into the air, and traveled a distance of almost 184 feet. Goddard continued his research for many years and developed ways to return the rockets using parachutes. Goddard is considered the father of modern rocketry.

In 1923 Hermann Oberth, a German, published a book about space travel using rockets. One German scientist who worked with Oberth was Dr. Wernher von Braun.

Dr. Wernher von Braun, *Sputnik*, and *Explorer I*

Wernher von Braun was born in Germany in 1912. As a youth, he read science fiction by Jules Verne and H. G. Wells and the science writings of Hermann Oberth. At age twenty, von Braun began working for the German army where he helped develop ballistic missiles. He received a Ph.D. in physics when he was twenty-two. During World War II, Dr. von Braun helped Germany develop the V-2 missile, which was used against Great Britain. When von Braun realized that Germany could not win World War II, he arranged for five

Pickering, van Allen, and von Braun with the Explorer I

hundred of the top scientists who worked for him to surrender to the Americans.

Von Braun came to the United States in 1945 under contract with the U.S. Army. He learned of Goddard's research and was impressed with it. In 1950 he and scientists working with him were sent to the Redstone Arsenal near Huntsville, Alabama, where they worked on the Jupiter ballistic missile for the U.S. Army. Throughout the 1950s, American scientists did rocket research for two reasons: defense and space exploration.

With the help of German scientists who had gone to the U.S.S.R. after World War II, the Soviets launched *Sputnik* on Friday, October 4, 1957. On that night in America, television viewers followed news about integration at Little Rock Central High School and enjoyed

Above: Close-Up of Explorer I
At Left: Explorer I *sits atop a Jupiter-C rocket.*

the premier of the new television show *Leave It to Beaver*.

In an effort to keep up with their Cold War enemies, the U.S. Army launched America's first satellite, *Explorer I*, early the next year. See photos at left. Those in charge of the project were Dr. William Pickering, Dr. James van Allen, and Dr. von Braun. They hold *Explorer I* over their heads in the photo above.

The Founding of the Marshall Space Flight Center

Much of the later success of the American space program was a result of the organization put in place by President Eisenhower in the 1950s. He signed the National Aeronautics and Space Act of 1958 in July. In October the National Aeronautics and Space Administration (NASA) was founded. In 1960 Dr. von Braun and his team of scientists were transferred from the Redstone Arsenal to NASA. Land at the Redstone Arsenal was set aside for the Marshall Space Flight Center (MSFC), NASA's first field center. The center was named for General George C. Marshall, who devised the Marshall Plan after World War II (see page 712). Wernher von Braun was named director of the center. In the photo at right, von Braun serves as President Eisenhower's guide during the center's dedication in September of 1960. Von Braun remained the director of MSFC until March 1970. In the photos below, he is shown with President John F. Kennedy in 1962; on a speaker's platform with President Lyndon Johnson when Johnson toured the facility in 1967; and talking with Vice President Hubert Humphrey during Humphrey's visit in 1967.

Von Braun and Eisenhower at MSFC, 1960

Von Braun and President John F. Kennedy at the Marshall facility in September of 1962.

Booster Rockets

One of the major contributions the Marshall Space Flight Center has made to the American space program has been the development of rockets. In the early years of manned space flight, astronauts traveled in small space capsules. At launch time, the space capsule sat atop a rocket. The rocket was used to boost the spaceship away from the earth's gravity.

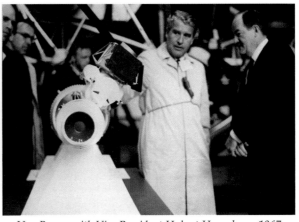

Von Braun and President Lyndon Johnson, 1967   *Von Braun with Vice President Hubert Humphrey, 1967*

Mercury, Gemini, and Apollo

Early NASA space programs had mythological names: Mercury, Gemini, and Apollo. Mercury spaceships took the first American astronauts into space. These missions proved that man could go into space and return safely. The first manned Mercury spaceship was propelled by a Mercury-Redstone rocket designed at MSFC.

When NASA began sending two astronauts in one spaceship, they designed capsules just large

Dr. Von Braun and President Kennedy, November 16, 1963

enough to squeeze in two astronauts and their equipment. This new phase of the space program was named Project Gemini, after the Gemini constellation which the Greeks thought looked like twins. Project Gemini helped NASA learn how a spacecraft could attach to (or dock with) another vehicle. It also proved that an astronaut could leave the spacecraft for a spacewalk and return to it. Gemini spacecraft were the first to have computers on board. The Titan rockets that propelled Gemini spacecraft had been designed as ballistic missiles during the 1950s.

The Apollo program took astronauts to the moon, where they explored and then returned safely to earth. The Saturn rockets used for Apollo were designed at Marshall. Dr. von Braun was the chief designer of the Saturn V, which was used as the booster rocket for the Apollo 11 mission, during which humans first walked on the moon. In the photo above, Dr. Wernher von Braun talks to President Kennedy about Saturn rockets. The photo was taken just six days before Kennedy was assassinated.

The U.S. Space and Rocket Center

Rocket Park at the U.S. Space and Rocket Center

The visitor center for the Marshall Space Flight Center is housed at the U.S. Space and Rocket Center, which opened in 1970 on land donated by the Redstone Arsenal. While he and other scientists were finishing the Saturn V to take Americans to the moon, Dr. von Braun was working on a permanent museum about the space program. Von Braun asked the Alabama legislature to pay for the construction of the Space and Rocket Center. In 1968 Alabama lawmakers and its citizens voted to construct the museum. Today von Braun's papers and thousands of space artifacts are housed in the U.S. Space and Rocket Center, which is also home to Space Camp. The camp began in 1982 and has provided astronaut training activities for more than 500,000 young people and adults from all fifty states and many foreign countries. Rocket Park, pictured on page 828, is a popular attraction at the center.

Other NASA Facilities

Before NASA was founded, several space, rocket, and missile research facilities in addition to Marshall existed around the country. Many of these became part of NASA, and additional NASA facilities have since been built. See the list of NASA facilities at right.

Through millennia man has looked upward in wonder at what God has created above us.

It is I who made the earth,
and created man upon it.
I stretched out the heavens with My hands
And I ordained all their host.
Isaiah 45:12

Activities for Lesson 132

Map Study – Complete the assignment for Lesson 132 on Map 3 "American Landmarks" in *Maps of America the Beautiful*.

Vocabulary – In your notebook, make a drawing for each of these words that illustrates what each one means: propellant, rocketry, ballistic missile, constellation, legislature. Write the correct word under each drawing. Check in a dictionary if you need help with their definitions.

Creative Writing – Write a poem of at least 16 lines about man's interest in the frontier of space throughout history.

NASA Facilities Around the Country

Alabama
Marshall Space Flight Center

California
Ames Research Center
Dryden Flight Research Center
Jet Propulsion Laboratory

District of Columbia
NASA Headquarters

Florida
Kennedy Space Center

Louisiana
Michoud Assembly Facility

Maryland
Goddard Space Flight Center

Mississippi
NASA Shared Services Center
Stennis Space Center

New Mexico
White Sands Test Facility

New York
Goddard Institute of Space Studies

Ohio
Glenn Research Center
Plum Brook Station

Texas
Johnson Space Center

Virginia
Langley Research Center
Wallops Flight Facility

West Virginia
IV and V Facility

Timeline – In *Timeline of America the Beautiful* next to 1960, write: The Marshall Space Flight Center becomes NASA's first field center.

Student Workbook or Lesson Review – If you are using one of these optional books, complete the assignment for Lesson 132.

American Astronauts

Bill Dana stands beside the X-15 after completing a mission in 1966.

Sending American astronauts into space has been a mission of NASA since its beginning in 1958. Astronauts began going into space in the 1960s. In the first half of the 1970s, NASA sent American astronauts on Apollo missions to the moon. In the last half of the decade, the agency designed space shuttles which could blast off from Cape Canaveral while attached to a rocket and land on dry ground like a glider (earlier spacecraft had been designed to land in the ocean). In this lesson, we learn about Americans who have left the earth to travel in space.

People working at NASA considered for a time using the term cosmonaut. This is the term that the Soviet space program chose to use. However, even before Soviet cosmonaut Yuri Gagarin became the first person to fly into space on April 12, 1961, those working in the American space program were already calling their future space travelers astronauts.

Though a Soviet cosmonaut was the first human being to orbit around the earth, it was an American astronaut who first set foot on the moon less than a decade later. The 1960s saw over twenty manned space missions. This lesson focuses on just a few of them, plus some missions from the 1970s.

Test Pilots

The first American jet, the Bell P-59, was invented in 1942. As faster jets and later rocket-

Engineers check a model of a supersonic aircraft before testing it in a supersonic wind tunnel, 1957.

powered planes were invented, brave pilots tested them. It was a dangerous job. Most testing was done at what is now Edwards Air Force Base in the southern California desert. Research test pilots who worked at NASA's Dryden Flight Research Center located on Edwards Air Force Base tested America's rocket-powered X-plane fleet. These tests gave NASA information they needed to launch manned spacecraft. Bill Dana, chief engineer at Dryden, and seven other test pilots flew the X-15 rocket plane out of the atmosphere. Dana and the X-15 are pictured above. Dana himself flew the X-15 sixteen times.

Great human achievements require the cooperation of many people. In the lower photo on page 830, engineers perform testing on a model of a supersonic aircraft in 1957 at what is now the Glenn Research Center in Cleveland, Ohio. Supersonic planes go faster than the speed of sound.

The Mercury 7

Shortly after NASA was founded, the agency asked 110 test pilots to volunteer for the manned space program. In April of 1959, it introduced its first seven astronauts, the

Front Row: Walter H. Schirra, Donald K. Slayton, John H. Glenn Jr., Scott Carpenter; Back Row: Alan B Shepard Jr., Virgil I. "Gus" Grissom, and L. Gordon Cooper

Mercury 7 above. Before they ever left the earth, Americans considered these men to be heroes. Throughout the 1960s, Americans gathered around their television sets whenever an astronaut climbed into a space capsule and rose high above the launching pad at Cape Canaveral, but their first space heroes were the Mercury 7: Walter Schirra, Donald Slayton, John Glenn, Scott Carpenter, Alan Shepard, Gus Grissom, and Gordon Cooper. Cape Canaveral was called Cape Kennedy from 1963 to 1973 in honor of President Kennedy.

John Glenn, Gus Grissom, and Alan Shepard stand in front of the Mercury-Redstone rocket.

The First American in Space

Alan B. Shepard Jr. said that when he was chosen as one of the Mercury 7, it was one of the happiest days of his life. Out of the Mercury 7, NASA picked three men, one of whom would be the first in space. Again Shepard was chosen, along with Gus Grissom and John Glenn. See picture at left. When Shepard found out he would be the very first American to go into space, he was again elated, but he soon felt sad for Grissom and Glenn.

On May 5, 1961, Shepard began one of the most memorable days of his life. Examine the photos at left, below, and on pages 832-833 as you read his story. Early that morning he sat down for breakfast with fellow astronaut John Glenn. Medical doctors checked his blood pressure, listened to his lungs and heartbeat, and took his temperature. A member of the NASA team helped him put on his pressurized spacesuit.

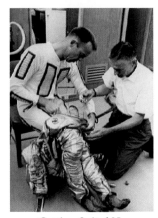

Medical Check

Breakfast with John Glenn

Getting Suited Up

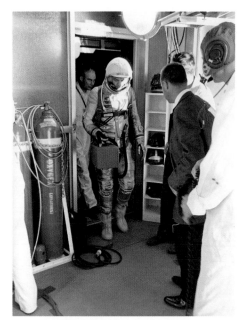

Shepard exits the elevator at the top of the service tower.

Gus Grissom wishes Alan Shepard a safe flight.

Shepard awaits takeoff.

Shepard rode an elevator to the top of the service tower. Fellow Mercury 7 astronaut Gus Grissom wished him a safe flight and Shepard climbed into the cramped *Freedom 7* space capsule that sat above what he called a beautiful rocket.

After the countdown, the rocket blasted off carrying *Freedom 7* away from the earth's gravitational pull. In the photo below, notice the arrows that point to the tiny space capsule at the top of the rocket and to the exhaust coming from the bottom of the rocket. The rocket carried *Freedom 7* high above the earth where the capsule separated from the rocket and headed into space. There Shepard saw the beautiful view of planet Earth shown below. He said that he saw the west coast of Florida, the Gulf of Mexico, and Lake Okeechobee before he re-entered earth's atmosphere.

After Shepard's fifteen-minute and twenty-two-second flight, the *Freedom 7* space capsule re-entered the atmosphere. As it fell to earth, its parachute opened. The capsule splashed down in the Atlantic Ocean. Shepard floated in the capsule until helicopters came to retrieve him. Shepard opened his hatch and was hoisted to safety. The crew then attached a cable to the capsule and lifted it from the ocean. NASA told the news media: "The astronaut reports that he is A-OK." "A-OK" has since become a popular phrase in American English.

The Mercury-Redstone rocket lifts Freedom 7.

The helicopter carried Shepard and the spaceship to the USS *Champlain* aircraft carrier, where an excited crew was waiting. President and Mrs. Kennedy, Vice President Johnson, and 45 million other Americans watched on television.

Shepard's View of Earth

Shepard is lifted from his Freedom 7 *space capsule.*

A Marine helicopter lifts Freedom 7 *from the Atlantic Ocean.*

Shepard and his spacecraft are brought to the waiting USS Champlain.

The crew of the USS Champlain *cheers as Shepard is brought to their vessel.*

Vice President Johnson, President and Mrs. Kennedy, and others watch on television.

Examining Freedom 7

Onboard the USS *Champlain*, Shepard examined his spacecraft. Later that day, he arrived in the Bahamas and was greeted by fellow Mercury 7 astronauts Donald Slayton and Gus Grissom. A few days later, President Kennedy awarded Shepard the NASA Distinguished Service Award, while Shepard's wife and mother and the other six members of the Mercury 7 stood around him. Eleven years later, Alan Shepard returned to space and walked on the moon.

Shepard is greeted by fellow astronauts.

Shepard's wife and mother watch as he receives the NASA Distinguished Service Award from President Kennedy.

The First American to Orbit the Earth

The second Mercury astronaut in space was Gus Grissom, who flew for fifteen minutes and thirty-seven seconds. His flight went well, but when he reached the Atlantic Ocean the hatch opened too quickly. Grissom escaped and was only in the water three or four minutes before he was rescued by helicopter. However, the spaceship was lost in the 15,000-foot-deep ocean.

Less than one year after Shepard's initial flight, John Glenn boarded *Friendship 7*, blasted off from Cape Canaveral, and began to orbit the earth, becoming the first American astronaut to do so. He orbited the earth three times. At top left, he relaxes onboard the USS *Randolph* after his flight.

Glenn soon left the space program and entered business. In 1974 he was elected to the United States Senate. In 1998, at the age of seventy-seven, he returned to space on the Space Shuttle *Discovery* and stayed for nine days. See photo at left. Glenn performed duties as a payload specialist. He also participated in research on how weightlessness affects the body of an older person. During the 1998 flight, he circled the earth 134 times — 131 more times than during his first flight.

John Glenn Onboard the USS Randolph *After His Successful Splashdown*

Astronaut John Glenn returns to space at age 77.

The First American to Walk in Space

Gemini 4 lifted off at Cape Kennedy on June 3, 1965, with its two-man crew, James A. McDivitt and Edward H. White II. Later that day, White made history when he floated out of the Gemini capsule into space, becoming the first American to "walk" in space. Below is the first photograph McDivitt took of White during the spacewalk. White was attached to the capsule by a twenty-five-foot umbilical cord. For the first three minutes, he propelled himself using a gas-powered gun. When the fuel ran out, he moved about by pulling on the umbilical cord and twisting his body around. White was a strong man who performed the experiment well. A spacewalk is also called an Extra-Vehicular Activity or EVA. White's EVA lasted twenty-three minutes. When he exited the spacecraft, he was over the Pacific Ocean. When he returned to the spacecraft, he was over the Gulf of Mexico. White later said that hearing the command to re-enter the space capsule was the saddest moment of his life.

During the flight, McDivitt and White were able to talk to their families, who were at Mission Control at the Johnson Space Center in Houston. The *Gemini 4* crew returned to earth on June 7. After their return to earth, the two astronauts communicated with President Johnson. See photos on page 835.

Ed White During His 1965 Spacewalk

White (left) and McDivitt listen to President Johnson just after their splashdown recovery from the Atlantic Ocean.

From Left to Right: Patricia McDivitt, Bonnie White, Patricia White, Flight Director Christopher Kraft, and Edward White

Merry Christmas from the Moon

In 1968 an estimated one billion people watched on television or listened on radio when the three-man crew of *Apollo 8* broadcast a Christmas Eve message while orbiting the moon. Frank Borman, James A. Lovell Jr., and William A. Anders had left earth on December 21. They were the first astronauts to leave earth's orbit. Though they did not land on the moon, on Christmas Eve they began to orbit around it. The Apollo 8 crew gave the people of the world a wonderful Christmas greeting. First, William Anders said:

> For all the people on Earth the crew of *Apollo 8* has a message we would like to send you. "In the beginnning God created the heaven and the earth. And the earth was without form, and void; and darkness was upon the face of the deep. And the Spirit of God moved upon the face of the waters. And God said, 'Let there be light': and there was light. And God saw the light, that it was good: and God divided the light from the darkness."

Then Jim Lovell said:

> "And God called the light Day, and the darkness he called Night. And the evening and the morning were the first day. And God said, let there be a firmament in the midst of the waters, and let it divide the waters from the waters. And God made the firmament, and divided the waters which were under the firmament from the waters which were above the firmament: and it was so. And God called the firmament Heaven. And the evening and the morning were the second day."

Finally, Frank Borman spoke, saying:

> "And God said, Let the waters under the heavens be gathered together unto one place, and let the dry land appear: and it was so. And God called the dry land Earth; and the gathering together of the waters called He Seas: and God saw that it was good."And from the crew of *Apollo 8*, we close with good night, good luck, a Merry Christmas, and God bless all of you—all of you on the good Earth.

In addition to their greeting, the *Apollo 8* crew sent a wonderful Christmas present to the people of the world—the first pictures that people on earth had ever seen of their home from so far away. On earth we can watch the sun rise in the morning and the moon rise at night. From the moon, the astronauts could see the earth rise. The earthrise below was taken on December 22. The crew returned to earth on December 27.

Earthrise at Christmas Time, December 22, 1968

Man Lands on the Moon

On July 16, 1969, President Richard Nixon invited a great champion of the U.S. space program, former President Lyndon Johnson, to come to Cape Kennedy for an historic launch. Eight years after President Kennedy's challenge, the time had come for Americans to land on the moon. Just seven months after the 1968 Christmas flight, *Apollo 11* blasted off with Commander Neil Armstrong and fellow astronauts Edwin "Buzz" Aldrin and Michael Collins on board. See their photo below. With them was a piece of cloth and a piece of wood from the Wright brothers flyer that had flown at Kitty Hawk on December 17, 1903. Notice Johnson in the center of the photo at the top of page 837. To his left is Vice President Agnew.

Apollo 11 Astronauts Neil Armstrong, Michael Collins, and Edwin "Buzz" Aldrin

After one and a half orbits around earth, the *Apollo 11* crew was given the command for "Translunar Injection." That meant, "Head for the moon!" Three days later the crew went into orbit around the moon. The following day Armstrong and Aldrin climbed into their lunar module, the *Eagle*. Michael Collins stayed aboard the command module *Columbia* and continued to orbit the moon while Armstrong and Aldrin flew down toward the moon's surface.

Armstrong saw boulders on the surface, so he had to pilot the ship manually away from them. The lunar module landed with only thirty seconds of its descent fuel remaining!

Former President Johnson and Vice President Agnew watch as Apollo 11 lifts off from Cape Kennedy.

Back on earth at Mission Control in Houston, anxious NASA co-workers waited. At 4:18 p.m. Eastern Daylight Time, Armstrong radioed: "Houston, Tranquility Base here. The *Eagle* has landed." Mission Control erupted in

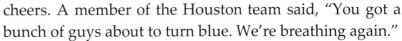

cheers. A member of the Houston team said, "You got a bunch of guys about to turn blue. We're breathing again."

Six hours and thirty-eight minutes later, Armstrong climbed down the *Eagle*'s ladder and, as he put the first human foot on the moon, said, "That's one small step for man, one giant leap for mankind."

Buzz Aldrin on the Eagle's *Ladder*

When Aldrin stepped out shortly after, he said "Magnificent desolation." For two and a half hours, Armstrong and Aldrin collected samples from the moon's surface and took these and other photographs.

When their tasks on the moon were completed, Armstrong and Aldrin climbed back aboard the *Eagle* and lifted off from the lunar surface. On the surface of the moon they left the legs of the *Eagle*. On the legs is a plaque which reads: "Here men from the planet Earth first set foot upon the moon. July 1969 A.D. We came in peace for all mankind." They also left an American flag, a patch

Buzz Aldrin on the Moon's Surface

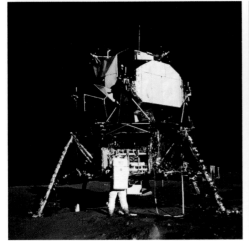

Buzz Aldrin and the Eagle

Neil Armstrong stands beside the flag the astronauts placed on the moon.

The Eagle *ascends from the moon's surface to dock with the* Columbia.

honoring astronauts who had died in an Apollo accident in 1967, and many footprints. Armstrong and Aldrin successfully docked the *Eagle* with the *Columbia* command module. See picture at left. On July 24, eight days, three hours, and eighteen minutes after they had left earth, the *Columbia* splashed down in the Pacific Ocean 825 miles from Hawaii. In the photo below, Mission Control in Houston, which had directed and monitored the flight, celebrates.

Officials at NASA were fearful of what the *Apollo 11* crew might have brought back with them from the moon, since no one had ever been there before. They wondered if there might be diseases on the moon. The crew was placed in a "Mobile Quarantine Facility," which was taken first to Hawaii and then to Houston. In the photo below, President Nixon speaks with them through the window. The astronauts stayed in the unit for two and a half weeks until medical doctors could be certain they were not bringing a deadly disease back to earth.

Mission Control in Houston celebrates when the Apollo 11 *mission is completed.*

President Nixon talks to the astronauts in their Mobile Quarantine Facility.

In 2001 Neil Armstrong praised the hundreds of thousands of people who worked behind the scenes on the *Apollo 11* mission. He said that each one had worked in such a way that if anything went wrong, it wouldn't be his or her fault.

Ten more astronauts visited the moon on other Apollo missions. On July 26, 1971, astronauts from the *Apollo 15* crew explored the lunar surface on a vehicle called a LEM (Lunar Excursion Module). *Apollo 17* left earth on December 7, 1972 for the last Apollo mission. The astronauts returned on December 19.

Other Space Missions of the 1970s

In 1973 NASA launched *Skylab*, an orbiting space laboratory. During the decade, three different crews performed research in the labs. In the photo at right, *Skylab* is in orbit above the Amazon River. One *Skylab* crew was in the space lab during Christmas. They used cans to create the Christmas tree at the top of page 839. The photo was taken on Christmas Eve in 1973. Skylab malfunctioned in 1979 and fell back to earth, landing in the Indian Ocean and western Australia.

Skylab

Skylab Christmas Tree Made from Cans, 1973

In 1970 the U.S. and U.S.S.R. space programs began planning for a joint space project. In 1975 American astronauts and Russian cosmonauts participated in the Apollo-Soyuz Test Project, in which an American spaceship and a Soviet spaceship linked up while in orbit around the earth. The astronauts carried out several joint projects. In the photo below, President Gerald Ford watches the crew on television while talking to them on a radio-telephone.

In the bottom photo, President Jimmy Carter gives the first Congressional Space Medal of Honor to Neil Armstrong. The era of rocket-boosted spacecrafts that returned to earth by splashing down into the ocean ended in the 1970s. In 1981 the space shuttle era began. The accomplishments of the Mercury, Gemini, and Apollo space programs and of those that came after them are awe-inspiring, but even more awe-inspiring are the creations of space and the God who created them.

When I consider Your heavens,
the work of Your fingers,
The moon and the stars, which You have ordained;
What is man that You take thought of him,
And the son of man that You care for him?
Pslam 8:3-4

Activities for Lesson 133

Thinking Biblically – Look again at the Christmas Eve message broadcast by the crew of *Apollo 8*. Write one page in your notebook about the new perspective the astronauts gained about the creations of God mentioned in their message.

Literature – Read "One Small Step" in *We the People*, page 175.

Timeline – In *Timeline of America the Beautiful* next to 1959, write: The first seven astronauts are chosen for the U.S. space program.

Family Activity – Complete American Space Firsts Poster. See instructions on page 978.

Student Workbook or Lesson Review – If you are using one of these optional books, complete the assignment for Lesson 133.

President Ford talks to the crew of the Apollo-Soyuz Test Project by way of a radio-telephone, July 18, 1975.

President Jimmy Carter gives the first Congressional Space Medal of Honor to Neil Armstrong, 1978.

God Created the Agricultural Lands of California

God created more than 1,680 kinds of soils in the coasts, deserts, foothills, mountains, and valleys of California. Many of these soils are excellent for agriculture. God also gave California a moderate climate, similar to the area around the Mediterranean Sea. This combination allows Californians to produce an amazing amount of food. California grows more than half of the fruits, vegetables, and nuts grown in the United States, even though it has only four percent of the nation's farmland!

Many of California's farms are in areas that require irrigation. California agriculture has grown as water has become available. In 1890 one million acres of crop land were irrigated. By 1930 irrigated cropland had increased five times. Today one out of every five gallons of water used for irrigation in America is used by California farmers.

Around 1960 California became America's number one state for agriculture. Since then it has continued to grow a wider variety of crops. In the 1970s, the state grew about two hundred different kinds. By 2000 it grew about 350 different crops. Since eating a wide variety of different kinds of foods is healthy for our bodies, it would be good to try a new California product every week. How long would it take to try each one of them? If the Great Plains is America's Breadbasket, then California is its Salad Bowl and the source for many other foods we have on our dinner tables. California's farmers supply food not only for America; they help to feed the world.

A Year-Round Growing Season and A Short Growing Season

Since four out of five of the nation's carrots are grown in California, there is a good chance that the carrots on your table in January were grown in California, even if you live as far away as Maine. This is true for many fresh foods. The climate God created in California makes it possible for some crops to grow there all through the year. Examples include mushrooms; fruits such as lemons and avocados; and vegetables such as artichokes, broccoli, cabbage, carrots, cauliflower, celery, lettuce, potatoes, and spinach.

Some crops, however, have a short season. Cherries are in season for just six weeks, from mid-May through June. Spanish missionaries brought sweet cherries to California many years ago. Today five different types are grown in the state: Bing, Rainier, Tulare, Brooks, and Garnet. God has placed great health-giving qualities in cherries. They are rich in B vitamins and minerals. They make our bones healthy and help reduce the risk of cancer and heart disease.

Farmers have learned that cherries will sometimes pop if water sits on them too long. When there has been a large amount of rain, growers dry their cherry trees using large fans or low-flying helicopters! Since most of California's cherries are grown not to be canned or frozen but to be sold as fresh produce, farmers have to work quickly. Cherries do not ripen off the tree, so farmers hire workers to hand pick them when they are ripe. They must be cooled immediately, so they are put in portable coolers while still in the orchard. The cherries are then quickly sorted and packed. Ideally, the cherry is picked off the tree just twenty-four hours before it arrives in the grocery store.

California is Number One

California produces more of the following fruits than any other state: apricots, avocados, Bartlett pears, bell peppers, cantaloupe, freestone peaches, honeydew melons, lemons, limes, nectarines, persimmons, plums, raspberries, strawberries, table grapes, tangelos, and tangerines. See California table grapes at right. California also leads the nation in growing these vegetables: asparagus, broccoli, Brussels sprouts, carrots, cauliflower, celery, eggplant, garlic, green onions, head

These plump, seedless, white Autumn King table grapes were grown in California. They ripen in late summer.

lettuce, leaf lettuce, Romaine lettuce, and spinach. As impressive as these lists are, California also grows ninety-nine percent or more of America's annual production of almonds, artichokes, clingstone peaches, dates, figs, raisins, kiwi, olives, pistachios, dried plums (also called prunes), pomegranates, and walnuts!

In addition to all these crops for which California ranks first in the nation, it ranks second in many crops. In 2008 it ranked second in the production of cabbage, cherries, chili peppers, pumpkins, sweet corn, squash, sweet potatoes, and watermelon.

U.S. Department of Agriculture geneticist Craig Ledbetter examines almonds in a test plot in California.

California Almonds

Of all the crops grown in California, the number one crop is almonds. See photo at left. California farmers began to plant many almond trees in the late 1960s. From the mid-sixties to the mid-eighties, the number of almond trees mature enough to bear fruit increased four hundred percent. Today California supplies three out of four of all the almonds in the world. Spain imports more California almonds than any other country. China, Germany, India, and the United Arab Emirates also buy many California almonds.

California Dried Plums and Raisins

Prunes and raisins are fruits preserved by drying, a food preservation method that dates back to Biblical times. In 1 Chronicles 16:3, King David gave everyone in Israel a raisin cake.

Six out of ten prunes produced in the world are from California. See photo at right. During the Gold Rush, French brothers Louis and Pierre Pellier brought a Petite d'Argen plum tree from France. They grafted it onto the rootstock of a wild American plum.

Plum Grown in California

In 1905 one California plum grower did not have enough workers to harvest his plums. He got five hundred monkeys, which he organized into gangs of fifty. Each gang had a person to oversee it. The harvest was successful, except for one detail. The monkeys ate the plums! Today a machine shakes the tree trunk and the plums fall onto a fabric sheet. A conveyor belt takes the fruit away. The plums are washed and weighed before being stacked onto trays. They are then rolled into tunnels to dry and become prunes. Afterwards, the prunes are sorted and steamed, the pits are removed, and they are put into packages.

According to legend, the first crop of raisins in California was produced by accident in 1873. When a heat wave hit vineyards in the Great Central Valley, most of the grapes dried while still on the vine. Three years later William Thompson, an immigrant from Scotland, began growing sweet, seedless grapes with thin skins. Ninety-five percent of the raisins grown in California today are made from Thompson seedless grapes. Other immigrants also greatly influenced this California crop. Armenian immigrants came to California in the late 1800s. Their culture has a long history of expertise in growing grapes. Many of California's modern grape growers are descendants of these Armenian settlers.

These grapes were grown in California. The center cluster of grapes has dried and become raisins.

Today grapes are removed from the vine while still in clusters. Workers then place the clusters on paper trays which are lying on the ground between the rows of grape vines. After two or three weeks of being dried by the sun, workers take the raisins out of the field for further drying and packaging. See photo at left.

Citrus Trees Come to California

When President Nixon was born, his family lived on a California lemon ranch. California grows most of America's lemons that are sold fresh. Lemons grown in Florida and Arizona are often used to make lemonade and lemon juice. Lemon growers have found an ingenious way to keep harmful snails off their trees. They put a copper ring around the tree trunk. When a snail's slime touches the copper, the snail receives an electrical shock.

The first citrus fruit seeds were brought to California by Spanish priests in 1769. A Spanish priest planned California's first large citrus grove in 1804. Native Americans living nearby planted it.

When people do not get enough Vitamin C, they get a disease called scurvy. Ship captains have for many years taken lemons on long voyages to keep their sailors healthy. When people flocked to California during the 1849 Gold Rush, many suffered from scurvy. The price of lemons rose to $1.00 each! That is a high price even today. Former fur trapper William Wolfskin reaped the benefits of those high prices. In 1840 he planted hundreds of orange and lemon seedlings on two acres of land. Those two acres are now part of Los Angeles.

By the time Wolfskin died in 1866, he had added many more acres of orange trees. His son Joseph took over his father's agribusiness. After the completion of the transcontinental railroad, Joseph Wolfskin sent a load of oranges east to St. Louis. Easterners enjoyed this new treat, and California citrus farmers gained a new market for their fruit.

Southern California Fruit Exchange worker puts crates of oranges into a refrigerated rail car in 1943.

Sunkist Citrus Fruits

Some farmers sell their products directly to consumers at farmer's markets, but most sell them to a wholesale company, which sells them to retail stores, which sell them to the consumer. People working for wholesale companies are sometimes called middlemen. In the late 1800s, citrus growers suffered because wholesale companies were making most of the money from the sale of oranges. In 1893 several growers formed the Southern California Fruit Exchange, a sort of wholesale company of their own called a co-op. In the photo at left, a man working for the co-op is putting crates of oranges into a refrigerated railcar. By 1908 this growers' co-op was calling its best fruit Sunkist. In the photo below, a woman is putting oranges into a crate labeled Sunkist. The growers started stamping their fruit with that name in 1926 and they continue to do so today.

In 1916 Sunkist started educating consumers on a new kind of beverage they could make from oranges—orange juice. In the 1920s, ships started taking California oranges and lemons through the Panama Canal and on to London, England. In 1966 Sunkist shipped 12,400,000 cartons of fresh fruit all over the world. When the Sunkist farmer cooperative celebrated its one hundredth anniversary in 1993, annual sales worldwide had reached 80,000,000 cartons per year!

A woman puts oranges into a crate labeled Sunkist.

843

Avocados, Romaine, and the Mother Navel

Six thousand California growers raise avocados. Unlike cherries, avocados ripen after they come off the tree. To harvest the fruit, workers climb ladders up to thirty feet tall and cut off the fruit using fourteen-foot-long clippers. When a worker has filled the bag on his shoulder with thirty to fifty pounds of fruit, he brings it down and puts it into a bin before climbing back up the ladder to get more.

California farmers have learned innovative ways to get produce to market as fresh as possible. For example, Romaine lettuce is grown along California's central coast. Workers take bag sealing machines into the lettuce fields. They cut the lettuce, bag it, and seal it right in the field.

In 1870 the California Commissioner of Agriculture gave three navel orange trees from Brazil to Luther and Eliza Tibbets who lived in Riverside, California. Five years later, the Tibbets harvested their first crop of navel oranges. Customers loved their sweet flavor. Since navel oranges have no seeds, citrus growers grow additional naval oranges by grafting a bud from a navel orange tree onto another citrus tree. By 1875 citrus growers were paying $5.00 for each navel orange bud. By 1900 California had 5.5 million navel orange trees! One of those first trees still grows in Riverside. It is called the Mother Navel.

The Great Central Valley

God shaped the interior of California into what is known as the Great Central Valley. The Central Valley is about 450 miles long and between forty and sixty miles wide. Its eighteen counties make up two fifths of the land area of the whole state. Seven of California's top ten agricultural counties are in the Great Central Valley.

The valley is home to dairy farms and ranches raising beef cows. California leads the nation in milk and cream production, and much of what the state produces comes from the valley. The Great Central Valley also has many vineyards. Over half of California's citrus is grown here

"All Races Serve the Crops in California"

The Library of Congress holds many photos by Depression-era photographer Dorothea Lange. The photos below were taken in 1938 and are in a collection entitled "All Races Serve the Crops in California." They are labeled as follows (clockwise, beginning at top left): "Filipinos working in pole peas," "from Texas," "Future voter and his Mexican Father," and "Pea picker from Texas."

and it is the center of the state's almond production. Growers in the valley also tend many cherry, peach, and plum orchards.

Most of California's rice is grown in the southern half of the Great Central Valley. In late spring, farmers flood their rice fields with four to six inches of water. Airplanes fly over the fields, dropping rice seed into the water. God causes the rice seeds to sprout. By fall He has caused them to grow into mature stalks. Farmers harvest the rice with a combine. The rice grains are sold for food. The stalks are also sold. They are used as a growing medium for mushrooms and as an component in fiberboard used for building construction. Many species of birds stop in the rice fields as they migrate from north to south. Mammals and amphibians live in them too.

California Farmers and Farm Workers

Though much of America's food is grown on giant farms owned by corporations, nine out of ten California farms are either family farms or farms owned by partners. The average farm is 347 acres, but six out of ten farms have less than fifty acres.

Immigrants have long been a source of workers for California farms. See box on page 844. In the late 1800s, most immigrant farm workers were Chinese. They were gradually replaced by Japanese, then immigrants from the Philippines, then immigrants from India, and then Mexico. Today's immigrant farm workers mainly come from Mexico and Central America.

God has provided the soils, sunshine, and water needed for California's crops. He has also given people strength and intellect to know how to use them:

> He who tills his land will have plenty of food,
> But he who follows empty pursuits will have poverty in plenty.
> Proverbs 28:19

Activities for Lesson 134

Thinking Biblically – Jesus told parables about vineyards. Read Matthew 20:1-16 and 21:28-45.

Map Study – Complete the assignment for Lesson 134 on Map 2 "God's Wonders" in *Maps of America the Beautiful*.

Literature – Read "The Story of the Navel Orange" in *We the People*, pages 176-177.

Timeline – In *Timeline of America the Beautiful* next to 1900, write: California has 5.5 million navel orange trees.

Student Workbook or Lesson Review – If you are using one of these optional books, complete the assignment for Lesson 134.

Mister Rogers, Neighbor to America's Children

Mister Rogers meets with President George W. Bush in 2002.

Fred McFeely Rogers began the television show *Mister Rogers' Neighborhood* in Pittsburgh, Pennsylvania, in 1968. Five years earlier, President John F. Kennedy established the highest award an American civilian can receive from the United States, the Presidential Medal of Freedom. President George W. Bush presented the Medal of Freedom to Fred Rogers in 2002. The text of the citation accompanying his medal reads:

Fred Rogers has entertained and educated children for more than thirty years through his extraordinary public television program, "Mister Rogers' Neighborhood." His program helps children understand caring, safety, and respect for others, and his legendary commitment to young people has been an enriching part of American life. The United States honors Fred Rogers for his dedication to the well-being of children, his faith, his family, and his community, and for a career that demonstrates the importance of kindness, compassion, and learning.

Fred Rogers was a devoted follower of Jesus Christ. At the heart of all he did was a firm belief in Jesus. A person who is familiar with teachings from the Bible can find many Biblical concepts as they watch *Mister Rogers' Neighborhood*.

Fred Rogers' pattern was to go to bed each night at 9:30 p.m. He awoke every morning at 5:00 a.m. He prayed for his family and his friends by name. He thanked God for people he had known before who had since passed away, and he read the Bible. At 7:30 a.m. he took a swim in a local swimming pool. Before diving in, he quietly sang in Latin a song a friend had taught him. In English, the words are: "Rejoice in the Lord. Rejoice in the Lord. Alleluia." When he arrived at the television studio to begin his workday, he prayed that God would let some word he said be His.

Fred's prayers were not all private ones. In 1992 he led a public prayer at the commencement exercises at Boston University. The cheering students were so excited about seeing their old childhood television friend that he had to calm them down so they could pray. He asked them to sing with him, "It's a Beautiful Day in the Neighborhood," a song that these television friends knew by heart.

Mister Rogers' Neighborhood

When parents turned on the television for their children to watch *Mister Rogers' Neighborhood*, the parents often sat down beside the children. They knew that lessons he taught their children were lessons they needed to learn and remember themselves. Many programs designed for children turn out to be harmful to them. Mister Rogers always sought simply to have a visit with those he called his "television neighbors." Always in his heart was Jesus' admonition to "love your neighbor as yourself."

The show had a simple format. It began with a view of a toy model of Mister Rogers' neighborhood. A trolley ran through the neighborhood as the show's theme song played in the background. The camera then went inside Mister Rogers' television house and panned to the front door. The smiling Mister Rogers walked into the room from outside, wearing a coat, a tie, and dress shoes, as he sang, "It's a beautiful day in the neighborhood." In his hand was often an object he wanted to show the children. He went to the closet to hang up his coat and pull out one of the hand-knit sweaters his mother had made for him. As he pulled the zipper up the front, he continued to sing, asking the children to be his neighbor and telling each listener that he had always wanted a neighbor "just like you." As he finished the song, he sat on a bench and changed into his tennis shoes.

Sitting on the bench, Mister Rogers told the children about what he had brought for them to see. He knew that children like to see things that are familiar to them. In many shows, Mister Rogers did familiar things, like go to the dentist or lie down to take a nap. As he did so, he talked to the children about what he was doing and mentioned things he knew they sometimes wondered. Gentle piano music often played in the background. In many ways, Mr. Rogers was demonstrating to children (and their parents) how to deal with life in a calm way.

Television shows often try to show children something new every few seconds, but not Mister Rogers. The pace of *Mister Rogers' Neighborhood* was always slow, so that children could think about what he was saying. He also wanted them to feel that he had plenty of time for each of them. He made simple things like flashlights seem marvelous. He was a master at creating a sense of wonder in children. Sometimes the things he did may have seemed childish to older viewers, but he was trying to show children that what they liked to do was not silly but very important.

Often, while Mister Rogers talked to his television neighbors, he was interrupted by a knock on the door. On his way to the door, he pulled back a curtain and peeked out the window to tell the children who the visitor was. Sometimes Mister Rogers was interrupted by a famous artist, musician, or other person he wanted his neighbors to meet. Sometimes Mister Rogers took his viewers out of his television house into the neighborhood or to the place where the famous person worked.

Often Mister McFeely, the Speedy Delivery man, came to bring Mister Rogers a delivery. In contrast to the slow-paced Mister Rogers, Mister McFeely was always in a big hurry. Many times Mister McFeely brought a movie that Mister Rogers would put in "Picture-Picture." Often the movie was about how people make something. Mister Rogers himself was very interested in all kinds of things, and he tried to pass his excitement on to the children. He was curious and he wanted the children to know that being curious was a good thing. He also wanted them to see that all people are important and that we depend on each other. If he was talking about a flashlight, for instance, he wanted the children to know about the people who work in factories to make flashlights. By showing children how important each person's job was, he was telling them that each person is valuable. Often Mister McFeely would take a pause from his busyness and watch "Picture-Picture" or talk to Mister Rogers about important things. Mister Rogers and Mister McFeely taught viewers that people who are different can still care about one another and be good friends.

One segment of each show was devoted to the Neighborhood of Make-Believe, where Mister Rogers' cast of puppets talked about the same things Mister Rogers had been talking about that day. The connection between Mister Rogers' television house and the Neighborhood of Make-Believe was a trolley, which Mister Rogers sent on its way in his television house. When the camera switched to Make-Believe, the first thing the children saw was the trolley coming out of a tunnel.

Each puppet was a creation of Mister Rogers' imagination. While the children watched what was happening in the Neighborhood of Make-Believe, Mister Rogers was backstage working as the puppeteer. He did the puppets' voices and made them move. Many puppets lived in Make-Believe, including the main characters, King Friday XIII, Queen Sara, Prince Tuesday, Daniel Striped Tiger, Henrietta Pussy Cat, X the Owl, and Lady Elaine Fairchilde. Humans lived there, too, including Handyman Negri and Lady Aberlin.

After some time in the Neighborhood of Make-Believe, the trolley returned to Mr. Rogers' television living room, where the viewers again spent time with Mr. Rogers.

When it was time for the show to end, Mister Rogers put things away in his television house, while talking to the children about the visit they had just had. He sat back on the bench and sang about how "it's such a good feeling to know you're alive," as he put his dress shoes back on, put his sweater back in the closet, and put his sport coat on again. He finished by talking a little more and letting the children know he would be back when the day (or week) was new. He finished by telling them, "You always make it a special day for me. You know how, by just your being yourself. That's right. People can like you just the way you are." Then he walked back out the door he had entered about half an hour before.

Modern-Day Main Street in Latrobe, Pennsylvania

The Childhood of Mister Rogers

Fred McFeely Rogers was born in 1928, forty miles from Pittsburgh in the small town of Latrobe, Pennsylvania, pictured at left. His father, James Hillis Rogers, was a successful and well-respected businessman. His mother, Nancy McFeely Rogers, was sweet and kind. Her father had also been a successful businessman. Both sides of Fred's family believed in staying close to their friends, relatives, and community. They also believed in serving others.

Fred grew up in a loving home. He enjoyed happy times singing while his mother played the piano, and at five years old he began to play himself. However, a few years of his childhood were sad. Western Pennsylvania had problems with air pollution because of its industries. Like some other children there, Fred suffered from childhood asthma, which often kept him indoors. As an only child who was often sick, he felt isolated from other people and found comfort in his grandfather, his mother's father, who used to tell him, "Freddie, you make my day very special." Fred Rogers always reminded his viewers that each of them was special. Mister McFeely, the Speedy Delivery man, was named for this grandfather, whose name was Fred McFeely. Instead of becoming bitter about his childhood sadness, Fred used his experiences to understand the feelings of children, and he devoted his adult life to blessing them.

When Fred was eleven years old, his parents adopted a daughter, Elaine (Fred Rogers later named one of his puppet characters Lady Elaine Fairchilde because he thought of his sister as a "fair child"). By the time he entered high school, Fred had become a good student and an excellent musician. He became popular and, by the time he was a senior, was so well-respected that his fellow students elected him to be the president of their student council.

The College Years of Mister Rogers

After high school, Fred Rogers went to Dartmouth College. After one year, he transferred to Rollins College in Winter Park, Florida, to study music. He planned to enter a Presbyterian seminary after graduating from Rollins and become a minister.

At Rollins, Fred met his future wife, Sara Joanne Byrd, a concert pianist. (She was called Joanne; when Fred later created his puppet characters, he used her first name for the wife of King Friday XIII, Queen Sara.) Mrs. Rogers later recalled the exceptional musical talents Fred already had during his college years and also how much fun he was.

Knowles Memorial Chapel, Rollins College

A trip home to Latrobe in 1951 changed the course of his future. While there he saw some television shows geared to children. He was appalled at the poor quality. He later said, "I got into television because I hated it so. And I thought, 'There's some way of using this fabulous instrument to nurture those who would watch and listen.'"

Mister Rogers Works in Television

In 1951 Fred Rogers graduated from Rollins College with a degree in music and got a job at the NBC television network in New York City. He worked as an assistant producer and a floor director. The following year he married his college sweetheart Joanne. In 1953 Fred learned that Pittsburgh was about to begin the first television station that would be owned by a community, WQED. He decided to go back to western Pennsylvania and work at this new station. His friends in New York were surprised because they believed he had a promising career there.

In Pittsburgh, Fred began to work on an hour-long program called *The Children's Corner* with Josie Carey as its host. He composed music, played the organ, and worked as a puppeteer. He developed puppet characters, including a tiger named Daniel, an owl named X, a pussycat named Henrietta, and two puppets named King Friday and Lady Elaine Fairchilde. The show won an award for the best local children's program in the country.

Fred's early years at WQED were very busy. He and Josie Carey traveled once a week to New York to do a live show there. He also attended Pittsburgh Theological Seminary and the University of Pittsburgh's Graduate School of Child Development. After spending eight years studying part-time at the seminary, Fred Rogers was ordained by the United Presbyterian Church in 1963. He was made an evangelist and charged to continue working with children and families through mass media.

Later that year Fred and Joanne moved to Canada, where he had been invited by their public broadcasting service to create a children's program. In Canada he worked for the first time in front of the television camera instead of just behind the scenes. He did a series that his employer titled MISTEROGERS. In 1966 Fred and Joanne decided they wanted to live and raise their two sons in Pittsburgh.

Mister Rogers Begins *Mister Rogers' Neighborhood*

Back in Pittsburgh, Fred returned to WQED, pictured below. There he began developing *Mister Rogers' Neighborhood*. At first the show aired on the Eastern Educational Network (EEN). One of the cities that saw *Mister Rogers' Neighborhood* on the EEN was Boston. Its public television station WGBH invited Fred and his *Mister Rogers' Neighborhood* crew to come there for an open house. Ten thousand people lined up outside the station to meet Mister Rogers. This was quite a surprise for the people at WGBH, who had expected about five hundred. Mister Rogers' popularity grew. National Educational Television (NET) began to carry the show in 1968. NET later became the Public Broadcasting Service (PBS). Now children all over the country could see the show. During the thirty-three years that Mister Rogers created his television show, he made almost nine hundred episodes.

WQED Headquarters in Pittsburgh, Pennsylvania

Mister Rogers: Activist, Composer, Author, and Speaker

Believing that television could be a tool for good, Mister Rogers continued to be saddened by the bad things shown on TV. By 1969 he had become so well-known that he was asked to testify about television before a Congressional committee. As he gave a powerful plea for better television, Congressmen and others in the room were brought to tears.

Mister Rogers composed over two hundred songs. He wrote many books for both children and parents. He received many honorary degrees and gave many speeches.

The year before his death, Mister Rogers spoke at Dartmouth College, where he had begun college fifty-six years before. He told a story about a child running a race in the Special Olympics. The child fell down and began to cry. Every one of the other runners stopped, turned around, and went back to comfort the crying child. The runners linked arms and walked to the finish line together. Mister Rogers told his listeners, "It's not the honors and the prizes and the fancy outsides of life which ultimately nourish our souls. It's the knowing that we can be trusted, that we never have to fear the truth, that the bedrock of our lives from which we make our choices is very good stuff."

Remembering Mister Rogers

Fred Rogers died at his home in Pittsburgh in 2003 at the age of 74, leaving a loving family including his wife Joanne, their sons James and John, three grandsons, and millions of neighbors.

Fred and Joanne Rogers had a long, loving marriage. She once said that her husband was her icon first, before he became an icon for millions of Americans. A classmate who knew them at Rollins College once attended a college reunion with them. She said that Fred was playing the piano when his wife came into the room late. He stopped playing and hurried over to give her a hug and a kiss.

Mister Rogers had many things to teach his viewers. Just reading a few of his song titles gives a glimpse of those lessons: "It's Such a Good Feeling," "Let's Think of Something to Do While We're Waiting," "You've Got to Do It," "You Can Never Go Down the Drain," and "What Do You Do with the Mad That You Feel?" One way to summarize how Mister Rogers saw people, especially children, is to read some more of his song titles: "Everybody's Fancy," "I'm Proud of You," "It's You I Like," "There Are Many Ways to Say I Love You," "You Are Special," "You're Growing," and "Won't You Be My Neighbor?"

Mister Rogers received many awards and honors during his lifetime. In 1996 *TV Guide* named him one of the top fifty stars of all time. In 1998 he received a Lifetime Achievement Award from the Academy of Television Arts and Sciences. His star was placed on the Hollywood Walk of Fame in 1998.

Family Communications Inc., which he founded in 1971, is now called The Fred Rogers Company. In 2008 the Fred M. Rogers Center opened at Saint Vincent College in Latrobe, Pennsylvania. It includes the Fred Rogers Center for Early Learning and Children's Media, an exhibit about Fred Rogers, as well as personal papers belonging to Mister Rogers. Mister Rogers helped plan the center before he died. One of its purposes is to continue his efforts for good television and other media, especially for young children.

In the Smithsonian's National Museum of American History is a red knit cardigan Mister Rogers wore. It is pictured at right. Mr. Rogers wore more than twenty-four different cardigan sweaters during his thirty-three years on the program. He said that his mother made one sweater a month for all the years he knew her. Each Christmas she gave each family member a sweater. She would ask them all what kind they wanted the next year and then turn to her son and say, "I know what kind you want, Freddy. You want the one with the zipper up the front."

Mister Rogers' Sweater
at the Smithsonian

Mister Fred McFeely Rogers tried to obey the two commandments that Jesus said were the most important, and he encouraged others to do the same:

You shall love the Lord your God with all your heart,
and with all your soul, and with all your mind.
This is the great and foremost commandment.
The second is like it, You shall love your neighbor as yourself.
On these two commandments depend the whole law and the Prophets.
Matthew 22:37-40

Activities for Lesson 135

Vocabulary – In your notebook, write your own definition for each of these words: citation, commencement, admonition, nurture, ordain. Look in the lesson for clues to the meaning of the words. When you are finished writing your definitions, look in a dictionary for comparison.

Creative Writing – Fred Rogers taught his young neighbors to use their imagination to confront childhood fears. What is something you feared when you were a young child? In your notebook, write a story of at least two pages with imaginary characters who acknowledge, confront, and learn about this same fear.

Timeline – In *Timeline of America the Beautiful* next to 1966, write: Mister Rogers moves to Pittsburgh and continues to work in television.

Student Workbook or Lesson Review – If you are using one of these optional books, complete the assignment for Lesson 135. If you are using the Lesson Review, take the quiz for Unit 27.

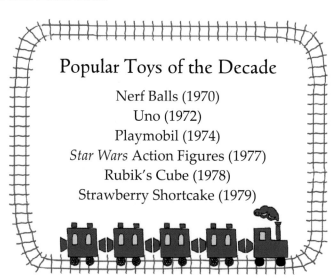

Popular Toys of the Decade

Nerf Balls (1970)
Uno (1972)
Playmobil (1974)
Star Wars Action Figures (1977)
Rubik's Cube (1978)
Strawberry Shortcake (1979)

The 1980s

World events that took place during the presidencies of Ronald Reagan and George Herbert Walker Bush amazed the world. Like other modern Presidents, Reagan founded a presidential library after leaving office. Washington's Mount Saint Helens erupted in 1980.

It continued to spew and sputter in the coming years. Bill Gates led the Microsoft software company, becoming one of the wealthiest men in the world. He and his wife decided to give much of their money away through the Bill and Melinda Gates Foundation. Many Americans went on a spending spree throughout the eighties. In 1992 Mall of America opened in Minnesota.

President Reagan on Air Force One, 1981

Lessons in Unit 28

Lesson 136 – Our American Story: The Reagan-Bush Years
Lesson 137 – An American Landmark: The Ronald Reagan Presidential
            Library and Museum
Lesson 138 – God's Wonders: God Created Mount Saint Helens
Lesson 139 – An American Biography: Bill Gates, Entrepreneur and Philanthropist
Lesson 140 – Daily Life: Shopping in America

Books Used in Unit 28

- *Maps of America the Beautiful*

- *Timeline of America the Beautiful*

- *We the People*

The Reagan-Bush Years

When the decade of the 1980s began, the U.S. economy was not doing well. The Americans that militant Muslims had taken hostage in Iran late in 1979 had still not been released. President Jimmy Carter was losing popularity. It is highly unusual for a President in office seeking re-election to be opposed by another member of his own political party. However, Senator Edward "Teddy" Kennedy, brother of President John F. Kennedy and Senator Robert Kennedy, campaigned to get the Democratic nomination in 1980. Carter was able to beat Kennedy in the Democratic primaries and was named the Democratic candidate at their convention.

Two of the Republicans who sought the Republican nomination were former California Governor Ronald Reagan and George Herbert Walker Bush, the Director of the Central Intelligence Agency (George Herbert Walker Bush is the father of George W. Bush, who was elected President in 2000). Reagan won the nomination and chose Bush as his running mate.

President Carter was very aware of America's problems and often talked about them. Ronald Reagan, on the other hand, was optimistic about America's future. He wanted to cut taxes to help the economy grow. He believed in a strong American military and a smaller government in Washington. American voters liked what they heard and elected Reagan and Bush.

President Carter continued to his last day in office trying to negotiate with officials in Iran to get the hostages released. On inauguration day, January 20, 1981, the hostages were released as President Reagan was being inaugurated.

President and Mrs. Reagan brought a more formal style to the presidency. Whereas President and Mrs. Carter had walked down Pennsylvania Avenue hand-in-hand four years before, President Reagan's inauguration was grand and stately. See President and Mrs. Reagan at left in the 1981 inaugural parade.

Ronald Reagan was sixty-nine years old when he was inaugurated, the oldest man ever to become President of the United States. Though some voters worried about his age, he proved his physical strength and mental alertness early in his presidency. An emotionally unstable man tried to assassinate President Reagan about a month after his

President and Mrs. Reagan in the 1981 Inaugural Parade

The Reagans leave the hospital after the assassination attempt.

inauguration. Reagan not only survived but regained his health. Through it all, he maintained a sense of humor. See Reagan leaving the hospital in the photo at left.

President Reagan appointed Sandra Day O'Connor to be the first woman justice on the Supreme Court. He worked with Congress to pass a major tax cut. Inflation went down and the economy slowly recovered, even though the Federal government spent billions more each year than it took in through taxes. The nation was pleased with Reagan's leadership and re-elected the Reagan-Bush team in 1984.

Space Shuttle *Columbia*

President Reagan was a great supporter of American space travel and research. On April 12, 1981, exactly twenty years after Russian cosmonaut Yuri Gagarin became the first human being to orbit the earth, America launched its first space shuttle, *Columbia*. See photo below. The *Columbia* was the first reusable spacecraft. Three years later, Sally K. Ride, an astrophysicist, became America's first female astronaut. About six weeks later, Air

Force Colonel Guion S. Bluford, an aerospace engineer, became America's first black astronaut.

Though NASA had many successes in the 1980s, it also experienced tragedy. In 1986 the *Challenger* space shuttle exploded just seconds after it launched, killing the seven astronauts on board. President Reagan, skilled at knowing what to say in many situations, comforted the nation when he spoke to the American people from the Oval Office after the *Challenger* accident. For two years, NASA did not send any more astronauts into space as they studied what had gone wrong with the *Challenger*.

Launch of Space Shuttle Columbia *on April 12, 1981*

Strength Against Communism

President Reagan worked to eliminate Communism. He believed it was morally wrong. During his presidency, the U.S. Central Intelligence Agency (CIA) trained citizens of Communist countries who wanted to work to overthrow their Communist governments. One group of rebels helped by the CIA was the Contras of Nicaragua, a country in Central America.

People who worked under President Reagan hurt his reputation in what came to be called the Iran-Contra Scandal. They secretly sold military equipment to Iran and gave some of the money to Nicaragua's Contras. Those who did this believed they were doing a good thing. At the time, Americans were being held hostage in Lebanon. The people making the secret deals thought that their actions would do two good things: encourage

Iran to help get the hostages freed and help overthrow the Communist government in Nicaragua. However, what they did was against the law. One Reagan adviser went to jail for six months as a result of these crimes.

Reagan strongly opposed Communism in the U.S.S.R. In a speech he made in 1983, he called the Soviet Union an "evil empire." See photo at right. However, President Reagan also wanted to

Reagan Giving His "Evil Empire" Speech, 1983

build a better relationship with the Soviet Union, knowing that this would make America safer. The Soviet leader at the time was Secretary General Mikhail Gorbachev. He too wanted improved relations between the two countries. Gorbachev knew that his country was spending too much money on their military, causing financial problems. Gorbachev, Reagan, and their advisors worked out an agreement to destroy some of both countries' nuclear weapons. President Reagan and Secretary General Gorbachev are pictured below in Moscow's Red Square. In the center below is the first page of a handwritten letter President Reagan sent to Gorbachev in 1985.

In 1987 President Reagan was invited to give a speech in front of the Berlin Wall. See photo at right below. Notice in the photograph that the wall is covered with graffiti.

Bush, Reagan, and Gorbachev, 1988

Towering up behind the wall is the Brandenburg Gate, a Berlin landmark dating back to 1791. During this historic speech, President Reagan gave the Soviet leader a challenge. Reagan said, "Mr. Gorbachev, tear down this wall!" In the photo above, Vice President George H. W. Bush, President Reagan, and Secretary General Gorbachev visit Governor's Island in New York City on a cold November day in 1988.

President Reagan completed two terms in office in January of 1989. Read about his life on the following pages.

Reagan and Gorbachev, 1988

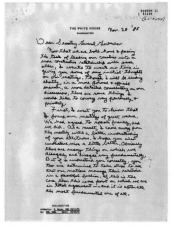

Letter from Reagan to Gorbachev

President Reagan speaks in front of the Berlin Wall in 1987.

Ronald Wilson Reagan
America's Fortieth President
January 20, 1981 - January 20, 1989

Parents John and Nelle Reagan and their two-year-old son Neil were living in a five-room apartment in Tampico, Illinois, when they welcomed ten-pound Ronald Wilson Reagan into the family on February 6, 1911. According to family legend, his father said this about his new baby boy: "He's a fat little Dutchman, but who knows, he might grow up to be President some day." Ronald Reagan carried traits from both parents into his adult life. John Reagan was a hard worker, a great storyteller, and a man who believed in the equality of every man and woman. Nelle Reagan believed deeply in prayer. She was very involved in the Disciples of Christ church. She believed that what happens to people is part of God's perfect plan. Nelle Reagan believed there was good in all people. She helped her family and friends, and also people at the local jail.

After several moves, the Reagan family settled in Dixon, Illinois, when Ronnie was nine. Two years later Ronald was baptized at his mother's church. While in high school, he became a lifeguard. In 1928 he enrolled in Eureka College, a small Christian school in the town of Eureka, Illinois. He continued to lifeguard during the summers and, by the end of seven summers, had rescued seventy-seven people. Ronald Reagan was an average student academically, but he excelled in football and acting (like his mother, who acted in local theater).

A few weeks after Ronald Reagan graduated from Eureka, he got a job as a radio announcer in Davenport, Iowa. In 1937 a Hollywood agent discovered his talents and offered him a seven-year contract working for the Warner Brothers company. That year Reagan made the first of more than fifty movies.

In 1940 Ronald Reagan married actress Jane Wyman. That same year, he portrayed football star George Gipp in the film *Knute Rockne, All American*, and gained his nickname, "The Gipper" (see page 599). When America entered World War II the following year, Reagan was drafted into the Army and was assigned to the Motion Picture Army Unit to make training films.

Reagan had joined the Screen Actors Guild (SAG) in 1937 and become a member of its board in 1941. In 1946 he became involved in a problem between SAG and another actors' union. The leader of the other group was a suspected Communist. Reagan's distrust of Communists began with this experience. Starting in 1947, Reagan served for five terms as president of SAG. As president of the union, he testified against Communists before the U.S. House of Representatives' Committee on Un-American Activities.

During their eight-year marriage, Jane gave birth to a daughter, Maureen, and a premature baby who died. They also adopted a son, Michael. Ronald and Jane divorced in 1948. In 1952 Reagan married actress Nancy Davis.

Ronald Reagan had been a Democrat for many years. In 1950 he had campaigned against Richard Nixon when Nixon ran for the U.S. Senate from California. However, in 1952 and 1956, Reagan led Democrats who supported Eisenhower in his presidential campaigns. In 1960 he gave more than two hundred speeches in favor of Republican candidate Richard Nixon. In 1962 he left the Democratic Party and became a Republican.

In 1954 Ronald Reagan was hired to host a Sunday evening television show, *General Electric Theater*. He was required to make appearances at GE factories, where he gave speeches. This gave him good experience, which he would later use in his political career. In 1964 he began to host a different television show, *Death Valley Days*.

In 1965 Reagan published an autobiography, *Where's the Rest of Me?* The following year he ran against the incumbent Democratic Governor of California and won by almost one million votes. While serving as Governor, Reagan cut the state budget by ten percent, which helped the state's financial difficulties. In 1968 he tried unsuccessfully to obtain the Republican nomination for President. In 1970 he was re-elected Governor of California. He did such a good job managing the state budget of California that he was able to give taxpayers a rebate. During the Watergate scandal, Reagan defended Nixon, until the evidence was so strong that he finally declared that Nixon had deceived the country.

After two terms as Governor, Reagan re-entered private life in 1975. He soon announced his decision to seek again the Republican presidential nomination. At the Republican National Convention, 47.4 percent of the delegates supported Reagan, but incumbent President Ford was chosen as the candidate. Reagan gave a speech at the convention, which was well-received by the delegates. Before seeking the presidential nomination again in 1980, Ronald Reagan wrote a weekly newspaper column, gave speeches, and worked at his California ranch.

After eight years in the White House, Ronald and Nancy Reagan returned to California. They divided their time between a new home in BelAir and their ranch. President Reagan left office with the highest approval rating of any President since Franklin Roosevelt. In 1989 Reagan was knighted by Queen Elizabeth II. He published his autobiography, *An American Life*. In 1993 Ronald Reagan was diagnosed with Alzheimer's disease, which Nancy Reagan later described as "the long goodbye."

Ronald Reagan died in 2004 at the age of 93. He was survived by his wife Nancy; son Michael; and by Patty and Ronald, the two children he had with Nancy. His daughter Maureen had died in 2001. The nation honored this admired President with a state funeral, in which he was lovingly remembered. His funeral procession is pictured at right. He remains one of America's most beloved and respected Presidents.

The Election of 1988

In 1988 the Republican Party nominated Vice President Bush as their presidential candidate. Bush chose Dan Quayle, a Senator from Indiana, as his running mate. The Democrats nominated Michael Dukakis, Governor of Massachusetts. Bush told Americans he wanted to see a "kinder, gentler America." He encouraged people to get involved with others, calling people who would do that "a thousand points of light." During the campaign, Bush declared that he would tell the Democrats in Congress, "Read my lips: no new taxes." In November of 1988, Vice President Bush became the first Vice President still in office to be elected President since Martin Van Buren was elected in 1836. See box at right.

> **President Bush and President Bush**
>
> America has had two Presidents named George Bush. One was George Herbert Walker Bush. The other was his son, George Walker Bush. Their names are almost exactly the same. As you read this lesson, remember that George Herbert Walker Bush became President in 1989 and his son George Walker Bush became President in 2001.

Answered Prayers

The changes that happened in the U.S.S.R. while Bush was President were beyond what many could hope or imagine. Christians had been praying for people behind the Iron Curtain (see page 711) for many years. The government of the Soviet Union was officially atheist, and Christians there were persecuted because of their beliefs. Missionaries had long been smuggling Bibles into Communist countries. Thousands of Christians behind the Iron Curtain had remained faithful even though many had suffered greatly.

Economic problems continued to get worse in those countries because the Communist economic system simply did not work. Citizens there became more dissatisfied with their governments. They wanted freedom.

In 1989 Gorbachev began to allow Soviet citizens more freedom. In March they voted in nationwide elections for the first time in the history of the U.S.S.R. They elected Gorbachev as their president. The next month he announced that the U.S.S.R. would be a democratic country!

The Soviet Union had long controlled smaller Communist countries in Eastern Europe. In June Poland elected Lech Walesa, a popular labor leader who believed in democratic principles, as their president. Soon the Eastern European countries of Hungary, Czechoslovakia, Bulgaria, and Romania forsook Communism and became democratic. It was Eisenhower's domino theory in reverse. These countries were not becoming Communist—they were becoming democratic.

On November 9, 1989, joyful Germans began to tear down the Berlin Wall. They were no longer afraid of the East Berlin police or the East German soldiers who now just stood by and watched them. Families and friends who had not been together since 1961 were reunited. In 1990 East and West Germany reunited under one government. In 1991 Gorbachev dissolved the Union of Soviet Socialist Republics, which divided into several independent, democratic nations, the largest of which was Russia. The Soviet Union was no more! American missionaries began going into the former U.S.S.R. and establishing churches. The Russian government even realized that Communism had left its citizens morally destitute and invited American missionaries to teach the Bible in its schools.

In 1990 the Communists were voted out of power in Nicaragua. Mikhail Gorbachev received the Nobel Peace Prize that year.

Trouble in the Middle East

As the Cold War ended, problems in the Middle East got worse. In 1990 the tiny country of Kuwait started producing more oil than it had in the past. This hurt the economy of the neighboring country of Iraq. Saddam Hussein, the Iraqi leader, sent military forces into Kuwait and declared it to be a new province of Iraq. President George H. W. Bush asked the United Nations to condemn what Saddam had done and to demand that he remove his troops. The U.N. Security Council voted formally to condemn Iraq.

In November, 1990, the U.N. Security Council approved using military force to make Iraqi forces leave Kuwait. President Bush did an excellent job of getting leaders of many nations to work together. With his leadership, thirty-two nations joined together in a coalition. In the photo below, Bush shares a laugh with Saudi Arabia's King Fahd while they meet together in the king's royal palace in November of 1990.

President George Herbert Walker Bush and King Fahd of Saudi Arabia share a laugh while Bush visits in Fahd's royal palace.

In early January of 1991, the U.S. Congress gave the President permission to order American troops to be part of a multi-nation military coalition which would force Iraqi troops out of Kuwait.

Saddam refused to remove his troops from Kuwait. On January 17, 1991, U.S. troops and others in the coalition began Operation Desert Storm to force the Iraqi military out of Kuwait. In the photo below, Bush speaks by phone with Egyptian President Hosni Mubarak the day before the operation was to begin.

At first coalition forces bombed military facilities within Iraq. In late February, American and coalition troops started sending in tanks and soldiers. By February 28, 1991, the coalition had completed its stated goal of pushing Iraqi forces out of Kuwait, so President Bush ordered a cease-fire after only one hundred hours of fighting. During the conflict, Saudi Arabia allowed American troops to be stationed in that country. In the center right photo, President Bush visits troops there. In the lower photo, Queen Elizabeth II and Prince Philip of the United Kingdom visit in the White House. The UK was a major part of the coalition.

President George Herbert Walker Bush speaks with Egyptian President Hosni Mubarak the day before Operation Desert Storm begins. Vice President Dan Quayle looks on.

President George Herbert Walker Bush meets with members of the U.S. military in Saudi Arabia.

Economic Troubles

The American economy again had major problems during Bush's presidency. The Federal government was spending much more than it received in taxes. To improve the economy, Bush made a compromise with Democrats in Congress, agreeing to cut spending and raise taxes. By agreeing to this, President Bush broke the promise he had made during the campaign. When he ran for re-election in 1992, the voters remembered this and held it against him.

During his time in office, Bush worked for civil rights for people with disabilities and worked for a cleaner environment. Read about the life of President George Herbert Walker Bush beginning on page 861.

Prince Philip, Barbara Bush, Queen Elizabeth II, President Bush, May, 1991

George Herbert Walker Bush
America's Forty-First President
January 20, 1989 - January 20, 1993

George Herbert Walker Bush was born to Prescott Sheldon and Dorothy Walker Bush in Milton, Massachusetts, in 1924. When George was young, his family moved to Greenwich, Connecticut. Prescott Bush was a wealthy banker and served as a Republican Senator from Connecticut from 1952 until 1963. Prescott and Dorothy Bush raised their children to be giving and to serve their fellow man. They also taught them to be humble.

During his high school years, George H. W. Bush went to a private boarding school in Massachusetts, where he excelled in athletics and was president of his senior class. During Christmas vacation in 1941, he met Barbara Pierce at a dance in Greenwich. On his eighteenth birthday in 1942, he graduated from high school and joined the United States Navy. Like Eisenhower, Kennedy, Johnson, Nixon, Ford, Carter, and Reagan, George Bush served in the U.S. military during World War II. He was America's last World War II veteran to become President. When he earned his pilot wings at age nineteen, he was the U.S. Navy's youngest pilot. Bush flew torpedo bombers. He came close to death when the Japanese shot his plane down over the Pacific Ocean. George bailed out and was soon rescued by an American submarine. He received the Distinguished Flying Cross for heroism under fire.

George Bush married Barbara Pierce early in 1945. They had six children: George Walker, born in 1946; Robin, born in 1949; John Ellis "Jeb," born in 1953; Neil, born in 1955; Marvin, born in 1956; and Dorothy "Doro," born in 1959. Their eldest daughter Robin died of leukemia when she was four years old.

In the fall of 1945, Bush entered Yale. After graduating with honors in 1948, he moved his wife and young son George to Texas, where he worked in the oil business. In 1963 Bush became the chairman of the Republican Party of Harris County, Texas. Three years later, he was elected to the U.S. House of Representatives, where he served for two terms.

In 1970 President Nixon nominated Bush as the U.S. Ambassador to the United Nations. In this position, Bush met many influential people from around the world. In 1973 Bush left the U.N. to serve as chairman of the Republican National Committee. He supported Nixon at the beginning of the Watergate scandal, but when he found out that Nixon had covered up evidence, Bush told Nixon that the Republican Party no longer supported him.

President Ford appointed George H. W. Bush as Chief of the United States Liaison Office in China. He served there for two years. In 1975 Ford appointed Bush as director of the Central Intelligence Agency. In 1980 Bush was elected Vice President of the United States. In the days before computers, people in business and government often kept names and addresses in a Rolodex, like the one at left. Each card had the name, address, and phone number of an individual or business. President Bush was known for his Rolodex where he kept a record of people he had met. His genuine caring for the people he met, his disciplined practice of keeping good records, and the high positions he held as a government servant prepared him to do a good job as President, especially when it came time to build a coalition before Operation Desert Storm.

Since leaving the presidency, President Bush has helped to raise hundreds of millions of dollars for good causes. He has served as honorary chairman of the Points of Light Institute and a life member of the M. D. Anderson Cancer Center Board of Visitors. George and Barbara Bush have served as honorary co-chairs of a coalition of cancer organizations, called C-Change. He has raised funds to help after several natural disasters, including Hurricane Katrina, Hurricane Ike, and a tsunami in Southeast Asia.

From 2006 to 2008, President Bush served as Chairman of the National Constitution Center in Philadelphia. The organization gave him a Liberty Medal in 2006. He has been active in The George Bush Presidential Library and Museum. He has also supported the George Bush School of Government and Public Service at Texas A&M University.

President Bush published his autobiography *Looking Forward* in 1987. He co-authored, with General Brent Scowcroft, *A World Transformed*, a book about how the Bush administration handled relations with other countries. In 2008 he published the diary he kept while serving as chief of the United States Liaison Office in China. It is entitled *The China Diary of George H. W. Bush: The Making of a Global President*.

George Bush has followed the teachings of his parents. He has a reputation as a decent, generous man who does what he believes is right. He is good at connecting with people and remains loyal to them. He and Barbara have a strong marriage and are very family-oriented. In

addition to family gatherings, their children, grandchildren, and extended family spend vacation time with them at their second home at Kennebunkport, Maine. The photo at left is their 1989 Christmas portrait.

Their son George served as Governor of Texas from 1995 to 2000 and served as the forty-third President of the United States from 2001 to 2009. From 1999 to 2007, their son Jeb was Governor of Florida.

Grandchildren are the crown of old men and the glory of sons is their fathers.
Proverbs 17:6

Activities for Lesson 136

Thinking Biblically – President George H. W. Bush encouraged people to become "a thousand points of light" by getting involved with others. Copy Matthew 5:14-16 into your notebook.

Vocabulary – Look up each of these words in a dictionary and read their definitions: militant, aerospace, graffiti, destitute, coalition.

Literature – Read "Every Human Life is Precious" in *We the People*, pages 178-179.

Timeline – In *Timeline of America the Beautiful* next to 1989, write: The Berlin Wall falls, signaling the end of the Cold War.

Student Workbook or Lesson Review – If you are using one of these optional books, complete the assignment for Lesson 136.

The Ronald Reagan Presidential Library and Museum

The doors of this library are open now and all are welcome. The judgment of history is left to you, the people.

President Ronald Reagan spoke the above words during his remarks at the dedication of the Ronald Reagan Presidential Library and Museum on November 4, 1991. Five American Presidents were present that day. It was the first time in American history that five Presidents were together at the same time. Each of their wives, as well as Lady Bird Johnson, President Johnson's widow, were also present. See photos at right and below. In President Carter's remarks that day, he said, "Under President Ronald Reagan the nation stayed strong and resolute and made possible the end of the Cold War."

Mrs. Johnson, President and Mrs. Carter, President and Mrs. Ford, President and Mrs. Nixon, President and Mrs. Reagan, President and Mrs. Bush

President Ford, President Nixon, President Bush, President Reagan, and President Carter

The other four Presidents honored President Reagan on that November day, even though President Reagan had campaigned against each of them during his long political career. Nixon and Reagan had both tried to gain the Republican nomination in 1968. He and Ford had both campaigned for the Republican nomination in 1976. In 1980 Reagan and George H. W. Bush had both tried to win the Republican nomination. After Reagan became the Republican candidate that year, he ran against and defeated Jimmy Carter in the presidential election.

The Ronald Reagan Presidential Library and Museum is located at 40 Presidential Drive in Simi Valley, California, halfway between Santa Barbara and Los Angeles. President Reagan liked mountaintops. His California ranch was located in the mountains, and he chose a one-hundred-acre mountaintop as the site of his $57 million library. To the west is a view of the Pacific Ocean and to the east are hills that were used for filming Westerns during the time that Reagan was a movie star. At the top of page 864 is a photograph of President and Mrs. Reagan as they break ground for the library on November 21, 1988, just two months before he left the presidency. Like other presidential libraries, the Ronald

President and Mrs. Reagan break ground for his presidential library, 1991.

Reagan Presidential Library and Museum serves both researchers and tourists. The complex houses the records of Reagan's presidency and displays of historic objects, including many personal items from his extraordinary life.

Below are two views of the library. The top photo was taken from the air. It shows the entire complex of buildings and a portion of the grounds. Visitors strolling the grounds can visit a replica of the South Lawn of the White House, a replica of the Rose Garden that is three-fourths the size of the one on the White House grounds, a piece of the Berlin Wall, and the memorial where President Reagan is buried. The large flat-roofed building at far right is the Air Force One Pavilion. The lower view is a close-up of the library taken from its courtyard.

Inside the buildings are the archives, museum galleries, a replica of the Oval Office, theaters where visitors can watch films about President Reagan's life, offices, and President and Mrs. Reagan's private apartment they used when visiting the library. The library hosts book signings, special holiday events, traveling exhibits, events sponsored by the Ronald Reagan Center for Public Affairs, and more. Individuals and groups can rent facilities at the library to use for gatherings. During the first twenty years it was open, ten million people visited the library.

The Ronald Reagan Presidential Library and Museum

Reagan presents Gorbachev with the first Ronald Reagan Freedom Medal, 1992.

In the photo at left, Reagan presents the first Ronald Reagan Freedom Medal to Mikhail Gorbachev in March of 1992 at the library. He also dedicated the Ronald Reagan Center for Public Affairs that day.

History of Presidential Libraries

During Franklin D. Roosevelt's second term as President, he sought the advice of historians to find the best way to protect items collected while he had been President. Roosevelt knew that historical objects and documents from previous Presidents had at times been lost, destroyed, allowed to decay, and even sold for profit. Roosevelt raised money to build a library where items from his presidency could be protected. When it was completed, it was given to the National Archives so it could belong to the American people. Every President who has served since Roosevelt has done the same. President

Hoover was alive during the development of the Roosevelt, Truman, and Eisenhower libraries. Hoover himself dedicated his own library in 1962, two years before his death.

The Reagan Archives

The photos on pages 864-867 are just ten of the 1.6 million photographs kept in the archives of the Reagan library. In addition to photographs, the archives protects 500,000 feet of motion picture film, tens of thousands of audio and video tapes, fifty million pages of documents, and more than 40,000 objects from Reagan's eight years as President. Here also are Reagan's speeches, documents about his political campaigns, and papers related to his time as Governor of California. University professors, elementary school students, newspaper reporters, and anyone else who is interested can visit the library's research room to see and use these records. Many may be copied, but the items cannot be checked out as at a regular library. Since these are historic objects, a library staff person must show visitors how to handle the artifacts and may stay and watch while people use them.

Replica of the Oval Office

Replica of the Oval Office at the Reagan Library

When George Washington was President, he lived first in New York City and later in Philadelphia. His home in Philadelphia had a room that was bowed on one end. President Washington stood at the bowed end with a circle of guests surrounding him so that he could greet each visitor from the same distance. In 1909 President William Howard Taft had the presidential office in the White House remodeled into an oval to honor President Washington.

While Franklin Roosevelt was President, he had the Oval Office moved to its current location in the West Wing of the White House. Each President, except Dwight D. Eisenhower and Jimmy Carter, has redecorated the office to reflect his personal tastes. Like several other presidential libraries, the Reagan Library has a replica of the Oval Office, decorated as it was while Reagan was President. See photo above. President Reagan decorated his office with earthy colors. He brought in Western art, including a collection of bronze sculptures, created by the famed Western artist Frederick Remington.

With the exception of Presidents Johnson, Nixon, and Ford, every President since Rutherford B. Hayes has used the Resolute desk, either in the Oval Office or in his private study. President Reagan used the desk in the Oval Office. He was six feet two inches tall, so he had a two-inch base added to the bottom of the desk to make it tall enough. On the desk, he placed two plaques, which read "It can be done" and "There's no limit to what a man can do or where he can go if he doesn't mind who gets the credit." Reagan was a fan of Jelly Belly jelly beans, so he placed a jar of those on his desk, too.

In the Oval Office replica is the real chair purchased for President Reagan to use in the White House. The Kittinger Company of Buffalo, New York made the chair by hand. The Kittinger Company, founded in 1866, also made the furniture reproductions used in

Reagan speaks to Americans from the Oval Office after the Challenger accident.

Colonial Williamsburg. In the photo at left, Reagan sits in the Kittinger chair as he speaks words of comfort to the American people after the *Challenger* accident.

The Air Force One Pavilion

President Ronald Reagan traveled over 660,000 miles on Air Force One, the presidential jet. In an effort to bring peace to the world, he traveled to twenty-six countries. He believed the best way to build better relations between America and the nations of the world was to meet face-to-face with their leaders. In an effort to connect with the people he served, he also traveled to forty-six states.

Inside the Air Force One Pavilion, pictured below, is the presidential jet that carried Presidents Nixon, Carter, Ford, Reagan, George H. W. Bush, Clinton, and George W. Bush. The plane, designated Air Force One 27000 is on permanent loan from the United States Air Force. For Reagan and other Presidents, this jet served as a flying White House. President Reagan hand-wrote speeches and signed laws in Air Force One. Visitors can tour inside the historic vehicle when they visit the pavilion.

Air Force One Inside the Pavilion

In addition to Air Force One, the pavilion also has a police motor cycle, a police car, one of Reagan's presidential limousines, and a Secret Service Chevrolet Suburban. The vehicles are lined up as if in a presidential motorcade.

A Portion of the Berlin Wall

The Berlin Wall separated a city. It separated families. It separated friends. It was a symbol of the Iron Curtain and the separation of Western Europe from Eastern Europe. In front of the wall was freedom; behind it was Communism, oppression, darkness, and pain. One enduring result of the presidencies of Reagan and Bush was the removal of the Berlin Wall. While Reagan was in Berlin to celebrate the city's 750th anniversary, he gave the speech in which he challenged Gorbachev to tear down the wall. Here is more of what he said in June of 1987:

> There is one sign the Soviets can make that would be unmistakable, that would advance dramatically the cause of freedom and peace. General Secretary Gorbachev, if you seek peace, if you seek prosperity for the Soviet Union and Eastern Europe, if you seek liberalization: Come here to this gate! Mr. Gorbachev, open this gate! Mr. Gorbachev, tear down this wall!

The speech was just one of many things Reagan did to bring freedom to America's Cold War enemies. He met with Gorbachev many times. Five years earlier Reagan had given another speech in Berlin. In the 1982 speech, he had asked, "Do Soviet leaders want to be remembered for a prison wall, ringed with barbed wire and with armed guards, whose weapons are aimed at their own civilians?"

Portion of the Berlin Wall

President George H. W. Bush's gentle leadership continued the efforts that President Reagan had begun. In November of 1989 the wall came down. The following April, the retired Ronald Reagan stood on the grounds of his presidential library beside the section of the Berlin Wall pictured at right. This nine-and-a-half-foot tall portion of the wall weighs 6,338 pounds. The large butterfly graffiti seen in the picture faced the free West. The eastern side of the wall is stark gray. On that April day, Reagan said: "Let our children and grandchildren come here and see this wall and reflect on what it meant to history. Let them understand that only vigilance and strength will deter tyranny."

The Reagan Memorial

The Reagan Memorial

After President Ronald Reagan died on June 5, 2004, he was buried at the library on June 11. The memorial pictured at left marks his grave and overlooks the Pacific Ocean. Inscribed on the wall are these words spoken by Reagan: "I know in my heart that man is good, that what is right will always eventually triumph and there is purpose and worth to each and every life."

In the day when God created man, He made him in the likeness of God.
Genesis 5:1

Activities for Lesson 137

Map Study – Complete the assignment for Lesson 137 on Map 3 "American Landmarks" in *Maps of America the Beautiful*.

Literature – Read "A National Loss" in *We the People*, pages 180-181.

Creative Writing – Imagine that you are a reporter who has been given the opportunity to interview the five Presidents that gathered for the dedication of the Ronald Reagan Presidential Library and Museum (pictured on page 863). In your notebook, compose ten questions that you would like to ask them.

Timeline – In *Timeline of America the Beautiful* next to 1991, write: The Reagan Library is dedicated.

Student Workbook or Lesson Review – If you are using one of these optional books, complete the assignment for Lesson 137.

God Created Mount Saint Helens

God is constantly reshaping planet Earth. He sends gentle rains that soften the ground. He makes glaciers move across the land, carving the ground beneath them. He sends ocean waves that change the shape of beaches. Sometimes God changes the earth slowly and gently, but sometimes He changes it quickly and powerfully. This is what happened on May 18, 1980, at Mount Saint Helens in southwestern Washington.

Mount Saint Helens before 1980

In Lesson 110 we learned about Captain George Vancouver, a British Navy captain who explored the waters around the Olympic peninsula. In 1792 Vancouver named Mount Saint Helens, one of the volcanoes in the Cascade Mountains, for the British Ambassador to Spain, Ambassador Alleyne Fitzherbert whose title was Baron Saint Helens.

Mount Saint Helens, the "Fuji of America"

Native Americans told early explorers about the fire and smoke that sometimes came out of the mountain. One native name for the mountain is Louwala-Clough, meaning "smoking mountain." The volcano shook and spewed several times in the 1800s, but after 1857 it became dormant.

By 1979, 500,000 people per year were boating, camping, fishing, and hiking at Spirit Lake, which lies at the base of the mountain. At 9,677 feet, Mount Saint Helens was not the tallest peak in the Cascades, but it was the one climbed most frequently. Its beauty, shape, and constant snow cover reminded people of Japan's tallest peak, so they called Mount Saint Helens the "Fuji of America." See the photo above.

United States Geological Survey

In 1879, during the presidency of Rutherford B. Hayes, the U.S. Congress established the United States Geological Survey (USGS). This Federal agency finds petroleum, gas, and minerals such as gold and silver. It also studies earthquakes and volcanoes. The USGS makes predictions about when earthquakes may occur and when volcanoes may erupt. In the late 1970s, two USGS geologists published a report which warned that Mount Saint Helens might come out of its dormant state, perhaps within the next twenty-five years.

God's Loving Care

God created everything and everyone on earth. In the Sermon on the Mount, Jesus used God's care of the lilies of the field and the birds of the air to illustrate how He takes care of all people. To illustrate that God knows and cares about what is happening in all of creation, Jesus said that God knows when a sparrow falls to the ground.

View of Mount Saint Helens and Spirit Lake

In Romans 8:28, the apostle Paul teaches us that God causes all things to work together for good for those who love God and are called according to His purpose. When we hear about something like a volcano, we may wonder how this can be part of God's plan. When something bad happens to us or to our families, we may wonder why and doubt whether God still loves us.

This small steam eruption occurred on Mount Saint Helens during the spring of 1980.

Scientists who study what has happened at Mount Saint Helens since 1980 have learned about how different parts of creation work together. They have been amazed at how quickly life returned to the mountain after the events of May 18, 1980. Looking back at how God brings about good after terrible events can help us trust Him the next time we experience something painful.

This photo taken on April 27, 1980, shows the bulge on Mount Saint Helens.

Paying Attention to Warnings

Between March 15 and March 19, many small earthquakes occurred at Mount Saint Helens. Then, on March 20, 1980, the mountain experienced an earthquake that measured 4.2 on the Richter scale. About a week later, a tiny eruption of steam came out of the mountain. During the next six weeks, the mountain trembled many times and steam continued to escape. A bulge appeared on the northern side of the volcano. Each day it grew as much as five feet. Notice the changes in Mount Saint Helens as illustrated in the photos above.

Parts of Mount Saint Helens were in Gifford Pinchot National Forest, one of America's oldest national forests. However, private corporations owned the top of the mountain and much of the forest land near it. Officials of the National Forest Service and the USGS worked together to prepare for the coming catastrophe and to figure out how to protect people from the danger. Officials warned tourists and people living in the area that they should leave. Television stations, radio stations, and newspapers across America reported stories about what was likely to happen at Mount Saint Helens. Some people took the warnings seriously and others did not. Some news reporters caused problems when they ridiculed officials and their warnings.

Federal lands around Mount Saint Helens were closed and people within an area called the red zone were ordered to leave. Local law enforcement personnel set up roadblocks to keep people out, but many found ways to get around the roadblocks. Logging companies cooperated in some ways. They helped keep the public off of their lands, but they insisted that their loggers continue working. The news story was so big that the Federal Aviation Agency had to set up a special office near Mount Saint Helens to keep news people from flying into the red zone.

How Volcanoes Erupt

When a volcano erupts, it sends gases and melted rock from beneath the earth's surface out through vents in the earth's crust. This melted rock is called magma or molten rock. Scientists believe that rock deep within the earth gets very hot and starts to melt. They believe the melted rock rises toward the surface of the earth because it is not as dense as solid rock.

This photo of Mount Saint Helens was taken from six miles away on May 17, 1980 the day before it erupted.

When magma comes out of a volcano and forms a sort of river of melted rock, it is called lava; but when magma explodes into pieces as it comes out of a volcano, it is called tephra. Tephra is made up of cinders (like you see flying up from a campfire), pumice (a type of rock), and volcanic ash (tiny pieces of magma that are smaller than .08 inches).

The bulge growing on the side of Mount Saint Helens was created by magma that was pushing on the surface of the mountain. By Saturday, May 17, the bulge had grown to over 450 feet. The above photo was taken that day.

Mount Saint Helens on May 18, 1980

May 18, 1980

On May 18, 1980, at 8:32 a.m. Pacific Daylight Time, Mount Saint Helens experienced an earthquake that registered 5.1 on the Richter scale. The bulge and the area around it slid down the mountain in the largest landslide that humans have ever recorded. This avalanche released pressure inside the mountain. The volcano erupted with a blast four hundred times more powerful than an atomic bomb. The eruption, which lasted nine hours, was heard more than seven hundred miles away. See photo at left.

The top of the mountain blew off, leaving a horseshoe-shaped crater more than one mile wide. The mountain lost 1,314 feet of its height. Ash and rock flew into the air. Some of the rocks were the size of large buildings. The landslide went into Spirit Lake, pushing millions of gallons of water down the mountain. Within the first three minutes after the blast began, 230 square miles of forest were either blown down or burned. Within fifteen minutes of the explosion, the cloud of volcanic ash and pumice was 80,000 feet high. This is twice as high as the usual altitude of a jet plane. By the afternoon, the ash cloud made the sky look like nighttime. Streetlights came on in surrounding towns.

As this helicopter tries to land on August 22, 1980, it stirs up ash.

By noon on May 18, ash was falling in Idaho. Over the next three days, wind blew ash across the United States, with noticeable ash in eleven states. By the end of fifteen days, the ash had circled around the Earth. If all the ash had been piled on a football field, it would have been 150 miles high. The eruption also created new lakes, including Castle Lake and Coldwater Lake.

This view of ash-covered Mount Saint Helens with its horseshoe-shaped crater was taken taken on September 16, 1980.

Eruptions continued from May into October. A July 22 explosion sent pumice and ash six to eleven miles in the sky; it could be seen one hundred miles away in Seattle, Washington. The photos at right illustrate the changes the eruptions caused at Mount Saint Helens. All three show some of the ash cover. The center photo shows the mountain's horseshoe-shaped crater and the bottom photo shows pumice stone.

On October 17, 1980, a USGS scientist examines pumice rocks produced by the volcano.

Victims and Heroes

Fifty-seven people died from the volcano. They were scientists, loggers, tourists, and reporters. Only a few were in the red zone. Many of the deaths could have been avoided if the red zone had been made larger. President Carter came quickly to visit the area and see the destruction.

Brave people performed many amazing rescues, mostly by helicopter. They saved 130 people. The ash was so thick that pilots had to reach out of the windows of the helicopters and wipe ash off their windshields. Realizing that they could see best if they looked out their side windows instead of their windshields, some pilots flew sideways. Eighty to ninety percent of helicopter pilots who flew rescue missions were Washington National Guardsmen. Some pilots were Vietnam veterans who had flown helicopters during the war. Their war experience helped them know how to fly into dangerous situations.

One Town's Experience

The little farm town of Ritzville, Washington (population 1,900), was two hundred miles away from Mount Saint Helens. At noon on May 18, when many residents were leaving church, they looked up and saw a black cloud of ash against a beautiful blue sky. Soon the skies grew dark and a light-gray ash began to fall like rain.

Since two major highways come near the town, Ritzville began to fill with people. With volcanic ash everywhere, car motors clogged with the ash. Roads were officially closed and many people were stranded. The local motel filled up. Total strangers shared rooms. The police asked churches, schools, and residents to help. That night 127 people slept in the Methodist church. About five hundred stayed in schools.

By the middle of the night, ash was four inches deep all over town. The next morning, town officials realized that the ash was actually tiny pieces of rock. It was heavy and could make roofs collapse. Volunteer firemen started removing ash from roofs all over town. Visitors ran out of cash, so the local bank cashed checks for them without asking questions.

By Thursday the state highway patrol came and led groups of travelers out of town. Then townspeople could concentrate on cleaning up their town. Ritzville scooped up about 780,000 tons of ash. They dumped it into an old gravel pit in the town.

The experience in Ritzville reveals some of the best of America. Again and again when disaster strikes, Americans band together to help those who are suffering. God blessed Ritzville by giving it one of its best wheat harvests ever after the volcano. The coating of ash helped hold in moisture needed by the wheat crop. Some of those stranded in Ritzville came back the next year for a reunion. One couple who got stranded had been thinking about getting a divorce. Instead, they decided to stay married and they later moved to Ritzville.

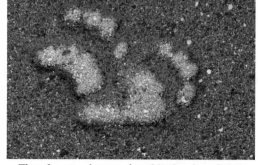

These bear tracks were found in October of 1980 in the ash near Mount Saint Helens.

Rebirth at Mount Saint Helens

Mount Saint Helens looked gray and dead after it erupted, but plants and animals were fruitful and multiplied fast. A few small trees that were buried under snow when the eruption occurred survived. Within a couple of weeks, spiders and scavenging beetles returned. Frogs, fish, and insects, plus burrowing animals like moles, pocket gophers, and ants, that had been hibernating underground on May 18, 1980, came out of their underground homes.

The pocket gophers were especially helpful to plants. God made these little animals constant diggers. As they dug in the ground at Mount Saint Helens, they mixed volcanic ash with the mountain's rich soil. Ants, beetles, and deer mice, along with the gophers, acted like tillers as they dug in the soil. A variety of small plants, shrubs, and trees took root quickly in the plowed-up soil. The seeds of the fireweed plant are like tiny parachutes. The wind spread these seeds on Mount Saint Helens; and by the summer of 1981, fireweed covered the hills around the volcano.

In 1982 an ecologist working at Mount Saint Helens spotted one blue lupine wildflower growing in a plain of pumice. It was surrounded by a ring of seedlings. The ecologist returned each year to see what was happening in a 200-square-yard plot surrounding that one lupine. Four years later, 16,000 lupines were growing there. Three years after that, there were 35,000. By 1990 twenty-seven species of plants were growing in that plot alone.

Volcanic ash poisoned the lakes, but algae, plankton, and freshwater crustaceans quickly returned, followed by frogs and salamanders. Large animals came back to Mount Saint Helens, too. Within a few weeks elk came to the mountain. See the photo on page 872 from October of 1980 taken after a bear left a track in the ash. Soon deer and coyotes came back, too.

Today more than 150 different species of wildflowers, shrubs, and trees grow at Mount Saint Helens. It is also brimming with birds and animals. The two NASA photos at right show how plants have returned to Mount Saint Helens. Compare the amount of green in the top photo taken in 1984 with the lower one taken in 2010.

NASA Photos of Mount Saint Helens:
Top Photo, 1984; Lower Photo, 2010

Continuing Eruptions

From October 1980 through 1986, Mount Saint Helens experienced seventeen lava eruptions that created a lava dome inside the Mount Saint Helens crater. Notice the dome in the 1982 photo below. In 1986 the dome's height reached 876 feet above the floor of the crater. Between 1986 and 2004, a 650-foot glacier formed in the crater atop Mount Saint Helens. Crater Glacier is the youngest glacier in North America.

In October 2004 Mount Saint Helens began to erupt again, with more than 1,000 small earthquakes a day. A new dome began to form. It divided Crater Glacier into east and west arms. The dome rose at a rate of about one dump truck load of material per second! By

Spirit Lake reflects Mount Saint Helens, May, 1982. Notice lava dome in the center of the crater. Steam is escaping from the lava dome.

2008, when Mount Saint Helens again rested, the dome was taller than New York's Empire State Building.

Visiting Mount Saint Helens

In 1982 Congress set aside 110,300 acres to establish the Mount Saint Helens National Volcanic Monument. The National Monument is part of Gifford

Pinchot National Forest. Scientists come to the monument to learn more about this amazing, active creation.

Mount Saint Helens has made this region even more famous. About 600,000 tourists visit here each year, more than came before the volcano erupted. In the year 2000, the twentieth anniversary of the eruption of Mount Saint Helens, visitors came from as far away as Israel and England. Tourists stop by visitor centers and hike U.S. Forest Service trails while they take in the beauty and wonder of the mountain. They must be careful when they visit the volcano. The crater rim is fragile and can break off, some spots are still hot, and avalanches and small explosions can happen at any time. Another way to see Mount Saint Helens is by helicopter. On a helicopter tour, visitors can see the crater, its dome, and Crater Glacier (see photo below); but this method can still be dangerous.

Though it was hard to see good at Mount Saint Helens on Sunday, May 18, 1980, God has done amazing things there over the years. The same was true when Jesus died on the Cross. At the time, it seemed nothing good could come out of it; but remember what happened to Jesus three days later!

The Lord is good,
A stronghold in the day of trouble,
And He knows those who
take refuge in Him.
Nahum 7

The Dome and the Western Arm of Crater Glacier
Inside the Crater at Mount Saint Helens, January 2006

Activities for Lesson 138

Thinking Biblically – Copy Psalm 46:1-3 into your notebook.

Map Study – Complete the assignment for Lesson 138 on Map 2 "God's Wonders" in *Maps of America the Beautiful*.

Vocabulary – Write five sentences in your notebook, using one of these words in each: dormant, corporation, pumice, altitude, crustacean. Check in a dictionary if you need help with their definitions.

Timeline – In *Timeline of America the Beautiful* next to 1980, write: Mount Saint Helens erupts.

Student Workbook or Lesson Review – If you are using one of these optional books, complete the assignment for Lesson 138.

Bill Gates, Entrepreneur and Philanthropist

Bill Gates Speaking at the Consumer Electronics Show in Las Vegas, Nevada, 2007

While Bill Gates was growing up, computers were big, expensive, and complicated to use. Today people around the world use them in their homes every day. For a computer to do what people want it to do, it must have software. Software is a computer program stored inside a computer. The computer itself is called hardware.

In 1975 Bill Gates of Seattle, Washington, pictured at left, co-founded the Microsoft Corporation, which became the world's largest software company. The innovative work of Microsoft has made possible much of what people are able to do on their computers today. Bill Gates' work with Microsoft made him one of the richest men in the world.

The Childhood of Bill Gates

William Henry Gates Jr. was a shy student at the University of Washington law school when he met fellow student Mary Maxwell. They married and had a daughter Kristianne. In 1955 Mary gave birth to their only son, William (Bill) Henry Gates III. They later had another daughter, Libby. William Henry Jr. became a successful Seattle attorney. While their children were growing up, the Gates lived an upper middle class lifestyle with a home in Seattle and a summer home on nearby Puget Sound.

William and Mary Gates raised a close family. As a child, Bill was especially close to his mother; and he remained so as an adult. Mary was devoted to rearing her children, helping her community, and working for charity. She served on the boards of several businesses, including a Seattle bank that her grandfather had founded. She served as a regent of the University of Washington. Mary often took Bill along when she did volunteer work.

As a child, Bill Gates enjoyed coordinating family sports at their summer house and playing board games, especially Risk. He was also very good at Monopoly. Young Bill Gates was an avid reader. He spent many hours studying encyclopedias and other reference books. When Bill was eleven or twelve years old, his parents worried about him because he sometimes seemed bored and was withdrawn from others. When he was thirteen, they sent him to Lakeside, an exclusive private school. There he did very well in math, science, drama, and English.

When Bill was thirteen years old, a computer company offered to let Lakeside students link to the company's computers from the school. Lakeside's Mothers Club purchased computer equipment with money they had earned through a rummage sale. Bill became fascinated with the machines and began to write computer programs. Paul Allen, another student at Lakeside who was two years older than Bill, shared his love of computers. Bill and Paul became friends.

In 1970 when Bill was fifteen and Paul was seventeen, the two developed a computer program called "Traf-o-Data," which earned them $20,000. Bill took a brief leave from high school to work on his business, but his parents insisted that he finish school. They wanted him to become a lawyer. Bill went back to high school and scored an astonishing 1590 out of 1600 on the SAT college entrance exam. He graduated from high school in 1973 and went to Harvard that fall.

From Harvard to Microsoft

At Harvard Bill continued his obsession with computers, finding them much more interesting than sleep or class. Still, he was able to cram information into his brain just in time to take tests and make pretty good grades. Bill's friend Paul Allen had gone to Washington State University for a while, but while Bill was at Harvard, Paul worked at Honeywell International Incorporated in nearby Boston. In the summer after his freshman year at Harvard, Bill went to work at Honeywell, too. After reading an article in a *Popular Electronics* magazine about the Altair 8800 mini-computer kit, Bill and Paul got in touch with the small company that made the Altair, offering to create a software program for the computer.

Bill returned to Harvard that fall. In Harvard's computer lab, Bill and Paul wrote software for the Altair. When Paul showed it to the company, they liked it and hired him. Paul Allen moved to New Mexico where the company was based. Bill soon dropped out of Harvard and joined Paul in New Mexico. In 1975 Bill and Paul formed a partnership they called Micro-Soft. They took the name from "micro-computer" and "software." It wasn't long before they dropped the hyphen. For a while they continued working for the company that made Altair, but after the company was sold they moved Microsoft to Bellevue, Washington, outside of Seattle.

Bill Gates Leads Microsoft to Success

In Seattle the two business partners hired twenty-three employees. These employees and the two owners all worked on everything. They all wrote software and they all worked at selling what they developed. In 1978, when Bill was only twenty-three years old, Microsoft brought in $2.5 million.

Bill was good at both developing software and managing a business. He became the leader in getting business for the company. He began traveling and often took his mother along. She was respected and had gotten to know many people through her years of service. It was through Mary Gates that Bill was introduced to the chairman of IBM. Mary and the chairman had served together on the national board of United Way International. It was a very important introduction. When IBM introduced its personal computer (PC), the computer used Microsoft software.

By 1981 Microsoft had grown from 25 to 128 employees and was bringing in $16 million per year. By 1983 three out of ten computers in the world were using Microsoft software. Paul Allen was diagnosed with Hodgkins disease, a form of cancer, in 1983 and resigned from Microsoft. Allen went through treatment and his cancer went into remission. Paul Allen made wise investments and also became one of the richest men in the world. He also became a philanthropist, giving large amounts to charity.

Microsoft continued to grow. In 1986, when Gates was thirty-one, he became a millionaire. The following year, shortly before his thirty-second birthday, he became a billionaire. He has remained one of the world's wealthiest men since that time.

Bill Gates Begins a Family

In 1989 thirty-seven-year-old Bill Gates noticed Melinda French, a twenty-eight-year-old Microsoft executive from Dallas, Texas. Melinda and Bill were married in Hawaii on New Year's Day of 1994. Just a few months later, Bill was heartbroken when he found out his mother was terminally ill. She died in June of that year.

A few months later, Bill and Melinda took some time off from work. They visited several countries in Europe and tried to get a new outlook on life. In 1996 they had their first child, a girl they named Jennifer Katharine. In 1997 the family moved into an earth-sheltered mansion on Lake Washington. A son, Rory John, was born in 1999. Another daughter, Phoebe Adele, was born in 2002.

Bill and Melinda Gates

The Bill and Melinda Gates Foundation

Melinda Gates encouraged her husband to do the work that his mother had done by serving others. Bill studied the lives of Andrew Carnegie and John D. Rockefeller to learn from their giving. In 1994 Bill founded the William H. Gates Foundation and later the Gates Learning Foundation. In 1995 he published *The Road Ahead* and in 1999 *Business @ the Speed of Thought*. Both became bestsellers and Gates donated the money he earned from book sales to non-profit organizations.

In 2000 Bill and Melinda merged their two foundations into the Bill and Melinda Gates Foundation. They gave the new foundation $28.8 billion when it began. Bill and Melinda became co-chairmen of the foundation. Bill stopped his day-to-day management of Microsoft the same year. He turned daily operation over to a college friend who had worked with him since 1980. Over the years Gates became more and more involved in the foundation. In June of 2008 he left full-time work at Microsoft, though he remained as chairman of the board and continued to work as an advisor for its most important projects. The purpose of the Bill and Melinda Gates Foundation is to help every person of the world have the chance to live a healthy, productive life. They pay for projects in the United States and around the world. They concentrate on improving health and education.

Bill Gates honors his parents daily. One way is by building a strong family himself. In 2009 Bill and Melinda Gates took their family on a European vacation. They took them to museums and historical sites. They taught them about the cultures of the places they visited. While they were in Europe, Bill tutored the children in science, especially in the physics of light, while Melinda tutored them in other subjects. In 2010 Bill, his father, and his young son Rory went on a trip together to Antarctica.

Bill serves others as his mother did. He chose his father to serve with Melinda and himself as a co-chairman of the Bill and Melinda Gates Foundation.

Honor your father and mother (which is the first commandment with a promise),
so that it may be well with you, and that you may live long on the earth.
Ephesians 6:2-3

Activities for Lesson 139

Thinking Biblically – Read Acts 20:35. Write a paragraph in your notebook reflecting on the concept, "It is more blessed to give than to receive."

Vocabulary – Copy these words in your notebook, each on a separate line: software, innovative, regent, avid, remission. Look up each word in the dictionary. Next to each word, write what part of speech it is, according to the way the word is used in the lesson.

Creative Writing – If you were a billionaire and started a foundation to give your money away, what charities or causes would you support? Make a list of at least ten in your notebook.

Timeline – In *Timeline of America the Beautiful* next to 1975, write: Bill Gates co-founds Microsoft.

Student Workbook or Lesson Review – If you are using one of these optional books, complete the assignment for Lesson 139.

In the 1980s . . .

- The Pac-Man video game apeared in video arcades in 1980.
- The Commodore 64 personal computer was introduced in 1982.
- Compact discs (CDs) were released in 1983.
- The first cell phones were used in Chicago in 1983.
- The wreck of the *Titanic* was found in 1985.
- The Nintendo Entertainment System was introduced in 1985.

Shopping in America

Americans shop. They shop a lot. Even families who grow their own food and make their own clothes need to buy seeds and fabric. How do Americans shop? They buy from organic farmers at local farmers' markets. They order from mail order catalogs. They shop online. They stroll the mall. They go to Walmart.

All Americans depend on other people buying. People who own their own businesses know this because they make an income when customers purchase what they sell. If your father is an engineer at a company that makes vacuum cleaners, your family depends on people buying those vacuum cleaners. If your father teaches at a state university, your family still depends on shopping. Your father depends on people going to stores, purchasing products, and paying sales tax on them, so the state will have money to pay your father's salary.

Shopping is a way to bless people. When you shop at a farmers' market, you are helping the farmer. You are also cutting down on air pollution because a truck doesn't have to bring the food from several states away. However, if you live in Louisiana and buy avocados from California, you are blessing the farmer in California and the truck drivers who brought them to your store. You are helping those truck drivers keep their jobs. In our shopping and in everything else we do in our daily lives, it is important to think about what we are doing to make sure that our choices honor God and bless people.

Shopping should not become an idol. "Shop 'til you drop!" was a slogan for many Americans in the 1980s, a decade known for its consumerism. Consumerism is an idea that the economy will be better if people buy more and more. During the eighties, people did just that. They rented storage buildings to keep their extra stuff. Many were fooled into thinking that they would be happier if they had lots of stuff. Let's explore how Americans shopped in the eighties and throughout the twentieth century.

Piggly Wiggly Grocery Store

Before 1916 grocery shoppers went into a store and told the clerk what they wanted to purchase. The clerk gathered the items for them. Clarence Saunders of Memphis, Tennessee, decided that this method wasted time and money. He opened a new store with shopping baskets and open shelves. He called it Piggly Wiggly. Customers could take items off the shelves, put them in a basket, and take them to the clerk to pay for them. It was considered revolutionary. Of course, the idea caught on and today's customers can hardly imagine another way to shop for groceries.

Shopping Downtown

Before the invention of shopping centers and malls, Americans shopped at a variety of stores along Main Street or around the town square of small towns or in the downtown shopping district of large cities. Downtown shoppers could visit department stores, men's clothing stores, ladies' dress shops, shoe stores, 5¢ & 10¢ stores, furniture stores, and more. After cars were invented, parking lots and multi-level parking structures were built downtown.

Department stores had many departments (or areas) in one store: jewelry, fabric, toys, ladies', men's, boys', girls', linens, china, music, and often a popular bargain basement. They had restaurants, where customers sometimes watched fashion shows. Many large cities had one or more department stores owned by local families. Each store had its own style. One example is the Harvey's department store in downtown Nashville, Tennessee. Its theme was carousel horses. The walls beside the escalator were decorated with real carousel horses, and on one floor was a full-size carousel for children to ride.

Shopping Centers and Shopping Malls

Downtown shopping districts grew slowly over the years, one store at a time. Shopping centers were invented after Americans began to drive cars. They were built in other parts

Tower at Country Club Plaza

of the city, on the outskirts of town, and in suburbs. In 1922 Country Club Plaza opened in Kansas City, Missouri. Like modern shopping centers, it had paved and lighted parking lots. Unlike downtown stores, it was built all at once and managed by one company, which rented space to a variety of businesses. See the Country Club Plaza tower at left.

As cars became more numerous, small strip shopping centers were built away from downtown. They usually had a supermarket and a drugstore, plus other shops. In the 1930s and 1940s, Sears, Roebuck and Company and Montgomery Ward began to build large stores away from the downtown shopping district, providing their own parking lots.

Some shopping centers used unusual stunts to get people to shop there. The Town and Country Shopping Center in Columbus, Ohio, once hired the elderly performer, Kay "Grandma Carver" Embrey of Mountain View, Missouri, to perform there. She dove ninety feet into a six-foot tank of flaming water! (Don't try this!) The shopping center also hosted square dances on the parking lot and had Santa Claus land in a helicopter. In the 1950s, downtown department stores started opening branches in shopping centers.

By the time Lyndon Johnson became President, America had 7,600 shopping centers. Most were near residential neighborhoods built after World War II. By 1972 the number of shopping centers had doubled. During 1976, the year that America celebrated its bicentennial, Faneuil Hall Marketplace opened in Boston and Water Tower Place opened on Michigan Avenue in Chicago. These two major shopping centers were built where Americans had once done most of their shopping—downtown.

During the 1980s, entrepreneurs built giant shopping malls. A combined total of 16,000 shopping centers and malls were built during the decade. In addition to having retail stores, malls expanded to include movie theaters, post offices, schools, libraries, museums, and entertainment. When the Gallup polling company researched shopping in America in 1990, they found that the average American visited malls or shopping centers about four times each month.

In 1990 a factory outlet shopping center named Sawgrass Mills opened in Sunrise, Florida. This two-million-square-foot center featured stores where manufacturers sold their products at discounted prices. Factory outlet malls quickly became popular.

In 1992 Mall of America opened in Bloomington, Minnesota. It combined hundreds of stores with an entertainment center and amusement park. The mall had 10,000 employees on the day it opened. Today forty million visitors go there each year.

Walmart

Kmart and Target opened their first stores in 1962. That same year, Sam Walton opened the first Walmart in Rogers, Arkansas. By the end of the 1960s, Walmart had fifteen stores. The first Walmart stores were relatively small, and they were built in small to medium-sized towns. By the end of the 1970s, the company had 276 stores in eleven states.

Walmart expanded greatly in the 1980s. At the beginning of the decade, its annual sales were $1 billion; in 1989 the figure was $26 billion, with stores in twenty-nine states. In 1987 Walmart used space technology when it completed the largest private satellite communication system in the United States. The Walmart Satellite Network linked all its stores and warehouses with its home office in Bentonville, Arkansas.

In 1991 Walmart expanded outside the U.S. when it opened a store in Mexico City. That year President George H. W. Bush presented Sam Walton the Presidential Medal of Freedom, just a few weeks before Walton died. Walmart has continued to expand in the United States. When the first Vermont Walmart opened in 1995, Walmart had expanded to all fifty states. By 1997 Walmart was the largest private employer in the United States. That year its annual sales reached over $100 billion for the first time. In 1999 the Walmart Corporation became the largest private employer in the world. By 2005 it had 3,800 stores in America and 3,800 stores in other countries. The following year, sales reached $345 billion.

Shopping from Home

Americans have been shopping at home since colonial days, when peddlers traveled from town to town. In 1888 Richard Sears began selling watches and jewelry through a mail order catalog. In the next few decades, the Sears, Roebuck and Company catalog sold sewing machines, musical instruments, eyeglasses, pianos, Edison's graphophone, buggies, kits for building houses, and many other products.

Through the years, American families have purchased goods from traveling salesmen who knocked on their doors trying to sell them everything from encyclopedias to vacuum cleaners. Traditionally, traveling salesmen were men who traveled from one town to another. House to house selling became a popular part-time job for women when they began to sell Avon makeup door to door. After World War II, suburban homemakers began inviting friends to home parties, where they bought plastic storage containers called Tupperware. Since then, Americans have bought toys, jewelry, books, make-up, kitchen gadgets, and more at home parties.

Home Shopping Network became America's first national television shopping network on July 1, 1985. During the presidency of George H. W. Bush, home shopping began to use an even newer technology when the World Wide Web was started. Throughout the

nineties, more and more individuals and businesses purchased computers and got connected to the Internet. As this happened, existing businesses and new entrepreneurs found ways to make Internet shopping one of the many ways that Americans shop.

Do not store up for yourselves treasures on earth,
where moth and rust destroy,
and where thieves break in and steal.
Matthew 6:19

Apple Computer Store in New York City

Activities for Lesson 140

Thinking Biblically – Copy Matthew 6:19-21 into your notebook.

Literature – Read "Bunny Brown and His Sister Sue Keeping Store" in *We the People*, pages 182-185.

Timeline – In *Timeline of America the Beautiful* next to 1992, write: Mall of America opens in Bloomington, Minnesota.

Family Activity – Conduct "Shopping in America" interviews. See pages 979-980 for instructions.

Student Workbook or Lesson Review – If you are using one of these optional books, complete the assignment for Lesson 140. If you are using the Lesson Review, take the quiz on Unit 28.

Popular Toys of the Decade

Trivial Pursuit (1982)
Cabbage Patch Dolls (1983)
Care Bears (1983)
My Little Pony (1983)
Transformers (1984)
Koosh Ball (1986)
Pictionary (1987)
Super Soaker (1989)

The 1990s

Arkansas Governor Bill Clinton became President in 1993. While he served as President, he awarded the Presidential Medal of Freedom to Marjory Stoneman Douglas, who helped protect the intricate Everglades that God created in Florida. In 1999 the U.S. Mint began producing coins for the 50 State Quarters program. President Clinton also awarded the Presidential Medal of Freedom to Millard Fuller, co-founder of Habitat for Humanity. The number of families choosing to homeschool grew rapidly during the decade of the 1990s.

Construction of the Weisman Art Museum in Minneapolis, Minnesota was completed in 1993.

Lessons in Unit 29

Lesson 141 – Our American Story: A President from Arkansas
Lesson 142 – God's Wonders: God Created the Everglades
Lesson 143 – An American Landmark: The U.S. Mint and Its Coins
Lesson 144 – An American Biography: The Volunteers of Habitat, Homebuilders for the Poor
Lesson 145 – Daily Life: Homeschooling in America

Books Used in Unit 29

- *Maps of America the Beautiful*

- *Timeline of America the Beautiful*

- *We the People*

- *Katy* by Mary Evelyn Notgrass

A President from Arkansas

President Bill Clinton and Vice President Al Gore on the White House Lawn, 1993

When the Persian Gulf War ended, President George H. W. Bush was very popular among the American public. Bush received the Republican nomination to run again for President with Dan Quayle as the Republican vice-presidential candidate. The Democrats nominated Arkansas Governor Bill Clinton for President and Tennessee Senator Al Gore for Vice President. Texas billionaire businessman H. Ross Perot ran as an independent with Vietnam veteran and former prisoner of war James Stockdale as his vice-presidential candidate. In the tight 1992 election, Clinton received only 43% of the popular vote, but a majority of the electoral votes.

Health Care Reform

Clinton chose health care reform as his top priority. He appointed his wife Hillary to head up a commission to propose changes to the health care system. She and other Democrats wanted the United States government to provide health insurance for all Americans. Neither Congress nor the American people supported the idea, and it was not approved.

President Clinton Discusses NAFTA with Former Presidents Gerald Ford, George H. W. Bush, and Jimmy Carter

NAFTA

In 1993 Congress passed the North American Free Trade Agreement (NAFTA). President George H. W. Bush had supported it and worked to get it passed. Clinton sought the advice of three former Presidents, as seen in the photo above. President Clinton signed the final bill. This agreement between Canada, the United States, and Mexico eventually did away with all tariffs and taxes for goods transported and sold between the three countries. NAFTA increased trade between America and its two neighbors. American company profits went up. However, many Americans lost their jobs because of NAFTA, which made it easy for U.S. companies to move their factories to Mexico, where workers usually earn less money than American workers. The photos on page 885 illustrate other national and international responsibilities President Clinton had during his time in office.

The Elections of 1994 and 1996

During the 1994 mid-term elections, Republicans gained enough seats to have majorities in both the House and the Senate. Republicans had not had a majority in both Houses since 1954. The election was historic because every Republican Senator and Congressman who ran for re-election won, while many Democrat incumbents lost.

Even though the Democrats suffered this great loss in 1994, Clinton ran for a second term as President in 1996 and was victorious. He was the first Democrat to be elected to the presidency twice since Franklin Roosevelt. Clinton defeated the Republican candidate, long-time Kansas Senator Bob Dole. The 73-year-old Dole had received a Purple Heart following an injury in World War II. He was the last veteran of World War II to run for President of the United States.

President Clinton and Pope John Paul II during the Pope's visit to Colorado.

President and First Lady Clinton meet with guests at an interfaith breakfast.

President Clinton speaks with Israeli Prime Minister Yitzhak Rabin while aboard Air Force One.

President and First Lady Clinton meet with King Juan Carlos and Queen Sofia of Spain.

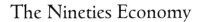

President Bill Clinton jogs with South Korean President Kim Young while on a visit to Seoul, South Korea.

The Nineties Economy

America recovered from the recession of the early 1990s and the economy grew rapidly. In 1998 the Federal government actually brought in more money than it spent, the first time this had happened since 1969. The value of stocks traded on the New York Stock Exchange grew, and Americans invested a large amount of money in businesses.

Illegal Immigration

Every American is an immigrant or a descendant of an immigrant. Immigrants from around the world have built our country, from the Native Americans who came many centuries ago, to the Russian Mennonites who brought their wheat seeds to Kansas, to the Scottish immigrant who brought Thompson grapes to California. America is a place where many people of the world want to live. Many wait for years to come here legally. However, during the 1990s, millions of immigrants came into America illegally. Most came looking for jobs. They wanted help from Federal, state, and local government programs. Many Americans believe that our government should make illegal immigrants return home and that it is too expensive to provide them with help from the government, when they do not pay the same taxes that many American citizens do. Other Americans believe they should be allowed to stay.

Muslim Terrorism

The Muslim religion (Islam) is based on the teachings of Mohammed, a man who lived in the Middle East from about 570 to 632 A.D. Islam is divided into many sects, some of which are violent. Muslim extremists took

USS Cole, *Showing Damage Caused by Terrorists*

Americans hostage in Iran while Carter was President. Muslims began to attack Americans again during the 1990s. A bomb exploded in the underground parking garage at the World Trade Center in New York City in 1993; six people died. In 1998 bombs exploded outside of U.S. embassies in the African countries of Kenya and Tanzania on the same day. This time two hundred people died. Two years later an American ship, the USS *Cole*, pictured above, was attacked while it was in a port in Yemen in the Middle East. Seventeen Americans died and thirty-nine were injured.

Tragedy in Oklahoma City

Two Americans committed a terrible act of terrorism in 1995 in Oklahoma City, Oklahoma. These two men set off a bomb outside a Federal office building, killing 198 people and injuring six hundred others. Evidently they were angry at the U.S. government and committed this cowardly act. In the photo at right, Staff Sergeant David Humphries, a military policeman with the Oklahoma National Guard, stands guard in front of the bombing site.

Sergeant Humphries Stands Guard in Oklahoma City

War on the Balkan Peninsula

Various ethnic groups live on Europe's Balkan peninsula. Before the Berlin Wall came down and the Soviet Union broke apart, countries on this peninsula included Greece to the south and the Communist countries of Yugoslavia, Albania, Bulgaria, and Romania to

US Air Force F-16C Fighting Falcons Fly Sorties to Support NATO During Conflict (A sortie is a military mission.)

the north. When the Communists lost control of these four countries, ethnic groups in Yugoslavia began to fight against each other. Yugoslavia divided into Bosnia-Herzegovina, Croatia, Kosovo, Macedonia, Montenegro, Serbia, and Slovenia. The Serbs were cruel to Muslims, especially in Bosnia-Herzegovina and Kosovo. In the 1990s, the United States and other members of the North Atlantic Treaty Organization (NATO) attacked the Serbs to protect the Muslims. See U.S. Air Force planes at left.

Seven Wonders of the Modern World

During President Clinton's first term in office, the American Society of Civil Engineers decided to choose seven engineering marvels from around the world and designate them the Seven Wonders of the Modern World. They asked experts from around the world to nominate places they believed were worthy of this honor. Wonders that American engineers designed included the Empire State Building in New York City, the Golden Gate Bridge in San Francisco, and the Panama Canal. The other Seven Wonders of the Modern World, according to the ASCE, are the Channel Tunnel, constructed between England and France beneath the English Channel; the CN Tower in Toronto, Canada; the Itaipu Dam on the border between Brazil and Paraguay; and the Netherlands North Sea Protection Works.

President Clinton Becomes the Second President in American History to Be Impeached

While President Clinton was Governor of Arkansas, he and his wife had become involved in a business project with other investors. The group was developing a large piece of land. The U.S. Department of Justice discovered possible illegal activity related to the project. The Justice Department investigator decided to find out if the Clintons had done anything wrong. In 1994 attorney Kenneth Starr became involved in the investigation of the Clintons. At the same time, a woman who once worked in Arkansas state government accused President Clinton of behaving improperly toward her.

While the Justice Department investigated her story, they found evidence that the President was behaving improperly at the White House with Monica Lewinsky, a young intern who worked there. A government intern is someone who is employed temporarily to get training and experience working in a government office.

The Justice Department decided to require President Clinton to give testimony under oath. When he gave his testimony, he did not mention Miss Lewinsky. News reporters found out about the President's alleged conduct with Miss Lewinsky (alleged conduct is an action that someone has been accused of but which has not been proven). At first the President stated strongly that he had not done anything wrong with Monica Lewinsky. But later he gave more testimony under oath and admitted that he had had an improper relationship with her. This second testimony under oath meant that the President had lied in his first testimony.

Kenneth Starr reported his findings to the U.S. House of Representatives in September of 1998. In December the House accused President Clinton of two crimes: perjury (not telling the truth while under oath) and obstruction of justice (doing wrong things to keep people from finding out the truth). The House impeached President Clinton for both of these crimes.

The U.S. Constitution declares that a President can be impeached for "high crimes and misdemeanors." People who supported the President said that his two crimes were morally wrong, but that they were not "high crimes and misdemeanors." Those who wanted him removed from the presidency said that his two crimes were "high crimes and misdemeanors."

When a President is impeached by the U.S. House of Representatives, the U.S. Senate must hold a trial. President Clinton's impeachment trial began on January 7, 1999, and lasted for five weeks. The Senate needed sixty-seven votes to remove the President from office. They voted forty-five to fifty-five on the charge of perjury and fifty to fifty on the obstruction of justice charge. President Clinton remained in office, but he lost a great deal of respect in the eyes of many American citizens. He apologized for his wrong actions.

On the last full day that President Clinton was in office, he made a deal with the Justice Department. He admitted that he had made false statements under oath during his first testimony. The President had to pay a fine. He also lost his license to practice law for five years. The Justice Department agreed that Clinton would not have to go to trial about his illegal actions after he left the presidency.

Read about President Clinton's life below.

William Jefferson Clinton
America's Forty-Second President
January 20, 1993 - January 20, 2001

William Jefferson Blythe III was born on August 19, 1946, to Virginia Cassidy Blythe in Hope, Arkansas. His father had died in an automobile accident three months earlier. Bill spent his early years in the home of his grandmother, Edith Cassidy, who taught him to be an avid reader when he was quite young. His mother was often in New Orleans taking nursing classes. In 1950 Virginia married car dealer Roger Clinton, who was an alcoholic. Roger, Virginia, and Bill moved to Hot Springs, Arkansas. During Bill's childhood, his mother often told him that he would someday be President.

When Bill was fifteen years old, his mother and stepfather divorced; but they remarried a few months later. As a teenager, Bill changed his name to William Jefferson Clinton. In high school, Bill was a good student and played saxophone in the school band. He loved gospel music and attended a Baptist church on Sundays, even though his parents did not. The principal of Hot Springs High School took a special interest in Bill and acted as a mentor. In high school, Bill was privileged to visit Washington, D.C., through an American Legion program. While there he met and shook hands with President Kennedy.

Clinton graduated from high school in 1964 and enrolled at Georgetown University in Washington, D.C.,where he studied international relations. While in college, Clinton worked as a clerk for a U.S. Senate committee. Just before he graduated, Clinton won a two-year Rhodes scholarship to study at Oxford University in England. After completing two years at Oxford, Clinton returned to America. He earned a law degree from Yale Law School in 1973. After graduation, he moved back to Arkansas to teach law at the University of Arkansas. In 1974 he ran for a seat in the U.S. House of Representatives, but lost. The following year Bill Clinton married Hillary Rodham, a fellow law student at Yale.

In 1976, at age thirty, Bill Clinton was elected as the Arkansas state attorney general. Two years later, he was elected Governor of Arkansas. Arkansas citizens did not approve of Clinton's performance as Governor, and he was not re-elected in 1980. The Clintons' only child was born that year, a daughter named Chelsea.

Clinton went to work at a Little Rock law firm and prepared to run for Governor again in 1982. During the campaign, he admitted mistakes he made during his first term. Voters gave him another chance. Clinton was elected in 1982 and continued in that office until he was inaugurated as President of the United States in 1993.

During the last year that President Clinton was in the White House, he and Hillary purchased a home in New York so that the First Lady could run for the U.S. Senate from that state. She was elected. Once out of office, Bill Clinton established an office in Harlem in New York City. President Clinton remained a popular speaker. He wrote his memoirs and opened his presidential library, the William J. Clinton Presidential Center in Little Rock. After Barack Obama was elected President, Obama named Hillary Clinton to be the U.S. Secretary of State.

Presidents and all Americans need to heed God's commands.

He has told you, O man, what is good;
And what does the Lord require of you
But to do justice, to love kindness,
And to walk humbly with your God?
Micah 6:8

Activities for Lesson 141

Thinking Biblically – Read Psalm 10 and reflect on the instances of oppression and violence you read about in this lesson.

Literature – Read "A Time for Healing" in *We the People*, pages 186-187, and chapters 1-2 in *Katy*.

Creative Writing – Write a one-page essay explaining your opinion about what the United States government should do about illegal immigrants.

Timeline – In *Timeline of America the Beautiful* next to 1993, write: The NAFTA agreement is approved by Congress.

Student Workbook or Lesson Review – If you are using one of these optional books, complete the assignment for Lesson 141.

God Created the Everglades

In south Florida, God created a place that is like no other on planet Earth. Its most obvious features are water and miles and miles of sawgrass, some reaching ten feet high. The first map that labeled the region "Everglades" was published in 1823. Native Americans had a more accurate name; they called it Pa-hay-Okee, which means "grassy waters." Perhaps the best name is the one used by conservationist Marjory Stoneman

Sunset in the Everglades

Douglas—river of grass. Douglas helped get a large portion of the Everglades set aside in a national park. See map below.

The Kissimmee River flows into Lake Okheechobe in southern Florida. From the lake, water meanders slowly toward the ocean, creeping along about one hundred feet per day, until its fresh water mingles with the salt waters of Florida Bay and the Gulf of Mexico.

The best way to travel through the Everglades is by airboat. In the photo at the top of page 891, Discovery Channel host Mike Rowe, a cameraman, and others travel by airboat through a portion of the Everglades region that is outside of the national park in Loxahatchee National Wildlife Refuge.

The Everglades are full of life. Here God has placed small communities of plants and animals that depend on the rocks, soils, water, air, and sun He provides for them. Many types of plants and animals combine in a complex environment. With both fresh and salt water, the Everglades is the only place in the world where alligators and crocodiles live side by side. It is home to nearly three hundred species of fish. Bird watchers come to the Everglades from around the world to see more than 350 species of birds. After John James Audubon saw the Everglades, he said that the flocks of wading birds were so thick overhead that they blocked out the light of the sun for some time.

Filming in the Sawgrass of the Loxahatchee National Wildlife Refuge on October 6, 2010

Freshwater Sloughs

A slough is soft, muddy ground. The average depth of Everglades sloughs is about six inches. The deepest waters in the Everglades flow through two freshwater sloughs, the larger Shark River Slough and the much smaller Taylor Slough to its east. See map. Both sloughs empty into Florida Bay. Smaller freshwater sloughs flow through the Big Cypress Swamp just north of the Everglades and empty into western Florida Bay and the waters of the Gulf of Mexico at Ten Thousand Islands. Many animals live here, with even more moving in during the dry season.

String-Lily (or Swamplily)

Freshwater Marl Prairies

Freshwater marl prairies border the sloughs. Marl refers to the kind of soil that exists in the Everglades. Pictured below is a portion of the vast freshwater sloughs and freshwater marl prairies. Since both are covered with sawgrass, it is hard to tell where the sloughs end and the marl prairies begin when looking at them

Apple Snail Eggs

from ground level. This is especially true during and after the summer rainy season when the prairies are under water. Apple snails, muskrats, deer, and alligators use this habitat. Notice the string-lily and apple snail eggs above. Deer of the Everglades eat string-lilies and birds eat apple snail eggs. See sloughs and prairies on the map on page 890.

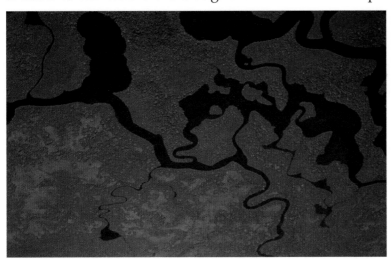

Aerial View of the Meandering River of Grass, Known as the Everglades

Sawgrass with Hardwood Hammocks

Florida Panther

Hardwood Hammocks

Hardwood hammocks are covered with dense forests of broad-leafed trees. Tropical trees such as mahogany, gumbo limbo, and cocoplums share space with temperate trees such as live oaks, red maples, and hackberries. These tall trees provide shade for air plants, ferns, mosses, orchids, and vines. Find hardwood hammocks on the map on page 890 and look at the photo at left.

The elevations of hardwood hammock islands are measured not in feet, but in inches. As plants die and decay, they release acid which dissolves the limestone around these miniature islands. This process creates little moats that keep the hardwoods from burning when natural fires come near. Tiny tree snails, white-tailed deer, opossums, raccoons, gray foxes, snakes, lizards, tree frogs, and bobcats live here, as does the rare Florida panther. See photo at left.

Pinelands

Limestone lies under the Everglades. These porous rock layers absorb large amounts of water. The slash pine trees of the pinelands can take root in the small amount of soil found in little pockets on top of this rock. Slash pines have thick bark which can withstand the natural fires that sometimes burn here. Fire keeps fast-growing hardwoods from growing, which gives the slow-growing pine seedlings a chance. Beneath the tall trees are diverse plant species, including many endemic ones. The cotton mouse, opossum, raccoon, pine warbler, reef gecko, and five-lined skink live in the pinelands. Find the pinelands on the map on page 890 and see photo at left.

Rock Pinelands

Cypress Heads

Cypress heads also look like tiny islands in the marl prairies, but they grow in low places filled with water. See picture at right. A cypress head has taller cypress trees growing in the center of a pond with shorter trees surrounding them. This growth pattern

Cypress Trees with Great Egret

makes these forests look like domes. Bald eagles like to perch in the tallest trees. Bobcats, otters, wild turkeys, and white-tailed deer live here.

Wood storks, herons, egrets, and white ibis feed on the abundant aquatic life in the waters under these trees. The wood stork, pictured at right, has unusual feeding habits. It sticks its beak in the water and then shuffles its feet to frighten fish. When the fish swim away, they hit the bird's sensitive beak, which quickly snaps up the bird's lunch. God provides wood stork families with 440 pounds of fish for each breeding season. That is the amount of food needed by a male, a female, and their babies.

Wood Stork

Periphyton

Floating around the stems of underwater plants in the Everglades are cylinder-shaped masses of life called periphyton. They look like sausages. Periphyton is made up mostly of algae, though as many as one hundred different tiny forms of life may be in each one. The periphyton is the first stage of the food chain of the Everglades. Tadpoles, salamanders, mosquito larva, and other small creatures eat the tiny living things in the periphyton. Frogs, small fish, and others make up the next stage. Big fish, birds, mammals, and some reptiles are next. The last stage of the food chain is the alligator.

The periphyton also helps the slough. The organisms take calcium out of the water and help convert it to marl, which falls to the bottom. Sawgrass extends its roots into the marl. Decaying sawgrass forms peat. Other plants grow in the peat. Dying plants in the tree islands dissolve marl and limestone.

Alligator Holes

The alligator is crucial to the Everglades ecosystem. See photo below. Using their feet and snouts, alligators dig out muck and vegetation from large holes in Everglades limestone. This clears out the water, making room for more fish. In the winter dry season, alligator holes become havens for Everglade life. Freshwater animals such as fish, turtles, and snails, move into alligator holes alongside their "host." Birds and mammals come, too. Occasionally the alligator makes a meal of one of his guests, but enough survive to repopulate the Everglades when summer thunderstorms begin.

Everglades Alligator

Alligator flags often live beside alligator holes. Lily pads often live on top of the holes. See the photos at right. Sometimes, as the pile of refuse the alligator dug out begins to decay, ferns, wildflowers, and trees take root in it and a tree island forms around the hole. Thousands of alligators live in the Everglades, partly because alligator mothers fiercely defend their young until they are one or two years old.

Beautiful Flowering Lily Pad

Mangrove Forests and Coastal Marshes

North America's largest mangrove forests are along the coastlines of the western and southern portions of the Everglades, where salt and fresh water mix. Here are red

Alligator Flag

mangroves, with their roots that look like stilts. See photo at left. Black mangroves and white mangroves grow here, too. Mangrove forests protect the Everglades from hurricanes. People enjoy canoeing in the intricate system of waterways that wind through them. Shrimp are harvested in these waters, and the forests are popular with fishermen.

Red Mangrove

Wading birds come here during the dry winter months. Many marine animals use the waters of the mangrove forests for their nurseries. Notice the vast mangrove forests along Lost Man's River in the photo at left. Scattered among the mangrove forests are coastal marshes. Find mangrove forests and coastal marshes on the map on page 890.

Florida Bay

Mangrove Forests Along Lost Man's River

Florida Bay, pictured at left, is home to porpoises, American crocodiles, and great white herons. Bald eagles, osprey, and other birds breed here. Huge numbers of wading birds feed here in the sea grasses on the bottom of the bay. At its deepest, Florida Bay is only nine feet deep. Scattered in the bay are about 100 keys (a key is a low islet). Corals and sponges live in some areas. Florida Bay is one of the best sport-fishing locations along America's east coast.

Florida Bay

Coastal Prairies

Cape Sable is northeast of Florida Bay (see map on page 890). Its coastline has wild beaches covered mainly with tiny shell fragments instead of sand. Beachcombers find whole shells and Native American artifacts here. They are permitted to carry home a few shells for personal use, but they may not carry away any artifacts. Bald eagles, egrets, gulls, ospreys, pelicans, and sandpipers nest, breed, and feed here. Loggerhead turtles nest here, too. Humans can get to these beaches only by boat.

Just inland from the beaches are hardwoods, cacti, and other plants. Beyond these are the coastal prairies with their very salty soils. Salt-tolerant grasses and red and black mangroves grow here. Among the animals living in the coastal prairies are marsh rabbits, which are also found in the Everglades' fresh water marshes and pinelands. Marsh rabbits are often seen swimming in the Everglades.

Marjory Stoneman Douglas in Front of Her Miami Home, Coconut Grove Cottage

Ernest F. Coe and Marjory Stoneman Douglas

The Everglades once extended all the way from Lake Okheechobe to the ocean, but much of it was drained in the early 1900s so that people could use it for farms. Edward Coe was a landscape architect. He loved the outdoors, especially the Everglades. For many years, he worked to have the remaining portion of the Everglades protected in a national park. Coe founded the Tropical Everglades National Park Association. By 1934 the group had convinced members of Congress that the area should become a park, but it was thirteen years before the park was officially established.

In 1915 Minnesota native Marjory Stoneman Douglas moved to Miami, Florida. She worked for her father, the first editor of the *Miami Herald* newspaper. After serving in the Red Cross in France, Belgium, Italy, and on the Balkan peninsula during World War I, Douglas returned to Miami. There she became fascinated with the Everglades. In 1947 she published *The Everglades: River of Grass*, in which she beautifully described the Everglades and its history. Her book helped people see that the Everglades was not a "worthless swamp," but a place of life and beauty.

As a result of the work of Douglas and others, President Truman signed legislation creating Everglades National Park on December 6, 1947. Until this time, America's national parks had been set aside for their beauty. Everglades National Park was the first park established because of its unique ecosystem. At 1.5 million acres, it is the largest national park east of the Mississippi River.

The Everglades: River of Grass had a great impact on the American conservation movement. Douglas continued to work for the preservation of the Everglades for the rest of her life. She received a visit from Queen Elizabeth II of Great Britain in 1991. Two years later, President Clinton awarded Douglas with the Presidential Medal of Freedom when she was 103. The Friends of the Everglades organization she founded in 1969 had 5,000

Osprey

Frog

Great Blue Heron

American Crocodile

American Alligator

members at the time of her death at age 108 in 1998. They continue her work to protect the Everglades.

At left are some of the many creatures that God has provided with homes in this delicately balanced and complex river of grass.

All the rivers flow into the sea, Yet the sea is not full.
To the place where the rivers flow, There they flow again.
Ecclesiastes 1:7

Activities for Lesson 142

Map Study – Complete the assignment for Lesson 142 on Map 2 "God's Wonders" in *Maps of America the Beautiful*.

Vocabulary – In your notebook, write a paragraph using all of these words: meander, slough, temperate, acid, endemic. Consult a dictionary if you need help with their definitions.

Literature – Read chapters 3-4 in *Katy*.

Timeline – In *Timeline of America the Beautiful* next to 1947, write: Everglades National Park is established.

Student Workbook or Lesson Review – If you are using one of these optional books, complete the assignment for Lesson 142.

The U.S. Mint and Its Coins

Americans are often discouraged about the amount of money the Federal government spends, but there is at least one Federal agency that makes money—literally! The U.S. Mint not only manufactures money, it actually makes a profit. The Mint makes America's coins, while the Bureau of Engraving and Printing in Washington, D.C. creates our paper currency.

"The Congress Shall Have the Power . . . to Coin Money."

With these words, the U.S. Constitution gave Congress the power to make (coin) money. On April 2, 1792, Congress passed the Coinage Act. It created a Federal department that was responsible for making coins. The Act also authorized the construction of the first Federal building, the U.S. Mint in Philadelphia. The noun "Mint" refers both to the governmental department and to the buildings where coins are made. When used as a verb, "mint" means to manufacture coins from metal.

President George Washington appointed a leading American scientist, David Rittenhouse, to be the first director of the U.S. Mint. The first U.S. coins made were 11,178 copper cents. The Mint soon made gold and silver coins, too. President Washington lived near the new Mint. It is believed that he donated part of his personal silver to make some of America's first silver coins.

In 1801 the U.S. Mint made its first large silver peace medals to give to Native American chiefs and warriors. They bore the image of President Jefferson, who sent some of these with Lewis and Clark on their great Voyage of Discovery. In addition to circulating coins, the U.S. Mint continues to make medals with images of each U.S. President. They are now called Presidential Medals. The Mint makes other medals, too, plus commemorative coins and a variety of collectible coins. At times it has also minted coins for other countries.

Circulating coins refers to money used for buying and selling, as opposed to coins kept because they are valuable or are in some way special to the owner. Money "circulates" when it passes from person to store to bank and back around again. Commemorative coins are ones made to honor a person or an event. The first U.S. commemorative coin was minted in 1892 to honor Christopher Columbus. A more recent commemorative coin is the Golden Dollar featuring Sacajawea and her son Jean Baptiste, released in 2000. All U.S. commemorative coins are legal tender; they can be used like other coins and paper bills.

Today the U.S. Mint has five locations: Washington, D.C.; Philadelphia, Pennsylvania; Denver, Colorado; San Francisco, California; and West Point, New York. The U.S. Mint is also responsible for the United States Bullion Depository at Fort Knox, Kentucky, where America keeps many of its reserves of precious metals. Visitors can tour the facilities in Philadelphia and Denver, the only U.S. Mint facilities that make circulating coins. The Philadelphia Mint is in its fourth facility. Built in 1969, it covers five acres of land.

U.S. Mint in Denver

The Denver Mint

In 1858 gold was discovered at the Platte River near what is now Denver, Colorado. Hundreds of miners, settlers, and shopkeepers moved there. Denver was founded the following year. In 1862 the U.S. Congress established a branch of the U.S. Mint in Denver. At first the Denver office was an assay office. The word assay has to do with deciding how pure or valuable something is. People brought gold dust and gold nuggets there to be melted, cast into bars, and then stamped to show weight and quality. By 1895 the Denver assay office was bringing in more than $5.6 million worth of gold and silver each year.

In 1904 the Federal government began building a grand and beautiful Italian Renaissance-style structure to be used as a new Mint facility in Denver. The building looks like a Florentine palace. See photos on this page. During its first operating year, it produced 167,371,035 gold and silver coins. Today it can produce over fifty million coins a day.

U.S. Coin Facts

- The U.S. Mint has minted half cent, cent, two-cent, three-cent, five-cent, half dime, dime, twenty-cent, quarter dollar, half dollar, and dollar coins. Gold coins with values different from these have also been minted.

The Denver Mint

- All U.S. coins are minted with a "coin turn," meaning that when the heads side image is right side up the tails side image is upside down. Officials at the Mint do not know why this was begun, but the practice is continued for the sake of tradition.

- In 1943, during World War II, pennies were minted from steel and coated with zinc to save copper for use in the war.

Inspecting Designs for Jefferson Nickels, 1938

- Several U.S. Coins have had images of U.S. Presidents. The Lincoln penny was first issued in 1909 to celebrate Lincoln's one hundredth birthday. George Washington's image first appeared on the quarter in 1932 to honor his two hundredth birthday. The first nickel with Thomas Jefferson's image was issued in 1938. In the photo above, people are inspecting designs for the Jefferson nickel. Franklin Roosevelt's likeness first appeared on the U.S. dime in 1946, less than one year after his death. Half-dollars with John F. Kennedy's image were issued in February of 1964, less than three months after Kennedy's death.

State Quarters Program

In 1997 the U.S. Congress passed and President Clinton signed a law authorizing the 50 State Quarters program. The law stated:

> The Congress finds that it is appropriate and timely to honor the unique Federal republic of 50 States that comprise the United States; and to promote the diffusion of knowledge among the youth of the United States about the individual States, their history and geography, and the rich diversity of the national heritage. . . .

From 1999 to 2008, quarters were minted for each of the fifty states. As illustrated above, George Washington's head continued to be on the obverse (or heads) side of each coin. Notice that all of the words usually found on the quarter, except "E Pluribus Unum," were included on the obverse side of these quarters so there would be room for special new state designs on the reverse (or tails) side.

Quarters honoring five states went into circulation each year. Quarters for the original thirteen colonies were issued in the order that they ratified the U.S. Constitution. The remaining thirty-seven state quarters were issued in the order that the states entered the Union. Each state quarter was minted for up to ten weeks and no longer. The Governor of each state was responsible for overseeing the design for his state's quarter. Many citizens offered suggestions to their Governors. After designs were submitted, the Department of the Treasury made the final decisions.

Americans had fun with the 50 State Quarters program. An estimated 147 million Americans collected them. Sculptors from various states copied the designs of some quarters: an ice sculpture in New York, a sand castle in New Hampshire, and a butter sculpture in Kansas.

When each state quarter was issued, a ceremony was held in that state. Thousands of Americans attended these ceremonies, but they did not always go smoothly. The Arizona quarter was unveiled at an outdoor ceremony when the temperature was 103 degrees. The South Dakota quarter was launched at an outdoor ceremony during a snowstorm. When it came time for Alaska's Governor Sarah Palin to attend the ceremony honoring the issue of the Alaska quarter, she couldn't come because she was in Ohio for the announcement that Republican candidate John McCain had chosen her for his vice-presidential running mate in the 2008 election.

The U.S. Mint made 34 billion state quarters. The Philadelphia Mint made just over half of them and the Denver Mint made the rest. The program earned the United States about 2.8 billion dollars, which went into the U.S. Treasury General Fund.

The words, "E Pluribus Unum," a Latin phrase meaning "out of many, one," is on the Great Seal of the United States and on all U.S. coins. Since America is one country with many states, these words are especially appropriate as part of the design for each state quarter. Below are pictures of the quarters with an explanation of each design. Notice that each coin includes the name of the state, the year it came into the Union, and the year the coin was issued.

State Quarters Issued in 1999

Delaware, 1787: The First State, Caesar Rodney — Caesar Rodney on horseback. Rodney was away from the Continental Congress on July 1, 1776, when the delegates prepared to vote about declaring independence from Great Britain. He hurried back to Philadelphia overnight on horseback to cast his vote the next day.

Pennsylvania, 1787: Virtue, Liberty, Independence — The "Commonwealth" statue which stands atop the Pennsylvania state capitol, an outline of the state, and a "keystone" representing Pennsylvania's central position in the original thirteen colonies.

New Jersey, 1787: Crossroads of the Revolution — General George Washington crossing the Delaware River during the American Revolution.

Georgia, 1788: Wisdom, Justice, Moderation — A state outline, plus a peach and sprigs of the live oak tree. Georgia has long been known for growing peaches.

Connecticut, 1788: The Charter Oak — The Charter Oak tree where early settlers hid their original colonial charter so that soldiers sent by Great Britain's King James II could not take it away.

State Quarters Issued in 2000

Massachusetts, 1788: The Bay State — An American Revolution minuteman and an outline of the state.

Maryland, 1788: The Old Line State — The Maryland Statehouse surrounded by clusters of white oak leaves. "Old Line" refers to Revolutionary War soldiers from Maryland.

South Carolina, 1788: The Palmetto State — A palmetto tree, Carolina wren, and yellow jessamine (the state tree, bird, and flower), with an outline of the state and a star for its state capital, Columbia.

New Hampshire, 1788: Live Free or Die, Old Man of the Mountain — The Old Man of the Mountain, a natural formation on the side of Franconia Mountain. The formation fell off in 2003, but the mountain remains an important New Hampshire landmark.

Virginia, 1788: Jamestown 1607-2007, Quadricentennial — Three ships, the *Susan Constant*, *Godspeed*, and *Discovery*, which brought the first English settlers to Jamestown.

State Quarters Issued in 2001

New York, 1788: Gateway to Freedom — The Statue of Liberty and the state outline with eleven stars, indicating that New York was the eleventh state.

North Carolina, 1789: First Flight — The Wright brothers' first flight in Kill Devil Hills, North Carolina.

Rhode Island, 1790: The Ocean State — A sailboat glides through Narragansett Bay, with the Pell Bridge in the background.

Vermont, 1791: Freedom and Unity — Camel's Hump Mountain, a beautiful peak that is still in its natural state, with a Vermonter, maple trees, and sap buckets in the foreground. Vermont is known for producing maple syrup.

Kentucky, 1792: "My Old Kentucky Home" — Federal Hill mansion and a thoroughbred racehorse behind a fence. Federal Hill mansion was the inspiration for Stephen Foster's song, "My Old Kentucky Home." Kentucky is known for its thoroughbred horses and horse racing, especially the Kentucky Derby.

State Quarters Issued in 2002

Tennessee, 1796: Musical Heritage — A fiddle, a trumpet, a guitar, a book of music, and three stars. Tennessee is famous for its many kinds of music. The three stars represent East, Middle, and West Tennessee.

Ohio, 1803: Birthplace of Aviation Pioneers — An early aircraft and an astronaut over a state outline. This design honors the Wright Brothers and Ohio's many astronauts.

Louisiana, 1812: Louisiana Purchase — A trumpet with musical notes, an outline of the Louisiana Purchase and the United States, and a pelican, the state bird. The trumpet represents New Orleans as the birthplace of jazz.

Indiana, 1816: Crossroads of America — A racecar over an outline of the state, plus nineteen stars, indicating that Indiana was the nineteenth state. The racecar represents the Indianapolis 500. Several Interstate highways go through Indiana.

Mississippi, 1817: The Magnolia State — Magnolias, the state flower of Mississippi.

State Quarters Issued in 2003

Illinois, 1818: The Land of Lincoln, 21st State/Century — Young Abraham Lincoln, an outline of the state, a farm scene, and an outline of the Chicago skyline. Surrounding the design are twenty-one stars, which signify that Illinois was the twenty-first state and that Illinois wants to be a leader in the twenty-first century. Abraham Lincoln moved to Illinois as a young man and was elected to the presidency from there.

Alabama, 1819: Spirit of Courage, Helen Keller (in Braille and English) — Helen Keller, an Alabama long leaf pine branch, and magnolias. Helen Keller was born in Alabama. She was blind and deaf. Her courage and accomplishments are an inspiration to many.

Maine, 1820 — Pemaquid Point Light on top of a granite coast with a schooner at sea. The Pemaquid Point Light was constructed in 1827.

Missouri, 1821: Corps of Discovery 1804-2004 — Lewis and Clark returning to St. Louis down the Missouri River. They are shown beneath the Jefferson National Expansion Memorial, known as the Gateway Arch.

Arkansas, 1836 — A mallard flying over a lake with rice stalks, and a diamond. Arkansas is known for duck hunting, its many rice fields, and diamond mining.

State Quarters Issued in 2004

Michigan, 1837: Great Lakes State — The Great Lakes and a state outline. The Great Lakes surround much of Michigan.

Florida, 1845: Gateway to Discovery — Sixteenth-century Spanish galleon and a space shuttle over a scene with sabal palm trees. In the 1500s, Spain discovered Florida; today Americans explore space from Cape Canaveral, Florida.

Texas, 1845: The Lone Star State — The Texas star over a state outline. A cowboy lariat encircles the design. The lariat symbolizes Texas' cattle and cowboy history.

Iowa, 1846: Foundation in Education, Grant Wood — A one-room schoolhouse with teacher and students planting a tree. The design is based on "Arbor Day," a painting by Iowa-born artist Grant Wood.

Wisconsin, 1848: Forward — The head of a cow, a round of cheese, and an ear of corn. These signify Wisconsin's importance as an agricultural state.

State Quarters Issued in 2005

California, 1850: John Muir, Yosemite Valley — Conservationist John Muir admires Yosemite Valley and Half Dome while a California condor flies overhead. John Muir helped Americans understand the need to protect beautiful places that God placed in America.

Minnesota, 1858: Land of 10,000 Lakes — Two people fish on a tree-lined Minnesota lake while a loon swims in the foreground, plus an outline of the state.

Oregon, 1859: Crater Lake — A portion of Crater Lake with Wizard Island and the Watchman and Hillman Peaks.

Kansas, 1861 — Buffalo and sunflower. Fields of sunflowers now grow in Kansas where herds of buffalo once roamed.

West Virginia, 1863: New River Gorge — New River and the New River Gorge Bridge. New River Gorge National River provides rugged, white-water canoeing through deep canyons.

State Quarters Issued in 2006

Nevada, 1864: The Silver State — Three wild horses, snow-capped mountains, the sunrise, and sagebrush. Nevada is known for silver mining and is home to thousands of wild horses.

Nebraska, 1867: Chimney Rock — An ox-drawn covered wagon carries pioneers by Chimney Rock.

Colorado, 1876: Colorful Colorado — The Rocky Mountains with evergreen trees.

North Dakota, 1889 — Grazing American bison in front of a sunset in the Badlands region.

South Dakota, 1889 — A Chinese ring-necked pheasant, the state bird, flies above Mount Rushmore National Memorial.

State Quarters Issued in 2007

Montana, 1889: Big Sky Country — A bison skull over a diverse Montana landscape.

Washington, 1889: The Evergreen State — A king salmon and Mount Rainier.

Idaho, 1890: Esto Perpetua (May It Be Forever) —A peregrine falcon and state outline.

Wyoming, 1890: The Equality State —A bucking horse and rider. Rodeos are popular in Wyoming. Wyoming was the first state to grant women the right to vote.

Utah, 1896: Crossroads of the West — Two locomotives moving toward the golden spike.

State Quarters Issued in 2008

Oklahoma, 1907 — Wildflowers with the state bird, the scissortail flycatcher, and the state wildflower, the Indian blanket.

New Mexico, 1912: Land of Enchantment — A Zia sun symbol over a state outline. The Zia are a Native American tribe who live in pueblos in New Mexico.

Arizona, 1912: The Grand Canyon State — The Grand Canyon and the state flower, the saguaro cactus.

Alaska, 1959: The Great Land — Grizzly bear with salmon and the North Star.

Hawaii, 1959: Ua mau ke ea o ka 'aina i ka pono ("The life of the land is perpetuated in righteousness.") — Hawaiian King Kamehameha I stretching his hand toward the eight major islands.

District of Columbia and U.S. Territories Quarters Program (2009)

The 50 State Quarters program was the most successful program in the history of the Mint. After its success, the U.S. Mint began the District of Columbia and United States Territories Quarters Program. These coins honor our national capital and the Commonwealth of Puerto Rico, Guam, American Samoa, the United States Virgin Islands, and the Northern Mariana Islands. All were issued in 2009. See the designs below.

District of Columbia: Justice for All, Duke Ellington — Composer and band leader Duke Ellington was from Washington, D.C.

Puerto Rico: Isla del Encanto ("Isle of Enchantment") — A sentry box and a hibiscus flower. The sentry box represents Puerto Rico's history and important location.

Guam: Guahan I Tanó ManChamorro ("Guam— Land of the Chamorro") — A proa and a latte stone. The proa is a boat built by the Chamorro people and a latte stone is used at the base of homes on Guam.

American Samoa: SAMOA MUAMUA LE ATUA ("Samoa, God is First") — An ava bowl (used for making the drink kava), a whisk, a staff, and a coconut tree on a shore.

U.S. Virgin Islands: United in Pride and Hope — Outlines of the three major islands; the yellow breast (or bananaquit), the territorial bird; and a Tyre palm tree.

Northern Mariana Islands — A limestone latte, a canoe (representing the great distances the native people have traveled by sea), two white fairy terns flying in unison, and a mwar (a lei worn on the head). The lei is made of these native plants: plueria, ylang ylang, peacock flowers, and teibwo (a Pacific basil).

America the Beautiful Quarters Program (2010)

In 2010 the U.S. Mint began issuing coins in its America the Beautiful Program. With George Washington on the front, the reverse sides of these quarters honor fifty-six places, one in each state and territory and the District of Columbia, issued in the order they were established as national sites. Concerning this program, U.S. Mint Director Ed Moy said:

> These new quarters will honor some of our most revered, treasured, and beautiful national sites—majestic and historic places located throughout the United States and its territories that truly make us "America the Beautiful." The designs will help reinvigorate interest in our national parks, forests, fish and wildlife refuges, and other national sites, as well as educate the public about their importance to us and our history.

Many of the national parks you have learned about in the God's Wonders lessons in *America the Beautiful* were chosen for these quarters. Among them are Yellowstone, Yosemite, and Grand Canyon National Parks. See images of these coins at right. Also included are Glacier, Olympic, Mount Rushmore, and Everglades National Parks and Gettysburg National Military Park.

Make sure that your character is free from the love of money,
being content with what you have;
for He Himself has said, "I will never desert you,
nor will I ever forsake you."
Hebrews 13:5

Activities for Lesson 143

Thinking Biblically – Jesus used a coin to teach the Pharisees an important lesson. Read Matthew 22:15-22.

Map Study – Complete the assignment for Lesson 143 on Map 3 "American Landmarks" in *Maps of America the Beautiful*.

Literature – Read chapters 5-6 in *Katy*.

Timeline – In *Timeline of America the Beautiful* next to 2000, write: The U.S. Mint introduces the Golden Dollar featuring Sacajawea.

Family Activity – Create your own Family Commemorative Coins. See pages 981-982.

Student Workbook or Lesson Review – If you are using one of these optional books, complete the assignment for Lesson 143.

The Volunteers of Habitat, Homebuilders for the Poor

Millard and Linda Fuller founded Habitat for Humanity International in 1976. Habitat is a Christian organization that helps poor people become homeowners and helps to repair and improve existing homes. In 1984 former President and Mrs. Jimmy Carter helped bring attention to Habitat when they began to volunteer with the organization. By 2010 Habitat for Humanity International had built more than 350,000 houses in 3,000 communities around the world, thereby providing safe housing for more than 1.75 million people.

Millard and Linda Fuller

Millard Fuller was born in Alabama in 1935. His mother died when he was three years old. He lived briefly with an aunt while his father grieved over a wife he loved deeply. When Millard was six years old, his father remarried. Mr. Fuller and his second wife eventually had two sons.

While Millard was young, his father bought a grocery store. Mr. Fuller later bought a four hundred acre farm. While growing up, Millard worked with his father, first in the grocery store and later as a partner in their father and son cattle business. After high school, Fuller studied at Auburn University, graduating with a degree in economics. He then attended law school at the University of Alabama. While in law school, Fuller married Linda Caldwell. Linda had grown up in the university town of Tuscaloosa, Alabama. She had one sister. Her family owned a local appliance store. Millard and Linda had four children: Christopher, Kim, Faith, and Georgia.

During law school, Millard Fuller started a business with fellow student Morris Dees. At first they sold Christmas trees and mistletoe. Later they imported Christmas wreaths from Italy and sold them to Boy Scouts, who used them in fundraising. The partners added more products to their line. After graduation, with income from both a law practice and the business, Millard Fuller became wealthy quickly. He was a millionaire by age twenty-nine.

Fuller spent so much time getting rich that his marriage and health suffered. At twenty-nine, he decided to stop and think about his values. He renewed his commitment to his marriage and to Christ. He and Linda made a bold decision. They sold their half of Fuller and Dees Marketing for one million dollars and gave the money to the poor. The Fullers decided to search for a new lifestyle. They moved to Georgia. There they got involved in providing housing for the poor. In 1973 the family moved to Zaire (now the Democratic Republic of the Congo) to try out the same idea there.

In 1976 the Fullers returned to Georgia. They met with close friends who were like-minded and formed Habitat for Humanity International.

People who volunteer with Habitat for Humanity are part of a team. Businesses and individuals donate materials to build or restore a home. Volunteers work alongside the people who will live in it. Habitat is not a hand-out. Those who live in a Habitat home pay a down payment and monthly mortgage payments. Future homeowners also provide hundreds of hours of labor for their own house and for the houses of others. See Fuller at right.

Millard Fuller, Co-Founder of Habitat for Humanity International

The people who purchase these low-cost homes do not pay any interest on their mortgages. Millard Fuller said that the idea of not charging interest to the new homeowners came from Exodus 22:25: "If you lend money to My people, to the poor among you, you are not to act as a creditor to him; you shall not charge him interest." Fuller called this the "economics of Jesus." The organization grew strong under the able leadership of Fuller, who traveled, spoke, raised funds, and volunteered on work sites. In the first five years, Habitat for Humanity built 342 houses.

A Boost from Jimmy and Rosalynn Carter

Three years after leaving the presidency, Jimmy Carter led a Habitat for Humanity project in New York City, called the Jimmy Carter Work Project. In 1984 the Carters and their forty-two fellow volunteers began renovating a six-story building, which provided homes for nineteen families. They returned to New York City the next year to complete the project. In 1986 the Carters worked with about 150 other volunteers to build a four-unit townhouse in Chicago. The Carters were among 235 volunteers who undertook "Miracle on 19th Street," building fourteen new homes in Charlotte, North Carolina, in 1987.

The Carter Work Project grew in 1988, when President and Mrs. Carter and two hundred other volunteers renovated a ten-unit row house in north Philadelphia, while 1,000 other volunteers completed twenty houses in Atlanta. In 1989 almost 1,000 volunteers, including President and Mrs. Carter, built six new homes and renovated eight others in Milwaukee, Wisconsin.

Carter Work Projects, 1990-2000

The Carter Work Project went outside the United States in 1990, when the Carters and approximately 2,000 volunteers built one hundred homes in Tijuana, Mexico, and seven in San Diego, California. In 1991 President and Mrs. Carter went to the Liberty City neighborhood in Miami, Florida, where they and more than four hundred volunteers built fourteen houses and a day care center.

The Carters worked with about 1,000 volunteers to complete ten homes in Washington, D.C., and restore ten row houses in Baltimore in 1992. The next year they joined over 1,100 volunteers to complete projects in Canada. They built eighteen houses in Winnipeg, Manitoba, and ten in Waterloo, Ontario.

In 1994 the Carter Work Project built thirty houses on the Cheyenne River Indian Reservation in Eagle Butte, South Dakota. More than 1,500 volunteers from thirty-nine states and five countries gathered with the Carters in 1995 to build twenty-one houses in the Watts/Willowbook community of Los Angeles. Watts had been the scene of rioting thirty years earlier during the turbulent sixties. The Carters took their work project to Europe in 1996. They and about five hundred other volunteers from twenty-three countries built ten houses in Vac, Hungary.

In the 1997 "Hammering in the Hills" project, the Carters and 3,300 volunteers built fifty-two homes in seven counties of Tennessee and Kentucky. In 1998 the Carters headed to Houston, Texas, where they and other volunteers built one hundred houses.

In 1999, when Carter was seventy-five years old, he and Rosalynn volunteered with 14,000 others from around the world to build 293 houses in the Philippines. Philippine President Joseph Estrada and former President Fidel Ramos were among the volunteers.

During the 2000 Carter Work Project, an abandoned apartment house in Harlem in New York City was converted into ten condominiums. One of the condos was the 100,000th Habitat home. Volunteers also built houses in Jacksonville, Florida, and in the Carters' hometown of Plains, Georgia, and in nearby Americus, Georgia.

Volunteers at the 2008 Gulf Coast Project: The Carters are standing in the front row.

Carter Work Projects, 2001-2010

South Korean President Kim Dae-Jung and about 9,000 volunteers joined the Carters to build 135 Habitat houses in South Korea in 2001. The following year the Carters joined thousands of volunteers who built one hundred houses in Durban, South Africa. When Habitat president Millard Fuller led the morning devotions on the first day, he encouraged the volunteers: "Let us love one another. Let us get to know the homeowners and love them and let them love us."

The communities of Anniston, Alabama; LaGrange, Georgia; and Valdosta, Georgia, gained ninety-two homes when the Carters and volunteers from around the world gathered for the 2003 Carter Work Project. The following year saw seventy-five houses built in Puebla, Mexico, and seventy-five in Veracruz, Mexico. In 2005 the Carters and others worked in Detroit and Benton Harbor, Michigan.

More than one hundred U.S. Navy sailors joined the Carters and 2,000 other volunteers in 2006 to construct one hundred homes in Lonavala, India. Thousands of volunteers gathered in Los Angeles and San Pedro, California, in 2007 to build thirty houses and restore dozens more. In 2008 the Carters and other volunteers worked on the Gulf Coast, building and repairing homes damaged three years before by Hurricane Katrina. See photo above. That year the annual Jimmy Carter Work Project was renamed the Jimmy and

Rosalynn Carter Work Project in order to recognize the great contributions of Rosalynn. The following year, the Carters and other volunteers worked on houses in Vietnam, Cambodia, Laos, Thailand, and the Sichuan Province of China.

In 2010 the Carters led 1,000 volunteers as they built, renovated, or repaired eighty-six homes in Washington, D.C.; Baltimore and Annapolis, Maryland; Minneapolis and St. Paul, Minnesota; and Birmingham, Alabama. The Carters began the week in Washington, D.C., where they were honored for their twenty-seven years as volunteers. Among the volunteers in Washington that week were students, faculty, and staff from Gallaudet University, a college for the deaf. On Wednesday they were in Minneapolis, working alongside Walter Mondale, Carter's Vice President. The next day, Mondale and the Carters worked in St. Paul. On Friday the Carters were in Birmingham. A father whose house was being constructed that week told President Carter that he was forty-nine years old and asked the President what advice he would give him. Carter placed his hand on the man's shoulder and said, "Well, I can tell you that I'd take care of my wife, I'd keep going to church, and I'd stay involved with Habitat." By 2010 President and Mrs. Carter had led week-long Habitat projects for twenty-seven consecutive years in the United States, Cambodia, Canada, China, Hungary, India, Laos, Mexico, the Philippines, South Africa, South Korea, Thailand, and Vietnam.

President Clinton awards Millard Fuller the Presidential Medal of Freedom, 1996

Fuller Receives Presidential Medal of Freedom

In 1996 President Clinton awarded Millard Fuller the Presidential Medal of Freedom. Clinton remarked: "Millard Fuller has done as much to make the dream of home ownership a reality in our country and throughout the world as any living person." Clinton also said, "I don't think it's an exaggeration to say that Millard Fuller has literally revolutionized the concept of philanthropy." Clinton himself has served as a Habitat volunteer. See photo above.

President and Mrs. Carter helped bring attention to the work being accomplished through Habitat, but under the leadership of Fuller, many other projects were also being completed around the world during the other fifty-one weeks of each year. Fuller led Habitat for Humanity International from 1976 to 2005. Under his leadership, the organization built 200,000 homes in one hundred countries.

In 2005 Millard and Linda Fuller were honored by being included on The Extra Mile Points of Light Volunteer Pathway in Washington, D.C. See medallion at right.

Millard Fuller passed away on February 3, 2009. He was seventy-four years old. Shortly

Fuller Medallion on The Points of Light Volunteer Pathway in Washington, D.C.

after his death, President Jimmy Carter called Fuller one of the most remarkable men he had ever known.

American Volunteers

Habitat Volunteers in Nashville, Tennessee

Thousands of Americans, like those pictured at right, volunteer each year to build Habitat houses in their hometowns. Other volunteers travel to the Carter Work Projects or to other Habitat sites throughout America and in other countries. They are simply Americans doing what so many Americans do: helping people in need.

People who volunteered at one Habitat project illustrate the kind of people who give their time. Volunteers there included a prison nurse from Kansas, a software consultant from San Diego, an air conditioner saleswoman from Florida, a female attorney who was volunteering for the fifteenth time, and the attorney's younger sister who was there for the first time. Another volunteer was seventy-four-year-old retiree Irving Hall from Albuquerque, New Mexico. He and his wife got involved with Habitat through their church. He said: "These are the final chapters of my life, and I want to do things that matter."

But whoever has the world's goods,
and sees his brother in need and closes his heart against him,
how does the love of God abide in him?
1 John 3:17

Activities for Lesson 144

Thinking Biblically – Read 2 Corinthians 9:6-15. Choose a section of two or three verses to copy into your notebook.

Vocabulary – In your notebook, write your own definition for each of these words: economics, marketing, mortgage, creditor, renovate. Look in the lesson for clues for the meaning of the words. When you are finished writing your definitions, look in a dictionary for comparison.

Literature – Read "Home" in *We the People*, page 188, and chapters 7-8 in *Katy*.

Creative Writing – In your notebook, write a short story of at least two pages about a family whose lives were transformed by the chance to own a Habitat for Humanity home.

Timeline – In *Timeline of America the Beautiful* next to 1976, write: Millard and Linda Fuller begin Habitat for Humanity International.

Student Workbook or Lesson Review – If you are using one of these optional books, complete the assignment for Lesson 144.

Homeschooling in America

A Homeschooling Family Sings Together

Babies are born completely dependent. They need parents to care for their hearts, souls, minds, and bodies. When God sent His Son to earth, He sent Him into a family who loved Him, cared for Him, and taught Him. For families to work as God intended, parents must lead their children well and children must follow well. Wise King Solomon wrote, "Hear, my son, your father's instruction and do not forsake your mother's teaching" (Proverbs 1:8). When Jesus was twelve years old, He went with Mary and Joseph to the temple in Jerusalem (see Luke 2:41-50). Afterwards:

> He went down with them and came to Nazareth, and He continued in
> subjection to them; and His mother treasured all these things in her heart.
> And Jesus kept increasing in wisdom and stature, and in favor with God
> and men. (Luke 2:51-52)

Though it may seem that modern public schools are normal, parents teaching their own children has been the normal way for most people for most of the world's history.

The purpose of the wise parent's teaching is to provide their children with the knowledge and skills they need in childhood, in adulthood, and in eternity. While Moses was reminding the Israelites of God's laws, he told them:

> These words, which I am commanding you today, shall be on your heart.
> You shall teach them diligently to your sons and shall talk of them when
> you sit in your house and when you walk by the way and when you lie
> down and when you rise up. (Deuteronomy 6:6-7)

Look again at Luke 2:51-52 above. Jesus grew in wisdom, in stature, and in favor with God and man. While growing up, He got wiser and taller. He learned and practiced what pleased God. He learned how to relate to people. Wise parents pass along the knowledge and wisdom learned in their own and previous generations to the children of the next generation—and wise children learn what those wise parents teach. Wise parents also make sure that their children have a wide circle of other wise adults to learn from as well.

A Look Back at the Traditional Education of Alaska's Inuit People

Let's look at how one group of Americans educated their children before public schools became common. The Inuit people of Alaska thrived in their environment by passing skills learned in one generation down to the children of the next. Inuit parents did not put their children out in the snow in mid-winter and leave them to figure out what to do. Since the children did not go away from home to go to school, they were with their parents.

The children learned first by watching what their parents did. They also learned by listening to stories told by their parents and their elders. Since the stories were about hunting and other activities that adults did, children learned about duties that would some day be theirs. As a child listened, he imagined. When it came time for him to use the skills he learned by watching and listening, he had already thought about the skills a great deal. The stories taught not only about what adults do, but also about the attitudes they had while they worked.

Praise was another important aspect of child training. When a young boy killed his first ptarmigan or rabbit, his parents told him to give it to his oldest female relative, perhaps his grandmother or great-grandmother. She praised him for his fine catch. The boy was then told to go to the homes of his relatives and friends to invite them for a feast. Together the women prepared a great feast with many dishes. They made the little ptarmigan or rabbit into a stew, which became the main dish. As the community ate the feast, they praised the young hunter and his catch. The boy learned about sharing and hard work. He learned that what he did had a great impact on his family and community. He learned that he must take responsibility seriously, because if he did not he could hurt those he loved.

The Inuit child was not the only person watching and listening. Adults in his or her life were watching and listening, too. When they could tell that the child was ready to practice a needed skill, they invited the child to accompany them in a task. This was quite different from the modern education approach of deciding that every child should learn multiplication tables or learn how to drive a car at a specific age. In Inuit culture, the child began practicing a skill when adults who loved him or her saw that the child was ready.

Watching, listening, receiving praise, and practicing. This is how Inuit children learned. They did not learn in scheduled hours at a school building. They learned as they watched and listened, as they sat in their houses, when they walked by the way, when they lay down, and when they rose up.

Compulsory Education

In the first centuries after Europeans began to settle in America, some parents taught their children at home, some used tutors, and some sent them to public or private schools. Many of America's most famous historical figures were homeschooled at least part of the time, including patriot Patrick Henry, First Lady Abigail Adams, Chief Justice John Jay, President John Quincy Adams, inventor Thomas Edison, and photographer Ansel Adams.

Before 1852 all American families had the freedom to educate their children as they thought best. That year the state of Massachusetts became the first state to pass a compulsory attendance law that required parents to send their children to school away from home. By 1918 all states had a compulsory attendance law. Once these laws were passed, almost all parents sent their children to either a public or a private school.

Some Americans who lived overseas working as missionaries or in some other occupation sent their children to boarding schools, but others taught them at home. An example of a child who learned at home under these circumstances was young Douglas MacArthur (see pages 529 and 713). Douglas, whose father was a general, grew up on various Army posts, so his mother taught him at home. One curriculum supplier for these families was the Calvert School in Baltimore, Maryland. Children who could not go to school because of illness also learned at home, as did children living in remote areas, like some parts of Alaska.

The Modern Homeschooling Movement

During the 1970s and 1980s, a few parents began to think again about educating their children at home. A small number decided to give homeschooling a try. As other parents heard what they were doing, they tried it, too. These parents were true pioneers. They had few options for curriculum. Some public school teachers saw themselves as experts and said that these parents were unqualified to teach their children. Some states made it very difficult for homeschooling parents. Government officials sometimes took legal action against them.

Still these homeschooling families persevered. They found creative ways to learn at home. Groups of parents founded support groups so that they could encourage one another. These groups began to hold local meetings. They started offering classes where children could learn together. They formed sports teams, bands, and choruses. They began 4-H clubs and started drama groups. See photos on this page and on page 915.

Parents worked to change state laws to make homeschooling legal. In time it became legal in all fifty states. Curriculum suppliers that had once refused to sell to homeschoolers sought their business, and new curriculum companies wrote material specifically for homeschoolers. Hardworking parents formed state organizations. These and some local and regional groups began hosting conventions, where parents could come together to learn how to improve their teaching skills. Conventions also began to organize curriculum fairs, where parents could choose from the growing variety of materials.

Homeschooling grew rapidly at the end of the 1990s and in the beginning of the twenty-first century. By 2008

A homeschool graduate leads homeschooled children in costume as they practice for a musical drama.

approximately 2,000,000 American children were being homeschooled.

Publicized Success

As more and more brave parents began to homeschool, their friends, relatives, and neighbors saw that homeschooling worked. They saw homeschooled children involved in church activities and in community sports teams and clubs. They saw them serving as volunteers and getting involved in political campaigns. They saw them succeed as adults.

Homeschoolers dress as favorite characters from Narnia.

Homeschooled children typically score higher on achievement tests than do children who go to public schools. They also score higher on college entrance exams like the ACT and SAT. Homeschooled children who have succeeded in highly-publicized competitions, such as the National Spelling Bee and the National Geography Bee, have brought national attention to homeschooling's successes.

The *Courier-Journal* of Louisville, Kentucky, sponsored the first National Spelling Bee in 1925. The Scripps media company became the sponsor in 1941. The competition has been held each year since 1925, except for three years during World War II. In 1997 Rebecca Sealfron of Brooklyn, New York, became the first homeschooler to win the National Spelling Bee. Since 1989 *National Geographic* magazine has sponsored a National Geography Bee. In 2002 ten-year-old Calvin McCarter from Michigan became the youngest person ever to win the competition. He was also the first winner who was homeschooled. Four of the top ten competitors that year were homeschoolers.

A homeschooling father and daughter celebrate her high school graduation.

True Success

Homeschooling parents want their children to live productive lives. They want them to experience joy. They want them to make good use of their talents. Ultimately, though, those who choose to homeschool for the purpose of raising children for God's glory want more than anything else for their children to live with God forever. All other goals pale in comparison. Some homeschoolers win the National Spelling Bee or the National Geography Bee; some receive full scholarships from Ivy League schools, become Rhodes Scholars, or are appointed to a military academy. God gives some of His children public honor and titles of distinction, but of utmost importance is that you honor your God and your parents by walking in purity and putting God first.

It is by his deeds that a lad distinguishes himself
If his conduct is pure and right.
Proverbs 20:11

Activities for Lesson 145

Vocabulary – Write five sentences in your notebook, using one of these words in each: stature, compulsory, patriot, curriculum, remote. Check in a dictionary if you need help with their definitions.

Literature – Read "Righteous Fundamentals" in *We the People*, page 189, and chapters 9-10 in *Katy*.

Creative Writing – Ask your parents what their goals are for your home education. In your notebook, write down in your own words what they said.

Timeline – In *Timeline of America the Beautiful* next to 2008, write: About 2 million children are being homeschooled in the United States.

Student Workbook or Lesson Review – If you are using one of these optional books, complete the assignment for Lesson 145. If you are using the Lesson Review, take the quiz for Unit 29.

Popular Toys of the Decade

Tickle-Me Elmo (1996)
Beanie Babies (1996)
Tamagotchi (1997)
Furby (1998)

In the 1990s . . .

- The Hubble Space Telescope was launched in 1990.
- Major League Baseball players went on strike in 1994. The World Series was not played that year.
- The Hale-Bopp comet was visible from earth in 1997.
- To save memory on computers, programmers in the twentieth century used only two digits when they entered data about a year. For example, 1971 was simply entered as 71. As the year 2000 approached, people became afraid that some computers would stop working at midnight on December 31, 1999, because the computers would "think" that the year 2000 was the year 1900. Companies spent billions of dollars to fix what became known as the Y2K bug (Y2K is short for Year 2000 and bug is a term used for a problem in a computer program). Many people were terribly frightened about the issue, fearing that communication, electrical, and other systems would break down, causing people to panic and become violent. They stored up food, water, and other supplies. The Y2K bug repairers did an excellent job. When the clock struck its last midnight of the 1990s, people celebrated, and there were no disasters.

America Enters
a New Millennium

The citizens of the United States live in a land that can truly be called America the Beautiful. Just a few months after President George Walker Bush was inaugurated, the country suffered an attack by terrorists. Again America asked God for His blessings and showed the world that it is not only our land that is beautiful—its people are, too. In America's time of crisis, Americans worked bravely to rescue, help, and comfort one another.

The Rocky Mountains inspired Katharine Lee Bates to write the song "America the Beautiful." America has had many song writers and musicians. Our country has given the world many new styles of music that were born right here. We end our study where our country began—on the Fourth of July. We see how Americans have celebrated this holiday through the years. May we in America always seek the God who blesses us. May we use wisely the America God has created, and may we do our part to keep America strong.

Lessons in Unit 30

Lesson 146 – Our American Story: The Digital Age
Lesson 147 – God's Wonders: God Created the Rocky Mountains
Lesson 148 – Daily Life: Making Music
Lesson 149 – An American Landmark: Music City, USA and the Ryman Auditorium
Lesson 150 – Daily Life: Celebrating the Fourth of July

Books Used in Unit 30

- *Maps of America the Beautiful*

- *Timeline of America the Beautiful*

- *We the People*

- *Katy* by Mary Evelyn Notgrass

*A train pulls coal cars across South Dakota
on September 16, 2009.*

The Digital Age

It is not surprising that in the months preceding New Year's Day 2000, the news was filled with stories about the Y2K bug (see page 916). America had truly entered a digital age, an age when information can be shared digitally.

People share words, messages, and information daily. One way is person-to-person. God used this method when He wanted to share His great love with us. He sent Jesus to earth as the living Word of God. Jesus was a message from God to people. We can also write messages down. God used this method, too, when He gave us the Bible.

As people in the 1800s learned ways to use electricity, they began to share information using telegraphs, telephones, photographs, and motion pictures. In the twentieth century, people used electricity to spread information on radio, television, and computers.

People made computers faster and faster and able to hold more and more information. They learned how to make them less and less expensive. Today digital electronics, including computers, cell phones, digital cameras, and other electronic devices, are cheap enough to be part of our daily lives. These devices bombard Americans with information, especially through the Internet, where we can learn about current events, history, science, medicine, music, literature, and much more. Information that we can find quickly on the Internet was once available only in big cities or universities or the libraries of wealthy people. Now it is available to people in tiny American towns and in remote villages in South America, Africa, or Asia.

The Controversial 2000 Election

As America prepared to enter the new millennium, the time came to elect a new President. The Democratic nominee was Vice President Al Gore. His running mate was Connecticut Senator Joe Lieberman, the first Jewish American chosen as a major party candidate for a national election. The Republican Party nominated George Walker Bush, Governor of Texas and son of former President George Herbert Walker Bush. His running mate was former Secretary of Defense Dick Cheney.

The election was very close. At midnight on election day, Americans did not know who their new President would be. They did not know the next day. In fact, it was more than a month before the election results were finalized.

Al Gore won a majority of the popular vote, but American presidential elections are not decided by popular vote. They are decided by electoral vote. The votes in the state of Florida were uncertain. If Gore won in Florida, he would receive its electoral votes and become President; but if Bush won in Florida, he would become the new President. It appeared that Bush had won in Florida, but there were problems with voting procedures in part of the state. Lawyers for both Bush and Gore took the matter to court. Finally on December 12, 2000, the U.S. Supreme Court ruled in a five to four decision that the votes in Florida would not be counted again. Out of the six million votes cast in Florida, Bush had 537 more votes than Gore, so he got the state's electoral votes and won the presidency with 271 electoral votes to Gore's 266.

Republicans won a majority in the U.S. House of Representatives. The Senate was evenly divided between Democrats and Republicans. However, the following June, one Republican Senator left the Republican Party and became an independent who usually voted with the Democrats.

Proud parents President and Mrs. George H. W. Bush watched as George W. Bush took the oath of office in January 2001. Not since John Quincy Adams was inaugurated in 1825 had the son of a former President become President. During his first months in office, Bush proposed and Congress passed large tax cuts. In August President Bush and more than twenty-five other current and former world leaders participated in a World Leaders Build project with Habitat for Humanity. President and Mrs. Bush worked with a crew constructing a home in Waco, Texas. That same week members of President Bush's staff volunteered in a Habitat project in Fairfax, Virginia, while President and Mrs. Carter worked in South Korea.

September 11, 2001

Just eight months after Bush took office, tragedy came to America. On September 11, 2001, nineteen Muslim terrorists carried out a pre-planned attack against the United States. They boarded four planes in American airports and then took over the planes while they were in flight. Terrorists on one plane crashed into one of the World Trade Center towers in New York City. A few minutes later another plane crashed into the other tower. A third plane was flown into the Pentagon building, the headquarters of the U.S. Department of Defense, just outside of Washington, D.C. Brave Americans in the fourth plane realized what was happening. They kept the terrorists from flying it into a fourth target. When the plane was just fifteen minutes from Washington, they made it crash in a field in Pennsylvania. It was likely heading for the White House or the U.S. Capitol.

An estimated 2,992 people died that day. All passengers on board all four planes were killed, including the terrorists. The Pentagon was badly damaged; 125 people lost their lives there. Over ninety percent of the deaths occurred in New York City, where casualties included 403 policemen and firefighters, who worked selflessly to rescue people trapped

A Cross Made from Pieces of the World Trade Center After the 9/11 Tragedy

inside the World Trade Center before the towers collapsed. The cross pictured at left was constructed from pieces of the World Trade Center.

The President's Day

President Bush awoke before dawn on September 11, 2001, read his Bible, and went on a four-mile run as was his usual routine. The President was in Florida where he was to visit an elementary school that morning. Like other Americans, when he heard that the first plane had crashed into the World Trade Center in New York City, he thought it was an accident. When the second plane hit the other tower, President Bush was sitting with second graders in the elementary school. He was quickly informed about what had happened. President Bush was rushed to Air Force One. On the way he told a Secret Service agent to make sure that his wife and daughters were protected.

The pilot of Air Force One quickly lifted the plane off the runway to take the President to safety. He flew along the Gulf Coast to head to Washington. Officials on the plane were worried that the plane would be attacked. The pilot asked for a guard to stand at the cockpit door. Secret Service agents made sure that everyone on the plane was supposed to be there. The pilot took the plane high above where jets normally fly. Officials decided to take the President to a secret underground command center in Nebraska. The pilot was afraid to talk to airport officials on the radio because other terrorists might intercept the message. Soon two military planes came to escort Air Force One.

All this time the President worried about the American people not knowing where he was, so he ordered that the plane land somewhere, so he could talk to them. It landed at Barksdale Air Force Base in Louisiana. In a brief address, he told the American people that America was being tested, but that it would pass the test.

Air Force One reached Offutt Air Force Base in Nebraska about 3:00 p.m. Bush and his team went into a red brick hut. Below it was the U.S. Strategic Command Underground Command Center. Bush stayed there for a time, but he soon decided that terrorists would not keep him out of Washington. He told the Air Force One crew to take him there. After his plane landed, Bush took the presidential helicopter to the White House. On the way, he flew by the severely-damaged Pentagon. Bush arrived at the White House nine hours after the attacks. He went on

President Bush Descends the Steps of Air Force One on September 11, 2001

television again to address the American people. He began, "Today our fellow citizens, our way of life, our very freedom came under attack in a series of deadly terrorist acts." Against the advice of his advisors, President Bush spent that first night in the White House. At bottom right on page 920 is a photo of Bush descending the steps of Air Force One on September 11, 2001.

Sorrow and Fear

Americans felt great sorrow and fear. Their hearts were filled with compassion for the families of people who had died. Many became afraid to travel. Businesses suffered economically, especially airlines, hotels, and other businesses related to travel. However, this attack on America resulted in a great outpouring of faith and patriotism. Scenes like those pictured at right and below were commonplace. Notice that the words "God Bless America!" are on a public school marquee.

Patriotic Scenes Following 9/11

America Fights Terrorists in Afghanistan

U.S. officials learned quickly that the al Qaeda terrorist group had planned the attack. Among the many people who helped the investigation was a flight attendant on one of the hijacked planes. She had called her airline's office and given them the seat numbers where her plane's hijackers were sitting, so that officials could know who they were. Al Qaeda's leader was Muslim extremist Osama bin Laden, who was training more terrorists while hiding in Afghanistan. President Bush announced that war had been declared on the

United States, and Congress gave him authority to fight a war against terrorism. NATO came to the aid of America. That fall a military force with troops from many nations began attacking terrorist bases in Afghanistan. The fighting lasted for many years. Some Afghans supported the efforts of American troops, but others fought against them. In the photo at right, U.S. soldiers and Afghan national soldiers meet with local Afghan villagers in 2002.

U. S. Soldiers, Afghan National Soldiers, and Afghan Villagers, 2002

War in Iraq

In 2003 the United States and other nations attacked Iraq. For many years its leader, Saddam Hussein, had supported terrorists. President Bush and other top officials also believed that the country was making very destructive weapons. The Iraqi military was defeated in just a few weeks. Saddam was eventually captured. America set to work rebuilding the country and helping it form a new democratic government. This turned out to be a costly process, because several groups fought for control in Iraq. Many Americans lost their lives in the continued fighting and many soldiers returned home with serious injuries. Many families suffered while the soldiers in their families served in Afghanistan and Iraq, some returning again and again.

Republican Gains in the Elections of 2002 and 2004

In the mid-term elections of 2002, the Republican Party gained even more seats in the House of Representatives. This election showed a vote of confidence for President Bush and his handling of the war on terrorism. Republicans also gained two seats in the U.S. Senate, which gave the party a majority.

In 2004 President Bush was again nominated by the Republican Party to run as its presidential candidate. The Democrats chose Massachusetts Senator John Kerry. Bush won a clear victory and the Republicans gained even more seats in the Senate and the House of Representatives.

President George W. Bush's Second Term in Office

During Bush's second term in office, the coast along the Gulf of Mexico was struck by a powerful hurricane, Hurricane Katrina. Communities in Mississippi along the coast were devastated as was the city of New Orleans, especially in the poorer sections of that large city. Victims looked toward their governments at the local, state, and Federal levels; but those governments did not handle the situation quickly or well. Thousands of people and many businesses moved away permanently from New Orleans and from other places along the Gulf.

As the wars in Afghanistan and Iraq dragged on, some Americans lost confidence in Bush and the Republicans. In the 2006 election, Democrats won a majority in both the House of Representatives and the Senate.

In late 2007, the American economy began to suffer. Banks had loaned people money for houses they really could not afford, and then the people could not make their payments. The price of gasoline increased greatly. Many businesses closed. This economic recession lasted from December of 2007 until June of 2009, making it the longest recession America had experienced since World War II. Unemployment was high and many American families suffered. Many Americans became unhappy with their elected Senators and Congressmen when they tried to help the economy by spending huge amounts to rescue large corporations that had made poor financial choices.

The war on terror was very expensive and the U.S. government went more deeply into debt during the Bush presidency. Though President Bush and the Republican Party had enjoyed wide support early in his presidency, that support dwindled as the war dragged on and the economic situation within the U.S. grew worse.

The Extra Mile

On October 14, 2005, President Bush's parents, along with the Points of Light Foundation, dedicated a new national monument called "The Extra Mile" next to the White House in Washington, D.C. The monument was begun to honor up to seventy Americans who have dedicated their lives to building service movements. President George H. W. Bush made remarks that day along with the only living honorees, Millard and Linda Fuller, founders of Habitat for Humanity International, and Eunice Kennedy Shriver, founder of the Special Olympics. Nearly fifty people who are related to honorees were in attendance, including descendants of nineteenth century African American leaders Frederick Douglass and Booker T. Washington.

Read about President George W. Bush's life below.

George Walker Bush
America's Forty-Third President
January 20, 2001 - January 20, 2009

George Walker Bush was born in 1946 to George and Barbara Bush as his father was finishing his sophomore year at Yale. They called their first baby "Georgie" so as not to get him confused with his dad. Georgie's first home was an apartment in a single-family house that had been converted into twelve apartments for veterans and their wives. All of those veterans had one child, except one, who had twins, so thirty-seven people lived in a home originally designed for one family. See the Bushes at right.

In 1948 the Bushes moved to Odessa, Texas, where they rented another apartment. They moved briefly to California, where a baby girl, Robin, was born. The Bush family then returned to Texas, where another son, Jeb, was born in 1953. When Georgie was seven years old, his sister

Robin died of leukemia. While Barbara Bush was at the hospital with her daughter before she died, Barbara's hair began to turn white. She was only twenty-eight years old.

Georgie and his mother became very close after Robin's death. Barbara was depressed, and Georgie decided it was his job to help cheer her up. George and Barbara had three more children: Neil, Marvin, and Dorothy. The family has always been very close.

Georgie Bush and his siblings grew up in Midland, Texas, where their father was a successful businessman in the petroleum industry. The younger George's favorite childhood activity was Little League Baseball. His father managed his team for three years. At school he loved to organize other boys so they could play baseball. George was the class clown and was once paddled for painting Elvis Presley sideburns on his face. The family moved to Houston before George went into the eighth grade. After one year in a private school there, he went to boarding school in Andover, Massachusetts. There he was a popular student.

Bush entered Yale in 1964. He graduated in 1968 and joined the Texas Air National Guard, where he trained as an F-102 pilot. During this time, he worked for Republicans in two political campaigns, one in Florida and another in Alabama. In 1973 at age twenty-seven, Bush entered Harvard Business School and was honorably discharged from the Guard that fall.

After receiving an M.B.A. degree, Bush returned to Texas to work in the oil business like his father. George remained a bachelor until a friend introduced him to school librarian Laura Welch at a backyard barbecue in 1977. Like George, she was from Midland, Texas. They married four months later. The couple has twin daughters, Barbara and Jenna.

Bush began to seek Christ after a conversation with Billy Graham in 1985. That same year he joined a Community Bible Study in Midland. He began to read God's Word and became a man of prayer. George ran unsuccessfully for the U.S. House of Representatives in 1978. He later sold his oil business, and in 1989 he helped buy the Texas Rangers major league baseball team with an investment of $600,000. He became the managing partner. Bush was respected by those who worked in the Ranger organization. Under his leadership, taxpayers built a beautiful new stadium. When Bush sold his interest in the team, he walked away with $15 million.

In 1994 George W. Bush was elected Governor of Texas. He did a good job as Governor; and when he ran for re-election in 1998, he won 239 of the 254 counties in Texas. From there, he went on to become President of the United States. On November 9, 2010, President Bush published his memoirs, *Decision Points.*

The Election of 2008

In the months before the 2008 election, many Republican and Democratic candidates worked to receive their party's presidential nomination. The two leading Democratic candidates were Illinois Senator Barack Obama and New York Senator Hillary Clinton, the former First Lady. The party chose Barack Obama as its nominee. Obama selected Delaware Senator Joseph Biden as his running mate. John McCain, a former POW in Vietnam, won the Republican nomination and, as mentioned on page 900, he chose Alaska Governor Sarah Palin as the vice-presidential candidate. Sarah Palin was only the second woman to be nominated for Vice President by a major party. The first was Geraldine Ferraro, the Democratic vice-presidential candidate in 1984. Obama soundly defeated McCain, becoming America's first African American President. The Democrats gained seats in both the Senate and the House. Obama appointed his chief Democratic rival Hillary Clinton as his Secretary of State.

The Obama Presidency

Soon after Barack Obama was inaugurated in 2009, he encouraged Congress to pass a huge spending program to try to help the economy. Congress passed these bills, but this spending put the United States government even deeper in debt. Under Obama's leadership, Congress also passed a major change to America's health care system, making the Federal government much more involved in health care. The President began to remove troops from Iraq and focused on fighting terrorism in Afghanistan.

Families of people who died in the terrorist attacks of September 11, 2001, worked for many years to establish September 11 as a National Day of Service and Remembrance. The first official National Day of Service and Remembrance was on September 11, 2010. Service projects were planned in all fifty states. President and Mrs. Obama volunteered that day at a Habitat for Humanity project in Washington, D.C.

Five Presidents: George H. W. Bush, Barack Obama, George W. Bush, Bill Clinton, and Jimmy Carter

Recent Elections

By the November 2010 election, many Americans were dissatisfied with President Obama and his fellow Democrats in Congress. In that election, the Democrats kept a small majority in the U.S. Senate, but Republicans gained more than sixty seats in the U.S. House of Representatives, giving them a majority. In the 2012 elections, Republicans kept their majority in the House, and Democrats retained control of the Senate. President Obama defeated Republican candidate Mitt Romney to win a second term as President.

Read about President Obama's life below.

Barack Hussein Obama II
America's Forty-Fourth President
January 20, 2009 -

Barack Obama was born in Hawaii in 1961. His parents were students at the University of Hawaii. His mother was Ann Dunham Obama, from Kansas; his father was from Kenya. Barack Sr. left Ann and Barack when the child was two years old and the couple divorced. Barack Sr. studied at Harvard, returned to Kenya, and later died in an automobile accident. After the divorce, Ann married Lolo Soetoro, another foreign student at the university. Ann and Lolo took Barack to Soetoro's home country of Indonesia when he was six years old. Barack attended both Catholic and Muslim schools there. When her son was ten years old, Ann sent him to live with her parents in Hawaii, where he could attend a prestigious private school. Barack attended Punahou School from grades five through twelve.

Obama moved to California to attend Occidental College in Los Angeles. After two years, he went to Columbia University in New York City. He graduated from Columbia in 1983 with a degree in political science. Barack Obama worked for one year as a researcher for a business consulting firm and then went to Chicago to become a community organizer for the poor on the city's South Side. In 1988 he entered Harvard Law School, where he excelled. That year he was baptized at Chicago's Trinity United Church of Christ, a large black congregation. For the 1990-1991 school year he served as president of the *Harvard Law Review*, the first African American to hold that position. While in law school, Obama worked one summer at a Chicago law firm. There he met Michelle Robinson, who supervised his work there. She was a native of Chicago and a graduate of Princeton University and Harvard Law School. They married in 1992 after a four-year courtship. The Obamas have two daughters. Malia was born in 1998 and Natasha, called "Sasha," in 2001. See the Obama family below.

Obama entered politics in 1992 when he directed a voter registration drive. After the election he began working with a civil rights law firm in Chicago and also taught at the University of Chicago Law School. In 1995 Barack Obama wrote a book about his personal struggle to be a black man though he was raised by whites without his African father. The following year he won election to the Illinois state senate. He was an active state senator for eight years, helping to get nearly three hundred bills passed. In 2000 he lost an election for the U.S. House of Representatives, but in 2004 he ran a successful campaign to become a U.S. Senator from Illinois. In 2008 Obama was elected President of the United States.

The Obama Family

President Obama speaks at a Pentagon Memorial, 2009.

Both Democrats and Republicans are humans who will fail us. Our trust must be in the God who created all of us.

It is better to take refuge in the Lord than to trust in man.
It is better to take refuge in the Lord than to trust in princes.
Psalm 118:8-9

Activities for Lesson 146

Vocabulary – Find each of these words in a dictionary: digital, bombard, terrorist, cockpit, marquee. Find the definition that corresponds to the way each word is used in this lesson. Copy the words and definitions into your notebook.

Literature – Read "Freedom and Fear At War" in *We the People*, pages 190-192, and chapters 11-12 in *Katy*.

Creative Writing – Interview your parents or grandparents about their 9/11 experience. Find out where they were when they heard the news and how the events impacted them personally. Write one to two pages in your notebook about what you learned.

Timeline – In *Timeline of America the Beautiful* next to 2003, write: American soldiers help rebuild Iraq and establish democracy.

Student Workbook or Lesson Review – If you are using one of these optional books, complete the assignment for Lesson 146.

God Created the Rocky Mountains

Lower Sand Creek Lake in Great Sand Dunes National Park

Black Canyon of the Gunnison National Park

View of the Rocky Mountains from Space

When explorers like Meriwether Lewis and William Clark, fur trappers like Jedediah Smith and Jim Bridger, and thousands of settlers set out across the Great American West, they encountered the beautiful Rocky Mountains, which were truly "purple mountain majesties" rising "above the fruited plain." Here God placed many of the tallest peaks of the lower forty-eight states. Along the top of the Rockies is the Continental Divide (also called the Great Divide). Flowing out of these mountains are the Arkansas, Colorado, Columbia, Missouri, Río Grande, and Snake Rivers. The mountains are dotted with lakes. The region is home to several national parks, including Black Canyon of the Gunnison National Park, established in 1999, and Great Sand Dunes National Park, established in 2000. Both are pictured at left.

The Rocky Mountain chain extends from the Canadian province of British Columbia to central New Mexico. When astronauts circle the earth, they can see the Rockies towering above the Great Plains to the east and the Great Basin and a valley called the Rocky Mountain Trench to the west. The NASA/Jet Propulsion Laboratory image at left was compiled using information collected during more than five hundred Space Shuttle orbits from 2000 to 2004. The data was collected during times when the skies were cloudless. Find the Rocky Mountains in the image.

Bighorn Canyon

Grand Teton Mountains with Sagebrush

Chesler Park in Canyonlands National Park

Curecanti National Recreation Area

The Northern Rockies

The Rockies can be divided into four sections: Canadian, Northern, Central, and Southern. We will only discuss the sections that are in the United States. The Northern Rockies are in northeastern Washington, northern Idaho, and western Montana. The Bitterroot Mountains, which Lewis and Clark found so difficult to cross, are in this region. Both Glacier National Park and the Bighorn Canyon National Recreation Area are in the Northern Rockies.

Bighorn Canyon National Recreation Area is along the border of Montana and Wyoming. The canyon ranges from 1,000 to 2,500 feet deep. Jedediah Smith, Jim Bridger, and other fur trappers once floated furs from Bighorn Canyon to the Yellowstone River. See Bighorn Canyon at top left. Wild horses, mule deer, mountain lions, bears, coyotes, and other mammals live here, as do snakes and more than two hundred species of birds. The wild horses here are believed to be descendants of Spanish horses. They are believed to be unique because no known horses of this breed still live in Spain.

The Central Rockies

The Central Rockies are in southern Montana, eastern Idaho, western Wyoming, and northeastern Utah. Yellowstone, Grand Teton, and Canyonlands National Parks are in the Central Rockies. See scenes from Grand Teton and Canyonlands National Parks at left.

The Southern Rockies

The tallest peaks in the Rocky Mountains are in the Southern Rockies, which extend from southern Wyoming, through Colorado, to central New Mexico. At 14,433 feet, Colorado's Mount Elbert is the highest mountain in the Rockies. Rocky Mountain, Black Canyon of the Gunnison, and Great Sand Dunes National

Rocky Mountain National Park

Mount Herard, Dunes, and Sandhill Cranes in Great Sand Dune National Park

Parks are in Colorado, as is Curecanti National Recreation Area. Rocky Mountain National Park, established in 1915, is pictured above. Morrow Point Reservoir in Curecanti National Recreation Area is pictured at lower left on page 928. Scenes from Great Sand Dunes National Park are pictured at right and below.

Sangre de Cristos Mountains and Dunes Blanketed with Snow

Thar's Gold in Them Thar Hills!

God placed many minerals inside the Rocky Mountains. Among them are coal, copper, gold, iron, lead, natural gas, petroleum, silver, zinc, and molybdenum. People have used minerals since the earliest days of creation. Over the centuries, they have learned new ways to use them. Molybdenum is a silver-white

Star Dune

Rocky Mountains with Dunes Taken from Space

Great Sand Dunes Tiger Beetle on Dune Sand

929

metal used to make steel stronger. Zinc is used to coat iron and steel so they will not rust. Zinc is also used to make brass and is a component of paint, rubber, TV screens, and fluorescent lights. The Rocky Mountain region has important mining centers in Colorado, Idaho, Montana, and Wyoming.

Life in the Rockies

Astronauts can see the earth from space, but when God looks down, He sees much more. "For He looked down from His holy height; from heaven the Lord gazed upon the earth" (Psalm 102:19). In the Sermon on the Mount, Jesus taught us that God cares for every living thing. Psalm 145:15b-16 says, "And You give them their food in due time. You open Your hand and satisfy the desire of every living thing." From heaven, God can see the living things He created in the Rocky Mountains; and He cares for each one of them. A few are pictured on page 930.

> For behold, He who forms mountains and creates the wind
> And declares to man what are His thoughts,
> He who makes dawn into darkness
> And treads on the high places of the earth,
> The Lord God of hosts is His name.
> Amos 4:13

Snow-Covered Pine and Cottonwoods in Bighorn Canyon National Park

Activities for Lesson 147

Thinking Biblically – Copy Psalm 36:5-6 in your notebook. Write a paragraph in your notebook about how God's righteousness is like the highest mountains.

Map Study – Complete the assignments for Lesson 147 on Map 2 "God's Wonders" and Map 30 "Rocky Mountains" in *Maps of America the Beautiful*.

Literature – Read "Ascending Long's Peak" in *We the People*, pages 193-195, and chapters 13-14 in *Katy*.

Church of the Transfiguration in Grand Teton National Park

Timeline – In *Timeline of America the Beautiful* next to 1915, write: Rocky Mountain National Park is established.

Student Workbook or Lesson Review – If you are using one of these optional books, complete the assignment for Lesson 147.

Page 930 Photos, Left Column: Yellow-Bellied Marmot, Gray Wolf, Long-Tailed Weasel, Sage Grouse (strutting), Wild Horses at Play, Broad-Tailed Hummingbird; Center Column: Alpine Forget-Me-Not, Sunflower Wooly Actinea, Mountain Harebell, Mountain Wood Lily, Pipsessewa, Mountain Globe Flower, Rocky Mountain Columbine, Gray Owlet, Fringe Gentian, Rocky Mountain Porcupines; Right Column: Pika, Otter on Ice, Red Fox, Beaver, Badger, Mountain Lion

Making Music

The first book printed in America, the *Bay Psalm Book*, was a book of songs. Its tunes were all from Europe. Some of America's first patriotic songs, "The Star-Spangled Banner," "Yankee Doodle," and "America," all had English tunes. However, it would not be long before America would be writing, singing, and playing her own songs.

Colonial Americans loved to sing at home and enjoyed going to singing schools held in churches. As pioneers began moving across the Appalachian Mountains, they carried the tradition of singing with them. "Down in the Valley" was a popular song on the frontier. When frontier men and women came to Christ during camp meetings and other revivals of the Second Great Awakening (see pages 235), they found comfort in southern folk hymns like "Amazing Grace" and "Wayfaring Stranger."

When young people got together for social events on the frontier, they sometimes enjoyed "play-party" games. These were especially popular among people who did not believe in dancing. Play-party games usually involved young people holding hands in a large circle, while they sang and skipped. A popular play-party game was "Skip to My Lou." The word "Lou" came to mean sweetheart in the South. The term comes from a Scottish word for love. As seen in the photo at right, the tradition continued into the 1900s.

Play-Party Game, Oklahoma, 1940

The Sacred Harp

Music teachers often teach students to sing by using the syllables DO, RE, MI, FA, SOL, LA, and TI to represent the seven notes of the musical scale. On the southern frontier, music teachers began to teach a shape note method of singing that had begun in New England. Though shape note teachers eventually developed seven different shapes, they originally taught only four: MI was a diamond, FA a right triangle, SOL an oval, and LA a rectangle. These singing schools became very popular. Some were held for three hours each night for one month.

In 1844 B. F. White and E. J. King published *The Sacred Harp*, a songbook with music printed in shape notes. The book has been revised and Sacred Harp singings are still held. Singers sit in a square facing one another, while a leader in the center marks time with his hand. Sacred Harp singings are not accompanied by a musical instrument.

Minstrel Shows and Stephen Foster

Stephen Foster

In the 1840s, four-man white quartets began touring the country performing minstrel shows. They blackened their faces and sang with a banjo, a tambourine, a fiddle, and castanets made of bone. Although these shows gave audiences a glimpse into African African culture, the white performers often made fun of black people.

Several American composers wrote music for these shows. One of the most popular minstrel songs was "Dixie." Others were "Buffalo Gals," "Wait for the Wagon," and "Polly Wolly Doodle." The shows became popular across America and even in Europe. By the mid-1800s, African Americans were also performing in minstrel shows.

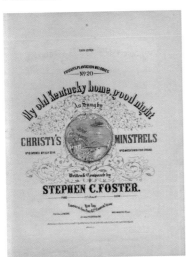

Perhaps the best-known American songwriter of the 1800s was Stephen Foster. See his picture above. Foster wrote more than two hundred songs, including ones for the popular Christy's Minstrels. Some of Foster's best-loved minstrel songs are "Oh, Susanna," "Camptown Races," "Old Folks at Home (Swanee River)," and "My Old Kentucky Home." The sheet music pictured at left is for "My Old Kentucky Home" as sung by Christy's Minstrels.

Songwriter Septimus Winner

Septimus Winner, the owner of a music store in Philadelphia, wrote several popular songs, including "Listen to the Mockingbird," "Whispering Hope," "Ten Little Indians," and "Where, Oh Where Has My Little Dog Gone?" Writing under a pen-name was common then; Winner used the name Alice Hawthorn as his pen-name for "Listen to the Mockingbird." Dick Milburn, a young and poor African American street performer, inspired Winner to write the song in 1856. Milburn, known as "Whistling Dick," played guitar and whistled. He often whistled like a mockingbird. It is estimated that twenty million copies of "Listen to the Mockingbird" sheet music were sold by 1905.

Sailing, Railroad, and Civil War Songs

Sailors and railroad builders sang while they worked; Civil War soldiers sang as they marched. A special sailor song was "Blow the Man Down." Forty-Niners who were wealthy enough to go to the California Gold Rush on ships around the tip of South America learned this song from the sailors. The song became popular in California. Widely-known and enjoyed railroad songs were "She'll Be Comin' 'Round the Mountain" and "I've Been Working on the Railroad."

During the Civil War, southerners sang songs like "Dixie" and "Goober Peas." Northerners sang "Battle Hymn of the Republic" and "Marching Through Georgia." "When Johnny Comes Marching Home" was also sung during the Civil War, but it became popular across the nation during the Spanish-American War.

African American Spirituals and the Fisk Jubilee Singers

Colonial churches sometimes sang using a method called "lining out." First the song leader chanted a line and then the congregation sang it. At other times the leader sang verses and the congregation sang words like "glory" and "hallelujah." "Lining out" is similar to African styles of singing. As African slaves became believers, they sang hymns in an African style. These came to be called Negro spirituals.

African American music became popular after the Civil War. *Slave Songs of the United States* was published in 1867. It included "Michael, Row the Boat Ashore" and "Roll, Jordan, Roll." In 1866 northern Christians worked with the Freedman's Bureau to found what is now Fisk University in Nashville, Tennessee. Its purpose was to educate former

slaves. A group of Fisk students was organized into a choral group called the Fisk Jubilee Singers, pictured at right. They toured nationally and internationally, even singing for royalty in Great Britain. They were immensely popular and introduced African American music to a broad audience. Thousands of African American vocalists have performed with the Fisk Jubilee Singers, a group which continues today.

Fisk Jubilee Singers

Barbershop Quartet Contest Poster

Barbershop Quartets

Traditional barbershop quartet music is sung by four male voices. It is sung acappella, meaning without the accompaniment of musical instruments. Each voice sings a different part. Parts include lead, tenor, baritone, and bass. The lyrics of barbershop music are easy to understand. Traditional costumes for a barbershop quartet include striped vests and straw hats. Handlebar mustaches are popular with barbershop quartets.

This singing style became popular in America in the late 1800s. The poster at left was created by the Works Progress Administration in 1936 to advertise a barbershop quartet contest in New York City's Central Park. One of the most famous barbershop quartets, the Buffalo Bills, were the International Quartet Champions in 1950. They performed in the Broadway musical *The Music Man*.

Vaudeville

Vaudeville was a form of stage entertainment with many kinds of performers, including acrobats, comedians, family acts, jugglers, magicians, musicians, and trained animals. Some of the first vaudeville acts were not respectable. New York actor and theater manager Tony Pastor helped make it a more acceptable form of entertainment after

934

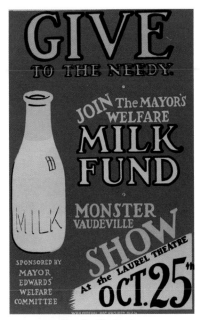
Vaudeville Poster

opening his own theater in New York in 1881. At the height of vaudeville's popularity in 1928, America had about 1,000 vaudeville theaters with a daily attendance of about 2,000,000 people. Popular vaudeville songs were "While Strolling Through the Park,""By the Light of the Silvery Moon," "In My Merry Oldsmobile," and "Sidewalks of New York" (also called "East Side, West Side"). At left is a late-1930s WPA advertisement for a vaudeville show held to benefit the poor in New York City.

Music Publishers in Tin Pan Alley

In the late 1800s, most of America's important music publishers were in Manhattan on West 28th Street between Broadway and Sixth Avenue. This area became known as "Tin Pan Alley." From 1880 to the late 1940s, publishing and selling sheet music was a big business. Before recorded music was available, people who lived all over the country could enjoy popular music by buying sheet music and playing it in their own homes. Since recorded music in the form of records and later tapes, CDs, and other technologies became widely available, a song has been judged popular if people have bought many recordings of it. A song's popularity was once measured by how many pieces of sheet music were sold.

Ragtime

Ragtime was a popular style of music published in Tin Pan Alley during the first decade of the twentieth century. Southern and midwestern African Americans were probably the first to play ragtime. It became especially popular in Missouri. One of the most famous ragtime tunes of the day was "Maple Leaf Rag" by Scott Joplin. Today more people are familiar with Joplin's song, "The Entertainer," a tune often played at piano recitals. Ragtime was so popular that people began to buy more pianos. Stores sold many pieces of ragtime sheet music. Sales of mechanical self-playing pianos, called player pianos, also rose, as did the musical rolls used in them. See diagram of a player piano at right.

Diagram of Player Piano

The Blues

Another music style developed by African Americans and published in Tin Pan Alley is called the blues. Composer W. C. Handy from Montgomery, Alabama, and singer Bessie Smith made this style popular. Bessie Smith was born in Chattanooga, Tennessee. Both her parents died before she was ten years old, so she and her brother began performing on Ninth Street in Chattanooga. Bessie sang and he played the guitar. In 1912 she joined a troupe of touring minstrels. In 1923 Smith recorded "Down Hearted Blues" for Columbia Records. It sold 800,000 copies and became the company's first big hit. She wrote many of her own songs. She made 156 recordings, including "Nobody Knows You When You're Down and Out." Louis Armstrong, who later became a popular jazz trumpeter, accompanied Smith on nine of her recordings.

Smith came to be called "The Empress of the Blues." She was five feet nine inches tall and weighed two hundred pounds. She wore satin gowns, long strands of pearls, feather boas, and headdresses when she performed. Her voice was so strong that she could be heard outside the theater, and this was before theaters used microphones!

W. C. Handy introduced the blues to people attending the World's Columbian Exposition in 1893. He moved to Memphis, Tennessee, before 1910. Blues music is often associated with Memphis, especially the city's Beale Street where many blues performers from the delta regions of western Mississippi and Tennessee played. Handy's first published song was "Memphis Blues," a campaign song he wrote for a Memphis politician. He also wrote "Beale Street Blues," recorded by Bessie Smith. Memphis became a major recording center for blues music. See sign for Blues City Cafe on Beale Street at top right. One of the most popular blues singers to come out of Memphis was B. B. King. He began recording in the 1940s and his popularity continued throughout the twentieth century.

Cafe Sign on Beale Street

W. C. Handy later moved to New York City where he continued his career in blues music. In 1941 he wrote his autobiography, *Father of the Blues*. See Handy statue at right.

W. C. Handy Statue in Florence, Alabama

Thomas Dorsey, Mahalia Jackson, and Gospel Music

Thomas Dorsey helped make American gospel music a popular American music form. This style of gospel music combines a blues style with a Christian message. Gospel music builds on the long history of both African American and white church music as it developed in America.

Dorsey grew up in Georgia. His father was a preacher and sharecropper, his mother a church organist. Dorsey was drawn to both Christian music and the blues, but especially the blues. His mother encouraged him to stick with Christian music.

While working as a blues musician in Chicago, a female singer sang Dorsey's "If You See My Savior," at a National Baptist Convention, an organization of African American Baptist churches. Afterwards the Ebenezer Baptist Church in Chicago hired Dorsey to form a chorus. The following year Pilgrim Baptist, Chicago's second largest church, hired him for the same purpose. Later that year, Dorsey's wife died while giving birth. While grieving his terrible loss, Dorsey wrote the song "Precious Lord, Take My Hand," which he said was given to him by God. The song had a Christian message with a blues style.

During the late 1930s and 1940s, Dorsey became the top gospel music composer. He worked with large choruses and with phenomenal gospel singer Mahalia Jackson, who had a rich and beautiful voice. Jackson was born in New Orleans. She was a devout believer. After moving to Chicago in the late 1920s, she became a member of the Greater Salem Baptist Church and a member of the Johnson Gospel Singers. She began recording in the 1930s. Her first major success was "Move Up a Little Higher," which she recorded in 1947. It sold one million copies. Jackson had her own gospel music television show on CBS in 1954. She became active in the civil rights movement and sang at the March on Washington in 1963. In 1968 she sang at the funeral of Dr. Martin Luther King Jr. (see pages 781 and 785). The Gospel Music Workshop of America was organized in 1968. It is the largest gospel music convention in the world.

Jazz, the Swing Era, and the Big Band Sound

In jazz music, musicians decide what to play while the song is being played. This is called improvisation. African American piano soloists played the first jazz at picnics and weddings. Jazz was also played at funerals. Players walked with mourners, playing slow dirges on the way to the cemetery and then upbeat marches on the way back. In the early 1900s, jazz became popular in New Orleans. Here jazz bands had either a cornet, trumpet, or violin which played the melody. It also had a clarinet, a trombone, a guitar or banjo, drums, and a string bass. When the bands marched, the string bass was replaced with a tuba. Jazz bands also included a piano if one was available.

Though jazz was rooted in the African American culture, the first jazz band to make a recording was a white band from New Orleans called The Original Dixieland Jazz Band. The band became popular across America and overseas. The most famous jazz

Jazz Great Louis Armstrong in Characteristic Poses

musician to come out of New Orleans was trumpet player Louis Armstrong. See photos above. He introduced a style of jazz band that featured a soloist. Armstrong excelled in trumpet and voice solos. Louis Armstrong improvised with both his trumpet and his voice. Armstrong also became a jazz composer as did African American jazz pianist Jelly Roll Morton. Armstrong and other New Orleans jazz musicians moved to Chicago. Chicago jazz bands also added a saxophone. Many jazz musicians from Chicago eventually carried their music to New York City.

Music styles change as new artists add their own personalities and ideas. In the 1930s and 1940s, some musicians began to play a variation of jazz called boogie woogie. Another variation on traditional jazz was the swing band or big band. Instead of one clarinet, one trombone, and so forth, the bands had sections with several musicians playing most instruments. One popular jazz composer who formed his own band was Duke Ellington

Jazz Pianist and Conductor Duke Ellington, 1943

Clarinetist and Conductor Benny Goodman with One of His Performers and Two Senators at the Capitol, 1939

Count Basie's Band at Chicago's Savoy Ballroom, 1941

from Washington, D.C. Two favorites among Ellington fans are "It Don't Mean a Thing if It Ain't Got That Swing" and "Take the 'A' Train." Other popular band leaders were Benny Goodman, Count Basie, Guy Lombardo, Lawrence Welk, and Tommy Dorsey (not to be confused with Thomas Dorsey). Duke Ellington and Benny Goodman are pictured above along with Count Basie's Band.

Glenn Miller was one of the top big band leaders. Miller played with other bands and even had his own band for a while before he finally came up with a unique blend of sounds and formed the famous Glenn Miller Orchestra. Hits that fans remember include "Tuxedo Junction," "Pennsylvania 6-5000," "Moonlight Serenade," and "Chattanooga Choo Choo."

Irving Berlin

Soloists

At the same time that jazz, swing, and big bands were popular, a number of soloists were also enjoying successful careers. The most popular jazz singer of the twentieth century was Ella Fitzgerald, called "The First Lady of Song." Fitzgerald entered a talent contest when she was a teenager and at the last minute decided to sing instead of dance. Someone who heard her that night was impressed and helped her begin a career. She was soon singing with a band. When Fitzgerald was twenty-one years old, she recorded a jazzy rendition of the nursery rhyme "A-Tisket, A-Tasket." It sold one million copies and made her famous. During a long career, Fitzgerald sang all over the world and sold over forty million albums.

Other soloists sang popular music, written by composers like Irving Berlin, pictured above. Popular music appeals to many different listeners. Berlin gave America some of its most treasured popular songs, including "God Bless America," "White Christmas," and "Count Your Blessings." Many popular singers hosted their own TV variety shows. A variety show has a variety of acts such as singing, dancing, and comedy. Bing Crosby, Dinah Shore, Frank Sinatra, Nat King Cole, Andy Williams, and Dean Martin all hosted their own shows. At the top of page 939 is a list of popular soloists with some of their top songs.

The Music of Aaron Copeland

This lesson has not emphasized music played by symphonic orchestras; but we must mention the uniquely American music of Aaron Copeland, who wove American folk music into his compositions. He composed *Billy the Kid* in 1938, *Rodeo* in 1942, and *Appalachian Spring* in 1944. *Appalachian Spring* included "'Tis a Gift to be Simple," a song originally sung by the Shakers beginning in 1848. The Shakers were a religious group who pulled away from society into a closed community.

Popular Soloists
Bing Crosby — "White Christmas"
Dinah Shore — "Dear Hearts and Gentle People"
Tennessee Ernie Ford — "Sixteen Tons," one of the biggest-selling songs in American history
Frank Sinatra — "New York, New York"
Nat King Cole — "Unforgettable"
Andy Williams — "Moon River"
Dean Martin — "Everybody Loves Somebody Sometime"
Perry Como — "Home for the Holidays"

Broadway Musicals

George M. Cohan was born in Rhode Island in 1878. He appeared on stage for the first time when he was nine years old. His family later formed a traveling vaudeville troupe called the Four Cohans, including George and his father, mother, and sister. George presented his first play on Broadway in New York when he was just twenty-one years old. His first successful Broadway production was *Little Johnny Jones*, which opened when Cohan was twenty-four. He played the character Yankee Doodle Boy. Cohan continued to write musicals for live theater, often casting himself as the lead actor. His plays were especially popular in the 1920s. One of his most popular musicals was *Forty-Five Minutes from Broadway*. Many of Cohan's patriotic songs are still popular today, including "Grand Old Flag" "I'm a Yankee Doodle Dandy," and the song that encouraged American troops in both World Wars, "Over There." Another Cohan song that remains popular is "Give My Regards to Broadway." Cohan is pictured above with the sheet music for "Over There."

George M. Cohan   *"Over There" Sheet Music*

Richard Rogers and Oscar Hammerstein II teamed up to write musicals in the 1940s. They are pictured at right with Irving Berlin. Their first popular Broadway musical, *Oklahoma*, opened in 1943. Other well-loved Rogers and Hammerstein musicals are *The King and I* and *The Sound of Music*. Many Hollywood movies were based on their Broadway musicals.

Rogers, Berlin, and Hammerstein

Rock and Roll

Rock and roll music became popular in the 1950s. Rock and roll bands and singers learned from jazz, blues, and gospel musicians of the previous decades. Then and now rock music appealed mostly to teenagers and young adults. Rock and roll's popularity grew as radio stations began to play the songs more and more. An early rock and roll hit was "Rock Around the Clock" by Bill Haley and the Comets.

Early rock and roll song lyrics were often very simple. Early rock music was simple, too. Soloists, duos, and bands performed rock and roll. Bands usually had a lead guitar, a rhythm guitar, a bass guitar, and drums. The bands were often called "combos." The list of stars over the past decades is long. One of rock's early stars was Elvis Presley, who had grown up under the influence of African American musicians in northern Mississippi and

Gates of Graceland, Home of Elvis Presley

Memphis, Tennessee. "Hound Dog" was one of his early hits. The gates to Presley's famed Graceland Estate in Memphis are pictured at left.

A hit by early star Pat Boone from Nashville, Tennessee, was "Love Letters in the Sand." The Beach Boys were one of several rock and roll groups who emphasized beaches and surfing. An early Beach Boy hit was "Surfin' USA." An early hit by the popular duo The Righteous Brothers was "You've Lost That Lovin' Feeling."

Both black and white entertainers performed rock and roll, but in the 1950s they usually appealed to segregated audiences. This segregation of listeners lessened in the 1960s as both black and white performers enjoyed popularity across America. As American rock and roll artists became popular in Great Britain, British groups started playing rock and roll, too. They in turn became a big influence in America. The wildly popular group the Beatles led this trend. Pictured at right is the Rock and Roll Hall of Fame in Cleveland, Ohio.

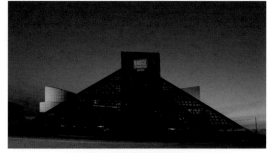
Rock and Roll Hall of Fame

Motown

In 1960 Berry Gordy began Motown Records in Detroit (Motown refers to Detroit as the "Motor City"). There Gordy recorded a style called rhythm and blues, or R and B. His first Motown hit was "Shop Around" by The Miracles. It sold one million records. During the next ten years, Motown Records had 110 songs that made it into the Top Ten list of hits. Motown artists included The Supremes, who sang "Stop in the Name of Love"; Stevie Wonder, who sang "Signed, Sealed, and Delivered"; and The Four Tops, who sang "I Can't Help Myself" ("Sugar Pie, Honey Bunch").

Gordy later began another record label called Gordy. The Temptations recorded on the Gordy label, which specialized in a music style called "soul music" or the "Motown Sound." Gordy hired Maxine Powell to work at Motown. Powell taught newcomers how to walk and talk like stars, training that helped talented singers become popular.

Folk Music

In the 1960s, radio stations began to play folk songs in addition to the popular rock and roll and Motown sounds. The new folk singers had a style similar to Woody Guthrie's songs from the 1940s. Guthrie's music and the folk music that became popular in the 1960s was often written and sung for the purpose of protesting. Woody Guthrie believed: "A folk song is what's wrong and how to fix it or it could be who's hungry and where their mouth is or who's out of work and where the job is or who's broke and where the money is or who's carrying a gun and where the peace is."

Woody Guthrie learned Western songs, Scottish folk tunes, and Indian songs from his father. His mother also enjoyed music. When many poor "Okies" from Oklahoma migrated to California during the Great Depression, Woody Guthrie was among them. He had been playing music for a few years by then and soon got a job on a radio station. There he sang "ole time" songs and original songs that he had written. He also talked to his listeners about things he would like to see changed.

After living in California, Guthrie moved to New York where he became friends with other folk singers like Burl Ives and Pete Seeger. Two aspects of Guthrie's time in New York seem very contradictory. He served in the U.S. Army and supported the U.S. effort in World War II, but he also came to believe Communist ideas.

Of the nearly 3,000 songs Guthrie wrote, "This Land is Your Land" is a favorite. Guthrie's friend Pete Seeger was also a songwriter. He wrote "If I Had a Hammer." Many children are familiar with folk singer Burl Ives through the Christmas television classic *Rudolph the Red-Nosed Reindeer*. The voice of the snowman who narrates the show and who sings "Silver and Gold" and "Rudolph the Red-Nosed Reindeer" is that of Burl Ives.

Some rock and roll bands sang a musical style called folk rock. The Byrds did a folk rock version of Seeger's "Turn, Turn, Turn," which is based on Ecclesiastes 3. In the box at right is a list of popular folk soloists and groups along with some of their hit recordings.

Folk Soloists and Groups

Bob Dylan — "Mr. Tamborine Man"
Judy Collins — "Amazing Grace"
John Denver — "Take Me Home, Country Roads"
Pete Seeger — "This Land is Your Land"
Joan Baez — "The Night They Drove Ole Dixie Down"
The Kingston Trio — "Where Have All the Flowers Gone?"
The Weavers — "On Top of Ole Smokey"
Peter, Paul, and Mary — "If I Had a Hammer"

Contemporary Christian

In the late 1960s and early 1970s, some young people pulled away from the rest of American culture and were called "hippies" or "flower children." Male and female hippies started to wear jeans and T-shirts. Sometimes the jeans were embroidered with flowers. Some of the women wore long, flowing dresses. Sandals were very popular. They often drove vehicles painted with flowers and peace symbols. These young people rejected the values of their parents and other older adults. Some became involved in using illegal drugs. Some moved into communes where they shared their possessions. Many protested the Vietnam War.

When some hippies realized that their lives were empty, they turned to Jesus. They were called "Jesus people." They started singing songs with Christian lyrics, but in the styles of rock and roll and folk songs. Contemporary Christian music grew out of the music sung and played by the Jesus people. Much of today's contemporary Christian music is recorded in Nashville, Tennessee.

But let all who take refuge in You be glad,
Let them ever sing for joy;
And may You shelter them,
That those who love Your name may exult in You.
Psalm 5:11

Activities for Lesson 148

Thinking Biblically – Write at least one page in your notebook about why you think God created music. Discuss the different ways people use and enjoy music and the ways music is a part of your own life.

Vocabulary – In your notebook, copy the sentences below, inserting one of these words in each: spiritual, acappella, vaudeville, popularity, sharecropper

1. We were amazed at the rich sound of the _____ choir.
2. The singer gained _____ after his Christmas concert.
3. During the Depression, Granddaddy was thankful to work even as a _____.
4. "Swing Low, Sweet Chariot" is a _____ that was sung by slaves.
5. The tap dancer who did magic tricks was a big hit at the _____ show.

Literature – Read "Songs of Septimus Winner" in *We the People*, pages 196-197, and chapters 15-16 in *Katy*.

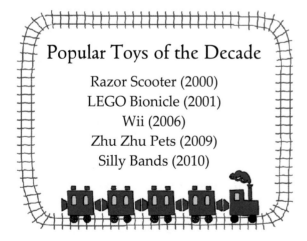

Popular Toys of the Decade

Razor Scooter (2000)
LEGO Bionicle (2001)
Wii (2006)
Zhu Zhu Pets (2009)
Silly Bands (2010)

Timeline – In *Timeline of America the Beautiful* next to 1968, write: The Gospel Music Workshop of America is organized.

Student Workbook or Lesson Review – If you are using one of these optional books, complete the assignment for Lesson 148.

Music City, USA and the Ryman Auditorium

Country music is another uniquely American style of music. It has its roots in the southern Appalachian Mountains. Beautiful harmonies echoed in these hills, where descendants of English, Scots, and Irish immigrants sang what was in their hearts and what had been passed down to them from past generations. Some songs were enjoyed by groups gathered for a church service, a corn shucking, or a dance, while others were sung at home. Much was sung acappella.

The songs sung at home were often ballads that originated in the British Isles. A ballad is a song that tells a story. Many have a dozen or two dozen verses. Ballads were sung throughout the South and in New England. In the early 1800s, British scholar Cecil Sharp traveled in the Appalachians gathering information for his 1932 book *English Folk-Songs from the Southern Appalachians*.

Uncle Alex Dunford of the Bogtrotters Band with His Fiddle, Galax, Virginia, c. 1940

The rich musical culture of the Appalachians spread beyond the mountains into other parts of the South as did their traditional way of talking, which has come to be called a southern accent.

Musicians Performing at Mountain Music Festival, Asheville, North Carolina, c. 1940

At the same time that people were enjoying traditional folk songs in the Appalachians, a beautiful instrumental tradition was growing as well. The favored instruments were fiddles and banjos, but also popular were the autoharp, harmonica, and dulcimer, in both the mountain and hammered styles. The fiddle was brought to America from England, Scotland, and Ireland; the banjo was based on African instruments. President Andrew Jackson used to enjoy dancing to the tunes of fiddles. Fiddling contests began in the late 1880s. They are still held today; and for many years have included buck dancing, square dancing, singing, and contests for players of other instruments. See photos above, at left, and on page 944.

The Carter Family

The technologies of radio and musical recordings brought southern Appalachian music into the homes of people across America. It was given several names: old time music, hillbilly music, mountain music, and finally, country music. Some of the first recordings of old time music were made in the 1920s. In July and August of 1927, the Victor Talking Machine Company from New Jersey brought

Musicians Performing at Mountain Music Festival, Asheville, North Carolina, c. 1940

recording equipment to Bristol, Tennessee, to record local music. One of the groups they recorded was the Carter Family, which included A. P. Carter, his wife Sara, and Sara's cousin Maybelle. They became very famous. The Carter Family's music continues to influence American music today. Three of their best-loved songs are "It Takes a Worried Man to Sing a Worried Song," "Keep on the Sunny Side," and "Will the Circle Be Unbroken?"

WSM, the Grand Ole Opry, and Roy Acuff

During the Great Depression, when people had less money to spend, they began to enjoy music they could hear on the radio for free. Radio stations hosted shows with live music. One of the most successful radio stations that aired country music was WSM in Nashville, Tennessee. It went on the air in October of 1925 and three months later started a musical show that featured country music. This show was eventually called the Grand Ole Opry. One of the earliest performers on the Opry was Roy Acuff, who was later called the "King of Country Music." One of Acuff's best-known songs was "Wabash Cannonball."

Early Grand Ole Opry shows were broadcast from Nashville's War Memorial Auditorium. In 1943 it was moved to the Ryman Auditorium. You will read about the Ryman Auditorium at the end of this lesson.

Uncle Dave Macon

Uncle Dave Macon from Middle Tennessee was the son of a Confederate captain. This former vaudeville performer became a favorite on the Opry. He sang beautifully, played the banjo superbly, and kept the audience laughing with his humor. Three of his most popular songs were "Keep My Skillet Good and Greasy," "Cripple Creek," and "How Beautiful Heaven Must Be." Macon, like many other country singers, included gospel songs in his performances.

Bill Monroe, the Father of Bluegrass

The bluegrass musical style grew out of country music. Mandolin-player Bill Monroe from Kentucky is recognized as the "Father of Bluegrass Music." Monroe played on the

Grand Ole Opry for the first time in 1939, when he was only twenty-eight years old. He played "Muleskinner Blues." People applauded until he played three encores.

In the 1940s, Bill Monroe began to write lyrics. His "Blue Moon of Kentucky" is a standard bluegrass song today. Monroe formed a band called the Blue Grass Boys with banjo-picker Earl Scruggs from North Carolina, singer and guitarist Lester Flatt from Tennessee, fiddler Chubby Wise from Florida, and bass player Cedric Rainwater, also from Florida. In 1995 President Clinton awarded Bill Monroe the Presidential Medal of Freedom. Monroe called bluegrass "music that matters." He said that it combines Scottish bagpipes, "ole-time fiddlin'," Methodist, Baptist, Holiness, blues, and jazz. He said it is "played from my heart to your heart." His funeral in 1996 was held at the Ryman Auditorium.

Flatt and Scruggs

After Lester Flatt and Earl Scruggs left the Blue Grass Boys, they formed a band called Flatt and Scruggs and the Foggy Mountain Boys. One of their most famous bluegrass tunes was "Foggy Mountain Breakdown." The Flatt and Scruggs band became famous nationwide by recording many songs, touring widely, and hosting their own segment of the Grand Ole Opry which was sponsored by the Martha White Flour Company. In 1962 the group recorded "The Ballad of Jed Clampett," the theme song for a popular television show, *The Beverly Hillbillies*. They also appeared on the television show several times.

Chet Atkins

Guitarist Chet Atkins first played on the Grand Ole Opry in 1946. Atkins became a world-class guitarist, had many hits, and was a regular performer on the Opry. He designed guitars for the Gibson guitar company; worked as a recording studio musician; played on the records of many other performers; and was a recording company executive. When he died in 2001, his funeral was held at the Ryman Auditorium.

Members of the Grand Ole Opry

One of the highest honors bestowed on a country music performer is membership in the Grand Ole Opry. Other performers may appear on stage at the Opry, but the following are some of the many performers who have been inducted as members of the Opry, along with songs that helped make them famous:

"Little" Jimmy Dickens – Dickens was the first Opry performer to circle the earth on a world tour. He entertained troops in Vietnam twice. He is known for his funny songs, like "May the Bird of Paradise Fly Up Your Nose."

Johnny Cash – Singer-songwriter Johnny Cash made his first recording at Sun Records in Memphis in 1955. See right. Rock stars Elvis Presley, Jerry Lee Lewis, and Carl Perkins also recorded at Sun Records. These four

Sun Records in Memphis, Tennessee

singer-musicians are the most famous to have recorded at Sun Records. During his career, Cash made over seventy record albums of original music. In 1968 Johnny Cash won a Grammy for "Folsom Prison Blues." In 1969 he began hosting *The Johnny Cash Show*, a television show filmed at the Ryman Auditorium. See Cash at right.

Johnny Cash with President Nixon

Loretta Lynn – Singer-songwriter Loretta Lynn has had sixty country hits. Some of her most famous lyrics are "When you're lookin' at me, you're lookin' at country."

Osborne Brothers – These real brothers grew up in Kentucky. In 1967 they recorded "Rocky Top."

Dolly Parton – In 1971 Dolly Parton recorded "Coat of Many Colors," about the poor family in which she grew up. One of Parton's many charitable efforts is providing books for young children through her Imagination Library programs in many states.

Riders in the Sky Perform in the Volcano Room at Cumberland Caverns in McMinnville, Tennessee, on January 29, 2011

Barbara Mandrell – Barbara Mandrell is one of country music's Mandrell sisters. In 1981 Barbara recorded "I Was Country When Country Wasn't Cool."

Gatlin Brothers – Family singing helped form the country style of music. Brothers Larry, Steve, and Rudy Gatlin have been singing together since 1976. They recorded the album *Family Gospel Favorites* in 2004.

Riders in the Sky – Songs about cowboys and the West became part of the country music style, which is also called Country and Western music. Country music songs with Western themes include "El Paso" by Marty Robbins and "Big Bad John" by Jimmy Dean. The talented group known as Riders in the Sky has recorded Western classics like "Tumbling Tumbleweed" and "Back in the Saddle Again," but are perhaps best known now for "Woody's Round-Up" from the movie *Toy Story 2*. See Riders in the Sky above.

Alan Jackson – Jackson voiced values felt by many Americans in his song "Small Town Southern Man."

Randy Travis – Randy Travis was inducted into the Grand Ole Opry in 1986. Two of his top hits are "Forever and Ever, Amen" and "Three Wooden Crosses."

Guitar on Broadway in Nashville

Music City, USA

Nashville, Tennessee, has earned the title Music City, USA. In addition to being the home of the Grand Ole Opry, many artists, both country and those from other music styles, record in its studios on Music Row. Many musicians come to Nashville hoping to become country stars. Some perform in one of the many live music venues along a street in Nashville named Broadway. On page 946, notice the giant guitar decorated with the faces of country stars. It was photographed on Broadway. In the center are Willie Nelson in a black hat, Hank Williams Sr. in a light hat, and Hank Williams Jr. in a black hat. Counter-clockwise from top left are Merle Haggard, Waylon Jennings, Patsy Cline, Loretta Lynn, Conway Twitty, Dolly Parton, Charlie Price, Johnny Cash, George Jones, and Tammy Wynette, all popular country stars.

The Ryman Auditorium

In 1885 riverboat captain Thomas Ryman, who had recently been converted to Christ, decided to build the Union Gospel Tabernacle as a place to hold revival meetings.

The first revival held at the Union Gospel Tabernacle was in 1890 before the structure was finished. A piece of canvas was placed over a hole in the unfinished roof. The building was completed two years later. Dwight L. Moody held a revival there in 1896. The sound quality (or acoustics) of the building were so wonderful, it came to be used for concerts. Two events there in 1893 were a lecture by Arctic explorer Robert Peary and a performance by the New York Symphony. William Jennings Bryan spoke there in 1897.

Pews are used as seating at the Ryman. The original capacity was 3,755 people. In 1897 a balcony was added for a Confederate Veterans Association reunion. This "Confederate Gallery," as it is still called, brought the seating capacity to 6,000.

Booker T. Washington lectured at the Ryman Auditorium in 1902. Captain Ryman died two years later. During his funeral at the Ryman, a minister asked those assembled to vote on whether to change the name of the Union Gospel Tabernacle to Ryman Auditorium. The audience responded with a standing ovation.

In 1907 Theodore Roosevelt lectured at the Ryman. John Philip Sousa and his band performed there the following year. Boy Scout founder Sir Robert Baden Powell lectured at the Ryman Auditorium in 1912. In 1913 Helen Keller and her teacher Anne Sullivan lectured there; later that year, the Fisk Jubilee Singers performed. Russian dancer Anna Pavlova performed at the Ryman the following year.

During World War I, Hollywood actors Charlie Chaplin, Douglas Fairbanks, and Mary Pickford spoke at the Ryman, encouraging the audience to buy savings bonds. Evangelist Billy Sunday held a revival at the Ryman shortly after the war.

Ryman Auditorium

The Ryman hosted vaudeville shows, Broadway plays, ballet performances, Shakespearean plays, and opera singers in the early decades of the twentieth century. In 1930 a German passion play (about Christ's crucifixion) was performed on the Ryman stage. In 1934 the Vienna Boys Choir performed there. Eleanor Roosevelt lectured at the Ryman Auditorium in 1938.

As mentioned previously, WSM radio moved the Grand Ole Opry to the Ryman Auditorium in 1943. For thirty-one years, country music fans from all over America and around the world traveled to Nashville to see a live Friday or Saturday night performance of the Opry, while millions listened to it on the radio. Though audiences continued to see other styles of entertainment at the Ryman, it was country music played on the Grand Ole Opry radio show that made it famous. A new, larger Opry House was built in 1974. President Nixon attended the first Grand Ole Opry held at the new Opry House. As seen in the photo at right, he sang and played the piano on stage that night.

The Ryman Auditorium fell into disrepair, but it was restored in the 1990s. Once again it is a popular music venue for many types of performances and a popular tourist destination.

Let the word of Christ richly dwell within you,
with all wisdom teaching and admonishing one another
with psalms and hymns and spiritual songs,
singing with thankfulness in your hearts to God.
Colossians 3:16

Nixon on the Opry Stage, 1974

Activities for Lesson 149

Map Study – Complete the assignment for Lesson 149 on Map 3 "American Landmarks" in *Maps of America the Beautiful*.

Vocabulary – In your notebook, make a drawing for each of these words that illustrates what it means: charitable, venue, acoustics, capacity, ovation. Write the correct word under each drawing. Check in a dictionary if you need help with their definitions.

Literature – Read "Songs of the Carter Family" in *We the People*, pages 198-199, and chapters 17-18 and Author's Note in *Katy*.

Creative Writing – Write a poem of twelve to sixteen lines that celebrates America's music.

Timeline – In *Timeline of America the Beautiful* next to 1943, write: The Grand Ole Opry is first performed at the Ryman Auditorium.

Student Workbook or Lesson Review – If you are using one of these optional books, complete the assignment for Lesson 149. If you are using the Lesson Review, answer the questions on *Katy*.

Celebrating the Fourth of July

Katharine Lee Bates was a poet and a professor of English literature at Wellesley College in Wellesley, Massachusetts, near Boston. In 1893 she made a trip to the Rocky Mountains of Colorado. While there she and other tourists gathered into a prairie wagon with the words, "Pike's Peak or Bust" painted across the back. Horses pulled the wagon part of the way up the side of Pike's Peak, and then mules pulled it to the top. Isn't it amazing that only ten years later, the Wright brothers were making their first flight in their airplane? Think of the changes since then. What an amazing century!

Miss Bates and her group expected to spend an hour and a half enjoying the view; but when two people became faint in the thin mountain air, everyone got back in the wagon and hurried down the mountain. Miss Bates remembered her time at the top of Pike's Peak as "one ecstatic gaze," but in that brief moment the first lines of a poem came to her:

Tacoma Park, Maryland, July 4, 1940

> *O beautiful for spacious skies,*
> *For amber waves of grain,*
> *For purple mountain majesty,*
> *Above the fruited plain.*

The poem "America the Beautiful" was first published two years later in the July 4, 1895, issue of the weekly newspaper *The Congregationalist*. Miss Bates made final additions to "America the Beautiful" in 1913. For many years the poem was sung to a variety of popular tunes. Often it was sung to "Auld Lang Syne." In 1926 the National Federation of Music Clubs sponsored a contest for people to write music for the poem. No winner was found, but people began more and more to sing it to a melody Samuel Augustus Ward had written in 1882. This is the tune we use today.

The Fourth of July is important to Americans. We have been celebrating Independence Day since the signing of the Declaration of Independence in 1776. Common activities in the earliest celebrations included listening to speeches, firing guns, watching military parades, listening to bands play, and reading the Declaration of Independence aloud.

Laura Ingalls Wilder wrote about Fourth of July celebrations in her books. In *Farmer Boy*, Almanzo and his family dressed in their best and celebrated Independence Day in nearby Malone, New York, which was decorated everywhere with flags. A crowd gathered in the square to listen to a prayer, a reading of the Declaration of Independence, and a band playing patriotic songs. Townspeople and their country neighbors joined to sing "The Star-Spangled Banner." Afterwards, Almanzo and his family enjoyed a picnic in the church yard. The festivities concluded with the firing of two cannons on the square. In *Little Town on the Prairie*, Laura tells of a celebration in De Smet, South Dakota. Pa, Laura, and Carrie walked to town, also dressed in their Sunday best. They heard firecrackers as they went along. Though Laura and Carrie knew the Declaration of Independence by heart, it gave them a "solemn, glorious feeling to hear the words" spoken by a townsman. De Smet citizens had taken up a collection to make a barrel of lemonade, a wonderful treat for the two girls. The biggest thrill of the day was a horse race on the prairie. Little did Laura know then that she would some day marry the winner, Almanzo Wilder.

Historic Fourth of July Events

On July 2, 1776, the Continental Congress adopted a resolution that America should become an independent country. The following day John Adams wrote a letter to his wife Abigail. Excited about what the Continental Congress had done, he told her that he believed July 2 would be celebrated for generations. He said that it should commemorated by "solemn acts of devotion to God Almighty." Adams told Abigail that it should be "solemnized" with pomp, parades, shows, games, guns, bells, bonfires, and illuminations "from one end of this continent to the other from this time forward forever more."

On the day that Adams wrote his letter to Abigail, Thomas Jefferson and the rest of the committee chosen to write the Declaration of Independence were busy finishing their work. On July 4, 1776, the Continental Congress adopted and signed it. Adams ably predicted what Americans would do to celebrate, though he thought they would celebrate the day of decision rather than the day the delegates voted to adopt the Declaration.

Two years later, on July 4, 1778, while Americans were fighting for their independence in the American Revolution, General George Washington told his Army to put green boughs on their hats and ordered that the artillery give salute. After becoming President, Washington gave a Fourth of July address in Lancaster, Pennsylvania, in 1791. In New York City, on July 4, 1800, a twenty-foot long by twenty-four-foot high model of Mount Vernon (Washington's home) was illuminated by several hundred lamps.

The first public Fourth of July reception held at the White House occurred in 1801 during the presidency of Thomas Jefferson. On July 4, 1804, Lewis and Clark and the Corps of Discovery fired a gun to begin the day and fired another at its close. This was the first known Fourth of July celebration west of the Mississippi River. When the Corps passed a creek with no name that day, they named it Independence Creek.

In 1821 future President John Quincy Adams, son of John Adams, read an original copy of the Declaration of Independence at the Capitol. Four years later, while serving as

President, he marched from the White House to the Capitol in a parade. Also in the parade was a stage mounted on wheels that represented the twenty-four states. In 1826, fifty years after the the Declaration was signed, Americans celebrated the "Jubilee of Freedom." Both John Adams and Thomas Jefferson died that day, Adams in Quincy, Massachusetts, and Jefferson at his Virginia home, Monticello. New York state emancipated its slaves on the Fourth of July in 1827. The following year in Baltimore, Maryland, Charles Carroll, the last man living who had signed the Declaration of Independence, participated in a ceremony to celebrate the beginning of the construction of the Baltimore and Ohio Railroad.

As mentioned in Lesson 29, on July 4, 1831, children first sang "America," also known as "My Country 'Tis of Thee," on the steps of the Park Street Church in Boston. In 1832 another President, James Monroe, died on the Fourth of July. In 1835 shoemaker George Robert Twelves Hewes was honored as the last survivor of the Boston Tea Party.

In 1848 the cornerstone of the Washington Monument was laid in Washington, D.C. On July 5, 1852, abolitionist Frederick Douglass gave a speech, "The Meaning of July Fourth for the Negro." In 1868 President Andrew Johnson issued an amnesty proclamation for people who had participated in the Civil War.

Future President Calvin Coolidge was born on the Fourth of July in 1872. The following year Mark Twain gave a Fourth of July speech in London. In 1876 in honor of the one-hundredth anniversary of the signing of the Declaration of Independence, large celebrations were held across America and in foreign countries. In 1881 Fourth of July celebrations were canceled and prayer meetings for the recently-wounded President James Garfield were held in their place. In 1899 all British warships in Plymouth, England (the port from which the Pilgrims left for America), flew flags while artillery gave a twenty-one gun salute.

Cover Illustration for Puck *Magazine, 1903*

The *Puck* magazine cover at right was created for its Fourth of July issue of 1903. In 1915, while World War I raged in Europe, William Jennings Bryan gave a speech in Philadelphia entitled "Universal Peace." In 1923 President Harding became the first President to celebrate the Fourth of July on the west coast. He gave an address to citizens of Portland, Oregon. He was initiated into the Cayuse tribe that day at the Oregon Trail Celebration. Special celebrations were held in 1926 to celebrate the 150th anniversary of the signing of the Declaration of Independence. Four years later the sixty-foot high sculpture of Washington's face was unveiled at Mount Rushmore on July 4.

Fireworks in most cities were canceled in 1942 because of blackouts due to World War II. In 1946 American soldiers occupying Germany and Japan celebrated with parades and artillery salutes, while Americans at home celebrated the first peacetime Fourth of July in five years. In 1959 the forty-nine star American flag waved for the first time, since Alaska had recently become a state. The following year the fifty star flag waved, following the addition of Hawaii. In 1964 a recording of the recently-slain President John F. Kennedy reading the Declaration of Independence was broadcast on radio. In 1975 President and Mrs. Ford participated in Independence Day festivities at Fort McHenry, Maryland, where the American flag inspired the writing of "The Star-Spangled Banner" in 1814.

In 1976 Americans celebrated two hundred years of freedom. At 2:00 p.m. Eastern time, the same time that the Declaration of Independence was signed in 1776, churches and citizens rang bells across the country. Hundreds of ships, including ones from twenty-two countries, sailed into New York harbor for Operation Sail. In Boston the USS *Constitution* fired her cannons for the first time in ninety-five years. That day 10,471 flags flew over the U.S. Capitol. President Gerald Ford gave an address at Valley Forge, Pennsylvania.

In 1981 President Reagan, who had recently been shot by a would-be assassin, left the hospital to watch fireworks on the National Mall. The following year astronauts Thomas K. Mattingly and Henry W. Hartsfield landed the space shuttle *Columbia* at Edwards Air Force Base in California. President Reagan gave a speech welcoming them home. In 1992 seven astronauts aboard the space shuttle *Columbia* unfurled an American flag and chanted "Happy Birthday, America!" In 1993 country music singer Johnny Cash honored American prisoners of war and those missing in action during the Vietnam War by reciting his poem "Ragged Old Flag" in Washington, D.C. In 1999, 112 people who had been born on the Fourth of July since 1900 gathered in front of Independence Hall, where their photograph was taken. It was called "Photo of the Century." On July 4, 2000, 150 tall sailing ships from more than twenty countries and twenty-four naval ships from around the world gathered in New York harbor for Operation Sail 2000. It was the largest number of ships ever to sail in one event. The line of naval ships alone was eleven miles long.

Just ten weeks before the September 11, 2001, terrorist attacks, public readings of the Declaration of Independence were held in many places across America, including the Old State House in Boston and the National Archives in Washington, D.C. The following July, celebrations were held across the country in spite of fears following the 9/11 terrorist attacks. American soldiers celebrated the Fourth of July in 2003 with a cookout at Saddam Hussein's palace that had been built in his hometown. The next year the cornerstone was laid for the new Freedom Tower, built on the site of the World Trade Center. The space shuttle *Discovery* was launched on the Fourth of July in 2006. That same year, soldiers who had been wounded in Iraq read aloud portions of the Declaration of Independence at a ceremony at the National Archives in Washington, D.C. In 2009 the crown of the Statue of Liberty opened to the public for the first time since being closed for security after 9/11.

Everyday Citizens Celebrate the Fourth of July

Across our land, Americans have found ways to celebrate their feelings of patriotism and their gratitude to God for allowing them to live in a rich, beautiful, and free land. We have found quiet ways to celebrate the Fourth of July—and ways that are not so quiet. We have celebrated with thousands of people and with only a few. Most Fourth of July celebrations are never written about in a history book. They are written instead on the hearts of those who shared them. Enjoy this scrapbook of Americans celebrating the Fourth of July.

America Celebrates!

Hats Off for the Pledge of Allegiance
Vale, Oregon, July 4, 1941

Deaf Children Sign
"The Star-Spangled Banner"
At St. Rica's School
in Cincinnati, Ohio, c. 1925

Brave American Legion Veterans
March in the Watertown, Wisconsin,
Parade on July 4, 1941

All Dressed Up
for the Pagent
Tacoma Park,
Maryland,
July 4, 1922

She Bought
a New Flag
for the Fourth!
Caldwell, Idaho,
July 4, 1941

My Fireworks Are Ready for
the Fourth! - July 3, 1906

A 4th of July Fair in Oregon

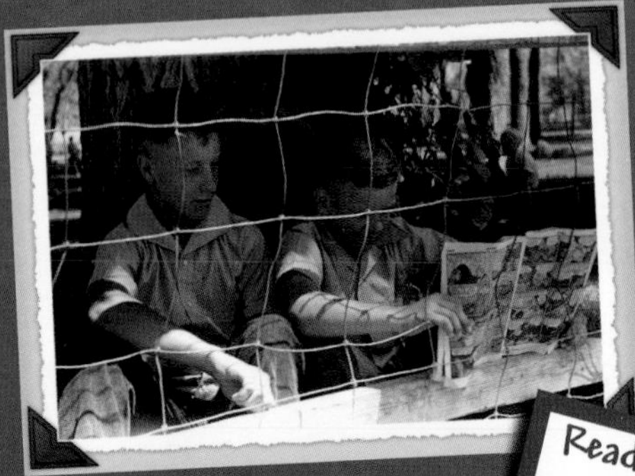

Riding the Merry-Go-Round With Daddy

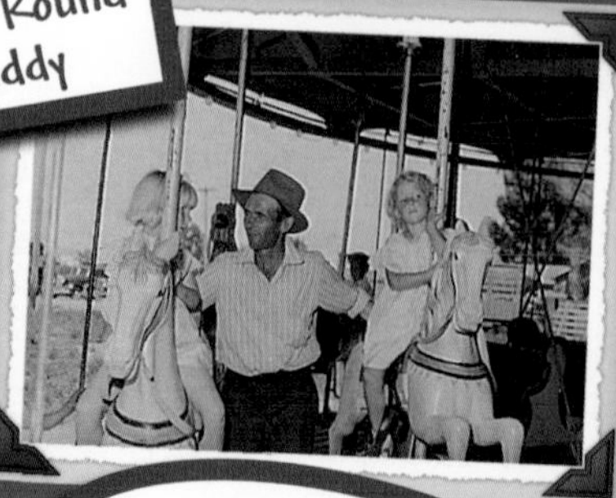

Reading The Funnies

Vale, Oregon

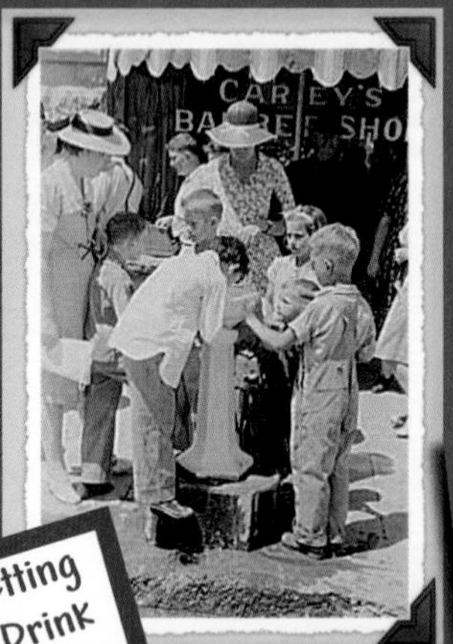

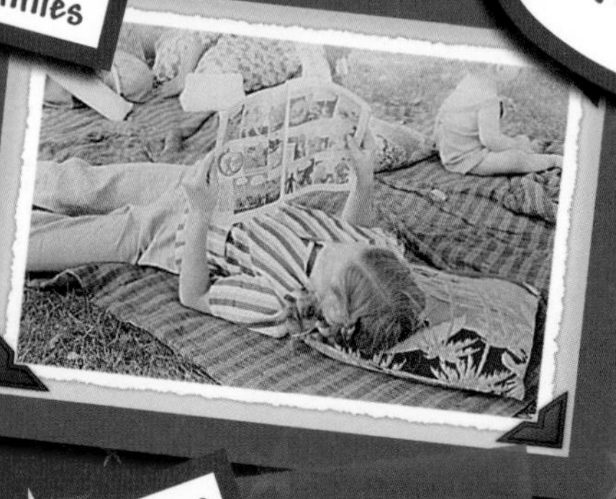

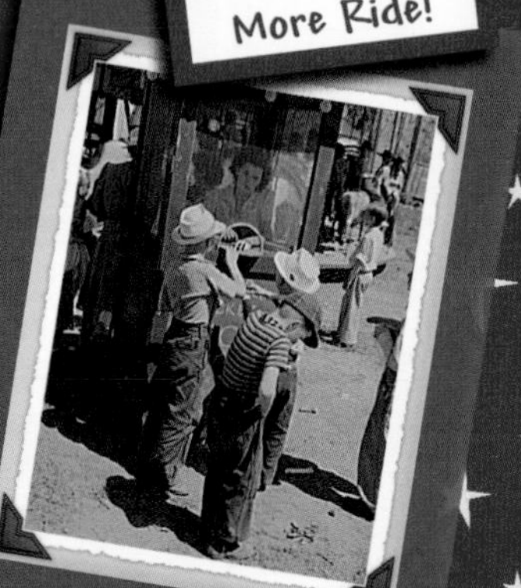

Getting a Drink from the Fountain

Going on a Pony Ride

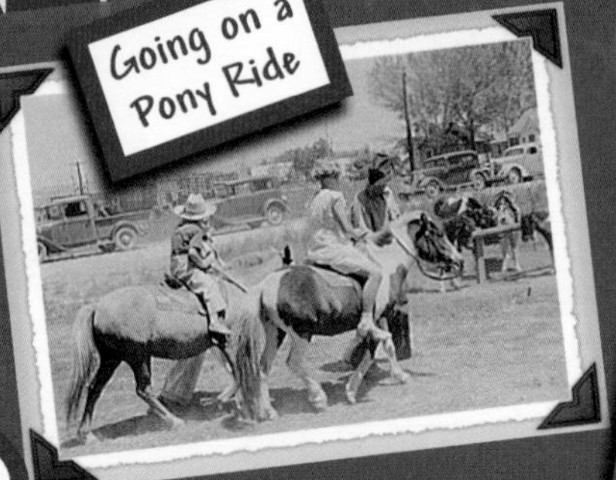

Finding a Nickel for One More Ride!

July 4, 1941

Riding a Float in the Parade

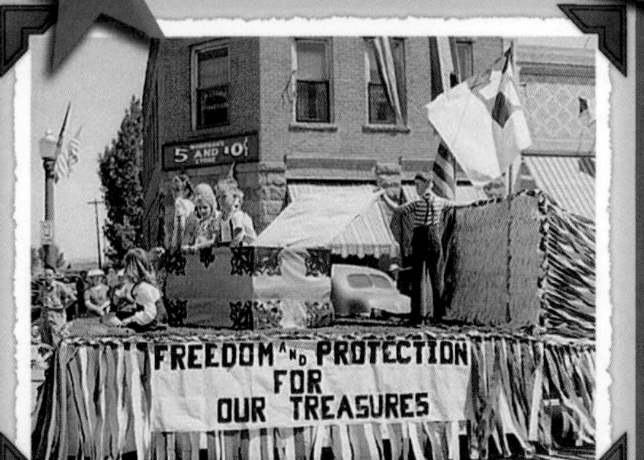

FREEDOM AND PROTECTION FOR OUR TREASURES

Riding the Ferris Wheel

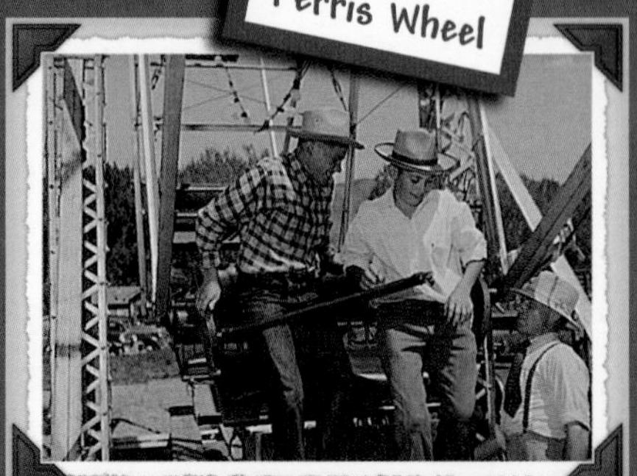

A Soap Box Derby

Salisbury, Maryland

Hoping to Win in "Bullet"

Who Will Win the Race?

July 4, 1940

Remembering Our Founders

Honoring the Women Who Helped to Found America

Honoring the Revolutionary Soldiers in New York City, July 4, 1911

Immigrants Celebrate the 4th

Immigrants from Sweden

Immigrants from Greece

New York City

Immigrants from Switzerland

Around 1908

Immigrants from China

Immigrants from Italy

Celebrating Around the Country

Just Fishing in Natchitoches, Louisiana, July 4, 1940

Eskimo Highkick, Nome, Alaska, July 4, 1915. 6 feet 5 inches!

At the Celebration in Asheville, Ohio, July 4, 1938

Native Americans Celebrate the 4th in New York City

Sharecropper Families Gather for a Picnic in Hill House, Mississippi, July 4, 1936

Playing Bingo in State College, Pennsylvania, July 4, 1941

Representing Troop 83 in Tacoma Park, Maryland, July 4, 1922

Enjoying Being Together in Vienna, Virginia, July 4, 1922

America the Beautiful

O beautiful for spacious skies,
For amber waves of grain,
For purple mountain majesties
Above the fruited plain!
America! America!
God shed His grace on thee,
And crown thy good with brotherhood
From sea to shining sea!

O beautiful for pilgrim feet
Whose stern, impassioned stress
A thoroughfare for freedom beat
Across the wilderness!
America! America!
God mend thine ev'ry flaw,
Confirm thy soul in self-control,
Thy liberty in law!

O beautiful for heroes prov'd
In liberating strife,
Who more than self their country loved,
And mercy more than life!
America! America!
May God thy gold refine
Till all success be nobleness,
And ev'ry gain divine!

O beautiful for patriot dream
That sees beyond the years
Thine alabaster cities gleam
Undimmed by human tears!
America! America!
God shed His grace on thee,
And crown thy good with brotherhood
From sea to shining sea!

Celebrating the Fourth at
Pismo Beach, California, 2010

Happy Birthday, America
Washington, D.C., 2007

Indeed may God shed His grace on America the Beautiful, both the land He created and the people He chose to live here. God's saving grace is available to us all through His Son, Jesus Christ.

The Word became flesh, and dwelt among us,
and we saw His glory, glory as of the only begotten from the Father,
full of grace and truth.
John 1:14

Activities for Lesson 150

Thinking Biblically – In your notebook, write a prayer of gratitude for the blessings you enjoy because you live in the United States of America.

Literature – Read "The Glorious Fourth" in *We the People*, pages 200-202.

Timeline – In *Timeline of America the Beautiful* next to 1895, write: The poem "America the Beautiful" is first published on July 4.

Family Activity – Have an America the Beautiful Party. See page 983 for instructions.

Student Workbook or Lesson Review – If you are using one of these optional books, complete the assignment for Lesson 150. If you are using the Lesson Review, take the quiz on Unit 30.

Family Activity for Unit 16

Homestead Map

Supplies

- 1 piece white poster board
- ruler
- pencil
- colored pencils

Instructions

You are going to make a map of an imaginary homestead, viewed directly from above. Your map should have a house, barn, shed, well, stream, road, garden, trees, pasture, fences, and fields for three different crops. You can add more details to your homestead if you wish. Think about where everything should be placed for the homestead to run smoothly.

Use the dull side of the poster board for your drawing. Use a ruler for the straight lines. Draw everything lightly with a regular pencil so that you can erase if needed.

Add color to your map with colored pencil. For large spaces such as fields and the road, you may just shade along the edges instead of coloring the entire area.

Make up a name for the family that lives on this homestead. Then make up a name for the town nearest their homestead. Choose one of the states with homestead claims listed in Lesson 78. Using the names you make up, write the title at the top of the poster like this one:

Elliott Family Homestead near Crazy Lizard, Nebraska

Thank You, Thomas Edison! Book

Supplies

- 22 sheets of multi-colored construction paper or photo scrapbooking paper
- camera
- printed photographs
- photo-safe adhesive
- markers
- hole punch
- yarn

Instructions

For this activity, you will make a book showing how the inventions of Thomas Edison benefit you and your family in your everyday lives.

1. Make a list of twenty common things that happen in your household that involve Thomas Edison's inventions of recorded sound, the electric light bulb, electrical wiring, and recorded moving pictures. Here are some ideas:

   listening to recorded music of any kind (in the car and at home)

   toys that talk or make sound

   lamps, ceiling light fixtures, and flashlights

   watching a movie or recorded TV

   using a movie camera

   anything that involves electricity: cooking with a stove or microwave, using a washer and dryer, computer, electric razor, vacuum, hair dryer, alarm clock, fans, charging cell phone

   using hot water (if water heater is electric)

   electric heating and cooling, etc.

2. Take photographs of different people in your family using or doing the things on your list. Try to include photographs of everyone who lives in your house. You can even use pets if they enjoy the inventions of Thomas Edison! Be creative about how you set up the photographs. Try to make the person and the object they are using fill up the picture without any extra wall space or furniture showing. Be careful of the lighting in your photos. If you are using a digital camera, you can re-take photos until you like the way they look.

3. Have the twenty pictures printed by a local photo printing service or print them at home.

4. Punch three holes in one of the short sides of one sheet of construction or scrapbooking paper (one inch in from the edge) for tying your book together. Using the first sheet as a guide, punch holes in all the sheets in the same places.

5. Design and decorate a cover for your book that includes the title "Thank You, Thomas Edison!" and "by: (your name)".

6. Attach one photograph per page in the center of the pieces of construction paper.

7. On the last sheet of construction paper, write:

Genius is 1% inspiration and 99% perspiration.
Thomas Edison

8. Cut three five-inch pieces of yarn and tie the book together through the punched holes.

Thomas Edison With One of the Engines He Invented

Family Activity for Unit 18

Sousa Band Concert

Supplies

- recording of the music of John Philip Sousa
- chairs
- paper
- computer and printer or markers/colored pencils
- refreshments

Instructions

1. Obtain a recording of the music of John Philip Sousa played by a band or orchestra. You might find a CD at a public or university library. There are are some recordings available online. Try the audio resources at the web site of the Marine Band (see www.notgrass.com/ablinks.php). You may also consider purchasing a recording of John Philip Sousa's marches to add to your family's library.

2. Choose the date, time, and place of your concert. Make 3 posters advertising your "Sousa Band Concert" with the date, time, and place—such as your family room or dining room. You can make the posters by hand or on the computer. Post them in different places around your house.

3. Design fancy tickets for the concert (by hand or on the computer) and give them to everyone in your family and anyone else you want to invite.

4. Make programs that say "Sousa Band Concert" with the date, time, and place. List all the Sousa selections that will be in the concert.

5. Write a few paragraphs about the life and work of John Philip Sousa to read aloud at the concert. Use the information in Lesson 89 and "Experiences of a Bandmaster" in *We the People*.

6. Prepare refreshments. Lemonade, crisp cookies (such as shortbread or vanilla wafers), and ice cream were popular choices in the early twentieth century.

7. Arrange chairs for the concert, a way to play the music, and a podium.

8. As people arrive for the concert, take the tickets and hand out the programs.

9. When everyone is seated, stand behind the podium, welcome everyone to the concert of Sousa's Band, read aloud the information you wrote about John Philip Sousa, and announce the first selection. Before you play each selection, announce the title.

10. After the last selection, thank everyone for coming and invite them to enjoy refreshments.

Paper Airplanes

Supplies

- paper
- instructions for making paper airplanes

Instructions

Find instructions in a book from the library or online (with a parent's supervision) for making several different kinds of paper airplanes. Have a fun family paper airplane festival. Observe how the airplanes fly and what attributes make them fly higher, longer, or straighter. You might want to decorate your favorite paper airplanes and give them names that celebrate the Wright brothers' achievement such as "The Kitty Hawk" or "1903 Express."

Hamentaschen

Ingredients

- 2 2/3 cups flour
- 1 1/2 teaspoons baking powder
- 1/4 teaspoon salt
- 1 1/2 sticks cold butter
- 2/3 cup sugar
- 1 egg
- 1 egg white
- 1 jar apricot preserves (or preserves of another fruit)

Parental Supervision Required

This project requires uses of an electrical applicance and the oven.

Please Note: Be careful. Some children may be allergic to recipe ingredients.

Instructions

Purim is a celebration of the escape of the Jewish people from Haman's evil plans, as told in the book of Esther. The first Purim and the establishment of an annual celebration is described in Esther 9:16-30. Purim is celebrated by Jewish immigrants in America with many customs and traditions, including making, eating, and sharing these delicious fruit-filled cookies called Hamentaschen ("Haman's pockets" in German). Hamentaschen are mentioned in *All-of-a-Kind Family* in the chapter titled "Purim Play." Make these traditional Jewish cookies; and while you eat them, enjoy a read-aloud of the book of Esther.

1. Place the flour, baking powder, and salt in a bowl. Using a wire whisk, mix them together.

2. If you have a food processor or stand mixer, place the flour mixture and the cold butter in the bowl and process until mixed. If you do not have one of these appliances, cut the butter into small pieces and rub and squeeze it into the flour until well mixed.

3. Crack two eggs into a separate bowl. With a large spoon, gently remove one of the egg yolks, taking care not to break it. Set the yolk aside. Add the sugar to the remaining egg and egg white. Stir until completely mixed.

4. Mix the flour/butter mixture and the egg/sugar mixture together, just until completely blended.

5. Divide the dough in half and shape each half into a disc. Wrap each disc in plastic wrap and chill for 30 minutes.

6. Preheat oven to 350 degrees.

7. Spread waxed paper (about 2 feet long) on a counter top and sprinkle with flour.

8. Place one disc of dough in the center of the waxed paper, and place another piece of waxed paper on top. Using a rolling pin, roll dough to an even 1/8″ thickness.

9. Use a round biscuit cutter (2½-3″ in diameter) to cut the dough into circles. Cut all the circles first, re-rolling dough scraps to cut more. Make sure you roll all the dough to a 1/8″ thickness.

10. Spoon a quarter-size drop of preserves onto the middle of a circle. Fold over each side to make the circle into a triangle. This is the tricky part: each side of the triangle is a small flap that should be over the adjoining flap on one side and under the adjoining flap on the other side. Refer to the pictures.

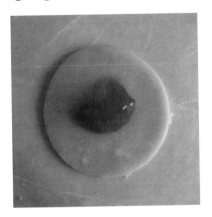
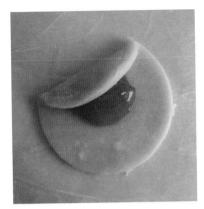
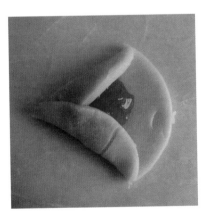
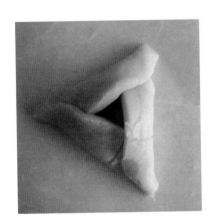

11. When the flaps are correctly placed, firmly squeeze each corner. Place on a lightly greased cookie sheet.

12. Continue with all dough circles, placing about 1 inch apart on the cookie sheet.

13. Bake for 14-15 minutes until cookies are golden brown. The preserves will start to bubble.

14. Remove baked cookies and place on waxed paper or a wire rack to cool.

15. Let cookies cool before you taste them—the preserves will be hot!

16. Using a 2-3/4″ cutter, this recipe makes about 36 cookies.

Cupcake Factory

Supplies

- 1 batch of 16-18 cupcakes (the yield of one cake mix)
- white frosting
- blue food coloring (if desired)
- 1 large bag (19.2 oz) of M&M chocolate candies
- 1 bag miniature marshmallows
- 2 large trays

Parental Supervision Required

This project requires uses of the oven.

Please Note: Be careful. Some children may be allergic to recipe ingredients.

Instructions

1. Bake the cupcakes according to cake mix box instructions or your favorite recipe, using cupcake papers. Allow to cool.

2. Tint the white frosting light blue by mixing in a few drops of food coloring (if desired).

3. Sort the M&Ms candies by color, with each color in a separate small bowl. Set the brown M&Ms aside to eat later; you will not need them for this project.

4. Set up the assembly line at the kitchen counter or at a table this way:

   - Station 1: Tray of plain cupcakes with bowl of frosting and spreader

   - Station 2: Bowl of yellow M&Ms

   - Station 3: Bowl of orange M&Ms

   - Station 4: Bowl of red M&Ms

   - Station 5: Bowl of green M&Ms

   - Station 6: Bowl of blue M&Ms

   - Station 7: Bowl of miniature marshmallows and tray for finished cupcakes

5. Assign each person in the family to a station. If you do not have enough people for each station, give one person stations 2 and 3, stations 4 and 5, or stations 6 and 7. Assign station 1 to the person with the most experience with frosting; that will be the most time-consuming station.

6. Decorate the cupcakes along the assembly line as shown in the photographs.

7. Enjoy eating your cupcakes! You might want to share them with another family and tell them about your cupcake factory.

4

1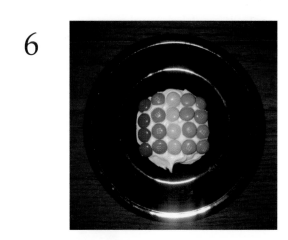

2

5

6

3

7

1930s Family Game and Treat Night

Supplies

- games
- treats

Instructions

Host a family game and treat night celebrating the 1930s! You can celebrate with your own family, or you may want to invite another family over to share the fun with you.

Play some or all of these games that were invented or became highly popular in the 1930s: Sorry, Monopoly, Scrabble, Bingo, and Pick-Up Sticks.

For treats, serve some of the enduringly popular candies that were introduced in the 1930s: Snickers, Nestlé's Crunch, 3 Musketeers, Kit Kat, and Tootsie Pops.

For a homemade treat, try Nestlé Toll House Chocolate Chip Cookies, which were invented in 1930. Ruth Wakefield and her husband Keith owned the Toll House Inn in Massachusetts. Her guests enjoyed her exceptional cooking and baking. One day Ruth was making Butter Drop Do Cookies and discovered she had run out of baker's chocolate. She decided to cut up a plain Nestlé's chocolate bar and mix it in. The guests loved the results!

Ruth published the recipe in several New England newspapers. Nestlé soon saw a dramatic leap in its chocolate bar sales in the region. The Nestlé company and Ruth Wakefield made an agreement: they could print her recipe on the chocolate bar wrapper and Nestlé would supply her with all the chocolate she could use. Nestlé began scoring their chocolate bars for easy cutting and even included a small chopper in the package. In 1939 Nestlé began selling packages of chocolate morsels to make it easier to bake. Visit www.notgrass.com/ablinks.php for a link to the classic recipe.

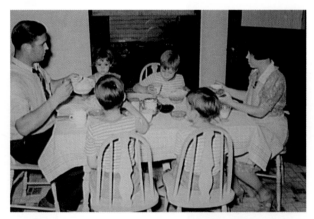

A Pennsylvania Family Gathers Around the Table, 1937

WWII Home Front Posters

Supplies

- ◆ pencil
- ◆ plain white paper
- ◆ white poster board
- ◆ markers or paints

Instructions

During World War II, the United States government used a myriad of posters to communicate important messages to Americans on the home front. The wide range of poster subjects included the following:

- ◆ joining the armed forces
- ◆ victory gardening
- ◆ buying war bonds
- ◆ joining the women's branches of the military
- ◆ not wasting food
- ◆ observing blackouts
- ◆ taking industrial war jobs
- ◆ car-pooling and avoiding unnecessary travel
- ◆ avoiding careless talk
- ◆ saving metal, rags, paper, and coal
- ◆ hard work rather than laziness in war jobs
- ◆ becoming a military nurse
- ◆ protecting American children
- ◆ American patriotism

Lesson 112 has several examples. For this activity, you will design and create a World War II poster. Use the plain white paper to make sketches of your poster ideas. Combine words and images to convey your message powerfully and memorably. You might come up with a catchy slogan similar to the famous "Loose Lips Sink Ships."

When you have decided how you want your poster to look, draw and letter it with pencil on the dull side of the poster board. When you are satisfied with your poster design, color it in using vibrant colors. Some parts of your drawing or lettering might look best outlined in black. Family members may want to make their own individual posters or may want to collaborate on a few posters.

Get Your Kicks on Route 66

Supplies

- four pieces of poster board
- one piece of plain white paper per person
- markers or crayons
- food (see suggestions below)

Instructions

The family road trip is long established as an important feature of American life. Nowhere is the road trip better epitomized than on the iconic Route 66. This activity involves planning and enjoying a "family road trip" party with a Route 66 theme. You may want to invite another family over to enjoy your Route 66 evening or simply enjoy the festivities as a family. Read these instructions completely to plan what to do before and during the party.

1) Route 66 Sign

From a piece of poster board, make a large Route 66 sign like the one pictured on page 429. Display the sign on the front door or another prominent place at your party. Now everyone "piles into the car" for a road trip on Route 66! In other words, sit around in your living room and pretend to buckle your seat belts and settle back for a long ride.

2) Classic Road Trip Games

Alphabet Game: Choose a category such as places, food, adjectives, famous people, book or movie titles, etc. Go through the alphabet in turn trying to think of an item in the chosen category that begins with each letter of the alphabet. For example, with four players, person 1 says, "Artichoke." Person 2 says, "Banana." Person 3 says, "Chips." Person 4 says, "Donut." Person 1 takes the next turn, saying a food that begins with the letter "E."

Twenty Questions: One person thinks of a person, place, or thing. Everyone else asks questions that can be answered "yes" or "no" to find out what it is, with a limit of 20 questions. If no one has correctly guessed the person, place, or thing after 20 questions, then the person must reveal the answer. If time permits, give each person a chance to be the one to think of something and answer questions.

Aunt Emma's Trunk: The first person says, "I packed Aunt Emma's trunk with a ____." A vegetable peeler? A sofa cushion? A broken bicycle? Whatever your imagination can come up with, and the sillier the better. The next person must remember what the first person packed and add an item. Play continues around the circle, each person adding an item (with a maximum of two words per item).

Each person begins with "I packed Aunt Emma's trunk with . . ." and recites all of the previous items before adding one of his own. When a player can't accurately recall all the items packed, he or she drops out of the game. The last person who successfully recites the whole list is the winner.

3) Museum

Create a silly museum in a bedroom on a table or bed. It could be a stuffed animal museum, pencil museum, sock museum, toy museum, or anything you can think of! Make a sign for the museum on a piece of poster board and post it on the bedroom door. Charge a very small admission fee, such as a nickel per person, or charge admission in play money.

4) Road Trip Sing-Along

Climb back into "the car" (the living room) to continue on your way! Gather some books of familiar American folk songs and children's songs. You can find such song books at your library. Sing your family's favorite just-for-fun songs.

5) Get Your Kicks Souvenir Shop

Create a just-for-fun souvenir shop. Your currency could be pennies or play money. You could sell candy and drinks, handmade Route 66 postcards, artwork, friendship bracelets, doorknob hangers, marbles, bouncy balls, fake bumper stickers, etc. Use your imagination! Make an attractive sign for the Get Your Kicks Souvenir Shop on a piece of poster board.

6) Route 66 Good Eats Diner

Make paper placemats that read "Route 66 Good Eats Diner" from plain white paper. Roll a fork, spoon, and knife in a paper napkin for each person. Write "Today's Special" and the menu you choose on a chalkboard or piece of poster board. Choose and prepare the menu for "Today's Special," (which is also the only meal available at the diner!). Choose a meal of traditional diner food, such as hamburgers or cheeseburgers, french fries, chili, grilled cheese or any other kind of sandwich, soup, and of course ice cream sundaes or milkshakes! Set the table with the placemats and wrapped silverware. Designate one person as the waiter or waitress who will don an apron, carry a pen and notepad, take drink orders, serve the drinks and food, and take away the empty dishes.

Don't forget to ask "Are we there yet?" often during the party and take lots of pictures along the way!

1950s Mini TV Puppet Stage

The introduction of the television into many American homes both reflected and shaped 1950s culture. Many shows for children that were popular during the 1950s used puppets, including *Romper Room*, *Captain Kangaroo*, and *Howdy Doody*. For this activity, you will make a mini 1950s-style TV that doubles as a mini puppet stage!

Supplies

- an extra-large empty cereal box
- clear 2" mailing tape
- brown craft wrapping paper
- silver or black duct tape
- piece of fabric slightly larger than your screen opening
- small piece corrugated cardboard
- white school glue
- 2 white or gray chenille stems ("pipe cleaners")
- finger puppets

> ## Parental Supervision Required
>
> This project requires use of scissors.

Instructions

1. Securely tape the opening of the cereal box closed with 2" mailing tape. Wrap the box like a gift with brown craft wrapping paper. Use 2" clear mailing tape to securely tape the wrapping paper. Make sure your paper fits as tightly as possible around the box.

2. Cut a piece of paper to the size you want for your screen opening. (The example shows a half sheet of 8.5 x 11" paper.) Lay the piece of paper in the middle of the box near the top on the side without tape. Trace around it.

3. Look closely at the picture of televisions on page 756. Notice that the screens have curved edges. Draw curved edges for your "screen" that fit just inside the rectangle you drew.

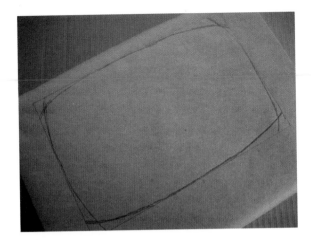

4. Carefully cut out the screen opening. (Cutting tip: use a point of your scissors to spear a hole in the center. Using a sawing motion, cut an approximately 4-inch slit. Use the slit as access to cut out the rest of the shape.)

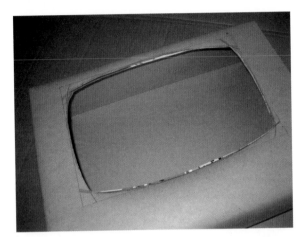

5. Neatly edge the screen opening with duct tape, using an individual strip of tape for each edge. As illustrated below, you will need to cut slits on one side of the tape so it can fit around the curved opening.

Duct tape with slits

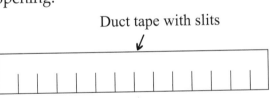

6. Find a circle about 3.5" diameter to trace two circles near the bottom of the back of the box. Cut out the circles, then edge with small pieces of duct tape. These are for your hands and puppets to enter the puppet stage.

7. Staple the piece of cloth along the top of your screen. (This will be tricky! Ask for a parent's help and don't staple your finger!)

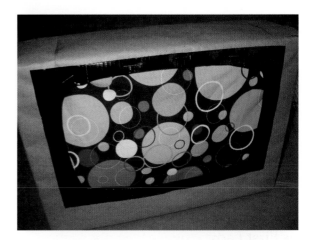

8. With corrugated cardboard, make two round dials, one for "volume" and one marked with numbers for "channels." (The examples are about 2 inches in diameter.) Glue them near the bottom corners of the front of your TV. Draw indicator arrows next to them.

9. Cut off about 2 inches from the ends of the chenille stems. Bend them as shown in the photo for antennas or "rabbit ears." Tape them to the top of the TV as shown.

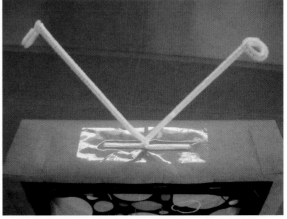

10. Gather or make finger or mini puppets. You can draw a character on paper, cut it out, and tape it to a popsicle stick or drinking straw. You can cut two finger-shaped pieces of felt, sew the rounded edges together, and draw faces and clothing on one side. You can cut the fingers from an old knitted glove and decorate with yarn hair and beads for eyes. With a parent's help, you can also find printable finger puppets online. Enjoy sharing puppet shows with your family and friends!

White House Family Research Project

Instructions

Many children have lived in the White House with their father as President and mother as First Lady. You learned about the Kennedy and Johnson families in Lesson 127. Choose a family that lived in the White House and research this family, using at least three different reliable sources for information. Write a report of 1-2 typed pages about the family, focusing on their family life while they lived in the White House.

Ask a parent to read a draft of your report and mark spelling and grammar errors and suggest improvements. Apply your parent's corrections and read over the report again at least twice to polish it for your final version. Include a page with your report listing the sources you used for information (books and their authors, articles and their authors, and websites.) Do not use the Internet without a parent's supervision.

Amy Carter moved into the White House at age nine when her father Jimmy Carter became President. Here she is pictured with her cat Misty Malarky Ying Yang.

American Space Firsts Poster

Supplies

- 1 piece of black poster board
- various colors of construction paper
- glue stick
- white school glue
- silver glitter
- scissors

> ### Parental Supervision Required
>
> This project requires use of scissors.

Instructions

1. Cut letters out of red, white, and blue paper to spell the words "American Space Firsts." (Hint: draw "bubble letters" and cut them out.) Glue the letters across the top of the poster board with a glue stick.

2. Cut at least 7 shapes of various sizes from different colors of construction paper, the largest about 6" in diameter, to represent space objects such as sun, moon, shuttle, planet, comet, satellite, etc.

3. Choose one American space first (first American satellite, first American jet, first American in space, etc.) for each shape. Write the "The First . . ." as a title at the top and write some details about the event underneath. You can find information in Lessons 132-133, books from the library, and Internet research (with a parent's help). You can add more space objects with information if you wish.

4. Scatter your objects on the poster board and glue them on with a glue stick.

5. In an area of the poster board that is still black, make a dot with white school glue. Sprinkle a small amount of silver glitter on the glue to make a "star." Add many stars in the black areas of the poster until you like the way it looks. Let the glue dry for 30 minutes. Carefully shake the excess glitter into a large garbage can.

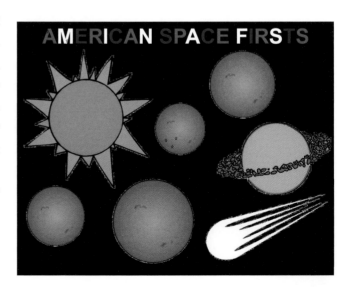

Shopping in America Interviews

Supplies

- audio or video recording device

For this activity, you will learn more about shopping in America by conducting three interviews: two interviews of shoppers and one interview of a person who works or has worked in a retail business.

Interview 1 and 2

Choose two adults you know who shop regularly, only one of whom may be your parent, for your first two interviews. Prepare a way to record the interviews with a recording device.

Carefully prepare your list of questions. Copy this list to have with you at the interviews:
- How often in an average week do you visit a store?
- What are your main considerations when shopping for groceries?
- What are your main considerations when shopping for non-grocery items (clothing, books, etc.)?
- How frequently do you buy from catalogs and online retailers?
- Do you sometimes choose shopping as a recreational activity? Why or why not?
- What are your favorite and least favorite stores? Why?
- How much do you think advertising affects what you purchase?
- *Add two or three questions of your own to this list.*

Conduct the interviews completely separately so that each interviewee has as much time as he or she desires to answer questions and feels free to give original responses. Try to make the interviewee feel comfortable and relaxed. Be familiar with all of your questions before the interview. As you ask questions, speak clearly and in a friendly manner, and give your interviewee plenty of time to answer. Do not interrupt or rush to the next question. Ask appropriate follow-up questions regarding their answers. Listen actively and respond briefly to their answers, but do not talk too much or add your own thoughts and opinions. Thank each interviewee for their time and responses when the interview is finished.

Interview 3

For your third interview, choose someone you know who currently works or has worked in a retail business, preferably someone who deals directly with the public. Conduct your third interview the same way as described above, but with the following questions:

- Would you please describe the company you work for and the store or stores they have?
- Would you please describe your position in the company?
- What companies provide the goods that are sold in your store?
- What are some common problems you encounter when dealing with customers?
- What are some store policies that help things run smoothly?
- What are the busiest times of day and times of the year at your store?
- What attributes make someone a good customer?
- *Add two or three questions of your own creation to this list.*

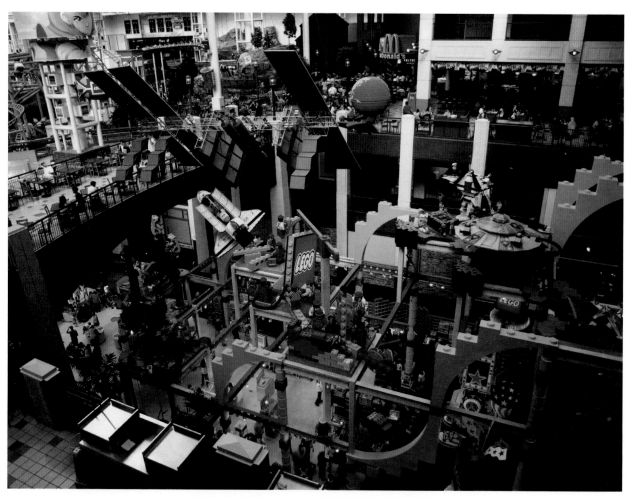

Inside the Mall of America, Bloomington, Minnesota

Family Commemorative Coins

The U.S. Mint produces coins for general circulation as well as special commemorative coins celebrating significant people and events in American history. The coins are given as special gifts and awards, and sometimes additional copies are minted for sale to the public. For this activity, you will create commemorative "coins" that celebrate special people and events in your family.

Supplies

- air-drying paintable clay (available at craft supply stores; Crayola is one brand available)
- a plastic disposable lid with sides, about 4 inches across (such as a lid from a large yogurt, cottage cheese, sour cream, or coffee container)
- waxed paper
- very sharp pencil
- gold or silver craft paint
- paintbrush

Instructions

1. Think about what special person or event in your family you would like to commemorate with your coin. Your coin could celebrate your grandparents or parents, a pet, a wedding or graduation, the birth of a sibling, or moving to a new house. Design both sides of your coin on paper. Include your initials and the year.

2. Press clay into the lid to form a coin shape. Fill the lid all the way to the top of the sides and make the clay smooth. Press hard to remove any seams or bumps.

3. Carefully peel the clay out of the lid and lay it on a piece of waxed paper. Gently smooth out any bumps or wrinkles.

4. Using a sharp pencil, draw and write your coin design for the front side (obverse). Be careful not to press so hard that your design goes through to the other side. Carefully remove any tiny bits of clay that scroll off as you etch your design. If you would like, you may use additional clay to make a relief (raised) design, like the heads on U.S. coins. If you want your coin to be hangable, use your pencil to make a hole all the way through the clay near the top of the design.

5. Lifting the edge of the waxed paper with one hand, carefully peel off your coin and turn it over. Use the pencil to etch your design on the back side (reverse). You might

want to make a design along the edge of your coin as well. (Notice how U.S. quarters have lines etched around the edge.) Be creative and think of other etching tools you could use to make designs in addition to the pencil.

6. Let the clay coin dry according to the clay package instructions. You might need to turn the coin over during the drying process.

7. When both sides of the coin are completely dry, paint one side and the edge with silver or gold paint. When the paint is dry, turn the coin over and paint the other side.

Mrs. Edness Wilkins, Secretary at the US Mint, with Her Coin Collection, 1938

America the Beautiful Party

Celebrate America the Beautiful and your completion of *America the Beautiful*!

- Each person in your family can dress up as a different famous American.
- Make your favorite American meal and Red, White, and Blue Cake for dessert (instructions below).
- Decorate your dining table in red, white, and blue.
- Display your *America the Beautiful* notebook, projects, and maps.
- Sing "The Star Spangled Banner" and read the Declaration of Independence or a poem about America.
- Talk about what you have learned studying this curriculum.
- Discuss some places in America you have seen and some you would like to visit.
- Use facts from the *America the Beautiful* books to make an "America the Beautiful Trivia Game." Write at least 30 questions and 30 answers on 60 index cards with a pencil (you may make as many pairs as you would like). Make an answer key. Use the cards to play "Unscramble." Shuffle and deal out all the question cards. Lay the answer cards face up in different locations around the room. At the word "Go" everyone tries to find the answers to his or her questions. The first person to find the correct answer cards to all of his or her question cards is the winner.

Red, White, and Blue Cake

Supplies:

- your favorite chocolate, white, or yellow cake, made from scratch or from a cake mix, baked and cooled in a 9" x 13" pan
- white icing of any kind
- strawberries
- blueberries

Parental Supervision Required

This project requires uses of the oven.

Please Note: Be careful. Some children may be allergic to recipe ingredients.

Instructions:

You may leave the cake in the pan or turn it out onto a tray. Ice the cake with white icing. Core and slice the strawberries. Decorate your cake with the berries to look like the U.S. flag. Make a rectangle of blueberries in the top left corner, leaving white space between the berries for the stars. Make stripes with strawberry slices, leaving white stripes in between. Serve immediately or within half an hour so the juices don't run.

Image Credits

Note: Numbers indicate the page numbers of images. The meanings of the letters t, m, b, l, and r are as follows: t - top of page; m - middle; b - bottom; l - left; r - right.

Alan Vernon (Flickr, CC-BY-2.0) 806b

Amy Selleck (Flickr, CC-BY-2.0) 802 (sunset)

Architect of the Capitol 630

Aturkus/Alan Turkus (Flickr, CC-BY-SA2.0) Front Cover (Manhattan)

Bdamon (Flickr, CC-BY-2.0) 801b

Beatnik Photos (Flickr, CC-BY-2.0) 980

Ben Demey (Flickr, CC-BY-2.0) 445t

Bethany Poore 967, 968, 974, 975, 976

Bruce Tuten (Flickr, CC-BY-2.0) 801m

Bureau of Land Management 448t

Charlene Notgrass 921tl/tr

Chensiyuan (CC-BY-SA-2.0) 474tr

Chris Garrison (Flickr, CC-BY-2.0) 909

Cornell University Library 439, 756tl

Dave Friedel (Flickr, CC-BY-2.0) 898tr

Dbking (Flickr, CC-BY-2.0) 911b

Dennymont (Flickr, CC-BY-2.0) 802 (balloon)

Domain Barnyard/Lori Tingey (Flickr, CC-BY-2.0) 875

Ebyabe (CC-BY-SA-3.0) 849

Eisenhower Library 744b, 745, 747m, 750m, 754 (Eisenhower family), 755 (Eisenhower parade), 774 (newspaper), 779m, 814bl

Federal Highway Administration 718 (all but Truman's car)

FirstBaptistNashville (Flickr, CC-BY-2.0) 911t

Franklin D. Roosevelt Presidential Library 637 (Roosevelt), 639t, 671, 674b, 677, 685m, 689, 690, 691, 692, 693, 694, 695, 696t, 712, 752 (Mrs. Roosevelt), 778t, 822bl

The Fuller Center for Housing 908b, 910

Gerald R. Ford Library 821t

George Bush Presidential Library 860, 861t, 862, 923br, 934br

Glennwilliamspdx/Glenn Scofield Williams (Flickr, CC-BY-2.0) 474br

Google Books 566, 568m/b

Gt8073a (Flickr, CC-BY-2.0) 898br

Harry S. Truman Library 710b, 713, 714 (Harry Truman, Margaret Truman), 718, 744t

Jdnx/Daniel Ramirez (Flickr, CC-BY-2.0) 654t

John F. Kennedy Presidential Library 780t, 788, 791m/b

John Morgan (Flickr, CC-BY-2.0) 801t

Jsorbieus (Flickr, CC-BY-2.0) Back Cover (church)

JupiterImages Front cover (fireworks, baseball player), 445b, 467, 469t, 470b, 483t, 492, 501t, 502t, 504, 526b, 530b, 565b, 586b, 588m, 599b, 609b, 638b, 639b, 648 (except map), 650b, 651, 652tr, bl, bm, br, 653, 664 (murres), 719t, 732, 738, 747b, 750b, 751 (all but bottom two), 756 (clothespins, bottles), 757, 770 (map), 783tr, 787, 798t/m/b, 800, 824, 852b, 861, 878, 879, 882b, 916, 918, 933t, 935b, 939tr, 942, 965, 978 (elements of poster)

Jurvetson/Steve Jurvetson (Flickr, CC-BY-2.0) 698

K. Kendall (Flickr, CC-BY-2.0) Front Cover (car)

Ken Koehler 723tr

Kjetil Ree (CC-BY-SA-3.0) 877

Kkimpel/Kathy Kimpel (Flickr, CC-BY-2.0) 842t

Larry D. Moore/Nv8200p (CC-BY-SA-3.0) 898bl

Leftrightworld/Jay Iwasaki (Flickr, CC-BY-2.0) 804

Sources

Information

Please note that websites listed in these sources were used in research to complete *America the Beautiful*, but they have not been reviewed to see if they are suitable for children:

Books

The American Song Treasury by Theodore Raph

Anniversary of the Highway System Recalls Eisenhower's Role as Catalyst by David A. Pfeiffer

Cornerstones of Freedom: The Golden Gate Bridge by Sharlene and Ted Nelson

The Early Book Illustrations of Norman Rockwell by Steven Lomazow, M.D.

The Faith of American Presidents, Daniel Mount

The First Battle: A Story of the Campaign of 1896 by William Jennings Bryan

I Never Had It Made: An Autobiography, Jackie Robinson

Shirley Temple: A Pictorial History of the World's Greatest Child Star by Rita Dubas

The Simple Faith of Mr. Rogers: Spiritual Insights from the World's Most Beloved Neighbor by Amy Hollingsworth

When John and Caroline Lived in the White House by Laurie Coulter

Businesses and Business Organizations

Burma Shave

California Dried Plum Board

Country Music Television

Dole Plantation

Glenn Miller Orchestra

Hasbro

Hershey's

International Council of Shopping Centers

Kimberly-Clark

Microsoft Corporation

Piggly Wiggly

Ryman Auditorium

Sears

Snack Food Association

Sunkist

Walmart

Encyclopedias

Britannica

Encarta Encyclopedia

Georgia Encyclopedia

Tennessee Encyclopedia

Federal, State, and Local Government Agencies

Architect of the Capitol

Cascade Volcano Observatory, United States Geological Survey

Golden Gate Bridge, Highway and Transportation District

Library of Congress

National Aeronautics and Space Administration

National Archives

National Institutes of Health

National Guard, State of Washington

National Park Service

Our Living Resources: Hawaii by Science Editor J. Michael Scott National Biological Service, Idaho Cooperative Fish and Wildlife Research Unit

Peace Corps

Utah Division of Wildlife Resources

Utah Geological Survey

United States Department of Transportation - Federal Highway Administration

United States Fish and Wildlife Service

United States Forest Service

United States Geological Survey

United States House of Representatives

Media

60 Minutes II

Life

National Geographic

National Public Radio

The New York Times

"Answers About World War II in New York, Parts, I, II, and III" by Richard Goldstein, September 29, October 1, October 4, 2010

"Babe Ruth and the World Series" by Joe Dorish, October. 23, 2010

"Marjory Douglas, Champion of Everglades, Dies at 108" by Richard Severo, May 15, 1998

Public Broadcasting System

Salt Lake Tribune

Saturday Evening Post

saturdayeveningpostcovers.com

www.seattlepi.com

The Seattle Times

"Warning and Response to the Mount St. Helens Eruption" by Thomas Frederick Saarinen and James L. Sell, May 18, 2000

Smithsonian

"Rising from the Ashes" by David B. Williams, May 2005

Sports Illustrated

Time
> "A Brief History of: The Oval Office" by Frances Romero Thursday, Nov. 13, 2008

USA Today
> "Billy Graham, Turning 92, Still Has a Sermon on His Heart," November 4, 2010

U.S. News and World Report
> 70th Anniversary Photo Essay [of Little Rock Central High School] (www.usnews.com)

The Washington Post

Organizations for the Arts, Education, History, Science, and Philanthropy

Academy of Achievement

Academy of Television Arts and Sciences

Bill and Melinda Gates Foundation

California Ag in the Classroom

Children's Television Workshop

Daughters of the American Revolution

Detroit Historical Society

The Eisenhower Foundation

Field Museum (Chicago)

Grand Ole Opry

Habitat for Humanity International

Historic Columbus Indiana, "The Drive In, Columbus Indiana: 'One Mile North On 31A' Memories," David Sechrest (www.historiccolumbusindiana.org)

Home School Legal Defense Association

Jackie Robinson Foundation

The John F. Kennedy Center for the Performing Arts

National Home Education Research Institute — Facts on Homeschooling (www.nheri.org)

Naval and History Heritage Command

New York Historical Society

Norman Rockwell Museum

Screen Actors Guild

Scripps National Spelling Bee

Smithsonian Institution

Songwriters Hall of Fame

Transportation Research Board, National Academy of Sciences

Presidential Libraries (In order of their presidencies)

Herbert Hoover Presidential Library and Museum

Franklin D. Roosevelt Presidential Library and Museum

Harry S. Truman Library and Museum

Dwight D. Eisenhower Presidential Library and Museum

John F. Kennedy Presidential Library and Museum

Lyndon Baines Johnson Library and Museum

Nixon Presidential Library and Museum

Gerald R. Ford Presidential Library and Museum

Jimmy Carter Library and Museum

Ronald Reagan Presidential Library

George Bush Presidential Library and Museum

William J. Clinton Presidential Library and Museum

George W. Bush Presidential Library

Special Interest Websites

www.alaskool.org (online materials about Alaska Native history, education, languages, and culture) — "Aspects of Traditional Inupiat Education" by Paul Ongtooguk. Information about education among Native Alaskans in Lesson 145 was obtained from this article.

www.biography.com (The Biography Channel)

www.extramile.us — The Extra Mile Points of Light Volunteer Pathway

www.history.com (The History Channel)

www.roadtraveler.com (a travel website)

www.thegatesnotes.com (Bill Gates' blog)

www.whitehousemuseum.org (an online White House museum)

Universities

American University Fourth of July Celebrations Database, Researched, Compiled, and Arranged by James R. Heintze

Andrews University, Department of Biology

Bryan College

City University of New York — American Social History Project at the Center for Media and Learning

George Mason University: Center for History and New Media

Harvard Business School

Rollins College

University of California — Whither California Agriculture, Up, Down or Out? Some Thoughts about the Future by Gionnini of the Foundation of Agricultural Economics

University of Hawaii Institute for Astronomy

University of Mississippi — Department of Music

University of Virginia — American Studies at the University of Virginia; Miller Center for Public Affairs

Vassar University

Weber State University Department of Botany

Wheaton College

Yale University — The Formation of Modern American Culture Since 1920, an American Studies Class by Professor Michael Denning

Websites Dedicated to Famous People

www.baberuth.com (Family of Babe Ruth and Babe Ruth League, Inc.)

www.billygraham.org

www.drmartinlutherkingjr.com

www.shirleytemple.com

www.woodieguthrie.org

Quotes

Mrs. Rogers' comment to her son Fred Rogers about his Christmas sweater on page 852: http://asp3.rollins.edu/olin/oldsite/archives/golden/rogers.htm

Norman Rockwell quote on page 763: Norman Rockwell Museum at www.nrm.org

Index

Pages 1-436 are in Part 1. Pages 437-983 are in Part 2.

Thank you for using *America the Beautiful!*

For more curriculum that teaches the heart, soul, and mind, visit www.notgrass.com.

Resources for Middle School and for All Ages

A Record of the Learning Lifestyle **by Charlene Notgrass**
A simple and effective record-keeping system that helps you focus on the most important things and feel good about what you are accomplishing each week. All ages.

Draw to Learn **by The Notgrass Family**
Art curriculum that helps children and adults hide God's word in their hearts. All ages.

Walking In Faith **by Mary Evelyn McCurdy**
A 30-lesson study of what the Bible says about faith. Ages 7-12.

Walking In Peace **by Mary Evelyn McCurdy**
A 30-lesson study of what the Bible says about faith. Ages 7-12.

Walking In Truth **by Mary Evelyn McCurdy**
A 30-lesson study of what the Bible says about truthfulness. Ages 7-12.

Celebrate the Savior **by Charlene Notgrass**
A 15-lesson study of the birth of Jesus and Christmas around the world. Ages 7-12.

Celebrate Thanksgiving **by Charlene Notgrass**
A 15-lesson study of the history and traditions of Thanksgiving. Ages 7-12.

Resources for High School

Exploring World History **by Ray Notgrass**
Study world history from Creation to the 21st century with history narrative, literature, and Bible integrated into one course. Three high school credits.

Exploring America **by Ray Notgrass**
Study American history from Columbus to the war in Iraq with history narrative, American literature, and Bible integrated into one course. Three high school credits.

Exploring Government **by Ray Notgrass**
Learn about Federal, state, and local government with an emphasis on the Biblical basis for government and on the U.S. Constitution. One semester for high school.

Exploring Economics **by Ray Notgrass**
Survey Biblical teachings on money and finance, get an overview of the economic history of the United States, find a clear explanation of terms and concepts used in economics, and study current issues in the national and world economies. One semester for high school.